a *Transaction/Society* reader

SOCIAL PSYCHOLOGY

edited by

Elliot Aronson · Robert Helmreich

The University of Texas at Austin

D. Van Nostrand Company

New York · Cincinnati · Toronto · London · Melbourne

D. Van Nostrand Company Regional Offices:
New York   Cincinnati   Milbrae

D. Van Nostrand Company International Offices:
London   Toronto   Melbourne

Library of Congress Catalog Card Number 73-2864
ISBN 0-442-20357-8

Published by D. Van Nostrand Company
450 West 33rd Street, New York, N.Y. 10001

Published simultaneously in Canada by
Van Nostrand Reinhold Ltd.

10 9 8 7 6 5 4 3 2

Picture Credits

Cover photograph, Shelly Rusten

ONE. SOCIALIZATION: 2, 27, George W. Gardner. 5, Dorka Raynor. 13, Wayne Miller, Magnum. 16, Hugh Rogers. 19, © Howard Harrison, 1969.

TWO. BELIEFS, ATTITUDES, AND CONVERSION: 30, James Marchael. 33, Bruce Davidson, Magnum. 40, Laurence Fink. 48, Mort Walker. 50, King Features Syndicate. 57, UFO International. 67, Eve Arnold, Magnum. 74, Shelly Rusten. 80, Bill Wingell.

THREE. INDIVIDUAL AND GROUP INFLUENCES ON BEHAVIOR: 84, 87, Erich Hartmann, Magnum. 93, Robert Osborn, from "On Leisure," © E. R. Squibb & Sons. 102, Bruce Davidson, Magnum. 117, Joshua Feigenbaum.

FOUR. CLOSED ENVIRONMENTS: 130, 151, National Aeronautics and Space Administration. 133, Pamela Harris-McLeod. 141, The Bettmann Archive. 157, Bruce Davidson, Magnum. 162, U. S. Navy.

FIVE. PREJUDICE AND SCAPEGOATING: 166, Charles Gatewood. 169, Ronny Jaques. 173, Paul Sequeira. 177, Constantine Manos, Magnum. 183 (detail), Laurence Fink. 190, Bruce Davidson, Magnum. 194, Charles Gatewood. 201, © 1972 George W. Gardner. 203, Declan Hunt, Black Star.

SIX. VIOLENCE, CONFLICT, AND CONFLICT RESOLUTION: 218, 221, George W. Gardner. 226, Paul Sequeira. 240, Burt Glinn, Magnum. 244, United Press International. 260, Elliott Erwitt, Magnum.

SEVEN. POLITICAL BEHAVIOR: 268, 285, United Press International. 270, Wayne Miller, Magnum. 280, Charles Harbutt, Magnum. 291, Inge Morath, Magnum.

Acknowledgments

"The Socialization of the Second Sex" by Jo Freeman: Excerpted from *Roles Women Play: Readings Toward Women's Liberation*, edited by Michelle Hoffnumn Garskof, published by Brooks Cole Publishing Company. Copyright © 1971 by Jo Freeman.

"Environmental Stress and the Maintenance of Self-Esteem" by Robert Helmreich and Roland Radloff: Adapted from a report prepared for the National Academy of Science—National Research Council Manned Spaceflight Isolation Study. The research was sponsored by contract N00014-67A-0126-0061 between the Office of Naval Research and Robert Helmreich, principal investigator.

"Psychosexual Development" by William Simon and John Gagnon: Excerpted from *Handbook of Socialization Theory and Research*, edited by David A. Goslin, copyright © 1969 by Rand-McNally & Company.

Foreword

The blunt truth is that there is no such thing as a trade book or a text book—but much more to the point, good books and bad books. It is with that in mind that this collection of articles, based on work previously published in the magazine *trans-Action/Society*, is being made available for the college and university communities.

It is our feeling at Transaction, shared by D. Van Nostrand Company and hopefully by readers of this book as well, that these analyses of social-psychological issues which first appeared in article form in *trans-Action/Society* are of sufficient interest and value to hold up over time and can become both part of the permanent learning experience of the student and, beyond that, part of the permanent corpus of solid materials by which the best of any field is deservedly judged. The text that has resulted from this compilation clearly demonstrates, we believe, the superiority of starting with real world problems, and searching out practical solutions. That the essays fall into generally established patterns of professional disciplines is more an accident than a necessity; it also demonstrates a growing awareness on the part of the basic areas of social science of their larger commitment to the amelioration of the human condition.

The demands upon scholarship and scientific judgment are always stringent—especially so in an era of booming scientific information, to the point of overload. The advantage of these studies is that in every paper there has been an effort to communicate the experience of the crisis of current social living. Yet, despite the sense of urgency these contributions exhibit, the editors have chosen them because they have withstood the test of time and match, if not exceed, in durable interest the best of available social science literature. This collection, then, attempts to address fundamental issues and in so doing add to the basic insights derived from a classical literature in the various fields of the social sciences.

Because of the concreteness of these writings, the editors have seen fit to develop a theoretical scaffold that links the specific essays themselves. As a result, the text can serve as a valuable series of core readings or as an adjunct anthology. There was nothing slap-dash or random about the selection process, the editing process, or the ideological process that went into this volume. It is our feeling that these essays represent the best in social science thinking and deserve the permanence granted by republication in book form.

The social scientists involved, both as editors and authors of this reader, have gone beyond observation, and have entered into the vital and difficult tasks of explanation and interpretation. The text has defined issues in a way that makes solutions possible. It has provided answers as well as asked the right questions. Thus, this book is dedicated not simply to highlighting social problems for students already inundated with such an awareness but, far more important, establishing guidelines for social solutions based on the social sciences.

Irving Louis Horowitz
Editor-in-Chief
trans-Action/Society

other *Transaction/Society* readers

Marriages and Families

edited by **Helena Z. Lopata**
Loyola University of Chicago

Politics/America

edited by **Walter Dean Burnham**
Massachusetts Institute of Technology

Contents

Preface

It is the editors' intention that this volume of essays fill a critical need in foundation courses in social psychology. That need as we see it is for a sound collection of lively reports that communicate the findings of contemporary social psychology while giving students an exposure to the men and women who practice this discipline and the insights and methodology they bring to their endeavors.

In his autobiography, the contemporary Russian poet Yevgeny Yevtushenko describes an incident that occurred immediately after he had finished reciting some of his poems to a group of factory workers during their lunch hour. An old woman, who had been listening so intently that she neglected even to eat her sandwich, approached the poet, wiped her eyes on the sleeve of her overalls, and gave him these words of encouragement: "Look for the truth in yourself and take it to the people. Look for the truth in people and store it in yourself" (Yevtushenko, 1964, p. 111).

Her advice might well be taken to heart by presentday students and researchers in social psychology. The social psychologist is in a unique position to find out things about human social interaction by systematically studying people, and he can then report these "truths" back to the people so that they might put them to use. Social psychology has, indeed, become increasingly adept at part of that dual task—the part that involves looking for the truth in people. Whether our technique of truth-gathering is the public opinion poll, the systematic observation of an event, or the laboratory experiment, we have been finding out a great many important things about people in society. We know much about propaganda, brainwashing, interpersonal attraction, conformity, prejudice, socialization and the like. We are gaining information about social phenomena that could be extremely useful in improving the human condition. But it is equally true that we have shown little enthusiasm for the other task mentioned by Yevtushenko's sage friend: we have failed badly in the task of examining this truth, mulling it over, making sense of it and taking it to the people. By and large, we social psychologists have not communicated our findings to masses of people; rather, we have tended to spend our time talking to each other—confining our communications, for the most part, to highly technical reports in relatively esoteric journals that are not readily available to the uninitiated.

As citizens, we can hardly afford this luxury. We are living in a fast-changing society where a knowledge of human interaction should not be confined to professionals; rather, it can be a vital asset for all of us, both as a means of increasing our understanding of what is going on in contemporary society and, hopefully, as a means of doing something to improve our state. The greater the number of people who can utilize whatever light social psychologists shed on contemporary events, the closer this country will be to becoming a truly informed democracy.

A recent example may clarify the point. In the aftermath of the 1971 Attica prison tragedy, there were many recriminations, charges and counter charges. Regardless of the side of the issue being argued, one thing was clear: the major focus of attention was on the nature of the people involved. There was a marked tendency to attribute brutality and sadism to the guards, psychopathy to the prisoners or callousness to the administrators. The danger of this kind of thinking rests on the fact that it suggests a rather simplistic solution to social problems. If we could only get "good," "decent," "kind" (or, depending on your persuasion, "tough," "no-nonsense") people to run the prisons, there would be no problem. Carried to the extreme, this line of reasoning would set, as the ultimate goal of social science, the development of personality tests which would tell us who is too sadistic, who is too cruel, who is too soft, etc. We could then prevent these people from serving as prison guards, keep them from running for political office or, in extreme cases, assign them to incarceration in an appropriate institution.

But the world is not that simple. In one of the social psychological essays anthologized here, Philip Zimbardo reports a striking piece of research showing what happens to ordinary human beings, like you or us, when they are placed in a simulated prison situation. In effect, after several days of playing the role of guards in the closed environment of a "prison," student volunteers began to behave like guards—with much of the viciousness commonly associated with guards. Other students, randomly assigned the role of prisoners, began thinking and behaving like prisoners—some rebellious, some docile. Zimbardo's research indicates that the situation itself has a tremendous impact on the way people will behave in prison. The behavior of prisoners and guards, in short, may be more a function of the kind of environment that exists in a prison than of the dispositional attributes of the individuals involved. For a more detailed discussion of this research, see the introduction to Part Four.

If information such as this were made more available to the public, both laymen and officials, it might affect the way society thinks about prison reform. If all the data of social psychology were made readily available, they might shape the way people think about the entire spectrum of social issues.

Society's need is for such information to be reported in a manner that, while remaining true to the subtleties and complexities of the research, can be easily understood by the nonprofessional. Teachers, especially, sense this need. And as teachers, both of us have been searching, in vain, for a collection of readings that would bring to the beginning student the flavor, excitement and implications of research projects without burying him under a load of jargon or forcing him to wallow in a swamp of unnecessary detail. In this volume, therefore, we have tried to edit and organize a number of reports from *trans-Action/Society* into a coherent unit. We have taken special pains to limit our collection to essays which are based upon high-quality research into issues that are of vital interest. The subject matter represents a wide range of topics, interests, disciplines and research methodologies. A single section may contain essays by a social psychologist, a political scientist and a sociologist, utilizing experimental methods, systematic observation or survey research. We think we have come up with a highly readable collection of articles by a group of distinguished scholars and researchers. In addition, we believe that, viewed as a whole, the volume presents a balanced and integrated picture of social psychology *of* and *for* the people of the seventies.

Elliot Aronson
Robert Helmreich

SOCIAL
PSYCHOLOGY

Socialization can be thought of as the process of "housebreaking" humans. The term refers to the learning of approved and acceptable patterns of behavior in the surrounding environment. Through socialization, we acquire values and attitudes and develop a moral code. Socialization includes such disparate phenomena as toilet training, the learning of language skills and the development of esthetic preferences. It also includes the transmission of sex roles (male and female) and modes of sexual behavior as well as the formation of political and ideological value systems.

Everyone with whom an individual has contact—direct or indirect—can be considered an agent of socialization. Parents typically play the most important roles in transmitting the norms and order of the surrounding world to their growing child. As an individual matures and his universe expands, siblings, peers, teachers, other adults and the communications media all influence his conception and internalization of the culture around him.

The mechanisms of socialization are those governing all behavior. The child is *rewarded* for performing in accordance with desired standards. He is *punished* for deviation from parental, peer or societal norms or for imperfect fulfillment of his assigned roles. He also acquires patterns of response by imitating the behavior of those in the environment who serve as models. The individual's need to maintain *consistency* in his beliefs and in his conception of himself also leads him to acquire some values and behaviors and to reject others.

Two important points should be kept in mind when considering socialization. The first is that socialization is an imperfect process in the sense that there is no one-to-one relationship between what is transmitted and what is internalized as a set of coherent, internally consistent values and skills. Misperceptions and distortions in the individual tend inevitably to color and transform the information and behaviors acquired,

Part One

Socialization

acquiring beliefs and behaviors from the cultural context

and this transformed culture is changed yet again in subsequent transmissions. Thus, within a framework of broad similarities, the socialization of each individual is unique. Even within the same family, children exposed to the same general environment may acquire very different ways of responding to the world. One child may be a "hippie radical," his sibling a policeman dedicated to preserving the status quo; another may be an aggressive Don Juan while his sibling is a timid recluse. Such variability in outcomes can lead a parent to ask "Where have I gone wrong?" Seeking the answer to the broader question of why such dramatic differences appear in the course of socialization is one of the great challenges of psychology.

A second point about socialization is that it is a continuing process—not simply the early inculcation of civilization into the barbaric child. The socialization of an individual is never complete and never irreversible. Formal education is certainly one of the most important aspects of socialization. We may also think of the individual as being socialized into college culture or the military, or into prison or social movements.

Many experiences constitute a *resocialization*, in which old values and behaviors are exchanged for new ones. Psychotherapy is often described in such terms, as a relearning of values and a replacement of maladaptive behaviors with more effective coping techniques.

Although the essays in this section deal with basic issues in socialization, many essays throughout the rest of the book, too, concern themselves with issues which are aspects of socialization or resocialization. This is particularly true of studies of conversion experiences (Part Two), gang behavior (Part Three) and reactions to total environments (Part Four).

In the first essay, immediately following, William Simon and John Gagnon discuss psychosexual development in American culture. They point out that sexual behavior is learned and that differences between sexes and social classes can be understood as a function of learning experiences. They provide illustrations of the pressures that shape an individual, and they show how human sexual behavior is far more complex than the simple unfolding of an instinctual, biological script.

In the second essay, Elliot Aronson reports research on the internalization of standards of behavior. Although strong external threats and punishments can cause people to behave in desired ways on a temporary basis, Aronson is interested in the processes through which an individual develops internal controls of his behavior which lead to more permanent effects. His thesis is that the need for consistency will cause the person to adopt attitudes and values consistent with his behavior. Thus, if a child is deterred from performing an undesirable act by a weak threat, he will attempt to justify his nonperformance by convincing himself that "I didn't really want to do that anyway."

Subsequent essays explore the results of socialization as it determines how the individual sees himself and how he adopts the sex roles deemed appropriate by society. While it seems banal to note that men and women are "different," and that some members of each sex are more "masculine" or "feminine" than others, the extent to which between- and within-sex differences are due to biology as opposed to socialization is a topic of serious concern and intensive investigation today. As demands for sexual equality and rectification of past sex-linked abuses increase, so does the need for sound data showing how socialization interacts with biology to produce differences in self-concept and role behavior. The three studies by Kurtz, Freeman and Barclay/Cusumano present some of the outcomes of socialization and explore some of the factors in socialization which may lead to different outcomes.

Richard M. Kurtz describes differences between individuals of different body types and how each type evaluates his or her own body. Kurtz reports that women like their bodies more than men and that, among men, those with muscular builds rate their bodies more highly than do those of other types. In many ways the reported findings reflect our cultural norms of what constitutes "good" and "attractive." To a large extent, individuals internalize these standards during socialization. The fact that notions of "desirable" characteristics are *learned* is shown by the existence of differences among cultures. Moreover, what cultures regard as attractive is not static; rather it tends to change over time.

Jo Freeman examines the patterns of socialization of females in American culture. She shows how child-rearing practices act upon the girl to produce those characteristics we consider "feminine," such as passivity, sensitivity, submission, indirectness and lower performance. She also points out that these are also the characteristics noted in "oppressed peoples" by students of prejudice. Her data emphasize the fact that many of the sex differences we attribute to biological factors may well be the result of sexist attitudes in our society.

Allen G. Barclay and D. R. Cusumano report on another aspect of sex-role socialization. They studied the "masculinity" of boys growing up with—and without—fathers. They found that boys who grew up in a home with an older male present score higher on a test assumed to measure "masculinity." These results emphasize the social learning present in even the most basic behaviors.

The studies in this Part typify the most prominent research methods employed by social psychologists. The research reported by Simon and Gagnon, for example, illustrates the type of information which can be obtained through *survey research.* This form of investigation involves asking a number of respondents to describe systematically their reactions or behavior. The goal of such research is to specify the characteristic patterns of behavior of particular populations or subgroups, such as race, sex, or social class. Survey research is an invaluable technique for the social scientist, one which provides essential baseline data for comparing groups and individuals. The major weaknesses of this type of research are that respondents may falsify or distort their answers to questions—especially to questions dealing with personal and sensitive matters—and that the sample of individuals chosen may not be representative of the larger population from which they were selected.

Research reported by Aronson, in the second essay, is an example of the *experimental approach* to psychological investigation. In experimental studies the investigator starts with a hypothesis derived from a theory of behavior and sets up a laboratory analog of a real situation. By controlling extraneous factors and varying a crucial element of the experimental environment, the investigator can make strong statements about causal relationships and can evaluate the correctness of theoretical formulations. The experiment is thus an essential tool in the development and refinement of theories of behavior. There are pitfalls in laboratory experimentation, however. One is that the experimenter may develop a laboratory model which does not accurately reflect his theoretical concerns. Another is that irrelevant and uncontrolled factors, rather than those he thinks he is investigating, may be causing the observed effects. Finally, there is always the danger that relationships reliably obtained in the laboratory may not generalize to the more complex situations found in the "real world."

The final three essays, dealing with sex roles, illustrate a third approach to the acquisition of data and the understanding of behavior: *correlational techniques.* In correlational research, which is non-experimental, the investigator assesses whether a certain trait or characteristic is present or varies as a function of another variable. For example, are scores on the masculinity test higher when a father is present than when he is absent? Or, in another correlational study, the researcher might test to see if higher scores on a measure of masculinity are associated with higher scores on a test of aggressiveness. Correlational research tells the investigator how strong the association is between two variables; it does not provide information about causal relationships. That is, knowing that two variables vary systematically with each other does not let us draw inferences about whether variations in one *cause* variations in the other. This has been a major limitation in social psychological research, since many phenomena occurring in natural situations can be studied only through correlational techniques. Recently, however, developments in statistics and computer technology have made it possible to draw some conclusions about cause and effect in correlational research. These advances may well add significantly to our understanding of social behavior.

The five studies in this Part, then, provide both a view of the complex topic of socialization and examples of the diverse approaches to research used by students of social psychology. No single approach provides a sure route to understanding, but through the application of all our methodologies, knowledge of the roots of social behavior is increasing rapidly.

Psychosexual Development

William Simon and John Gagnon

Erik Erikson has observed that, prior to Sigmund Freud, "sexologists" tended to believe that sexual capacities appeared suddenly with the onset of adolescence. Sexuality followed those external evidences of physiological change that occurred concurrent with or just after puberty. Psycho-

analysis changed all that. In Freud's view, libido—the generation of psychosexual energies—should be viewed as a fundamental element of human experience at least beginning with birth, and possibly before that. Libido, therefore, is essential, a biological constant to be coped with at all levels of individual, social, and cultural development. The truth of this received wisdom, that is, that sexual development is a continuous contest between biological drive and cultural restraint should be seriously questioned. Obviously sexuality has roots in biological processes, but so do many other capacities including many that involve physical and mental competence and vigor. There is, however, abundant evidence that the final states which these capacities attain escape the rigid impress of biology. This independence of biological constraint is rarely claimed for the area of sexuality, but we would like to argue that the sexual is precisely that realm where the sociocultural forms most completely dominate biological influences.

It is difficult to get data that might shed much light on the earliest aspects of these questions: Adults are hardly equipped with total recall and the pre-verbal or primitively verbal child does not have ability to report accurately on his own internal state. But it seems obvious—and it is a basic assumption of this paper—that with the beginnings of adolescence many new factors come into play, and to emphasize a straight-line developmental continuity with infant and childhood experiences may be seriously misleading. In particular, it is dangerous to assume that because some childhood behavior appears sexual to adults, it must be sexual. An infant or a child engaged in genital play (even if orgasm is observed) can in no sense be seen as experiencing the complex set of feelings that accompanies adult or even adolescent masturbation.

Therefore, the authors reject the unproven assumption that "powerful" psychosexual drives are fixed biological attributes. More importantly, we reject the even more dubious assumption that sexual capacities or experiences tend to translate immediately into a kind of universal "knowing" or innate wisdom—that sexuality has a magical ability, possessed by no other capacity, that allows biological drives to be expressed directly in psychosocial and social behaviors.

The prevailing image of sexuality—particularly that of the Freudian tradition—is that of an intense, high-pressure drive that forces a person to seek physical sexual gratification, a drive that expresses itself indirectly if it cannot be expressed directly. The available data suggest to us a different picture—one that shows either lower levels of intensity, or, at least, greater variability. We find that there are many social situations or life-roles in which reduced sex activity or even deliberate celibacy is undertaken with little evidence that the libido has shifted in compensation to some other sphere.

A part of the legacy of Freud is that we have all become remarkably adept at discovering "sexual" elements in nonsexual behavior and symbolism. What we suggest instead (following Kenneth Burke's three-decade-old insight) is

the reverse—that sexual behavior can often express and serve nonsexual motives.

No Play Without A Script

We see sexual behavior therefore as *scripted* behavior, not the masked expression of a primordial drive. The individual can learn sexual behavior as he or she learns other behavior—through scripts that in this case give the self, other persons, and situations erotic abilities or content. Desire, privacy, opportunity, and propinquity with an attractive member of the opposite sex are not, in themselves, enough; in ordinary circumstances, nothing sexual will occur unless one or both actors organize these elements into an appropriate script. The very concern with foreplay in sex suggests this. From one point of view, foreplay may be defined as merely progressive physical excitement generated by touching naturally erogenous zones. The authors have referred to this conception elsewhere as the "rubbing of two sticks together to make a fire" model. It would seem to be more valuable to see this activity as symbolically invested behavior through which the body is eroticized and through which mute, inarticulate motions and gestures are translated into a sociosexual drama.

A belief in the sociocultural dominance of sexual behavior finds support in cross-cultural research as well as in data restricted to the United States. Psychosexual development is universal—but it takes many forms and tempos. People in different cultures construct their scripts differently; and in our own society, different segments of the population act out different psychosexual dramas—something much less likely to occur if they were all reacting more or less blindly to the same superordinate urge. The most marked differences occur, of course, between male and female patterns of sexual behavior. Obviously, some of this is due to biological differences, including differences in hormonal functions at different ages. But the significance of social scripts predominate; the recent work of Masters and Johnson, for example, clearly points to far greater orgasmic capacities on the part of females than our culture would lead us to suspect. And within each sex—especially among men—different social and economic groups have different patterns.

Let us examine some of these variations, and see if we can decipher the scripts.

Childhood

Whether one agrees with Freud or not, it is obvious that we do not become sexual all at once. There is continuity with the past. Even infant experiences can strongly influence later sexual development.

But continuity is not causality. Childhood experiences (even those that appear sexual) will in all likelihood be influential not because they are intrinsically sexual, but because they can affect a number of developmental trends, *including* the sexual. What situations in infancy—or even early childhood—can be called psychosexual in any sense other than that of creating potentials?

The key term, therefore, must remain potentiation. In infancy, we can locate some of the experiences (or sensations) that will bring about a sense of the body and its capacities for pleasure and discomfort and those that will influence the child's ability to relate to others. It is possible, of course, that through these primitive experiences, ranges are being established—but they are very broad and overlapping. Moreover, if these are profound experiences to the child—and they may well be that—they are not expressions of biological necessity, but of the earliest forms of social learning.

In childhood, after infancy there is what appears to be some real sex play. About half of all adults report that they did engage in some form of sex play as children; and the total who actually did may be half again as many. But, however the adult interprets it later, what did it mean to the child at the time? One suspects that, as in much of childhood role-playing, their sense of the adult meanings attributed to the behavior is fragmentary and ill-formed. Many of the adults recall that, at the time, they were concerned with being found out. But here, too, were they concerned because of the real content of sex play, or because of the mystery and the lure of the forbidden that so often enchant the child? The child may be assimilating outside information about sex for which, at the time, he has no real internal correlate or understanding.

A small number of persons do have sociosexual activity during preadolescence—most of it initiated by adults. But for the majority of these, little apparently follows from it. Without appropriate sexual scripts, the experience remains unassimilated—at least in adult terms. For some, it is clear, a severe reaction may follow from falling "victim" to the sexuality of an adult—but, again, does this reaction come from the sexual act itself or from the social response, the strong reactions of others? (There is some evidence that early sexual activity of this sort is associated with deviant adjustments in later life. But this, too, may not be the result of sexual experiences in themselves so much as the consequence of having fallen out of the social main stream and, therefore, of running greater risks of isolation and alienation.)

In short, relatively few become truly active sexually before adolescence. And when they do (for girls more often than boys), it is seldom immediately related to sexual feelings or gratifications but is a use of sex for nonsexual goals and purposes. The "seductive" Lolita is rare; but she is significant: She illustrates a more general pattern of psycho-sexual development—a commitment to the social relationships linked to sex before one can really grasp the social meaning of the physical relationships.

Of great importance are the values (or feelings, or images) that children pick up as being related to sex. Although we talk a lot about sexuality, as though trying to exorcise the demon of shame, learning about sex in our society is in large part learning about guilt; and learning how to manage sexuality commonly involves learning how to manage guilt. An important source of guilt in children comes from the imputation to them by adults of sexual appetites or abilities that they may not have, but that they learn, however imperfectly, to pretend they have. The gestural concomitants of sexual modesty are learned early. For instance, when do girls learn to sit or pick up objects with their knees together? When do they learn that the bust must be covered? However, since this behavior is learned unlinked to later adult sexual performances, what children must make of all this is very mysterious.

The learning of sex roles, or sex identities, involves many things that are remote from actual sexual experience, or that become involved with sexuality only after puberty. Masculinity or femininity, their meaning and postures, are rehearsed before adolescence in many nonsexual ways.

A number of scholars have pointed, for instance, to the importance of aggressive, deference, dependency, and dominance behavior in childhood. Jerome Kagan and Howard Moss have found that aggressive behavior in males and dependency in females are relatively stable aspects of development. But what is social role, and what is biology? They found that when aggressive behavior occurred among girls, it tended to appear most often among those from well-educated families that were more tolerant of deviation. Curiously, they also reported that "it was impossible to predict the character of adult sexuality in women from their pre-adolescent and early adolescent behavior," and that "erotic activity is more anxiety-arousing for females than for males," because "the traditional ego ideal for women dictates inhibition of sexual impulses."

The belief in the importance of early sex-role learning for boys can be viewed in two ways. First, it may directly indicate an early sexual capacity in male children. Or, second, early masculine identification may merely be an appropriate framework within which the sexual impulse (salient with puberty) and the socially available sexual scripts (or accepted patterns of sexual behavior) can most conveniently find expression. Our bias, of course, is toward the second.

But, as Kagan and Moss also noted, the sex role learned by the child does not reliably predict how he will act sexually as an adult. This finding also can be interpreted in the same two alternative ways. Where sexuality is viewed as a biological constant which struggles to express itself, the female sex role learning can be interpreted as the successful repression of sexual impulses. The other interpretation suggests that the difference lies not in learning how to handle a pre-existent sexuality, but in learning how to *be* sexual. Differences between men and women, therefore, will have consequences both for *what* is done sexually, as well as *when*.

Once again, we prefer the latter interpretation, and some recent work that we have done with lesbians supports it. We observed that many of the major elements of their sex lives—the start of actual genital sexual behavior, the onset and frequency of masturbation, the time of entry in sociosexual patterns, the number of partners, and the reports of feelings of sexual deprivation—were for these homosexual women almost identical with those of ordinary women. Since sexuality would seem to be more important for lesbians—after all, they sacrifice much in order to follow their own sexual pathways—this is surprising. We concluded that the primary factor was something both categories of women share—the sex-role learning that occurs before sexuality itself becomes significant.

Social class also appears significant, more for boys than girls. Sex-role learning may vary by class; lower-class boys are supposed to be more aggressive and put much greater emphasis on early heterosexuality. The middle and upper classes tend to tolerate more deviance from traditional attitudes regarding appropriate male sex-role performances.

Given all these circumstances, it seems rather naive to think of sexuality as a constant pressure, with a peculiar necessity all its own. For us, the crucial period of childhood has significance not because of sexual occurrences, but because of nonsexual developments that will provide the names and judgments for later encounters with sexuality.

Adolescence

The actual beginnings and endings of adolescence are vague. Generally, the beginning marks the first time society, as such, acknowledges that the individual has sexual capacity. Training in the postures and rhetoric of the sexual experience is now accelerated. Most important, the adolescent begins to regard those about him (particularly his peers, but also adults) as sexual actors and finds confirmation from others for this view.

For some, as noted, adolescent sexual experience begins before they are considered adolescents. Kinsey reports that a tenth of his female sample and a fifth of his male sample had experienced orgasm through masturbation by age 12. But still, for the vast majority, despite some casual play and exploration that post-Freudians might view as masked sexuality, sexual experience begins with adolescence. Even

those who have had prior experience find that it acquires new meanings with adolescence. They now relate such meanings to both larger spheres of social life and greater senses of self. For example, it is not uncommon during the transition between childhood and adolescence for boys and, more rarely, girls to report arousal and orgasm while doing things not manifestly sexual—climbing trees, sliding down bannisters, or other activities that involve genital contact— without defining them as sexual. Often they do not even take it seriously enough to try to explore or repeat what was, in all likelihood, a pleasurable experience.

Adolescent sexual development, therefore, really represents the beginning of adult sexuality. It marks a definite break with what went on before. Not only will future experiences occur in new and more complex contexts, but they will be conceived of as explicitly sexual and thereby begin to complicate social relationships. The need to manage sexuality will rise not only from physical needs and desires, but also from the new implications of personal relationships. Playing, or associating, with members of the opposite sex now acquires different meanings.

At adolescence, changes in the developments of boys and girls diverge and must be considered separately. The one thing both share at this point is a reinforcement of their new status by a dramatic biological event—for girls, menstruation, and for boys, the discovery of the ability to ejaculate. But here they part. For boys, the beginning of a commitment to sexuality is primarily genital; within two years of puberty all but a relatively few have had the experience of orgasm, almost universally brought about by masturbation. The corresponding organizing event for girls is not genitally sexual but social: they have arrived at an age where they will learn role performances linked with proximity to marriage. In contrast to boys, only two-thirds of girls will report ever having masturbated (and, characteristically, the frequency is much less). For women, it is not until the late twenties that the incidence of orgasm from any source reaches that of boys at age 16. In fact, significantly, about half of the females who masturbate do so only after having experienced orgasm in some situation involving others. This contrast points to a basic distinction between the developmental processes for males and females: males move from privatized personal sexuality to sociosexuality; females do the reverse and at a later stage in the life cycle.

The Turned-On Boys

We have worked hard to demonstrate the dominance of social, psychological, and cultural influences over the biological; now, dealing with adolescent boys, we must briefly reverse course. There is much evidence that the early male sexual impulses—again, initially through masturbation—

are linked to physiological changes, to high hormonal inpnts during puberty. This produces an organism that, to put it simply, is more easily turned on. Male adolescents report frequent erections, often without apparent stimulation of any kind. Even so, though there is greater biological sensitization and hence masturbation is more likely, the meaning, organization, and continuance of this activity still tends to be subordinate to social and psychological factors.

Masturbation provokes guilt and anxiety among most adolescent boys. This is not likely to change in spite of more "enlightened" rhetoric and discourse on the subject (generally, we have shifted from stark warnings of mental, moral, and physical damage to vague counsels against nonsocial or "inappropriate" behavior). However, it may be that this very guilt and anxiety gives the sexual experience an intensity of feeling that is often attributed to sex itself.

Such guilt and anxiety do not follow simply from social disapproval. Rather, they seem to come from several sources, including the difficulty the boy has in presenting himself as a sexual being to his immediate family, particularly his parents. Another source is the fantasies or plans associated with masturbation—fantasies about doing sexual "things" to others or having others do sexual "things" to oneself; or having to learn and rehearse available but proscribed sexual scripts or patterns of behavior. And, of course, some guilt and anxiety center around the general disapproval of masturbation. After the early period of adolescence, in fact, most youths will not admit to their peers that they did or do it.

Nevertheless, masturbation is for most adolescent boys the major sexual activity, and they engage in it fairly frequently. It is an extremely positive and gratifying experience to them. Such an introduction to sexuality can lead to a capacity for detached sex activity—activity whose only sustaining motive is sexual. This may be the hallmark of male sexuality in our society.

Of the three sources of guilt and anxiety mentioned, the first—how to manage both sexuality and an attachment to family members—probably cuts across class lines. But the others should show remarkable class differences. The second one, how to manage a fairly elaborate and exotic fantasy life during masturbation, should be confined most typically to the higher classes, who are more experienced and adept at dealing with symbols. (It is possible, in fact, that this behavior, which girls rarely engage in, plays a role in the processes by which middle-class boys catch up with girls in measures of achievement and creativity and, by the end of adolescence, move out in front. However, this is only a hypothesis.)

The ability to fantasize during masturbation implies certain broad consequences. One is a tendency to see large parts of the environment in an erotic light, as well as the ability to respond, sexually and perhaps poetically, to many visual and auditory stimuli. We might also expect both a capacity and need for fairly elaborate forms of sexual activity. Further, since masturbatory fantasies generally deal with relationships and acts leading to coitus, they should also reinforce a developing capacity for heterosociality.

The third source of guilt and anxiety—the alleged "unmanliness" of masturbation—should more directly concern the lower-class male adolescent. ("Manliness" has always been an important value for lower-class males.) In these groups, social life is more often segregated by sex, and there are, generally, fewer rewarding social experiences from other sources. The adolescent therefore moves into heterosexual—if not heterosocial—relationships sooner than his middle-class counterparts. Sexual segregation makes it easier for him than for the middle-class boy to learn that he does not have to love everything he desires, and therefore to come more naturally to casual, if not exploitative, relationships. The second condition—fewer social rewards that his fellows would respect—should lead to an exaggerated concern for proving masculinity by direct displays of physical prowess, aggression, and visible sexual success. And these three, of course, may be mutually reinforcing.

In a sense, the lower-class male is the first to reach "sexual maturity" as defined by the Freudians. That is, he is generally the first to become aggressively heterosexual and exclusively genital. This characteristic, in fact, is a distinguishing difference between lower-class males and those above them socially.

But one consequence is that although their sex lives are almost exclusively heterosexual, they remain homosocial. They have intercourse with females, but the standards and the audience they refer to are those of their male fellows. Middle-class boys shift predominantly to coitus at a significantly later time. They, too, need and tend to have homosocial elements in their sexual lives. But their fantasies, their ability to symbolize, and their social training in a world in which distinctions between masculinity and femininity are less sharply drawn, allow them to withdraw more easily from an all-male world. This difference between social classes obviously has important consequences for stable adult relationships.

One thing common in male experience during adolescence is that while it provides much opportunity for sexual commitment, in one form or another, there is little training in how to handle emotional relations with girls. The imagery and rhetoric of romantic love is all around us; we are immersed in it. But whereas much is undoubtedly absorbed by the adolescent, he is not likely to tie it closely to his sexuality. In fact, such a connection might be inhibiting, as indicated by the survival of the "bad-girl-who-does" and "good-girl-who-doesn't" distinction. This is important to keep in mind as we turn to the female side of the story.

With the Girls

In contrast to males, female sexual development during adolescence is so similar in all classes that it is easy to suspect that it is solely determined by biology. But, while girls do not have the same level of hormonal sensitization to sexuality at puberty as adolescent boys, there is little evidence of a biological or social inhibitor either. The "equipment" for sexual pleasure is clearly present by puberty, but tends not to be used by many females of any class. Masturbation rates are fairly low, and among those who do masturbate, fairly infrequent. Arousal from "sexual" materials or situations happens seldom, and exceedingly few girls report feeling sexually deprived during adolescence.

Basically, girls in our society are not encouraged to be sexual—and may be strongly discouraged from being so. Most of us accept the fact that while "bad boy" can mean many things, "bad girl" almost exclusively implies sexual delinquency. It is both difficult and dangerous for an adolescent girl to become too active sexually. As Joseph Rheingold puts it, where men need only fear sexual failure, women must fear both success and failure.

Does this long period of relative sexual inactivity among girls come from repression of an elemental drive, or merely from a failure to learn how to be sexual? The answers have important implications for their later sexual development. If it is repression, the path to a fuller sexuality must pass through processes of loss of inhibitions, during which the girl unlearns, in varying degrees, attitudes and values that block the expression of natural internal feelings. It also implies that the quest for ways to express directly sexual behavior and feelings that had been expressed nonsexually is secondary and of considerably less significance.

On the other hand, the "learning" answer suggests that women create or invent a capacity for sexual behavior, learning how and when to be aroused and how and when to respond. This approach implies greater flexibility; unlike the repression view, it makes sexuality both more and less than a basic force that may break loose at any time in strange or costly ways. The learning approach also lessens the power of sexuality altogether; all at once, particular kinds of sex activities need no longer be defined as either "healthy" or "sick." Lastly, subjectively, this approach appeals to the authors because it describes female sexuality in terms that seem less like a mere projection of male sexuality.

If sexual activity by adolescent girls assumes less specific forms than with boys, that does not mean that sexual learning and training do not occur. Curiously, though girls are, as a group, far less active sexually than boys, they receive far more training in self-consciously viewing themselves—and in viewing boys—as desirable mates. This is particularly true in recent years. Females begin early in adolescence to define attractiveness, at least partially, in sexual terms. We suspect that the use of sexual attractiveness for nonsexual purposes that marked our preadolescent "seductress" now begins to characterize many girls. Talcott Parsons' description of how the wife "uses" sex to bind the husband to the family, although harsh, may be quite accurate. More generally, in keeping with the childbearing and child-raising function of women, the development of a sexual role seems to involve a need to include in that role more than pleasure.

To round out the picture of the difference between the sexes, girls appear to be well-trained precisely in that area in which boys are poorly trained—that is, a belief in and a capacity for intense, emotionally-charged relationships and the language of romantic love. When girls during this period describe having been aroused sexually, they more often report it as a response to romantic, rather than erotic, words and actions.

In later adolescence, as dates, parties, and other sociosexual activities increase, boys—committed to sexuality and relatively untrained in the language and actions of romantic love—interact with girls, committed to romantic love and relatively untrained in sexuality. Dating and courtship may well be considered processes in which each sex trains the other in what each wants and expects. What data is available suggests that this exchange system does not always work very smoothly. Thus, ironically, it is not uncommon to find that the boy becomes emotionally involved with his partner and therefore lets up on trying to seduce her, at the same time that the girl comes to feel that the boy's affection is genuine and therefore that sexual intimacy is more permissible.

In our recent study of college students, we found that boys typically had intercourse with their first coital partners one to three times, while with girls it was ten or more. Clearly, for the majority of females first intercourse becomes possible only in stable relationships or in those with strong bonds.

"Woman, What Does She Want?"

The male experience does conform to the general Freudian expectation that there is a developmental movement from a predominantly genital sexual commitment to a loving relationship with another person. But this movement is, in effect, reversed for females, with love or affection often a necessary precondition for intercourse. No wonder, therefore, that Freud had great difficulty understanding female sexuality—recall the concluding line in his great essay on women: "Woman, what does she want?" This "error"—the assumption that female sexuality is similar to or a mirror image of that of the male—may come from the fact that so many of those who constructed the theory were men. With Freud, in addition, we must remember the very concept of sexuality essential to most of nineteenth century Europe—it was an elemental beast that had to be curbed.

It has been noted that there are very few class differences in sexuality among females, far fewer than among males. One difference, however, is very relevant to this discussion —the age of first intercourse. This varies inversely with social class—that is, the higher the class, the later the age of first intercourse—a relationship that is also true of first marriage. The correlation between these two ages suggest the necessary social and emotional linkage between courtship and the entrance into sexual activity on the part of women. A second difference, perhaps only indirectly related to social class, has to do with educational achievement: here, a sharp border line seems to separate from all other women those who have or have had graduate or professional work. If sexual success may be measured by the percentage of sex acts that culminate in orgasm, graduate and professional women are the most sexually successful women in the nation.

Why? One possible interpretation derives from the work of Abraham Maslow: Women who get so far in higher education are more likely to be more aggressive, perhaps to have strong needs to dominate; both these characteristics are associated with heightened sexuality. Another, more general interpretation would be that in a society in which girls are expected primarily to become wives and mothers, going on to graduate school represents a kind of deviancy —a failure of, or alienation from, normal female social adjustment. In effect, then, it would be this flawed socialization—not biology—that produced both commitment toward advanced training and toward heightened sexuality.

For both males and females, increasingly greater involvement in the social aspects of sexuality—"socializing" with the opposite sex—may be one factor that marks the end of adolescence. We know little about this transition, especially among noncollege boys and girls; but our present feeling is that sexuality plays an important role in it. First, sociosexuality is important in family formation and also in learning the roles and obligations involved in being an adult. Second, and more fundamental, late adolescence is when a youth is seeking, and experimenting toward finding, his identity—who and what he is and will be; and sociosexual activity is the one aspect of this exploration that we associate particularly with late adolescence.

Young people are particularly vulnerable at this time.

This may be partly due to the fact that society has difficulty protecting the adolescent from the consequences of sexual behavior that it pretends he is not engaged in. But, more importantly, it may be because, at all ages, we all have great problems in discussing our sexual feelings and experiences in personal terms. These, in turn, make it extremely difficult to get support from others for an adolescent's experiments toward trying to invent his sexual self. We suspect that success or failure in the discovery or management of sexual identity may have consequences in personal development far beyond merely the sexual sphere —perhaps in confidence and feelings of self-worth, belonging, competence, guilt, force of personality, and so on.

Adulthood

In our society, all but a few ultimately marry. Handling sexual commitments inside marriage makes up the larger part of adult experience. Again, we have too little data for firm findings. The data we do have come largely from studies of broken and troubled marriages, and we do not know to what extent sexual problems in such marriages exceed those of intact marriages. It is possible that, because we have assumed that sex is important in most people's lives, we have exaggerated its importance in holding marriages together. Also, it is quite possible that, once people are married, sexuality declines relatively, becoming less important than other gratifications (such as domesticity or parenthood); or it may be that these other gratifications can minimize the effect of sexual dissatisfaction. Further, it may be possible that individuals learn to get sexual gratification, or an equivalent, from activities that are nonsexual, or only partially sexual.

The sexual desires and commitments of males are the main determinants of the rate of sexual activity in our society. Men are most interested in intercourse in the early years of marriage—woman's interest peaks much later; nonetheless, coital rates decline steadily throughout marriage. This decline derives from many things, only one of which is decline in biological capacity. With many men, it is more difficult to relate sexually to a wife who is pregnant or a mother. Lower-class adult men receive less support and plaudits from their male friends for married sexual performance than they did as single adolescents; and we might also add the lower-class disadvantage of less training in the use of auxiliary or symbolic sexually stimulating materials. For middle-class men, the decline is not as steep, owing perhaps to their greater ability to find stimulation from auxiliary sources, such as literature, movies, music, and romantic or erotic conversation. It should be further noted that for about 30 percent of college-educated men, masturbation continues regularly during marriage, even when the wife is available.

An additional (if unknown) proportion do not physically masturbate, but derive additional excitement from the fantasies that accompany intercourse.

But even middle-class sexual activity declines more rapidly than bodily changes can account for. Perhaps the ways males learn to be sexual in our society make it very difficult to keep it up at a high level with the same woman for a long time. However, this may not be vital in maintaining the family, or even in the man's personal sense of well-being, because, as previously suggested, sexual dissatisfaction may become less important as other satisfactions increase. Therefore, it need seldom result in crisis.

About half of all married men and a quarter of all married women will have intercourse outside of marriage at one time or another. For women, infidelity seems to have been on the increase since the turn of the century— at the same time that their rates of orgasm have been increasing. It is possible that the very nature of female sexuality is changing. Work being done now may give us new light on this. For men, there are strong social-class differences—the lower class accounts for most extramarital activity, especially during the early years of marriage. We have observed that it is difficult for a lower-class man to acquire the appreciation of his fellows for married intercourse; extramarital sex, of course, is another matter.

In general, we feel that far from sexual needs affecting other adult concerns, the reverse may be true: adult sexual activity may become that aspect of a person's life most often used to act out other needs. There are some data that suggest this. Men who have trouble handling authority relationships at work more often have dreams about homosexuality; some others, under heavy stress on the job, have been shown to have more frequent episodic homosexual experiences. Such phenomena as the rise of sadomasochistic practices and experiments in group sex may also be tied to nonsexual tensions, the use of sex for nonsexual purposes.

It is only fairly recently in the history of man that he has been able to begin to understand that his own time and place do not embody some eternal principle or necessity, but are only dots on a continuum. It is difficult for many to believe that man can change, and is changing, in important ways. This conservative view is evident even in contemporary behavioral science; and a conception of man as having relatively constant sexual needs has become part of it. In an ever-changing world, it is perhaps comforting to think that man's sexuality does not change very much, and therefore is relatively easily explained. We cannot accept this. Instead, we have attempted to offer a description of sexual development as a variable social invention—an invention that in itself explains little, and requires much continuing explanation.

Threat and Obedience

Elliot Aronson

Most psychologists, parents, and employers have learned that if one wants a rat, a pigeon, a four-year-old child, a college sophomore, or a factory worker to do something, good results can usually be attained by rewarding "good" behavior or by threatening to punish "bad" behavior. Ice cream cones, spankings, food pellets, electric shocks, ridicule, flunking grades, high salaries—these have all been used successfully to control the behavior of children, laboratory animals, or adult humans. Generally, the larger the reward or the more severe the threat of punishment, the greater the likelihood of compliance.

But to induce compliance by rewards and punishments is terribly inefficient, because in order to ensure continued compliance, rewards or punishment must also be continued indefinitely—and often in increasing doses. The indulgent mother must keep doling out candy, the tough foreman can never relax. It would be much more efficient and desirable if society could somehow induce people to enjoy doing things that must be done, and refrain from doing those things that society considers undesirable. For example, few people would run a stop sign if a policeman always stood alongside, pencil conspicuously poised, ready to issue a costly ticket. But it would be more efficient if all drivers could be persuaded to quit running through stop signs, policeman or no.

Such a technique of persuasion—or self-persuasion—is quite possible. It can be derived from Leon Festinger's theory of "cognitive dissonance" which states, briefly, that when a person simultaneously holds two incompatible ideas (cognitions), dissonance occurs. This creates internal tension. Such tension is unpleasant, and the individual tries to diminish it by reducing the dissonance. This can be done by changing one idea (cognition) or the other to bring them closer together and make them more compatible.

For example, suppose one man lies to another. He knows there is a great disparity between what he believes true and what he has said. If he considers himself to be a basically truthful person, dissonance is set up. One way for him to reduce it is to rationalize—to convince himself that it wasn't such a big lie after all, and therefore closer to the truth than it seemed. This involves changing prior attitudes and beliefs. An even better technique to diminish dissonance is to justify the lie, since the amount of dissonance depends on the strength of his motives (what caused him to lie in the first place?). The greater the pressure and need to lie, the less the dissonance. For example, if he told a small lie to save a life, or to become very wealthy, he will experience little dissonance—the consequences help justify the act. "All right," he can say in effect, "so I told a lie—but it was worth it." His basic attitudes have not changed; he still sees himself as the same truthful person, adapting to exceptional circumstances.

But if he receives little or no reward for lying, he will have a great deal of dissonance, and will much more likely change his prior attitudes ("It wasn't such a big lie") to cut down the tension.

Several experiments in the last few years support this idea: people who tell a lie—say things they do not think right—and get only *small* rewards for them, undergo *greater* changes in attitude than those who tell the *same* lies for *large* rewards.

TO BEAT OR NOT TO BEAT

A few years ago (1963), Merrill Carlsmith and I applied dissonance theory to the problem of punishment, in an attempt to understand the relationship between degree of punishment and extent of attitude change. We reasoned that if you threaten to punish a person for a particular action, the more severe the threat, the greater the likelihood that he will refrain from the activity—while you are there watching him. But if you reduced the threat, you might succeed in producing a more permanent change in behavior through inducing a dislike of that activity.

For example, suppose you have a young child who likes to beat up his little brother and you want him to stop. Probably the best way to get him to stop is to threaten to hit him and hit him hard. The more severe the threat, the greater likelihood that he will stop, at that moment, *while you're watching him*. However, he may very well hit his brother again as soon as you turn your back.

But suppose instead that you threaten him with a very mild punishment—a punishment which is just barely severe enough to get him to stop aggressing at that time. In either case—under threat of severe punishment or of mild—the child is experiencing dissonance—he is aware that he is not beating up on his little brother while also aware that he wants to. When the little brother is present, the child has the urge to beat him up and, when he refrains, he asks himself in effect, "How come I'm not beating up my little brother?" Under severe threat he has a ready answer: "I know damn well why I'm not beating up my little brother. I'm not beating him up because if I do, that giant standing over there (my father) is going to knock the hell out of me." In effect, the severe threat of punishment has provided the child with justifications for not beating up his brother, *at that moment, while he's being watched*.

But consider the child in the mild threat situation; he experiences dissonance too. He asks himself, in effect, "How come I'm not beating up my little brother?" But the difference is that he doesn't have a good answer—because the threat (loss of candy, for example) was so mild that it does not provide complete justification for staying stopped. In this situation he continues to experience dissonance. There is no simple way for him to reduce it by blaming his inaction on a severe threat. He must, therefore, find reasons consonant with not hitting his little brother. He can, for instance, try to convince himself that he really doesn't like to beat his brother up, that he didn't want to do it in the first place.

In sum, Carlsmith and I suggested that one way to get a person to inhibit an activity is to get him to devalue it—and one way to get him to devalue it is to stop him in the first place with a mild threat rather than a severe one.

In our experiment, for ethical reasons, we did not try to manipulate basic values like aggression (beating up brothers). Instead, we chose a much more mundane value—toy preference. We first asked children to rate the attractiveness of several toys; then we chose one that a child considered to be quite attractive, and we told him he couldn't play with it. With one experimental group we threatened mild punishment for transgression—"I would be a little annoyed"; with the other, we threatened severe punishment—"I would be very angry. I would have to take all of my toys and go home and never come back again. I would think you were just a baby." After that, we left the room and allowed the children to play with the other toys—and perhaps to resist the temptation to play with the forbidden one. On returning to the room, we remeasured the attractiveness of all of the toys. We found that those children who were forbidden to play with a toy under a threat of mild punishment now derogated the toy. Those children under a severe threat did not derogate it.

Subsequent experiments have confirmed and extended our conclusion. In one recent experiment, Elizabeth Anne Turner and John C. Wright (1965) have confirmed our finding. In addition, they have shown clearly that derogation of the crucial toy occurs in the mild threat (high dissonance) situation in spite of a strong general tendency for children to overemphasize the attractiveness of a toy with which they have had little experience. That is, while they refrained from playing with the crucial toy, they *were* playing with other toys. The crucial toy was rated as less attractive (relative to the others) in spite of the fact that they tended to become satiated with the others. In a control situation where no threats were used, but the crucial toy was simply concealed from the children, they rated it *more* attractive than the others. Thus, not only did Turner and Wright show that a mild threat induces children to derogate the toy, they also showed that this dissonance effect is a very powerful one—powerful enough to overcome the appeal of that toy's novelty.

THE EFFECTIVE THREAT

Carlsmith and I originally reasoned that dissonance through insufficient threat of punishment would produce a long-lasting effect—because the individual *himself* was induced to derogate the activity. The child ceased playing with a toy, not because someone told him it was not fun, but because he convinced *himself* that it was not fun. But we did not design our experiment to provide for a thorough test of derogation over time. However, Jonathan L. Freedman has recently (1965) produced striking evidence confirming our speculations about the long-lasting effect of a mild threat. In his experiment, he repeated our procedure with minor changes. The crucial toy was by far the most attractive to all the children; it was one of those super-duper battery powered robots which hurls bombs against a child's enemies. The other toys were trivial by comparison. Freedman forbade the children to play with the mechanical robot, using mild threats for some and severe for others.

After some twenty-three to sixty-four days had elapsed, different experimenters came to the classroom under totally unrelated circumstances to administer a psychological test. They tested the students in the same room that was used by Freedman—the original toys were rather carelessly strewn about. After each experimenter had administered one test to a child, she told him that she would have to score it and might want to ask him some questions about it later—and while he was waiting, if he wanted to, he could amuse himself by playing with some of the toys lying around. The second experimenters, of course, did not know what part each child had played in Freedman's study.

The results were clear and exciting. Of twenty-one children under mild threat, only six played with the crucial toy; of the twenty-one under severe threat, fourteen played with it. The results are highly significant. The effect of a *single mild threat* was not only strong enough to lower the attractiveness of a preferred toy (as in the Aronson-Carlsmith experiment), it also was powerful enough to inhibit their playing with that toy as much as sixty-four days later!

The effects demonstrated in these experiments may very well apply beyond mere toy preference, to more basic and important values. For example, a parent might have more success in controlling aggressiveness in a child if he used threats of mild rather than severe punishment. By doing this, he might help the child convince himself that aggression is undesirable and so bring about a lasting change in his behavior. Studies in child development suggest clearly that parents who use severe punishment to stop a child's aggression do not succeed in curtailing it. In fact, aggressiveness in children increases directly with the severity of parental punishment. The more harshly a parent treats a child, the more aggressive he becomes, at least outside of the home.

On the other hand, although there appears to be no obvious reason why the results of these experiments cannot be replicated using more important value systems, caution is dictated in generalizing beyond the actual data until such replications are forthcoming. Moreover, the practical application of these results hinges upon the subtle problem of finding precisely the correct amount of threatened punishment—a threat which is severe enough to induce momentary compliance and yet mild enough to provide inadequate justification for that compliance. In the experiments described here, 100 percent compliance was achieved with the use of a very mild threat. My guess is that this high degree of compliance was aided by the fact that the experimenters were strangers; children are known not to comply as readily to the requests of their parents as to those of strangers.

Clearly, more research is needed before we can determine whether these techniques can bring about either a more efficient, more civilized society or an Orwellian nightmare.

Body Image– Male & Female

Richard M. Kurtz

The human body has been an object of study ever since the time of Hippocrates. Many investigators, for example, have suggested that there are connections between a person's body shape and his temperament and behavior. Thus people who tend to be fat were supposed to be phlegmatic; middle-girthed, muscular mesomorphs were supposed to be inclined toward extroversion, and to make up the majority of criminals.

But what impression do we get of our *own* bodies, and how does this affect our self-images, our feelings of worth and virility, our happiness and our behavior? In spite of the psychological importance of the answers

to such questions, very few people have ever done research in this area.

Now it seems reasonable to postulate that a person is concerned, often absorbed, with these impressions and attitudes about the appearance of his body. It also seems reasonable that he would judge these impressions along three major dimensions:

■ First, *value*. Is his body, as he sees it, a "good" or "bad" kind of body? *How* good or bad?

■ Second, *potency*. Would he consider it strong or weak, and *how* strong or weak?

■ Third, *activity*. Does he look upon himself, and his body build, as essentially an active or passive kind of body, and *how* active or passive?

These questions were put to my subjects—89 men and 80 women, all young, white college students, and most of them middle class. Using a seven-point scale, they were asked to rate themselves on 30 different body concepts, such as "size of my arms," and "color of my hair." The results were broken down according to sex, according to the general size of the subject (large, medium, small), according to the subject's general build (leptomorph—thin and narrow; mesomorph—medium muscular; eurymorph—wide and squat).

From my findings it seems plain that people—especially women—do have general, global attitudes toward their body builds, and that they do have opinions about whether their bodies are good or bad, strong or weak, active or passive.

As is evident to almost everybody, men and women are built differently, and are aware of the difference—although there is some overlap, especially these days. Women especially are aware of their distinguishing characteristics, and in considerably greater detail than men.

A person's attitudes and expectations about his body are, as a matter of fact, closely related to his sex. Our society seems far more conscious and more admiring of the female form than of the male. Judging by advertisements, for instance, it must be impossible to sell cars, Coca-cola, yens, and blood tonic unless a girl in a bathing suit goes along.

A great awareness about one's bodily appearance is obviously more acceptable in women than men—a finding supported by common observation. It is part of being a woman in our society to try to "be attractive"—to focus attention on the parts of the body that are well-proportioned and sexually stimulating, and to try to play down attention on those that are not. Men are not supposed to take such an obvious and active interest in their bodily appearances.

Women Like Their Bodies More Than Men Do

It seems logical, then, to hypothesize that a woman has a more clearly differentiated body concept than a man—that women draw finer distinctions between the qualities of parts of their figures than men do about theirs. This hypothesis turned out to be true. Consistent with this, women tend to value their bodies more than

men do; they tend to show more approval of what their full-length mirrors tell them.

This finding clearly contradicts the psychoanalytic theory that women have a lower evaluation of their bodies than men because of "penis envy." The women in this study, whatever their secret and suppressed feelings might be, and whatever the findings of other cultures, indicated that they had a *higher* evaluation of their bodies.

On the other hand, since muscular strength, aggression, and dominance are considered desirable, masculine characteristics, men should rate their bodies higher in potency than women do—and this was confirmed.

Among men the large mesomorphs—being not fat or thin, and inclined toward muscle—liked their own bodies better than all other male types did. They also thought themselves the most active. This fits in with our conventional idea of the he-man. But this picture, especially for potency, was not consistent down the line. Thus, large mesomorphs and small mesomorphs thought their bodies more potent than did any of the varieties thin men (leptomorphs). But so did the large and medium euryomorphs, the squat men—more so, in fact, than the medium mesomorphs did! These findings are tentative, and seem a little confused. But what they may indicate is that men not only associate potency with physical strength, but also with sheer bulk—reflected by a similar association, or confusion, in the English language, in which "stout" can be used to mean either fat or strong, but always means bulky.

Among women, the large, thin leptomorphs liked their bodies more than all other types liked theirs. The eurymorphs—usually broad-hipped, big-breasted—generally saw their bodies as more potent. Again, whether this self-evaluation came from an association of bulk with strength, or whether "potency" was considered symbolic of sexual or reproductive capacity in women, must be left for a future study. But however potent the fat women were, the thin women considered themselves most desirable, an opinion generally shared in our nation.

Several investigators have shown that college and non-college men and women tend to look down upon the thin and the stout in favor of the mesomorphs, to attribute more undesirable personality attributes to people with extreme body builds. In people's stereotypes, the skinny are usually pinched and mean, and the fat are usually gluttonous, unattractive, and insensitive. Do leptomorphs and eurymorphs themselves consider their body builds less desirable? The men do; but the women, as noted, do not.

Investigators seem to agree that the eurymorph—being broad and usually overweight—is basically more passive, calm, and lethargic. His opposite number—the thin, narrow leptomorph—is often characterized as active, excitable, and tense, with a faster reaction time. Logically, I expected the leptomorphs to judge themselves as more active than the eurymorphs. But this, strangely enough, was not true—for either sex.

Now, in American society it is apparent that height is related to how people feel about their bodies. Consider the demand of small men for shoes that will increase their height. In our culture, height in men, among other physical characteristics, is associated with dominance, self-confidence, and leadership. Many women admire tall men because they can look up to them. Shortness of stature is seen by most people as a liability for a man. And a large body size is seen by many as reflecting an image of dominance and strength. People of large body size are therefore assumed to be more powerful than small people.

Build and Size Differ in Relevance

Generally, this hypothesis checked out. But there were distinct and significant sexual variations. Tall, thin men put the lowest values on their bodies; tall, thin females the *highest*. And, as previously mentioned, though the large, male mesomorphs had the greatest belief in the potency of their type of body build, with women it was the large, fat eurymorphs who did. In other words, body build and body size do not have parallel relevance for men and women.

Instead of discussing all the results of this study, however, I would rather discuss what it missed—to indicate future directions for possible research.

No straightforward attitude measure can begin to reveal the complexity and richness of the feelings—conscious and unconscious—that people have about their bodies. One sure way to lose the personal and individual is to analyze central tendencies between *groups,* as has been done in this study. This may be experimentally necessary—but we should understand what we are losing. Perhaps we can restore some of this richness through depth interviews, or projective techniques.

And what of a person's attitudes and fantasies about the *inside* of his body, and its products? How does this affect his overall view of what he, and his body, are?

It is also clear that the body dimensions used in this study are not the last word in precision. Might not the actual amount of fat, and its distribution, have more meaning for a person's attitude toward his body than simply the designation of "leptomorph" or "eurymorph?" Futher, white college students 18 to 23 years old are obviously not a representative population. In this group there was little significant difference in the findings because of the age spread—but middle-aged and poor people almost certainly regard their bodies differently. The middle-aged—especially women—might well have shown greater dissatisfaction with their appearances, and lower ratings on potency and activity.

Perhaps to some extent we all live in the past. Do middle-aged people tend to see themselves as straighter, thinner, and less gray—as they were in earlier days and in old photographs? Paul Schilder has speculated that the rapid physical changes during puberty and adolescence may result in a body-concept lag, with the changing body outstripping the mind's grasp of it. Puberty usually does disturb a teenager's attitudes and impressions. Anna Freud has reported that many adolescents develop a sharp increase in puritanical and ascetic attitudes toward their bodies—perhaps indicating a lack of acceptance of the changes, and perhaps also indicating a lower evaluation of their bodies. But this was not explored in my study.

And what of race? Do Negroes have the same attitudes toward their bodies as whites have? Do many really think that black is beautiful, or have they—as Erik Erikson believes—internalized white standards to the extent of downgrading their own distinctive bodily traits? (A recent survey found that whites often consider Negroes "bad," "potent," and "passive.")

To what extent do a person's body attitudes affect—or become associated with—his other concepts about himself? Does the large, male mesomorph, the physical cock-of-the-walk, also tend to regard himself as superior in intellect, athletics, creative ability—to consider himself Abraham Maslow's all-round superior being?

This study, unfortunately, has not been able to answer these questions. It *has* demonstrated that people do have total body impressions that have important consequences. It has shown that, for the population tested, there are meaningful and often complex relationships between these attitudes and sex, body size, and body build. And perhaps it has also demonstrated that down this path of discovery—relating how people see their bodies with how they see themselves—may lie some rich field of understanding not yet explored.

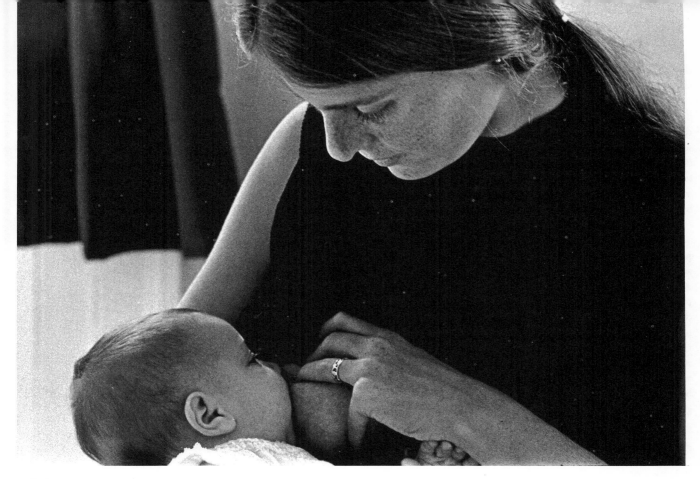

The Social Construction of the Second Sex

Jo Freeman

The passivity that is the essential characteristic of the "feminine" woman is a trait that develops in her from the earliest years. But it is wrong to assert a biological datum is concerned; it is in fact a destiny imposed upon her by her teachers and by society.

Simone de Beauvoir

During the last 30 years social science has paid scant attention to women, confining its explorations of humanity to the male. Research has generally reinforced the popular mythology that women are essentially nurturant, expressive, passive and men instrumental, active, aggressive. Social scientists have tended to justify these stereotypes rather than analyze their origins, their value or their effect.

The result of this trend has been a social science that is more a mechanism of social control than of social inquiry. Rather than trying to analyze why, it has only described what. Rather than exploring how men and women came to be the way they are, it has taken their condition as irrevocably given and sought to explain this on the basis of "biological" differences.

Nonetheless, the assumption that psychology recapitulates physiology has begun to crack. William Masters and Virginia Johnson shattered the myth of woman's natural sexual passivity—on which her psychological passivity was claimed to rest. Research is just beginning in other areas, and while evidence is being accumulated, new interpretations of the old data are being explored. What these new interpretations say is that women are the way they are because they've been trained to be that way—their motivations as well as their alternatives have been channelled by society.

This motivation is controlled through the socialization process. Women are raised to want to fill the social roles in which society needs them. They are trained to model themselves after the accepted image and to meet as individuals the expectations that are held for women as a group. Therefore, to understand how most women are socialized we must first understand how they see themselves and are seen by others. Several studies have been done on this.

One thorough study asked men and women to choose out of a long list of adjectives those that most closely applied to themselves. The results showed that women strongly felt that they could accurately be described as uncertain, anxious, nervous, hasty, careless, fearful, dull, childish, helpless, sorry, timid, clumsy, stupid, silly and domestic. On the more positive side women felt they were understanding, tender, sympathetic, pure, generous, affectionate, loving, moral, kind, grateful and patient. This is not a very favorable self-image, but it does correspond fairly well to the myths about what women are like. The image has some "nice" qualities, but they are not the ones normally required for the kinds of achievement to which society gives its highest rewards.

Gross Distortions

Now, one can justifiably question both the idea of achievement and the qualities necessary for it, but this is not the place to do so. The fact remains that these standards are widely accepted and that women have been told they do not meet them. My purpose here, then, is to look at the socialization process as a mechanism to keep them from doing so. All people are socialized to meet the social expectations held for them, and only when this process fails to work (as is currently happening on several fronts) is it at all questioned.

When we look at the *results* of female socialization we find a strong similarity between what our society labels, even extols, as the typical "feminine" character structure and that of oppressed peoples in this country and elsewhere. In his classic study on *The Nature of Prejudice*, Gordon Allport devotes a chapter to "Traits Due to Victimization." Included are such personality characteristics as sensitivity, submission, fantasies of power, desire for protection, indirectness, ingratiation, petty revenge and sabotage, sympathy, extremes of both self and group hatred and self and group glorification, display of flashy status symbols, compassion for the underprivileged, identification with the dominant group's norms and passivity. Allport was

primarily concerned with Jews and Negroes, but his characterization is disturbingly congruent with the general profile of girls that Lewis Terman and Leona Tyler draw after a very thorough review of the literature on sex differences among young children. For girls, they listed such traits as sensitivity, conformity to social pressures, response to environment, ease of social control, ingratiation, sympathy, low levels of aspiration, compassion for the underprivileged and anxiety. They found that girls compared to boys were more nervous, unstable, neurotic, socially dependent, submissive, had less self-confidence, lower opinions of themselves and of girls in general, and were more timid, emotional, ministrative, fearful and passive.

Girls' perceptions of themselves were also distorted. Although girls make consistently better school grades than boys until late high school, their opinion of themselves grows progressively worse with age and their opinion of boys and boys' abilities grows better. Boys, however, have an increasingly better opinion of themselves and worse opinion of girls as they grow older.

These distortions become so gross that, according to Phillip Goldberg in an article in this magazine, by the time girls reach college they have become prejudiced against women. He gave college girls sets of booklets containing six identical professional articles in traditional male, female and neutral fields. The articles were identical, but the names of the authors were not. For example, an article in one set would bear the name John T. McKay, and in another set the same article would be by-lined Joan T. McKay. Each booklet contained three articles by "women" and three by "men." Questions at the end of each article asked the students to rate the articles on value, persuasiveness and profundity and the authors for style and competence. The male authors fared better on every dimension, even such "feminine" areas as art history and dietetics. Goldberg concluded that "women are prejudiced against female professionals and, regardless of the actual accomplishments of these professionals, will firmly refuse to recognize them as the equals of their male colleagues."

This combination of group self-hate and a distortion of perceptions to justify that group self-hate is precisely typical of a minority group character structure. It has been noted time and time again. Kenneth and Mamie Clark's finding of the same pattern in Negro children in segregated schools contributed to the 1954 Supreme Court decision that outlawed such schools. These traits, as well as the others typical of the "feminine" stereotype, have been found in the Indians under British rule, in the Algerians under the French and in black Americans. It would seem, then, that being "feminine" is related to low social status.

This pattern repeats itself even within cultures. In giving Thematic Apperception Tests to women in Japanese villages, George De Vos discovered that those from fishing villages, where the status position of women was higher than in farming communities, were more assertive, not as guilt-ridden and were more willing to ignore the traditional pattern of arranged marriages in favor of love marriages.

In Terman's famous 50-year study of the gifted, a comparison of those men who conspicuously failed to fulfill their early promise with those who did, showed that the successful had more self-confidence, fewer background disabilities and were less nervous and emotionally unstable. But, he concluded, "the disadvantages associated with lower social home status appeared to present the outstanding handicap."

Sexual Characteristics

The fact that women do have lower social status than men in our society and that both sexes tend to value men, and male characteristics, values and activities more highly than those of women, has been noted by many authorities. What has not been done is to make the connection between this status and its accompanying personality. The failure to analyze the effects and the causes of lower social status among women is surprising in light of the many efforts that have been made to uncover distinct psychological differences between men and women to account for the tremendous disparity in their social production and creativity. The Goldberg study implies that even if women did achieve on a par with men it would not be perceived or accepted as such and that a woman's work must be of a much higher quality than that of a man to be given the same recognition. But these circumstances alone, or the fact that it is the male definition of achievement which is applied, are not sufficient to account for the relative failure of women to achieve. So research has turned to male-female differences.

Most of this research, in the Freudian tradition, has focused on finding the psychological and developmental differences supposedly inherent in feminine nature and function. Despite all these efforts, the general findings of psychological testing indicate only that individual differences are greater than sex differences. In other words, sex is just one of the many characteristics that define a human being.

An examination of the work done on intellectual differences between the sexes discloses some interesting patterns, however. First of all, the statistics themselves show some regularity. Most conclusions of what is typical of one sex or the other are founded upon the performances of two-thirds of the subjects. For example, two-thirds of all boys do better on the math section of the College Board Exam than they do on the verbal section, and two-thirds of the girls do better on the verbal than the math. Robert Bales' studies show a similar distribution when he concludes that in small groups men are the task-oriented leaders and women are the social-emotional leaders. Not all tests show this two-thirds differential, but it is the mean about which most results of the ability tests cluster. Sex is an easily visible, differentiable and testable criterion on which to draw conclusions; but it doesn't explain the one-third that do not fit. The only characteristic virtually all women seem to have in common, besides their anatomy, is their lower social status.

Secondly, girls get off to a very good start. They begin speaking, reading and counting sooner. They articulate more clearly and put words into sentences earlier. They have fewer reading and stuttering problems. Girls are even better in math in the early school years. Consistent sex differences in favor of boys do not appear until high school age. Here another pattern begins to develop.

During high school, girls' performance in school and on ability tests begins to drop, sometimes drastically. Although well over half of all high-school graduates are girls, significantly less than half of all college students are girls. Presumably, this should mean that a higher percentage of the better female students go on to higher education, but their performance vis-a-vis boys' continues to decline.

Only Men Excel

Girls start off better than boys and end up worse. This change in their performance occurs at a very significant point in time. It happens when their status changes or, to be more precise, when girls become aware of what their adult status is supposed to be. It is during adolescence that peer group pressures to be "feminine" or "masculine" increase and the conceptions of what is "feminine" and "masculine" become more narrow. It is also at this time that there is a personal drive for conformity. And one of the norms of our culture to which a girl learns to conform is that only men excel. This was evident in Beatrice Lipinski's study on *Sex-Role Conflict and Achievement Motivation in College Women* which showed that thematic pictures depicting males as central characters elicited significantly more achievement imagery than those with females in them. One need only recall Asch's experiments to see how peer group pressures, armed only with our rigid ideas about "feminity" and "masculinity" could lead to a decline in girls' performance. Asch found that some 33 percent of his subjects would go contrary to the evidence of their own senses about something as tangible as the comparative length of two lines when their judgements were at variance with those made by the other group members. All but a handful of the other 67 percent experienced tremendous trauma in trying to stick to their correct perceptions.

When we move to something as intangible as sex role behavior and to social sanctions far greater than the displeasure of a group of unknown experimental stooges we can get an idea of how stifling social expectations can be. A corollary of the notion that only men can excel is the cultural norm that a girl should not appear too smart or surpass boys in anything. Again, the pressures to conform, so prevalent in adolescence, prompt girls to believe that the development of their minds will have, only negative results. These pressures even affect the supposedly unchangeable IQ scores. Corresponding with the drive for social acceptance, girls' IQs drop below those of boys during high school, rise slightly if they go to college and go into a steady and consistent decline when and if they become full-time housewives.

These are not the only consequences. Negative self-conceptions have negative effects. They stifle motivation and channel energies into areas more likely to get some positive social rewards. The clincher comes when the very people (women) who have been subjected to these pressures are condemned for not having striven for the highest rewards society has to offer.

A good example of this double bind is what psychologists call the "need for achievement." Achievement motivation in male college sophomores has been studied extensively. In women it has barely been looked at. The reason for this is that women didn't fit the model social scientists set up to explain achievement in men. Nonetheless, some theories have been put forward which suggest that the real situation is not that women do not have achievement motivation but that this motivation is directed differently than that of men. In fact, the achievement orientation of both sexes goes precisely where it is socially directed—educational achievement for boys and marriage achievement for girls.

After considerable research on the question James Pierce concluded that "girls see that to achieve in life as adult females they need to achieve in non-academic ways, that is, attaining the social graces, achieving beauty in person and dress, finding a desirable social status, marrying the right man. This is the successful adult woman . . . Their achievement motivations are directed toward realizing personal goals through their relationship with men . . . Girls who are following the normal course of development are most likely to seek adult status through marriage at an early age."

Achievement for women is adult status through marriage, not success in the usual use of the word. One might postulate that both kinds of success might be possible, particularly for the highly achievement-oriented woman. But in fact the two are more often perceived as contradictory; success in one is seen to preclude success in the other.

Matina Horner recently completed a study at the University of Michigan from which she postulated a psychological barrier to achievement in women. She administered a test in which she asked undergraduates to complete the sentence, "After first term finals Anne finds herself at the top of her medical school class," with a story of their own. A similar one for a male control group used a masculine name. The results were scored for imagery of fear of success and Horner found that 65 percent of the women and only 10 percent of the men demonstrated a definite "motive to avoid success." She explained the results by hypothesizing that the prospect of success, or situations in which success or failure is a relevant dimension, are perceived as, and in fact do, have negative consequences for women.

While many of the choices and attitudes of woman are determined by peer and cultural pressures, many other sex differences appear too early to be much affected by peer groups and are not directly related to sex role attributes.

Analytic Children

One such sex difference is spatial perception, or the ability to visualize objects out of their context. This is a test in which boys do better, though differences are usually not discernible before the early school years. Other tests, such as the Embedded Figures and the Rod and Frame Tests, likewise favor boys. They indicate that boys perceive more analytically while girls are more contextual. Again, however, this ability to "break set" or be "field independent" also does not seem to appear until after the fourth or fifth year.

According to Eleanor Maccoby, this contextual mode of perception common to women is a distinct disadvantage for scientific production: "Girls on the average develop a somewhat different way of handling incoming information—their thinking is less analytic, more global, and more perservative [sic] —and this kind of thinking may serve very well for many kinds of functioning but it is not the kind of thinking most conducive to high-level intellectual productivity, especially in science."

Several social psychologists have postulated that the key

developmental characteristic of analytic thinking is what is called early "independence and mastery training," or as one group of researchers put it, "whether and how soon a child is encouraged to assume initiative, to take responsibility for himself, and to solve problems by himself, rather than rely on others for the direction of his activities." In other words, analytically inclined children are those who have not been subject to what Urie Bronfenbrenner calls "oversocialization," and there is a good deal of indirect evidence that such is the case. D.M. Levy has observed that "overprotected" boys tend to develop intellectually like girls. Bing found that those girls who were good at spatial tasks were those whose mothers left them alone to solve the problems by themselves while the mothers of verbally inclined daughters insisted on helping them. H.A. Witkin similarly found that mothers of analytic children had encouraged their initiative while mothers of nonanalytic children had encouraged dependence and discouraged self-assertion. One writer commented on these studies that "this is to be expected, for the independent child is less likely to accept superficial appearances of objects without exploring them for himself, while the dependent child will be afraid to reach out on his own, and will accept appearances without question. In other words, the independent child is likely to be more active, not only psychologically but physically, and the physically active child will naturally have more kinesthetic experience with spatial relationships in his environment."

The qualities associated with independence training also have an effect on IQ. I.W. Sontag did a longitudinal study in which he compared children whose IQs had improved with those whose IQs had declined with age. He discovered that the child with increasing IQ was competitive, self-assertive, independent and dominant in interaction with other children. Children with declining IQs were passive, shy and dependent.

Maccoby commented on this study that "the characteristics associated with a rising IQ are not very feminine characteristics." When one of the people working on the Sontag study was asked about what kind of developmental history was necessary to make a girl into an intellectual person, he replied, "The simplest way to put it is that she must be a tomboy at some point in her childhood."

However, analytic abilities are not the only ones that are valued in our society. Being person-oriented and contextual in perception are very valuable attributes for many fields where, nevertheless, very few women are found. Such characteristics are also valuable in the arts and some of the social sciences. But while women do succeed here more than in the sciences, their achievement is still not equivalent to that of men. One explanation of this, of course, is the study by Horner which established a "motive to avoid success" among women. But when one looks further it appears that there is an earlier cause here as well.

Sons and Daughters

The very same early independence and mastery training which has such a beneficial effect on analytic thinking also determines the extent of one's achievement orientation. Although comparative studies of parental treatment of boys and girls are not extensive, those that have been made indicate that the traditional practices applied to girls are very different from those applied to boys. Girls receive more affection, more protectiveness, more control and more restrictions. Boys are subjected to more achievement demands and higher expectations. In short, while girls are not always encouraged to be dependent per se, they are usually not encouraged to be independent and physically active. As Bronfenbrenner put it, "Such findings indicate that the differential treatment of the two sexes reflects in part a difference in goals. With sons, socialization seems to focus primarily on directing and constraining the boys' impact on the environment. With daughters, the aim is rather to protect the girl from the impact of environment. The boy is being prepared to mold his world, the girl to be molded by it."

Bronfenbrenner concludes that the crucial variable is the differential treatment by the father, and "in fact, it is the father who is especially likely to treat children of the two sexes differently." His extremes of affection and of authority are both deleterious. Not only do his high degrees of nurturance and protectiveness toward girls result in "oversocialization" but "the presence of strong paternal . . . power, is particularly debilitating. In short, boys thrive in a patriarchal context, girls in a matriarchal one."

Bronfenbrenner's observations receive indirect support from Elizabeth Douvan who noted that "part-time jobs of mothers have a beneficial effect on adolescent children, particularly daughters. This reflects the fact that adolescents may receive too much mothering."

Anxiety

The importance of mothers, as well as mothering, was pointed out by Kagan and Moss. In looking at the kinds of role models that mothers provide for developing daughters, they discovered that it is those women who are looked upon as unfeminine whose daughters tend to achieve intellectually. These mothers are "aggressive and competitive women who were critical of their daughters and presented themselves to their daughters as intellectually competitive and aggressive role models. It is reasonable to assume that the girls identified with these intellectually aggressive women who valued mastery behavior."

To sum up, there seems to be some evidence that the sexes have been differentially socialized with different training practices, for different goals and with different results. If David McClelland is right in all the relationships he finds between child-rearing practices, in particular independence and mastery training, achievement motivations scores of individuals tested, actual achievement of individuals and, indeed, the economic growth of whole societies, there is no longer much question as to why the historical achievement of women has been so low. In fact, with the dependency training they receive so early in life, the wonder is that they have achieved so much.

But this is not the whole story. Maccoby, in her discussion of the relationship of independence training to analytic abilities, notes that the girl who does not succumb to overprotection and develop the appropriate personality and behavior for her sex has a major price to pay—a price in anxiety. Some anxiety is beneficial to creative thinking, but high or sustained levels of it are damaging. Anxiety is particularly manifest in college women, and of course they are the ones who experience the most conflict between their current—intellectual—activities and expectations about their future—unintellectual—careers.

Maccoby feels that "it is this anxiety which helps to account for the lack of productivity among those women who do make intellectual careers." The combination of social pressures, role expectations and parental training together tells "something of a horror story. It would appear that even when a woman is suitably endowed intellectually and develops the right temperament and habits of thought to make use of her endowment, she must be fleet of foot indeed to scale the hurdles society has erected for her and to remain a whole and happy person while continuing to follow her intellectual bent."

The reasons for this horror story must by now be clearly evident. Traditionally, women have been defined as passive creatures, sexually, physically and mentally. Their roles have been limited to the passive, dependent, auxiliary ones, and they have been trained from birth to fit these roles. However, those qualities by which one succeeds in this society are active ones. Achievement orientation, intellectuality, analytic ability all require a certain amount of aggression.

As long as women were convinced that these qualities were beyond them, that they would be much happier if they stayed in their place, they remained quiescent under the paternalistic system of Western civilization. But paternalism was a pre-industrial scheme of life, and its yoke was partially broken by the industrial revolution. With this loosening up of the social order, the talents of women began to appear.

In the eighteenth century it was held that no woman had ever produced anything worthwhile in literature with the possible exception of Sappho. But in the first half of the nineteenth century, feminine writers of genius flooded the literary scene. It wasn't until the end of the nineteenth century that women scientists of note appeared and still later that women philosophers were found.

Lords at Home

In pre-industrial societies, the family was the basic unit of social and economic organization, and women held a significant and functional role within it. This, coupled with the high birth and death rates of those times, gave women more than enough to do within the home. It was the center of production, and women could be both at home and in the world at the same time. But the industrial revolution, along with decreased infant mortality, increased life span and changes in economic organization, has all but destroyed the family as the economic unit. Technological advances have taken men out of the home, and now those functions traditionally defined as female are being taken out also. For the first time in human history women have had to devote themselves to being full-time mothers in order to have enough to do.

Conceptions of society have also changed. At one time, authoritiarian hierarchies were the norm, and paternalism was reflective of a general social authoritarian attitude. While it is impossible to do retroactive studies on feudalistic society, we do know that authoritarianism as a personality trait does correlate strongly with a rigid conception of sex roles, and with ethnocentrism. We also know from ethnological data that, As W.N. Stephens wrote, there is a "parallel between family relationships and the larger social hierarchy. Autocratic societies have autocratic families. As the king rules his subjects and the nobles subjugate and exploit the commoners, so does husband tend to lord it over wife, father rule over son."

According to Roy D'Andrade, "another variable that appears to affect the distribution of authority and deference between the sexes is the degree to which men rather than women control and mediate property." He presented evidence that showed a direct correlation between the extent to which inheritance, succession and descent-group membership were patrilineal and the degree of subjection of women.

Even today, the equality of the sexes in the family is often reflective of the economic quality of the partners. In a Detroit sample, Robert Blood and D.M. Wolfe found that the relative power of the wife was low if she did not work and increased with her economic contribution to the family. "The employment of women affects the power structure of the family by equalizing the resources of husband and wife. A working wife's husband listens to her more, and she listens to herself more. She expresses herself and has more opinions. Instead of looking up into her husband's eyes and worshipping him, she levels with him, compromising on the issues at hand. Thus her power increases and, relatively speaking, the husband's falls."

William J. Goode also noted this pattern but said it varied inversely with class status. Toward the upper strata wives are not only less likely to work but when they do they contribute a smaller percentage of the total family income than is true in the lower classes. Reuben Hill went so far as to say "Money is a source of power that supports male dominance in the family . . . Money belongs to him who earns it not to her who spends it, since he who earns it may withhold it." Phyllis Hallenbeck feels more than just economic resources are involved but does conclude that there is a balance of power in every family which affects "every other aspect of the marriage—division of labor, amount of adaptation necessary for either spouse, methods used to resolve conflicts, and so forth." Blood feels the economic situation affects the whole family structure. "Daughters of working mothers are more independent, more self-reliant, more aggressive, more dominant, and more disobedient. Such girls are no longer meek, mild, submissive, and feminine like 'little ladies' ought to be. They are rough and tough, actively express their ideas, and refuse to take anything from anybody else . . . Because their mothers have set an example, the daughters get up the courage and the desire to earn money as well. They take more part-time jobs after school and more jobs during summer vacation."

Sex and Work

Herbert Barry, M.K. Bacon and Irvin Child did an ethno-historiographic analysis which provides some further insights into the origins of male dominance. After examining the ethnographic reports of 110 cultures, they concluded that large sexual differentiation and male superiority occur concurrently and in "an economy that places a high premium on the superior strength and superior development of motor skills requiring strength, which characterize the male." It is those societies in which great physical strength and mobility are required for survival, in which hunting and herding, or warfare, play an important role, that the male, as the physically stronger and more mobile sex, tends to dominate.

Although there are a few tasks which virtually every society assigns only to men or women, there is a great deal of overlap for most jobs. Virtually every task, even in the most primitive societies, can be performed by either men or women. Equally important, what is defined as a man's task in one society may well be classified as a woman's job in another. Nonetheless, the sexual division of labor is much more narrow than dictated by physical limitations, and what any one culture defines as a woman's job will seldom be performed by a man and vice versa. It seems that what originated as a division of labor based upon the necessities of survival has spilled over into many other areas and lasted long past the time of its social value. Where male strength and mobility have been crucial to social survival, male dominance and the aura of male superiority have been the strongest. The latter has been incorporated into the value structure and attained an existence of its own.

Thus, male superiority has not ceased with an end to the need for male strength. As Goode pointed out, there is one consistent element in the assignment of jobs to the sexes, even in modern societies: "Whatever the strictly male tasks are, they are defined as *more honorific* [emphasis his] . . .Moreover, the tasks of control, management, decision, appeals to the gods—in short the higher level jobs that typically do not require strength, speed or traveling far from home—are male jobs."

He goes on to comment that "this element suggests that the sexual divisions of labor within family and society, come perilously close to the racial or caste restrictions in some modern countries. That is, the low-ranking race, caste, or sex is defined as not being able to do certain types of prestigious work, but it is also considered a violation of propriety if they do. Obviously, if women really cannot do various kinds of male tasks, no moral or ethical prohibition would be necessary to keep them from it."

Companionship

These sex role differences may have served a natural function at one time, but it is doubtful that they still do so.

The characteristics we observe in women and men today are a result of socialization practices developed for the survival of a primitive society. The value structure of male superiority is a reflection of the primitive orientations and values. But social and economic conditions have changed drastically since these values were developed. Technology has reduced to almost nothing the importance of muscular strength. In fact, the warlike attitude that goes along with an idealization of physical strength and dominance is coming to be seen as dreadfully dangerous. The value of large families has also come to be questioned. The result of all these changes is that the traditional sex roles and the traditional family structures have become dysfunctional.

To some extent, patterns of child rearing have also changed. Bronfenbrenner reports that at least middle-class parents are raising both boys and girls much the same. He noted that over a 50-year period middle-class parents have been developing a "more acceptant, equalitarian relationship with their children." With an increase in the family's social position, the patterns of parental treatment of children begin to converge. He likewise noted that a similar phenomenon is beginning to develop in lower-class parents and that equality of treatment is slowly working its way down the social ladder.

These changes in patterns of child rearing correlate with changes in relationships within the family. Both are moving toward a less hierarchical and more egalitarian pattern of living. As Blood has pointed out, "today we may be on the verge of a new phase in American family history, when the companionship family is beginning to manifest itself. One distinguishing characteristic of this family is the dual employment of husband and wife . . . Employment emancipates women from domination by their husbands and, secondarily, raises their daughters from inferiority to their brothers . . . The classic differences between masculinity and femininity are disappearing as both sexes in the adult generation take on the same roles in the labor market . . . The roles of men and women are converging for both adults and children. As a result the family will be far less segregated internally, far less stratified into different age generations and different sexes. The old asymmetry of male dominated, female-serviced family life is being replaced by a new symmetry."

Leftover Definitions

All these data indicate that several trends are converging at about the same time. Our value structure has changed from an authoritarian one to a more democratic one, though our social structure has not yet caught up. Social attitudes begin in the family; only a democratic family can raise children to be citizens in a democratic society. The social and economic organization of society which kept women in the home has likewise changed. The home is no longer the center of society. The primary male and female functions have left it, and there is no longer any major reason for maintaining the large sex role differentiations that the home supported. The value placed on physical strength, which reinforced the dominance of men, and the male superiority attitudes that this generated have also become dysfunctional. It is the mind, not the body, that society needs now, and woman's mind is the equal of man's. The pill has liberated women from the uncertainty of childbearing, and with it the necessity of being attached to a man for economic support. But our attitudes toward women, and toward the family, have not changed. There is a distinct "cultural lag." Definitions of the family, conceptions of women and ideas about social function are left over from an era when they were necessary for social survival. They have persisted into an era in which they are no longer viable. The result can only be called severe role dysfunctionality for women.

The necessary relief for this dysfunctionality must come through changes in the social and economic organization of society and in social attitudes that will permit women to play a full and equal part in the social order. With this must come changes in the family, so that men and women are not only equal but can raise their children in a democratic atmosphere. These changes will not come easily, nor will they come through the simple evolution of social trends. Trends do not move all in the same direction or at the same rate. To the extent that changes are dysfunctional with each other they create problems. These problems will be solved not by complacency but by conscious human direction. Only in this way can we have a real say in the shape of our future and the shape of our lives.

Testing Masculinity in Boys without Fathers

Allan G. Barclay and D.R. Cusumano

For many years, psychiatrists and psychologists have suspected that the boy who grows up with no father or father-figure at home may not be able to establish a firm masculine identity. Without a man around the house, goes the reasoning, a boy will have no model to emulate in developing masculine patterns of behavior. Instead, he will emulate the only adult model he has—his mother—and thus have the problem of feminine, "cross-sex," identification.

But how can we tell whether this predicted problem really occurs? To the casual observer, most adolescent boys from fatherless homes seem just as masculine as other boys.

To find out whether "father-absent" boys really tend to be less masculine than other boys, we must first decide that some behavior indicates masculinity, then measure the prevalence of that behavior among the two groups of boys. In a study we conducted, we chose what psychologists call "field-independent" behavior as our main measure of masculinity.

"Field-dependency" refers to the extent to which a person's perceptions are, or are not, influenced by his surrounding environment. One measure of field-dependency is the rod-and-frame test. The subject sits in a darkened room and faces a luminous rod inside a luminous frame. Both the rod and frame are tilted. The subject's task is to adjust the rod to a vertical position, vertical *not* to the tilted frame but to himself and to the rest of the room. Those who succeed, those who are autonomous enough to resist the influence of the tilted frame, are said to be field-independent. Those who cannot set the rod straight, who *are* influenced by the tilted frame, are field dependent.

A person's performance on the rod-and-frame test seems closely tied to traditional ideas of masculinity and femininity. The field-independent people tend to be analytic and aggressive—in short, rather masculine. The field-dependent people tend to be more passive—and thus more feminine. Field-independent people are the enterprising ones who make things happen; field-dependent people are the ones things happen *to*.

Now, a perceptual test of this sort should tap a very basic orientation—one formed very early in life and carefully hidden beneath later layers of consciously-acquired masculine behavior. So, if our theory is correct, father-absent boys should show high scores for field-dependency.

To find out whether fatherless boys would, in fact, display an overtly masculine identity combined with a deeply-buried feminine identity, we took 20 Negro high-school boys and 20 white high-school boys and gave them three tests.

The 40 boys were divided into two groups: 20 (10 of each race) who came from homes in which the father had been absent since the subject was 5; and 20 (also equally divided) who had had fathers at home while they were growing up.

The first two tests were straightforward measures of overt masculinity—they were based on the boys' own description of themselves and their interests. The Gough Femininity Scale, part of the California Psychological Inventory, measures interest patterns. It focuses on the difference between traditionally masculine interests (such as hunting and body-contact sports) and feminine pastimes (such as cooking). On this first test, both groups of boys showed a similar number of overtly masculine interests.

Then came a semantic-differential test. The subjects were asked to rate themselves, their fathers, and their mothers on a series of 24 adjective pairs that had definite sex-role connotations—active or passive, rugged or delicate, dominant or submissive, and similar pairs. These psychological profiles of fathers, mothers, and sons were then compared, to see whether the subject thought he was more like his father or like his mother. Again, both groups of boys clearly identified themselves with their fathers.

The fact that boys with fathers and boys without fathers both scored about the same on these two preliminary measures of masculinity fits in with what we would expect to find from casual observation—that both groups *seem* about equally interested in football, cars, girls, and other traditional pursuits of the American male adolescent. But we should keep in mind that these tests are not difficult to fake, consciously or unconsciously. The interests listed in the first test, and the adjectives listed in the second, have rather obvious connections with masculinity or femininity —so the boy worried about his own masculinity may try to give answers that will *appear* as masculine as possible. These tests may reveal the boy not as he is, but as he would *like* to be. And his daily behavior may reflect the same pose.

The rod-and-frame test administered next was an attempt to get beneath this he-man facade and tap a boy's true orientation. In this test, the relation of the task to sex-role identification is *not* obvious. What's more, even if the subject knew what the "masculine" response would be, he would have a hard time giving it (setting the rod vertical) if his perceptions really were distorted by the tilting frame.

Each subject tried to adjust the rod to a vertical position eight times—four times with the frame tilted 28 degrees to the left and four with it tilted 28 degrees to the right. Each time, we recorded the number of degrees the rod deviated from perfect vertical. Then we averaged all eight trial scores together to get a mean response. A high score would indicate a field-dependent, feminine orientation, while a low score would indicate a field-independent, masculine orientation.

The "father-absent" boys made *higher, more field-dependent, and hence more feminine,* scores than the boys with fathers.

Interpreting the results of these experiments, we arrive at conclusions that confirm our original hypothesis: Boys who lack a father in the home are likely to be confused about their sexual identity. The fact that father-absent boys appeared just as masculine as the others on the preliminary, superficial tests of sexual identity can be viewed as evidence of a compensatory drive toward hyper-masculinity in this group. They develop exaggeratedly masculine interests and characteristics in the effort to compensate for what they sense to be missing. The results of the rod-and-frame test bear out this interpretation. This more probing test would

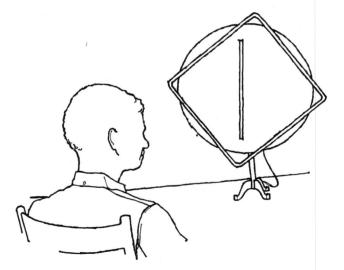

The Passive Negro Boy

Surprisingly, the Negro boys in our study made significantly higher, more field-dependent scores than the white boys. How can we account for this finding?

Of course, more Negroes than whites live in female-headed households, without a full-time husband and father. Thus more Negro boys than white fall into the "father-absent" category. But in this study, the number of Negro and white boys with and without fathers was the same, and the Negroes *still* came out with higher, more feminine scores.

One possible answer: The much-discussed "demasculinization" of the Negro male may begin very early in life. And it may be caused by very general features of the Negro subculture that will touch a boy whether he has a father at home or not. Here the concept of field-dependency is especially relevant. At the core of field-dependent orientation is passivity. Most Negro boys—that vast majority who do *not* grow up to be militant black-power activists—may well grow up with the feeling that any real initiative on their part is wasted effort. They can't change the system, they may feel, so why fight it?

This lack of interest in practical, goal-directed action is why observers have labeled Negro culture "expressive" (in contrast with "instrumental," or goal-directed behavior).

seem to give a more accurate picture of the subject than the first two tests.

Our conclusions are in agreement with the results of other studies. J.H. Rohrer and M.S. Edmonson discovered that when boys raised solely by women are forced into competition with other males, they tend to employ rather feminine tactics.

In another particularly intriguing piece of research, Rohrer and Edmonson found that the fantasies of father-absent boys have many feminine qualities. A father-absent boy might be less likely to dream of *making* a million dollars than of having the money simply fall into his lap. He would dream not of becoming a great industrial tycoon, but of holding a winning lottery ticket, being befriended by a wealthy benefactor, or being left a fortune by a distant relative. Clearly, there is a similarity between this sort of passive fantasy and the passivity that marks field-dependent behavior.

In sum, boys from fatherless homes may try to cover up their sex-role confusion by a compulsive denial of anything that smacks of femininity. They may make a football jersey or a motorcycling jacket into a cloak of masculinity. But the experimental evidence of our study, and of the other research just mentioned, points firmly to one conclusion—that these boys do tend to relate to their surroundings in the passive way that our society has, at least until now, considered typically feminine.

During socialization, as we have seen in Part One, we develop systems of basic beliefs and attitudes. These beliefs and attitudes govern much of our behavior and serve to integrate our perception of the world we live in. Just as our own attitudes bring order to our existence, the knowledge of another's attitudes gives us considerable accuracy in predicting how he will react and behave in given situations. However, in much the same way that socialization is a continuing process of change and development, the formation, maintenance and modification of attitudes are dynamic, ongoing phenomena in every individual. We speak of attitude and belief "systems" because individual attitudes exist not in isolation but rather in interaction with other elements of a person's cognitive world. Our attitudes about politicians and political parties, for example, cannot exist independent of our beliefs about civil liberties, law and order, and welfare. New information is processed, accepted or rejected as a function of its congruence or incongruence with existing attitudes and beliefs.

Most social psychologists accept the theoretical notion that there is a tendency toward cognitive consistency among humans (see, for example, Aronson's essay in Part One). This striving for consistency leads us to accept more readily that information which is consistent with existing attitudes than that which is at variance. As a result, the modification of attitudes is not the relatively simple task of changing a single element but rather one of altering the relationships among a number of related attitudes. Research has shown that the change of one attitude results in the compensatory modification of related attitudes. Because of this, for a person to modify an attitude, means that he must undergo a difficult and painful reassessment. Thus, considerable resistance to the change of established attitudes is a normal and inevitable characteristic of our cognitive universe. While the reluctance to

Part Two

Beliefs, Attitudes, and Conversion

maintaining and changing one's values

change attitudes causes us to see others as stubborn, pig-headed and impervious to logic, it also enables us to achieve considerable success in forecasting others' reactions.

Nevertheless, attitudes and beliefs do change. Moreover, much of our life is devoted to attempts to alter the attitudes of those around us. On a subtle level, education can be seen in part as a process of attitude formation and modification. At the other extreme, advertising and political campaigning represent overt (and sometimes blatant) attempts to manipulate attitudes. World leaders and ordinary citizens alike are concerned with the process of attitude change and often experiment with techniques for producing it. Although much practical and theoretical knowledge has been gained, the unknown still looms larger than the known, suggesting that the study of attitude change will undoubtedly remain a central topic in social psychology.

The levels of attitude change are many. At the deepest level a person can dramatically alter his fundamental outlooks and behaviors. Such a deep and abiding change can best be described as a *conversion* experience. In conversion, not just one but a constellation of attitudes important to the individual undergo significant alteration. Conversion is often thought of in terms of the sudden espousal of deep religious belief, but it also frequently involves commitment to a political or social movement. What is characteristic of all conversion experiences is that the individual becomes resocialized into the ways of a movement—a process which can involve a dramatic reorganization of life style and personal relationships. Examples of such dramatic conversions abound in modern society; consider the swinging skeptic who suddenly embraces a conservative religious movement, the apolitical student who becomes radicalized, the career army officer who becomes an avid peace demonstrator.

The essays in Part Two deal with a variety of beliefs and attitudes. They consider the structure and function of attitudes and attitude systems as well as the processes and results of change. Milton Rokeach provides an excellent introduction by describing four types of beliefs held by people: A) *primitive beliefs* about the nature of reality; B) *beliefs based on deep personal experience;* C) *beliefs accepted from authorities;* and D) *peripheral beliefs* derived from authorities; and E) *inconsequential beliefs*. Rokeach discusses the relative difficulty in changing the various types of beliefs and describes the approaches of advertisers to belief modification.

Approaching attitude systems from another angle, Bennett Berger next examines hippie morality. He concludes that the moral system attributed to hippie culture represents neither the development of a new code of values nor the collapse of conventional ethics. He sees it rather as a restatement of many long-held beliefs. The fact that a minority of individuals restating and reliving a set of long-standing beliefs can focus and polarize opinions shows that, when a number of people share beliefs which deviate from those of the majority, this deviation can be perceived as a threat to the existence of the dominant group. Such perceptions foster the development of prejudice, which will be examined in Part Five (see especially the essay on "The Condemnation and Persecution of Hippies" for a discussion of prejudice against that group).

Arthur Berger next contrasts attitudes in two cultures—Italian and American. His methodological approach consists of inferring the values of a culture from an examination of the content of its popular media. Looking at the themes found in Italian and American comic strips, Berger found that Italian comics show a much greater deference for established authority than do American comics. Berger's technique of diagnosing the norms of a group from the content of its media has been applied to a number of cultures and societies, where it has provided useful insights into the concerns and standards of diverse populations.

Rita Simon presents an experimental study of the effects of media publicity on judgments of guilt and innocence. The influence of TV, radio and newspaper publicity on the ability of a defendant to receive a fair trial from an unbiased jury has been hotly debated recently, during a time of sensational trials with political overtones. Simon's findings are reassuring as she concludes that, although sensational publicity does indeed prejudice opinions, these opinions are reversible under conditions where individuals are instructed to consider only objective evidence. However, before dismissing this issue as resolved, we must remember that one cannot conclude that the results of a particular laboratory investigation accurately reflect the conditions prevailing in the more complex environment of everyday life.

Flying saucer cultists who accept the notion that the earth is visited by unidentified flying objects and who belong to clubs composed of believers are subjected to scrutiny by H. Taylor Buckner. Through studying those who share such a deviant belief, we gain insight into the functional value of belief systems. Those who belong to flying saucer clubs tend to be old, alone and seeking some form of escape. Belief and participation in the broad activities of such an organization provide excitement and hope for many whose lives would otherwise contain neither.

The last three essays in this section deal generally with conversion experiences and describe the predisposition and reactions of those committing themselves to a militant social or religious group. Two common threads run through all the descriptions of conversion: that dedication to a movement involves the reorganization of many attitudes and behavior patterns, and that members of groups can and must provide strong social support for each other in order to maintain commitment to the goals of the movement—especially in the face of hostile outsiders.

Robert Coles gives a very personal description of his involvement in the civil rights movement of the sixties. From an initial research orientation, Coles became an active and effective worker in the field. He describes the stresses and frustrations which accompany attempts to change the behavior and values of a society. John Howard reports the characteristics and experiences of those who adopt the Black Muslim religion. The faith offers an ascetic and productive way of life to its members, proclaims a dogma of hope for a better future with black superiority and provides strong social support for its members.

Finally, Anita Micossi discusses conversion to the women's liberation movement. The attitudes of American society in general and typical socialization practices (described in Freeman's Part One essay) result in an unequal and often inferior status for women. These pressures can result in women accepting the notion of inferiority and sharing the societal stereotype (as shown by Philip Goldberg in Part Five). Micossi presents the backgrounds of women who have rejected the societal view of the female and who are working for equality. As with other social movements, efforts are directed toward changing the attitudes and behavior of others and toward the resocialization of converts. Like Black Muslims, members of women's liberation groups provide social support for one another in the face of hostile outsiders.

The concept of attitude is the most central aspect of social psychology. Each of the essays in this Part illustrates the importance of attitude systems for the individual and the social pressures which can reinforce or modify beliefs. Although the studies presented here are grouped under the heading of beliefs and attitudes, in a broader sense all of the essays in this book could be classified as studies of attitudes and behavior.

The Consumer's Changing Image

Milton Rokeach

Advertisers are not the only ones who try to shape and change beliefs, attitudes and behavior of others into forms more congenial for themselves. Many people—professionals and non-professionals, idealists and angle-shooters, working for pay or for love—are fascinated by the theory and practice of influencing others. Psychotherapists, teachers, missionaries, politicians, salesmen, lobbyists, con-men, parents, and wives all qualify by this definition.

But this does not mean that the advertising man

wants to change the same kinds of beliefs as, say, the therapist or politician. Every human being has many different sorts of beliefs, and every advanced society seems to have encouraged the growth of different kinds of persuaders who specialize in trying to change some beliefs and not others. Like the go-getting salesman in "The Music Man" you have to know the territory, and what you want to accomplish.

We have thus far isolated five kinds of beliefs in our work at Michigan State University. This work is part of a larger, ongoing program of research extending over the past decade on the nature of man's systems of belief, how such systems are formed, organized, and modified, and how they differ from one person to the next.

The five kinds of beliefs may be represented by five concentric circles with the key beliefs at the center and the more inconsequential along the outer circle. To help keep track of them let me call the innermost beliefs Type A, which is then followed by Type B, and so on, until we get to Type E along the outside circle.

Primitive Beliefs

At the core are Type A — primitive — beliefs. These we all share with one another about the nature of physical reality, social reality and the self. For example, *I believe I am working at a typewriter. I believe my name is Milton Rokeach.* I hope nobody answers that if I believe these statements I'll believe anything, because I might become very disturbed about his sanity. And worse, if several people were to genuinely challenge these beliefs, I might become even more disturbed about my own sanity.

Type A beliefs are fundamental, taken for granted axioms which are not subject to controversy because we believe them implicitly—and believe that everyone else believes them. Our evidence shows that they are more resistant to change than any other type of belief—and that we become extremely upset when they are brought into serious question. Nothing would shake our world more thoroughly for instance than doubt about our very identity. Therefore, at the risk of sounding dog-

matic, I hope there is not too much argument on the matter: I *am* Milton Rokeach.

Beliefs of Deep Personal Experience

A second kind of primitive belief—Type B—is also extremely resistant to change though it does not depend on social support or consensus. Instead it arises from deep personal experience. Type B beliefs are incontrovertible, and we believe them regardless of whether anyone else believes them. Many of these unshakeable beliefs about ourselves and some of these self-conceptions are positive ones —Type B+—and some are negative—Type B—. The positive ones represent complimentary beliefs about what we are and can do, and the negative ones represent beliefs about our fears and anxieties, so deeply felt that we believe then without question.

Regardless of what others may think, and may even be unkind enough to tell us, we usually believe ourselves fundamentally intelligent and rational, able and competent, kind and charitable. If we do not always believe ourselves overwhelmingly benign —we have mirrors, most of us—we usually are nevertheless sure that there is at least some quality of grace or charm—the golden gleam of sterling worth shining however dimly in our eyes—which makes us *attractive* to ourselves and others, whatever that may mean. Type B+ beliefs represent our positive self-images—and guide our ambitions and resolves to become even better, greater, wiser, and nobler than we already are.

But many of us also have the Type B— beliefs— negative self-conceptions—which we also cling to regardless of whether others may agree with us. We are often beset by phobias, compulsions, and obsessions. We have neurotic doubts and anxieties about self-worth, self-identity, and self-competence. These are the kinds of primitive beliefs which we wish we were rid of, and it is these Type B— beliefs which the psychotherapist is often asked to change. Other specialized persuaders are generally not trained or interested in changing Type B— beliefs—though they may be interested in exploiting them.

Authority Beliefs

A third kind of belief—Type C—we call authority beliefs—beliefs that we all have about which authorities to accept and trust and which not to trust. Many facts of physical and social reality have alternative interpretations, are socially controversial, or are not capable of being personally verified or experienced. All men need to identify with authorities who will help them to decide what is good or bad, true or untrue, sanctified or evil—what to believe and what not to believe. Is Communism good or bad? Is there a God or isn't there? How do we know the French Revolution actually took place? Who told us? What about evolution?

No man can personally ascertain all truth, so he believes in his parents, teachers, priests, political leaders, scientists or whoever—and he will often take their word for many things. Each of us decides which authorities are trustworthy and which are not, and we look to those we believe in for information about what is (and is not) true and beautiful, and good for us.

Peripheral Beliefs

A fourth kind of belief—Type D—we call peripheral beliefs, *derived* from the authorities we identify with. For example, a devout Catholic has certain beliefs about birth control and divorce because he has taken them over from his prime authority. I believe Jupiter has 12 moons not because I have seen them but because I trust authorities who have seen them. I am prepared to change my belief about Jupiter's moons when the authorities I trust change their teachings. If they became discredited, or were replaced, I might change my authorities—or beliefs —accordingly.

Inconsequential Beliefs

Finally, there is a fifth class—Type E—which I call inconsequential beliefs. If they change, the total system is not altered in any significant way. I believe that I can get a better shave from one brand of razor blade than another; that a vacation at the beach is more enjoyable than one in the mountains; that Sophia Loren is prettier than Elizabeth Taylor. If you undermine those beliefs, however, it doesn't neccessarily follow that I will have a nervous breakdown, or take to drink, or convert to Zen Buddhism. I might actually be better off for changing to another brand of razor blades, and be grateful that you persuaded me. As for the change to Elizabeth Taylor—under present circumstances that too is, alas, inconsequential.

Types of Beliefs	Definition	Examples
Type A Primitive Beliefs	A belief which is uncontroversial because everyone in a position to know believes it too.	I believe this is a typewriter. I believe the sun rises in the east. I believe my name is Milton Rokeach.
Type B+ Primitive Beliefs	A belief which is uncontroversial because I continue to believe it regardless of what others may think.	I believe I am intelligent. I believe I am rational. I believe I am a kind person.
Type B—		I believe I am abnormal. I believe others cannot be trusted. I believe I am no good.
Type C Authority Beliefs	Beliefs about which authorities can and cannot be trusted.	The Church, the President, Einstein, scientists, parents, and the like.
Type D Peripheral Beliefs	Beliefs which are derived from authority.	I believe divorce is immoral. I believe Jupiter has twelve moons.
Type E Inconsequential beliefs	Beliefs which, if changed, leave other beliefs unaffected.	I believe a vacation at the beach is more enjoyable than one in the mountains. I believe Sophia Loren is prettier than Elizabeth Taylor.

To briefly summarize: every person's total system of beliefs ranges in importance from the inconsequential, through the peripheral, to authority beliefs and, finally, at the core, to primitive beliefs which are extremely resistant to change because they do not at all depend on social support—or because, paradoxically, they enjoy universal social support. All these kinds of beliefs, considered together, are organized into a remarkable piece of architecture—the belief *system*. It has definable content and definable structure. And it has a job to do: it helps the individual adjust and survive by building up his positive self-image and minimizing his negative self-image. Every person has a need to know himself and his world as much as possible—and also, when necessary, a need *not* to know himself and his world. The total belief system must serve both functions simultaneously.

Changing Beliefs

What objective evidence is there that these five kinds of beliefs really exist? The best evidence—acquired in collaboration with my colleagues Dr. Joseph Reyher and Dr. Richard Wiseman at Michigan State University—comes from a study in which we tried to change these beliefs through hypnotic suggestion. The results obtained are quite clear. All five kinds changed under hypnosis. But, as expected, the amount of change varied with centrality. The primitive beliefs—Types A and B—changed the least; beliefs about authority—Type C—changed more; peripheral beliefs—Type D—changed yet more; and inconsequential beliefs — Type E—changed the most.

The results also show that beliefs are interdependent: changing one leads to changes in others. Changes in Types A and B exerted the greatest effects; changes in Type C beliefs exerted less; changes in Type D exerted even less; and, finally, changing Type E, the ones most easy to change, had the least effect on other beliefs.

Now we can obtain a clearer picture of what society's specialized persuaders are trying to do. As far as I know none of them are trying to change Type A, the most central and fundamental kind of belief. But, as noted, the professional psychotherapist tries to change the second kind of primitive belief. The psychotherapist wants to help rid us of

negative self-conceptions—Type B– beliefs—and to strengthen positive self-conceptions — Type B+ beliefs.

What kind of beliefs are other specialized persuaders—the political and religious partisans and ideologists of various stripes—mostly concerned with? I suggest that they focus mainly on Type C and Type D—authority and peripheral beliefs.

Psychologically, where the purpose of the advertising man has been to meet competition, he has concentrated on Type E—inconsequential—beliefs; where his primary purpose has been to give information, he has concentrated on Type D—peripheral—beliefs. *The more competitive the advertising the more it addresses itself to the psychologically inconsequential beliefs about the relative merits of different brands.*

Unique Characters

Some interesting implications follow. Not the least of the reasons for the peculiar problems and embarrassments of advertising—those even beyond the exorcising powers of liquor and psychoanalysis —comes from the great disparity between the minor consequence (to the consumer) of the beliefs advertising men must alter, and the great economic consequence (to the advertisers) that they be altered. It is difficult for the advertising man, psychologically, to keep much of a "positive self-image" when most of his talents, labors, and time are earnestly devoted to trying to convince housewives that one brand of paper tissue is "better" than another. On the other hand, an advertising man can often acquire real evangelistic zeal merely by contemplating the economic consequences to himself, his client, and his company if he does *not* so convince the housewife. Enter the ulcer and the couch. Enter also the highly organized and persuasive rationalizations by which advertising men justify their calling.

True enough, inconsequential beliefs are generally easier to change than other kinds—but this does not mean that the consumer will sit still and let someone change them for him. We resist changing *all* our beliefs because we gain comfort in clinging to the familiar; and because our total beliefs, as suggested, serve highly important functions for

36

us. So the advertising man, while he has a certain advantage over those persuaders who specialize on central beliefs, still must find economical ways to change the "less consequential." He may try to do this by trying to convince the innocent consumer that the advantages to be gained by changing brands *are* important ("the difference *does* make a difference") and that *deeper,* more central beliefs and needs will thereby be satisfied. The advertising industry has often been successful at this—sometimes "miraculously" so.

The Advertiser's Goal

How do advertising men do this? Mostly by implying that the inconsequential beliefs and the consequential are really dependent on each other. Theoretically it is possible to associate inconsequential beliefs with even the most central and vital beliefs and needs (Pavlov's dogs came to "believe" that a ringing bell meant food, so when the bell rang they salivated) but the advertising industry does not use all these combinations with equal frequency. The most common associations are those between the inconsequential (Type E) and the authority beliefs (Type C)—as in testimonials—and between the inconsequential (Type E) and primitive beliefs (Type B—).

"Body Odor!" the old Lifebuoy ads shouted, and the psychologically insecure and inadequate immediately became uncomfortable and apprehensive. If they detected nothing else they did smell their own primtive fears, guilt-feelings, and insecurities. Modern, more sophisticated ads do it more gently: they urge ladies worried about looking insufficiently feminine to "dream" of appearing in public without their blouses—an embarrassment from which a Maidenform Bra stands ready to rescue them with glory.

Why should these combinations—inconsequential and authority beliefs, inconsequential and primitive beliefs—come up more often than other possibilities? I suspect it is because the advertising industry has been heavily influenced by two theories in psychology—behaviorism and psychoanalysis—having in common an image of man as a fundamentally irrational creature, helplessly pushed around on the one hand by guilt, anxiety, self-doubt, and other neurotic self-conceptions (B- beliefs); and on the other hand the unresisting victim of external stimuli which, through reward and punishment, condition him to form arbitrary associations.

Advertising has borrowed from psychoanalysis its laws of association, and from behaviorism its principles of conditioning. Psychoanalyisis tells what to associate with what, and behaviorism tells how to stamp it in. I suggest that it is because the advertising profession believes in the image of irrational man that the inconsequential beliefs have been so often associated with the authority beliefs and with the primitive beliefs. In doing so, advertisers have been roundly criticized—to my mind with justice—for a style of advertising which encourages conformity, which is exploitative, debasing, lacking in taste, and insulting to the dignity of man.

Given the facts of our industrial society and given what Harry C. Groome, writing in the *Saturday Review,* has called the *inevitability* of advertising, the advertising man's general strategy of associating the psychologically inconsequential with the consequential is probably the only one open to him. But it is now possible at least to explore systematically the other combinations to see where they might lead. What would an ad look like which tried to associate an inconsequential belief with a primitive belief which we all share—a Type A belief?

Water Off a Duck's Back

I recall having seen only one example of such an advertisement—it caught my eye as no advertisement has in many years. It is an advertisement for *London Fog*: "How to keep water off a duck's back," appearing in *The New Yorker*, September 7, 1963, p. 138, showing a duck wearing a *London Fog* raincoat. Children especially seem to find great delight in this picture. Here we see an inconsequential belief about a particular brand of raincoat associated with a primitive physical belief about the fundamental nature of a certain animal—a duck. Our primitive belief about the stark-naked duck is momentarily violated; our sanity is threatened and it is virtually impossible to turn away from the ad until belief is somehow re-established or restored to its original state. In the process the viewer is entertained and *London Fog* gains attention. Whether *London Fog* also gains customers of course remains to be seen.

Similarly, the television program *Candid Camera* often entertains mass audiences by having them watch what happens when there is a momentary disruption of a person's primitive beliefs about physical and social reality. I am rather surprised that the advertising industry has not consciously applied some of the *Candid Camera* ideas for its own uses.

Many psychological considerations favor increasing emphasis on associating inconsequential beliefs and the *positive* conceptions we strive to have of ourselves—Type B+.

Since World War II an increasing number of distinguished psychologists have revolted against the image of Irrational Man built by behaviorism and classical psychoanalysis. Contemporary psychoanalysts talk more and more about man's freedom of choice—the conflict-free sphere of ego functioning. The Gestalt psychologists have emphasized for a long time man's search for meaning, understanding, and organization; Carl Rogers has described the drive for growth and maturity within all individuals; Abraham Maslow has familiarized us with man's need for self-actualization; Gordon Allport and the existentialists talk about "being and becoming"; and Robert White, Harlow, Berlyne, Festinger, and many others have pointed to the fact that man has a *need to know, to understand,* and *to be competent.* I would say that the major way in which contemporary psychology differs from the psychology of 20 years ago is that Man is now seen to be not only a *rationalizing* creature but also a *rational* creature—curious, exploratory and receptive to new ideas.

He is not a helpless chip on a turbulent stream, but a reasoning being capable of decision, wanting fulfillment, resenting manipulation, and with some control over his destiny. This changing image of man is represented by the Type B+ beliefs—the positive self-image.

Images of Man

I can see the beginnings—if only the very barest beginnings—of the use of this image of man in modern ads—and it will surprise you to learn which ads I have in mind: the Pepto-Bismol and Anacin ads. As a result of them, millions of Americans walking around right now must think that their stomachs are hollow dumbbells standing on end; and their minds, like suburban houses, are composed of split-level, empty compartments with little art or amenity. The picture of man presented is over-simplified, degraded, patronizing and insulting. Nevertheless it does concede that consumers—the ones with belly-aches and head-aches anyway—are entitled to some explanation of their physical troubles. It isn't much—advertisers haven't departed far from their original pessimism about man—but it is something.

But it is certainly not enough. If we learned that our children were being taught such conceptions of the stomach or head we would demand that their teachers be immediately fired for incompetence. Why should the advertising man be allowed to exploit for money the consumer's legitimate need to understand his belly-aches and head-aches?

Is there not a better example of the advertising industry's changing conception of man? I think there is. David Ogilvy expressed a more dignified and respectful view of the consumer at a conference we attended on creativity early in 1962; he has reiterated this view in his recently-published book *Confessions of an Advertising Man* and in his advertisements on Puerto Rico and on travel in the United States and abroad. Of course this dignified man does not emerge in all his famous advertisements—his Schweppes and Rolls-Royce ads, for instance, depend on snobbery, and do him no particular credit. But his travel ads at least try to associate the inconsequential with a self that tries to become better-realized, better-rounded, and more open to experience. These ads say that man has fundamental worth and possibility; they hold out a dignified promise to let the consumer be and become.

Irrational Image Predominates

But whatever the signs and portents, the irrational image of man still predominates in the advertising world. The more inconsequential the benefits of one brand over a competitor's the more desperately the industry has harangued and nagged and irritated its mass audience. It is not easy work to convince indifferent people that psychologically insignificant matters are all that important.

The fact that advertising attracts such highly talented people, pays them such fabulous salaries, and puts them under such terrific pressure—these can all be attributed to the kinds of beliefs it specializes in changing. Consequently, no wonder the advertising profession is among the most guilt-ridden, anxiety-ridden, ulcer-ridden, and death-ridden professions in America.

The advertising man's image of the consumer requires revision, not only to bring it into line with the newer, broader, and prouder image of man now prominent in psychology, but out of justice to his own self-respect. It is a well-established principle psychologically, socially, and historically, that no man degrades another without degrading himself. If the advertising man can bring himself to change this, he will not only gain new regard for that so often underrated and dehumanized American on whom he is so dependent—the consumer—but for his profession and himself as well.

Hippie Morality— More Old than New

Bennett M. Berger

For a few months I've been going around the San Francisco Bay Area asking hippies what the New Morality is all about, and for more than a few months I've been reading and listening to their sympathizers and spokesmen, present and former: Paul Goodman, Edgar Friedenberg, Herbert Marcuse, Norman O. Brown, John Seeley, Alan Watts, Tim Leary, and Ken Kesey, among others. I read the *East Village Other* and the *Berkeley Barb,* and the *San Francisco Oracle* (when I can bear to), and I've been doing more than my share of cafe-sitting, digging the moral feeling of the young as it comes across through their talk. On the basis of this—forgive the expression—data, it would be very easy to argue (as I will) that there isn't much, if any, New Morality around, and certainly none that warrants upper-case letters (although how unprecedented or unheard of a morality must be to be regarded as "new" is a question too difficult for me to attempt to answer here).

But the conclusion that there isn't much new morality around is one I am reluctant to come to, because it almost inevitably functions as a put-down of various activities, some of which I actually want to encourage. Thus I am confronted with the very old problem of whether to speak

the truth when it may have undesired consequences. To love the truth is no doubt a great virtue; but to love to speak the truth is a small vanity, and I should like to be very explicit that it is my vanity that constrains me to risk dampening the ardor of some of those who belong to a movement, which in many respects I admire, by attempting to speak the truth about it. People whose spirit may rest on an erroneous conviction that they are doing something new and revolutionary may be unhappy when told that they are (only) the most recent expression of what is by now an old tradition, even if it is, as I believe, an important and honorable tradition as well.

Bohemian Doctrine

More than 30 years ago (a "generation," as Karl Mannheim reckoned social time, two generations as José Ortega y Gasset reckoned it, and three, four, or more as contemporary journalists and other grabbers of the main literary chance reckon it), the literary critic Malcolm Cowley wrote *Exile's Return,* a book about the experience of American literary expatriates in Europe in the 1920s. In it he treats to some extent the history of bohemianism, starting back in the middle of the 19th century with that important document of bohemian history, Henry Murger's *Scenes of Bohemian Life.* By 1920, Cowley says, bohemia had a relatively formal doctrine, "a system of ideas that could be roughly summarized as follows" (and as I go through these eight basic ideas, please keep in mind the hippies— and the fact that these ideas were formulated 33 years ago about phenomena that were then more than a hundred years old):

■ The first point in the bohemian doctrine is what Cowley calls "The idea of salvation by the child.—Each of us at birth has special potentialities which are slowly crushed and destroyed by a standardized society and mechanical modes of teaching. If a new educational system can be introduced, one by which children are encouraged to develop their own personalities, to [listen!] blossom freely like flowers, then the world will be saved by this new, free generation." The analogues here are hippie innocence (more on this later), flower power, and the educational revolution.

■ "The idea of self-expression.—Each man's, each woman's, purpose in life is to express himself, to realize his full individuality through creative work and beautiful living in beautiful surroundings." This, I believe, is identical with the hippies' moral injunction to "do your thing."

■ "The idea of paganism.—The body is a temple in which there is nothing unclean, a shrine to be adorned for the ritual of love." Contemporary paganism, by no means limited to the hippies but especially prevalent among them, is manifest in the overpowering eroticism that their scene exudes: the prevalence of female flesh (toe, ankle, belly, breast, and thigh) and male symbols of strength (beards, boots, denim, buckles, motorcycles), or the gentler and more restrained versions of these, or the by-now hardly controversial assumption that fucking will help set you free.

■ "The idea of living for the moment.—It is stupid to pile up treasures that we can enjoy only in old age. . . . Better to seize the moment as it comes. . . . Better to live extravagantly . . . 'burn [your] candle at both ends. . . .' " Today, this might be formulated as something like being super WOW where the action is in the NOW generation, who, like, know what's happening and where it's at. (It was a gentle English cleric who said many years ago that the man who marries the spirit of his own age is likely to be a widower in the next. Prophets of rapid social change, please take notice.)

■ "The idea of liberty.—Every law . . . that prevents self-expression or the full enjoyment of the moment should be shattered and abolished. Puritanism is the great enemy." Today, this is manifest in the movement to legalize marihuana, to render ecstasy respectable (dancing in the park, orgiastic sex, turning everybody on, etc.), and to demonstrate the absurdity of laws against acts that harm no one and the hypocrisy of those who insist on the enforcement of these laws.

■ "The idea of female equality.—Women should be the economic and moral equals of men . . . same pay . . . same working conditions, the same opportunity for drinking, smoking, taking or dismissing lovers." For the hippies, insistence on equality in smoking and the taking and dismissing of lovers is already quaint, and drinking is increasingly irrelevant. But the theme of sexual equality is still important with respect to cultural differences between the sexes, and evident in the insistence that men may be gentle and women aggressive, and in the merging of sexually related symbols of adornment (long hair, beads, bells, colorful clothes, and so on).

■ Hippies often tell me that it is really quite difficult, if not impossible, to understand their scene without appreciating the importance of psychedelic drugs in it. Although I am inclined to believe this, the importance of mind-expansion in the bohemian doctrine was plain to Cowley 33

years ago. The references are dated but the main point of his seventh basic idea is unmistakable: "The idea of psychological adjustment.—We are unhappy because . . . we are repressed." To Cowley, the then-contemporary version of the doctrine prescribed that repression could and should be overcome by Freudian analysis, or by the mystic qualities of George Ivanovich Gurdjieff's psycho-physical disciplining, or by *a daily dose of thyroid.* Today, repression may be uptightness or "game reality," and it is not Freud but Reich, not thyroid but LSD, not Gurdjieff but yoga, I Ching, *The Book of the Dead,* or some other meditational means of transcending the realities that hang one up.

■ Cowley's final point in the bohemian doctrine is the old romantic love of the exotic. "The idea of changing place.— 'They do things better in . . .' " (you name it). At some times the wisdom of old cultures has been affirmed, at other times, wild and primitive places—anything that will break the puritan shackles. Paris, Mexico, Tahiti, Tangier, Big Sur. The contemporary hippie fascination with American Indians has a triple attraction: They were oppressed, they were nobly savage, and by a symbolic act of identification they became a part of one's American collective unconscious, reachable under the influence of drugs.

No Put-Down of Hippies

Hippie morality, then, at least that part of it perceivable from the outside, seems to be only the most recent expression of a long tradition. Having said this, I don't want to just leave it there, because if my saying that the morality isn't new functions as a put-down of what it actually is, then my statement is misleading. Let me try to clarify what I am getting at.

Some months ago I gave a talk on "black culture" to what I then mistakenly thought was the usual sort of polite, university-extension audience of culture-hungry schoolteachers and social workers—in this case, many of them Negro. I argued—tentatively, without much conviction, in the dispassionate style I have argued so far in this article—that although the idea of black culture seemed useful to me as a myth to bind Negroes together in a way that would enhance their ability to press their political demands, there seemed to be little in what the nationalists and other militants were touting as "black culture" that couldn't be understood as a combination of Southern regional patterns, evangelical Christianity, and lower-class patterns of the metropolitan ghetto. I had hardly finished when I found myself facing an angry and shouting group of people who felt they had been insulted, and who, in other circumstances, might simply have killed me as an enemy of the people (I am not being melodramatic). Later, it was pointed out to me that black culture was in the process of being formed, and if I didn't see it, that was because I didn't know where it was at (both of which may be true). Besides, my implying that there wasn't any was likely not only to weaken the myth but to impede the actual growth and development of the reality—which made me an enemy.

Strength in Numbers

The logical form of this problem is an old one for sociologists who deal with issues of public resonance: the problem of self-fulfilling and self-denying assertions. So although I do not see among the hippies any system of values that warrants the pretentious solemnity of the phrase "New Morality," I believe that moralities old *and* new rise and fall in part through self-fulfilling and self-denying processes that may be activated by descriptive statements innocent of prescriptive intent. But knowing this destroys the possibility of innocence for those who make statements that affect outcomes they are interested in. There are, that is, always potentially ascendant, deviant, or subterranean moralities around, the numbers of whose adherents are subject to expansion or contraction partly on the basis of how persuasively the morality is talked up or down, glamorized or mystified, vitalized or stultified, and its prevalence exaggerated or minimized. Such processes affect the rigor with which sanctions are or are not applied, and therefore obstruct or facilitate not merely moral deviance but the prospect that deviance will become legitimate and proclaim its own propriety. Joseph Conrad, that famous Polish sociologist, used as an epigraph for his very sociological *Lord Jim* the following words: "It is certain that my conviction increases the moment another soul will believe it."

Hippie morality is not new, but I think that more souls are believing it. The proportions of the age-grade may not be any larger, but the absolute numbers are enormous— for two very good and rather new reasons. First, there is the unprecedented, colossal size of the cohort between, say, 13 and 25, even a small percentage of which produces very large numbers indeed. Second, this cohort of morally deviant youth has been further swelled by the group known as "teeny-boppers"—pre-adolescents and early adolescents who have not, to my knowledge, previously played any significant role in bohemian movements. Their presence on the contemporary scene is, I think, a function of the institutionalization of adolescence, not simply as the traditional

"transitional stage," but as a major period of life. This period may last as long as 20 years, and therefore evokes its own orientational phenomena and behavior, which we have learned to understand as "anticipatory socialization."

In addition to the hippies' large numbers, their peculiar visibility is playing an important part in the gradual legitimation of their traditionally subterranean morality. Exactly *un*like Michael Harrington's invisible poor, the hippies are unequally distributed in ways that magnify their visibility. They are concentrated—segregated in universities, or recently out of them and into the bohemian ghettos of the more glamorous big cities. They are colorful, disturbing, and always newsworthy. Moreover, they have a substantial press of their own and radio stations that play their music almost exclusively. And not only are many of them the children of relatively affluent and influential people, but they have their sympathizers (secret and not so secret) in the universities, and let's not forget the ballet, and in the mass media.

How do I know the bohemian morality is gradually being legitimated? I don't for sure, but when John Lennon said the Beatles were more popular than Jesus—something that probably wasn't even quite true—he got away with it, *and helped make it truer by getting away with it.* There's better evidence. Take sex, which in this country seems to be the quintessence of morality. More important and more reliable than survey data reporting premarital sexual experience are the revealing attitudes of more or less official moral spokesmen. Hollywood films, for example, are as good an indicator of acceptable morality as one is likely to find (appealing, as their producers say they must, to mass sentiments), and these films not only affirm unmarried sex but even suggest that your life may be ruined by the decision *not* to climb into bed with the person you love. It is still news when Christian ministers refuse to condemn unchastity, but it makes the inside pages now, and it is not nearly so startling an event as it was a few years ago. And now, finally, the topic is ready for discussion in the public schools: *Is premarital intercourse wrong?* William Graham Sumner gave us the answer: The moment the mores are questioned, they have lost their authority. And when they are questioned publicly by official representatives of the major institutions, they not only have lost their authority but are ready to be replaced—not, let me repeat, by a "New Morality" but by an old one that has been underground, and that now, like Yeats' rough beast, its hour come round at last, slouches toward Bethlehem to be born.

So what else is new? Well, several things that express traditional bohemian virtues in so fresh, unusual, and potentially consequential a manner that they are worth noting.

■ A few words about hippie innocence. Clearly, the symbols of childhood and innocence are very much *in*: flowers, ice cream, kites, beads, bells, bubbles, and feathers, and sitting on the ground, like Indians, or legs outstretched in front of one, like Charlie Brown and his friends (perhaps reflecting the guilelessness of the prose styles of Paul Goodman and Alan Watts?). Just recently, hippie innocence was a major theme in a CBS documentary oddly titled "The Hippie Temptation." CBS (Harry Reasoner, that is) disapproved, pointing out that the innocence is used in a hostile way (a girl taunts an annoyed policeman by insistently offering him flowers), and concluding with the (smug?) observation that people who can grow beards and make love ought to go beyond innocence to wisdom. What CBS apparently chose to ignore (and I say "chose" because it seems so obvious) was the fact that innocence *as* wisdom and the child *as* moral leader are two ideas that go back a couple of thousand years to very respectable sources. Harry Reasoner, a man with a usually reliable sense of irony, also chose to ignore the irony of network TV prescribing wisdom—and to the "TV generation"! Of *course*, hippie innocence is provocative; it angers the police, it angers CBS, and it is potentially consequential because authority finds it difficult to fight. Wisdom might be a good antidote, but there's very little wisdom around (and more people pleading incompetence to preach it). There's only sophistication, and not too much of that.

■ Another interesting development in the hippie milieu is the panhandling. It's interesting because of its relation to the innocence theme, and because of the peculiar moral relevance of the interaction. The approach is usually the standard "Do you have any spare change?" But it is often consciously winsome and "charming." A teen-age girl, for example, asks me to lend her 15 cents for an ice-cream cone, then asks for 2 cents more so she can have the ice cream in a sugar cone. The mood of the interaction is different from skid-row panhandling, where the bum plays humble and subservient, thus allowing his mark to feel generous or powerful—or even contemptuous—which is what the giver gets in return for giving. Hippie panhandling is innocent, offhand, as if to say "You've got it and can spare it, I haven't; all men are brothers, and if you don't give, you're a kind of fink; or, if you think it's principle that prevents you from giving, it reveals only your uptightness about money, your enslavement to an obsolete ethic about

the virtue of *earning* what you get." Indeed, one of the things one may learn from being approached is the shocking discovery that one *does* truly believe in that virtue. Whatever the specific character of one's response, the people I have spoken to invariably find it obscurely disturbing, an occasion for reflection, and this is important.

■ The hippies have also played an important role in the gradual institutionalization of the use of formerly obscene and other taboo language in public, even on ceremonial occasions. This trend is part of the general eroticization of public life, from print, to advertising, to film, to styles of dress and undress, and it has within it the potential for changing the quality of public life through its effect on spoken rhetoric, which may help reclaim the language from the depths to which public speech has sunk it. Lenny Bruce was a prophet of this trend. The so-called filthy-speech movement at Berkeley in the summer of 1965 is well-known, and so are the rather severe sanctions invoked against the offenders. What is not so well-known is that, shortly after this controversy, the university sponsored a poetry conference on the campus. For almost a whole week, there were daily and nightly readings, by, among others, several of the more successful beat poets of the '50s, as well as by many very young and relatively unknown hippie poets. I remember sitting in the hallowed halls of Wheeler Auditorium and the only slightly less hallowed Dwinelle Hall, amidst little old ladies with knitting, suburban housewives from Orinda, and cashmere-sweatered undergraduates holding tight to their boyfriends' hands. And I remember listening to Allen Ginsberg rhapsodize about waking up with his cock in the mouth of his friend Peter Orlovsky; I remember listening to other poets wax eloquent about cunnilinctus and about what they repeatedly insisted upon calling "fucking." Now, because I am a sociologist as well as a person interested in poetry, I remember not only sitting and listening to the poets, but I also remember observing that the ladies hardly looked up from their knitting and the undergraduates listened raptly (with that almost oppressive quiet reminiscent of museums), and I heard neither a titter nor a gasp of shock. I saw no outraged exits, and not an indignant word in the press that week about pornography or obscenity. Nor was I aware of any other complaints against the use of university facilities for such goings-on—although the organizer of the conference told me, when I spoke to him about it later, that there had been one or two letters of complaint. One or two. And, I must confess, it is the improbability of negative sanctions that encourages me, here, to contribute to the tendency I am describing, that is, to *show* you my point rather than argue it: that formerly taboo language is increasingly used in public, and that, yes, Virginia, it is erotic. Nor is the poetry conference the only example at hand. As Bay Area residents well know, Lenore Kandel's *The Love Book,* shortly after being banned by the San Francisco police, was read aloud at a mass meeting of faculty and students at San Francisco State. And I have been told by the cast of *The Beard*—a one-act play that had a long run in San Francisco before its New York opening, which uses all the four-letter words and winds up with an act of cunnilinctus on stage—that their performances on campuses before college groups have been invariably successful: The audiences laugh in the funny places, not in the dirty ones. Only the Saturday night audiences in their San Francisco theater still leave a good deal to be desired.

■ The music (rock, folk-rock, etc.), of course, is new, but I will not discuss it at any length except to point to some features of it that I think may have important social consequences. First of all, the lyrics of many of the songs are—for the first time in the history of popular music in this country—lyrics that a thoughtful person of some sensibility and taste can sing without embarrassment. Think of it! Intelligent people singing popular songs seriously! Cole Porter was an exception to the rule of banality. Bob Dylan is not an exception because there is no longer a rule. Dylan is no great poet; he's not even a very good one. But he *is* a poet in a country where lyricists have usually been versifiers rather than poets. Second, I am struck by the fact that few, if any, of the traditional popular baritones sing rock well, or sing good rock well, or sing rock at all. It seems apparent that rock songs are not made for deep or mature voices; there is a prevalence of high, reedy, thin, sometimes even falsetto male voices—indeed, when listening to rock songs, one often finds it difficult to tell the difference between a male and a female voice. Enunciation, when it can be understood at all, is often childlike, sometimes even infantile. Postures tend to be limp, and facial expressions unformed and vulnerable. All this tends to identify the music with an age-group and a life-style, a distinctive kind of music for a distinctive kind of people— music that outsiders may admire, if they do, only as a tourist admires an exotic scene, but closer intimacy with which exposes one to the dangers of infection by other aspects of the life-style. Finally, there is the fact that rock groups typically do their own material almost exclusively,

something—as far as I know—unprecedented in American popular music. And even when a song is very successful, other groups do not generally perform it. This may well express the importance of the idea of authenticity in the subculture, that doing your thing should be doing *your* thing, which would discourage a rock group from doing something that wasn't "theirs."

It is, of course, easy to deflate the authenticity balloon by pointing out that certain "things" can be authentically evil, and that doing *your* thing can be indirectly damaging to lots of people, including yourself. Qualifications, then, are necessary, but they are not usually made by moralists; the great moral dicta are typically stated in absolute terms, and never with all of the qualifications necessary to live with them. The commandment prohibiting homicide does not, after all, say except in self-defense, or except at the order of the commander-in-chief; and we all know that we may be pardoned our inability to honor our mothers and fathers if they push heroin in the high-school cafeteria.

This brings me to the question of the value of the not-so-new hippie morality. Unfortunately, we sociologists are among those least likely to speak with sympathy about expressive morality, because, of all data, data on morality reveal the greatest disparity between the point of view of the participant and that of the observer. The participant sees consummation, whereas we observers typically treat expressive morality as social facts whose prime significance lies in the institutional functions they facilitate or obstruct. As sociologists, we avoid moral discourse and resist indulging our moral feelings—because our scientific education has taught us that all moralities are ultimately arbitrary, and as men of science we have learned to abhor arbitrariness. Moralists frequently embarrass or bore sociologists: Their moralists' passion keeps demanding a like response from us, whereas *our* impulse is to look only for latent functions. But, like Philoctetes, the moralist has a magic bow as well as a festering wound, for one of the important manifest functions of the moralist's passion is to define or affirm or redefine the standards with reference to which expressive satisfactions are achieved. And to the extent that scientists get expressive satisfactions through their work, these standards are never irrelevant.

The closest that sociologists usually get to real moral judgment is when they invoke comparative data as a source or norms to appraise morally relevant situations. This angers and frustrates moralists, because their mission is utopian. In moral discourse, reliance on norms of evaluation derived from comparative data leaves one impotent to affect the standards in terms of which the evaluations are made; it renders one morally acted upon rather than morally active. For moralists, the invocation of comparative norms is irrelevant. If the moralists appear fanatical, intransigent, and unreasonable, it is because they must believe that moral feeling is not negotiable, that half a consummation is no consummation at all. It makes no difference that Americans are freer than Peruvians or Iranians and more humane than Guatemalans or Guineans; in terms of some current moral vision of human possibility, America may still stink. Where expressive values rather than facts or judicious estimates are at stake, the utopian standard is more relevant than the comparative norm, and therefore sociologists make poor moral leaders. Let me conclude with an old Jewish joke that may clarify this somewhat. Jake says, "So nu, Sam, how's your wife?" And Sam says, "Compared to what?" It's funny because of the inappropriateness of the comparative norm. How, then, is the hippie morality? Compared to what? No worse than anybody else's, better than many, but still not good enough.

Authority in the Comics

Arthur A. Berger

In the last few months there has been what might be called a "comic craze." It started with the discovery that Batman was "camp." Batman's enormous success on television, spread to the stage with Superman and led to such things as Jules Feiffer's anthology of "classic episodes" called *The Great Comic Book Heroes.* If the comics are ". . . a basic expression of American culture (and a) reflection of the predominant values in the life of the United States," as social psychologist William Albig put it in *Modern Public Opinion,* then perhaps we should take a better look at them than we have done in the past.

Because comic strips are popular in other countries, they furnish a very useful means for comparing attitudes and values. I recently made a study of some representative American and Italian comics (*fumetti* in Italian) and discovered that they reveal profoundly different attitudes toward the subject of authority.

For example, let us examine how the "military" is treated in American and Italian comics. The differences are so striking as to suggest that there are fundamental differences between the two cultures in general.

The great Italian "anti-military" comic hero is Marmittone (1928) by Bruno Angoletta. Like many of the earlier Italian comics, it is very simply drawn with rather stiff, wooden figures, plain backgrounds and dialogue in the form of rhymed verse (which appears in captions underneath the drawings). As in most comics, the dialogue isn't really necessary; it only adds details, although the rhyme and humor of the poetry are very amusing to children.

Marmittone is an extremely enthusiastic and zealous soldier who, as a result of bungling or bad luck, always ends up behind bars. Most of his adventures involve accidentally discomfiting officers or their friends and being reprimanded by being sent to the guardhouse. Marmittone is not rebellious at all. Indeed, he is just the opposite—he *respects authority figures.* He exhibits no desire to "cross" them, and if it were not for the fact that he is "jinxed" or perhaps even "doomed," he would be a model soldier. The only thing negative in the comic strip is that the hero, for whom we have affection and sympathy, ends ups in prison—a dark, empty room into which a symbolic ray of light is always seen filtering. It thus seems that *something* must be wrong if Marmittone, a good-willed hero, can end up in jail. But no direct attack is made on the officers; they are only obliquely ridiculed, and always at the *expense* of the hero.

In American "anti-military" comics such as Mort Walker's Beetle Bailey the attack is more direct. In this strip, currently one of the most popular in America, the common soldier consistently engages in the battle of wits with his superiors and generally emerges victorious. The sergeant and the captain in Beetle Bailey are both relatively sympathetic antagonists whose cupidity and stupidity endear them to the reader. It is the enlisted men who have the "upper hand" most of the time because they have the brains and because *authority is not seen as valid.* The sergeant is a good-natured, boisterous glutton, and the lieutenant is foolish and childish.

What's more, the ridicule is pictorial. In one episode, for example, the sergeant is seen coming through the "chow" line. He has a tray loaded with steaks, potatoes, salad, etc. "Wait," he says to the mess sergeant, "I don't have any celery." He also doesn't have any ice cream but the mess sergeant tells him there is no room on his tray and adds that there is "no coming through the line twice." The dilemma is solved by stuffing celery in the sergeant's ears and ice cream in his mouth. He thus "succeeds" but at the price of becoming a clown.

A contemporary Italian military strip dealing with the adventures of Gibernetta and Gedeone is somewhat closer to Beetle Bailey, though it retains the humorous poetry captions of Marmittone, and still has a reverential and respectful attitude toward authority. Rather than ending in prison as Marmittone always does, Gibernetta and Gedeone generally are awarded medals. The "fall guy" or the victim is the sergeant who blunders and suffers for it. Since receiving a medal is seen as a proper reward for the heroes, then the officers, the real authority figures, are still seen as *legitimate.* The sergeant, who is only instrumental in executing the wishes of the officers is also, we must remember, an enlisted man who has risen—but he is still not a true authority figure.

Possibly the artist who draws the strip, Cimpiani, was influenced by Walker, for his hero, Gibernetta, at times

looks strikingly like Beetle. He has the same round head, his hair sticks out wildly from under his cap, his legs are thin and like toothpicks (this applies to all Cimpiani's characters) ; the only real difference is that you can see Gibernetta's eyes, whereas Beetle's are usually hidden under his cap.

Few of the "classic" Italian comics (such as Bonaventura, Bilbolbul, Pier Cloruro, or Pampurio) have the highly stylized, toothpick limbs and big feet that you find in Disney characters, such as Mickey Mouse. Both this kind of stylization and exaggeration and the realistic, "draftsman" type *fumetti* (which aren't usually comic) are more or less American innovations, and fairly recent ones at that. Mickey Mouse dates from 1928 and "draftsman" style *fumetti* from Milton Caniff's Terry and the Pirates, 1934.

Mickey Mouse, Model Citizen

Mickey Mouse, known as Topolino in Italy, is probably the most important comic strip figure in Italy. He is the hero of at least one weekly magazine, *Topolino,* and a monthly one, *Almanac of Topolino.* Both magazines contain Donald Duck and other Disney characters and have some adventures that are written specifically for the Italian public. Almost 30 percent of the readers are between 16 and 34 years of age, which suggests that a good many of the fathers of children reading Topolino also read it. (The weekly edition has a circulation of 260,000 copies and *Almanacco* has a circulation of 140,000 copies per month.)

The Disney characters have a "supra-national" appeal because they are simple animals and indulge in slapstick-filled cops-and-robber chases and activities amusing to all children. Donald Duck, Mickey Mouse, and their friends have also inspired a host of imitators so that there is now a comical cartoon character for almost every animal that exists.

But why should a mouse be so popular with children? Possibly because the mouse is a small, defenseless, and "household" creature that most children have seen, with whom they can empathize, and of whom they need not be afraid.

Historically, Mickey Mouse is a descendant of the mouse Ignatz in one of the greatest American comics, Krazy Kat, which flourished between 1911 and 1944 (until Herriman, its creator, died). But Krazy Kat was very different from Mickey Mouse. Ignatz Mouse was a decidedly *anti-social character,* constantly in rebellion against society, whereas Mickey Mouse is well adjusted, internalizes the values of his society, and is on the side of "law and order." He is comforting to children since he shows that submitting oneself to the values of a given order ends in well-being, rewards, and acceptance.

In the older "classics" of Italian and American comic repertoires, we find another interesting pair of "anti-social" animals, the American mule, Maud (1906), and the Italian goat, Barbacucco (1909).

Both animals are pitted against human beings—the goat butts people and the mule kicks them, but there is an important difference in the consequences. While Maud always ends up "victorious," the goat's actions always come to nothing. For example, he will butt a tree in which a boy and a girl are sitting and the fruit will fall down, which they then eat. On the other hand, all attempts to "tame" Maud, the ornery mule, are useless and people who try are most always defeated, though they might have momentary and temporary successes.

**Marmittone adesso si
che sa l'uso degli sci!**

Marmittone finds out what skis are for!

**Sul nevaio pianeggiante
tien gia un passo lesto - andante;**

On the flat snow he is fast—but not speedy;

**ma se scende da un'altura
par che voli addirittura!**

If he comes down hill he looks like he is flying!

**Ma un di sai che gli e accaduto!
Nel tenente si e abbattuto.**

Do you know what happened one day!
He ran into the lieutenant.

**e successo ahime il soqquadro
che si vede in questo quadro!**

All this turmoil took place and
you can see it in this picture!

**"Anche l'uso degli sci
riconduce ad esser qui!"**

"The use of skis also brings people here."

Que Sera, Sera

Maud is a rebel who succeeds; Barbacucco is a rebel who does not, and perhaps, in a strange way, they mirror two different attitudes: the American type of self-sufficient individualism and the Italian idea that somehow the "given order of society" is too strong to be bucked, that things are "fated." Whether the fates are smiling or not is beside the point, for if things are ultimately fated, individual initiative and efforts are of no great importance—"whatever will be will be."

Probably the best example of this reliance "on the gods" is the famous Italian comic hero, Bonaventura, who started amusing children in 1917. Graphically, Bonaventura is typically "old school" Italian—the figures are stiff and crudely drawn, little attention is paid to landscape (which is highly stylized and greatly over-simplified), there is not much expression on the faces of the characters, there is much fantasy, and the dialogue is given in rhymed verse captions.

Things do not *always* turn out well for Bonaventura (which means "good adventures" or "good luck"). When he instigates actions and activities—such as trying to drive a car or trying to become a social lion—things turn out badly for him and he generally retreats and goes back to simpler ways and more secure activities. It is only by chance (even the malicious acts of his nemeses are chance events) that potential "disasters" turn out well for him, and he earns his *milione* (fortune). Thus, at the end of an episode in which Bonaventura tries to drive automobiles, with calamitous results, he decides that from now on he will walk; or at the end of an adventure in which he tries to "enter society," he decides that society is full of delusions and that he will remain with his sweet and good family. For reasons such as these, I think we can call Bonaventura a decidedly *conservative* character, or one who embodies a conservative outlook toward experience.

This, in turn, suggests that Bonaventura isn't as optimistic a strip as is commonly believed in Italy. Bonaventura's "rebellions" against the more cloying aspects of family life or the limitations of being a pedestrian end in defeat. And even when he gets his *milione* it is generally the result of a freak occurrence, it is always rather "miraculous." Individual initiative is played down and luck is all; the best of all possible rewards is seen as money. Bonaventura is a materialist who emphasizes for readers that the only way to become a success in the world is through a miracle—not a particularly hopeful outlook.

The Democratic 'Little King'

There are several other comparisons between American and Italian comics that suggest differences in attitudes toward royalty and aristocracies and the treatment of the "mischievous" child.

Soglow's "The Little King," which started appearing in 1934, is very close to the classical Italian comic in style, but far different in attitude. The king, a fat dwarf who has a big mustache, always wears his crown and generally an ermine robe. But he is humanized. He fetches the milk in the morning, he rushes to bargain clearances in department stores, and is generally shown to be "just like anyone else." He is made into a good democrat, and there is no suggestion of any divinity "that doth hedge a king." Indeed, both the title of the strip, "The Little King" and the fact that he is mute, indicate this.

Rubino's "Lola and Lalla" is much different. Here, Lola, the daughter of a rich man (we have an aristocracy of wealth here), is always elaborately dressed and quite vicious toward Lalla, her social inferior. Lalla is always shown in "modest but clean" clothing, decidedly inferior to that of Lola. As a result of being pushed around by Lola, however, she ends up with more beautiful clothing. Generally this is accomplished by having some sticky substance fall on Lalla to which flower blossoms become attached.

Here the aristocracy, as represented by Lola, is seen as vicious and brutal, repulsing any attempt by the common people (Lalla) to be friendly or to gain recognition. Social class is shown by clothing, as in "The Little King." But whereas the king is warm and very human, as we might expect from a democratic American king, the European aristocracy is demonic and insists that the people "know their place." Social mobility is impossible and any attempts

at it are repulsed. Even Lola's dog, conventionally a friendly animal, is shown as nasty and cold, corrupted, we imagine, by his relationship with Lola and the "upper classes."

KRAZY KAT

A similar attitude in Italian comics deals with "naughty" children. That is, in many of the episodes the mischievous child is caught and punished; the price of rebellion is a spanking or some kind of humiliation. This is different from many American comics, in which the child often succeeds.

Take, for example, Rubino's remarkable strips Pierino and Quadratino, who appeared from 1909 on. Pierino is a little boy who is always trying to get rid of his doll, but never succeeds. He buries it, he gives it away, he throws it down the chimney—but no matter, it keeps coming back. Generally in the last panel the same shaft of light that fell on Marmittone in jail now falls on Pierino, although in this case the ray of light probably symbolizes internalized conscience rather than socially "objectionable" activities.

Quadratino is a boy whose head is a cube. His escapades generally result in his head getting changed in shape, so that the fact that he has committed "crimes" becomes visible. There is much distortion in the strip and a good deal of plane geometry. But the moral of Quadratino (and of Pierino) is that bad boys always get caught or, in more general terms, *rebellion against properly constituted authority is perilous and futile*.

It might be objected that Hans and Fritz, the Katzenjammer Kids also usually end up being punished, and this is true. But there is an important difference to be noted between the endings in the Katzenjammer Kids and in Rubino's strips. Generally, the pranks of Hans and Fritz are successful and cause a great deal of discomfort to the adults against whom they are directed. Thus, the pranks are successful as pranks. It is only the fact that adults, having a monopoly on force, can get their revenge—and do so—that pales the victories of the kids (and tans their hides).

Let me summarize the underlying psychological and social attitudes in these comics and which I am hypothesizing might be broadly accepted cultural values:

ITALIAN COMICS

Character	Attitude to Authority
Marmittone (1928-1953)	respects constituted authority, zealous, but jinxed
Gibernetta (contemporary)	respects authority
Barbacucco (1910-1924)	unsuccessful in his rebellion against people
Bonaventura (1917-1965)	bad luck turns out miraculously for the best, conservative approach to experience
Lola and Lalla (1910-1913)	interaction between classes impossible, upper classes seen as demonic
Quadratino (1910)	rebellion against authority (adult world) seen as futile
Pierino (1909)	

AMERICAN COMICS

Character	Attitude to Authority
Beetle Bailey (1953-present)	authority not recognized as valid
Mickey Mouse (1928-present)	values of the given order are valid
Ignatz Mouse (1913-44)	anti-social and rebellious
Maud (1906)	anti-social and rebellious (successfully)
Little King (1934-present)	democratic "King"—no different from anyone else
Katzenjammer Kids (1898-present)	rebellion against adult world successful in short run, but often has bad consequences

These Italian comics reflect a basically conservative approach toward experience and society. Authority is generally portrayed as valid and rebellion against it as futile. Social mobility must depend on miracles in a rigid and hierarchical society in which all attempts to climb are brusquely repulsed.

The American comics described here suggested, on the other hand, an irreverential approach toward authority. Authority is often invalid, and not necessarily worthy of respect. So there is much more anti-social and rebellious activity, which is seen as possibly successful. Mickey Mouse is the only conformist of the group; but then Mickey, as I have already pointed out, is also very popular in Italy.

These conclusions are, of course, tentative—they have been drawn from a rather limited reading of a rather small group of comics. On the other hand, these comics cover a wide range in time and concept, and some of them can rightly be considered to be classics. Moreover, I did not choose them because they dealt with authority, but merely tried to compare comics that were similar in time and subject (for instance, Maud and Barbacucco). I found that with a number of important strip characters the outstanding difference revolved around the way authority was treated.

It is, I think, much more than coincidence that these values found in the comic strips parallel closely what social scientists and skilled observers have had to say for a long time about the different attitudes toward authority in the

United States and other countries. For example, De Tocqueville said in *Democracy in America:*

> To the European, a public officer represents a superior force: to an American, he represents a right. In America, then, it may be said that no one renders obedience to man, but to justice and law. If the opinion which the citizen entertains of himself is exaggerated, it is at least salutory; he unhesitatingly confides in his own powers, which appear to him to be all-sufficient.

Recently, Glen H. Elder Jr. studied family authoritarianism in five countries and found that Italy was most authoritarian country and America the least authoritarian one. This would suggest, then, that comics accurately reflect values and are worthy of more serious attention.

Murder, Juries, and the Press

Rita James Simon

Can newspaper accounts of a murder case prejudice a jury and deny a fair trial to the accused? This is the issue confronting the Supreme Court as it ponders the appeal of Dr. Sam Sheppard in one of the longest and most sensational murder cases in recent history.

In the summer of 1954 the body of a young housewife named Marilyn Sheppard was discovered in a suburban home near Cleveland, Ohio. While the police were gathering evidence in the case, the members of the editorial board of the *Cleveland Press* became convinced that they knew who the murderer was. On July 30 the *Press* ran a banner headline that demanded:

WHY ISN'T SAM SHEPPARD IN JAIL?

Osteopathic physician Sam Sheppard, the victim's husband, was arrested later that same afternoon. Dr. Sheppard's trial was front-page news across the country; daily reports ran in every paper and flickered on every TV screen from coast to coast. A mob of reporters recorded every word for an eager public. Dr. Sheppard was convicted and sentenced to life imprisonment.

From his cell in an Ohio penitentiary, Dr. Sheppard appealed to the Ohio courts again and again to set him free; he claimed that the reportage of his arrest and trial had prejudiced the jurors against him. When his appeal was turned down by the Ohio Supreme Court, Sheppard turned to the federal courts. Ten years after his conviction, US District Court Judge Carl A. Weinman, declaring that "inflammatory" reporting had made Sheppard's trial "a mockery of justice," unlocked the doors of Sheppard's prison. Judge Weinman's view was not shared by his colleagues; in May 1965, the US Court of Appeals in Cincinnati reversed his decision. Sheppard's lawyers appealed to the Supreme Court, and the court has heard the case. Dr. Sam is out of jail pending a decision.

The issue raised by the Sheppard case is not new. The Supreme Court has, in a few cases, reversed convictions where flagrant publicity has clearly prejudiced the jury against the defendant. But the court has been hesitant about making a general statement on the effects of pre-trial news coverage because cases like Sam Sheppard's present a constitutional dilemma; the defendant's guarantee of a fair trial seems to collide with another basic constitutional right— the right of the press to be free of constraint in reporting the news. The British judiciary is convinced that the defendant's rights are the most important consideration; British judges can cite publishers, editors, or agents of a newspaper for contempt if they publish any information about an accused before it is disclosed at his trial.

American newspaper representatives like Alfred Friendly, vice president and associate editor of the *Washington Post,* argue that restrictions on freedom of the press are a greater danger to our liberties than any harm that is or might be created by trial publicity. Sponsors of Senate Bill 290 (which would give federal courts the power to cite for contempt anyone who distributed improper information to the press) insist that the right of an accused to a fair trial must be protected by whatever measures are necessary.

The weighing of the conflicting constitutional values is up to the nine justices. But there is a factual question which ought to be settled before binding legal decisions are made: Are juries really prejudiced by pre-trial news reports? Once a juror has read a news report or seen a TV newscast about a defendant, can he put that information aside and reach a verdict solely on the evidence he hears in court? Or is a juror's verdict indelibly influenced by the reports that bombard him before (and sometimes during) the trial?

My colleagues and I have completed a pilot study in which we conducted a fictional trial to find out how jurors react to newspaper publicity.

First, we wrote two newspaper accounts of the same murder—one as it would be played by a conservative paper like the *New York Times,* the other as the sensational tabloids would handle it. The conservative stories carried a sober account of the murder, as it would run on three successive days, with headlines of modest size (above right):

YOUNG CHICAGO WOMAN KILLED IN APARTMENT

TWO ARRESTED IN SOCIALITE MURDER CASE

NEW EVIDENCE REVEALED IN HYDE CASE

On the sensational stories the headlines (in much larger type, above left) read:

WOMAN SLASHED TO DEATH IN APARTMENT

COPS NAB TWO FOR HYDE KNIFE SLAYING

KNIFE DISCOVERED IN MURDERERS' ROOMS

The sensational stories gave all the gory details of the

crime, and revealed the fact that one of the fictional accused, "Fred Kessler," had "a long standing criminal record." The first story mentioned his record; the second reported his release from prison at Joliet in 1957; the third preceded every mention of his name with the phrase "ex-convict." The fictional co-defendant was "Bill Anderson."

For experimental subjects in Champaign and Urbana, Illinois, we turned to the list of registered voters, the source used in most large cities to select people for jury duty. We

differentiate between the two defendants and were less likely to find either of them guilty.

We then conducted the second half of our experiment—and vital changes occurred. Our mock jurors listened to a tape-recording we had made of the "trial" of Fred Kessler

Knife Discovered In Murderers' Rooms

NEW EVIDENCE REVEALED IN HYDE CASE

wrote to every fortieth name on the list, a total of 825 people, describing the problem of trial publicity and asking for the cooperation in our study. We found 97 willing subjects.

At a meeting, we gave the sensational news stories to 51 of our subjects and the conservative clippings to the other 56. When they finished reading, we handed out ballots and asked for a verdict on the guilt or innocence of the accused. The results indicate that people *are* influenced by what they read, and that sensational news coverage has more influence than more sober accounts:

SENSATIONAL	% guilty	% not guilty	% no opinion
Kessler	67	21	12
Anderson	53	33	14
CONSERVATIVE	% guilty	% not guilty	% no opinion
Kessler	37	39	24
Anderson	37	39	24

As these figures indicate, the subjects who read the sensational stories were more likely to believe Kessler guilty than the subjects who saw the conservative account. Subjects who read the conservative stories were more likely to suspend judgment (24 percent had no opinion about the guilt or innocence of either defendant) than those who read sensational accounts (only 12 percent had no opinion about Kessler's guilt, 14 percent about Anderson's). The subjects who read the conservative reports did not

and his co-defendant, Bill Anderson. The recording begins with this admonition from the presiding judge:

Before the trial begins we ask that you lay aside any opinion that you may have formed about the case and that you listen to the testimony and to the attorneys' closing statements with an open mind. The decision that you reach should be based on the evidence presented during the trial—not on the speculation of newspapers.

The "trial" itself began with opening statements from the two attorneys, followed by three witnesses for the prosecution and four for the defense. Since Kessler did not take the stand, there could be no reference during the proceedings to his criminal record. After each attorney made his closing statement, the judge instructed the jurors in the law they were to apply, and told them that if the defendants were found guilty they could receive the death sentence. Once again we asked our jurors to come to individual decisions. (This was not a "verdict" in that the jury did not discuss the trial proceedings.) This was the crucial vote, held in a situation approximating what happens to actual jurors in a real courtroom. Here are the results:

SENSATIONAL	% guilty	% not guilty	% no opinion
Kessler	25	73	2
Anderson	25	73	2
CONSERVATIVE	% guilty	% not guilty	% no opinion
Kessler	22	78	—
Anderson	22	78	—

The most striking finding is that *after they had heard the trial, most of our jurors changed their minds and found the defendants innocent.* This is true regardless of which version of the story the jurors had read before the trial. On the basis of news accounts alone, 67 percent of those who had seen the sensational account were persuaded that Fred Kessler was guilty; after the trial, only 25 percent voted to convict Kessler. These jurors seem to have taken the judge's admonition very seriously. They were able to put out of their minds the material they had read, and to reach a verdict solely on the basis of what they heard at the trial.

Would jurors serving in a real trial do the same?

We believe they would. Our findings gibe with the results of experiments on jury behavior conducted by the University of Chicago Law School a few years ago. As part of a large scale study of the jury system, the Chicago Law School ran an experiment involving automobile negligence actions. The point of the experiment was to see whether juries could disregard (when they were instructed to do so) information they had heard about the insurance status of the people involved in an accident. The accident case was heard by a number of experimental juries, and their deliberations were recorded. The recordings show that jurors instructed to disregard insurance information made noticeably fewer references to the defendant's insurance status than jurors who were not so instructed, and that the references they did make were more likely to be neutral in their implications for the verdict.

There must be a special word of caution about the findings reported in this study. The persons who agreed to participate in it were not representative of the general population. They were primarily upper middle class; about two-thirds of them were business and professional people with a college education. They are not, then, typical of the average jury. They are, however, typical of what is called a "blue-ribbon" jury, and in all fairness we feel entitled to point out that it is a blue-ribbon jury that usually decides cases (like the Sheppard case) that are likely to receive extensive pre-trial publicity.

Our preliminary study indicates that the dangers of pre-trial publicity may have been exaggerated. If these results can be reproduced in a larger sample and in communities of different sizes and in different locations, they would provide strong support for those who warn against the restriction of the freedom of the press to report trial news.

Flying Saucers are for People

H. Taylor Buckner

The flood of recent flying saucer reports is still under investigation, so we don't yet know whether or not earth is being visited by creatures from outer space. But the recent UFO phenomenon recalls a period only a few years ago when hundreds of such reports were made annually and thousands of people become convinced that something from out there was paying a visit down here.

Yet the flying saucer might just as well be a flying Rorschach test, considering the social impact made by all the headlines and strange stories about observers from other worlds. A few officials of the Federal Aviation Agency, the air force, and the Department of Defense continue to check out reports of Unidentified Flying Objects (UFO), such as those two months ago, but for all the furore of the immediate postwar years there are few private organizations of any size that support the notion, or the hope, that earth is being visited by men from outer space.

Although there are only a few flying saucer associations founded by flying saucer believers (or flying saucerians), their development and change over a short period of time is a dramatic illustration of what happens to certain kinds of occult organizations. Most groups dispensing occult wisdom have a delimited body of knowledge which changes little over time: astrology, spiritualism, faith healing; some method of restricting membership to true believers; and some control over, and evaluation of, the conformity of its members. But since there are no externally verifiable facts about the UFO—from Venus? from Mars? benefactors of mankind? a danger to civilization?—none of the many interpretations saucerians give can be refuted. Therefore, flying saucer clubs do not operate with the same restrictions as the customary cult. Indeed, over the years they have turned into "open door" cults, embracing many kinds of people with no direct interest in saucers at all.

Popular excitement about UFO had three main periods: a period of sensitization from 1947 to 1951; a period of hysteria in 1952; and a period of secondary hysteria following Sputnik in the last months of 1957. Many people who saw flying saucers were in all other ways quite normal.

As a result many of them to this day are unwilling to completely reject the idea that there is "something up there."

When Kenneth Arnold saw some lights from his airplane near Mount Ranier in June, 1947, he gave them the happy name of "flying saucers." This concrete name defined a previously undefined class of phenomena, and people began fitting their experiences to it. From 1947 through 1951 reports of flying saucers came in at a rate of 100 to 200 a year. During this period of sensitization the public at large came to be aware of the word flying saucer, and to be unsure of its reality or meaning. On May 20, 1950, 94 percent of respondents to an American Institute of Public Opinion poll, claimed to have heard of flying saucers. The largest portion of these people said they didn't know what they were, and those who thought they knew guessed wildly.

From April to July of 1952 *Life* magazine and the United States Air Force managed to trigger a flying saucer hysteria. On April 7 *Life* printed an article which argued that the flying saucers came from another planet. Then the air force began to report seeing flying saucers. Through a series of incredible public relations blunders which ranged from giving official sanction to wild reports, to advancing patently absurd "explanations," the air force managed to fan the hysteria. By the end of 1952, 1,501 sightings had been reported for the year.

The hysteria fell away rapidly, though not to the low level of the sensitizing period, and was briefly revived when people began looking at the sky after Sputnik went up in October, 1957. This ended the phase of popular excitement. There are still people who report seeing flying saucers, but their numbers are quite small, though there are occasional flare-ups such as the March reports.

LITTLE GREEN MEN

A new phase, overlapping the first, then began—the phase of occult colonization. It consisted, in brief, of people who reported not that they had seen something in the sky, but that they had personal contact with beings from another planet who were piloting the flying saucers. This is

clearly quite a different phenomenon. Defining the situation in occult terms began in 1950 with the publication of two books—including the first mention of little green men —Frank Skully's *Behind the Flying Saucers* and Gerald Heard's *Is Another World Watching?*

A publication explosion hit the flying saucer field in 1953 and 1954—ten books claiming contact with the flying saucers were published. These books found a ready audience of interested people who, after the hysteria of 1952 had passed

were still wondering what flying saucers were. Many people read the books; few believed them. But some people were convinced. Who were they? I think that they were people who were already believers in the occult and psychic.

People who believed the flying saucer books began, in 1955 and 1956, to band together in flying saucer clubs and to hold flying saucer conventions. A chain of saucer clubs, Understanding Incorporated, was started in 1956. With the existence of this public, a number of magazines devoted to flying saucers began publication. This was a period of great growth for flying saucer organizations. The existence of flying saucer clubs meant that there was a ready market for lectures given by those who had been contacted by flying saucers. It became common for them to go from club to club telling of their "experiences" with the "space brothers." This pattern persists, though in greatly modified form, to this day.

The social world of the occult "seeker" is a very unusual one. The seeker moves in a world populated by astral spirits, cosmic truths, astrologers, mystery schools, lost continents, magic healing, human "auras," "second comings," telepathy, and vibrations. A typical occult seeker will probably have been a Rosicrucian, a member of Mankind United, a Theosophist, and also a member of four or five smaller specific cults. The pattern of membership is one of continuous movement from one idea to another. Seekers stay with a cult until they are satisfied that they can learn no more from it, or that it has nothing to offer, and then they move on.

THE SPACE SEEKERS

Seekers know one another from various meetings over the years, and there is an occult social world which contains all of the various occult philosophies, and all the people who restlessly move from one to another of them. Any new philosophy can gain a large first-time audience simply by letting it be known among the seekers that it exists. There are very few occult philosophies, however, which are so well organized as to keep the interest of the seeker over many years. If the seeker doesn't feel that he is learning anything, or that something is being hidden from him, he will move on.

The flying saucer movement started as just another distinct occult philosophy but it gradually changed and is now an "open door" cult, with room for diverse beliefs. How did this come about?

The most important single fact about the flying saucer clubs I have had contact with is that they were organized by people who were already functioning within the occult social world. One particular club which I have followed for several years, and whose records I have been able to examine, is typical. Its organizer was a late-middle-aged lady whose formal education had ended with the fourth grade. She used the title "Reverend" which she was given by a man who claims the title himself, but who had been

taken to task by the State of California for dispensing titles for a fee. She had been a member of Mankind United before the war and had been president of the Theosophist Club. She was familiar with all of the other major occult philosophies. When she decided that the new field of flying saucers was of more than passing interest, after reading some of the volumes of the publication explosion, she decided to start a club. Apparently this was entirely on her own as no other organizations of any size existed then.

She rented a small hall for the first meeting, and immediately ran into difficulty. The owner objected to having "Flying Saucer" on his bulletin board. The name was changed to "Space-Craft Club." She then mailed out postcards "to her friends." Her friends, of course, were people she knew from her contacts in the world of occult seekers.

To the first meeting in February 1956 35 people came. The first three meetings consisted of quite straight-forward flying saucer information. The fourth meeting was on "Space People in the Bible," which is not an unusual topic as, according to one version, Jesus Christ was (and is) a saucer pilot.

The flying saucer clubs were organized around a fairly simple idea. In brief, it is that intelligent beings from other planets, disturbed by mankind's development of atomic energy, have appeared above earth in flying saucers with the intent of saving man from himself. In its original formulation, the flying saucer is a material object which operates on magnetic energy and is free of the laws of acceleration and inertia. It also "vibrates," in some way so that it can disappear into the fourth, fifth, or sixth dimension.

The pilots bring a new message to the men of earth which is roughly "do unto others as you would have them do unto you." Even space people seem to have a norm of reciprocity.

Given all of its ramifications and variations this is not a very complex revelation, and the occult seekers who joined the club were probably soon able to look elsewhere for new revelations. The response of the club was to tie flying saucers up with occultism of various types. Thus flying saucers were supposed to be the way of travel between Atlantis and Venus and between Mu and Venus. Also flying saucers are supposed to travel between various astral levels—thus the ascended spirits of one's departed relatives can talk to earth over a radio-like communications system from a flying saucer.

FLYING RORSCHACH BLOTS

When varied occult beliefs like this one become diffused throughout a social world it becomes very difficult to determine what is distinctively a property of flying saucers. The flying saucer thus becomes a Rorschach blot. Anyone with an occult line to sell can hook it up to flying saucers in some way and have it accepted in the flying saucer club.

For several years this took place with speakers moving around the Understanding Incorporated lecture circuit with progressively further-out connections with flying saucers. Then, around 1960, a strange thing began to happen. The audience in the flying saucer clubs began to lose interest in flying saucer sightings. A common remark was "we all know about that." Which implies that they were no longer interested in hearing about it. In the terms used by club members, "we have advanced" from those elementary insights to more complex insights. These more complex insights were the various occult philosophies with which everyone was already familiar. The occult lines were presented from the flying saucer platform in a non-exclusive fashion with no particular emphasis on one line or another. For many seekers the seeking was over. They could stay in one place and have the various lines of the occult world paraded before them without having to move from one group to another.

The personal characteristics of the audience are of particular significance because they relate to the survival of the flying saucer organization. (My data have been gathered by observation over a period of three years of attendance at conventions, including one year of continuous attendance at meetings with sporadic attendance of meetings during three other years.)

■ The members are old. The average age is probably around 65 and there are very few people under 50. Most of the members, perhaps 90 percent of the regulars, are women. The ordinary meeting, then, will have an audience which is at least 80 percent composed of women over 50 years old.

■ Most of the members seem to be widowed or single. There are very few couples who attend, but there are a few people who attend who are married to non-believers who do not attend.

■ The socio-economic status of the members seems to be in the upper-working class and lower-middle class with, perhaps, a greater dispersion downward than upward.

■ The formal education level of most members is quite low. Consequently, although they spend all their time learning, and they consider themselves "students," they do not learn things in an ordered and disciplined way, but build up chunks of disconnected knowledge which they cannot bring to bear on a problem, and which they cannot systematize.

■ The physical health of the audience appears to be bad, even worse than would be accounted for by the high average age. Many members are deaf, many have very poor vision, many walk with the aid of sticks and many more display obvious physical handicaps of other types.

■ By any conventional definition the mental health level of the audience is quite low. Hallucinations are quite common, though people may be drawn to the environment by the fact that "seeing things" is accepted as a mark of special sensitivity. Many symptoms of serious illness are displayed.

The audience, as a group, has a norm of "anything goes" in several areas. No behavior and no ideas, except those in bad taste, are considered illegitimate. All human defects are treated with kindness, even to the extent of completely disrupting a meeting, so that a late-arriving person with hearing difficulties can be given a front row seat.

The flying saucer clubs have difficulties as organizations. Having few members who are explicitly interested in flying saucers is one thing. But having an audience that on one level is willing to learn about anything occult, but that would gradually drift away if only one line were emphasized; and on another level having an audience that will drift away if they don't feel that they are being benefited, is quite another. It poses problems for the person who must choose the speakers: they must always have something "new" to say and it must be helpful. The club has no line of its own to sell that is so important as to exclude any other even contradictory line. Enclosed in a recent newsletter was the following statement which illustrates the latitude given to other lines:

The "Bay City" Space-Craft Club, as such, may not always share the views of extra and varied statements placed in the envelope for distribution, but the Club is always ready to serve its patrons, in any plan that will build a "Better World" for the present and future generations.

In the past this open door policy has been wide enough to include socialism, Birchism, peace, retirement plans, anti-communism, new-age economics, and the saucerians' own Universal Party, all at more or less the same time. In addition to political lines where contradictory characteristics may be clear, occult and assorted lines have included:

Lemurianism, astrology, Rosicrucianism, Yoga, Baha'i, Christian Yoga, Unity, Divine Precepts, UFOlogy, health food, ascended masters, the Master Aetherius, technical metaphysics, Negro history, color healing, free energy, Akashic records, celestial music, and hypnotism. The strain toward variety is clear.

GOOD LINES FOR BETTER WORLDS

But unrestrained variety is chaotic and would lead to a small average attendance as any single line may attract a fairly specific audience. A decision must be made whether or not to present a line, and the decision is made in large part on the basis of whether it will attract an audience. Some things, such as political lines, can be presented in a convention where people will sit still for them, but could not be presented in a meeting, where no one would come. The founding of the Universal Party, the saucerians' very own political party drew exactly eleven people, six of whom had set it up, four members of the "audience," and me. Attendance like that doesn't pay the rent.

The characteristics of the audience affect what they want to hear. Time after time the "good" speakers are the healers. Anything which has to do with physical disease draws a good-sized audience, and if the speaker presents a line of magic healing with mental power the audience will be large and interested. The healers on the Understanding lecture trail are all con-men of some talent, and they use the flying saucer club platform to make their public pitch for private and expensive treatments or therapy. Thus given limited amounts of money in the hands of saucerians, healing speakers are a self limiting group.

When there is a flare-up of sightings as there was in March, any speaker, even a conventional saucerian, can draw a large audience. At a late March meeting I attended, so many people came, including many college student observers, that the hall was overfilled, and the extra room that was opened up was soon filled as well. The speaker gave a fairly conventional speech linking saucers to the hollow earth theory, planetary reincarnation, our collective descent from Lucifer's hoard, and a reincarnated "master" saucer pilot. Even though this was familiar to most of the regular audience, it might serve to recruit some of those who attended because of the Michigan sightings. So flying saucer clubs will never become exclusively devoted to healing speakers, but they will probably continue to drift toward an exclusive interest in the magic healing of the problems —social, economic, political, physical, and mental—of the aged.

The flying saucer clubs have maintained themselves in the face of the loss of interest in flying saucers by choosing a goal so general, building a better world, that it can legitimate anything. Then, drifting with the interests of the audience, the organizations manage to survive. They are not prospering, however. It takes more than drift to build.

A Psychiatrist Joins the Movement

Robert Coles

"When I go near a voting registrar in Mississippi I feel I'm dueling with the whole history of my race and the white race. It gets you just like that, in your bones. You're not just a person who is scared. You're doing something for the books; for history, too." (A Negro student civil rights worker.)

My involvement with the civil rights movement, like that of many people now in it, both Negro and white, did not come suddenly. I think what developed in my mind is similar to what has happened in the lives of many thousands, a gradual awakening.

During the late 1950's I was in charge of the neuro-psychiatric service of an Air Force hospital located in Mississippi. I became interested in racial matters because demonstrations started breaking out all around me. In 1960, I avidly read the newspaper accounts of school desegregation in New Orleans, and of the ordeal of four six-year-old Negro girls daily facing disorder and danger in the streets, and then isolation in the classrooms.

Previously, as a psychiatric resident in Boston I had been interested in "medical" stress, specifically in the effects of acute, paralytic poliomyelitis on children. Now I decided to find out how Negro children survived this new kind of social stress—going through mobs to get an education.

After a few months of work, however, I realized that the standard methods of investigation, including field interviews, were simply not sufficient. Although I learned how to establish contact with Negroes suspicious of my intentions and fearful of my white skin—and also how to approach white children, with their distrustful, if polite, parents—I was primarily an observer. To do meaningful research on the sit-in movement and other civil rights activity I found that another approach would be neces-sary—one more active, risky, and committing than any I had ever attempted. I would have to join "the movement."

A TIME FOR TESTING

I first came to the Atlanta office of SNCC (Student Non-Violent Coordinating Committee, often called "Snick") in late 1961. I was studying Atlanta's first episode of school desegregation and a sixteen-year-old Negro boy whom I knew particularly well suggested I visit "the office." The student sit-in movement at that time was in its infancy; the SNCC office had been in existence only a few months.

Right off I met up with doubts and suspicions. What did I, a doctor, and a psychiatrist, want there? (Today, four years later, things are different. Many doctors and social scientists are busy working with civil rights groups. Many have been sought out and welcomed by the demonstrators. But it was not always that way, and a residue of suspicion remains; it is still not easy to gain the trust of many.)

I was told then that if I wanted to help I could work stamping envelopes or typing. If anyone wanted to talk with me, or I with anyone, that would be allowed. It seemed a good idea to me, a good way to get to know the students and learn how they spent their time and managed their tasks. Also it might help to dissolve the distrust felt toward me, an older, white, middle-class professional man, and a psychiatrist to boot.

It took months for us to relax with one another. But when that had happened, there was no question about what I should do. They decided that others could stamp envelopes. I would be their physician and psychiatrist. As such, I heard their various medical and emotional complaints, and offered what treatment I could. I did so quite informally, in many places and many ways. At times I kept fairly regular "hours," using the office to talk with the students. At other times I followed them "into the field." At the request of attorneys I visited them in jails, to appraise their survival under often unjust and wretched conditions. Finally, when the Mississippi Summer Project of 1964 to increase voter registration was being organized, I took part in its planning, the orientation period of two weeks in Oxford, Ohio, and the operations as they unfolded in Mississippi.

Isolated forays had been made into Mississippi before. Several leaders of the 1964 project had already experienced the threats, jailings, beatings, and injuries that go hand in hand with trying to work for the voting rights of Negroes in that state. The segregationists in those towns are so solidly established, and their living is so effectively removed from the will or practices of the rest of the nation, that centuries seem to separate one from the other.

Before the Summer Project began the SNCC youths traveled over the country making their plans known and discussing them with students, sympathetic educators, and religious and political leaders. By the spring of 1964 recruitment on campuses was well on its way, and plans were firm for a preliminary, two week period of orientation followed by a summer's work likely to bring hundreds of students converging on dozens of Negro communities.

Even before Oxford I had noted that the students interested in the project seemed consistently serious, dedicated, and well aware of the serious implications of the kind of work they were asking to do. Every effort was made to acquaint them with the hard facts of life facing the Negro citizens of that state, and the firm conviction of its leading white citizens that no change could occur. Some students decided well before the orientation meeting that the risk to life or limb was not only real and substantial, but too much for them. Some of these students were afraid, others insufficiently concerned about civil rights. "I thought it might be an *interesting* summer," one college junior told me, "but I frankly don't care enough to risk my life."

The real time when motivations were tested and responses to fear and tension were quite apparent came at Oxford, Ohio, where for two weeks, on the lovely campus of Western College for Women, about 400 college students assembled to learn about their coming summer, and once and for all decide whether it would suit their wishes and capacities. I can only suggest the background here: the constant presence of reporters and television cameras; the anxiety in the nation and over the world; the threats spoken in Mississippi. Within a few days three members of the project disappeared in Mississippi. First their death seemed an increasing likelihood, then a certainty. Such a grim general atmosphere became for each volunteer a specific confrontation: going to Mississippi meant the concrete, explicit risk of death.

The veterans also were under strain. Some Negro Southerners resented outsiders even as they welcomed and needed them—and particularly white and relatively privileged ones. Many were afraid, not as they had been before in their comparative isolation and powerlessness, but in the face of the new significance that had come upon their struggle, and the tensions, rivalries, and fears of the increasing organizational life which accompanied it. Some felt guilty. Did they have the right to ask aid of others, knowing—as only those who have fought for civil rights in a small town in the Delta can possibly know—the fateful hazards and gambles attached to the work, the constant jeopardy of its achievement?

Within all of the students—veterans and new volunteers—lived the slowly awakening conscience of much of their country. Yet, there were really few people or groups giving them clear support. Even many morally sympathetic people felt hesitant, doubtful, or fearful before their actions as they slowly took shape. Nor were these volunteers simply lonely or isolated from the approval of others. An aroused conscience does not automatically generate the will to change things. Even given the will, such events in the life of the mind as fear, inertia, the onset of rationalizations and denials—or the legitimate rise of feelings of helplessness or despair before the magnitude of a difficult ordeal—combine to stay action, to spread doubt, to start anxieties in motion that can become paralyzing worries, suspicions, or tensions between people.

It was thus apparent from the very beginning that each one of this tiny handful of young people, a fraction of 1 percent of the college population of this country, would have to come to some conclusion—even if in his private thoughts, fantasies, or dreams—about why he was taking on this kind of summer, and how he expected to manage it.

They hassled and argued with their guilt and self-doubt, the racking accusations, the continual analysis of motives which bespeak inner uncertainty coming to grips with outer uncertainty. Many of them wondered whether they were hopelessly "neurotic" or "masochistic," doing the right thing for the wrong reasons. Some could resolve such conflicts quickly; others did so only with difficulty, or only over time, or only with the help of a person or event which somehow "made it all clear."

For example, during one long, heated meeting a young Negro woman from Mississippi replied to a series of remarks which largely reflected apprehension and hesitation with the following words, spoken with a gentleness and simplicity which only added to their force:

I've been listening to you all for two hours and I suppose if I didn't get up to speak you might be talking two days or two years from now about whether you should go and what will happen when you do. But I'm going to tell you something: I don't want to know why you're here. I want to know what's taken you so long to come; and I want to be *thankful* you're here.

THE TROUBLE WITH RACE

Another issue besides those of anticipatory fear or personal motivation was that of racial attitudes. The very problem summoning them to Mississippi was also part of their own problem as a group of white and Negro Americans with widely different backgrounds and experiences. For many of the white volunteers this was the first time they would be living on "equal" terms both physically and psychologically with Negroes; living with them as a preparatory group in Ohio, and then in the Negro quarters of Southern towns and villages under the strongly disapproving eye of a white society. The common nervousness of all concerned, from poor Southern Negroes to wealthy Northern whites (there were Southern whites and Northern Negroes there, too) was variously expressed: in sly avoidance, in forced, awkward encounters at meal time, in humorous exchanges while watching television, in all the ways that people find to meet and accommodate themselves to one another.

There were some medical and psychiatric problems of a serious nature, requiring the usual clinical diagnostic work-up and finally a decision about the person's fitness for the project. We encountered three youths near psychosis—one suspicious and withdrawn, the other two clearly near panic. It was of interest that they were referred by the students themselves as a bit odd or seemingly "troubled" or "distracted" and in need of help. They were willing to leave the project, in fact pleased to do it for medical reasons.

A more difficult few to evaluate were those with "neurotic" personalities or "character disorders." Five students knew they were "in trouble," realized that however well they had managed before, they were headed for serious difficulty under the stresses likely in Mississippi. Three of them sought us out fairly quickly, and were helped to leave without excessive guilt or sense of failure. Two others were spotted by their roommates or friends, and similarly helped to decide upon departure from the project. They themselves had wanted to see us, hesitating out of guilt at abandoning their summer's objectives. Three of these five had previously been in treatment for depression, anxiety, or phobias. The other two were of rather rigid, brittle makeup, each of them attached to an orderly, punctual kind of living. They were bothered by the "confusion" of Oxford—that is, the lack of precise timing for meetings, the tendency for lectures and discussions necessarily to carry on so long as there were intense preoccupations and uncertainties to be aired. Their distress showed them and us that the similar but even more marked disorder (and consequent need for flexibility) of active social struggle was not for them.

Over-all, we were struck at how successfully the students kept their spirits high, their resolve undiminished. The orientation session was to instruct the students in what they would be doing, and where; to help them get to know one another, and form some cohesive bond; to prepare them for the challenge and problems ahead, by lectures, demonstrations, and even films; and to filter and select out those not quite suited. The terrible news from Philadelphia, Mississippi, revealed how effectively these aims had been accomplished.

After the killings at Philadelphia, there was a noticeable increase in the consultations made. We worked almost round the clock. Minor medical complaints, bruises, cuts, aches, and pains came in higher numbers—we thought because many students were doubtful of their strength of body and mind to face their own possible Philadelphias. There was an increase in those openly anxious, fearful, or unable to sleep. Yet the general drift of those tense hours and days was toward a final consolidation of the entire group of several hundred youths. They assembled in song and prayer, in silent marches, in circular, hand-holding communication and recital of their determination to proceed. The emotional power and support of those songs can hardly be conveyed. One has to be there, feel the strength and reassurance of the words, the melodies, the young people united in saying and singing.

WHY THEY DO IT

Looking back, what did I find as I worked alongside, but not quite in the midst of, these young Americans both in 1964 and in the summer of 1965?

Initially I wanted to know why civil rights workers undertook such obviously dangerous tasks. Then, I wanted to know how, in fact, they survived. They are a diverse lot, embracing a wide range of personality types and social, cultural, and economic backgrounds. Traditional psychiatric classifications are not really very helpful in thinking of these youths, though Freud's psychodynamic view of the mind does give insight into the essential conflicts facing them. What united them—poor, rural Negro youth and rich urban white ones; neat, slow-acting, earnestly thoughtful ones and untidy, dramatic, moody ones—was a common willingness to dedicate energy and, in some cases, life itself, to an ideal. Whatever first brought them there—elementary self-interest, or defiance, or wish for adventure, or rebellion—they found themselves facing the same questions and the same ordeal. I have heard again and again:

"However we got into the movement, it's the same in jail and the same with the police or the Klan." There are many ways to be defiant, adventurous, or rebellious that are less idealistic and dangerous than civil rights work.

I have learned that there are definite phases in the adjustment of civil rights workers to their jobs. First, the transition from "ordinary" life: whether the volunteer comes from a wealthy home and a first-rate Eastern college, or is a high school drop-out reared in a sharecropper cabin, the confusions and dangers of social protest soon become forcibly clear. Jailings are always possible; harassment by local people (including law-enforcement officials) is constant. The civil rights worker lives in a climate of apprehension. The routine of school and work disappear. Periods of boredom and inactivity alternate with hectic, chaotic, exceedingly tense episodes of protest or activity. The worker must accommodate himself to this life, using whatever mental defenses can help him.

Quite common at this time are the so-called psychosomatic complaints: headaches, colds, sore muscles, back pain, stomach pains, skin disorders. In my experience their incidence can almost be graphed, reaching a fast peak in the first days and weeks of the volunteer's exposure to his new life. Even those who commit themselves to a short spell of participation may, all through it, remark upon a pain in this limb, a little disorder in that organ.

Why physical symptoms? Evidence of psychiatric pathology is noticeably absent at this time. Fear and anxiety are stubbornly denied. Any doubts about the wisdom of a particular activity or the danger involved in carrying it out must be overlooked. The novice realizes he is inexperienced and he eagerly wishes to be accepted by his new-found companions. Thus, in the two-week orientation session that preceded the Mississippi Project, another physician and I were kept busy day and night with basically healthy youths who were afraid, but also afraid to be afraid. In our society a sore back is unlikely to suggest a judgment of cowardice.

The attitude of the youth (or, indeed, the older participant) toward the "outside" world also begins to change fairly quickly after his involvement in civil rights work. Usually he is exposed to danger, or at the very least isolated from many others in our society. Particularly in the South, he is likely to find himself in a relatively small group, constantly scorned or harassed by everyone from the police to various frightened and aroused citizens. His common response is to pull himself closer to his fellow volunteers and further away from "others." I heard one civil rights worker a 32-year-old white, middle-class school teacher, put it this way:

After a few days you throw out a lot of baggage, your habits and expectations, from running water and inside plumbing to brushing your teeth regularly; and you become "men against the sea"—a small group rowing against odds that are sometimes heavy. . . . You think of yourself as removed from a lot you once took for granted; when I go past a bank or a restaurant now, it's like I'm looking into another world. . . . I guess, in a nutshell, you become an outsider.

Many had never been South, had never been face-to-face with the kinds of poverty they now lived with intimately, had never had to contend with the gap in social and cultural customs between them and their Negro hosts and the equally significant gulf that separated them from the white people of the state. It may be one thing to read of poverty in the Delta; it is another matter to enter a sharecropper's cabin and live there—eat and sleep there, attempt to make conversation there. Here are the recorded words of one volunteer, summing up for many:

It's like I never could have imagined. I read all the books, but they don't tell you what to say when you're left with a family and you're there to help them, but you find they're scared stiff of you, and pretty soon you're scared of them. . . . They treated me as if I was some strange god, and I mean a dangerous one as well as a good one. They tried to be nice, but they were so respectful; and I kept trying to be equal with them, because that's what we were there to do. . . . Well, it was awkward as hell. First I told them not to call me "Sir." Then I could see they couldn't help it . . . and I stopped trying to pretend, too. I didn't like being without running water and good toilet facilities; and I didn't like some of their food either. It was too fried and greasy. . . . Well, we grew accustomed to one another, and then we'd slip up once in a while, let our guard down; *really* let it down, like getting annoyed, or just plain speaking the truth of how we felt. . . . And the work we did was what made a go of it for us.

That same volunteer described the other part of his difficult accommodation as follows:

You know, at first I thought, "Who cares about the whites? They're blind, and we'll just show them the light." Well, it's not that simple. You go down town to mail a letter, or buy some razor blades, and they stare at you, and make you feel like an enemy spy. . . . It's not the way we dress. They call us beatnik if we don't wear a tie in 100 degree weather, when they don't *themselves*. Look at the way the klansmen dress; not just "on duty" but "off duty," with sweatshirts and khakis just like ours. . . . What you slowly begin to realize is that they're not just enemies. They're *you*, in a different society; or what you're struggling with yourself. . . . So, sometimes I feel lonely for them; just to have a good talk with them. It's easier in ways than with the people I'm with. All I have to do, though, is think about what the whole system of segregation does to half of those in it, and I lose that idea pretty fast. . . .

With such isolation comes, in many instances, scorn or even hate for the world that has been left (in the case of whites) or challenged (in the case of Negroes). Detachment from the world being picketed or in various ways defied or confronted requires from many the price of strict criticism of that world. "You have to become a little bitter and sour," one summed it up.

SURVIVAL AND CHANGE

In time several modes of "adjustment" occur, as these earnest, mostly hardworking people come to terms with the hard life they have chosen. Many of them become exhausted, victims of real "battle fatigue." They become tired and moody. They lose interest in their work, or even leave it. On the other hand, they may stay, unaware of just how weary and sulky they feel, and consequently at the mercy of their own unacknowledged despair, or rage, or sense of frustration.

Some manage to survive this syndrome of fatigue and eventually consolidate their involvement in "the movement." They face their exhaustion and prevail over it. They take "vacations" and return strengthened. They turn to psychiatrists or psychologists, to friends, relatives, or ministers, "talking out" their experiences and in the process determining their own future. If they "go back" they usually do so "the wiser," that is less grandly hopeful and expectant, more accurately if painfully aware of how difficult social change can be—for those effecting it as well as those experiencing it. If their aims are more cautious, their capacity to endure is perhaps greater.

Many do not go back. A year or two, even a summer, is all they can take of heat and humidity, fear and brutality, doubt and ambiguity. "You sweat it out a summer," a Northern college student, a Negro, told me "and you leave wondering whether anything you did makes any difference. You can't help wondering what will happen when you're gone; whether the people will settle right back to their old ways, the whites and Negroes both."

For some the decision to leave comes from more than personal fatigue; they recognize that to remain not only time and energy must be spent. Often enough good-will must yield to fierce determination, and the worker senses his kindly feelings giving way to an increasing cynicism. Toward the end of the Mississippi Project one college girl remarked:

If I stay here much longer, I'll become hard. That's what happens. You get so tired and angry that you become like the enemy you're fighting, and anything goes to win. You lose patience with anyone that's not right square on your side, the liberals and the moderates and "the good people" caught in the middle, and the Negroes who won't cooperate or are indifferent. They all become enemies . . . I've never realized how *soon* you can become bitter or change your mind and your perspective, if the pressure on you is great enough.

While some may flee such a threat to their own values or ideals, others stay, and the lives of such people have their own natural history. As noted, such civil rights workers become tired and depressed. A second point of separation occurs then, some leaving permanently, some leaving for a while to come back refreshed, and some never really giving up the daily struggle.

Those in this last group, in my experience, present a recognizable and characteristic clinical picture. I use the word "clinical" with some hesitation, fearful of dubbing such a word upon the actions and attitudes of brave and hard-working young men and women. Yet, I think it fair to say that there are some civil rights workers in whom long and hard exposure to the stresses of their kind of work has produced more than a temporary period of "battle fatigue." Fixed anger and suspicion plague them. They lose not only perspective and humor, but they begin to distrust the intentions and aspirations of others, so that fewer and fewer people, even among their own co-workers can be trusted. Hate and its moral and psychological equivalents appear: scorn for newcomers in civil rights, distrust of anyone, black or white, connected ever so slightly or innocently with the "power structure."

In five years, by the way, I have heard the term "power structure" spread from a specific description (of social and political institutions) to an indiscriminate word thrown about in anger so willingly and arbitrarily as to lose all its meaning and value. If I have second-thoughts about this or that idea, I am selling out to the "power structure." If I wonder and shudder at the spectacle of arrogance in myself and my fellow civil rights workers, I am heeding the rationalizations or seductions of the "power structure." If I worry about my job, my family, this comfort or that private interest, I am in danger of being "processed" by the "power structure."

BITTER FRUIT

Smaller and smaller are the number of those whose motives can be genuinely trusted, whose actions are above reproach. Angrier and angrier become the discussions between some of the veteran fighters and the newer recruits. It is not simply a matter of nerves shaken, tempers for a while let loose. I am describing those for whom anxiety, depression, and misgivings of one sort or another have turned to chronic withdrawal, uncompromising suspiciousness and a readiness of soreness, even for hate, that is destructive to every goal espoused by the movement.

How many are so affected, and how seriously do they threaten the others with whom they work? It is hard to say precisely, but I would suggest that working strongly to minimize the influences of such people is necessary to the continuing success of the over-all cause of civil rights, not to mention the very value of work in that cause.

It is, for example, hard to justify complete bitterness in the face of what has happened these past few years in the South. Not simply the Civil Rights Laws of 1964 and 1965, but the thrust of the poverty program have all been felt throughout the region, and not only by a few Negro middle-class citizens. I spent a portion of the summer of 1965 as a consultant to Operation Head-Start, and particularly its program in Mississippi.

While there I met up again with many of the volunteers I had come to know the previous summer during the Mississippi Project. Yes, some of them were wiser, wearier, less flushed with that mixture of excitement and single-minded devotion I saw in many of them as they had prepared, in Oxford, Ohio, for the Mississippi Project. However clear it was to them a year later that Mississippi's segregation had not yielded to their courage, their freedom schools and voter registration drives, it was also clear to them that the state *had* changed. Its schools *were* desegregating. (I lived in the state in 1960 when few indeed thought school desegregation would come to Mississippi by 1965.) Its major hotels and motels, restaurants, and movie chains were also open to all.

I remember the Freedom Riders setting off in 1961; I have their tape-recorded descriptions of Jackson's police in 1961. Jackson's police in 1965 were reported by some to

be brutal; yet all agreed their behavior *was* different, decidedly so. Social changes such as Mississippi has seen in the past five years cannot escape the notice of civil rights workers no matter how tired and overworked and frustrated they are. "Just when I really get fed up, I see enough real hope, real change to keep me going," I heard from a young Ivy Leaguer, a resident of the Delta for over a year.

The psychological adjustment of volunteers who return to school is by no means an easy one. Consider the differences between school life on American campuses and life as some college students have known it recently in the deep South. From safe class rooms and comfortable dormitories they have gone to rural cabins, many of them as primitive as there are in America, and done so to face constant danger.

I have seen quiet, even timid young men become vigorous teachers, shrewd organizers, and adaptive fighters in what often has been, in many senses, a real war—between sheriffs and the police on the one hand and students on the other, between angry white mobs and determined Negro and white demonstrators.

The list of accomplishments wrought by these young workers is more than impressive, or even stirring. Confronted with what many of them have shown they can do, what they *will* do, the puzzled psychiatrist begins to wonder about the human mind: what accounts for such resourcefulness and ethical development? I cannot frankly say that I ever would have been able to predict the courage and ability I have seen these youths demonstrate. Is it not time for us in medicine and psychiatry to acknowledge more than the vague "influence" of "environmental factors" upon man's health and state of mind?

As a doctor privileged as much by accident as reasons within his own life to see the actions of many of these people, as well as get to know them as individuals, I am thankful that my clinical impressions are what they are. I would frankly worry hard were there not a puzzling diversity to these youths, and to their manner of behavior and survival. Either I would be doing them an injustice, not seeing the many truths of their many lives in the interests of my own tidy, categorical inclinations; or they themselves would be indeed united and similar—an ideology, in behavior, in professed aims.

We have seen such uniform, mass youth movements in our time; I find it significant and a cause for gratitude that for five years—while their ambitions had deepened and broadened—the overwhelming majority of these civil rights workers have refused to march to any such cadence.

The Making of
a Black Muslim

John R. Howard

You were black enough to get in here. You had the courage
to stay. Now be man enough to follow the honorable Elijah
Muhammad. You have tried the devil's way. Now try the way
of the Messenger.

Minister William X, in a West
Coast Black Muslim mosque

The Lost-Found Nation of Islam in the Wilderness of
North America, commonly known as the Black Muslim
movement, claims a small but fanatically devoted membership among the Negroes of our major cities. The way

of the "Messenger" is rigorous for those who follow it.
The man or woman who becomes a Muslim accepts not only
an ideology but an all-encompassing code that amounts
to a way of life.

A good Muslim does a full day's work on an empty
stomach. When he finally has his one meal of the day in
the evening, it can include no pork, nor can he have drink
before or a cigarette after; strict dietary rules are standard
procedure, and liquor and smoking are forbidden under any
circumstances. His recreation is likely to consist of reading

the Koran or participating in a demanding round of temple-centered activities, running public meetings or aggressively proselytizing on the streets by selling the Muslim newspaper, *Muhammad Speaks*.

Despite allegations of Muslim violence (adverse publicity from the slaying of Malcolm X supports the erroneous notion that Muslims preach violence), the member's life is basically ascetic. Why then in a non-ascetic, hedonistically-oriented society do people become Muslims? What is the life of a Muslim like? These are questions I asked in research among West Coast members. Specifically, I wanted to know:

■ What perspective on life makes membership in such an organization attractive?

■ Under what conditions does the potential recruit develop those perspectives?

■ How does he happen to come to the door of the temple for his first meeting?

■ The Black Muslims are a deviant organization even within the Negro community; the parents or friends of many members strongly objected to their joining. So how does the recruit handle pressures that might erode his allegiance to the organization and its beliefs?

Presenting my questions as an effort to "learn the truth" about the organization, I was able to conduct depth interviews with 19 West Coast recruits, following them through the process of their commitment to the Nation of Islam.

Two main points of appeal emerged—black nationalism and an emphasis on self-help. Some recruits were attracted

---

"The white man can blow up a church and kill four children, and the black man worries that an organization which tells you not to just take it is teaching hate."—Muhammad Kabah

---

primarily by the first, and some by the second. The 14 interviewees who joined the organization for its aggressive black nationalism will be called "Muslim militants." The remaining five, who were attracted more by its emphasis on hard work and rigid personal morality, may be aptly termed "Protestant Ethic Muslims."

Muslim Militants: Beating the Devil

Of the 14 Muslim militants, some came from the South, some from border states, and some from the North. All lived in California at the time of the interviews; some migrated to the state as adults, others were brought out by their families as children. They varied in age from 24 to 46, and in education from a few years of grade school to four years of college. Regardless of these substantial differences in background, there were certain broad similarities among them.

At some point, each one had experiences that led away from the institutionally-bound ties and commitments that lend stability to most people's lives. Nine had been engaged in semi-legal or criminal activities. Two had been in the military, not as a career but as a way of postponing the decision of what to do for a living. None had a stable marital history. All of them were acutely aware of being outsiders by the standards of the larger society—and all had come to focus on race bias as the factor which denied them more conventional alternatives.

Leroy X came to California in his late teens, just before World War II:

I grew up in Kansas City, Missouri, and Missouri was a segregated state. Negroes in Kansas City were always restricted to the menial jobs. I came out here in 1940 and tried to get a job as a waiter. I was a trained waiter, but they weren't hiring any Negroes as waiters in any of the downtown hotels or restaurants. The best I could do was busboy, and they fired me from that when they found out I wasn't Filipino.

Leroy X was drafted, and after a short but stormy career was given a discharge as being psychologically unfit.

I tried to get a job, but I couldn't so I started stealing. There was nothing else to do—I couldn't live on air. The peckerwoods didn't seem to give a damn whether I lived or died. They wouldn't hire me and didn't seem to worry how I was going to stay alive. I started stealing.

I could get you anything you wanted—a car, drugs, women, jewelry. Crime is a business like any other. I started off stealing myself. I wound up filling orders and getting rid of stuff. I did that for fifteen years. In between I did a little time. I did time for things I never thought of doing and went free for things I really did.

In my business you had no friends, only associates, and not very close ones at that. . . . I had plenty of money. I could get anything I wanted without working for it. It wasn't enough, though.

Bernard X grew up in New York City:

As a kid . . . you always have dreams—fantasies—of yourself doing something later—being a big name singer or something that makes you outstanding. But you never draw the connection between where you are and how you're going to get there. I had to—I can't say exactly when, 13, 14, 15, 16. I saw I was nowhere and had no way of getting anywhere.

Race feeling is always with you. You always know about The Man but I don't think it is real, really real, until you have to deal with it in terms of what you are going to do with your own life. That's when you feel it. If you just disliked him before—you begin to hate him when you see him blocking you in your life. I think then a sense of inevitability hits you and you see you're not going to make it out—up—away—anywhere—and you see The Man's part in the whole thing, that's when you begin to think thoughts about him.

Frederick 2X became involved fairly early in a criminal subculture. His father obtained a "poor man's divorce" by deserting the family. His mother had children by other men. Only a tenuous sense of belonging to a family existed. He was picked up by the police for various offenses several times before reaching his teens. The police patrolling his neighborhood eventually restricted him to a two-block area. There was, of course, no legal basis for this, but he was manhandled if seen outside that area by any policeman who knew him. He graduated in his late teens from "pot" to "shooting shit" and eventually spent time in Lexington.

William 2X, formerly a shoeshine boy, related the development of his perspective this way:

You know how they always talk about us running after white women. There have always been a lot of [white] servicemen in this town—half of them would get around to asking me to get a woman for them. Some of them right out, some of them backing into it, laughing and joking and letting me know how much they were my friend, building up to asking me where they could find some woman. After a while I began to get them for them. I ran women—both black and white. . . . What I hated was they wanted me to do something for them [find women] and hated me for doing it. They figure "any nigger must know where to find it. . . ."

Things Begin to Add Up

Amos X grew up in an all-Negro town in Oklahoma and attended a Negro college. Because of this, he had almost no contact with whites during his formative years.

One of my aunts lived in Tulsa. I went to see her once when I was in college. I walked up to the front door of the house where she worked. She really got excited and told me if I came to see her anymore to come around to the back. But that didn't mean much to me at the time.

It is only in looking back on it that all these things begin to add up.

After graduating from college, Amos joined the Marines. There he began to "see how they [the whites] really felt" about him; by the end of his tour, he had concluded that "the white man is the greatest liar, the greatest cheat, the greatest hypocrite on earth." Alienated and disillusioned, he turned to professional gambling. Then, in an attempt at a more conventional way of life, he married and took a job teaching school.

I taught English. Now I'm no expert in the slave masters' language, but I knew the way those kids talked after being in school eight and nine years was ridiculous. They said things like "mens" for "men." I drilled them and pretty soon some of them at least in class began to sound like they had been inside a school. Now the principal taught a senior class in English and his kids talked as bad as mine. When I began to straighten out his kids also he felt I was criticizing him. . . . That little black man was afraid of the [white] superintendent and all those teachers were afraid. They had a little more than other so-called Negroes and didn't give a damn about those black children they were teaching. Those were the wages of honesty. It's one thing to want to do an honest job and another thing to be able to. . . .

With the collapse of his career as a public school teacher and the break-up of his marriage, Amos went to California, where he was introduced to the Muslim movement.

I first heard about them [the Muslims] in 1961. There was a debate here between a Muslim and a Christian minister. The Muslims said all the things about Christianity which I had been thinking but which I had never heard anyone say before. He tore the minister up.

Finding an organization that aggressively rejected the white man and the white man's religion, Amos found his own point of view crystallized. He joined without hesitation.

Norman Maghid first heard of the Muslims while he was in prison.

I ran into one of the Brothers selling the paper about two weeks after I got out and asked him about the meetings. Whether a guy could just go and walk in. He told me about the meetings so I made it around on a Wednesday evening. I wasn't even bugged when they searched me. When they asked me about taking out my letter [joining the organization] I took one out. They seemed to know what they were talking about. I never believed in nonviolence and love my enemies, especially when my enemies don't love me.

Muhammad Soule Kabah, born into a family of debt-ridden Texas sharecroppers, was recruited into the Nation of Islam after moving to California.

I read a series of articles in the Los Angeles *Herald Dispatch,* an exchange between Minister Henry and a Christian minister. It confirmed what my grandfather had told me about my African heritage, that I had nothing to be ashamed of, that there were six thousand books on mathematics in the Library of the University of Timbucktoo while Europeans were still wearing skins. Also my father had taught me never to kow-tow to whites. My own father had fallen away. My parents didn't want me to join the Nation. They said they taught hate. That's funny isn't it? The white man can blow up a church and kill four children and the black man worries that an organization which tells you not to just take it is teaching hate.

Protestant Ethic Muslims: Up by Black Bootstraps

The Protestant Ethic Muslims all came from backgrounds with a strong tradition of Negro self-help. In two cases, the recruit's parents had been followers of Marcus Garvey; another recruit explicitly endorsed the beliefs of Booker T. Washington; and the remaining two, coming from upwardly mobile families, were firm in the belief that Negroes could achieve higher status if they were willing to work for it.

When asked what had appealed to him about the Muslims, Norman X replied:

They thought that black people should do something for themselves. I was running this small place [a photography shop] and trying to get by. I've stuck with this place even when it was paying me barely enough to eat. Things always improve and I don't have to go to the white man for anything.

Ernestine X stressed similar reasons for joining the Muslims.

You learned to stand up straight and do something for yourself. You learn to be a lady at all times—to keep your house clean—to teach your children good manners. There is not a girl in the M-G-T who does not know how to cook and sew. The children are very respectful; they speak only when they are spoken to. There is no such thing as letting your children talk back to you the way some people believe. The one thing they feel is the

Negroes' downfall is men and sex for the women, and women and sex for the men, and they frown on sex completely unless you are married.

Despite their middle-class attitudes in many areas, Protestant Ethic Muslims denounced moderate, traditional civil rights organizations such as the NAACP, just as vigorously as the militant Muslims did. Norman X said that he had once belonged to the NAACP but had dropped out.

They spent most of their time planning the annual brotherhood dinner. Besides it was mostly whites—whites and the colored doctors and lawyers who wanted to be white. As far as most Negroes were concerned they might as well not have existed.

Lindsey X, who had owned and run his own upholstery shop for more than 30 years, viewed the conventional black bourgeoisie with equal resentment.

I never belonged to the NAACP. What they wanted never seemed real to me. I think Negroes should create jobs for themselves rather than going begging for them. That's why I never supported CORE.

In this respect Norman and Lindsey were in full accord with the more militant Amos X, who asserted:

They [the NAACP and CORE] help just one class of people. . . . Let something happen to a doctor and they are right there; but if something happens to Old Mose on the corner, you can't find them.

The interviews made it clear that most of the Protestant Ethic Muslims had joined the Nation because, at some point, they began to feel the need of organizational support for their personal systems of value. For Norman and Lindsey, it was an attempt to stop what they considered their own backsliding after coming to California. Both mentioned drinking to excess and indulging in what they regarded as a profligate way of life. Guilt feelings apparently led them to seek Muslim support in returning to more enterprising habits.

Commitment to Deviance

The Nation of Islam is a deviant organization. As such it is subject to public scorn and ridicule. Thus it faces the problem of consolidating the recruit's allegiance in an environment where substantial pressures operate to erode this allegiance. How does it deal with this problem?

The structural characteristics of the Nation tend to insulate the member from the hostility of the larger society and thus contribute to the organization's survival. To begin with, the ritual of joining the organization itself stresses commitment without questions.

At the end of the general address at a temple meeting, the minister asks those nonmembers present who are "interested in learning more about Islam" to step to the

---

"The NAACP spent most of their time planning the annual brotherhood dinner. Besides it was mostly whites—whites and the colored doctors and lawyers who wanted to be white. As far as most Negroes were concerned they might as well not have existed."—Norman X

---

back of the temple. There they are given three blank sheets of ordinary stationery and a form letter addressed to Elijah Muhammad in Chicago:

> Dear Savior Allah, Our Deliverer:
> I have attended the Teachings of Islam, two or three times, as taught by one of your ministers. I believe in it. I bear witness that there is no God but Thee. And, that Muhammad is Thy Servant and Apostle. I desire to reclaim my Own. Please give me my Original name. My slave name is as follows:

The applicant is instructed to copy this letter verbatim on each of the three sheets of paper, giving his own name and address unabbreviated at the bottom. If he fails to copy the letter perfectly, he must repeat the whole task. No explanation is given for any of these requirements.

Formal acceptance of his letter makes the new member a Muslim, but in name only. Real commitment to the Nation of Islam comes gradually—for example, the personal commitment expressed when a chain smoker gives up cigarettes in accordance with the Muslim rules even though he knows that he could smoke unobserved. "It's not that easy to do these things," Stanley X said of the various forms of abstinence practiced by Muslims. "It takes will and discipline and time, . . . but you're a much better person after you do." Calvin X told of periodic backsliding in the beginning, but added, "Once I got into the thing deep, then I stuck with it."

This commitment and the new regimen that goes with it have been credited with effecting dramatic personality changes in many members, freeing alcoholics from the bottle and drug addicts from the needle. It can be argued, however, that the organization does not change the member's fundamental orientation. To put it somewhat differently, given needs and impulses can be expressed in a variety of ways; thus, a man may give vent to his sadism by beating up strangers in an alley or by joining the police force and beating them up in the back room of the station.

"Getting into the thing deep" for a Muslim usually comes in three stages:

■ Participation in organizational activities—selling the Muslim newspaper, dining at the Muslim restaurant, attending and helping run Muslim meetings.

■ Isolation from non-Muslim social contacts—drifting away from former friends and associates because of divergent attitudes or simply because of the time consumed in Muslim activities.

■ Assimilation of the ideology—marking full commitment, when a Muslim has so absorbed the organization's doctrines that he automatically uses them to guide his own behavior and to interpret what happens in the world around him.

The fact that the organization can provide a full social life furthers isolation from non-Muslims. Participation is

---

"There was a debate between a Muslim and a Christian minister. The Muslim said all the things about Christianity which I had been thinking. He tore the minister up."—Amos X

---

not wholly a matter of drudgery, of tramping the streets to sell the paper and studying the ideology. The organization presents programs of entertainment for its members and the public. For example, in two West Coast cities a Negro theatrical troupe called the Touring Artists put on two plays, "Jubilee Day" and "Don't You Want to Be Free." Although there was a high element of humor in both plays, the basic themes—white brutality and hypocrisy and the necessity of developing Negro self-respect and courage— were consonant with the organization's perspective. Thus the organization makes it possible for a member to satisfy his need for diversion without going outside to do so. At the same time, it continually reaches him with its message through the didactic element in such entertainment.

Carl X's experiences were typical of the recruit's growing commitment to the Nation. When asked what his friends had thought when he first joined, he replied: "They thought I was crazy. They said, 'Man, how can you believe all that stuff?' " He then commented that he no longer saw much of them, and added:

> When you start going to the temple four or five times a week and selling the newspaper you do not have time for people who are not doing these things. We drifted—the

friends I had—we drifted apart. . . . All the friends I have now are in the Nation. Another Brother and I get together regularly and read the Koran and other books, then ask each other questions on them like, "What is Allah's greatest weapon? The truth. What is the devil's greatest weapon? The truth. The devil keeps it hidden from men. Allah reveals it to man." We read and talk about the things we read and try to sharpen our thinking. I couldn't do that with my old friends.

Spelled out, the "stuff" that Carl X had come to believe, the official Muslim ideology, is this:

■ The so-called Negro, the American black man, is lost in ignorance. He is unaware of his own past history and the future role which history has destined him to play.

■ Elijah Muhammad has come as the Messenger of Allah to awaken the American black man.

■ The American black man finds himself now in a lowly state, but that was not always his condition.

■ The Original Man, the first men to populate the earth, were non-white. They enjoyed a high level of culture and reached high peaks of achievement.

■ A little over 6,000 years ago a black scientist named Yakub, after considerable work, produced a mutant, a new race, the white race.

■ This new race was inferior mentally, physically, and morally to the black race. Their very whiteness, the very mark of their difference from the black race, was an indication of their physical degeneracy and moral depravity.

■ Allah, in anger at Yakub's work, ordained that the white race should rule for a fixed amount of time and that the black man should suffer and by his suffering gain a greater appreciation of his own spiritual worth by comparing himself to the whites.

■ The time of white dominance is drawing near its end. It is foreordained that this race shall perish, and with its destruction the havoc, terror, and brutality which it has spread throughout the world shall disappear.

■ The major task facing the Nation of Islam is to awaken the American black man to his destiny, to acquaint him with the course of history.

■ The Nation of Islam in pursuing this task must battle against false prophets, in particular those who call for integration. Integration is a plot of the white race to forestall its own doom. The black bourgeoisie, bought off by a few paltry favors and attempting to ingratiate themselves with the whites, seek to spread this pernicious doctrine among so-called Negroes.

■ The Nation of Islam must encourage the American black man to begin now to assume his proper role by wresting economic control from the whites. The American black man must gain control over his own economic fortunes by going into business for himself and becoming economically strong.

■ The Nation of Islam must encourage the so-called Negro to give up those habits which have been spread among them by the whites as part of the effort to keep them weak, diseased, and demoralized. The so-called Negro must give up such white-fostered dissolute habits as drinking, smoking, and eating improper foods. The so-called Negro must prepare himself in mind and body for the task of wresting control from the whites.

■ The Nation of Islam must encourage the so-called Negro to seek now his own land within the continental United States. This is due him and frees him from the pernicious influence of the whites.

The Problem of Defection

Commitment to the Nation can diminish as well as grow. Four of the members I interviewed later defected. Why?

These four cases can be explained in terms of a weak point in the structure of the Nation. The organization has no effective mechanisms for handling grievances among the rank and file. Its logic accounts for this. Muslim doctrine assumes that there is a single, ultimate system of truth. Elijah Muhammad and, by delegation, his ministers are in possession of this truth. Thus only Elijah Muhammad himself can say whether a minister is doing an adequate job. The result is the implicit view that there is nothing to be adjudicated between the hierarchy and its rank and file.

Grievances arise, however. The four defectors were, for various reasons, all dissatisfied with Minister Gerard X. Since there were no formal mechanisms within the organization for expressing their dissatisfaction, the only solution was to withdraw.

For most members, however, the pattern is one of steadily growing involvement. And once the ideology is fully absorbed, there is virtually no such thing as dispute or counterevidence. If a civil rights bill is not passed, this proves the viciousness of whites in refusing to recognize Negro rights. If the same bill *is* passed, it merely proves the duplicity of whites in trying to hide their viciousness.

The ideology also provides a coherent theory of causation, provided one is willing to accept its basic assumptions. Norman X interpreted his victory over his wife in a court case as a sign of Allah's favor. Morris X used it to account for the day-to-day fortunes of his associates.

Minister X had some trouble. He was sick for a long time. He almost died. I think Allah was punishing him. He didn't run the temple right. Now the Brothers make mistakes. Everyone does—but Minister X used to abuse them at the meetings. It was more a personal thing. He had a little power and it went to his head. Allah struck him down and I think he learned a little humility.

When a man reasons in this fashion, he has become a fully committed member of the Nation of Islam. His life revolves around temple-centered activities, his friends are all fellow Muslims, and he sees his own world—usually the world of an urban slum dweller—through the framework of a very powerful myth. He is still doing penance for the sins of Yakub, but the millennium is at hand. He has only to prepare.

The Nation of Islam does not in any real sense convert members. Rather it attracts Negroes who have already, through their own experiences in white America, developed a perspective congruent with that of the Muslim movement. The recruit comes to the door of the temple with the essence of his ideas already formed. The Black Muslims only give this disaffection a voice.

Conversion to Women's Lib

Anita Lynn Micossi

The image of woman in art and literature reflects the general image of woman in society; at once debased and unreasonably glorified. Unlike the blacks, who until recently were all but invisible in Western art and literature, women are nearly ubiquitous. But when men write of women they are usually either looking down to the whore or up to the goddess—rarely across to another human being. And when she writes about herself the view is much the same: she's either apologizing for her weakness or exalting some "natural" triumph like the "maternal instinct."

But between the Madonna and the harlot is a vast middle ground where humans realize most of their "humanness," and of the women in the movement whom I talked with, all do. As will doubtless be apparent, I, too, subscribe to the beliefs and outlook of Women's Liberation, but my aim here is not to make any converts. It is rather to describe who gets converted to Women's Lib and how and why. First, though, a word about what it is they get converted to.

Briefly, the basic assertion of the Movement is that a problem exists and that it is social in character. The problem is the general oppression of all women, and this oppression is seen as qualitatively different from the dismal (to some) "human condition." Although the consequences of the oppression are peculiar to women, it resembles the dilemma of all subjugated groups and has a dual nature: the woman's predicament demands new concepts and analyses. Accordingly, Women's Liberation has developed an elaborate philosophy to define and articulate its insights. Of course, not all women who identify with Women's Liberation wholeheartedly subscribe to all its views, but many do,

and this is what concerns those who wish to expose the mythology of woman; in particular this is what concerns today's movement for Women's Liberation. In sifting through the layers of fantasy and fiction, Women's Liberation has uncovered the intangibles of this oppressive condition as well as material evidence. And in trying to relate these discoveries to others it has found that understanding can only come with nurturing, motherhood and domesticity. The "traditional woman" gives of herself to the exclusion of personal ambition, desire or need.

The potential convert to Women's Liberation must recog-

thetical to the traditional role, expanded the range of possibilities for these women in their own minds despite conflicting pressures from school, the media, relatives and the parents themselves to conform to the Feminine Mystique.

Some women were influenced by the example of others who had rejected the constricting image of womanhood in their own lives. One woman describes reading Simone de Beauvoir at age 16 and becoming then and there committed to the feminist perspective. Another grew up with idols like Margaret Sanger, who proved that a woman could do and be more than a mother and domestic. Many others flatly denounced the model of the traditional female closest to them:

> I became committed to a career at any early age because I didn't want to be like my mother.

> I identified with my father [a Ph.D. in physics] because my mother was regarded as the family idiot.

> I associate going crazy with not having a career or meaningful project. Mother had a breakdown and was institutionalized.

These women, even at a very early age, sensed their mothers' dissatisfaction and associated it with their uninspiring lives as housewives. The closest alternative model was the father with his career, his "public world."

Displays of intelligence and academic achievement opened up additional options. One woman was highly precocious as a child, and her parents indulged her interests in books and poetry while letting her out of household chores. Another joined an "anticlique clique" of intellectuals in high school, disdaining the social life of adolescents where girls are expected to play dumb. For several women, intelligence and scholarly excellence became the principal measures of self-esteem, to the exclusion of other "more female" measures like sexiness, popularity and clothes. They rarely if ever played dumb for the sake of appearing more "feminine."

nize that there are other alternatives to self-fulfillment than this. Among all the women I interviewed, these other alternatives were available because they all had intelligence, higher education and exposure to upwardly mobile goal orientations. Most had parents who encouraged careers and advanced schooling. One woman was "treated like a son" by her father who was a lawyer and who expected his girl to be like him and have a "public world." Another woman, the second oldest sibling with two brothers, "was definitely my father's favorite, and he encouraged me to be a doctor." This encouragement of ambition and success, clearly anti-

This kind of evidence raises the possibility that significant alternatives to the traditional role of women may be available only to those with an achievement-oriented class background and with access to educational institutions that first, structural and material discrimination, with its economic, social, legal, and cultural forms, and second, the subjective and psychological participation of women in their own abuse. The subjective aspect is the result of the material condition and reinforces it: a condition of slavery preceded the "happy slave mentality."

From this common belief, modern feminists take off in

various directions. Some elaborate the problem in Marxist analyses. Others take a more moderate stance. But whatever the political style, the essential point remains consistent and universal: a woman faces unique obstacles in realizing her full human worth, and these obstacles are rooted in the depths of her consciousness as well as in the society around her.

The Background

Who are the converts? Based on my own participation in the Women's Liberation movement over the past year and on a series of biographical interviews I recently conducted in and around an urban university community, I can say that they are a disparate group. My own subjects came from working-class, middle-class and upper-class backgrounds; their ages went from 19 to 41; they were married, single and divorced; they were with and without children of various age levels; and they were of different religious and ethnic origins. I found them strikingly similar in only two ways: all are Caucasian and all have at least some college education. This probably reflects more the bias of the movement than of my sampling. Although the message is rapidly spreading throughout the country, the origins and continuing centers of Women's Liberation activity are in large urban and university areas. Nevertheless, on the chance that my own sample was too constricted, I worked with another woman, Diane D'Agostino, who, using similar techniques, talked with feminists in groups and with interests different from my ten subjects.

What are some of the conditions that predispose a woman to conversion to Women's Lib? Each biography is a unique account of how and when self-images and levels of self-consciousness matured. Not only do these psychological developments occur at different points in the biographies of different individuals but the order in which they appear varies. For example, some of the women grew up with a political problem-solving perspective. Others had long experienced all the preconditions for conversion, except for a political perspective, which they didn't acquire until college. But this is an idiosyncratic matter of timing. That apart, I believe I can describe the conditions that are both necessary and sufficient for conversion to the beliefs and perspective of Women's Lib.

The first is that a woman must have alternative modes of self-expression and self-esteem beyond the prescribed female sex role. As Betty Friedan, Simone de Beauvoir and others have described it, this traditional role labels the female as inherently passive, weak-willed, frivolous, irrational, emotional, intellectually and physically inferior and depen-

dent. With these imputed characteristics, self-fulfillment will develop and affirm their intelligence. If true, this would of course mean that lower-class women are unlikely prospects for conversion. The demands of the black movement, however, have shown that such middle-class values have indeed filtered down into the lower class, although the avenues of realizing these goals have yet to be sufficiently opened. But if and when equal advantage and access are extended to poor and minority groups, then lower-class women will also be exposed to the contradictions of a society that "educates" their minds while encouraging only mindless sorts of self-fulfillment.

Once a woman has a notion, however vague and unarticulated, that housewife-motherhood is not the sole measure of her being, she still needs to see and feel the *discrepancies* between her actual circumstances and her potential, her aspirations and her self-image. This can come about in a number of ways, but a fairly common pattern is that of a woman, aged 40, who had performed brilliantly throughout high school and college and who got most of her self-esteem from personal achievements. She married and felt obliged "as a good wife" to have a child even though she had begun graduate school. Forced into a conventional feminine role which was out of phase with her ambitions and intellectual pursuits, she felt "trapped and suffocated" This resulted in guilt and anxiety about conflicting expectations.

Another woman voices a complaint common to females in New Left politics: "Women get fucked over in the movement." She describes the incongruence between the humane and egalitarian programs espoused by male leaders and their actual treatment of "movement chicks." While expected to do the political "shit work," these girls are systematically excluded from policy decision making and strategy planning. Like their housewife counterparts, they are forced into a supportive and passive position vis a vis the male leadership.

Not only do women sense discrepancies between what they know they can do and what others will actually allow them to do, they also sense the injustices caused by arbitrarily assigning sex role obligations and attributes:

I realized in high school that something was amiss and that "equality" was in fact unilateral giving.

My mother put me in a double bind with her contradictory advice: "You're inferior, but do it anyway." To me this meant, "make up for it" [her inferiority].

It always freaked me out that I would have to change *my* name when I got married. I was surprised to find out that taking one's husband's name was only a custom and not necessarily legal. I don't think many people are aware of that.

I used to wish that I'd been born a man or a moron. An intelligent woman is a contradiction in terms and creates situations very painful to live with.

This last remark is typical. The woman grew up with conflicting and, in a sense, mutually exclusive images of herself. On the one hand, she used her mind and was praised for it. On the other, she was taught that women are by nature passive, inferior and intellectually feeble. When people address only the latter image, this woman has sound reason to feel pushed and hauled between her felt potential and the acceptable means of realizing it. Such women may not doubt their intelligence (any more so than a man), but they are made to doubt the legitimacy of having and showing that intelligence.

The tension and frustration that arise out of felt discrepancies are a very common predicament. Almost all women, be they housewives or workers in a discriminatory job market, feel at one time or another disillusioned and unhappy. What sets Women's Liberation converts apart is their definitions of the problem and their ways of dealing with it. Which brings us to the third precondition of conversion: political problem-solving perspective.

There are many perspectives from which to define a problem, among them the psychiatric, the political, the technological-scientific and the religious. The belief system of Women's Liberation locates the source of problems in the social structure and wishes to change the system as its solution. This kind of program is inherently political. And for an individual to get behind this particular political view she must have some knowledge of, if not experience with, the potential of political solutions in general. It's not surprising then that the Women's Liberation Movement grew up around university centers, where we find high concentrations of political activity, at least in the past decade.

Few of the women I talked with came from homes where there was a lot of heavy political interest. The more frequent pattern is a political "awakening" after the individual has left home for college. Getting out from under parental control permits exploring and experimenting with new ideas. Some women describe being politically "awakened" in activist confrontation, others in discussions of radical thought. One older woman didn't become educated in politics until after she married an active Socialist. Several women talked about involvement at an earlier age, but usually in spite of, rather than because of, parents' involvement or apathy:

My father, being a diplomat, implicitly supported U.S. imperialism. . . . At age 16 I became a Socialist . . . and engaged my parents in political arguments at every meal. I was known as the high school iconoclast. . . . My battles were essentially over school issues like anti-dress legislation. I fought this because the dress laws were directed primarily against lower-class girls in the school who didn't conform to middle-class standards.

Only one woman came from an "activist" home. And her political manner of solving problems was evident as early as grammar school:

I was disliked by my teachers and regarded as a troublemaker. . . . I remember leading a strike against singing Christmas carols in class. After all, it was an all-Jewish school.

The political outlook with its notions of power, dissent, rights and tactics might seem to be readily available only to the highly educated and informed. This implies that the Women's Liberation movement can only appeal to an educated elite who have access to this perspective directly. Indeed, research shows that education is positively correlated with political participation. However, while direct experience with the approach may be essential for early converts, once there is a solid base of the committed, the active political education of others is possible. And already we see the movement reaching out to the politically isolated, like suburban housewives, not only to "raise consciousness" but to educate these women to the mode of problem solving as well.

Nonconformity

A fourth predisposing condition is a biographical *pattern of defiance* vis-a-vis tradition. Among all the women I interviewed, alternative frameworks and models emerged which enlarged their view and allowed them to reject orthodox behavior. An excellent illustration is provided by a woman who grew up in Utah in a very religious and authoritarian Mormon family. She didn't know any "troublemakers" or deviants who might have encouraged her to rebel, and all her siblings were obedient and faithful. But she had since earliest childhood immersed herself in a private world of books. The exposure to alternative symbolic and moral orders in these books and the critical spirit engendered by reading undermined the legitimacy of Mormonism for her and prompted her to reject it. "[The] rejection of Mormonism gave me moral courage to reject other things I thought were foolish," and she describes her subsequent nonconformity and beatnik life style.

Another woman had a scholarly grandfather who never had to work and was instead indulged by the family to pursue his studies. With him as a model she soon realized that her intellectual activity was far more important than any household responsibilities. So when all the other women at home were doing chores she withdrew to read and write poetry. She saw the usual preoccupations of a young girl like sewing, cooking and housekeeping as stupid wastes of time and refused to have any part of it.

The alternative frames of reference are quite varied in the sample, though books and an intellectual environment outside the home are most often named. The targets of defiance include most of the cherished bastions of orthodoxy from religion (no one is any longer a believer, though most had been raised with a faith) to sex (none of the single girls are virgins, and the divorced ones freely take lovers) to drugs (almost everyone has experimented with illegal drugs). I should add, however, that the people these women associate with now do not judge their behavior as deviant. Nevertheless, the women themselves are perfectly aware that their life styles do offend "general community standards." This is dramatized by how they relate to their parents and relatives, "guardians of the old values." Some simply keep their activities hidden; others describe the "training in tolerance" that they have subjected their parents to ("If you want to see me at all, you'll have to take me as I am").

There are a number of possible explanations for this pattern of defiance. An obvious one is the role of college life in encouraging experimentation and tolerating rebelliousness. However, most of the women were pretty defiant before coming to college. As a matter of fact, almost all felt some degree of contempt for "acceptable" behavior by the time they were adolescents. The libertarian university environment simply allowed the fuller expression of prior inclinations.

Another explanation is the lack of parental control. But such control was overwhelming in some cases, while totally absent or ineffective in others. A third conceivable explanation is the bravado of youth in general and of this generation in particular. Yet I talked with individuals from three generations and discovered that although the youngest women are the most anti-traditional in acts of daring characteristic of youth today (for example, drugs) all of the women regardless of age have to some extent rejected certain traditional practices and mores of the society.

Conversion

Although various other social situations may serve as the medium of conversion, the most common is the small group. Quite often, a significant event or encounter in the individual's life will intensify her feelings of anxiety and frustration and move her to join a group. It might be the birth of a child, job discrimination, divorce, social or physical dislocation or a particular book.

Often organized through a local office, these groups of about ten meet once a week at a private home. Someone who has already experienced conversion is usually present, but her leadership position is minimized. The idea is for spontaneous discussion to carry the group to a natural and unmanipulated awakening.

The first step is the articulation of the problem. Participants share anecdotes about their own encounters with discrimination and relate their vague feelings of discrepancy. In these conversations the problem becomes defined as social rather than personal:

Talking with other women made me realize that it wasn't me personally, but me as a woman.

The group facilitated the externalization of my individual anxieties onto the situation.

One can transfer the fault from oneself to the situation, and this can be accomplished alone on an "intellectual level," but to make that feeling "real" one needs a group. . . . Collective awareness is necessary for the transformation of individual problems into social issues.

Once the problem has been articulated and defined, the group begins to explore its character. Props may be used to expose subtleties and clarify its peculiar features: books, articles, movies, statistical reports, advertising layouts—anything that reinforces the belief system, either explicitly or by parading the Feminine Mystique in some offensive way. In this way, the sex role is revealed as an arbitrary and impersonal pattern of constraints, obligations and "privileges." How and why it is oppressive, individually and collectively, is unmasked. Although each small group makes the discovery on its own, there is a rhetoric—the language of Women's Liberation—common to each cell. Women eagerly adopt it because it describes vividly feelings which have remained buried and unspoken for such a long time. The rhetoric is important also because it puts the problem in a social context and in doing so provides a basis for collective mobilization. For example, many women when they first probe their discontent in the small group characterize the men around them as "somehow unfair" or "vaguely condescending" or "selfish and unresponsive." The vocabulary of Women's Liberation labels this behavior as "chauvinistic" and indicative of a general belief by men in their innate superiority. It interprets the oppression of an individual woman by an individual man in a larger social and psychological context. In this way, a personally hopeless and isolated situation is identified with collective struggle. It's not surprising that newcomers frequently sense an invigorating optimism after their first few meetings.

As the problem is considered in increasing detail and complexity, the actual "change in consciousness" gradually occurs. In essence this means a process of discernible, if uneven, increase in self-awareness. Minor setbacks may occur, usually when group reinforcement is absent, but although the process of self-awareness may have to be repeated, it's never entirely reversible: once a woman has adopted a new perspective and absorbed a new vocabulary, even her disavowal of it is defined in its very terms. Regression or backsliding is then seen as a "female cop-out."

The new self-awareness usually produces striking insights, some indication that a change in perspective has occurred. Domestic tasks, for example, traditionally accepted as "women's work," come to be seen as "slave labor." "Chivalrous concessions" are now perceived as part of a game in which the woman must eventually pay up—usually with herself. As one woman remembers:

I was asked out on a date by this friend of mine. It may sound trivial, but I haven't been on a real, prearranged formal type date in two or three years. Well, he blew my mind. Picked me up, brought me flowers, put on my coat, opened doors—the whole scene. What knocked me out was that several years ago I really dug this sort of attention from a strange guy. It made me feel all soft and helpless. But when it happened the other night it put me uptight. I really felt like it was a conspiracy. I kept waiting for his hand to find my knee or something. I guess I was overreacting because he was a nice fellow, and I knew I could handle anything he tried. But the whole evening brought home to me all the games and undercurrents of dating. He's supposed to do a,b,c. In return you're expected to give into his advances, or you're a bitch. I flashed on all those painful "kiss-at-the-front-door" scenes. Even if he's a creep you are somehow cheating him if you don't pay up at the end of the evening.

Once a woman becomes aware of the nature of the traditional role, she cannot act as before. And this is a painful jolt for the converted woman. The extent to which our lives are played out through sex roles is considerable. And when suddenly a woman invalidates these roles for herself she becomes disoriented, and normal interaction is disrupted. Her identity must be reconstituted, new forms of action constructed and people and objects in her environment reassessed.

Accompanying a rise in self-awareness, therefore, is a process of redefinition of self, significant others and society, all of which complement and reinforce her fresh perceptions of reality. A prime target for reevaluation is the convert's own past. For example:

I've always been a superior student, and for years teachers and counselors have supported my fantasies that I was "meant for something important." But this image was always ambivalent. Sure, I was good. But my education and future didn't have the urgency attached to it that the futures of men around me did. My parents considered it a self-indulgent luxury, and I began to feel guilty about my ambitions. I remember my father being disappointed—almost angry!—with me for taking advanced courses in science and math in high school instead of more "useful" things like typing and shorthand. I was hurt and confused by his attitude. I shrugged it off as part of his general hostility to intellectualism. But as I look back to those dinner table fights it all begins to make sense. He pulled the same thing on my younger sister. But now that my younger brother is in high school you should see his appreciation of physics and trig!

At the time, this woman felt that her ambitions were perhaps "unnatural," but she now sees her father's lack of positive reinforcement as a prejudice against her sex.

Looking at herself and past in this new way is followed by a rise in self-esteem. A woman begins to like herself more. This happens because the self-hatred that comes with failure and disappointment is hurled outward in a liberating catharsis. Society is held to blame for much of her frustration. And freed from guilt and self-doubt, converts often remark on their "new strength," an exhilarating feeling of "wholeness" or "a greater sense of myself and my potential."

In one of the small groups in which I participate, a young mother described a recent experience at a party:

I was talking about Women's Liberation with one of the other girls, and all of a sudden there was silence in the room, and I became the center of attention. So I started rapping down the position of the movement. The guys made snide remarks, and the women were pretty quiet. Later on some of the women came up to me and said they agreed with a lot of the things I'd said. I guess they were too intimidated to speak up when their men were in hearing distance.

I asked how she felt about being the center of attention in such a hostile situation:

I always felt incompetent about talking on any subject. I never knew enough to hold my own with any confidence. Then I realized that I really had learned a lot about Women's Liberation. Something that interested people. So I had something that I knew about and felt strongly and confident about. I enjoy talking Women's Liberation. Hostile remarks only confirm and strengthen my position.

Concomitant with a reassessment of self is the redefinition of significant others. For example, men are judged first as a class, of unaware and generally belligerent opponents, and then individually according to the flagrancy of their own chauvinism:

When I became conscious I couldn't be friends with men anymore. . . . But I like my husband, although he's hardly liberated.

I think all men are chauvinists; they just display it differ-

ently. . . . Each man must become aware of his chauvinism and agree to work on it.

My allies are women, my enemies are men. For men the world is more just, and they just can't understand our problem. I don't trust them.

I don't get along with most men because I don't shuffle anymore.

A striking change in attitude towards other women also occurs. Formerly competitors on the man market, they now are recognized as "sisters" in a common effort:

You shouldn't reject or despise "dragon ladies" but pull them into the struggle—make them aware.

I hadn't any close female friends before. But having an all-women group is good. We can be whole people with one another. . . . and I've become sensitized to women in general as people.

I have greater respect for women. . . . All females are potentially salvageable.

I generally feel better about myself around women. I don't have much self-confidence, so I need to be around people who treat me as an equal. Most men don't.

This increase in esteem for members of one's own sex is a measure of the increase in self-esteem (again, similar to the black experience) and demonstrates how relations with the world reflect one's relations to and image of self.

This point is further illustrated by the way in which society is redefined. On the one hand, institutions such as the university, government, legal system, occupational structure and the church are appraised according to their support of the traditional sex role and their manifestations of discrimination:

I identify more with students than with [male] colleagues. We are both in a system where we don't make the rules and are patronized. (40-year-old professor)

The job market ruins you. It doesn't make any difference if you are charming, attractive and unaggressive. You're damned if you're masculine or feminine. They'll use whatever traits you have to evaluate you negatively.

On the other hand, the cultural ideals for women, marriage and maternity, are demoted from necessary and sufficient to supplementary means of fulfillment:

I used to believe that if a woman wasn't married she wasn't a person. . . . If I had the chance, I wouldn't get married again. (A 41 year old, twice married)

I always assumed that I would have children. Now I no longer feel that I have to in order to be happy. (25-year-old single student)

How have I changed? I used to think that maybe in a year I will have met the man I am going to marry. He'll know everything about everything I'm interested in. Actually he would be bigger and better than me. I wanted to live vicariously. He would have dark hair and be very handsome—very sexy. All the other women wanted him, but he chose me. The "real one." Always I would say to myself, "Is this him?" This view has only faded over the last ten months. (19-year-old student)

More in this spirit, a Berkeley Women's Liberation position paper comments:

> Now, with birth control, higher education for women, and the Movement itself, it's becoming clear that the institution of marriage, like so many others is an anachronism. For the unmarried woman it offers only a sanctioned security and the promise of love. The married woman knows that love is, at its best, an inadequate reward for her unnecessary and bizarre heritage of oppression.

In addition to this qualification of the female role, the converted woman becomes sensitized to any presentations of the cultural ideal in the media. The television situation-comedy isn't funny anymore, but just another example of how the "scatterbrained, whining housewife stereotype" is perpetuated. And the jingle that proclaims "You've come a long way, baby" only intensifies a convert's disgust with the image of woman as sex object and consumer, the final blow coming with the word "baby" and its presumptuous intimacy. Movement women find it difficult to keep a sense of humor in the face of such crass condescension, and the constant insensitivity to them as "human beings" only fires up indignation. As one woman put it:

> I can hardly go to a movie anymore. I used to be able to laugh along with the dumb blonde and dizzy housewives. But now it's clear that these ludicrous stereotypes are the justifications men use to keep women down. It's like seeing an old Amos and Andy show. Not so funny anymore.

The complex process of redefinition described here does not occur in a vacuum. As a woman begins to see herself and the world differently, her behavior must change to align with these new images. By the same token, her new behavior modifies the whole character of her relations with others. At first this means disorientation: the old clues of interaction are gone, and new ones based on mutual agreement haven't yet evolved. A married woman faces the dilemma in perhaps the most acute and continual way. One of the married women I interviewed describes the problems she and her husband have trying to "create new roles for ourselves everday." She has redefined the husband-wife roles out of the master-slave/provider-nurterer mold. That means an equal sharing of household and child care responsibilities. For a woman trained to cook and clean her way through life and a man trained to bring home the bacon to a spotless domicile and bouncy offspring, this is no small readjustment:

> I get angry about feeling "grateful" when D is so "co-operative." . . . We fight every week about a woman's thing. I'm getting tired of having to point out to him something that's so obvious to me, like what around the house needs attention.

Division of labor in the house may be a small point on which husband and wife relate. But the disorientation reflected in this attempt to fashion new patterns of behavior is symptomatic of a more pervasive difficulty.

> I always felt good about the fact that D and I could relate about anything. But now I feel that there is no way to relate on the women's issues. Fights result from my having a higher level of consciousness about personal things.

She is not exactly the same woman he married, for she sees herself in a radically new way. And the relationship must respond to this or collapse under the strain of unresolved ambiguity. I note with relief, however, that those couples who do take the trouble to carve out new roles are much happier in the long run, since both partners have freer range of expression.

This is an extreme example of how interpersonal relations may be influenced by conversion. More casual relationships feel fewer repercussions. But the comprehensiveness of the perspective affects almost all spheres of almost any relationship.

Since Women's Liberation ideology is still very much a minority position and generally considered deviant, most of the convert's casual social contacts will be with nonsupportive people. In fact, a rather unsavory stereotype has already captured the public imagination, and it is this image more often than not that a movement woman must contend with. The best self-defense in such encounters is for the convert to neutralize these pejorative labels, as well as the abusive labelers. One way of doing so is to deny responsibility by deflecting the blame. For instance, a woman accused of being a "feminist bitch" responds:

> You're damn right I'm a bitch. But show me a choice. If a woman doesn't lay down some shit around here, she's going to sit in a passive little heap and get dumped on all the time.

She feels compelled to act in a way—loud, aggressive, domineering—that deviates from expected feminine behavior. But she also feel righteously justified in abrogating responsibility for her actions. Another way of meeting criticism, of course, is to deny its validity. For example, part of the program of Women's Liberation calls for freeing the woman of full-time child care duties by establishing day care collectives. Some critics denounce this as a neglect of duty, selfish at best, "unnatural" at worst. An ordinary woman would be crushed by the intimation that she is being a "bad mother" (an incredibly powerful social control). But the individual with a Liberationist perspective undercuts the label by exposing the tyrannical ideal which demands that she organize her life completely around the lives of others, total neglecting her own needs and desires. She further defuses the label by pointing out the advantages to the child in having several adult role models and numerous playmates at hand. If anything, in her own mind, "deviance" from "maternal norms" makes her a better mother.

Some women under attack may simply appeal to "circumstances." They don't deny that they may be committing injustices, but these, they say, are justifiable. An instance of this is the allegation by some women that all men without reservation are "chauvinist pigs." For the movement it earns a label of "man haters," and for some "innocent" men it may involve such unwarranted punishments as economic reprisals, emotional withdrawals or sexual boycotts. The stereotype doesn't affect those women who really do hate men and for those who don't, they slough off any guilt by seeing the "injury" as justifiable when balanced against men's calculated dehumanization of all females.

Another technique of self-defense is to shift the focus of attention from one's own alleged deviance to that of one's opponents. When a movement woman is called frigid or promiscuous or homosexual, depending on your source, she can and often does counter by playing on the insecurity and guilt of the labelers and claiming that they are only revealing their own sexual inadequacies and disappointments. This usually shuts them up.

After a woman has defined and explored the problem, expanded her level of consciousness and reevaluated her past life and present environment, a fifth and final step in the process of conversion is required: she must actively *display her commitments.* The new way she interacts with others, as elaborated above, is part of this. But some form of collective action is also necessary. Such struggle not only "builds and reinforces consciousness" but also confirms the social nature of the problem. The individual may choose to work within the system or to overthrow it. She may join an organization or "action group" with a specific focus (self-defense, abortion laws, professional discrimination), or her own small group may undertake a project. She may educate and proselytize or engage in mass demonstrations and strikes. Whatever the modus operandi, she will not slip into isolation and "try to make it on my own." That's the kind of "private battle" put down by Women's Liberation as ineffective and self-defeating, for it requires a woman to become a man and fight in his world, on his terms.

The more intensive the interaction with Liberation women and involvement with movement activities, the greater the personal growth and commitment. This boundless character is not surprising when one realizes that, for many adherents, Women's Liberation is not just a political cause but a medium through which they discover and mobilize their human potential—and to this there is no limit.

Man is a social animal who cannot escape the influence of the individuals and groups surrounding him. From infancy until death he is subjected to pressures (often conflicting) to one group or another and to adopt some attitudes while rejecting others. At the same time, his behavior is influenced, directly or indirectly, by the behavior of individuals around him.

In Part One we looked at socialization and the pressures placed on the individual to adopt the values and behavior patterns considered appropriate to his sex and social groups. As the essays there made evident, the resultant characteristics are the products of social influence. Part Two provided illustrations of the forces acting to maintain or change attitudes. In Part Three, following, the authors deal more specifically with the types of influence that individuals and groups bring to bear on a person.

The study of interpersonal influence has long been a focal point of social psychological research, as it transcends all other areas of social behavior. The topics under which the vast literature of social influence are categorized include attitude change, group dynamics, leadership, interpersonal attraction and conformity.

Charles A. Kiesler's research, reported directly following, is in the main tradition of experimental social psychology. He is concerned with conformity to group opinion and the effects of being committed to further contact with groups. Keisler finds that the more committed an individual is to continuing his interaction with a group, the more likely he is to conform and to change those attitudes that conflict with the norms of the group. His research method involves creating groups for experimental purposes and manipulating relevant dimensions of the group experience such as the amount of future contact expected, the goals of the group, and the specific reactions of the group members to the individual. This type of laboratory experiment provides excellent control over the experiences of the in-

Part Three

Individual and Group Influences on Behavior

responding to interpersonal dynamics

84

dividual; variations of this type of design are widely used. The unknown factor is whether the reactions noted in the short duration, artificially constructed, laboratory group are the same as those found in ongoing, natural groups. We have already remarked that, although findings from the experimental laboratory have proved quite robust in their applicability to the "real world," one cannot and must not assume a precise one-to-one equivalence between what happens in the experiment and the world.

In the second essay, Edward E. Jones reports on tactics employed by individuals to gain the favor of others; he also discusses the end results of such attempts at ingratiation. This research, too, is based on laboratory experiments where precise control can be maintained—in this case, control over influence attempts. Jones, however, also incorporates suggestions by practitioners of ingratiation in everyday life, such as those of Dale Carnegie, as well as reports from observers of social interaction such as Erving Goffman. An important point in this research is to distinguish conscious efforts at influence from the indirect manipulation which results simply from social interaction. Jones isolates three general tactics of ingratiation: 1) *other-enhancement*—the building up of the target through praise or flattery; 2) *conformity*—expressing attitudes and behavior in ways approved by the target; and 3) *self-presentation*—presenting oneself in the most favorable way without appearing boastful or threatening. All of these stratagems run the risk of backfiring if the target person perceives them as insincere attempts to gain favor or advantage.

Eugene Weinstein also deals with the tactics of direct influence. He describes the techniques used to gain power and credibility in exchanges with others. These include: 1) the *pre-interpretation* of information by such phrases as "There's nothing personal about this"; 2) *post-interpretations* like "I'm just telling you what's been said—I don't necessarily agree with it"; 3) *motive revelations* including such altruistic intents as "I'm only doing this for your own good"; and 4) *identity conformation*, revealing that a higher authority holds the same view—"Just the other day I was talking to the President and he agreed completely." As Weinstein notes, these ploys may be unconscious or may be used consciously as systematic attempts to influence others. In either case, such stratagems are acquired during the course of socialization in our society.

James A. Vaughan and Bernard M. Bass describe laboratory research of another type—the simulation study. Their goal was to investigate the effects of different organizational structures on the satisfaction and productivity of employees in business settings. The authors might have attempted to find businesses which were organized in a variety of different ways; they then could have correlated organization type with satisfaction and productivity. Vaughan and Bass argue, however, that the business world is so complex that it is extremely difficult to isolate the effects of any given variable or factor. They set up, instead, a business game in which various organizations could be simulated and the outcomes to players could be statistically controlled. The simulation of business through games provides one means of investigating specific hypotheses about organizations. In the study described here, two types of organization were contrasted: 1) the *bottoms-up* arrangement where the organization is split into subsystems responsible for various aspects of production, with operators, planners and coordinators all sharing in decision-making and responsibility; and 2) the *top-down* organization with a pyramidal structure and a formal hierarchy for responsibility and decision-making. Vaughan and Bass found a tendency for the bottoms-up organization to be more productive and better liked by participants in a first study, but noticed somewhat different results when the game was run again with older and more experienced participants. They provide some interesting insights into the reasons for these differences. Their findings point out again that researchers must be cautious in assuming that the results gained from one group will apply equally to other types of people and organizations.

A different approach to research is taken by Walter B. Miller. He deals with the structure and internal forces operating in adolescent gangs. His approach is that of the *ethnographer*, the trained outsider who observes and records the behavior of a particular social group. This technique has long been used by anthropologists and sociologists but is clearly applicable to psychological research and is consequently becoming more widely used by social psychologists. In this essay, conclusions from the observation of several gangs over a ten-year period are summarized. Such a study is important because the gang is a powerful social environment in which strong forces operate on the individual and is accordingly an excellent setting in which to study conformity, deviation, leadership and social control. It is also important because of its longitudinal nature; that is, much psychological research of necessity deals with the responses of individuals during a brief period of time. Accordingly, studies which follow individuals or groups over long durations provide much-needed information on stability and processes of change. Miller reports that adolescent gangs are not only highly prevalent in lower-class urban areas today but have existed in American cities since the early nineteenth century. Although there is great variability in the organization and activities of gangs, the value of membership for the individual is similar across all gangs. As Miller puts it, the gang is a "flexible and adaptable training instrument for imparting vital knowledge concerning the value of individual competence, the appropriate limits of law-violating behavior, the uses and abuses of authority, and the skills of interpersonal relations."

The final essay, by Charles and Rebecca Palson, is another ethnographic investigation, this time using the technique of participant observation. The authors set out to study the phenomenon of mate-swapping or "swinging" among married couples. They decided that the only way they could obtain the information they sought was through participation in swinging. Thus, they spent 18 months swinging and recording their observations of the behaviors encountered. They found marked differences in the behav-

ior of beginners and experienced swingers. Neophyte swingers, for example, are generally driven more by curiosity and are more concerned with sex than with the personalities of the other swingers. More experienced participants, on the other hand, tend to be more selective and more concerned with the individuation of self and others. Contrary to many conclusions advanced about swinging, this report suggests that swinging does not inevitably result in jealousy and marital breakdown but may often succeed in strengthening marriages. The Palsons also speculate that economic prosperity is a necessary condition for increased sexual freedom and that worsening economic conditions could result in a great decline in the incidence of swinging.

While the essays in this Part produce very different types of data, and represent a variety of approaches to understanding and evaluating human behavior, all are useful in adding to our knowledge of the variety of influences on social behavior.

Conformity and Commitment

Charles A. Kiesler

Should I go along with the group?

We have all confronted this question, consciously or not, in one form or another at some time in our multiple relationships with groups at work, in school, in social life, at play, even in the bosom of the family. Will we conform to go along with what others think is right?

People often talk of conformity in the abstract—and like sin in the abstract, they are usually against it. But men face *concrete* situations and decisions every day, often under considerable pressure. What do they do? When will a man change his attitudes and behavior to adjust? To what extent will he change them? What does conformity in this context actually mean? The word conformity implies one of three views of adaptive behavior:

■ The first view (the most popular) holds that conformity is an enduring personality characteristic—that organization men are essentially born, not made, so their seduction to conformity comes without strain.

■ The second view holds that conformist behavior is a kind of tactic—a superficial "going along with the crowd" because of necessity or temporary advantage—without essential change of private opinion.

■ The third is something of a middle ground, although closer to the second. It holds that a conforming individual may actually come to change his private as well as his public opinions and attitudes as a result of continued disagreement with the group; and that this change will last.

In the first view, the natural conformer will try to be

like others in most things, finding his satisfactions and support not in personal uniqueness or integrity but in a group identification. There is a germ of truth in this belief. People do wish to be "correct" and in agreement. To some extent we all look to others to validate our opinions. We tend to pick up our cues on proper behavior and personal worth from others. This influence is pervasive and important. After all, the great majority of people conform in rules and customs or our civilization would be impossible.

However, there is little evidence that mankind tends to polarize around two distinct breeds, conformist and non-conformist. People vary in their dependence on, or independence of, the opinions and attitudes of others. They vary in their internal needs and in their perceptions. Thus conformity depends not only on personality and experience, but also on how we analyze our situations.

The second and third views shift emphasis from personality to the situation and how it is perceived.

The second type of conformer goes along with the crowd overtly—while keeping his real disagreement private from the group in question. He is not convinced—he merely pretends he is, whether for convenience or to serve some higher goal. For instance, if a subject in an experiment is told that he and the group would be given $50 if they agreed on some issue, agreement will usually come soon enough.

Does She or Doesn't She?

This second view of conformity is called *compliance*. Its forms and rationalizations are many. People may want to be tactful and considerate, and so pretend to believe things they do not; they may want to get something unpleasant over with as soon as possible; they may be animated by greed or malice; or, as with Galileo disavowing belief in the Copernican theory before church authorities (while, legend has it, muttering to himself, "It's true all the same"), they may simply consider that a certain amount of lip service is a necessary price for peace and the chance to go one's own way in most things. A complier, among friends, may express very different opinions from those he expresses before the group with which he complies.

There has been much research on compliance, most notably that of Solomon Asch and his associates. In Asch's experiments subjects were shown two lines and asked which was longer. When alone, they almost never made a mistake. But in the rigged company of others who insisted that the shorter was longer, one-third went along. Presumably they still believed their eyes, and only their public, but not their private, opinions conformed.

The third view, a logical next step after compliance, has most concerned my students and myself in the last several years. It states that not only the overt opinion, but the private one as well, can be changed as a result of disagreement. Certain consequences follow that would not follow from compliance alone and that do not depend on the presence of the group. If a person changes his opinion, his behavior and attitudes will be changed whether the group is around or not. And this change should last.

Of course, people do not change their opinions easily. They must be motivated to do it. Research has shown that one important motivation is approval—if someone feels that others generally agree with him and find him attractive, he is likely to adjust his opinions to theirs on some issue.

But prior research did not prepare us for a finding in

A NOTE ON THE STUDY

This article represents the culmination of a series of studies on consistency, conformity, and commitment. However, it deals primarily with two recent studies.

The first of these, conducted by myself and Lee H. Corbin in 1965, used 180 volunteers, sorted into six-man discussion groups as part of the requirements of an introductory psychology course. Subjects did not know each other personally. They were told of interest by the (fictitious) American Institute for Small Group Research in how strangers worked out certain tasks. They were supposed to rate 10 abstract paintings which, they were told, had previously been rated by experts; theoretically, the individuals and group that came closest to the experts would win cash prizes. Half were made to feel that they would continue with the same group through four sessions; the other half were made to understand that the composition of their groups could and might change and that in time each would have some choice about who would be included in his final group analysis. Half, therefore, felt they would be continuing on with the others, with the problems in adjustment and conformity that this might entail; and the other half should, theoretically, have felt more free of this continuing social pressure.

The second major study, conducted by myself, Mark Zanna, and James De Salvo at Yale and published in 1966, was quite similar in design and procedure. The subjects, however, were 198 high school boys who volunteered to take part in five- and six-man discussion groups. They had been recruited from newspaper advertisements and record shops and did not know one another.

The final study mentioned in this article, by myself, Sara Kiesler, and Michael Pallak, is still in process, and data analyses are not yet complete. Its findings, therefore, while very suggestive, are still tentative.

our own work that is more important to us. Our experiments have shown that *commitment*—in this case the expectation by a person that he must continue working and associating with a particular group—is also a major factor in opinion change and conformity to that group's standards. (Elsewhere J. Sakumura and I have defined commitment as "a pledging or binding of the individual to behavioral acts." This is a perfectly reasonable, if somewhat limited, view of commitment, and could include more subjective meanings, such as dedication or resolve. We have evidence that commitment is not, in and of itself, a motivation to change or resistance to change; but the *effect* of commitment is to make particular cognitions, or perceptions, more resistant to change.)

Let us briefly review the complicated experimental procedure that led to this outcome.

The subjects, all volunteers, were told that they would be assigned to discussion groups designed to test how strangers can work together for common goals. Each was told he had to return for four successive one-hour sessions. However, some were told they would continue with the same groups for all sessions (were, in effect, committed to them) while others were told they would be switched later to different groups and had no anticipation of working with the same people all the time.

After a session each privately gave his "first impressions" of the others. He also discussed and ranked various objects by his preferences, including some modern paintings. Each subject was then given bogus information about how others rated him ("Perhaps you would like to see what others thought of you. . . .").

Thus some are told that others find them very attractive, average, or unattractive. All subjects are told that the others disagree with their rankings of the objects. Then each is asked to rerank the objects—" . . . just for the institute; the group will never see them."

Note that every relevant variable is manipulated: the anticipation of continuing with the group; the extent of disagreement; how attractive the group finds each one. The individuals were completely taken in, very serious about cooperating, and unaware that they were being manipulated. (After the experiment the subjects were informed of its purpose, and the manipulation was explained. We found them intrigued, interested, and not offended.)

Under such controlled and cooperative circumstances we could be precise about what factors produced our results and confident that the results could be reliably applied to others. Our studies also demonstrated that:

—the less others like us, the less we like them;
—the less we like them, the less they affect our opinions.

The more we impressed upon a subject that the group didn't like him, the more he indicated that he didn't like them either, and the less he changed his opinion to conform with what we told him theirs was. This much was predictable from other work. However, we found an important exception created by the factor of *commitment*. Results were not the same in those cases when the person was committed to continue associating with the same group.

A committed person—like the noncommitted—generally modified his own opinions when he felt there was a high expression of attraction from the others. They both also modified them, though somewhat less, when the attraction was moderate. *But at the extreme—when least attracted— the committed person (but not the uncommitted) changed his opinions almost as much as the highly attracted did!*

This fascinating finding is not easily accounted for in current psychological theory. The subject does not like the group; they apparently do not like him; yet they have large influence on him. It is passive influence—they do not overtly try to influence him at all, yet they do. Only the individual knows that he disagrees; the group, presumably, does not know he disagrees and would never know unless he brought it up himself. It is a safe position for him to be in, to disagree as much as he pleases privately without external consequence. Yet his opinion changes to meet what he has been told theirs is.

But this is true only if he must continue with the group. If he is not so committed the group does not influence him at all, and the relationship between attraction and opinion change proceeds in the predictable straight line.

Further, this opinion change is stable—it lasts. But the obvious suspicion that anyone capable of such change must be a well-oiled weathervane, swinging around to accommodate any new wind, is wrong.

The Deviate Ally

This was well illustrated when we told the committed but low-attracted person that he had an ally (a "deviate ally") who agreed with his original opinion in spite of the rest of the group. Previous studies have demonstrated that if a person who disagrees with a group finds he has even one ally, he will stick by his guns and hold out. But with the committed, low-attracted person it depended on *when* he found out about this ally. If he found out before he had changed his opinion, he stood fast, as expected— opinion change under these circumstances was near zero.

But if he found out *after* he had accepted and expressed his new opinion, the ally had little effect. Moreover, he tended to resent this new-found "friend" and even to build up an active dislike for him. Of those who found out about this ally early, before change, 58 percent liked him best in the group. But of those who discovered him late, after change, only 14 percent said they liked him best, and 13 percent said they liked him least.

Let us analyze the implications of this finding a little further. First, they definitely limit the concept that greater attraction must inevitably lead to greater private acceptance; they illustrate at least one significant condition under which it does not. Second, they illustrate how important commitment is for understanding the behavior of groups and of individuals within groups. Commitment obviously can make a difference in attitudes, conclusions, and behavior generally.

It must be reemphasized that commitment makes this difference only when there is very little (or even negative) attraction to the group—the person doesn't like them or the situation, and he doesn't want to keep on, but feels he must. Obviously, therefore, this change of attitude is not what the subject really prefers—it is used only when all other avenues of psychological escape are closed off.

How can we account for this reversal—which seems contrary not only to prior research but to "common sense" as well?

This process can loosely be described in the following way: If a person feels out of harmony with some others or with a group, he has certain alternative methods of response for self-protection or counterattack. He can reject the group—decide to have nothing to do with it, and break off as soon as possible. Or he can devalue it—say that its opinions, importance, and members are of no particular consequence, not worth agreeing with.

There is some evidence that people will act this way if they do not feel bound to continue with the others. But these alternatives are not available to someone who is committed. He must somehow make his peace with them—and with his own concept of himself as someone who acts from conviction.

Appeasement and Aggravation

This is not peace at any price. It is not bland and superficial conformity. As our findings indicate, the important peace is within the subject himself. Also, it takes the long view—it considers consequences for the whole length of the commitment. A person not committed to continue can afford to practice "appeasement"—to bend to immediate pressures in the hope that they will pass. The committed must be much more cautious.

Thus commitment does not only and always tend toward agreement and the easing of tensions. It can lead as well toward sharpened conflict *in the short term,* if this seems necessary for long-term benefits. People who must cooperate cannot forever sweep unpleasant things under the rug.

For instance, how should an individual react to someone else's unpleasant habits or overbearing manners? He can pretend to ignore them once or a very few times. But what if they must keep associating? He may face the same problem at each meeting—aggravated by time and apparent acceptance. This *would* be appeasement in its classical form.

I am now collaborating with Sara Kiesler and Michael Pallak on a series of experiments designed to answer such questions. Specifically, how will people react to a social faux pas made by another? Folklore—in fact, many of the precepts of formal etiquette—suggest we try to save the offender's "face" and "gloss things over" when he is annoying or embarrassing us.

Our data analyses are not yet complete. But so far we have found what we expected. The *un*committed will tend to ignore the faux pas in a private confrontation with the offender; but something very different occurs among people who must continue association. Committed subjects were quite blunt about privately calling the offender's attention to his acts, reproving him, trying to get him to change. They apparently feel compelled to face the problem *now,* rather than keep on suffering from it.

We often notice parallel behavior between husband and wife, people who could hardly be more closely committed. They may reprove each other for acts that each would tolerate without comment from strangers. We usually consider this a sign of breakdown of marriage ties. But could not, as our studies imply, something of the reverse also sometimes be true—a desire to clear away potential sources of friction to make for an easier and more sincere relationship?

It is unfortunate that the effects of commitment have not been given more study, and we can hope that more research will come soon. Any factor that can influence people to change convictions and attitudes is a major force in human behavior and must be reckoned with.

Flattery Will Get You Somewhere

Edward E. Jones

Dale Carnegie, author of *How to Win Friends and Influence People,* was enraged at the implication that he would advocate using compliments just to get something out of people: "Great God Almighty!!! If we are so contemptibly selfish that we can't radiate a little happiness and pass on a bit of honest appreciation without trying to screw something out of the other person in return—if our souls are no bigger than sour crab apples, we shall meet with the failure we so richly deserve." The chapter containing this observation (entitled "How to Make People Like You Instantly") is composed of anecdotes describing precisely how complimenters *do* gain advantages. The message is clearly stated in other chapters as well: success in one's chosen line of work may be dramatically furthered by practicing the arts of ingratiation along the way.

Carnegie is not the only advocate of "applied human relations" who has had trouble distinguishing between the legitimate and illegitimate in social behavior. In certain business and political circles, for example, "sincere" is used as a synonym for agreeable. Self-serving flattery is usually deplored—but when does "honest appreciation" become flattery? Everyone likes a cooperative, agreeable attitude, but where is the line between manipulative conformity and self-effacing compromise? Many see great evil in ingratiation; Milton considered it hypocrisy, which he called "the only evil that walks invisible, except to God alone." Norman Vincent Peale, on the other hand, is much more tolerant; he considers pleasantness a mark of Christian virtue, from which peace of mind and prosperity flow naturally—and rightly.

Between these two extremes we find the charmingly honest Lord Chesterfield:

Vanity . . . is, perhaps, the most universal principle of human actions . . . if a man has a mind to be thought wiser, and a woman handsomer than they really are, their error is a comfortable one for themselves, and an innocent one with regard to other people; and I would rather make them my friends, by indulging them, than my enemies by endeavoring (in that to no purpose) to undeceive them.

Adlai Stevenson was also willing to counsel moderation with the remark, after being given a glowing introduction, "I have sometimes said that flattery is all right if you don't inhale."

What is custom and what is manipulation depends on time, place, the society, and often the individual. In those cultures where fulsome compliments are the norm, like the more traditional groups in Japan, anything less may be considered insulting. On the other hand, in many masculine circles in our own society praise is considered an affectation—a man who pays compliments easily will be thought untrustworthy or effeminate.

Most theories of social structure make the strong assumption that persons adjust their actions to what is generally accepted and expected. Ingratiation can be defined as impression-management which stretches or exploits these expectations or norms. Acts of ingratiation are designed to increase an individual's attractiveness beyond the value of what he really can offer to his target. Ingratiation is the illegitimate—the seamy—side of interpersonal communication.

BREAKING THE SOCIAL CONTRACT

But how do we determine when behavior is "legitimate"? Relationships and associations involve, in normal circumstances, an unstated contract between the actors. Different authorities describe this contract in different ways. Sociologist Erving Goffman, in his book *The Presentation of Self in Everyday Life,* emphasizes what he calls "ritual elements" in social interaction. Goffman believes that not only does communication take place in its usual sense but the communicators also engage in a "performance"—each transmits and receives clues about his definition of the situation, his view of himself, and his evaluation of the other. Mutual adjustment occurs. *Perhaps most important, the actors enter into a silent compact to help each other save face.* Each becomes involved in "face-work"—give-and-take actions that smooth over potentially embarrassing threats, lend mutual support, and make for coherent and consistent performances. Each person has a "defensive orientation toward saving his own face and a protective orientation toward saving the other's face."

Within this frame of reference, the ingratiator may be seen as exploiting this contract while seeming to support it. He neither violates the contract openly, nor merely fulfills it. Rather, he keeps sending out reassuring signals that he accepts the terms of the contract; but all the while he is actually working toward other goals.

To put it in slightly different terms: while relying on his target to stick to the rule that each should get out of a relationship what he brings to it, the ingratiator deliberately violates the rule himself in hopes of gaining a one-sided advantage. By definition, ingratiation occurs when a person cannot or does not want to offer as much as he hopes to get from the other, so he tries to make his "offer" appear more valuable by fancy packaging, misrepresenting how much he brings to the relationship, or advertising the effort or cost involved in his contribution. For instance, the worker may apply himself with greatest industry when he expects the supervisor to appear momentarily, he may try to convince others that his job is more difficult than it really is, or attempt to convince his boss that it requires considerable experience or specialized education.

While the dependent member of a relationship has more to gain from successful ingratiation than the more powerful member, the latter may be also quite concerned about his image. It has often been noted that men rising in organizations tend to lose the spontaneity of old relationships and certainty about the loyalty and reliability of old colleagues. In spite of their increasing power, they are dependent on subordinates for signs of their own effectiveness and—perhaps as a way of hedging their bets—they will use ingratiating tactics to increase morale and performance.

Ingratiation raises important problems in human relations and self-knowledge. Much of our understanding of the world around us, and of ourselves, comes to us indirectly through the impressions we get from others. In particular, self-evaluation is to a large extent determined by how others judge us—personal qualities like friendliness,

respectability, or moral worth can only be assessed by social means or mirrored in the reactions of others. Since ingratiation subverts this response, it is a threat to normal interaction and to reliable information. Like the traditional Hollywood producer and his yes-men, the executive surrounded by ingratiators may find himself adrift in a sea of uncertainties in which the only markers are the selfish interests of his advisers.

Ingratiation takes three general tactical forms.

■ OTHER-ENHANCEMENT. The ingratiator may try to elicit favorable reactions to himself by building up his target. At the extreme this involves obvious flattery; but there are also more subtle and indirect ways. The ingratiator may, for instance, concentrate on playing up the real strong points of the target, passing over or playing down the weak ones.

The ultimate design is to convince the target that the ingratiator thinks highly of him. We tend to like those who like us. Sometimes, however, the tactics are not simple or direct. The higher the target's regard for himself, the less he needs the ingratiator's praise, and the more he accepts it as obvious and routine. Targets may prefer praise, as Lord Chesterfield puts it, "upon those points where they wish to excel, and yet are doubtful whether they do or not. . . . The late Sir Robert Walpole, who was certainly an able man, was little open to flattery upon that head . . . but his prevailing weakness was, to be thought to have a polite and happy turn of gallantry; of which he had undoubtedly less than any man living . . . (and) those who had any penetration—applied to it with success."

■ CONFORMITY. People tend to like those whose values and beliefs appear similar to their own. Again, however, the relationship is not always direct. The ingratiator must seem sincere. His agreement must seem to be arrived at independently, for no ulterior purpose. The tactical conformer might be wise to disagree on non-essentials in order to underline the "independence" and value of his agreement on essentials. Agreement may be more valued if it seems to result from a *change* in opinion, made at some psychological cost, seeming to reflect a sincere change of conviction.

■ SELF-PRESENTATION is the explicit description or presentation of oneself in such a way as to become attractive to the target. This includes avoiding those characteristics the target might consider unpleasant, and subtly emphasizing those he might approve. The ingratiator walks a tightrope: he must boast without seeming to, since open boasting is frowned on in our society; he must "be" those things his target considers ideal for his situation, and yet appear

Osborn

sincere; he must seem admirable to the target and yet not a threat. He may have to ride a paradox—to be both self-enhancing and self-deprecating at the same time. This may not be difficult for someone with strong and obvious credentials—someone widely acknowledged to be the best in his field may gain by not mentioning it, and instead acknowledging his all-too-human failings. But those with dubious credentials must be more blatant in advertising their strengths.

In sum, in each of these classes the main problem of the ingratiator is to seem sincere and yet impressive and engaging. It is also better if his tactics and stated opinions support some pet but not universally admired or accepted ideas of the target.

Little research has been done on ingratiation. To carry the inspection of the subject beyond anecdote and intuition, we conducted a number of experiments in which college student subjects were given strong or weak incentives to make themselves attractive to a particular target. Sometimes targets knew that the ingratiators were dependent on them for benefits and therefore had selfish reasons to be attract-

ive; sometimes they did not know. In other experiments, subjects were exposed to ingratiating overtures by others and their impressions of these others were assessed.

One experiment, designed to test ingratiation tactics in an organizational hierarchy, used as subjects seventy-nine male volunteers from the Naval ROTC unit at Duke University. Pairs of freshmen (low-status) and pairs of upperclassmen (high-status) were brought together in units of four. Each subject in the experimental condition (designed to promote ingratiation) was told that the purpose of the study was to find out if "compatible groups provide a better setting in which to test leadership potential than do incompatible groups." The experimenter's instructions continued: "For this reason I hope that you will make a special effort to gain (the other's) liking and respect, always remembering your position as commander (or subordinate)." With the remaining subjects, in the control condition, emphasis was on the importance of obtaining *valid* information: "We are not especially concerned with whether you end up liking each other or not. . . . We are interested only in how well you can do in reaching a clear impression of the other person."

Another experiment used fifty male volunteers from the introductory psychology course at the University of North Carolina in what was supposed to be a game designed to simulate a business situation. An experimental accomplice, presented as a graduate student from the School of Business Administration, was introduced as the "supervisor," conducting and scoring the games. Actually, the "business games" were used to discover and measure ingratiation tactics which might be used to gain advantage in comparable professional or business contexts.

From the results of the experiments thus far completed *there is no doubt that the average undergraduate behaves differently when he wants to be liked than when he wants only to be accurate in presenting himself socially.*

Specifically, let us break down the results in terms of the three major types of ingratiation tactics.

SELF-PRESENTATION. Generally, when instructed to try to make a good impression, our subjects played up their strong points and played down their weaknesses. (These varied according to the situation.) However, there were a few significant exceptions:

■ In a status hierachy, tactics vary according to the ingratiator's position. In the ROTC experiment, the lower-classmen usually inflated only those qualities they considered unimportant. Apparently they felt that to inflate the important qualities might make them seem pushy, and perhaps even threatening. Upper-classmen became more modest about all qualities. They felt secure, and their high status was obvious because of age and rank—therefore they did not feel it necessary to assert superiority. Modesty, we infer, helped them build up the impression of friendliness toward the lower ranks, which they considered desirable.

■ Who and what the target is influences how the ingratiator describes himself. In the business games, those trying to impress the supervisor favorably emphasized their competence and respectability rather than their geniality. "Attractiveness" can, therefore, be sought by emphasizing what is more desired in a given situation—perhaps efficiency, perhaps compatibility, perhaps trustworthiness or integrity. If the ingratiator knows that the target is aware of his dependence, his tactics are apt to be subtle or devious. He may very well deprecate himself in those areas he does not consider important in order to build up his credibility in areas he *does* consider important. If, however, the ingratiator believes the target is innocent enough to accept him at face value, he will be tempted to pull out all stops.

CONFORMITY. Perhaps the clearest research finding was that, to be successful, ingratiation must result in greater public agreement with the target's stated opinions. (Hamlet asked Polonius, "Do you see yonder cloud that's almost in the shape of a camel?" "By the mass, and 'tis like a camel, indeed." "Methinks it is like a weasel." "It is backed like a weasel." "Or like a whale?" "Very like a whale.")

Such conformity was true of both high-status and low-status students—with some significant differences. The low status freshmen conformed more on relevant than irrelevant items. Upper-classmen conformed more on the irrelevant than the relevant—presumably they were eager to appear good fellows, but not at the price of compromising any essential source of power or responsibility.

Further, as the business games showed, an ingratiator will cut the cloth of his agreement to fit the back of what is important to his target. If the target clearly values tact, cooperation, and getting along with others, the ingratiator will understand that the strategic use of agreement will probably result in personal advantage. Subjects were quick to reach this conclusion and to act on it, in contrast to their show of independence when the target appeared to be austerely concerned with the productivity of subordinates rather than the congeniality of their views.

When the ingratiator happens to agree closely with the target anyway, there is some evidence that too much agreement is deliberately avoided. Actually, agreement is almost never total. In most of the experimental cases of conformity, the ingratiator's final stated view were a compromise between his original opinion and that of his target. He might be described as avoiding extreme disagreement rather than seeking close agreement; nevertheless, the evidence is clear that expressed opinions are influenced by a desire to create a good impression.

OTHER-ENHANCEMENT. In this tactical area the results were quite inconclusive. There was some evidence that low-status subjects, after being instructed concerning the importance of compatibility with their superiors, were more complimentary than when operating under instructions to be accurate. High-status subjects did not show this same tendency to flatter more under conditions stressing compatibility. On the other hand, they were more inclined to view the low status complimenter as insincere in a final private judgment, when the instructions stressed compatibility. The low status subjects showed no such suspicions of their superiors.

THE BOUNDS OF VANITY

Our experiments have answered a few questions and

posed many more which may be profitably studied. Among the more important questions raised:

■ Given the ethical barriers to deceit and social manipulation, what *are* the modes of rationalization or self-justification in ingratiation? How does the ingratiator keep his self-respect? Though our data consistently revealed differences between experimental (compatibility) and control (accuracy) conditions, we were unable to detect any intent to win favor, or the *conscious* adoption of attraction-gaining strategies.

■ How are power differences affected by ingratiation tactics? Does ingratiation by the follower subvert or augment the power of the leader?

■ How precisely do the distortions of ingratiation affect our perceptions of ourselves and others?

■ What of the psychology of favor-giving as part of ingratiation? When does it help and when does it hurt the ingratiator? Is it possible that sometimes targets will like us more if we let *them* do favors for *us?* Why might this be so?

There remains the problem of defining ingratiation. Microscopic examination of ingratiating behavior keeps revealing an evanescent "something" that in any given case can be identified under more familiar headings such as: social conformity, deference to status, establishing credibility. It is my contention, however, that the concept of ingratiation links together various kinds of communicative acts that would otherwise be separately viewed and studied. By recognizing that there is a strategic side to social interaction, we open to examination the forms in which one person presents his "face" to another, when that other occupies an important position in his scheme of things.

Perhaps by acknowledging that ingratiation is part of the human condition, we may bring its facets into the light of day. As psychologists, if not as moralists, we may in this vein, admire Lord Chesterfield's candor:

Vanity is, perhaps, the most universal principle of human actions. . . . If my insatiable thirst for popularity, applause, and admiration made me do some silly things on the one hand, it made me, on the other hand, do almost all the right things that I did. . . . With the men I was a Proteus, and assumed every shape to please them all: among the gay, I was the gayest; among the grave, the gravest; and I never omitted the least attention to good breeding, to the least offices of friendship, that could either please or attach them to me. . . .

The Applied Art of One-Downmanship

Eugene A. Weinstein

"I hope you won't take this personally . . ."

"Of course I'm not as good at this as you are, but . . ."

"I've given this a lot of thought, and believe me it's for the best interests of everybody, including you . . ."

All these conversational gambits are common in everyone's social vocabulary; nevertheless, they illustrate a very important and too little understood phenomenon—the everyday tactics of getting what you want from others while keeping them willing to go along with you.

Erving Goffman in *The Presentation of Self in Everyday Life,* sees the encounters between human beings as having unspoken social rules and regulations. The participants must reach a "working consensus"—a tacit agreement about what "rights" should be honored, and what rules should be observed (though not necessarily believed in). Goffman sees social intercourse as a kind of performance in which the "actors" must ad-lib their way through changing situations; form, stability, and a loose set of rules must be obeyed if the consensus is to continue.

Four conditions, each depending on those preceding, must be satisfied for a working consensus to develop—and for a successful social performance to be staged:

■ Each participant must indicate his willingness to listen to the others.

■ At least some of the participants must indicate they have something to accomplish and the methods they intend to use.

■ The limits to their intentions, and to their actions, must be implied.

■ These implications cannot be openly denied by anyone. If a working consensus is to be established and maintained, no "actor" can deny another's chance to pursue his goals by his chosen methods.

Generally, who the actor is, and what he stands for, are vital to the justification of his claim that he is entitled to use the encounter to pursue his personal goals. Because of this the working consensus must include unspoken agreement about who *every* participant is, and what *each* stands for—their social identities. Not only the identity the actor claims for himself, but those he may openly assign to the others must be mutually acceptable.

Each actor has two problems in social encounters: while he tries to achieve his own goal he must, at the same time, keep the others bound into the relationship. To the universal cry of "What's in it for me?" the actor must offer something acceptable—in order to increase his chances of getting what's in it for him. Often, the bargain offered the other is recognition that he is entitled to an identity in the situation he is known to value. While this give-and-take is going on it is therefore particularly important that "face" be mutually respected—and that conflicts do not result in personal antagonisms that can break down the relationship.

To formalize and slightly extend some of Goffman's ideas —to emphasize the role of personal purpose—let us examine further the precise techniques in use (with appropriate jargon to keep it all sounding scientific).

WORDS ABOUT WORDS

To accomplish anything speech must have the favorable impact on the listener that the speaker intends—or hopes for. To try to make sure it does, the speaker can add to the message certain phrases which tell the listener what the message is supposed to mean. Such phrases can be called *communication about communication*.

Suppose an act or statement can have several meanings to a listener, some favorable and others unfavorable. One way to make sure he does not get the wrong meaning is to tell him what meaning he is supposed to get—in other words a *pre-interpretation*. "There's nothing personal about this . . ." is a common pre-interpretation. So are: "objectively speaking . . ." and "Be sure not to take this the wrong way. . . ."

A not uncommon ploy is to start with a *preinterpretation* that asserts that nothing detrimental is intended. This allows the speaker, then, to insult the other at will: "I think you've done a great job and I don't want you to get me wrong, but . . ."

Not all communication about communication need occur before the message; it can also come after. Sometimes it's evident that the listener got the "wrong" meaning; then the speaker may want to rush in and straighten him out. So he uses a *post-interpretation:* "I'm just telling you what's being said—I don't necessarily agree with it." "Now don't misunderstand and think I said. . . ."

The double function of communication about communication—getting your desire while keeping everybody else happy, or at least cooperative—is not always easily accomplished. Sometimes the speaker knows that his message or action may fall flat no matter what he says about it. He may try, then, to separate the listener's personal evaluation of him from the negative effects of the message or action by apologizing ahead of time. He uses a *pre-apology* "I haven't had the chance to read up on this yet . . ." and, "Just speaking off the top of my head, since we have to make a fast decision . . ." are examples that ask others not to downgrade the actor if his act comes below expectations. "I'm really not in practice, but I'll try . . ." asks a little less: that the others not judge the performance too strictly.

The pre-apology is good also for securing a "vote of confidence"—approval even before the action is attempted. This is called "fishing." "I'm really not very good at it," the new lady golfer demurs, and the rest of the foursome (she hopes) immediately choruses, "Oh, of course you are. You're good at everything."

When a pre-interpretation or a post-interpretation reveal causes for one's actions, they are *motive revelations.* If the actor wants to take responsibility and credit for his act, he uses the *personalized* form. If he wants to get off the hook (he was a helpless victim of circumstances) he uses a depersonalized form. A personalized motive revelation identifies the speaker firmly with the good things in the message, or at least with the good intentions implicit in bringing the message: "I'm mentioning this because I think you'd be pleased to know . . ." Depersonalized, it separates him from the bad things: "I didn't want this to happen, but you know what the boss is like when he makes up his mind . . ." The depersonalized motive revelation is, in short, an alibi.

The difference between them becomes most evident in responses to requests. When someone makes a request, he implies that both he and it are worthy of consideration. Denial entails risks on both sides. In consequence, elaborate feelers, and lines of action and reaction, are set up.

One way for a requester to minimize risk is to ask for something without seeming to—to keep the lines of retreat wide open: "It would be very nice if . . ." Assent in such cases tends to take the form of a personalized motive revelation: "Of course, I'd be happy to . . ." The asker can then counter with, "But I don't really want to impose . . . ," a very useful gambit. It serves as a preapology and, at the same time, puts the other in the role of defending the reasonableness of the request—so that before he quite knows what has happened he is urging the requester to accept what was requested. "Oh no, no trouble at all . . . that's perfectly all right . . . don't even mention it . . ."

Depersonalized forms predominate in the opposite tactic —when denying requests. The denier can't be blamed for denial when he demonstrates that he did the best he could. Nor is the requester liable to feel as personally rejected. Usually the matter was simply beyond the denier's control: he was too busy, his wife was sick, the fates were against him. For example; "I only have one vote on that committee. I did the best I could, but I didn't have a chance."

A further refinement is the *altruistic motive revelation*. The request was turned down or the deed was done for the *other's own good*. "No, I didn't put in your name for that apartment, but that was only because I know they don't accept Negroes or children and I just wanted to save you embarrassment." Unless the person using the altruistic form has close personal ties with us or is generally recognized to be in a superior position with superior information (for instance, a physician during illness) he can seem offensively patronizing. Parents however, always know what is best for their children, and often enough it turns out to be exactly opposite what the children want. Children, like adults, learn to be suspicious of such claims, and to discount them.

Altruistic statements are one of a large number of tactics useful in enhancing credibility—a person who has our best interests at heart presumably wouldn't lie to us. We can trust him. Credibility then shifts from the message itself to the preface—to the actor's statement of pious intent. If you reject the message then you reject his statement that he is acting sincerely, and you reject him too.

A similar pattern occurs in the "display of involvement." The actor, by the loudness and tone of his voice, inflections, gestures, and expression, indicates the intensity and sincerity of his feeling and concern for what he is saying and doing. He really *means* it—how can you doubt that? "Do you real-ly think I'd lie to you when it means so much to me too?" If you make it evident, however politely, that you do think so, you are calling him a fraud, and destroying his identity. He has proferred his heart's gold, and you have called it brass. Doubters will often hold back open expression of doubt because it runs a great risk of breaking up the consensus. But display of involvement, sincere or not, is always risky. Unless carefully managed it invites suspicion: "The lady doth protest too much, methinks."

A final tactic in the same vein can be called *identity conformation*. The actor establishes his credibility and importance by the "droppings" of authority—name dropping, place dropping, experience dropping—even if they may actually be irrelevant. "I have been in this business for twenty-five years . . ." "Back at Harvard we used to . . ." "I knew Lyndon when he was a congressman, and even then . . ."

If we ask what tactics are most apt to be used in a particular situation, the best prediction is, those that seem most likely to be successful—to get a person what he wants while still preserving his relationship with the others. One reason for this is conscious selection of tactics (and many are so selected). Who does not remember planning ahead for an encounter, deciding in advance what would be the best impression to try to make, the best tone to strike, the best tactic to take?

But not all efforts are or can be conscious. Many things we do, the prefaces we use, the deferences we show, are not because we clearly see their tactical advantage but because we have learned they are appropriate—and learned this as a normal part of growing up as a member of society. We may use them in order to satisfy, in our own eyes, our personal values about tactfulness—not particularly because we recognize that they help to keep others bound into a relationship so we can get them to do what we want.

Putting the Business World into a Test Tube

James A. Vaughan and Bernard M. Bass

Quite clearly, the way a business operation is organized helps determine how efficient that business will be and how satisfied its staff will be. But how can anyone determine how effective different kinds of business organizations really are? What about entirely theoretical business organizations—ones that have never existed? How, in fact, can the operations of *any* sort of organization—not just business—be studied under laboratory conditions?

We have found that "business games" are one very promising approach. In real life, it is difficult to gauge the effects of a company's organization—because of the extreme complexity of business operations and because of the near impossibility of isolating what should be measured. Though simulations cannot reproduce real-life operations in *every* detail, they often make it possible to make such measurements.

Using this method of attack, we recently completed two studies comparing the effectiveness of two types of organizational structure—types we call *bottoms-up* and *top-down*. We asked some of the same questions that measure effectiveness in any organization. How well does the organization function and produce—and, if it is a business, how much profit does it make? What about the personal satisfaction of the employees? Are they happy to be there? Will they stay on and perform well?

The business game used in our studies is called UPPOE (University of Pittsburgh Production Organization Exercise). Unlike many simulations, it does not use a computer. UPPOE resembles an actual manufacturing and marketing industry. In contrast with computerized games, real work is done, and in an organized fashion. Participants actually produce "products"—miniature I-beams—simulated by cutting and stapling IBM cards together according to given specifications. These I-beams are then sold, competitively, in a market of supply and demand, sales being influenced by factors like advertising, prices, and company history and reputation. The major difference between our market and a real one is that with ours the money transactions have no real value.

UPPOE is not a completely faithful simulation of any particular real-life industry, but decisions made by the participants do have real effects on the game's outcome. Personnel are able to learn from these decisions and modify their actions accordingly. In other words, success does *not* depend on chance, but on manufacturing and marketing efficiency, organizational ability, and individual satisfaction.

The organization and management of real people and real resources results in real-life problems. For example, labor-management problems result from the fact that the management team supervises real workers.

Then too, competition is basic to UPPOE—not only in the marketplace, but even in regard to the labor supply. Each company must try to hold the workers it begins with and, if possible, attract others.

To further simulate real-life businesses, game participants must follow certain rules. For example, no more than a third of a company's personnel are allowed to meet simultaneously. This rule forces the game participants to devise formal communication procedures, just as physical distance and sheer numbers force real-life organizations to formalize communications.

There is also a clear distinction in the game between managers and wage earners: Managers are not permitted to engage in any activity directly related to production. Thus, in emergencies the managers cannot pitch in and help the workers with actual production.

All companies, at the end of each production period, are required to complete public financial statements, which provide a quick and easy means of comparing their progress.

The number of people required to run a company in the game can vary, from eight to 20. In both of the game-runs reported here, there were 16 people in each company: eight managers and eight wage earners.

In the pilot study we conducted, two organizational forms were compared. Both were the products of a brainstorming exercise involving about 12 social scientists attending a Social Science of Organizations Seminar at the University of Pittsburgh. We presented the organizational problem to this group and asked them to come up with two distinctly different organizational designs, one "bottoms-up" and the other "top-down." Murray Horwitz and Paul Lawrence of Harvard were the primary designers of the bottoms-up management organization, and Harold J. Leavitt of Stanford and Ralph Stogdill of Ohio State were the primary designers of the top-down arrangement.

The *bottoms-up* organizational arrangement emphasizes the functions to be performed and the subsystems set up to perform these functions and integrate them into the production cycle—rather than the comparative authority, responsibilities, and status of individual staff members. This arrangement places its major subsystems at the top of the organization and is characterized by:
—multiple membership in subsystems—operators, planners, coordinators;
—the various functions that relate subsystems to one another;
—access to needed resources, like money;
—access to information about the limitations of the personnel and the general organization;
—approximate equity of reward to personnel; and
—available internal mechanisms to alter and restructure each subsystem as necessary.

In the game, the duties and responsibilities of operators, planners, and coordinators were detailed—but no individual was considered to be the overall director of the organization. Nor did the job titles or descriptions keep the personnel confined in pigeonholes. They shared duties and decision-making as the circumstances, and their abilities, required and allowed. Virtually all decision-making was done in groups. (One real-life organization that has many elements of such a bottoms-up structure is Non-linear Systems of Del Mar, Calif.)

The *top-down* organization, by contrast, has the pyramidal structure typical of large business corporations. The two aims of its designers were:
—to establish a line organization capable of (1) sensing outside opportunities, hazards, and pressures; and (2) controlling and coordinating operations with maximum efficiency;
—to establish staff services capable of providing a continuous diagnosis of internal conditions and rapidly correcting imbalances, dissatisfactions, and malfunctions.

It is probably fair to say that the bottoms-up organization was designed to be maximally responsive to the needs and characteristics of its members, while the top-down design was meant to maximize the organization's response to external pressures and needs. Stogdill and Lawrence came to Pittsburgh, explained the designs to the 96 graduate business students participating in the first study, and consulted with them during the all-day run of UPPOE. In the morning, three bottoms-up companies (with 16 men each) competed with three top-down companies. In the afternoon, the companies were reorganized: the managers of a top-down morning company became the workers for a bottoms-up company. Thus we really had six bottoms-up companies to compare with six top-down companies. The comparison is not clean, however, because of the movement of people and because of a significant "learning effect"—we found that all the afternoon companies performed better than all the morning companies.

Financially, the bottoms-up companies very clearly outperformed the top-down companies. This is true whether we compare all companies at once or treat the morning and afternoon groups separately. For example, the average net worth of the afternoon bottoms-up companies was $20,977, compared with $15,456 for the top-down companies—a significant difference.

With regard to staff satisfaction, as in most real companies, managers virtually always reported more satisfaction than workers. In addition, bottoms-up managers and workers were consistently more satisfied than their top-down counterparts. This was in response to a questionnaire that asked about:

—satisfaction with company operations;
—clarity of company goals;
—opportunity to make own decisions;
—feeling ease in expressing one's views;
—extent to which authority matched responsibility; and
—feeling conflict of interest with other workers.

Interestingly, the incomes of the bottoms-up workers were generally greater than those of workers in the top-down companies. The spread between high and low was greater in the top-down: Executive income was greater, but the average worker did not fare so well.

A second study of the same two organizational designs

was completed one year later. The subjects were again graduate business students, but this time we used night as well as day students. The night students held full-time jobs in industry and were, on the average, eight to ten years older than the men in the day group. Since we could not resist comparing the performance of the experienced, older, night students with the performance of the day students, we assigned them to separate teams rather than mixing them in the same companies. The result was six teams composed of day students, and two composed of night students. All teams had 16 men.

In retrospect, we believe that we muddied the waters—that the separation of night and day students obscured or diluted the top-down versus bottoms-up comparison we had hoped to make.

In any case, comparing the financial performance of the eight bottoms-up companies in this study with the eight top-down ones, we found that dollar outcomes slightly favored the bottoms-up group. Its average net worth was $19,821, whereas the top-down average was $18,582. For the night group alone, the difference was greater: $24,477 for the bottoms-up and $22,139 for the top-down. Both night companies performed significantly better than the day groups, with a mean net worth of $23,308 as compared with $17,506. This reflected, most likely, the greater age and experience of the night students.

With regard to attitudes, however, the top-down participants reported slightly more satisfaction with overall operations than the bottoms-up participants did. This finding does not agree with that of the first study. Probably, however, it too reflects the participation of the night students, who were more familiar with, and felt more at home in, the real business world, which is predominantly top-down.

Therefore, the clearest thing that emerged from this second study is that the students with greatest experience in the real business world performed significantly better than the others.

The dollar incomes—in the first study significantly, in the second one slightly—favored the bottoms-up organization. Still, we cannot definitely conclude that this design is really more efficient that the top-down design. One great and continuing difficulty with such studies is that we can seldom be sure that we are really measuring what we are trying to measure. For instance, interviews with some bottoms-up participants revealed that their companies, in actual practice, seemed to them to operate more like top-down firms!

In short, extensive and close monitoring is essential. If we must use simulations instead of real life, we must also make them reflect real-life patterns as closely as possible. Ideally, management-control systems need to develop gradually, as in real life, so that players cannot depart from designs without it being evident to the experimenter that a departure is occurring.

Our experience also suggests that the attitudes of the participants toward the organization are as important as the structure itself. If they don't like it, or can't believe in it, they simply won't give it a chance to function properly. They must regard the design they are asked to work with as a potentially efficient one—even if it is unfamiliar, contrasts with their experiences in real organizations, and reflects a management philosophy they disapprove of.

Finally, business games like UPPOE are too dependent on such things as good working relations and freedom from small human errors. That is, UPPOE is more sensitive to minor human failings and conflicts than the typical real-life firm, where business goes on despite such imperfections. These problems need careful thought if such studies are to be worthwhile.

In any case, what seems to us to have been demonstrated by these studies is that business games are valuable tools for studying organizational structures, both real and projected—and that, with proper precautions, much profitable use can be made of such simulations.

White Gangs Walter B. Miller

If one thinks about street corner gangs at all these days, it is probably in the roseate glow of *West Side Story,* itself the last flowering of a literary and journalistic concern that goes back at least to the late 40's. Those were the days when it seemed that the streets of every city in the country had become dark battlefields where small armies of young men engaged their honor in terrible trials of combat, clashing fiercely and suddenly, then retiring to the warm succor of their girl cohorts. The forward to a 1958 collection of short stories, *The Young Punks.* captures a bit of the flavor:

These are the stories behind today's terrifying headlines—about a strange new frightening cult that has grown up in our midst. Every writer whose work is included in this book tells the truth. These kids are tough. Here are knife-carrying killers, and thirteen-year-old street walkers who could give the most hardened call-girl lessons. These kids pride themselves on their "ethics": never go chicken, even if it means knifing your own friend in the back. Never rat on a guy who wears your gang colors, unless he rats on you first. Old men on crutches are fair game. If a chick plays you for a sucker, blacken her eyes and walk away fast.

Today, the one-time devotee of this sort of stuff might be excused for wondering where they went, the Amboy Dukes and all those other adolescent warriors and lovers who so excited his fancy a decade ago. The answer, as we shall see, is quite simple—nowhere. The street gangs are still there, out on the corner where they always were.

The fact is that the urban adolescent street gang is as old as the American city. Henry Adams, in his *Education*, describes in vivid detail the gang fights between the Northsiders and Southsiders on Boston Common in the 1840's. An observer in 1856 Brooklyn writes: " . . . at any and all hours there are multitudes of boys . . . congregated on the corners of the streets, idle in their habits, dissolute in their conduct, profane and obscene in their conversation, gross and vulgar in their manners. If a female passes one of the groups she is shocked by what she sees and hears. . . . " The Red Raiders of Boston have hung out on the same corner at least since the 1930's; similarly, gang fighting between the Tops and Bottoms in West Philadelphia, which started in the 30's, is still continuing in 1969.

Despite this historical continuity, each new generation tends to perceive the street gang as a new phenomenon generated by particular contemporary conditions and destined to vanish as these conditions vanish. Gangs in the 1910's and 20's were attributed to the cultural dislocations and community disorganization accompanying the mass immigration of foreigners; in the 30's to the enforced idleness and economic pressures produced by the Great Depression; in the 50's to the emotional disturbance of parents and children caused by the increased stresses and tensions of modern life. At present, the existence of gangs is widely attributed to a range of social injustices: racial discrimination, unequal educational and work opportunities, resentment over inequalities in the distribution of wealth and privilege in an affluent society, and the ineffective or oppressive policies of service agencies such as the police and the schools.

There is also a fairly substantial school of thought that holds that the street gangs are disappearing or have already disappeared. In New York City, the stage of so many real and fictional gang dramas of the 50's and early 60's, *The Times* sounded their death-knell as long ago as 1966. Very often, the passing of the gang is explained by the notion that young people in the slums have converted their gang-forming propensities into various substitute activities. They have been knocked out by narcotics, or they have been "politicized" in ways that consume their energies in radical or reform movements, or their members have become involved in "constructive" commercial activities, or enrolled in publicly financed education and/or work-training programs.

As has often been the case, these explanations are usually based on very shaky factual grounds and derived from rather parochial, not to say self-serving, perspectives. For street gangs are not only still widespread in United States cities, but some of them appear to have again taken up "gang warfare" on a scale that is equal to or greater than the phenomenon that received so much attention from the media in the 1950's.

In Chicago, street gangs operating in the classic formations of that city—War Lords, High Supremes, Cobra Stones—accounted for 33 killings and 252 injuries during the first six months of 1969. Philadelphia has experienced a wave of gang violence that has probably resulted in more murders in a shorter period of time than during any equivalent phase of the "fighting gang" era in New York. Police estimate that about 80 gangs comprising about 5,000 members are "active" in the city, and that about 20 are engaged in combat. Social agencies put the total estimated number of gangs at 200, with about 80 in the "most hostile" category. Between October 1962 and December 1968, gang members were reportedly involved in 257 shootings, 250 stabbings and 205 "rumbles." In the period between January 1968 and June 1969, 54 homicides and over 520 injuries were attributed to armed battles between gangs. Of the murder victims, all but eight were known to be affiliated with street gangs. The assailants ranged in age from 13 to 20, with 70 percent of them between 16 and 18 years old. Most of these gangs are designated by the name of the major corner where they hang out, the 12th and Poplar Streeters, or the 21 W's (for 21st and Westmoreland). Others bear traditional names such as the Centaurs, Morroccos and Pagans.

Gangs also continue to be active in Boston. In a single 90-minute period on May 10, 1969, one of the two channels of the Boston Police radio reported 38 incidents involving gangs, or one every 2½ minutes. This included two gang fights. Simultaneous field observation in several white lower-class neighborhoods turned up evidence that gangs were congregating at numerous street corners throughout the area.

Although most of these gangs are similar to the classic types to be described in what follows, as of this summer the national press had virtually ignored the revival of gang violence. *Time* magazine did include a brief mention of "casual mayhem" in its June 27 issue, but none of the 38 incidents in Boston on May 10 was reported even in the local papers. It seems most likely, however, that if all this had been going on in New York City, where most of the media have their headquarters, a spate of newspaper features, magazine articles and television "specials" would have created the impression that the country was being engulfed by a "new" wave of gang warfare. Instead, most people seem to persist in the belief that the gangs have disappeared or that they have been radically transformed.

This anomalous situation is partly a consequence of the problem of defining what a gang is (and we will offer a definition at the end of our discussion of two specific gangs), but it is also testimony to the fact that this enduring aspect of the lives of urban slum youth remains complex and poorly understood. It is hoped that the following examination of the Bandits and the Outlaws—both of Midcity—will clarify at least some of the many open questions about street corner gangs in American cities.

Midcity, which was the location of our 10-year gang study project (1954-64), is not really a city at all, but a portion of a large one, here called Port City. Midcity is a predominantly lower-class community with a relatively high rate of crime, in which both criminal behavior and a characteristic set of conditions—low-skill occupations, little education, low-rent dwellings, and many others—appeared as relatively stable and persisting features of a developed way of life. How did street gangs fit into this picture?

In common with most major cities during this period, there were many gangs in Midcity, but they varied widely in size, sex composition, stability and range of activities. There were about 50 Midcity street corners that served as hangouts for local adolescents. Fifteen of these were "major" corners, in that they were rallying points for the full range of a gang's membership, while the remaining 35 were "minor," meaning that in general fewer groups of smaller size habitually hung out there.

In all, for Midcity in this period, 3,650 out of 5,740, or 64 percent, of Midcity boys habitually hung out at a particular corner and could therefore be considered members of a particular gang. For girls, the figure is 1,125 out of 6,250, or 18 percent. These estimates also suggest that something like 35 percent of Midcity's boys, and 80 percent of its girls, did *not* hang out. What can be said about them? What made them different from the approximately 65 percent of the boys and 20 percent of the girls who did hang out?

Indirect evidence appears to show that the practice of hanging out with a gang was more prevalent among lower-status adolescents, and that many of those who were not known to hang out lived in middle-class or lower-class I (the higher range of the lower-class) areas. At the same time, however, it is evident that a fair proportion of higher-status youngsters also hung out. The question of status, and its relation to gang membership and gang behavior is very complex, but it should be borne in mind as we now take a closer look at the gangs we studied.

The Bandit Neighborhood

Between the Civil War and World War II, the Bandit neighborhood was well-known throughout the city as a colorful and close-knit community of Irish laborers. Moving to a flat in one of its ubiquitous three-decker frame tenements represented an important step up for the impoverished potato-famine immigrants who had initially settled in the crowded slums of central Port City. By the 1810's the second generation of Irish settlers had produced a spirited and energetic group of athletes and politicos, some of whom achieved national prominence.

Those residents of the Bandit neighborhood who shared in some degree the drive, vitality and capability of these famous men assumed steady and fairly remunerative positions in the political, legal and civil service world of Port City, and left the neighborhood for residential areas whose green lawns and single houses represented for them what Midcity had represented for their fathers and grandfathers. Those who lacked these qualities remained in the Bandit neighborhood, and at the outset of World War II made up a stable and relatively homogeneous community of low-skilled Irish laborers.

The Bandit neighborhood was directly adjacent to Midcity's major shopping district, and was spotted with bars, poolrooms and dance halls that served as meeting places for an active neighborhood social life. Within two blocks of the Bandits' hanging-out corner were the Old Erin and New Hibernia dance halls, and numerous drinking establishments bearing names such as the Shamrock, Murphy and Donoghue's, and the Emerald Bar and Grill.

A number of developments following World War II disrupted the physical and social shape of the Bandit community. A mammoth federally-financed housing project sliced through and blocked off the existing network of streets and razed the regular rows of wooden tenements. The neighborhood's small manufacturing plants were progressively diminished by the growth of a few large establishments, and by the 1950's the physical face of the neighborhood was dominated by three large and growing plants. As these plants expanded they bought off many of the properties which had not been taken by the housing project, demolished buildings, and converted them into acres of black-topped parking lots for their employees.

During this period, the parents of the Bandit corner gang members stubbornly held on to the decreasing number of low-rent, deteriorating, private dwelling units. Although the Bandits' major hanging corner was almost surrounded by the housing project, virtually none of the gang members lived there. For these families, residence in the housing project would have entailed a degree of financial stability and restrained behavior that they were unable or unwilling to assume, for the corner gang members of the Bandit neighborhood were the scions of men and women who occupied the lowest social level in Midcity. For them low rent was a passion, freedom to drink and to behave drunkenly a sacred privilege, sporadic employment a fact of life, and the social welfare and law-enforcement agencies of the state, partners of one's existence.

The Bandit Corner was subject to field observation for about three years—from June 1954 to May 1957. Hanging out on the corner during this period were six distinct but related gang subdivisions. There were four male groups: The Brigands, aged approximately 18 to 21 at the start of the study period; the Senior Bandits, aged 16 to 18; the Junior Bandits, 14 to 16, and the Midget Bandits, 12 to 14. There were also two distinct female subdivisions: The Bandettes, 14 to 16, and the Little Bandettes, 12 to 14.

The physical and psychic center of the Bandit corner was Sam's Variety Store, the owner and sole employee of which was not Sam but Ben, his son. Ben's father had founded the store in the 1920's, the heyday of the Irish laboring class in the Bandit neighborhood. When his father died, Ben took over the store, but did not change its name. Ben was a stocky, round-faced Jew in his middle 50's, who looked upon the whole of the Bandit neighborhood as his personal fief and bounden responsibility—a sacred legacy from his father. He knew everybody and was concerned with everybody; through his store passed a constant stream of customers and noncustomers of all ages and both sexes. In a space not much larger than that of a fair-sized bedroom Ben managed to crowd a phone booth, a juke box, a pinball machine, a space heater, counters, shelves and stock, and an assorted variety of patrons. During one 15-minute period on an average day Ben would supply $1.37 worth of groceries to 11-year-old Carol Donovan and enter the sum on her mother's page in the "tab" book, agree to extend Mrs. Thebodeau's already extended credit until her A.D.C. check arrived, bandage and solace the three-year-old Negro girl who came crying to him with a cut forefinger, and shoo into the street a covey of Junior Bandits whose altercation over a pinball score was impeding customer traffic and augmenting an already substantial level of din.

Ben was a bachelor, and while he had adopted the whole of the Bandit neighborhood as his extended family, he had taken on the 200 adolescents who hung out on the Bandit corner as his most immediate sons and daughters. Ben knew the background and present circumstances of every Bandit, and followed their lives with intense interest and concern. Ben's corner-gang progeny were a fast-moving and mercurial lot, and he watched over their adventures and misadventures with a curious mixture of indignation, solicitude, disgust, and sympathy. Ben's outlook on the affairs of the world was never bland; he held and freely voiced strong opinions on a wide variety of issues, prominent among which was the behavior and misbehavior of the younger generation.

This particular concern was given ample scope for attention by the young Bandits who congregated in and around his store. Of all the gangs studied, the Bandits were the most consistently and determinedly criminal, and central to Ben's concerns was how each one stood with regard to "trouble." In this respect, developments were seldom meager. By the time they reached the age of 18, every one of the 32 active members of the Senior Bandits had appeared in court at least once, and some many times; 28 of the 32 boys had been committed to a correctional institution and 16 had spent at least one term in confinement.

Ben's stout arm swept the expanse of pavement which fronted his store. "I'll tell ya, I give up on these kids. In all the years I been here, I never seen a worse bunch. You know what they should do? They should put up a big platform with one of them stocks right out there, and as soon as a kid gets in trouble, into the stocks with 'im. Then they'd straighten out. The way it is now, the kid tells a sob story to some soft-hearted cop or social worker, and pretty soon he's back at the same old thing. See that guy just comin' over here? That's what I mean. He's hopeless. Mark my word, he's gonna end up in the electric chair."

The Senior Bandit who entered the store came directly to Ben. "Hey, Ben, I just quit my job at the shoe factory. They don't pay ya nothin', and they got some wise guy nephew of the owner who thinks he can kick everyone around. I just got fed up. I ain't gonna tell Ma for awhile, she'll be mad." Ben's concern was evident. "Digger, ya just gotta learn you can't keep actin' smart to every boss ya have. And $1.30 an hour ain't bad pay at all for a 17-year-old boy. Look, I'll lend ya 10 bucks so ya can give 5 to ya Ma, and she won't know."

In their dealings with Ben, the Bandits, for their part, were in turn hostile and affectionate, cordial and sullen, open and reserved. They clearly regarded Ben's as "their" store. This meant, among other things, exclusive possession of the right to make trouble within its confines. At least three times during the observation period corner boys from outside neighborhoods entered the store obviously bent on stealing or creating a disturbance. On each occasion these outsiders were efficiently and forcefully removed by nearby Bandits, who then waxed indignant at the temerity of "outside" kids daring to consider Ben's as a target of illegal activity. One consequence, then, of Ben's seigneurial relationship to the Bandits was that his store was unusually well protected against theft, armed and otherwise, which presented a constant hazard to the small-store owner in Midcity.

On the other hand, the Bandits guarded jealously their own right to raise hell in Ben's. On one occasion, several Senior Bandits came into the store with a cache of pistol bullets and proceeded to empty the powder from one of the bullets onto the pinball machine and to ignite the powder. When Ben ordered them out they continued operations on the front sidewalk by wrapping gunpowder in newspaper and igniting it. Finally they set fire to a wad of paper containing two live bullets which exploded and narrowly missed local residents sitting on nearby doorsteps.

Such behavior, while calculated to bedevil Ben and perhaps to retaliate for a recent scolding or ejection, posed no real threat to him or his store; the same boys during this period were actively engaged in serious thefts from similar stores in other neighborhoods. For the most part, the behavior of the Bandits in and around the store involved the characteristic activities of hanging out. In warm weather the Bandits sat outside the store on the sidewalk or door-stoops playing cards, gambling, drinking, talking to one another and to the Bandettes. In cooler weather they moved into the store as the hour and space permitted, and there played the pinball machine for such cash payoffs as Ben saw fit to render, danced with the Bandettes to juke box records, and engaged in general horseplay.

While Ben's was the Bandits' favorite hangout, they did frequent other hanging locales, mostly within a few blocks of the corner. Among these was a park directly adjacent to the housing project where the boys played football and baseball in season. At night the park provided a favored locale for activities such as beer drinking and lovemaking,

neither of which particularly endeared them to the adult residents of the project, who not infrequently summoned the police to clear the park of late-night revellers. Other areas of congregation in the local neighborhood were a nearby delicatessen ("the Delly"), a pool hall, and the apartments of those Bandettes whose parents happened to be away. The Bandits also ran their own dances at the Old Erin and New Hibernia, but they had to conceal their identity as Bandits when renting these dance halls, since the proprietors had learned that the rental fees were scarcely sufficient to compensate for the chaos inevitably attending the conduct of a Bandit dance.

The Bandits were able to find other sources of entertainment in the central business district of Port City. While most of the Bandits and Bandettes were too young to gain admission to the numerous downtown cafes with their rock 'n' roll bands, they were able to find amusement in going to the movies (sneaking in whenever possible), playing the coin machines in the penny arcades and shoplifting from the downtown department stores. Sometimes, as a kind of diversion, small groups of Bandits spent the day in town job-hunting, with little serious intention of finding work.

One especially favored form of downtown entertainment was the court trial. Members of the Junior and Senior Bandits performed as on-stage participants in some 250 court trials during a four-year period. Most trials involving juveniles were conducted in nearby Midcity Court as private proceedings, but the older Bandits had adopted as routine procedure the practice of appealing their local court sentences to the Superior Court located in downtown Port City. When the appeal was successful, it was the occasion for as large a turnout of gang members as could be mustered, and the Bandits were a rapt and vitally interested audience. Afterwards, the gang held long and animated discussions about the severity or leniency of the sentence and other, finer points of legal procedure. The hearings provided not only an absorbing form of free entertainment, but also invaluable knowledge about court functioning, appropriate defendant behavior, and the predilections of particular judges—knowledge that would serve the spectators well when their own turn to star inevitably arrived.

The Senior Bandits

The Senior Bandits, the second oldest of the four male gang subdivisions hanging out on the Bandit corner, were under intensive observation for a period of 20 months.

At the start of this period the boys ranged in age from 15 to 17 (average age 16.3) and at the end, 17 to 19 (average age 18.1). The core group of the Senior Bandits numbered 32 boys.

Most of the gang members were Catholic, the majority of Irish background; several were Italian or French Canadian, and a few were English or Scotch Protestants. The gang contained two sets of brothers and several cousins, and about one third of the boys had relatives in other subdivisions. These included a brother in the Midgets, six brothers in the Juniors, and three in the Marauders.

The educational and occupational circumstances of the Senior Bandits were remarkably like those of their parents. Some seven years after the end of the intensive study period, when the average age of the Bandits was 25, 23 out of the 27 gang members whose occupations were known held jobs ordinarily classified in the bottom two occupational categories of the United States census. Twenty-one were classified as "laborer," holding jobs such as roofer, stock boy, and trucker's helper. Of 24 fathers whose occupations were known, 18, or 83 percent, held jobs in the same bottom two occupational categories as their sons; 17 were described as "laborer," holding jobs such as furniture mover and roofer. Fathers even held jobs of similar kinds and in similar proportions to those of their sons, e.g., construction laborers: sons 30 percent, fathers 25 percent; factory laborers: sons 15 percent, fathers 21 percent. Clearly the Senior Bandits were not rising above their fathers' status. In fact, there were indications of a slight decline, even taking account of the younger age of the sons. Two of the boys' fathers held jobs in "public safety" services—one policeman and one fireman; another had worked for a time in the "white collar" position of a salesclerk at Sears; a fourth had risen to the rank of Chief Petty Officer in the Merchant Marine. Four of the fathers, in other words, had attained relatively elevated positions, while the sons produced only one policeman.

The education of the Senior Bandits was consistent with their occupational status. Of 29 boys whose educational experience was known, 27 dropped out of school in the eighth, ninth, or tenth grades, having reached the age of 16. Two did complete high school, and one of these was reputed to have taken some post-high-school training in a local technical school. None entered college. It should be remarked that this record occurred not in a backward rural community of the 1800's, nor in a black community, but in the 1950's in a predominantly white neighborhood of a metropolis that took pride in being one of the major educational centers of the world.

Since only two of the Senior Bandits were still in school during the study, almost all of the boys held full-time jobs at some time during the contact period. But despite financial needs, pressure from parents and parole officers and other incentives to get work, the Senior Bandits found jobs slowly, accepted them reluctantly, and quit them with little provocation.

The Senior Bandits were clearly the most criminal of the seven gangs we studied most closely. For example, by the time he had reached the age of 18 the average Senior Bandit had been charged with offenses in court an average of 7.6 times; this compared with an average rate of 2.7 for all five male gangs, and added up to a total of almost 250 separate charges for the gang as a whole. A year after our intensive contact with the group, 100 percent of the Senior Bandits had been arrested at least once, compared with an average arrest figure of 45 percent for all groups. During the 20-month contact period, just about half of the Senior Bandits were on probation or parole for some period of time.

Law Violation, Cliques and Leadership

To a greater degree than in any of the other gangs we studied, crime as an occupation and preoccupation played a central role in the lives of the Senior Bandits. Prominent among recurrent topics of discussion were thefts successfully executed, fights recently engaged in, and the current status of gang members who were in the process of passing through the successive states of arrest, appearing in court, being sentenced, appealing, re-appealing and so on. Although none of the crimes of the Senior Bandits merited front-page headlines when we were close to them, a number of their more colorful exploits did receive newspaper attention, and the stories were carefully clipped and left in Ben's store for circulation among the gang members. Newspaper citations functioned for the Senior Bandits somewhat as do press notices for actors; gang members who made the papers were elated and granted prestige; those who did not were often disappointed; participants and non-participants who failed to see the stories felt cheated.

The majority of their crimes were thefts. The Senior Bandits were thieves *par excellence,* and their thievery was imaginative, colorful, and varied. Most thefts were from stores. Included among these was a department store theft of watches, jewelry and clothing for use as family Christmas presents; a daylight raid on a supermarket for food and refreshments needed for a beach outing; a daytime burglary of an antique store, in which eight gang members, in the presence of the owner, stole a Samurai sword and French duelling pistols. The gang also engaged in car theft. One summer several Bandits stole a car to visit girl friends who were working at a summer resort. Sixty miles north of Port City, hailed by police for exceeding speed limits, they raced away at speeds of up to 100 miles an hour, overturned the car, and were hospitalized for injuries. In another instance, Bandits stole a car in an effort to return a drunken companion to his home and avoid the police; when this car stalled they stole a second one parked in front of its owner's house; the owner ran out and fired several shots at the thieves, which, however, failed to forestall the theft.

The frequency of Senior Bandit crimes, along with the relative seriousness of their offenses, resulted in a high rate of arrest and confinement. During the contact period somewhat over 40 percent of the gang members were confined in correctional institutions, with terms averaging 11 months per boy. The average Senior Bandit spent approximately one month out of four in a correctional facility. This circumstance prompted one of the Bandettes to remark, "Ya know, them guys got a new place to hang—the reformatory. That bunch is never together—one halfa them don't even know the other half. . . . "

This appraisal, while based on fact, failed to recognize an important feature of gang relationships. With institutional confinement a frequent and predictable event, the Senior Bandits employed a set of devices to maintain a high degree of group solidarity. Lines of communication between corner and institution were kept open by frequent visits by those on the outside, during which inmates were brought food, money and cigarettes as well as news of the neighborhood and other correctional facilities. One Midcity social worker claimed that the institutionalized boys knew what was going on in the neighborhood before most neighborhood residents. The Bandits also developed well-established methods for arranging and carrying out institutional escape by those gang members who were so inclined. Details of escapes were arranged in the course of visits and inter-inmate contacts; escapees were provided by fellow gang members with equipment such as ropes to scale prison walls and getaway cars. The homes of one's gang fellows were also made available as hideouts. Given this set of arrangements, the Bandits carried out several

highly successful escapes, and one succeeded in executing the first escape in the history of a maximum security installation.

The means by which the Senior Bandits achieved group cohesion in spite of recurrent incarcerations of key members merit further consideration—both because they are of interest in their own right, and because they throw light on important relationships between leadership, group structure, and the motivation of criminal behavior. Despite the assertion that "one halfa them guys don't know the other half," the Senior Bandits were a solidaristic associational unit, with clear group boundaries and definite criteria for differentiating those who were "one of us" from those who were not. It was still said of an accepted group member that "he hangs with us"—even when the boy had been away from the corner in an institution for a year or more. Incarcerated leaders, in particular, were referred to frequently and in terms of admiration and respect.

The system used by the Senior Bandits to maintain solidarity and reliable leadership arrangements incorporated three major devices: the diffusion of authority, anticipation of contingencies, and interchangeability of roles. The recurring absence from the corner of varying numbers of gang members inhibited the formation of a set of relatively stable cliques of the kind found in the other gangs we studied intensively. What was fairly stable, instead, was a set of "classes" of members, each of which could include different individuals at different times. The relative size of these classes was fairly constant, and a member of one class could move to another to take the place of a member who had been removed by institutionalization.

The four major classes of gang members could be called key leaders, standby leaders, primary followers, and secondary followers. During the intensive contact period the gang contained five key leaders—boys whose accomplishments had earned them the right to command; six standby leaders—boys prepared to step into leadership positions when key leaders were institutionalized; eight primary followers—boys who hung out regularly and who were the most dependable followers of current leaders; and 13 secondary followers—boys who hung out less regularly and who tended to adapt their allegiances to particular leadership situations.

Predictably, given the dominant role of criminal activity among the Senior Bandits, leadership and followership were significantly related to criminal involvement. Each of the five key leaders had demonstrated unusual ability in criminal activity; in this respect the Senior Bandits differed from the other gangs, each of which included at least one leader whose position was based in whole or in part on a commitment to a law-abiding course of action. One of the Senior Bandits' key leaders was especially respected for his daring and adeptness in theft; another, who stole infrequently relative to other leaders, for his courage, stamina and resourcefulness as a fighter. The other three leaders had proven themselves in both theft and fighting, with theft the more important basis of eminence.

Confinement statistics show that gang members who were closest to leadership positions were also the most active in crime. They also suggest, however, that maintaining a system of leadership on this basis poses special problems. The more criminally active a gang member, the greater the likelihood that he would be apprehended and removed from the neighborhood, thus substantially diminishing his opportunities to convert earned prestige into operative leadership. How was it possible, then, for the Senior Bandits to maintain effective leadership arrangements? They utilized a remarkably efficient system whose several features were ingenious and deftly contrived.

First, the recognition by the Bandits of five key leaders— a relatively large number for a gang of 32 members—served as a form of insurance against being left without leadership. It was most unlikely that all five would be incarcerated at the same time, particularly since collective crimes were generally executed by one or possibly two leaders along with several of their followers. During one relatively brief part of the contact period, four of the key leaders were confined simultaneously, but over the full period the average number confined at any one time was two. One Bandit key leader expressed his conviction that exclusive reliance on a single leader was unwise: " . . . since we been hangin' out [at Ben's corner] we ain't had no leader. Other kids got a leader of the gang. Like up in Cornerville, they always got one kid who's the big boss . . . so far we ain't did that, and I don't think we ever will. We talk about 'Smiley and his boys,' or 'Digger and his clique,' and like that. . . . "

It is clear that for this Bandit the term "leader" carried the connotation of a single and all-powerful gang lord, which was not applicable to the diffuse and decentralized leadership arrangements of the Bandits. It is also significant that the gangs of Cornerville which he used as an example were Italian gangs whose rate of criminal involvement was relatively low. The "one big boss" type of leadership found in these gangs derives from the "Caesar" or "Il Duce"

pattern so well established in Italian culture, and it was workable for Cornerville gangs because the gangs and their leaders were sufficiently law-abiding and/or sufficiently capable of evading arrest as to make the removal of the leader an improbable event.

A second feature of Bandit leadership, the use of "standby" leaders, made possible a relatively stable balance among the several cliques. When the key leader of his clique was present in the area, the standby leader assumed a subordinate role and did not initiate action; if and when the key leader was committed to an institution, the standby was ready to assume leadership. He knew, however, that he was expected to relinquish this position on the return of the key leader. By this device each of the five major cliques was assured some form of leadership even when key leaders were absent, and could maintain its form, identity and influence vis-a-vis other cliques.

A third device that enabled the gang to maintain a relatively stable leadership and clique structure involved the phenomenon of "optimal" criminal involvement. Since excellence in crime was the major basis of gang leadership, it might be expected that some of those who aspired to leadership would assume that there was a simple and direct relationship between crime and leadership: the more crime, the more prestige; the more prestige, the stronger the basis of authority. The flaw in this simple formula was in fact recognized by the actual key leaders: in striving for maximal criminal involvement, one also incurred the maximum risk of incarceration. But leadership involved more than gaining prestige through crime; one had to be personally involved with other gang members for sufficiently extended periods to exploit won prestige through wooing followers, initiating noncriminal as well as criminal activities, and effecting working relationships with other leaders. Newly-returned key leaders as well as the less criminally-active class of standby leaders tended to step up their involvement in criminal activity on assuming or reassuming leadership positions in order to solidify their positions, but they also tended to diminish such involvement once this was achieved.

One fairly evident weakness in so flexible and fluid a system of cliques and leadership was the danger that violent and possibly disruptive internal conflict might erupt among key leaders who were competing for followers, or standby leaders who were reluctant to relinquish their positions. There was, in fact, surprisingly little overt conflict of any kind among Bandit leaders. On their release from confinement, leaders were welcomed with enthusiasm and appropriate observances both by their followers and by other leaders. They took the center of the stage as they recounted to rapt listeners their institutional experiences, the circumstances of those still confined, and new developments in policies, personnel and politics at the correctional school.

When they were together Bandit leaders dealt with one another gingerly, warily and with evident respect. On one occasion a standby leader, who was less criminally active than the returning key leader, offered little resistance to being displaced, but did serve his replacement with the warning that a resumption of his former high rate of crime would soon result in commitment both of himself and his clique. On another occasion one of the toughest of the Senior Bandits (later sentenced to an extended term in an adult institution for ringleading a major prison riot), returned to the corner to find that another leader had taken over not only some of his key followers but his steady girl friend as well. Instead of taking on his rival in an angry and perhaps violent confrontation, he reacted quite mildly, venting his hostility in the form of sarcastic teasing, calculated to needle but not to incite. In the place of a direct challenge, the newly returned key leader set about to regain his followers and his girl by actively throwing himself back into criminal activity. This course of action—competing for followers by successful performance in prestigious activities rather than by brute-force confrontation—was standard practice among the Senior Bandits.

The Junior Bandits

The leadership system of the Junior Bandits was, if anything, even farther removed from the "one big boss" pattern than was the "multi-leader power-balance" system of the Seniors. An intricate arrangement of cliques and leadership enabled this subdivision of the gang to contain within it a variety of individuals and cliques with different and often conflicting orientations.

Leadership for particular activities was provided as the occasion arose by boys whose competence in that activity had been established. Leadership was thus flexible, shifting, and adaptable to changing group circumstances. Insofar as there was a measure of relatively concentrated authority, it was invested in a collectivity rather than an individual. The several "situational" leaders of the dominant clique constituted what was in effect a kind of ruling council, which arrived at its decisions through a process of extended collective discussion generally involving all concerned. Those who were to execute a plan of action thereby took part in the process by which it was developed.

A final feature of this system concerns the boy who was recognized as "the leader" of the Junior Bandits. When the gang formed a club to expedite involvement in athletic activities, he was chosen its president. Although he was an accepted member of the dominant clique, he did not, on the surface, seem to possess any particular qualifications for this position. He was mild-mannered, unassertive, and consistently refused to take a definite stand on outstanding issues, let alone taking the initiative in implementing policy. He appeared to follow rather than to lead. One night when the leaders of the two subordinate factions became infuriated with one another in the course of a dispute, he trailed both boys around for several hours, begging them to calm down and reconcile their differences. On another occasion the gang was on the verge of splitting into irreconcilable factions over a financial issue. One group accused another of stealing club funds; the accusation was hotly denied; angry recriminations arose that swept in a variety of dissatisfactions with the club and its conduct. In the course of this melee, the leader of one faction, the "bad boys," complained bitterly about the refusal of the president to take sides or assume any initiative in resolving the dispute, and called for a new election. This was agreed to and the election was held—with the result that the "weak" president was re-elected by a decisive majority, and was reinstated in office amidst emotional outbursts of acclaim and reaffirmation of the unity of the gang.

It was thus evident that the majority of gang members, despite temporary periods of anger over particular issues, recognized on some level the true function performed by a "weak" leader. Given the fact that the gang included a set of cliques with differing orientations and conflicting notions, and a set of leaders whose authority was limited to specific areas, the maintenance of gang cohesion required some special mechanisms. One was the device of the "weak" leader. It is most unlikely that a forceful or dominant person could have controlled the sanctions that would enable him to coerce the strong-willed factions into compliance. The very fact that the "weak" leader refused to take sides and was noncommittal on key issues made him acceptable to the conflicting interests represented in the gang. Further, along with the boy's nonassertive demeanor went a real talent for mediation.

The Outlaw Neighborhood

The Outlaw street corner was less than a mile from that of the Bandits, and like the Bandits, the Outlaws were white, Catholic, and predominantly Irish, with a few Italians and Irish-Italians. But their social status, in the middle range of the lower class, was sufficiently higher than that of the Bandits to be reflected in significant differences in both their gang and family life. The neighborhood environment also was quite different.

Still, the Outlaws hung out on a classic corner—complete with drug store, variety store, a neighborhood bar (Callahan's Bar and Grill), a pool hall, and several other small businesses such as a laundromat. The corner was within one block of a large park, a convenient locale for card games, lovemaking, and athletic practice. Most residents of the Outlaw neighborhood were oblivious to the deafening roar of the elevated train that periodically rattled the houses and stores of Midcity Avenue, which formed one street of the Outlaw corner. There was no housing project in the Outlaw neighborhood, and none of the Outlaws were project residents. Most of their families rented one level of one of the three-decker wooden tenements which were common in the area; a few owned their own homes.

In the mid-1950's, however, the Outlaw neighborhood underwent significant changes as Negroes began moving in. Most of the white residents, gradually and with reluctance, left their homes and moved out to the first fringe of Port City's residential suburbs, abandoning the area to the Negroes.

Prior to this time the Outlaw corner had been a hanging locale for many years. The Outlaw name and corner dated from at least the late 1920's, and perhaps earlier. One local boy who was not an Outlaw observed disgruntledly that anyone who started a fight with an Outlaw would end up fighting son, father, and grandfather, since all were or had been members of the gang. A somewhat drunken and sentimental Outlaw, speaking at a farewell banquet for their field worker, declared impassionedly that any infant born into an Outlaw family was destined from birth to wear the Outlaw jacket.

One consequence of the fact that Outlaws had hung out on the same corner for many years was that the group that congregated there during the 30-month observation period included a full complement of age-graded subdivisions. Another consequence was that the subdivisions were closely connected by kinship. There were six clearly differentiated subdivisions on the corner: the Marauders, boys in their late teens and early twenties; the Senior Outlaws, boys between 16 and 18; the Junior Outlaws, 14 to 16; and the Midget Outlaws, 11 to 13. There were also two girls groups, the Outlawettes and the Little Outlawettes.

The number of Outlaws in all subdivisions totalled slightly over 200 persons, ranging in age, approximately, from 10 to 25 years.

The cohesiveness of the Outlaws, during the 1950's, was enhanced in no small measure by an adult who, like Ben for the Bandits, played a central role in the Outlaws' lives. This was Rosa—the owner of the variety store which was their principal hangout—a stout, unmarried woman of about 40 who was, in effect, the street-corner mother of all 200 Outlaws.

The Junior Outlaws

The Junior Outlaws, numbering 24 active members, were the third oldest of the four male subdivisions on the Outlaw Corner, ranging in age from 14 to 16. Consistent with their middle-range lower-class status, the boys' fathers were employed in such jobs as bricklayer, mechanic, chauffeur, milk deliveryman; but a small minority of these men had attained somewhat higher positions, one being the owner of a small electroplating shop and the other rising to the position of plant superintendent. The educational status of the Junior Outlaws was higher than that of the Bandit gangs, but lower than that of their older brother gang, the Senior Outlaws.

With regard to law violations, the Junior Outlaws, as one might expect from their status and age, were considerably less criminal than the lower-status Bandits, but considerably more so than the Senior Outlaws. They ranked third among the five male gangs in illegal involvement during the observation period (25 involvements per 10 boys per 10 months), which was well below the second-ranking Senior Bandits (54.2) and well above the fourth-ranking Negro Kings (13.9). Nevertheless, the two-and-a-half-year period during which we observed the Juniors was for them, as for other boys of their status and age group, a time of substantial increase in the frequency and seriousness of illegal behavior. An account of the events of this time provides some insight into the process by which age-related influences engender criminality. It also provides another variation on the issue, already discussed in the case of the Bandits, of the relation of leadership to criminality.

It is clear from the case of the Bandits that gang affairs were ordered not by autocratic ganglords, but rather through a subtle and intricate interplay between leadership and a set of elements such as personal competency, intra-gang divisions and law violation. The case of the Junior Outlaws is particularly dramatic in this regard, since the observation period found them at the critical age when boys of this social-status level are faced with a serious decision—the amount of weight to be granted to law-violating behavior as a basis of prestige. Because there were in the Junior Outlaws two cliques, each of which was committed quite clearly to opposing alternatives, the interplay of the various elements over time emerges with some vividness, and echoes the classic morality play wherein forces of good and evil are locked in mortal combat over the souls of the uncommitted.

At the start of the observation period, the Juniors, 13-, 14- and 15-year-olds, looked and acted for the most part like "nice young kids." By the end of the period both their voices and general demeanor had undergone a striking change. Their appearance, as they hung out in front of Rosa's store, was that of rough corner boys, and the series of thefts, fights and drinking bouts which had occurred during the intervening two-and-one-half years was the substance behind that appearance. When we first contacted them, the Juniors comprised three main cliques; seven boys associated primarily with a "good boy" who was quite explicitly oriented to law-abiding behavior; a second clique of seven boys associated with a "bad boy" who was just starting to pursue prestige through drinking and auto theft; and a third, less-frequently congregating group, who took a relatively neutral position with respect to the issue of violative behavior.

The leader of the "good boy" clique played an active part in the law-abiding activities of the gang, and was elected president of the formal club organized by the Juniors. This club at first included members of all three cliques; however, one of the first acts of the club members, dominated by the "good boy" leader and his supporters, was to vote out of membership the leader of the "bad boy" clique. Nevertheless, the "bad boy" leader and his followers continued to hang out on the corner with the other Juniors, and from this vantage point attempted to gain influence over the uncommitted boys as well as members of the "good boy" clique. His efforts proved unsuccessful, however, since during this period athletic prowess served for the majority of the Juniors as a basis of greater prestige than criminal behavior. Disgruntled by this failure, the "bad boy" leader took his followers and moved to a new hanging corner, about two blocks away from the traditional one.

From there, a tangible symbol of the ideological split within the Juniors, the "bad boy" leader continued his campaign to wean away the followers of the "good boy" leader, trying to persuade them to leave the old corner for the new. At the same time, behavior at the "bad boy" cor-

ner became increasingly delinquent, with, among other things, much noisy drinking and thefts of nearby cars. These incidents produced complaints by local residents that resulted in several police raids on the corner, and served to increase the antagonism between what now had become hostile factions. Determined to assert their separateness, the "bad boy" faction began to drink and create disturbances in Rosa's store, became hostile to her when she censured them, and finally stayed away from the store altogether.

The antagonism between the two factions finally became sufficiently intense to bring about a most unusual circumstance—plans for an actual gang fight, a "jam" of the type characteristic of rival gangs. The time and place for the battle were agreed on. But no one from either side showed up. A second battle site was selected. Again the combatants failed to appear. From the point of view of intragang relations, both the plan for the gang fight and its failure to materialize were significant. The fact that a physical fight between members of the same subdivision was actually projected showed that factional hostility over the issue of law violation had reached an unusual degree of bitterness; the fact that the planned encounters did not in fact occur indicated a realization that actual physical combat might well lead to an irreversible split.

A reunification of the hostile factions did not take place for almost a year, however. During this time changes occurred in both factions which had the net effect of blunting the sharpness of the ideological issue dividing them. Discouraged by his failure to win over the majority of the Outlaws to the cause of law-violation as a major badge of prestige, the leader of the "bad boy" clique began to hang out less frequently. At the same time, the eight "uncommitted" members of the Junior Outlaws, now moving toward their middle teens, began to gravitate toward the "bad boy" corner—attracted by the excitement and risk of its activities. More of the Juniors than ever before became involved in illegal drinking and petty theft. This trend became sufficiently pronounced to draw in members of the "good boy" clique, and the influence of the "good boy" leader diminished to the point where he could count on the loyalty only of his own brother and two other boys. In desperation, sensing the all-but-irresistible appeal of illegality for his erstwhile followers, he increased the tempo of his own delinquent behavior in a last-ditch effort to win them back. All in vain. Even his own brother deserted the regular Outlaw corner, although he did not go so far as to join the "bad boys" on theirs.

112

Disillusioned, the "good boy" leader took a night job that sharply curtailed the time he was able to devote to gang activities. Members of the "bad boy" clique now began a series of maneuvers aimed at gaining control of the formal club. Finally, about two months before the close of the 30-month contact period, a core member of the "bad boy" clique was elected to the club presidency. In effect, the proponents of illegality as a major basis of prestige had won the long struggle for dominance of the Junior Outlaws. But this achievement, while on the surface a clear victory for the "bad boy" faction, was in fact a far more subtle process of mutual accommodation.

The actions of each of the opposing sides accorded quite directly with their expressed convictions; each member of the "bad boy" faction averaged about 17 known illegal acts during the observation period, compared to a figure of about two per boy for the "good boy" faction. However, in the face of these sharp differences in both actions and sentiments respecting illegality, the two factions shared important common orientations. Most importantly, they shared the conviction that the issue of violative behavior as a basis of prestige was a paramount one, and one that required a choice. Moreover, both sides remained uncertain as to whether the choice they made was the correct one.

The behavior of both factions provides evidence of a fundamental ambivalence with respect to the "demanded" nature of delinquent behavior. The gradual withdrawal of support by followers of the "good boy" leader and the movement toward violative behavior of the previously "neutral" clique attest to a compelling conviction that prestige gained through law-abiding endeavor alone could not, at this age, suffice. Even more significant was the criminal experience of the "good boy" leader. As the prime exponent of law-abiding behavior, he might have been expected to serve as an exemplar in this respect. In fact, the opposite was true; his rate of illegal involvement was the highest of all the boys in his clique, and had been so even before his abortive attempt to regain his followers by a final burst of delinquency. This circumstance probably derived from his realization that a leader acceptable to both factions (which he wanted to be) would have to show proficiency in activities recognized by both as conferring prestige.

To Be a Man

It is equally clear, by the same token, that members of the "bad boy" faction were less than serenely confident in their commitment to law-violation as an ideal. Once they had won power in the club they did not keep as their leader the boy who had been the dominant figure on the "bad boy" corner, and who was without question the most criminally active of the Junior Outlaws, but instead elected as president another boy who was also criminally active, but considerably less so. Moreover, in the presence of older gang members, Seniors and Marauders, the "bad boy" clique was far more subdued, less obstreperous, and far less ardent in their advocacy of crime as an ideal. There was little question that they were sensitive to and responsive to negative reactions by others to their behavior.

It is noteworthy that members of both factions adhered more firmly to the "law-violation" and "law-abiding" positions on the level of abstract ideology than on the level of actual practice. This would suggest that the existence of the opposing ideologies and their corresponding factions served important functions both for individual gang members and for the group as a whole. Being in the same orbit as the "bad boys" made it possible for the "good boys" to reap some of the rewards of violative behavior without undergoing its risks; the presence of the "good boys" imposed restraints on the "bad" that they themselves desired, and helped protect them from dangerous excesses. The behavior and ideals of the "good boys" satisfied for both factions that component of their basic orientation that said "violation of the law is wrong and should be punished;" the behavior and ideals of the "bad boys" that component that said "one cannot earn manhood without some involvement in criminal activity."

It is instructive to compare the stress and turmoil attending the struggle for dominance of the Junior Outlaws with the leadership circumstances of the Senior Bandits. In this gang, older and of lower social status (lower-class III), competition for leadership had little to do with a choice between law-abiding and law-violating philosophies, but rather with the issue of which of a number of competing leaders was *best* able to demonstrate prowess in illegal activity. This virtual absence of effective pressures against delinquency contrasts sharply with the situation of the Junior Outlaws. During the year-long struggle between its "good" and "bad" factions, the Juniors were exposed to constant pressures, both internal and external to the gang, to refrain from illegality. External sources included Rosa, whom the boys loved and respected; a local youth worker whom they held in high esteem; their older brother gangs, whose frequent admonitions to the "little kids" to "straighten out" and "keep clean" were attended with utmost seriousness. Within the gang itself the "good boy" leader served as a consistent and persuasive advocate of a law-abiding course of action. In addition, most of the boys' parents deplored their misbehavior and urged them to keep out of trouble.

In the face of all these pressures from persons of no small importance in the lives of the Juniors, the final triumph of the proponents of illegality, however tempered, assumes added significance. What was it that impelled the "bad boy" faction? There was a quality of defiance about much of their delinquency, as if they were saying—"We know perfectly well that what we are doing is regarded as wrong, legally and morally; we also know that it violates the wishes and standards of many whose good opinion we value; yet, if we are to sustain our self-respect and our honor as males we *must,* at this stage of our lives, engage in criminal behavior." In light of the experience of the Junior Outlaws, one can scarcely argue that their delinquency sprang from any inability to distinguish right from wrong, or out of any simple conformity to a set of parochial standards that just happened to differ from those of the legal code or the adult middle class. Their delinquent behavior was engendered by a highly complex interplay of forces, including, among other elements, the fact that they were males, were in the middle range of the lower class and of critical importance in the present instance, were moving through the age period when the attainment of manhood was of the utmost concern.

In the younger gang just discussed, the Junior Outlaws, leadership and clique structure reflected an intense struggle between advocates and opponents of law-violation as a prime basis of prestige.

The Senior Outlaws

Leadership in the older Senior Outlaws reflected a resolution of the law-conformity versus law-violation conflict, but with different results. Although the gang was not under direct observation during their earlier adolescence, what we know of the Juniors, along with evidence that the Senior Outlaws themselves had been more criminal when younger, would suggest that the gang had in fact undergone a similar struggle, and that the proponents of conformity to the law had won.

In any case, the events of the observation period made it clear that the Senior Outlaws sought "rep" as a gang primarily through effective execution of legitimate enterprises such as athletics, dances, and other non-violative activities. In line with this objective, they maintained a consistent concern with the "good name" of the gang and with "keeping out of trouble" in the face of constant and ubiquitous

temptations. For example, they attempted (without much success) to establish friendly relations with the senior priest of their parish—in contrast with the Junior Outlaws, who were on very bad terms with the local church. At one point during the contact period when belligerent Bandits, claiming that the Outlaws had attacked one of the Midget Bandits, vowed to "wipe out every Outlaw jacket in Midcity," the Senior Outlaws were concerned not only with the threat of attack but also with the threat to their reputation. "That does it," said one boy, "I knew we'd get into something. There goes the good name of the Outlaws."

Leadership and clique arrangements in the Senior Outlaws reflected three conditions, each related in some way to the relatively low stress on criminal activity: the stability of gang membership (members were rarely removed from the area by institutional confinement), the absence of significant conflict over the prestige and criminality issue, and the importance placed on legitimate collective activities. The Senior Bandits were the most unified of the gangs we observed directly; there were no important cleavages or factions; even the distinction between more-active and less-active members was less pronounced than in the other gangs.

But as in the other gangs, leadership among the Senior Outlaws was collective and situational. There were four key leaders, each of whom assumed authority in his own sphere of competence. As in the case of the Bandit gangs there was little overt competition among leaders; when differences arose between the leadership and the rank and file, the several leaders tended to support one another. In one significant respect, however, Outlaw leadership differed from that of the other gangs; authority was exercised more firmly and accepted more readily. Those in charge of collective enterprises generally issued commands after the manner of a tough army sergeant or work-gang boss. Although obedience to such commands was frequently less than flawless, the leadership style of Outlaw leaders approximated the "snap-to-it" approach of organizations that control firmer sanctions than do most corner gangs. Compared to the near-chaotic behavior of their younger brother gang, the organizational practices of the Senior appeared as a model of efficiency. The "authoritarian" mode of leadership was particularly characteristic of one boy, whose prerogatives were somewhat more generalized than those of the other leaders. While he was far from an undisputed "boss," holding instead a kind of *primus inter pares* position, he was as close to a "boss" as anything found among the direct-observation gangs.

His special position derived from the fact that he showed superior capability in an unusually wide range of activities, and this permitted him wider authority than the other leaders. One might have expected, in a gang oriented predominantly to law-abiding activity, that this leader would serve as an exemplar of legitimacy and rank among the most law-abiding. This was not the case. He was, in fact, one of the most criminal of the Senior Outlaws, being among the relatively few who had "done time." He was a hard drinker, an able street-fighter, a skilled football strategist and team leader, an accomplished dancer and smooth ladies' man. His leadership position was based not on his capacity to best exemplify the law-abiding orientation of the gang, but on his capabilities in a variety of activities, violative and non-violative. Thus, even in the gang most concerned with "keeping clean," excellence in crime still constituted one important basis of prestige. Competence as such rather than the legitimacy of one's activities provided the major basis of authority.

We still have to ask, however, why leadership among the Senior Outlaws was more forceful than in the other gangs. One reason emerges by comparison with the "weak leader" situation of the Junior Bandits. Younger and of lower social status, their factional conflict over the law-violation-and-prestige issue was sufficiently intense so that only a leader without an explicit commitment to either side could be acceptable to both. The Seniors, older and of higher status, had developed a good degree of intragang consensus on this issue, and showed little factionalism. They could thus accept a relatively strong leader without jeopardizing gang unity.

A second reason also involves differences in age and social status, but as these relate to the world of work. In contrast to the younger gangs, whose perspectives more directly revolved around the subculture of adolescence and its specific concerns, the Senior Outlaws at age 19 were on the threshold of adult work, and some in fact were actively engaged in it. In contrast to the lower-status gangs whose orientation to gainful employment was not and never would be as "responsible" as that of the Outlaws, the activities of the Seniors as gang members more directly reflected and anticipated the requirements and conditions of the adult occupational roles they would soon assume.

Of considerable importance in the prospective occupational world of the Outlaws was, and is, the capacity to give and take orders in the execution of collective enterprises. Unlike the Bandits, few of whom would ever occupy other than subordinate positions, the Outlaws belonged to that sector of society which provides the men who exercise direct authority over groups of laborers or blue collar workers. The self-executed collective activities of the gang—organized athletics, recreational projects, fund-raising activities—provided a training ground for the practice of organizational skills—planning organized enterprises, working together in their conduct, executing the directives of legitimate superiors. It also provided a training ground wherein those boys with the requisite talents could learn and practice the difficult art of exercising authority effectively over lower-class men. By the time they had reached the age of 20, the leaders of the Outlaws had experienced in the gang many of the problems and responsibilities confronting the army sergeant, the police lieutenant and the factory foreman.

The nature and techniques of leadership in the Senior Outlaws had relevance not only to their own gang but to the Junior Outlaws as well. Relations between the Junior and Senior Outlaws were the closest of all the intensive-contact gang subdivisions. The Seniors kept a close watch on their younger fellows, and served them in a variety of ways, as athletic coaches, advisers, mediators and arbiters. The older gang followed the factional conflicts of the Juniors with close attention, and were not above intervening when conflict reached sufficient intensity or threatened their own interests. The dominant leader of the Seniors was particularly concerned with the behavior of the Juniors; at one point, lecturing them about their disorderly conduct in Rosa's store, he remarked, "I don't hang with you guys, but I know what you do. . . . " The Seniors did not, however, succeed in either preventing the near-breakup of the Junior Outlaws or slowing their move toward law-breaking activities.

The Prevalence of Gangs

The subtle and intricately contrived relations among cliques, leadership and crime in the four subdivisions of the Bandits and Outlaws reveal the gang as an ordered and adaptive form of association, and its members as able and rational human beings. The fascinating pattern of intergang variation within a basic framework illustrates vividly the compelling influences of differences in age and social status on crime, leadership and other forms of behavior—even when these differences are surprisingly small. The experiences of Midcity gang members show that the gang serves the lower-class adolescent as a flexible and adaptable training instrument for imparting vital knowledge concerning the value of individual competence, the appropriate limits of law-violating behavior, the uses and abuses of authority, and the skills of interpersonal relations. From this perspective, the street gang appears not as a casual or transient manifestation that emerges intermittently in response to unique and passing social conditions, but rather as a stable associational form, coordinate with and complementary to the family, and as an intrinsic part of the way of life of the urban low-status community.

How then can one account for the widespread conception of gangs as somehow popping up and then disappearing again? One critical reason concerns the way one defines what a gang is. Many observers, both scholars and non-scholars, often use a *sine qua non* to sort out "real" gangs from near-gangs, pseudo-gangs, and non-gangs. Among the more common of these single criteria are: autocratic one-man leadership, some "absolute" degree of solidarity or stable membership, a predominant involvement in violent conflict with other gangs, claim to a rigidly defined turf, or participation in activities thought to pose a threat to other sectors of the community. Reaction to groups lacking the *sine qua non* is often expressed with a dismissive "Oh, them. That's not a *gang*. That's just a bunch of kids out on the corner."

On the Corner Again

For many people there are no gangs if there is no gang warfare. It's that simple. For them, as for all those who concentrate on the "threatening" nature of the gang, the phenomenon is defined in terms of the degree of "problem" it poses: A group whose "problematic" behavior is hard to ignore is a gang; one less problematic is not. But what some people see as a problem may not appear so to others. In Philadelphia, for example, the police reckoned there were 80 gangs, of which 20 were at war; while social workers estimated there were 200 gangs, of which 80 were "most hostile." Obviously, the social workers' 80 "most hostile" gangs were the same as the 80 "gangs" of the police. The additional 120 groups defined as gangs by the social workers were seen as such because they were thought to be appropriate objects of social work; but to the police they were not sufficiently troublesome to require consistent police attention, and were not therefore defined as gangs.

In view of this sort of confusion, let me state our definition of what a gang is. A gang is a group of urban adolescents who congregate recurrently at one or more nonresidential locales, with continued affiliation based on self-defined criteria of inclusion and exclusion. Recruitment, customary places of assembly and ranging areas are based in a specific territory, over some portion of which limited use and occupancy rights are claimed. Membership both in the gang as a whole and in its subgroups is determined on the basis of age! The group maintains a versatile repertoire of activities, with hanging out, mating, recreational and illegal activity being of central importance; and it is internally differentiated on the basis of authority, prestige, personality and clique-formation.

The main reason that people have consistently mistaken the prevalence of gangs is the widespread tendency to define them as gangs on the basis of the presence or absence of one or two characteristics that are thought to be essential to the "true" gang. Changes in the forms or frequencies or particular characteristics, such as leadership, involvement in fighting, or modes of organization, are seen not as normal variations over time and space, but rather as signs of the emergence or disappearance of the gangs themselves. Our work does not support this view; instead, our evidence indicates that the core characteristics of the gang vary continuously from place to place and from time to time without negating the existence of the gang. Gangs may be larger or smaller, named or nameless, modestly or extensively differentiated, more or less active in gang fighting, stronger or weaker in leadership, black, white, yellow or brown, without affecting their identity as gangs. So long as groups of adolescents gather periodically outside the home, frequent a particular territory, restrict membership by age and other criteria, pursue a variety of activities, and maintain differences in authority and prestige—so long will the gang continue to exist as a basic associational form.

Swinging in Wedlock

Charles and Rebecca Palson

Since the later 1960s, an increasing number of middle-class couples have turned to mate swapping or "swinging" as an alternative to strictly monogamous marriage. That is, married couples (or unmarried couples with an apparently stable relationship) willingly and knowingly relinquish sexual rights to their own mates so that others may temporarily enjoy these rights. This phenomenon, which is fairly recent in its openness and proportions, provides an opportunity of testing, on a large scale, the traditional theories about the consequences of extramarital sexual activity. It has often been assumed that sexual infidelity, where all the concerned parties know of it, results to some

degree in jealousy. The intensity of jealousy is thought to increase in proportion to the amount of real or imagined emotional involvement on the part of the unfaithful member of the couple. Conversely, the more "purely physical" the infidelity, the less likely that there will be any jealousy. Thus it is often hypothesized that where marital stability coexists with infidelity, the character of the extramarital involvement is relatively depersonalized.

In the film *Bob and Carol and Ted and Alice*, Bob finds Carol, his wife, entertaining another man in their bedroom. Although he had previously told her that he was having an affair, and they had agreed in principle that she too could have affairs, he is obviously shaken by the reality. Nervously trying to reassure himself, he asks, "Well, it's just *sex*, isn't it? I mean, you don't *love* him?" In other words, Bob attempts to avoid feelings of jealousy by believing that Carol's affair involves only depersonalized sex in contrast to their own relationship of love.

In his book, *Group Sex*, Gilbert Bartell offers the same hypothesis about those people he calls "organization swingers:"

> They are terrified of the idea that involvement might take place. They take comfort from the fact that if they swing with a couple only once or at most twice, the chances of running into a marriage-threatening involvement are small.

These swingers, who can be described as organizational only in the sense that they tend to use swinger magazines or special swinging nightclubs to make their contacts, are mostly beginners who *may* act in ways that approximate Bartell's description. Near the end of the book, however, he mentions some couples he interviewed whom he calls dropouts. These people either had never desired depersonalized swinging or had passed through a depersonalized stage but now preferred some degree of emotional involvement and long-term friendship from their swinging relationships. Bartell does not explain how these couples continue to keep stable relationships and can remain free of jealousy, but the fact that such couples exist indicates that depersonalization is not the only way to jealousy-free swinging.

Our involvement with the subject has been partly a personal one, and this requires some introductory explanation. In September 1969, we read an article about swinging and became fascinated by the questions it raised about sex and the American family. Did this practice signal the beginning of the breakup of the family? Or was it a way to inject new life into marriage as the authors of the article suggested? How do people go about swinging and why? We contemplated these and many other questions but, not knowing any swingers, we could arrive at only very limited answers. It seemed to us that the only way to find out what we wanted to know was to participate ourselves. In one way this seemed natural because anthropologists have traditionally lived with the people they have studied. But our curiosity about swinging at that time was more personal than professional, and we knew that ultimately our participation would have personal consequences, although we had no idea what their nature might be. We had to decide whether exploration of this particular unknown was worth the risk of changing the perfectly sound and gratifying relationship which we had built during the previous three-and-a-half years. Finally, our misgivings gave way to curiosity and we wrote off to some couples who advertised in a national swinger's magazine.

Although, like most beginners, we were excited about swinging, we were nervous too. We didn't know what swinging in reality was like or what "rules" there were, if any. In general, however, we found those first experiences not only enjoyable from a personal point of view, but stimulating intellectually. It was then that we decided to study swinging as anthropologists. But, like many anthropologists who use participant observation as a method of study, we could never completely divorce ourselves from the personal aspects of our subject.

The method of participant observation is sometimes criticized as being too subjective. In an area such as sex, where experiences are highly individual and personal, we feel that participant observation can yield results even more thorough and disciplined than the more so-called objective methods. Most of our important insights into the nature of swinging could only have been found by actually experiencing some of the same things that our informants did. Had we not participated, we would not have known how to question them about many central aspects of their experience.

This article presents the results of our 18-month, participant observation study of 136 swingers. We made our contacts in three ways. First, we reached couples through swinger magazines. These are magazines devoted almost exclusively to ads placed by swingers for the purpose of contacting other interested couples and/or singles. Many, although not all, of the couples we contacted in this way seemed to be beginners who had not yet found people with whom they were interested in forming long-term relationships. Second, we were introduced to couples through personal networks. Couples whom we knew would pass our name on to others, sometimes explicitly because they wanted our study to be a success. Third, some couples contacted us as a result of lectures or papers we presented, to volunteer themselves as informants. It should be noted that we did not investigate the swingers' bars, although second-hand reports from couples we met who had used them for making contacts seem to indicate that these couples did not significantly differ from those who do not use the bars. Our informants came from Pennsylvania, New Jersey, New York, Massachusetts, Louisiana, California, Florida and Illinois. They were mostly middle class, although ten could be classified as working class.

Usually we interviewed couples in very informal settings, and these interviews were often indistinguishable from ordinary conversation that swingers might have about themselves and their activities. After each session we would return home, discuss the conversation and write notes on our observations. Later several couples volunteered to tape interviews, enabling us to check the accuracy of the field notes we had taken previously.

In spite of our efforts to find informants from as many different sources as possible, we can in no way guarantee the representativeness of our sample. It should be emphasized that statistics are practically useless in the study of swingers because of insurmountable sampling problems. We therefore avoided the statistical approach and instead focused the investigation on problems of a nonstatistical nature. The information we obtained enabled us to understand and describe the kinds of cultural symbols—a "symbolic calculus," if you will—that swingers must use to effectively navigate social situations with other swingers. This symbolic calculus organizes widely varying experiences into a coherent whole, enabling swingers to understand and evaluate each social situation in which they find themselves. They can thereby define the choices available to them and the desirability of each. Our research goal, then, was to describe the symbols that infuse meaning into the experiences of all the swingers that we contacted.

Unlike Bartell, we had no difficulty finding couples who either wanted to have or had succeeded in having some degree of emotional involvement and long-term friendship within a swinging context. In fact, many of them explained to us that depersonalization simply brought them no satisfaction. In observing such couples with their friends it was evident that they had formed close and enduring relationships. They host each other's children on weekends, celebrate birthdays together, take vacations together and, in general, do what close friends usually do. It should be noted that there is no way of ascertaining the numbers of couples who have actually succeeded in finding close friends through swinging. In fact, they may be underrepresented because they tend to retreat into their own small circle of friends and dislike using swinger magazines to find other couples. Thus they are more difficult to contact.

In order to see how swingers are able to form such relationships it is necessary to understand not how they avoid jealousy, but how they deal with its causes. Insecurity and fear of being replaced are the major ingredients in any experience with jealousy. An effective defense against jealousy, then, would include a way to guarantee one's irreplaceability as a mate. If, for example, a wife knows that she is unlike any other woman her husband has ever met or ever will meet, and if they have a satisfying relationship in which they have invested much time and emotion, she can rest assured that no other relationship her husband has can threaten her. If, on the other hand, a woman feels that the continuance of her marital relationship depends on how well she cooks, cleans and makes love, jealousy is more likely to occur, because she realizes that any number of women could fill the same role, perhaps better than she.

Similarly, a man who feels that the continuance of his wife's loyalty depends on how well he provides financial security will be apt to feel more jealousy because many men could perform the same function. To one degree or another, many swingers naturally develop towards a more secure kind of marital relationship, a tendency we call *individuation*. Among the couples we contacted, individuation was achieved for the most part at a level that precluded jealousy. And we found that, to the extent that couples did not individuate, either jealousy occurred or swinging had to take other, less flexible forms in order to prevent it.

We found evidence of individuation in two areas. First, we found that patterns of behavior at gatherings of swingers who had passed the beginning stages were thoroughly pervaded by individuation. Second, we found that by following changes in a couple's attitudes toward themselves, both as individuals and as a couple and toward other swingers, a trend of increasing individuation could be observed.

Individuating Behavior at Gatherings

When we first entered the swinging scene, we hypothesized that swinging must be characterized by a set of implicit and explicit rules or patterns of behavior. But every time we thought we had discovered a pattern, another encounter quickly invalidated it. We finally had to conclude that any particular swinging gathering is characterized by any one of a number of forms, whatever best suits the individuals involved. The ideal, as in nonswinging situations, is for the initiation of sexual interaction to appear to develop naturally—preferably in a nonverbal way. But with four or more people involved and all the signaling and cross-signaling of intentions that must take place, this ideal can only be approached in most cases. The initiation may begin with little or no socializing, much socializing with sex later on as a natural outgrowth of the good feelings thus created, or some mixture in-between. Socializing is of the variety found at many types of nonswinging gatherings. The sexual interaction itself may be "open" where couples participate in the same room or "closet" where couples pair off in separate rooms. In open swinging, a "pretzel," "flesh pile" or "scene" may take place, all terms which signify groups of more than two people having sex with each other. Like Bartell, we found that females are much more likely to participate in homosexuality—probably near 100 percent—while very few men participate in homosexuality. Younger people tend to be much more accepting about the latter.

All of this flexibility can be summed up by saying that swingers consider an ideal gathering one in which everyone can express themselves as individuals *and* appreciate others for doing the same. If even one person fails to have an enjoyable experience in these terms, the gathering is that much less enjoyable for everyone.

An important consequence of this "do your own thing" ethic is that sexual experiences are talked about as a primarily personal matter. Conversely they are not evaluated according to a general standard. Thus one hears about "bad experiences" rather than "bad swingers." This is not to say that swingers are not aware of general sexual competence, but only that it is largely irrelevant to their appreciation of other people. As one informant said:

Technique is not that much. If she's all right, I don't care if she's technically terrible—if I think she's a beautiful person, she can't be that bad.

Beginners may make certain mistakes if they do not individuate. They may, for example, take on the "social director" role. This kind of person insists that a party become the materialization of his own fantasies without regard for anyone else's wishes. This can make the situation very uncomfortable for everyone else unless someone can get him to stop. Or, a nervous beginner may feel compelled to look around to find out what to do and, as a result, will imitate someone else. This imitation can be disturbing to others for two reasons. First, the imitator may not be enjoying himself. Second, he may be competing with someone else by comparing the effects of the same activity on their different partners. In either case, he is not involved with perceiving and satisfying the individual needs of his own partner. This would also be true in the case of the person who regularly imitates his or her own previous behavior, making an unchanging formula for interaction, no matter who he is with. Swingers generally consider such behavior insensitive and/or insincere.

Modification of Attitudes

Beginners tend to approximate the popular stereotype of sex-starved deviates. A 50-year-old woman described one of her beginning experiences this way:

It was one after another, and really, after a point it didn't make any difference *who* it was. It was just one great big prick after another. And I *never* experienced anything like that in my whole life. I have never had an experience like that with quite so many. I think in the course of three hours I must have had 11 or 12 men, and one greater than the next. It just kept on getting better every time. It snowballed.

The manner in which she describes her experience exemplifies the attitudes of both male and female beginners. They are not likely to develop a long lasting friendship with one or a small number of couples, and they focus much more on sex than the personalities involved. Frequently, they will be more interested in larger parties where individual personality differences are blurred by the number of people.

Simple curiosity seems to be the reason for this attitude. As one beginner told us, "Sometimes, we get titillated with them as people, knowing in the long run that it won't work out." It seems that because the beginner has been prevented so often from satisfying his curiosity through sexual liaisons in "straight" life, an important goal of early swinging is to satisfy this curiosity about people in general. This goal is apt to take precedence over any other for quite some time. Thus, even if a couple sincerely hopes to find long-lasting friendships, their desire to "move on" is apt to win out at first.

Bartell has asserted that both personality shallowness and jealousy are always responsible for this focus on sex and the search for new faces. For the most part, neither of these factors is necessarily responsible. First, the very same couples who appear shallow in fact may develop friendships later on. Second, as we shall see below, some couples who focus almost exclusively on sex nevertheless experience jealousy and must take certain precautions. On the other hand, some swingers *do* couple-hop because of jealousy. The Races, for example, dislike swinging with a couple more than once or twice because of the jealousy that arises each time. Very often only one member is jealous of the other's involvement but the jealousy will be hidden. Pride may prevent each from admitting jealousy for quite some time. Each partner may feel that to admit jealousy would be to admit a weakness and instead will feign disinterest in a particular couple to avoid another meeting.

This stage of swinging eventually stops in almost all cases we know of, probably because the superficial curiosity about people in general is satisfied. Women are usually responsible for the change, probably because they have been raised to reject superficial sexual relationships. Sometimes this is precipitated by a bad experience when, for example, a man is particularly rough or inconsiderate in some way. Sometimes a man will be the first to suggest a change because of erection problems which seem to be caused in some cases by a general lack of interest in superficial sexual contacts. In other words, once his general curiosity is satisfied, he can no longer sustain enough interest to be aroused.

The termination of the curiosity stage and the beginning of a stage of relative selectivity is characterized by increasing individuation of self and others. Among men this change manifests itself in the nature of fantasies that give interest to the sexual experience. The statement of one male informant exemplifies the change:

Now, I don't fantasize much. There's too much reality to fantasize, too much sex and sex realities we've experienced. So there is not too much that I *can* fantasize with. I just remember the good times we've actually had.

Instead of fantasies being what one would wish to happen,

they are instead a kind of reliving of pleasant past experiences with particular people. Also, some informants have noticed that where their previous fantasies had been impersonal, they eventually became tied to specific people with whom pleasant sexual experiences had been shared.

Increasing individuation is also noticeable in beginners' changing perceptions of certain problems that arise in swinging situations. Many male swingers have difficulty with erections at one time or another. Initially, this can be quite ego shattering. The reason for this trauma is not difficult to understand. Most Americans believe that the mere sight of a nude, sexually available woman should arouse a man almost instantly. A male who fails to be aroused may interpret this as a sign of his hitherto unknown impotency. But if he is not too discouraged by this first experience he may eventually find the real reasons. He may realize that he does not find some women attractive mentally and/or physically even though they are sexually available. He learns to recognize when he is being deliberately though subtly discouraged by a woman. He may discover that he dislikes certain situational factors. For example, he may find that he likes only open or only closet swinging or that he cannot relax sufficiently to perform after a hard day's work. Once a swinger realizes that his physical responses may very well be due to elements that inhere to the individual relationship rather than to an innate sexual inadequacy, he has arrived at a very different conception of sexual relationships. He is better able to see women as human beings to whom he may be attracted as personalities rather than as objects to be exploited for their sexual potential. In our terms, he can now more successfully individuate his relationships with women.

Women must cope with problems of a slightly different nature when they begin to swing. Their difficulties develop mostly because of their tendency to place decorum above the expression of their own individual desires in social situations. This tendency manifests itself from the time the husband suggests swinging. Many women seem to swing merely because their husbands want to rather than because of their own positive feelings on the matter. This should not be interpreted to mean that wives participate against their will, but only that as in most recreational activity, the male provides the initial impetus that she can then choose to go along with or reject. Her lack of positive initiative may express itself in the quality of her interaction. She is apt to swing with a man not because he manifests particular attributes that she appreciates, but because he lacks any traits that she finds outright objectionable. One woman describes one of her first experiences this way:

As I recall, I did not find him particularly appealing, but he was nice, and that was OK. He actually embarrassed me a bit because he was so shy and such a kind of nonperson.

This is not to say that women do not enjoy their experiences once they begin participating. The same woman remarks about her first experience in this way:

Somehow, it was the situation that made the demand. I got turned on, although I hadn't anticipated a thing up to that point. In fact, I still have a hard time accounting for my excitement that first time and the good time which I did actually have.

In fact, it sometimes happens at this stage that women become more enthusiastic about swinging than men, much to the latter's embarrassment.

Their enjoyment, however, seems to result from the same kind of psychology that is likely to propel them into swinging in the first place, the desire to please men. Hence, like her nonswinging counterparts, a woman in swinging will judge herself in terms of her desirability and her attractiveness to men much more than thinking about her own individuality in relation to others.

After swinging for awhile, however, her wish to be desired and to satisfy can no longer be as generalized because it becomes apparent that she is indeed desired by many men, and thus she has no need to prove it to herself. In order to make the experience meaningful, she arrives at a point where she feels that she must begin to actually refuse the advances of many men. This means that she must learn to define her own preferences more clearly and to learn to act on these preferences, an experience that many women rarely have because they have learned to rely on their husbands to make these kinds of decisions in social situations. In short, a woman learns to individuate both herself and others in the second stage of swinging.

Another change that swingers mention concerns their feelings towards their mates. They say that since they started swinging they communicate better than they did before. Such couples, who previously had a stable but uninteresting or stale marriage ("like brother and sister without the blood"), say that swinging has recreated the romantic feelings they once had for each other. These feelings seem to find concrete expression in an increasing satisfaction with the sexual aspects of the marital relationship, if not in an actual increase in sexual intercourse. This is almost always experienced by older couples in terms of feeling younger.

An explanation for this change, again, involves the individuation process. Marriage can grow stale if a couple loses a sense of appreciation of each other's individuality. A husband may look too much like an ordinary husband, a wife like an ordinary wife. This can happen easily especially when a couple's circumstances (job, children and so forth) necessitate a great deal of routinization of their life together. Such couples find in swinging the rare opportunity to escape from the routine roles that must be assumed in everyday life. In this setting individual differences receive attention and appreciation and, because of this, married couples can again see and appreciate their own distinct individuality, thus reactivating their romantic feelings for each other.

It is interesting to note that, those couples who do not answer in this way almost always experience jealousy, not romanticization, as a result of swinging. This is the case with one couple we interviewed, each of whom insists that the other is "better than anyone else," although it was clear by their jealousy of each other that neither was entirely confident of this.

Individuation, then, pervades the swinging scene and plays an important role in minimizing jealousy. But it alone cannot guarantee the control of jealousy—because there is always the possibility that a person will appreciate and be equally attracted to two unique individuals. Clearly, individuation must be complemented with something more if the marriage is to be effectively distinguished from other extramarital relationships.

This "something else" is compatibility. Two individuals who perceive and appreciate each other's individuality may nevertheless make poor living mates unless they are compatible. Compatibility is a kind of superindividuation. It requires not only the perception and appreciation of uniqueness, but the inclusion of this in the solutions to any problems that confront the relationship. Each partner must have the willingness and the ability to consider his or her mate's needs, desires and attitudes, when making the basic decisions that affect them both. This is viewed as something that people must work to achieve, as indicated by the phrase, "He failed in his marriage."

Unlike swinging, then, marriage requires a great deal of day-to-day giving and taking, and an emotional investment that increases with the years. Because such an investment is not given up easily, it provides another important safeguard against jealousy.

The dimension of marital compatibility often shows itself in swinging situations. If and when serious problems are encountered by one marriage partner, it is expected that the other partner will take primary responsibility for doing what is necessary. One couple, for example, was at a gathering, each sitting with their swinging partners. It was the first time they had ever tried pot, and the wife suddenly became hysterical. The man she was with quickly relinquished his place to her husband, who was expected to take primary responsibility for comforting his wife, although everyone was concerned about her. Another example can occur when a man has erection problems. If he is obviously miserable, it is considered wrong for his wife to ignore his condition, although we have heard of a few cases where this has happened. His wife may go to his side and they will decide to go home or she may simply act worried and less than completely enthusiastic, thus evincing some minimal

concern for her husband. In other words, the married couple is still distinguished as the most compatible partners and remains therefore the primary problem-solving unit.

The importance of compatibility also shows up in certain situations where a couple decides that they must stop swinging. In several cases reported to us, couples who had been married two years or less found that swinging tended to disrupt their marital relationship. We ourselves encountered three couples who had been married for under one year and had not lived together before marriage. All three had difficulties as a result of swinging, and one is now divorced. These couples evidently had not had the time to build up the emotional investment so necessary to a compatible marriage.

It is clear, then, that to the degree that couples individuate and are compatible, jealousy presents no major problems. Conversely, when these conditions are not satisfied, disruptive jealousy can result.

There are, however, some interesting exceptions. For a few couples who seem to place little emphasis on individuation, marital compatibility is an issue which remains chronically unresolved. Compatibility for them is a quality to be constantly demonstrated rather than a fact of life to be more or less taken for granted. Hence, every give-and-take becomes an issue.

These couples focus on the mechanics of sexual competence rather than on personal relationships. These are the people who will talk about "good swingers" and "bad swingers" rather than good and bad experiences. One of these husbands once commented:

Some people say there's no such thing as a good lay and a bad lay. But in my experience that just isn't true. I remember this one woman I went with for a long time. She was just a bad lay. No matter what I did, she was just lousy!

In other words, his bad lay is everyone's bad lay. One of his friends expressed it differently. He didn't understand why some swingers were so concerned with compatibility; he felt it was the sex that was important—and simply "having a good time."

Because they do not consider individuation important, these couples tend to approximate most closely the popular stereotypes of swingers as desiring only "pure sex." Swinging for these couples is primarily a matter of sexual interaction. Consequently, they are chiefly interested in seeing how sexually competent a couple is before they decide whether or not to develop a friendship. Competence may be defined in any or all of a number of ways. Endurance, size of penis, foreplay competence—all may be used to assess competence during the actual sexual interaction whether it be a large open party or a smaller gathering.

It is clear, then, that such couples perceive sex in a way

that individuators find uncongenial or even repugnant. When we first observed and interviewed them, we interpreted their behavior as the beginning stage of promiscuity that new couples may go through. But when we asked, we would find that they had been swinging frequently for a period of two years, much too long to be considered inexperienced. How, we asked ourselves, could such couples avoid jealousy, if they regularly evaluated sexual partners against a common standard? It seemed to us that a husband or wife in such a situation could conceivably be replaced some day by a "better lay," especially if the issue of marital compatibility remained somewhat unresolved. Yet these couples did not appear to experience any disruptive jealousy as a result of swinging. We found that they are able to accomplish this by instituting special, somewhat less flexible arrangements for swinging. First, they are invariably exclusive open swingers. That is, sexual interaction must take place in the same room. This tends to reduce any emotional involvement in one interaction. They think that closet swinging (swinging in separate rooms) is "no better than cheating." They clearly worry about the possibility of emotional infidelity more than individuators. An insistence on open swinging reduces the possibility of emotional involvement, and with it, the reason for jealousy. Second, they try to control the swinging situation as much as possible. So, for example, they are much more likely to insist on being hosts. And they also desire to state their sexual preferences ahead of time, thereby insuring that nothing very spontaneous and unpredictable can happen. Third, the women are more likely to desire female homosexuality and more aggressively so. This often results in the women experiencing more emotional involvement with each other than with the men, which is more acceptable because it does not threaten the marital relationship.

Conclusion: The Social Significance of Swinging

A full explanation of the reasons for the rise in popularity of swinging cannot be made adequately within the space of this article. But we would like to sketch briefly some of our findings in order to apply a corrective to the rather optimistic view which swingers have of swinging, the view which we have presented in this article.

A glance at the recent history of Western civilization reveals the locus of an adequate explanation. In the U.S.A. during this century, an increase in sexual freedom has always been followed by periods of relatively greater sexual repression. The flappers of the 1920's were followed by the more conservative women of the 1930's, and the freer female role of World War II was superseded by a wave of conservatism that sent women flocking back to the home. And, finally, in the 1960's, Americans have witnessed un-

precedented heights of sexual freedom in this country. In its level of intensity, this last period is most analogous to what occurred in Germany during the 1920's and early 1930's. The interesting thing about these ebbs and flows in sexual freedom is that they correlate quite closely with certain kinds of economic developments. In these cases, where sexual freedom appears as a general trend in the population, it is clearly a function of factors which are beyond the immediate control of individuals. Such factors as investment flows, limited resources, fluctuations in world markets, and so forth, all events that seem isolated from the arena of intimacy which people carve for themselves, are in fact very much a part of their most personal relationships.

Three questions present themselves. First, what is the nature of the social conditions which surround swinging? Second, what is the relationship between those conditions and the consciousness of individual swingers? And finally, why should the two have anything to do with each other?

Taking last things first, for a moment, it is important to consider swinging as a social event which seems appropriate to the participants. By "appropriate" we mean that it makes sense to them in terms of how they see their relationships to other people, in terms of their conceptions of social reality, and in terms of their notions about value. These ideas appear rational only in so far as they seem to address themselves to the objective realities which people face in their day to day existence.

An interesting example of the relationship between objective reality and morality is the effect which Germany's great inflation during the 1920's had on the morality of the Berlin middle class. Otto Freidrich in his book *Before the Deluge* interviews a woman who vividly describes the effect of this economic development:

> Yes, the inflation was by far the most important event of this period. The inflation wiped out the savings of the entire middle class, but those are just words. You have to realize what that *meant*. There was not a single girl in the entire German middle class who could get *married* without her father paying a dowry. Even the maids—they never spent a penny of their wages. They saved and saved so that they could get married. When money became worthless, it destroyed the whole system for getting married, and so it destroyed the whole idea of remaining chaste until marriage.
>
> The rich had never lived up to their own standards, of course, and the poor had different standards anyway, but the middle class, by and large, obeyed the rules. Not every girl was a virgin when she was married, but it was

FIVE TYPES OF SWINGING COUPLES:
The Eversearches, the Closefriends, the Snares, the Races and the Successes

The following are composite case histories of five swinging couples. Although each case history is closely tied to one couple whom we knew fairly well, the case itself is more generalized to represent at least a few couples we have met. To check the accuracy of our perceptions of these different types of couples, we showed these case histories to five couples. All recognized other swinging couples whom they had also met.

Two problems present themselves here—the representativeness of the individual cases and the comprehensiveness of the five cases taken as a whole. In regard to the former, there is no way to know what proportion of swingers represent each case. In fact, to judge proportions from our sample might very well be misleading. This is because couples such as the Eversearches use swinging media and are therefore more visible and easier to contact, while couples like the Closefriends are very difficult to locate because they stay within their own circle of close friends. Hence, even though the Eversearches probably represent a higher proportion of our sample, this in no way tells us about the actual proportion of Eversearch types. In regard to the question of comprehensiveness, these case histories are only meant to intuitively represent the possible range of types. Many couples may better be seen as a mixture of types, and some types of couples may not be represented at all.

Jack and Jeanine Eversearch

Jack and Jeanine grew up in the same small town. They went to the same schools and the same church. In their sophomore year of high school they began to go steady. Just before she was to graduate, Jeanine, to her dismay, became pregnant, and her parents, experiencing a similar reaction, finally decided on abortion. They wanted her to go to college, enlarge her experiences, and perhaps find some other marriage prospect than the rather placid Jack.

At college, however, the two continued to see each other frequently. Jeanine occasionally went out with other men, but never felt as comfortable with them as she did with Jack. Jack never went out with anyone but Jeanine, mainly because his shyness prevented him from meeting other girls. It was predictable that the two would marry the June they graduated.

Five years and two children later, Jack and Jeanine were living much as they always had, in a new suburban home, close to their families. Life had become a routine of barbecues and bridge parties on weekends and children to get ready for school during the week, marked by occasional special events like a church social or a ride in the country. To all appearances, they seemed to have a model marriage.

But their marriage had actually changed, so gradually that the shift was almost imperceptible. Like most married couples, they had experienced a waning of sexual interest from time to time. But in their case, the troughs had lengthened until sex had become a perfunctory gesture, something they did just because they were married. As Jeanine said, "We didn't fight, because there was nothing to fight about. We just felt the inevitability of being together for the rest of our lives—something like brother and sister without the blood."

They had used the church before in a social way; they turned to it now for inspiration. Their congregation had recently acquired a new pastor, a sincere and intelligent man, whom almost everyone liked.

But the home situation continued to disintegrate. Jeanine, on her own there most of the day, found the situation intolerable and decided to seek help from the pastor:

I knew something was wrong but it was too vague to talk about very clearly. I just kept stammering about how . . . things weren't what they used to be. But I couldn't say exactly why. In fact, I was so fuzzy that I was afraid he'd misunderstand me and that instead of advice I'd get a lecture about how God is the source of all meaning in life or something like that. So, when he started telling me about the problems that he and his wife had, I was quite surprised but also delighted.

They continued to meet as friends, and it became apparent that the pastor needed Jeanine for personal comfort and support as much as she needed him. This led to an affair, which lasted until Jack came home unexpectedly early from work one day three months later.

After the initial shock faded, Jack was left with a feeling of total inadequacy:

I guess I thought that if Jeanine wanted to sleep with someone else, that meant I had disappointed her. I felt that my inability to rise in the company reflected on our marriage and on her choice of me as a husband—which didn't do my ego any good.

The episode proved fortunate, because it provided them with a reason to talk about their problems, and with the channels of communication open once more, their marriage began to seem fulfilling again. Their sexual interest in each other returned:

We started doing things in bed that we'd always been curious about but had never bothered to try or had been too embarrassed to mention. There were many nights when we couldn't wait to get into bed.

About a year after Jeanine's affair ended, they started discussing the possibility of swinging. But when they thought of it seriously, they realized that not one other couple they knew would be willing partners. Jack had heard of swingers' magazines, gave the local smut peddler a try, and brought one home.

They examined the magazine for hours, wondering about the people who had placed the ads and looking at the pictures. Finally, caution gave way to curiosity, and they answered four of the more conservative ads. Within a few weeks they had received encouraging answers from all four.

Jack and Jeanine found their first swinging experience very pleasant. They felt nervous at first when they were greeted at the door by the other couple because they did not know what to expect. Nevertheless, they enjoyed themselves enough to agree to swing when it was suggested by their hosts. Having their fantasies and desires come true in the bedroom was intensely pleasurable to them both, and when they returned home they longed to share their elation with someone else, but could think of no one who would not be shocked. So they called the other couple back and told *them* what a good time they'd had.

Encouraged by this first happy experience, the Eversearches began to swing with practically every couple they could contact. Lately, they have become more selective, but they still devote some time to contacting and meeting new people.

Looking back, both feel that swinging has changed them. Before, Jack had always gone along with the men he knew, accepting, at least verbally, their values, attitudes and behavior:

It bugs me now that I have to play some kind of he-man role all the time. I never used to notice it. You know how guys are always talking about this girl and how they would like to get her in bed? Well . . . I'm not interested in just sex anymore—I mean, I want to have someone I like, not just a writhing body.

Jeanine feels similarly:

All of a sudden it seems I have more insight into everybody, into how they interact with each other. Maybe because we've met so many different kinds of people. And I have to be very careful that I don't express some of my liberal views. Sometimes, I really want to tell our nonswinging friends about our new life—but then I'm sure they wouldn't understand.

Mike and Maryann Closefriend

Mike and Maryann are 30 and 25 years old and have been married five years. They originally met when Mike, then an advanced graduate student, gave a lecture about inner-city family structure to a group of volunteer social workers. Maryann was in the audience and asked several penetrating questions. After the talk, she approached him to find out more. They were immediately attracted to each other and started going out frequently. After about six months they rented an apartment together, and when Mike got his Ph.D. in social science a year later, they married and moved to the East Coast, where he had obtained a teaching post.

Their early life together seemed an experience of endless enjoyment. They went camping on weekends, took pottery classes, and were lucky in meeting several people whose outlook on life was similar to theirs, with whom they developed close relationships. These friends have helped not only in practical things, such as moving or house painting, but in emotional crises. When, for example, Mike and Maryann seemed to be on the verge of breaking up about two years ago, their friends helped to smooth things over by acting as amateur psychologists.

The Closefriends don't remember exactly how they started swinging. Mike says it was "just a natural consequence of our friendship—our feeling for our friends." They remember some nudity at their parties before they swung, mostly unplanned. People took off their clothes because of the heat or just because they felt more comfortable that way. Sometimes they engaged in sexual play of various kinds, and this led to intercourse as a natural part of these occasions. Sometimes just two people felt like swinging, and sometimes everyone. If the former was the case, people could just watch, or if the couple wanted privacy, they went to another room. And sometimes no one felt like swinging, and the subject was never brought up.

For the Closefriends, swinging seems to be a natural outgrowth of the way they approached marriage and friendship, and the way they feel about and relate to people in general. As Maryann puts it:

I guess it has to do with our basic belief in the totality of sharing and the kind of dialogue that we have with each other. Our no-holds-barred, no secrets kind of relationship produces such a lovely kind of glow that we just naturally like to share it with our friends. Our having close relationships with people is actually like having a second marriage. Not that we would all want to live together, although that might be possible some day. Some of the men, for example, couldn't live with me—we would be incompatible—but that doesn't make us any less desirable to each other.

Paul and Georgia Snare

When Paul met Georgia, he had been married about a year and was beginning to find his wife Serita both boring and demanding. A handsome young man, Paul had led an exciting life as a bachelor and found the daily routine of marriage very depressing:

I felt awfully trapped. . . . It just got worse and worse until I couldn't see going home anymore. I bought a motorcycle and joined up with a bunch of guys pretty much like me. We'd ride around all night so we wouldn't have to go home to our old ladies.

Georgia was a salesgirl in the drug-store next door to the camera shop where Paul worked. He used to drop by daily for cigarettes and a chat, and they became friendly. Paul even made a few passes, but Georgia knew he already had a wife and refused his attentions. Unused to this kind of treatment, Paul took her refusals as a challenge and became quite serious in his efforts to persuade her to go out with him. Finally, when Paul and Serita got a formal separation, Georgia accepted his invitations, and they began to date steadily.

Georgia became pregnant about three months before Paul's divorce was due to come through, so they were married the week after the decree became final. At first things went well. Georgia stayed home and took care of the small house in the suburbs that Paul had bought for her, and the marriage ran smoothly for about six months, until the baby came. Then Paul began to feel trapped again, "going to work every day, coming home to dinner and going to bed. I didn't want it to happen again but it did."

Paul resorted to outside affairs, but found them unsatisfactory because they took too much time and money, and "it just wasn't worth all the lying." He suggested to Georgia the possibility of swinging with some friends of theirs, pointing out that he loved her but that "every man needs a bit of variety." Georgia initially thought the idea was crazy, but Paul persisted and finally persuaded her to try it.

Persuading their friends, however, was another matter. They didn't want to come right out and proposition them, so they decided on seduction as the method of persuasion. They would

"date" a couple each weekend, and go dancing to provide an excuse for body contact. Paul would get increasingly intimate with the wife, and if the husband followed his example, Georgia would accept his advances.

They decided their first couple would be their old friends Bill and Jean. Everything went as planned for a while until Bill became suspicious and asked Paul to explain his attentions to Jean. When Paul did so, the couple became upset and left almost immediately.

Somewhat depressed by the loss of their friends, Paul and Georgia tried another couple they knew, but this time they enacted their plan more slowly. It took about six months, but it worked, and they continued to swing with the couple exclusively for about a year, until they discovered swinging magazines and began making new contacts through them.

Neither of the Snares have any problems with jealousy, and agree that this is because "we are so good in bed with each other that no one could really compete." From time to time Paul even brings home girls he has met; Georgia doesn't get jealous "just so long as he introduces them to me first and they do their thing in my house." For her part, Georgia has discovered that she likes women too and regularly brings home girls from a nearby homosexual bar. "Men," she says, "are good for sex, but it isn't in their nature to be able to give the kind of affection a woman needs." Georgia's activities don't worry Paul a bit:

A woman couldn't provide the kind of support I do. They just don't know how to get along in the world without a man. A lot of these lesbians she meets are really irresponsible and would never be able to take care of the kid.

Swinging has affected Georgia's self-confidence as well as changing her sex habits. She now feels much more confident in social situations, a change that occurred after she began making

her own choices about whom she would swing with. At first, she had let Paul make all the decisions:

If he liked the woman, then I would swing with the man. But it got so I couldn't stand it anymore. I had to make it with so many creeps! I just got sick of it after a while. Paul kept getting the good deals and I never found anybody I liked. Finally, I just had to insist on my rights!

Paul agrees that this is good and points out that one swinger they know constantly forces his wife to swing with men she has no desire for, and as a result their marriage is slowly disintegrating. He credits swinging with saving his own marriage with Georgia and thinks that, had he known about it before, it could have saved his first marriage too.

Frank and Helen Race

Frank and Helen met at a well-known West Coast university where both were top-ranked graduate students in bio-chemistry. Both were from Jewish backgrounds, strongly oriented toward academic achievement.

Frank, largely because of his parents' urging, had excelled in high school, both academically and in extracurricular activities. After high school, he enlisted in the marines, was commissioned after OCS training and commanded one of the best units on his base. Ultimately, he became dissatisfied with the life of a marine officer and left to attend college, where he finished his bachelor degree in three years, graduated with honors and went on to graduate school.

As a child, Helen had experienced much the same kind of pressure. Her father, an excellent musician, dominated the family and drove her endlessly. She began piano lessons at age four and remembers that he was always at her shoulder to scold her when she made a mistake. She was able to end music lessons only because she attended a college where no facilities were available, leaving her free to devote all her time to the study of biochemistry, which she much preferred.

Helen and Frank married during their third year of graduate school. It seemed a perfect match—two fine scholars with identical interests, who could work as a team. For the next four years they did work closely together on their respective Ph.D. dissertations, which were published and became well known in the field. Despite this success, however, they could not find jobs with prestige schools and had to take posts at a less well known institution.

They settled into their professional lives, both publishing as much as possible in the hope of eventually gaining positions at a more prestigious university. They worked together closely, constantly seeking each other's help and proffering severe criticisms. If either published more than the other during the year, the "underpublished" one would experience intense jealousy. Realizing this disruptive competition was a serious threat to their marriage, they sought help from a psychotherapist and from group therapy sessions.

The most important thing Frank and Helen learned about themselves in therapy was that by making their relationship competitive they had forfeited their appreciation of each other as individuals. They also discovered another element in their lives, which Frank links directly to their decision to take up swinging:

> I told Helen that I missed terribly the experiences that other men had as kids. I was always too busy with school to ever have a good time dating. I only had a date once in high school, for the senior prom, and I had only had one girl friend in college. I felt that a whole stage of my life was totally absent. I wanted to do those things that I had missed out on—then maybe I'd feel more able to cope with our

problems. Much to my surprise, Helen felt she too had missed out.

Like the Eversearches, the Races met their first couple through an ad in a swinger publication. Their first meeting, however, was somewhat unpleasant. Frank felt jealous because he feared the man might be sexually better than he. He did not tell Helen this, however, but simply refused to return, on the grounds that he had not enjoyed the woman. Helen suspected Frank was in fact jealous, and many arguments ensued.

The Races have been swinging for about three years and average one contact every two or three months, a rate of frequency considerably lower than usual. Both agree that they have a lot of difficulty with jealousy. If, for example, they meet a couple and Helen is very attracted to the man, Frank will invariably insist he does not find the woman desirable. They have come to realize that the one who exercises the veto is probably jealous of the good time the other has had or is about to have and thus insists on breaking off the threatening relationship. They also realize that swinging may not be the best way to use their leisure time—but somehow they can't give up the hope that they may find the experiences they missed as young people.

Glen and Andrea Success

Glen and Andrea were married shortly before the end of the war, immediately after Glen graduated with a Ph.D. in biology. Because he felt that teaching at a university would be financially limiting, he found a job with a medical supply manufacturing company, which promised him a high-ranking executive position in the future. He has stayed with the company for nearly 20 years, rising to positions of increased responsibility.

Five years after he had begun work, Andrea and Glen were able to afford a luxurious suburban home. Well settled into their house and community, they

started their family. Andrea enjoyed motherhood and raised her two boys and a girl as model children:

> There wasn't a thing we couldn't do. Glen and I traveled all over the States and Europe. We even went to Australia. We had bought ourselves a lovely house, we had a fine marriage and wonderful, healthy children. We had many fine friends too.

Glen claims it was this unusual good luck that eventually turned them to swinging. About seven years ago, they began to feel they had achieved everything that people usually want and anything else would be anticlimactic:

> We knew one couple with whom we could talk about anything and everything, and we did! One conversation especially, I think, led to our considering swinging. We were talking about success and trying to define exactly what it meant. Andrea and I thought it was something like having all the money you need and a good marriage. They said that if that was true, then we already had everything we would ever want. . . . Later on, when I thought about what he'd said, I got a funny kind of hollow feeling. Forty-five, I said to myself, and at the end of the line.

In this state of mind Glen got the idea that swinging might be a way out. He and Andrea spent about a month discussing the possibility and finally decided to try it out. Their first meeting with another couple was disturbing for them both, but they continued to look for more satisfactory people. If the second meeting had been equally bad, they probably would have given up the whole idea. But it ended pleasantly in a friendship that lasted about three years.

At first they had to rely on contacts from the *National Enquirer*, but about a year after they started swinging their local newspaper began running ads on the lines of "Modern couple interested in meeting the same. Box 1023." About ten of these ads appeared during the brief period before the paper found out what they were for and ceased to accept any more. By then Glen and Andrea had contacted all the couples who had advertised. These people, in turn, knew other swingers whom they had either met through national publications or had initiated themselves. Soon a large network began to form.

Glen applied his organizational talents to the swinging scene and was soon arranging parties for couples he felt would be compatible, spending his own money to rent halls for get-togethers. Many couples started coming to him with their problems, and to help them out, he arranged for a doctor to direct group discussions dealing with typical swinging problems. He even contacted lawyers whom he knew personally to protect "his swingers," as he was beginning to call them, should they have any difficulties with the law. In fact, the Successes knew so many couples that other swingers began to rely on them as a kind of dating service that could arrange for either quiet evenings or major parties.

The Successes feel that in swinging they have finally found an activity which offers lasting interest and stimulation. Says Andrea:

Glen and I have done everything—I don't just mean sex. Just doing things doesn't really appeal to us anymore. But swinging has managed to hold our attention for a long time. If you give me a choice between going to South America, nightclubbing or swinging, I think swinging is the most satisfying and interesting.

Why? Glen says:

I think it's because in swinging you can see people for who they really are—as individuals, without the masks they have to wear most of the time. In a way, I guess I never knew people before, and I'm amazed at the variety. Maybe that's why swinging holds my interest—everybody is different, a challenge to get to know.

generally accepted that one *should* be. But what happened from the inflation was that the girls learned that virginity didn't matter any more. The women were liberated.

It may seem odd to think of a person confronting his system of values and suddenly finding it obsolete, but that is exactly what happened to many of the swingers we talked to. This was reflected not only in their comments to us but in their approach to swinging as beginners. Couples who seemed otherwise very cautious and conservative would often persist through one, two, or as many as six perfectly horrendous initial experiences, absolutely determined to find a compatible couple. Such tenacity is remarkable in that these couples, like many middle class Americans, were prone to form strong opinions on the basis of their own personal experience. In addition to persistence, another important indicator of swingers' needs to modify their value systems is their stated satisfaction with swinging as a new life style. Generally, these couples feel that swinging benefits them not only as a form of entertainment but as an activity which boosts their self confidence, enlarges their understanding of others, and helps them shed their "hypocritical" attitudes.

The fact that swingers say they feel better about themselves as a result of swinging indicates that swinging and the ideology that goes along with it are more appropriate to the present conditions of their existence than were the values which these couples held previous to swinging. The question is, what were these new "facts of life" which the middle class had to deal with in the middle sixties?

Two related developments occurring during this period which affected practically every member of this society were rising inflation and increased speculation. By speculation we refer to the massive shift in investments away from increasingly productive capacity into such areas as land speculation, conglomerate building, defense production, and insurance and various other "service industries."

Where inflation did not result in outright cuts in the real, disposable income of the middle class, it at least generated considerable anxiety. Many women were forced onto the job market in order to help maintain their familial standard of living, abruptly threatened by the unexpectedly high cost of buying or keeping up a home, of financing a college education, or of paying taxes. Many young couples began to restrict the size of their families because they feared that they would not be able to provide adequately for their children. These couples felt that under such circumstances child rearing would prove a singularly unrewarding experience, both for themselves and their children.

This movement away from traditional forms of adulthood, which included marriage and a family, was exacerbated by the speculative trend in the economy which made it necessary. Far from causing anxiety, the new life styles were often viewed as being desirable. For they expressed the kind of human relationships inherent in a society where the economy runs on speculation and non-productive enterprise. In such an atmosphere, all social forms associated with production begin to seem less and less appropriate.

Swinging as an ideology addresses itself to the new conditions which the middle class faces as the result of economic stagnation. Before swinging, the nature of relations between husband and wife had more or less reflected the role of the family as an important biological and social reproductive unit of society. That is, the ideal of monogamous sexual relationships, realized even in the institution of cheating, reflected the notion that the family unit existed not only for rearing children but for the maintenance of the sexual division of labor. Husband and wife formed an interdependent productive whole that was crucial to the continuance of the society. Swinging breaks with the past in that it does not reflect any productive relation to society whatsoever. Sex within the context of swinging at its best merely symbolizes a loosely defined friendship. As one swinger told us, "It's all a lot of fun, but it sure is irrelevant to anything." This notion of "sex for fun" as many have called it does not confine itself to swinging, however. The trend towards a revivification of marriage through romance essentially returns fun and adventure to the marriage, replacing or dominating the old productive functions.

In essence, swinging helps a couple adjust their self conceptions so that they are more in tune with the surrounding conditions generated by social breakdown and decay. As a successful adaptation, however, swinging can in no way address itself to solving those problems.

The prisoner locked behind bars and the mental patient confined to a hospital ward are totally immersed in their social and physical surroundings. The term *closed* or *total environment* is loosely applied to settings where inhabitants are in close contact with one another, share the same physical environment and find it difficult or impossible to extricate themselves from their situation. While prisons and mental hospitals are usually described as representative total environments, the criteria noted above can apply to a much wider range of situations in which persons can find themselves, voluntarily or involuntarily. Included would be such diverse settings as military units, spacecraft, undersea habitats, Antarctic stations and monasteries. Although less cut off from outside contact than the examples cited above, communes and small towns often approach total environments in their impact on the individual.

Total environments bring maximum social influence to bear on their members. The types of pressures discussed in the preceding Parts operate most powerfully when the individual spends all of his time in a unitary environment. Pressures to conform and to adopt the beliefs and attitudes of the group are high. The pressures are intensified when the individual cannot easily leave the environment—as in the case of a prisoner, a patient or an astronaut in space. Typically, the group and/or leaders of the social organization in a total environment have the power to punish deviant members through psychological sanctions such as condemnation or ostracism or through physical retribution. In most cases the psychological force has more impact than physical punishment; the mere threat of psychological pressure produces a high degree of behavioral control. Many of the psychological processes in closed environments seem to be the same whether the individual is an eager, highly screened volunteer or a completely unwilling prisoner or patient.

The first two essays in this Part deal with

**living
in a
sealed-off
society**

the mental hospital and its effect on patients. Ailon Shiloh, first, describes the varied response of patients to a progressive mental hospital. He finds that some patients make a complete adjustment to the patterns of life in the institution and hold no desire for or expectation of returning to outside society. Other patients see their incarceration as temporary and hope for release. The crucial point is that a total institution purportedly aimed at healing and returning the ill to society can, through its social power over inmates, become a necessary and sufficient end in itself. Thus, a total environment can exert enormous influence toward covert goals quite different from those it explicitly espouses.

Eugene Talbot and Stuart C. Miller, in the next essay, describe a very different organization for a mental hospital—one in which patients are given primary responsibility for running the institution. Here the explicit goal of treatment and recovery and the implicit organization of the institution are congruent; accordingly, the development of socialized "permanent patients" such as those described by Shiloh is rare. Contrasting the two studies shows how strongly the dynamics of a total institution can influence its inhabitants and how subtle the forces can be within such a setting.

David W. Plath and Yoshie Sugihara, in contrast, look at social pressure and the responses to such pressure by Japanese villagers. We have noted that isolated villages can develop many of the characteristics of total environments. In the Japanese village studied, a group of villagers were ostracized by their neighbors, in the sense that they were almost completely cut off from communication and interchange with their peers. This treatment represents perhaps the most extreme form of psychological pressure possible in a closed environment. Interestingly, the response of those cut off from one total environment was to develop another which functioned very effectively. In the case reported, the reaction of the isolates was to develop a commune composed of the rejected individuals in the village.

In the next essay, William W. Haythorn and Irwin Altman report on a laboratory investigation of reactions to a total environment. They placed pairs of volunteer subjects in completely self-contained environments without outside contact and observed their behavior in this isolated mini-world. A crucial part of their research design was the assessment of personality characteristics and the matching of pairs of subjects before isolation. By using this experimental strategy, they were able to investigate not only what individual characteristics facilitated adjustment to a total and isolated environment, but also what combinations of individuals were most and least likely to adapt to total lack of outside contact. Subjects were measured on four dimensions of personality: 1) the *need for achievement*—or task orientation, 2) the *need for dominance*—the desire to control or dominate others, 3) the *need for affiliation*—a desire for affection and the company of others, and 4) the *need for dogmatism*—the belief that one's own opinions are the only important and correct ones. Some pairs contained individuals who were both high on these traits, other pairs were composed of one subject scoring high on a trait and another who scored low. Haythorn and Altman found that the "mix" of personalities did indeed influence performance and the quality of social interaction. Greatest difficulties were experienced by pairs where both men scored high on dominance and by pairs where one man had a great need for achievement and the other had little need to excel. Other pairings led to different kinds of reactions. These effects, however, were far more pronounced when individuals were in a total environment than when they spent only a part of their time together. Although highly complex, this type of research can provide invaluable information on social interaction and patterns of adjustment. When such laboratory investigations are followed by observations of natural groups, understanding of social processes can advance rapidly.

Robert Helmreich and Roland Radloff discuss the relationship between the stresses of isolated and dangerous environments and the maintenance of a sense of personal worth (self-esteem) in the next essay. They argue that exposure to stress reduces one's perception of being able to cope with new or existing situations and hence lowers his self-esteem. The authors present a cost-reward model designed to evaluate the relative difficulties in adjustment that can be expected in various environments. Their model is based on defining the costs incurred by participation in various situations relative to the rewards to be gained from that participation. Costs represent all negative aspects of an environment, such as danger, separation, discomfort, while rewards represent the positive benefits available, such as money, fame, job satisfaction. Applying these concepts to the problem of long-duration spaceflight, they argue that the customary rewards for being an astronaut, such as fame and public honors, are likely to decrease as spaceflight becomes more commonplace while the costs, in terms of danger, discomfort and isolation, will probably remain relatively high and constant. One solution they suggest is composing crews in such a way that each member would serve both as a teacher in the area of his expertise and as a student of other disciplines. They feel that such work interdependence can provide many intrinsic rewards and, thus, greater overall satisfaction for a crew.

The final essay, by Philip G. Zimbardo, discusses an environment which Helmreich and Radloff would define as extremely high in costs and extremely low in rewards—the prison. This report is important for several reasons. One is that Zimbardo draws powerful conclusions about the failure of the prison system and the dehumanizing effects of confinement on both inmates and those who supervise them. Another reason revolves around the vital questions Zimbardo's research raises about the ethicality of psychological experimentation. In his attempt to understand the psychology of prisons, Zimbardo created a prison by screening volunteers and assigning them by coin toss to be either prisoners or guards for a two-week simulation of a prison. All volunteers were psychologically normal, male college students. The researchers found their "mock prison" such a powerful and frightening experience that they had to terminate the experiment after six days because of the extreme stress experienced by virtually all of the participants.

Zimbardo draws two major conclusions from his research. The first is that individual behavior is primarily under the control of situational factors rather than personality traits. This is shown by the fact that normal, intelligent young men altered their behavior so drastically as a function of the simulated prison environment. The second conclusion, with regard to prisons, is that the mere assigning of labels such as "prisoner" or "guard" in our system is sufficient to elicit pathological behavior. He argues that "the prison situation, as presently arranged, is guaranteed to generate severe enough pathological reactions in both guards and prisoners as to debase their humanity, lower their feelings of self-worth, and make it difficult for them to be a part of a society outside of their prison." This is a damning indictment of the penal system and a compelling argument for prison reform.

While the results of the study are clear, the ethical issues involved in Zimbardo's research are far more complex. The issue is whether the psychologist is morally justified in causing physical or psychological discomfort in subjects participating in laboratory research. Although there is disagreement among research psychologists, one generally accepted ethical standard is that research subjects should not be exposed to any situation which causes extreme physical or psychological discomfort or which can result in irrevers-

ible physical or psychological changes. While the physical discomforts of the "prisoners" are obvious, the more serious issues relate to the psychological effects of being a subject in the study. The most important ethical concern is the fact that "prisoners" and "guards" alike discovered the indisputable, negative fact that they could become brutalized, dehumanized and totally unconcerned about the welfare of others during a brief simulation of prison life. But the ethical question is not one-sided. To a large extent, the researcher has an ethical obligation to society, which directs him toward pursuing important questions to the best of his ability as a scientist. If Zimbardo had decided *not* to undertake the study out of his concern for the welfare of his subjects, might he not have been turning his back on the welfare of society as a whole? The sociopsychological researcher is constantly in an ethical dilemma—attempting to find out things that may be useful to society without doing violence to his experimental subjects.

Zimbardo's research is an interesting case in point. His results have been reported to the Judiciary Committee of the United States House of Representatives and presented to the American people on a national television network. The research could well play a role in efforts to achieve a reorganization of our prison system. Again, this fact highlights the most difficult ethical question. *Is the experimenter justified in causing suffering on the part of a few if many may benefit from the results of the research?* There is no pat answer to the question nor is there a formula which can be applied to judge the relative importance of factors in a particular study. The researcher can only agonize with his own conscience and social concerns, seeking and accepting the counsel of his colleagues before deciding whether to undertake an investigation. This is probably the most painful aspect of psychological research. As a consumer of research, the reader should undertake his own evaluation of the ethicality of all research he encounters.

The study of closed environments can add to our understanding not only of total situations like those described but also to our comprehension of the social forces in everyday life. If one common theme can be isolated from the disparate environments considered in this section, it is that human behavior is so much a function of the individual's situation that more effort should be expended on changing negative environments than on changing human nature.

Sanctuary or Prison—

Responses to Life in a Mental Hospital

Ailon Shiloh

It is unlikely that very many mental hospitals remain of the kind described 20 years ago by Ivan Belknap. At that time, hundreds of patients slept—winter and summer—on windswept porches or on bare concrete floors. All of the buildings were old, crowded, and hazardous. The food was tasteless to begin with and cold when served. The total daily budget per patient was 47 cents. On any day, patients had one chance in 280 of seeing a doctor. The basic therapy consisted of allowing the patients to sit on benches and stare at the blank walls.

That hospital represented the worst aspects of the custodial approach to treating the mentally ill, an approach requiring only that patients be kept alive and out of the way. While few hospitals would dare to provide that sort of barbaric custody nowadays, my own research in a large public mental hospital suggests that less obvious but no less pernicious aspects of the custodial approach are still central to mental hospitals today.

What does the custodial approach do to patients? Clifford W. Beers has caught it in an aphorism: "Madmen are too often man-made." Lucy Ozarin reached a similar conclusion: "After visiting 35 mental hospitals, the writer has formed the strong conviction that much of the pathological behavior of patients is a result of their hospital experience rather than a manifestation of their mental illness."

Many observers have tried to make sense of this phenomenon, but perhaps the best theoretical work on the meaning of the custodial approach has been that of Erving Goffman. In *Asylums,* Goffman used his research in a mental hospital to develop a theory of the world of the "total institution," a category that includes not only mental hospitals, but prison, the armed services, and so on. Goffman focused on the world of the inmate and the ways in which he transforms his experience with the social world of the hospital into a "structure of the self."

Goffman's major research was a one-year field study of St. Elizabeth's Hospital in Washington, D.C. Since he wanted to give an anthropologist's detailed description of patient life, he did not employ measurements and controls—which, in addition, would have undermined his rapport with the patients and staff. I have employed much the same method in my study of a Veterans Administration hospital.

Goffman defined the total institution as a place of residence and work where a number of individuals in similar situations are cut off from the wider society and lead an enclosed, formally administered life. The key fact of the total institution is that many human needs of whole blocs of people are under bureaucratic control. In the total institution, there is a basic cleavage between the small managing groups (the staff, in the case of a hospital) and the large managed group (the inmates, or patients).

The staff is concerned with surveillance; the inmates with conformity. Each group sees the other in terms of narrow, hostile stereotypes. Their association is marked by misunderstanding and mistrust. Communications from inmates to staff are channeled and controlled by the lower staff with the knowledge and consent of the higher staff. Communications from staff to inmates are also restricted. Characteristically, inmates are excluded from knowing any decisions taken as to their fates, a fact that provides the staff with a further basis for distance from and control over the inmates. All of these restrictions, Goffman believes, help maintain the mutually antagonistic stereotypes.

This split between staff and inmates is one major aspect of the total institution. Other considerations stressed by Goffman are the nature of the staff's work —their lack of motivation can lead to demoralization and to extreme boredom—and the relationship of the institution to the inmate's families, who are incompatible with the aims of the total institution. All of these factors are particularly important when the institution uses a custodial approach, when it may have no intention of releasing the inmates.

Goffman, having suggested the key features of the total institution, goes on to discuss the ways in which the inmates are "programmed." This process is fairly standardized. The new inmate is subjected to a series of abasements, degradations, humiliations, and profanations of his self. The institutional machinery examines, identifies, and codes him. He is stripped of his possessions and provided with institutional clothing. He is given tests of obedience and placed under a strict surveillance program to teach him how to behave in his new role.

Particularly during this initial period, the inmate's life is controlled from above by regulations, judgments, and sanctions. He must learn to follow the rules unthinkingly. If he does, he will be paid off in privileges —a better room, a little more privacy, a kind word from an attendant, an appointment with a physician. Also clearly communicated to the patients are the punishments for not following the rules. Not only are his privileges removed, but he may also suffer ridicule, beatings, threats, isolation, or difficulty of access to professional help.

Clearly, therapy is not the primary aim of the custodial mental hospital. And if that were not enough, Goffman also shows, the inmate must make a persistent, conscientious effort just to stay out of trouble. Yet this same effort provides the inmate with important—and sometimes critical—evidence that he still has some control over his environment.

How does the inmate adapt to the total institution?

Goffman suggests that a person may choose at least three lines of adaptations:

■ He may drastically curtail his interaction with others —what Goffman calls the "situational withdrawal" or "regression line."

■ He may deliberately challenge the institution by refusing to cooperate—the "intransigent line."

■ He may fully accept the values and roles assigned him by the institution—the "colonization line."

Because the institution *is* total, Goffman believes that the intransigent line has to be temporary. He suggests that the regression line is also unsatisfactory: Too frequently it is irreversible.

Yet the staff may be embarrassed by inmates who take the colonization line. When an inmate admits having found a "home," and never having had it so good, staff members may sense that they are being used, or that their custodial role has become all too apparent.

Goffman believes that the colonization line appeals mostly to lower-class patients who have lived in orphanages, reformatories, or other total institutions; or who have grown up in authoritarian homes. These patient have been prepared for their roles as inmates in a total institution. Any attempt on the part of the staff to make the lives of such inmates more bearable may increase the likelihood that they will be colonized.

That is the theory, or at least a sketch of it.

Now, what of the people I studied in the Veterans Administration Hospital in Downey, Ill.?

Downey is 35 miles north of the Chicago Loop. The V.A. hospital there has 2487 beds. It is the largest of the 40 neuropsychiatric hospitals run by the V.A., and one of the largest mental institutions in the country. The hospital's annual budget is more than $13 million, or $15.37 per patient per day, which is about three times the average daily expenditure per patient in U.S. public mental hospitals.

At the time I studied the patients of Downey, 42 percent had been admitted with disabilities connected with their military service, and 58 percent had disabilities stemming from other sources.

In all, my study took five months. By the time it was completed I had interview data from 560 patients, more than half of the men in the open psychiatric wards of the hospital. My core interviewers were two female patients, both former army nurses. Three sets of interviews were given. First: 250 depth interviews about critical aspects of the hospital, for which both closed-end questions, and 10 prepared drawings, were used to elicit answers. Second: 210 guided interviews, with both open and closed questions, to go further into critical aspects of the hospital's operations and into the patient's perceptions of them. Third: 100 guided interviews, with open and closed questions, to find out what the patients thought about alternatives to remaining in the mental hospital.

There were two strikingly different kinds of patients in the hospital—this was the central finding from an analysis of the interviews. About 40 percent simply did not want to leave. In Goffman's terms, they had been colonized—or perhaps overcolonized. These inmates I call the *institutionalized*. Another 25 percent had hopes and expectations of being released. These—whose response does not quite match any of Goffman's categories—I call the *non*institutionalized.

The remaining one-third of the patients either did not fall into either of these categories or shared characteristics of both. In what follows, I shall concentrate on the first two categories, which encompass two-thirds of the interviewed sample.

Many patients could be placed in one of these categories almost as soon as the interview with them began. Institutionalized patients were passive and silent, given to rambling or disjointed answers, and quick to lapse into apathy or noncooperation. Many were frightened by the interview. "Is this material going to be used against me?" they asked. A more characteristic response was, "I'm going to leave the hospital when I decide to and no damn test is going to run me out!"

*Non*institutionalized patients were far more articulate. They were interested in the study and pleased to have been included in it. Many *non*institutionalized patients dropped by my office sometime after their interviews to inquire about the findings. They gave full and coherent replies to questions and straightforward descriptions of the drawings.

Perhaps the class differences between the two groups throw some light on their opposite responses to the interviews. The institutionalized patients had, for the most part, been born and raised in poor urban centers. Their parents were often immigrants or first-generation Americans; their fathers were laborers or semi-skilled workers. These patients had rarely completed high school and usually held jobs with little security. They were usually single, separated, or divorced, and often lived away from their parents, brothers, sisters, and the like. Compared to the *non*institutionalized patients, they were older and had spent more time in hospitals.

The *non*institutionalized inmates had been raised in diverse settings, urban and rural. Their parents usually were second-generation Americans, at least, and upper-lower to middle class. Most of these inmates were high-school graduates; some had college experience. Most had good, secure jobs. Compared to the other patients, they were more likely to be married and less likely to have had marital problems. Those who unmarried or separated were more likely to be living with their nuclear families. These inmates were also younger, and had usually been in mental hospitals for periods totaling fewer than two years.

Patients' Attitudes Make the Difference

Particularly wide differences between the institutionalized and *non*institutionalized inmates showed up in their ages, occupations, family arrangements, and lengths of residence in mental hospitals. The medical diagnosis that had led to an inmate's hospitalization proved to be of limited significance in determining his general profile, which strengthens the view that these profiles themselves represent reactions to the *institution*, not aspects of mental illness. All in all, a patient's attitude toward his hospitalization most clearly demonstrated the difference between the institutionalized and the *non*institutionalized inmates.

Institutionalized patients considered themselves simply cut off from the outside. They viewed their friends and family in a distant, "I-it" relationship. Downey Hospital was "home" for them. These patients, however, did not seem to identify with the people in the sketches of hospital scenes that were shown to them.

"They" were mowing the lawn.

"He" was in the locked ward.

TV is good for "them."

For *non*instutionalized patients, their hospitalization was an unfortunate but temporary state. They were oriented toward the outside world and viewed outside friends and family in a close "I-thou" relationship. Downey was never referred to as "home." Further, *non*institutionalized patients rapidly identified with the person or situation in each sketch and used personal pronouns, "I," "me," "we," "us."

Institutionalized patients were well aware of the

The Growth of the Custodial Ethic

If my findings at Downey and the theories of Goffman and other researchers apply generally, then a great deal of money is being spent in this country to *store* the mentally ill, as opposed to treating them and helping them return to society. This is what the custodial ethic really means. Where did it come from?

J. Sanbourne Bockoven maintains that the 1830's and 1840's were a golden age of *moral* treatment of mental patients—when they were treated with dignity and considered as guests, and when hospital discharge rates were at an all-time high. This moral treatment did not necessarily consist of any set of therapeutic measures. The assumption was that the recuperative powers of the patient would assert themselves and, if not obstructed, lead to his recovery. Hospitals were small, and the superintendents and staff shared their patients' daily life and living conditions.

But during the second half of the 19th century, the increasing population, particularly of immigrants, exerted such pressure upon mental hospitals that they grew rapidly in size. The physician became an administrator, remote from staff and patients. Attitudes toward patients were altered. As Milton Greenblatt, Richard H. York, and Esther Lucille Brown have written, "Physicians of colonial ancestry who were filled with compassion for the mentally ill who had a similar heritage were often revolted by the 'ignorant uncouth insane foreign paupers . . .' "

As these critical changes in attitudes and size were taking place, there was a general abandonment of moral treatment in favor of a concentration on the organic factors supposedly causing mental illness. At the same time, the philosophy of keeping patients in custody became dominant. The custodial approach thus arose with the arrival of patients who closely resemble those I have called the institutionalized, while moral treatment was reserved for those who match, less closely, those I have defined as *non*institutionalized.

As the Final Report of the Joint Commission on Mental Illness and Health put it, "By the beginning of the 20th century, the profile of the 'state asylum for the incurably insane' was stereotyped, both professionally and socially—it was an institution where hopeless cases were put away for good." This, of course, led to the sort of barbarities discussed in the opening of this article, for when patients are put away for good, it is for the good of society more than for the good of the patient.

Yet, as my investigation of Downey indicates, even after the reforms in the treatment of inmates that have come in the last 25 years, custodial attitudes have remained.

A.S.

material comforts of the hospital—the good food, clean beds, warm rooms, the free television, movies, and live shows—but at the same time spoke of its essential loneliness and its negative emotional aspects.

These patients spoke only occasionally of the hospital's therapeutic techniques or contributions to their mental health. Instead, they emphasized the punishment, the locked ward or electric-shock treatment, and the need to "keep out of the way" of the doctors and their staff.

Institutionalized patients seemed to see the hospital as a substitute for an old-age home, an old-soldier's home, a poorhouse. They were willing to endure the various disadvantages of the hospital only because they did not consider it a hospital.

The goal of the institutionalized inmates was security, and to achieve it there were recognized avenues of adaptation: to become occupied with certain minimal chores and thus ensure a secure role for oneself; to engage in all that was required of the patient, with a minimum of effort or participation; to just blend into the background and stay out of the way; or all of these at once.

The institutionalized patients could easily ignore the sports program. The staff was so busy that meetings between patient and doctor could be kept to a minimum, which often meant never. The workshops were useful places where one could be left alone by keeping "busy." Work details were perhaps unpleasant, but not too high a price to pay for the material returns. The day rooms and recreational facilities were a source of unlimited free pleasure. It was not wise to attract unfavorable attention—say, by sitting on the bed during the day—because of the possible punishment.

Leaving the hospital, or even going out on a pass, were not meaningful positive concepts for the institutionalized patients. Downey was their home, and it was large enough to provide for all of their needs.

*Non*institutionalized patients were also conscious of the material comforts of the hospital, but they tended to view them as the normal services of a modern hospital. They were more conscious of and more outspoken about the hospital's therapeutic techniques, and often evaluated specific programs or personnel. Like the institutionalized patients, they believed that the locked wards and electric-shock treatment were forms of punishment administered to recalcitrant patients.

*Non*institutionalized patients did not consider the hospital a substitute for an old-age home, an old-soldier's home, or a poorhouse, and they were critical of and most unwilling to endure the disadvantages of the hospital. To them the sports program was a possible aspect of their therapy, but the workshops and work details were onerous, untherapeutic chores. They, too, considered it unwise to attract unfavorable attention, and were resentful that it might be followed by punishment.

Leaving the hospital and going out on passes were quite meaningful to them: These events enabled them to renew their "normal" family and friendship ties. Downey, even with its day rooms and recreational program, by no means catered to all of their needs.

The responses to the guided interview in the second phase of the study also showed this essential dichotomy in the way the patients saw the mental institution.

The majority of the institutionalized patients were unable or unwilling to say who or what in Downey was most or least helpful to them. The *non*institutionalized patients *were* willing and able. They even volunteered criticism of specific aspects of the therapeutic program and showed clear awareness of the negative side of their experience in the hospital.

*Non*institutionalized patients, asked about the closed ward, replied promptly and clearly that they did not think that it helped them, and that they did not think all new patients should have to undergo such an experience. They questioned the therapeutic value of the closed ward and said it should be used only in extreme cases, and then only for short periods.

Institutionalized patients, on the other hand, thought that being in a closed ward had helped them; they saw nothing wrong with having all patients placed in a closed ward upon their entering the hospital; they accepted the idea that the closed ward had a useful purpose; and they did not believe that closed wards should be abolished.

Almost all of the patients, when asked about their friends in the hospital, replied that they were often lonely and had few or no close friends. This perceived, and apparently accepted, social isolation on the part of these patients could be a direct reflection of their adaptation to the local culture, or a continuation of their pre-hospitalization social behavior.

The respondents in this phase of the study were then asked if they wanted to leave the hospital and, if so, what they were doing about it. While all of the *non*institutionalized patients replied promptly and emphatically in the affirmative to the first question, institutionalized patients showed a greater range of responses. Some refused to acknowledge the question, ignored it, or were noncommittal; others replied in the straight negative. The few institutionalized patients who said they wanted to leave nonetheless contemplated discharge only in the vague future, when the weather was better, or only if en route to another hospital or institution. Very few in either group showed any clear perception of a way that they, as patients, could appreciably hasten their hospital discharge.

Most of the *non*institutionalized patients, when asked what they liked about the hospital, were cautious or neutral, or even had nothing at all favorable to say. Those who had something good to say were almost always thinking of therapy. The institutionalized, however, spoke enthusiastically about the hospital's material comforts, recreational facilities, and the like. The *non*institutionalized were quite ready to air their complaints about Downey, while the institutionalized shied away from a question about what they disliked about the hospital.

If Patients Ran the Hospital

The patients were asked what changes they would make in the hospital if they were in charge. Most of the institutionalized patients were unable to see themselves in authority and found it difficult to answer the question. *Non*institutionalized patients were amused with the idea, but suggested corrections for the problems or complaints that they had previously mentioned.

What was their idea of a good doctor and a good nurse? Institutionalized patients found it difficult, or were reluctant, to provide answers; the *non*institutionalized patients volunteered a wide range of perceptions.

Yet the institutionalized patients, when asked what was their idea of a good patient, were more able to promptly volunteer criteria (essentially those of the total institution), while the *non*institutionalized patients were more uncertain and hesitant in their replies. The institutionalized inmates emphasized proper behavior; the *non*institutionalized spoke about cooperating with therapy.

Finally, the patients were asked what type of help they believed patients needed after leaving the hospital. Institutionalized patients were essentially finance-oriented; *non*institutionalized patients, again, were essentially therapy-oriented.

These basic differences between institutionalized and *non*institutionalized patients were further corroborated by the findings from the third phase of the study, in which 100 patients were asked a series of questions about other therapeutic solutions that the V.A. offers its mental patients.

Institutionalized patients, when asked the neutral question of how long they had been in this or other mental hospitals, replied, perhaps understandably, with vague remarks. *Non*institutionalized patients replied more promptly and specifically.

Institutionalized patients, asked if they considered it healthy to remain in a mental hospital for a long time, saw nothing essentially unhealthy in such a situation. *Non*institutionalized patients saw it as essentially undesirable, as interfering with therapy.

The inmates were then asked if there were some patients in the hospital who were not mentally ill. Across the board, patients from both groups said Yes. When asked who such patients were, it was the institutionalized patients who were better at identifying them. Asked if such patients could be discharged elsewhere, again the majority of the respondents, irrespective of their profile, replied Yes.

The essential difference between the institutionalized and the *non*institutionalized patients appeared clearest in the way they volunteered possible alternatives to remaining in Downey, places where patients in good mental health might go if discharged. *Non*institutionalized patients said such patients could go home; institutionalized patients said that they could go to other types of institutions.

The patients were asked about three V.A. alternatives to the hospital—nursing homes, foster homes, and group-placement homes. These questions highlighted a serious lack of communication between the V.A. and the patients. Few patients showed any clear awareness of these programs, and knew of them only in negative or questionable stereotypes. Using these stereotypes, *non*institutionalized patients had a qualified but positive perception of these homes as paths to ultimate discharge, while institutionalized patients were negative or doubtful.

The Downey program that permits trial visits home was better known to the patients, but again the dichotomy persisted. The *non*institutionalized patients were quite positive as to its therapeutic value, and the institutionalized patients were quite as skeptical and negative.

The night hospital and day hospital were then raised as other solutions to the inmates remaining fulltime patients. *Non*institutionalized inmates expressed general ignorance of such hospitals, but perceived their possible positive therapeutic role; institutionalized patients maintained a consistently more cautious and negative attitude. There did seem to be a tendency for the institutionalized patients to favor the night hospital, which provides full evening hospital privileges with a greater amount of freedom during the day.

*Non*institutionalized patients, asked their opinion of the large-sized mental hospital as a therapeutic aid, indicated an awareness that the patient can too easily become depersonalized and lost; the institutionalized patients praised the anonymity of the large hospital and its extensive recreation resources.

The Finite Approach to Hospitalization

The succeeding question concerned the "finite" approach to mental-hospital hospitalization—that, at first, patients be admitted into such a mental hospital only for a definite period of time, perhaps a week or month. This, of course, runs counter to the custodial ethic.

Institutionalized patients did not agree, and argued for continued indefinite hospitalization; *non*institutionalized patients were less certain in their replies, but thought the finite approach could be far more therapeutic than the indefinite hospitalization process, with its apparent aimlessness.

When asked whether they agreed that, instead of going directly into the mental hospital, people should have the option of entering local mental-health clinics, neither institutionalized nor *non*institutionalized patients were enthusiastic. Institutionalized patients were likely to perceive the mental-health clinic as a possible block to hospitalization, while *non*institutionalized patients emphasized the general unavailability of such clinics. As with other solutions to remaining in the hospital, both kinds of patients had an unclear idea of what a mental-health clinic was or could do, and they were cautious to negative about it.

Finally, the patients in this last phase of the study were asked their views of how they themselves might fare once discharged from Downey. Institutionalized patients simply did not think they would ever be discharged, while *non*institutionalized patients were optimistic. But though the latter expected to be discharged, they were very uncertain as to when this might be. They expected to return home upon discharge, but were worried about their ability to return to a full role as an economic provider. Furthermore, *non*institutionalized patients did not show any clear knowledge of the resources within the hospital or community that might help them. They were as unaware of the help that they might get after they left the hospital as they were of the resources in therapy that were available within the hospital—another failure in communication between patients and staff.

Today, even the magnitude of the mental-health problem is unclear. In the United States, according to the National Association for Mental Health, at least one person in every ten—over 19 million people in all—manifests some form of mental or emotional illness that needs psychiatric treatment.

During 1962, over one and a half billion dollars was spent on the care and treatment of patients in state, county, and federal mental hospitals. Over one million people were treated. At any one time, there are more people hospitalized with mental illness than with all other diseases combined. Yet by no means do those hospitalized as mentally ill approximate the total population of the mentally ill.

What I have found at Downey—which is not contradicted by other, less extensive investigations of mental hospitals elsewhere—is that this well-funded and well-staffed institution is, in many ways, simply not functioning as a mental hospital.

Despite the essentially exploratory nature of my study, the remarkable finding has emerged that a sizable body of patients (perhaps 40 percent or more) do not want to leave the mental hospital. For a variety of reasons—social, economic, and even, perhaps, medical—the Downey V.A. mental hospital is home for them. Despite their perception of the mental hospital's limitations, of its hardship, loneliness, and even fear, the institutionalized patients still see Downey as the best solution to their problem. As one such patient put it, "It's still better than skid row."

For the institutionalized 40 percent, Downey is an old-soldiers' home with comfortable appointments, but with the constant danger of punishment for stepping out of line. The institutionalized *may* need an institution in order to function, but many of them are at Downey because they do not want to leave, not because they are mentally ill. And those who *are* mentally ill are not yearning after a cure that would require them to leave.

The *non*institutionalized 25 percent have the opposite problem with Downey. They want out, yet they cannot find the therapy they seek because the hospital is run for the institutionalized mass of patients. Unlike the institutionalized—who in many cases have no other place to go—the *non*institutionalized have a shelter outside the hospital to return to, but difficulty getting there.

What I question is the waste of public funds; the time and energy of the medical staff wasted on the reluctant institutionalized patients; and the tragic waste of the *non*institutionalized patients who are eager for a cure that seems a long time in coming. Downey and hospitals like it are not curing the institutionalized patients. Might not another home be found for them, to free the *non*institutionalized patients for treatment, and to make room for those others on the long waiting lists of mental hospitals—who might also be just as ready to be cured if room were made for them?

The Mental Hospital as a Sane Society

Eugene Talbot and Stuart C. Miller

When a person enters a psychiatric hospital it is because he feels, or others do, that his behavior has become so deviant as to be threatening. The threat may be to himself, to the people with whom he comes in contact, or to the generally accepted social order; and the reaction to this threat creates around him an atmosphere so fearful, aggressive, or even irrational, that his own disturbed state is perpetuated or made worse. In such an atmosphere the positive aspects of psychotherapy are undermined, and it becomes important to find a new setting within which treatment can take place.

On admission to the hospital, what does he find? Frequently, nothing but a cotton-padded milieu that emphasizes his fragility, incompetence, bizarreness, and incomprehensibility. He is valued not as a person, but solely as a patient. He is prevented from being himself—an individual with preferences, interests, and abilities—because both his fellow-patients and the hospital staff stress to an overwhelming degree his ineptness, his helpessness, and his deviancy. Thus, he begins to see himself, and is seen by others, almost exclusively as a "mental patient," to be cared for, protected, and pitied. He is not expected, nor does he expect himself, to have any value as a contributing member of any group or society.

These side effects of hospitalization and psychotherapy, which contribute heavily to an exclusively "patient identity," are decidedly antitherapeutic. In such a hospital situation, deviancy is normal and normality is deviant, so that a patient entering the hospital is encouraged further to succumb to deviancy. He accepts illness as the norm. He develops the magical expectation that he will be cured by a staff of omnipotent doctors and nurses. His isolation from the usual expectations and demands of society drives him further into himself (the *Magic Mountain* effect"). If the hospital emphasizes individual psychotherapy, a "cult of psyche" develops, with concentration on intrapsychic processes that substitute for productive activities and interests. Spontaneity worship leads the patient to believe that deviant thinking and deviant social codes give him special, superior access to insight and creativity. His time perspective dims, resulting in the decline of interest in planning for the future, or in organizing and scheduling activities. Patients lose the ability to judge time limits for a particular achievement.

Only by deliberately developing a hospital program based

141

on principles designed to eliminate, or at least minimize, these effects, can we protect people from sinking into an abyss of passivity and accepting a "patient identity."

This is what we have been trying to do at the Austen Riggs Center. We recognize that if the psychiatric hospital is to be an appropriate setting where psychologically disturbed people can receive treatment, it must provide a special sub-society in which the patient can find relief from those pressures in the family, at work, at school, and in society at large, which perpetuate his defensiveness and lack of adaptability.

This sub-society can provide levels of social demand and expectation appropriate to the patients' abilities to work, to socialize, to plan, to learn, and in general to assume a multitude of social positions and responsibilities even while living in a psychiatric hospital. It can maintain a reciprocal balance with the patients, so that a patient can expect a rational response even to his "irrational" behavior from other patients and staff members. When this sub-society permits the optimal use of its patients' abilities and capacities—those which have not been disrupted by his illness—then the mental hospital becomes a sane society.

ONE PATIENT, ONE VOTE

The Austen Riggs Center is an open, private psychiatric hospital specializing in the treatment of borderline psychotic patients, all of whom are in intensive psychoanalytic psychotherapy. Over the past fifteen years it has evolved into a community in which patients and staff share administrative responsibility and authority. There is a resident patient population of forty-two, with approximately equal numbers of men and women, who range in age from eighteen to about fifty-five years. The majority are under thirty. The patients have actively collaborated with the staff to set and enforce standards of behavior, as well as to devise social inventions to enable the hospital society to run smoothly. Each patient is a citizen in the hospital community, with the privileges and responsibilities that accrue to the position of a citizen. He votes for representatives to various agencies; votes on policies and procedures affecting community life; and is expected to exercise his rights as a citizen and to abide by the agreed-on customs, rules, and laws.

Patients are the principal administrators of a work program in which all patients are required to perform a daily job, one that would otherwise have to be done by hospital personnel, including some aspects of housekeeping, maintenance of grounds and buildings, construction, repair, and secretarial work. Patients who fail to meet a work assign-

ment must answer to a designated agency of patients and staff.

All patients live in a building that resembles a country inn. Each cares for his own room and decides for himself how he will spend his leisure time. There is no segregation by age, sex, or diagnosis. Any behavior that is socially acceptable, such as parties with drinking in moderation, tournaments, dating, and so on, is an accepted part of life in the hospital. Thus, life within the hospital incorporates many of the social expectations and responsibilities of life outside.

In order to create a community where patients can have an image of themselves as worthwhile, responsible, and productive people, we formulated these general principles:

- Both patients and staff can, and indeed should, value socially appropriate and productive behavior.
- Regressive and bizarre behavior, though it may occur, is not inevitable; nor is it something to be either valued or despised. Rather, such behavior can be reacted to on the basis of its social, as well as its personal, meaning.
- Adult and socially responsible behavior can be expected from patients, and opportunities for such behavior can be provided within the hospital community.

We have implemented these principles through the particular kind of social, political, administrative, and therapeutic organization of our hospital society. All our organizations are based on the general principle that various people and various groups may have relatively undisputed, clear-cut authority and responsibility about issues, events, rules, and decisions that affect them directly. Where two or more groups are affected, the authority and responsibility overlap and are cooperatively apportioned.

For example, in the area of leisure time activity, recreation by patients is left entirely to the patients themselves. The staff makes no attempt to prescribe, or even suggest (unless the patients ask) how such activity should be conducted. As far as the work program is concerned, the actual administration is mainly the responsibility of the patients who schedule the work, although they are helped by a committee composed of both patients and staff.

In matters that relate to psychotherapy or medical administration, responsibility and authority reside with the staff.

When patients act threateningly, bizarrely, defiantly, or deviantly in any way they are not punished, humored, or ignored in this hospital community. Patients and staff have learned to tolerate and therefore deal with deviant behavior that would, in society at large, lead to social ostracism. For example, if a patient acts in some peculiar or threatening way, so that other patients are frightened or offended by his behavior, he is referred to the Community Committee. This is a social agency composed of half-a-dozen patient members, a psychotherapy staff member, and a nurse. It reviews with him the reasons why he was referred to the committee, tries to show him what he was doing wrong and the consequences of his acts, and points out the personal meaning of potential alienation from his peers. One or several such meetings allow the patient to remain a participating member of the community, instead of isolating him or forcing him to isolate himself—which would probably only repeat the relationship between him and his environment before he entered the hospital. If that relationship were permitted to repeat itself, the patient's defensiveness and poor adaptation might be reinforced to such an extent that treatment within the hospital society could be undermined.

Early in the development of our community program, the staff met to evaluate some psychiatric movies for use in talks with PTA's and other groups in our area of Massachusetts. We invited the patients to view and discuss the films with us. Most of the staff had strong reservations about the wisdom of "mixed meetings" on any subject. They feared that transferences would get all smudged up and the purity of the one-to-one therapeutic relation would be sullied. Nevertheless, almost every patient attended the movies and most took part in two lively discussions. One patient, reflecting the feelings of many, remarked that taking part had been "a promotion from second-class citizen."

Respect for the collective ability of the patient group to assess problems accurately and solve them constructively has increased greatly in the course of time, but it had to be earned again and again before the staff could trust the patients very far (and before patients could trust patients to assume some responsibility for one another). We went through every possible permutation of mistrust, including patients mistrusting the staff and some of the therapy staff mistrusting their colleagues who appeared to be deluding themselves into a futile, or even dangerous, collaboration with the patients.

How has this collaboration worked out for patients?

In 1952, when the patients were queried about the possibility of their assuming responsibility and authority to deal with other patients who offended them, they responded with a petition that read, "I am not in favor of any administrative power being vested in any patient or patients over the other patients."

Four years later, in 1956, another petition, reflecting quite a different attitude, was sent to the staff. It began as follows:

In the spirit of improving the affirmative tone of the Riggs community, we wish to make a proposal for cooperative work, the proceeds from which will go into a Riggs Center Patients' Fund. . . .

Their proposal laid the foundation for our present work program.

A patient-staff committee, formed to draw up a code of behavior for patients (consisting of six patients elected by the patients and two nurses and two psychotherapists appointed by the medical director), was once invited to present the results of its deliberations at the annual meeting of the Riggs board of trustees. The meeting was to be held in the staff conference room, which patients usually entered only for clinical conferences. Acutely aware of the new and different role they were about to play, the patients anxiously discussed seating arrangements for two hours, until finally someone said, "Let's forget we're neurotic for one night, and sit at the conference table." Everyone relaxed and the meeting was extremely successful, with the trustees having an opportunity to observe patient-staff interaction, instead of hearing reports about it.

Some years ago, at the annual patient and staff Fourth of July picnic, several patients organized a baby-sitting service for the many children who attended. Out of this grew a year-round nursery school that has continued ever since. Patients run it, under the supervision of a professional nursery school teacher; their wards are both children of staff members and children from town.

COMMITTEE OF HIS PEERS

At a typical meeting of the Community Committee last year Marty, a 20-year-old patient, was called in for breaking bottles and dishes and marching angrily through the common rooms in a way that frightened and offended other patients. Marty told the committee he had been gripped by a need to smash things—a feeling that had been building up for a long time—and he just couldn't stop himself. "Besides," he said, "nobody made a move to stop me." Marty then admitted that if anyone had tried to stop him there would have been a fight. Further, he felt that it was a good thing to get his feelings out. However, he criticized the few people who had futilely tried to intervene, saying they had treated him like a baby, which only made him angrier.

The committee members observed that Marty was not fully aware of how much he had frightened other patients, and that he might have found other means for expressing his feelings than smashing dishes. Finally, one patient said, "Marty, you're asking for the right to behave like a child, but you want to be treated like an adult." Marty shrugged and replied, "You're really putting me down with that," and he visibly relaxed. His subsequent behavior moderated considerably. He was less afraid to ask for help, and other patients were less fearful about approaching him even when he seemed to be "wigging out."

There was no attempt at the committee meeting to explore the background of the personality dynamics that had caused the episode. This was left for Marty's psychotherapy, where not only the genetic causes but transference implications would be fruitfully discussed. Since Marty was not forced to cope with people who counter-reacted irrationally and fearfully, he could see that his inner conflicts were the driving force for his impulsive destructive feelings and behavior, and could keep his attention on the roots of his internal problems. As he came to understand the relation of his problems to his actions within the hospital community, he tried out and tested such relationships in other situations. For example, he asked the other patients not to permit his friend Sally to remain isolated and aloof from community life: he believed her isolation prevented her from getting the fullest benefit from treatment. As a result, Sally was actively sought out to participate in the work program and to attend subsequent meetings, much to her satisfaction and to the gratification of the whole community. Responsible intervention by a patient on behalf of another was shown to be mutually beneficial.

The socializing process within the hospital community gives individual psychotherapy its best chance to succeed because patients can view themselves as responsible adults even while struggling with severe inner conflicts and come to understand what is considered appropriate behavior in society and what revelations are appropriate in society.

A Case of Ostracism— and Its Unusual Aftermath

David W. Plath and Yoshie Sugihara

Shinkyō, in the village of Kasama about 35 miles from Osaka, Japan, has become widely known in recent years. For it is a communal society that has been successful, one that has—despite enormous hostility—endured and prospered.

Communal living—the sharing of resources, produce, and living experiences in a closely knit community—has been engaged in by many groups, for many reasons, all over the world and throughout history. Examples are the early Christian communities and the modern Communist collectives. What makes Shinkyō so unusual is that this communal society is non-ideological and non-missionary; in fact, its establishment was not even premeditated. Shinkyō began for negative reasons—because its founding members were ostracized.

In village Japan, organized ostracism is called *mura-hachibu*, or "village eight-parts." According to tradition, neighborly village social interaction consists of 10 parts, including the right to such near-necessities as disaster relief and the use of common land. When a family is ostracized, it will be deprived (at least in theory) of eight of these ten parts.

To have them restored, the head of the household must repent, persuade a village influential to stand as guarantor, and then make appropriate restitution. In Shinkyō, the offenders would not repent.

Shinkyō, and its success, were due in major part to the personality and work of its founder and dominant figure, Masutarō Ozaki.

The ostracism fell on four families at once, and they gave one another support; one alone would hardly have been able to stand up against its force. And they held together because of their trust, respect, and affection for Ozaki, who came to be called their *Sensei,* or revered leader.

Ozaki Sensei was born in 1900, at Kasama, the second son of a fairly prosperous farmer. Like most Kasama families, the Ozakis were ardent supporters of the Tenri church, one of the oldest and strongest of the more than 250 modern-era "new religions" of Japan. For several years, Ozaki himself served as a missionary, but then grew discouraged about Tenri's claims to healing powers—and disgusted by what he saw as the religion's milking of contributions from the poor and credulous. Eventually he refused to accept contributions for Tenri. Not long after, he destroyed the altar of his Osaka mission and persuaded four Kasama families (including his elder brother's) to do the same.

This was the official reason why Ozaki Sensei and the families were ostracized. Below the surface, however, was a covert power struggle between Ozaki and his childhood friend Iwazō Seki, then (1937) the foremost leader in Kasama. Seki reported Ozaki and the four families to the rural police—for criminal irreverence (the smashed altar) and abandoning a corpse (they had buried a man without religious rites, as directed in his will).

The police would not file charges. Thereupon the Seki faction called for *mura-hachibu.*

What happened next is best described by Mrs. Yoshie Sugihara, who joined Ozaki Sensei in the Shinkyō venture and later became his second wife. The following is translated and condensed from the fifth chapter of her book on the history of Shinkyō (Shunjusha Press, Tokyo, 1962):

On August 10, the Seki faction, having talked with the people of the Eastern section (which included Sensei's home), assembled them in the Mission, and summoned Sensei there. As they had planned, one after another the Seki faction roundly denounced him.

"You're a troublemaker who's disturbing the peace of the village."

"Have you managed to do anything but disrespectful work like burning up the gods?"

"Didn't you cheat an old man and hold a funeral that as much as threw away the corpse?"

"If these things are going to keep on and on we've got to consider what'll happen to the village. What in hell are you thinking of?"

In short they meant to close in on him, count up and review his "crimes" to date. They probably calculated that once he was faced by the power of the majority even the obstinate Ozaki would humble himself.

But Sensei wasn't bothered a bit. "If you mean the altar affair or that about Kunimatsu's burial," he said, "weren't they done only after everybody had talked them over and agreed to them? You talk about disrupting the village, but aren't those who go crying to the cops and secretly pull strings the real disturbers of the 'peace of the village'? They're right here among us. Do you want me to name names, or let it go at that?"

As Sensei spoke out so sharply and glared around, the gabbling assembly fell silent. Everybody had a guilty conscience. They hadn't foreseen that "Poke in the brush and the snakes come out"; they were completely flustered and didn't say another word.

Sensei said, "Well then, it's better that I hold off naming names for this meeting. I have nothing more to say, so it's best for you all to discuss it by yourselves." He hurried out, and not a single man tried to stop him.

But the gang was as persistent as could be. The next day, the 11th, a summons came for Hisajirō Yamanaka and Sei'ichi Mitani [members of the offending families]. First the gang surrounded Yamanaka and made him sit alone in the center.

"Break off with Ozaki!"

"If a good farmer like you tags along with a dangerous drifter like Ozaki," they said, "what do you think's going to happen in the future? We don't say you've done wrong, but break off with Ozaki today at this meeting and we'll see that you get a voice in village affairs." Such was their carrot-and-stick strategy. Knowing what had happened the day before with Ozaki Sensei, Yamanaka perceived the danger in the situation and was, as he put it, "scared silly." If he refused their demands here, what would come next? Considering how the gang operated, he could expect the worst.

But as Yamanaka himself told me later, "Before I thought about being hurt or helped or anything else I lost my temper at Seki and the rest of that gang, with their stinking proud attitude and their trying to force things their way; and I couldn't help what I did."

Yamanaka lifted his face and said to them, "He hasn't done a thing wrong. What he says is right. I won't leave him even if it kills me."

Next Mitani was called in and given exactly the same grilling. But Mitani also refused then and there, and said firmly that he would go along with Ozaki.

"We can't put up with people who've got the mad idea that they'll stick together to the death"—this was their reason for village ostracism. Of course we didn't have any way of knowing when and how it was decided; and there was no formal announcement. Nobody, not even a relative, was permitted to speak to any member of the four families; and a stiff rule was made that anybody who spoke even once would be fined 100 yen [equal to $100 at that time].

Becoming Nonpersons

The members of the four families were treated as if they didn't exist. They were stripped of all human rights. City people can't even imagine what a painful position you're put in when you suffer village ostracism.

Hemmed in by the ostracism, the four families had to resort to any means they could find in order just to keep alive during the war. [The war with China began on July 7, 1937.]

The influence of the China war gradually reached out. Recruits began to leave.

Saying farewell to a recruit was held to be a citizen's duty; neglecting it would be the same as treason. Eventually, unable to stand it, [members of the ostracized families] slipped out to discuss the situation with Sensei in Osaka.

"Out of respect for the red sash the right thing to do is to see off the recruit. Just go ahead and join the farewell party."

At a signal from firecrackers, the recruit, his family and kin, and the villagers assemble in the grounds of the community guardian shrine. The people just pass coldly by the four families, nobody says a word.

"This . . . it's a going-away present for the soldier. Couldn't you hand it to him for us?"

With a sour face Teijirō says, "We can't accept anything like this from people who've been ousted from the village."

Recruits continued to leave one after another, but eventually we couldn't take any more of it and we quit with the eighth one.

Instead we all eagerly poured our energy into our farm work.

The Eve. In Kasama this is the greatest event of the whole year, and a day for rest and relaxation.

Almost two months had passed in ostracism by the first of November 1937, when the Eve came around. By then all contact between the four families and the villagers had been completely cut off, starting with the farewell parties and extending to weddings, death-day anniversaries, and all other celebrations.

That day at Sensei's home we pounded ricecakes and prepared a feast just like anybody else. And the following day all the members of the four families, old and young, male and female, carried the feast and the ricecakes and fled to Hirao Saime. Hirao Saime is the boundary between Kasama and a place in Uda county called Hirao. The Yamanakas have a field there. In that field the families held their festival and "relaxation."

We had brought hoes and spades and rakes along with the feast. The innocent children had a good time eating the feast and the ricecakes; the old folks complained and sobbed regrets about "such an Eve"; and the men gritted their teeth, said nothing, and swung their hoes. We didn't care how much fun the villagers were having. We sowed radishes. Then we clasped hands firmly and vowed to each other that we would work together with all our might. And it was this that happened to become the first step toward our communal production and communal living.

Actually, having been ostracized, their ties with the villagers broken, freed from various rights and duties, the four families couldn't avoid strengthening their own bonds, like it or not, in order to make a living. For example they helped each other weed paddy, going from one's fields to another's. From time to time relatives of the four families came to us on the sly and asked us to tell them the reason for the ostracism. But we refused to discuss it, telling them as Sensei had instructed, "If that's what you want to know, instead of asking us you'd better go ask the village big shots."

When the Eve was past we entered the November harvest season. However, in the village they were saying they would not lend the community-owned rice-huller to the four families. The four families went right out, pooled their money in equal shares, and bought a huller and a thresher.

Once they had been refused the use of the huller even though they were members of the association, the four families requested repayment of their capital shares in the farmers' cooperative. The village went into an uproar. People came to offer compromises. The mayor came, the police came, and the head of the neighborhood association came. Finally even Iwazō Seki himself came. Sensei refused bluntly, telling them: "This isn't the kind of dispute you 'compromise.' We didn't start any fight so there's no issue over which we have to come to terms. We've simply been ostracized, and we're content to accept that. Instead of coming here you should go see those poor people in the village who are following the ostracism resolution without knowing anything about it, and ask them to tell you the origins of the reason for our being ostracized."

The Seki faction wouldn't agree to make public the reason for the ostracism. So the deliberate attempts to compromise and reconcile the parties could only end in separating them again. Sensei and the four families grew all the more strong in their desire to take up communal production.

When the autumn collective harvest was done, in December the four families turned to baking charcoal. At first each family dug its own oven, cut its own wood and made it into charcoal. We helped each other only with the baking. But efficiency was rotten this way. So from the second firing onward we collectivized thoroughly. That is, we baked everything in one oven on one hill.

Beginning the Communal Life

As the new year dawned we had a suggestion—from nobody in particular—that we build a meeting place where all of us could gather at ease. For one thing, we also could get Ozaki Sensei to live there. The site we chose was "Obatake," one of the Ozaki family's fields. It was one of those lonely edge-of-the-village places where at night the foxes and badgers come and go.

The house was not finished until November. Sensei's family and mine were already living communally in Osaka, and because of matters connected with my husband's job Sensei's wife and I decided to take turns for a while coming to the Obatake House. People gossiped about it viciously as "wife-swapping," but by that time we no longer were paying attention to what they said about us.

Once we had the Obatake House, everybody would come gather and talk things over both before going out on communal labor and again after the work was done. Not long after that we began to eat together, each of us bringing food from his home. Next we began to use the bath together.

Once we had a communal kitchen, the women and children also began to take their meals there. Eight of us already were living in the house—Sensei, his wife (or myself), his wife's parents and their two children, my child, and Ritarō's child. At meals we were joined by four Yamanakas (husband, wife, and two children); four Mitanis (same); and two Imanishis. We managed the meals by pooling our money and our own produce.

My job was to cook and to take care of clothing for the eight children. One day when I planned to wash the eight nemaki [sleeping kimono], my hand reached out and grabbed my own child's nemaki first. Once I noticed, I blinked in surprise. I'd had no bad intentions. Without thinking about it at all, sometime or other I'd gotten into the habit of doing it that way. But if somebody else were to see it, well, it would look like selfish concern for my own child. If they said I lack impartiality, what could I say? Warning myself that anything like this is absolutely out when you're working and living communally, I let go of my child's nemaki and began washing them in order from the end of the rack. Much ado about nothing, maybe, but after all we didn't have a single pattern to follow then for the communal way of life we were starting. Only after we hit against various problems in reality would we begin to catch on. We always had to remember to be on the alert for the chance that what seemed to be a trifle might turn into a major issue that could rock the whole basis of our common life. For me this was a great discovery.

Again, when I passed out the children's snacks, I was thinking to myself: "It would be good if my child got the best-looking piece." The children had no way of knowing what I had in mind; innocent beings that they are, they were just yelling for joy. I came to my senses, and once again I felt that a mother's instinct was actually repulsive and could lead to mistakes here.

All we had been thinking of was: what can we do to make communal labor more efficient and economical? and what can we do to make an effective comeback from ostracism? That was the goal of our daily strug-gles, though no doubt deep in everybody's heart there was a feeling all along that if we were to work communally we ought to be together as much as possible. Then we wouldn't be lonely and it would be equally convenient for all. That's why it wasn't unnatural at all that we began planning together to move and re-build all the homes in a way that would be convenient for everybody and at the same time suitable for communal life.

As each wife set aside her field clothes and tied on a white apron, and tried her hand at cooking for a group without the meddlesome interference of a moth-er-in-law, she found a change, gain, and excitement that she hadn't expected. Once you tried it, it could even be fun.

As we were doing these things we definitely gave birth to what I'd call a new style of life. Slowly we had begun to change—especially the women—and to feel that we'd be far better off finding satisfaction in our daily communal life than fretting about family wealth, and so on, in a future that we couldn't count on any-way.

But surely there was no reason to expect that every-thing would go smoothly. I have to admit that the others could not (any more easily than I could) break away from bonds to dependents or from the instinctive selfishness you feel for kinsmen; and that there was an unseen suspiciousness and sense of competition at work among us. For example, the duty cook would bring her own child to stay with her in the kitchen, and even if she didn't go so far as to make anything special for the child she might leave her own serving untouched and give it to the child. We hadn't particularly talked about it, but it turned out that every one of us was doing the same thing. And we were jealously suspicious about the partiality that other mothers might be show-ing towards their children. The children themselves caught on too, and each of them began to wait im-patiently for his mother to take the kitchen duty. Under these conditions communal life would not work. Ignore them and we probably would end up separating again.

At this point Sensei suggested that the children trade off and sleep with somebody else's parents. At first glance it looked like a bright idea, but in fact a child who happened to wake in the night and realize that the person sleeping next to him was not his mother but "some auntie or other" would start bawling out loud and wouldn't quit. The temporary mother-for-the-night was really in a fix. But no matter how angry it made her, when she realized that her child probably was annoying some other mother too, she just had to set aside her feelings and do something to quiet the one with her. As these experiences accumulated, the idea of playing favorite with your child disappeared of its own accord.

In the early stages the men on cattle duty were just like the women on kitchen duty: Each favored his own pet ox, giving it extra feed or being more careful about cleaning its pen. But he couldn't avoid having a guilty conscience as he did it. The men say that one day when one of them spoke out about it and they realized that they all were worried about it, they had mixed feelings of strangeness and shame.

Then Sensei suggested that we sell off the four oxen in order to do away with these feelings. The four families agreed, sold the oxen and bought different ones in their place. That way the notion of which ox was whose no longer applied. For good or bad all of them had to be treated with equal care. This was how the oxen came to be our first common property.

Except for rice we brought everything under communal control, without partitions, and everybody was free to carry home as much as he needed. The need for anyone to carry food home gradually decreased as our communal cooking gradually was done on a more complete scale.

Sharing the Rice

But rice remained the exception. Since rice is the one thing you can readily change into cash it can't be pooled, we thought. Sensei said again and again: "If you all haven't the guts to go on helping each other in any and every way, then how about apologizing to the village right now and getting the ostracism removed?"

The four families said they'd die before they'd do that now anymore. "Well then," Sensei told them, "if you feel that way about apologizing to the village, a little thing like putting all your rice into one bin isn't anything at all, is it?" This took place a number of times, and in the end we eventually were able to bring rice, too, under communal control.

After that came the question of communal bathing. By farm village custom, the women would not enter the bath until all the men were finished. But it wasted time and was uneconomical on fuel, so we revised it and let anybody who was free, man or woman, use the bath. Before long the men also began to enter without embarrassment while women were in the tub, and in a very natural way we developed a practice of group bathing.

Common use of the chests and the clothing also began spontaneously. It wasn't that we had figured out how sensible it might be to rationalize our clothing habits. We merely set out with the idea that by putting things together it would be handy and there'd be no waste. For example, in the first chest we would put all the men's dress over-kimono, in the second chest the women's going-out kimono, in the third all of our everyday clothes—so it was easy to use them in common.

On New Year's Day of 1940 we moved into our new building while its walls were still only rough-plastered. We called it the Cookhouse.

The Cookhouse had four bedrooms on the second floor, and four bedrooms and two guest rooms downstairs. In addition it had a bath, washroom, pantry, kitchen, 20-by-30-foot wood-floored dining room, and a dirt-floored dining room. We even ran pipes to the kitchen, bath, and washroom. We heard that the villagers were spreading rumors that "if they could put in facilities like that, they must've gotten money from Russia."

But in fact the only reason why we had enough labor to build it was that we didn't celebrate Midsummer or New Year's, and we didn't take any days off.

And this was how from 1939 into 1940 we completed laying the main foundations for our communal life.

Ostracism as a technique of social control is not peculiar to Japan, although Japanese villages and small groups are notorious for favoring it. Well-documented cases are rare, however, and even more rare are cases in which the people ostracized proved capable of fighting back.

Shinkyō's development under Masutarō Ozaki calls up many parallels with American "backwoods utopias" of the 19th century, particularly with the Oneida community under John Humphrey Noyes. At the same time, its step-by-step collectivization process in the late 1930s is surprisingly similar to what was carried out in rural China in the early years of the Peoples' Republic.

In 1943 the Shinkyō people decided to move to Manchukuo. In August of 1945, the loss of the war obliged them to return to Kasama.

In the reconstruction years they took in some destitute acquaintances from Manchukuo, one of whom was skilled in making *tatami,* the rice-straw mats that carpet Japanese dwellings. Gradually Shinkyō turned from farming to tatami-manufacturing, and within a decade became one of the largest and most mechanized establishments in the country. Part of the profits have been put back into improving the plant, another part into creating a collective standard of living well above that of the ordinary Japanese villager. (For example, in 1965 eight of the founders went on a jet holiday to Taiwan and Hong Kong.) Still another part of the profits are given to various kinds of public service. Shinkyō has made massive donations for improving schools, roads, and other public facilities in Kasama—Seki is dead, and the ostracism has long been ended. For several years the Shinkyō people have regularly cared for two or three juvenile parolees, and this year they expect to open a center for the care of feeble-minded children.

Ozaki refuses to proselytize or propagandize, although the mass media frequently publicize him as a sort of peasant sage. He receives an average of three letters a day from people all over Japan wanting to join the community, but he responds to each by urging the sender to strive harder in his own situation. "People say it's utopia or Communism or a lot of other things," he said to me once. "But for us it's just the way of life we happened to develop together. If people can learn from it to get rid of some stupid old customs, well and good. But the lesson in Shinkyō is that if they really want reform, they need to start at home."

Another lesson is that *mura-hachibu* in village Japan is dying. Under postwar human-rights codes, it is illegal. Today discrimination must take a more subtle course. But even when *mura-hachibu* was strong, the history of Shinkyō indicates that it was not necessarily fatal. Confronted, with proper leadership and enough people willing to work together and determined not to submit, it actually provided a spur to new cooperative forms, and a better life. Without *mura-hachibu,* there would have been no Shinkyō.

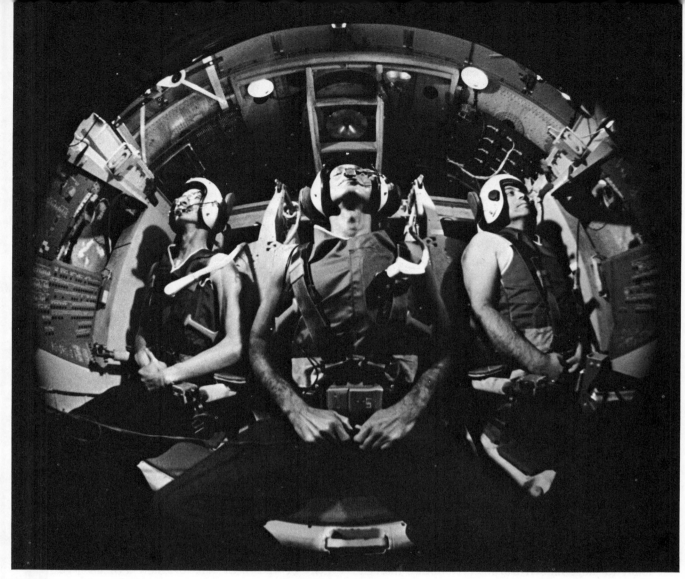

Together in Isolation

William W. Haythorn
and Irwin Altman

When Admiral Richard E. Byrd "wintered over" at an advanced weather station close to the South Pole in 1934-1935, he decided to go it alone because he felt that two could hardly be cooped up together for five months without seriously threatening each other's existence. He understood very well that he would face stresses of complete isolation. But isolation *with* another man—with all the personal con-

flicts and irritations that would inevitably result—seemed worse to Byrd.

The terrors of isolation are well known to explorers, prospectors, wardens, lighthousekeepers—and, more recently, submariners, Arctic weather and radar station operators, and astronauts. Our earliest prisons were built so that the sinner might have solitude in which to meditate on and repent his sins; but they produced more suicides and psychotics than repentant sinners. "Cabin fever" and "going stir-crazy" are still potent expressions for the effects of loneliness.

A variety of psychological strains—apart from any physical dangers—are created when small groups are isolated from their fellows and confined to limited spaces, such as undersea stations and space capsules. Chief among these strains are *stimulus reduction, social isolation,* and *interpersonal conflict.*

■ Research on *stimulus reduction* shows that man needs a minimum level of stimulation—and variety of stimuli—to survive and retain his faculties. People confined to dark, quiet chambers—the traditional "solitary confinement" of the prisoner, or the sound-proof room used for training astronauts—often display bizarre stress and anxiety symptoms, including hallucinations, delusions, apathy, and the fear of losing sanity. Their performance deteriorates. In fact, recent evidence suggests that important changes may actually occur in the nervous system that will persist for some time after the isolate comes back to the normal world. Men in lonely military stations have shown similar reactions, if to a lesser degree. Men simply may not be built to adapt well to a closed-in world with too little stimulus or variety.

■ *Social isolation* creates other problems. Man is a social animal. He needs other people; he gets emotional support from them; he understands and tests reality, and his feelings and beliefs, in large part through his interactions with them. Confined to a small group, his opportunity to get what he needs are strongly limited, and this can lead to frustration, dissatisfaction, and increased irritability. Without the normal ability to judge himself and his performance through the reactions of others, the accuracy and stability of his performance must fall, his emotional responses become less appropriate, and he may even become confused about what he really believes.

■ In isolation, *interpersonal conflict* becomes exaggerated —and there is less chance to go outside to blow off steam or escape from the difficulties of adjustment. In these circumstances irritations are likely to accumulate to the point of explosion. Such frictions are reported in histories of isolated groups almost without exception. In many instances, such conflicts have resulted in breaking up the group—even murder. Taken together, existing research and other evidence indicates that explorers of the future— in space and underseas—face socio-psychological hazards that may equal the physical threats of new environments.

Who Is the Good Adjustor?

From the available literature, mostly anecdotal descriptions of what presumably took place in such environments as Arctic stations, we get some general descriptions of the persons who adjust well to isolation—and of those who do not. In temperament the poor adjustor to isolation is anxious, restless, individualistic. He wants a lot of activity and an ever-changing environment. He is intolerant of whatever he doesn't like. But the good adjustor *is* tolerant—of others, of authority, of tedium. He is more conformist, much less likely to do something considered against regulations, improper, or illegal.

But "good adjustor," of course, is a relative term; all men suffer in isolation. Even a good adjustor cannot be locked into a space capsule with just anybody—or even with just any other good adjustor. So what kinds of people can get along together with the least amount of open friction in isolation? What kinds can accomplish most work when locked up together? What kinds simply sentence one another to mutual tedium?

The literature on group composition, though not addressed specifically to isolated groups, sheds some light on interpersonal stresses and adjustments. It indicates that compatibility and team coordination can be strongly affected by proper choices of group members. A large variety of group characteristics have been examined, but for two-man teams they can be generally classified as:

—*competitive,* in which both cannot be mutually satisfied, as when both seek to dominate;

—*congruent,* in which both have similar needs, which can be satisfied from the same source, as when both like classical music, similar foods, or the same topics of conversation—or when both want to achieve a common goal;

—*complementary,* in which the needs are different, but mutually satisfied in the same situation, as when one likes to lead and one to be led, one is dependent and one likes to help others.

But ordinary group behavior is not necessarily the same as isolated group behavior. Specifically, what happens when pairs of men are locked together around the clock that would not happen if they were merely fellow workers or roommates who went their own ways at night? To answer this question the literature was not enough; a controlled experiment was necessary.

Eighteen pairs of men—young sailors in boot training —were selected to meet certain conditions of compatibility, in order to determine how much of the stress of isolation could be relieved by properly matching personalities. They were tested and rated in four personality dimensions:

■ Need for *achievement.* This was defined as the desire or need to accomplish some overall goal—a task-orientation, or work-orientation.

■ Need for *dominance:* the need or desire for control over others, for individual prominence—a self-orientation.

■ Need for *affiliation:* the need and desire for affection, and association with others.

■ Need for *dogmatism:* the need to believe that one's own opinions and ideas are the only important ones; an inability to tolerate dissent; ethnocentric personality.

They were then matched in such a way that in one-third of the pairs both men were high in each of these dimensions, in one-third both were low, and in the final third one was high and one low.

Each pair in the experimental group was confined to a small room (12 feet by 12 feet) and isolated from outside contacts for 10 days. They were given a certain amount of work to do on a fixed schedule, but they were free to talk, read, play cards and checkers for several hours each day. They were not free to communicate in any way with the outside. They had no mail, radios, watches, or calendars.

The control group, composed of similar pairs, followed the same work schedule in identical rooms—but they slept in their regular Navy barracks, ate at the base mess, and were allowed to leave work for short breaks. In the evening they could use base recreation facilities.

The findings of the experiment will be presented in several categories:

■ *Territoriality*—the degree and intensity of the tendency to stake out certain areas, positions, and pieces of furniture as being exclusively one's own and off limits to others.

■ *Disclosure*—the intimacy with which each person confided in his partner and the extent of the confidence.

■ *Performance*—how well each personality type, in each condition of matching and environment did his tasks.

■ *Personality interaction and social behavior*—how well the different pairings got along with each other.

This Land Is My Land

Many animals show a possessiveness about specific objects and places that has been called "territoriality." Early in the spring, for instance, male robins stake out individual areas to receive mates and will fight any other males that try to enter. Very little scientific evidence on territoriality exists for humans, but many parallels have been marked, and a few anthropological and social-psychological studies suggest that it operates in men. For instance, delinquent gangs fight to protect their "turf." Anthropologist Jules Henry in *Culture Against Man* describes a dreadful scene in a home for aged paupers in which the inmates, stripped of possessions and dignity, still fought to protect their final refuge of identification—their beds.

Possessiveness about pieces of furniture and equipment has been cited as one cause of friction in isolated groups. Through one-way glass we observed our experimental isolated pairs and control pairs to see how true this was, and whether and to what extent it really affected both the isolation and the clash of personalities.

We predicted that the isolates would be much more particular about staking claims to specific beds, chairs, and sides of the table than the non-isolated. This turned out to be true. Isolates established preferences for their beds quickly and definitely, with little intrusion into each other's sleeping space. This separation eased a little with time but not very much. Since beds are highly personal objects with fixed geographic locations, but chairs are non-personal and movable, territoriality about chairs and place at table developed more slowly, but it was definite after a few days.

The reverse pattern held for the non-isolates: they established early preferences for chairs and place at table, which declined with time, and relatively little personal preferences for bunks at first, but this increased with time.

Getting to Know You

We had anticipated that the isolated pairs would, over time, confide much more personal information to each other than those who left every evening and that this would increasingly include intimate information—in other words, both greater breadth *and* depth of disclosure. Literature about isolated groups had suggested that people use each other as sources of stimulation—and that they might use disclosure to speed up acquaintanceship.

Results, obtained from questionnaires, were pretty much as predicted. Isolated pairs gave each other more personal information of every kind, both intimate and non-intimate, than non-isolates. In contrast, the controls confided in each other about as much as they usually did with men in their regular training company, but much less than with their best friends. Confidences by isolates to their roommates, both intimate and general, were considerably greater than they gave to the usual barracks acquaintance. While less than "best friends," they could be considered the equivalent of relations with close friends.

It appeared that such extremely close contact and dependency produced pressures to learn about each other rapidly—a situation that does not necessarily lead to permanence (much like a fragile "summer romance," with too little time spent in "courtship"). The results showed that more intimate information is exchanged only after a certain amount of less intimate information has been sampled—as though the total information about a person is padded around a central core like the layers of an onion, and the social penetration process consists of cutting a wedge through the layers. Isolates did not achieve broad exchange at these deeper levels.

Were these greater exchanges due merely to the greater amount of time spent together? Not entirely. Observers reported that during free periods isolates generally talked, socialized, and played together more than non-isolates. They were rated as being more friendly, showing more social initiative, than the controls. There were exceptions, of course (as discussed below), and the pattern did vary somewhat with time. But, generally, the isolates seemed to be trying harder to get to know each other, realizing perhaps that they had little alternative.

Records were also kept of the extent to which the men engaged in solitary or joint activities. Isolated pairs at first, as noted, did many things together, but gradually drew apart, spending more time in solitary activities such as reading or lying on their bunks. It appeared as though isolates began to draw a "cocoon" around themselves as the pattern of isolation became firmly fixed, withdrawing into their own territories and dealing with each other less and less. This same "cocooning" has been reported in groups kept isolated by nature. The non-isolates, in contrast, started out spending more and more of their time alone, but this declined in the last days as joint activity increased.

Toil and Trouble

Questionnaire responses and performance scores on various tasks indicated that the isolated pairs experienced greater stress than the non-isolated—but nonetheless performed better. It has been known for many years that moderate levels of stress generally result in better performance. Nobody worked hard in the Garden of Eden.

But nobody can get much work done in the middle of combat either. Isolated pairs had far more trouble and personal conflict than controls. Two pairs were unable to complete the 10 days in the room, though it was comfortable enough, air-conditioned, and in no way physically threatening. Two other pairs showed great hostility—including extreme verbal abuse and some actual fighting. In one pair it reached such a pitch that the experimenters—who monitored the rooms day and night—had to step in to keep it from getting worse or being repeated. These results reflect closely not only the effects of isolation but the interactions of the personalities involved, exaggerated and made more dramatic by isolation.

As noted, one of the chief interests of the study was to determine the effects of the various combinations of different personalities. The characteristics—need for dominance, dogmatism, affiliation, and achievement—had been chosen because they had proved useful in previous studies of small groups. For every personality characteristic, at least one combination was incompatible. Two dominant men in the same room would be obviously incompatible. Those with different ways of thinking would not agree on how to face mutual problems; those with different needs for affiliation would expect contrasting things from each other, leading to a tense "climate" (the cool, laconic, independent man would obviously irk and be irked by the gregarious, loud, dependent one); and dissimilar needs to achieve could easily convince one man that the other was lazy, and the other that the first was an "eager beaver" "bucking" for promotion.

Of the four groups that had the most trouble, including the severe arguments and fighting, three pairs were both high in dominance, and two were strongly contrasting in their need for achievement—proving the hypothesis that putting together in isolation two domineering men, or one who was a driving "go-getter" and one who was not, would very likely lead to trouble. Territoriality was much more strongly marked in these incompatibles than in other isolated pairs.

However, "in isolation" is an important qualifier. Among the controls, who went home every evening, though there was obvious tension, fighting did not break out, and incompatibles actually performed better than the compatible—once more demonstrating the idea that a certain amount of tension is desirable for good performance.

While these two incompatible combinations showed similarity in conflict and territoriality, they also showed a fundamental difference. The high dominance pairs worked, played (and argued) together a lot—they could be termed active, competitive, and volatile, and their arguments were part of this picture. But those incompatible in achievement, when duty or circumstance did not force them into confrontation, tended to withdraw and avoid each other when they could.

The dogmatic isolates (who believed that only their opinions were worth considering) also had a lot of active social interchange, including arguments—but they were not so concerned with private territories.

But the isolated pairs with contrasting needs for affiliation were the most consistently passive and withdrawn of the lot, staking out private preserves to which they could retreat from each other. In this way they resembled closely those pairs with incompatible achievement needs. Generally, they had relatively subdued, quiet and private relationships, where members bore one another in relative silence, at a distance, and from their own territories. Their method of adjustment to incompatibility was social withdrawal—movement *away* from one another. This is in strong contrast with dominance incompatibility, which led to a noisy, volatile, aggressive relationship—movement *against* one another.

The Self and the Social

Perhaps these differences and similarities in personality adjustments and clashes can be better understood if we take the analysis a step further. Dominance and dogmatism are *egocentric* qualities—they reflect primary concern for the self—whether in relation to other persons (dominance) or to ideas and/or things (dogmatism). Need for affiliation and need for achievement are *sociocentric* qualities—they reflect concern for joint relationships between the self and others (affiliation) and as members of a group striving for a common goal outside the self (achievement).

The high dominance pair is competitive because each is trying to get the other to do what he wants. The highly dogmatic person regards his view as the only important one, whether in personal beliefs or in organization and performance of mutual tasks; and his partner is not likely to take this arrogance quietly.

Those with high need for affiliation, on the other hand, satisfy themselves *by* satisfying others, working to set up close and friendly relationships; and, similarly, a man with a strong need to achieve will work closely and enthusiastically with another who is in pursuit of the same goal. Thus self-fulfillment is achieved through joint effort, helping each other. In both need for affiliation and achievement the focus is more on what a person does *for others* than it is with either dominance or dogmatism. Where the pair is incompatible for affiliation or achievement—that is, a high affiliator or achiever combined with a low one—they are incongruent rather than competitive or conflicting. They are frustrated more by the situation than the person—by what the other *doesn't* do rather than by what he does. Eager to cooperate, they depend on parallel eagerness. Faced by apathy, non-cooperation, or unfriendliness, they retreat and try to go their own ways. On the other hand the dominant or dogmatic do not really want cooperation (though they may use the word)—they want acquiescence.

This study demonstates clearly that the stresses of isolation are considerably affected by the relations between personality types. Good adjustment may decrease or modify stress in constructive ways; bad adjustment may increase, exaggerate, or complicate it, sometimes in destructive ways.

Should interpersonal conflict therefore be avoided in today's space capsules, Antarctic stations, and sea labs? No. It can enliven an existence of otherwise deadly and crippling monotony. It can produce better performance. The questions we now have to answer are: How much stress? What kinds? How to assure that proper matches are made?

Environmental Stress and the Maintenance of Self-Esteem

Robert Helmreich and Roland Radloff

How is self-esteem affected by environmental stress? How do feelings of self-worth affect man's adaptation to prolonged confinement in a total environment such as a space station, undersea habitat or isolated research station? There is an extensive literature on both the nature and the effects of environmental stress and on the antecedents and correlates of self-esteem, but few empirical studies have related stress to the maintenance of self-esteem.

Psychologists have yet to provide a generally accepted definition of psychological stress. For the purposes of this discussion, however, stressful environments will be defined as situations in which adjustment is difficult or impossible but in which motivation is very strong. Both field and laboratory investigations have specified a number of environmental factors which interfere with adjustment and are generally accepted as being stressful. These factors include physical danger (threat of injury or death), isolation, soli-

tude, crowding, noise, heat, cold, exotic breathing gases, lack of privacy, monotony and personality incompatibility. In few, if any, of the studies in the literature is only a single stress factor present. Even in laboratory simulations, a combination of environmental stresses typically acts on the subject while field environments usually contain a multiplicity of stressors.

One can tentatively propose a list of environmental stresses which are likely to be present in greater or lesser degree on a long duration, manned spaceflight. This list would probably include isolation (from family and society), physical danger (of death or injury from accident, equipment malfunction or prolonged exposure to an exotic environment), crowding and lack of privacy, monotony and inevitability (that is, no option to withdraw from the situation).

Although some exceptions can be noted, it is a safe

generalization to assert that a high intensity of or prolonged exposure to any of the conditions noted above will lead to difficulty in adjustment and decrements in performance. Although it has been proposed that moderate levels of arousal from stress (particularly stress from physical threat) may lead to facilitation of performance, the degradation of performance under extreme or prolonged stress is not questioned.

Stress researchers have had little success in developing equations to predict individual reactions to environmental stress. Relationships found in one population or stress situation fail to generalize to other settings. Examining the results of laboratory and simulation studies of stress, confinement and isolation leads to conclusions about man's capacity for tolerating stress very different from those reached through examination of field studies of exposure to stressful environments. In laboratory studies, where

conditions are typically less extreme than those in real life settings, investigators note high frequencies of failure to complete experimental confinement because of excessive emotional strain, large decrements in performance and profound interpersonal conflict. In contrast, successful confrontations with extreme stress have been noted in combat, exploration parties, paratroop training and saturation diving.

In our own research during the Navy's SEALAB II project where three teams of divers lived under extremely stressful conditions on the ocean floor 200 feet under water, we found that Aquanauts' adaptation and performance were excellent. More recently, we studied the reactions of ten teams of Scientist-Aquanauts who lived in an undersea habitat in the Virgin Islands during Project TEKTITE 2. Again, despite wide individual differences, we found an outstanding overall level of performance and extremely positive interpersonal relationships in a very demanding environment. In other words, a projection from laboratory and simulation studies of environmental stress would lead to the patently false prediction that humans could not successfully tolerate the high stress found in many natural environments.

The only safe conclusion from the literature on environmental stress is that one cannot accurately predict the decrease in performance and adjustment which will be produced in any given situation from the results of the exposure of other populations to stress. In other words, generality appears to be minimal and consideration of stresses alone can probably provide little useful information for assessing reactions to a situation such as a long-duration manned spaceflight.

For the purposes of this discussion, self-esteem will be defined as the evaluation an individual typically reaches and maintains regarding his personal worth. This self-definition expresses a judgment of approval or disapproval and is a global, personal conclusion about overall ability, morality and worthiness. Self-esteem so defined is a subjective appraisal by the individual of his own value as a human being.

Most research dealing with self-esteem has dealt with it as a chronic or enduring individual characteristic; that is, a person is seen as acquiring a pervasive conception of his self-worth during socialization which later influences his reactions to a wide variety of social and environmental stimuli. Level of self-esteem is usually assessed by means of paper and pencil tests and the results of such tests related to social or performance variables. Representative studies have found that chronic self-esteem influences persuasibility, interpersonal attraction, morality, academic performance, sociometric choices, leadership, affiliation and compliance.

Another less extensively pursued line of research consists of manipulating the self-esteem of the subject, usually by giving him false feedback about the results of psychological tests, feedback designed to raise or lower the individual's feelings of personal competence. The results of such studies indicate that although self-esteem appears to be one of the more enduring individual characteristics, it can be manipulated successfully by relatively weak laboratory techniques and that these manipulations can significantly influence social behavior.

The theoretical importance of the self-concept for the consideration of adjustment and performance under stress lies not only in the effects of chronic self-esteem on stress reactions but also in the possibility that exposure to environmental stress may in itself manipulate (lower) self-esteem. This has been proposed by several clinical observers of reactions to physical threat stress. In a 1945 study of combat pilots, R. R. Grinker and J. P. Spiegel reported that the basic effect of combat was a loss of self-confidence concerning personal invulnerability. The same reaction has been seen among survivors of natural disasters and among bombing victims.

Although the above formulations deal with reactions to the threat of physical injury, Irving Janis has proposed that the same basic attitude change "may develop if a highly stressful and frustrating life situation continues for a long time. The relentless accumulation of stresses day after day lowers the person's stress tolerance to the point where he begins to react to every minor stress as though it were a serious threat."

It is our proposal that such continued exposure to environmental stresses serves to lower an individual's self-esteem by reducing his feelings of competence in dealing with his physical and social environment. No experimental data are currently available to support these hypotheses, although several studies exploring this proposition are under way at The University of Texas at Austin.

If environmental stress does indeed lower an individual's self-esteem or sense of competence, then assessments of probable reactions to a stressful environment should take into account behavior associated with low (or lowered) self-esteem—particularly greater dependency on both peers and leaders, heightened persuasibility and impaired performance. Indeed, it has been suggested that an individual with low or lowered self-esteem may (because of needs to maintain cognitive consistency) behave in maladaptive and self-defeating ways because such behavior is most consistent with his low self-evaluation. Elliot Aronson and his colleagues have found that those with experimentally lowered self-concepts are more likely to cheat when given an opportunity and that those convinced of their lack of ability at a task will tend to alter their performance downward to make it consistent with their assumed incompetence. These findings suggest that a major goal of those exposing individuals to environmental stresses should be to explore and devise means to aid in the maintenance of a stable and high self-concept.

In an attempt to resolve the seeming paradox between the excellent performance and adjustment found in many extremely stressful natural environments and the negative reactions in much less stressful laboratory settings, we have extended Thibaut and Kelley's formulation of social interaction (presented in their 1959 book, *The Social Psychology of Groups*) into a cost-reward model of the desirability of various groups.

Briefly, the model is based on the concepts of costs, rewards and outcomes. Costs can be defined as the sum total of all stimuli which a person perceives as positive components of the total environment. The outcomes or consequences of any environment for an individual can be stated in terms of the rewards received and the costs incurred by participation. Thibaut and Kelley have proposed two standards by which the acceptability of outcomes for an individual can be judged. These are the comparison level (CL) and the comparison level of alternatives (CL[alt]). An individual's CL(alt) is the relative standard used to judge whether or not he wishes to remain in a situation. The alternatives are other situations in which a person could be at a given time. Thus the CL defines whether a person's outcomes are better than, worse than or equal to his expectations, while the CL(alt) indicates the relative attractiveness of other possible environments.

Considering the cost-reward characteristics of laboratory studies of groups under stress, such environments are, in contrast with such life situations as spaceflight, relatively low in both costs and rewards. In most laboratory and simulation studies, there is little or no physical danger although crowding and isolation may be present. Rewards in laboratory studies are also typically low. Normally the only rewards found are those gained from testing equipment in simulation work, contribution to scientific knowledge or receiving financial incentives.

In facing hazardous and demanding natural environments through such activities as diving, spaceflight or exploration, there is characteristically a great sense of exhilaration over accomplishment of unique and outstanding feats or making important scientific or technical discoveries. In Figure 1 various groups are placed on a cost-reward matrix. This figure may serve to provide a schematic representation of cost-reward concepts.

It should be possible to apply the cost-reward conceptualization to attempt to isolate problems connected with long-duration spaceflight as well as those in the rather similar situation of prolonged isolation underwater during extended saturation dives, and to relate these formulations to the question of self-esteem maintenance.

It is clear that a confined spacecraft during extended duration spaceflight and a diving capsule on a prolonged saturation dive represent high-cost environments. Both are characterized by isolation, crowding and physical danger.

Another common and important factor is the irrevocability of commitment to the situation. The disaffected astronaut or aquanaut cannot resign or opt out of the situation. Thus, the situation meets Erving Goffman's definition of a "total environment." This contrasts with the bored or disturbed subject in a laboratory or simulation study who can typically terminate his confinement at will.

Astronauts and aquanauts have, at least in missions conducted to date, perceived their environments as providing high rewards. Several factors have contributed to the experience having high reward value. Among these were a sense of pioneering, fame, career benefits and pride in unique achievement.

If the cost-reward interpretation is correct, adjustment and performance were high in these early diving and space adventures because (in part due to their pioneering status) the rewards were high and immediate enough to place the experience in the upper left side of the matrix (Figure 1). In other words, high subjective rewards seem to have fostered a sense of competence and kept self-esteem and motivation high. Because of this, performance and adjustment seem to have been less impaired by the high stresses present than would be predicted by considering only the objective stressors.

This maintenance of a high level of self-esteem and perceived competence seems to be characteristic of the early phases of many ventures where a select group faces new challenges. However, while objective costs in such ventures as space exploration and diving probably remain relatively stable, rewards tend to be much more subject to change. The sense of personal achievement associated with early ventures and the recognition from peers and from society at large will diminish rapidly as projects continue. The hundredth or thousandth man to achieve a given feat cannot be accorded the same recognition as the first man to accomplish it, no matter how difficult and dangerous that feat. Along with the decline in rewards associated with a sense of personal achievement and recognition by society at large, the rewards from a warm and supportive peer group may change from plus to zero or even to a minus value depending upon the nature of group interaction. Thus, attitudes and perceptions and interpersonal relationships which are very favorable in pioneering phases of groups in challenging environments may be altered rapidly so that they no longer compensate for the costs which may remain at a relatively high level.

An indication of the development of this phenomenon may be seen in the great differences in public acclaim and

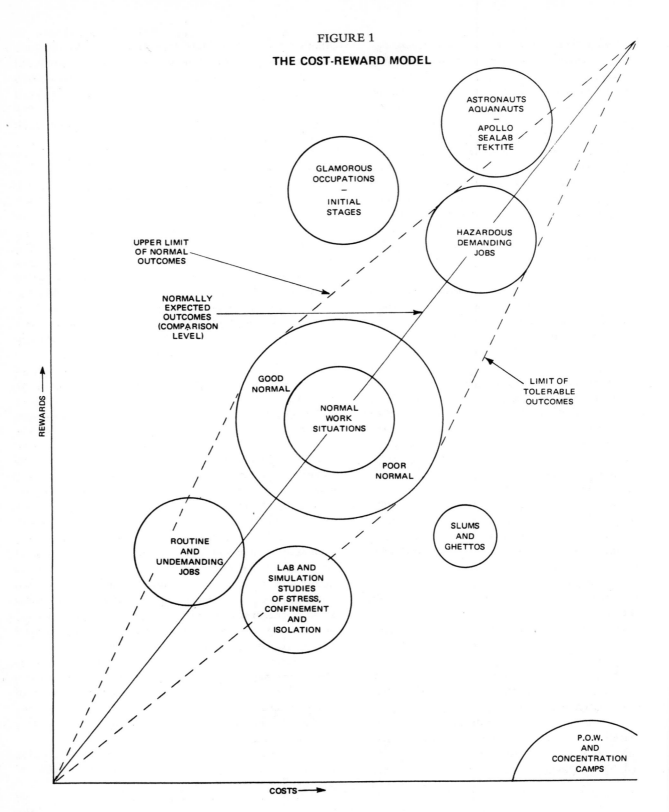

FIGURE 1

THE COST-REWARD MODEL

interest displayed toward the first explorers on the moon (Apollo XI) and the next groups (Apollo XII-XVII). Indeed, as the Apollo program progressed, the public responded with increasing apathy. Concurrent with diminished public acclaim, several instances of attempts by Astronauts to reap financial gain from their flights were noted.

This shift in cost-reward ratios is a crucial problem for all maturing systems. It presents a potentially serious situation for an extremely long project such as interplanetary spaceflight which might last almost two years. On such a mission, external rewards (i.e., from society) would be a long time coming while isolation, confinement and crowding would be prolonged beyond those of almost any project yet undertaken. Thus, the probability of an unfavorable cost-reward ratio would appear to be rather high on such a mission.

For mature projects (projects beyond the pioneering phase), greater emphasis should be given to within-group rewards for crews. The same suggestion should also apply to long-duration spaceflight where the crew will be isolated from society for an extremely long period of time.

The problem, then, would seem to be to select individuals who can maintain a high level of self-esteem as a sense of personal competence and fulfillment while enduring the high costs imposed by an exotic environment. The person most likely to achieve such a state would appear to be a person who can generate his own sense of rewards and accomplishments from the performance of tasks related to the mission. In other words, the person most apt to adjust successfully would be one more concerned with intrinsic (personal or group-derived) rewards than with extrinsic, societally donated rewards. To draw a crude analogy, the individual who finds it more rewarding to view the stars from a spacecraft window than to receive a medal and a tickertape parade should be better able to maintain his self-esteem on a prolonged mission.

It is also likely that an individual with a high and stable self-concept will be less likely to experience threat and a lowering of self-esteem in the face of profound environmental stress. Of importance also is the possible effect on the individual's self-esteem of prolonged, intense group interactions during prolonged, intense contact on a mission.

Group cohesion and compatability will undoubtedly be influenced by the perceived rewards being received by each group member. Studies of successful natural groups indicate that where rewards are high, individuals of widely differing personality types can successfully interact for long periods and can form highly cohesive groups.

Obviously, it is very difficult, if not impossible, to eliminate all potentially negative influences on social interaction. It appears that a more productive strategy would be to accentuate potentially positive influences. Such an approach would have as its goal the creation of a group in which naturally occurring social reinforcements are maximized. Work is of vital importance in exotic environments. Therefore, it is essential that each man have a job of abiding personal interest and involvement. However, very few persons are capable of working for extended periods of time without some form of recognition, regardless of personal involvement. In exotic environments such recognition must be provided within the group. Thus, it is necessary that each group member understand and value the contributions of each other man. Under these conditions, men can exchange essential reinforcements.

Let us propose one possible model of such a social system. Consider a team conducting scientific research in an exotic environment. This team might be composed of a number of scientists, each with a different area or sub-area of expertise. If investigations are planned so that each man requires the collaboration of one or more other group members, then the probability of mutual reinforcement is maximized. In effect each man is both a teacher and a student of others. In successful educational experiences, the self-concepts of both teacher and learner are enhanced and strengthened.

Opposing this model to the conventional static procedure of selecting individuals for stressful environments on the basis of such things as personality traits, biographical information and performance in training, we are proposing increased emphasis on structuring a dynamic situation which has a potential for maximizing intrinsic rewards for each member. Providing for a symbiotic teacher-learner relationship seems to be one feasible solution to the problem of prolonged isolation.

The Psychological Power and Pathology of Imprisonment

Philip G. Zimbardo

I was recently released from solitary confinement after being held therein for 37 months [months!]. A silent system was imposed upon me and to even whisper to the man in the next cell resulted in being beaten by guards, sprayed with chemical mace, blackjacked, stomped and thrown into a strip-cell naked to sleep on a concrete floor without bedding, covering, wash basin or even a toilet. The floor served as toilet and bed, and even there the silent system was enforced. To let a moan escape your lips because of the pain and discomfort . . . resulted in another beating. I spent not days, but months there during my 37 months in solitary. . . . I have filed every writ possible against the administrative acts of brutality. The state courts have all denied the petitions. Because of my refusal to let the things die down and forget all that happened during my 37 months in solitary . . . I am the most hated prisoner in [this] penitentiary, and called a "hard-core incorrigible."

Maybe I am an incorrigible, but if true, it's because I would rather die than to accept being treated as less than a human being. I have never complained of my prison sentence as being unjustified except through legal means of appeals. I have never put a knife on a guard's throat and demanded my release. I know that thieves must be punished and I don't justify stealing, even though I am a thief myself. But now I don't think I will be a thief when I am released. No, I'm not rehabilitated. It's just that I no longer think of becoming wealthy by stealing. I now only think of killing—killing those who have beaten me and treated me as if I were a dog. I hope and pray for the sake of my own soul and future life of freedom that I am able to overcome the bitterness and hatred which eats daily at my soul, but I know to overcome it will not be easy.

This eloquent plea for prison reform—for humane treatment of human beings, for the basic dignity that is the right of every American—came to me secretly in a letter from a prisoner who cannot be identified because he is still in a state correctional institution. He sent it to me because he read of an experiment I recently conducted at Stanford University. In an attempt to understand just what it means psychologically to be a prisoner or a prison guard, Craig Haney, Curt Banks, Dave Jaffe and I created our own prison. We carefully screened over 70 volunteers who answered an ad in a Palo Alto city newspaper and ended up with about two dozen young men who were selected to be part of this study. They were mature, emotionally stable, normal, intelligent college students from middle-class homes throughout the United States and Canada. They appeared to represent the cream of the crop of this generation. None had any criminal record and all were relatively homogeneous on many dimensions initially.

Half were arbitrarily designated as prisoners by a flip of a coin, the others as guards. These were the roles they were to play in our simulated prison. The guards were made aware of the potential seriousness and danger of the situation and their own vulnerability. They made up their own formal rules for maintaining law, order and respect, and were generally free to improvise new ones during their eight-hour, three-man shifts. The prisoners were unexpectedly picked up at their homes by a city policeman in a squad car, searched, handcuffed, fingerprinted, booked at the Palo Alto station house and taken blindfolded to our jail. There they were stripped, deloused, put into a uniform, given a number and put into a cell with two other prisoners where they expected to live for the next two weeks. The pay was good ($15 a day) and their motivation was to make money.

We observed and recorded on videotape the events that occurred in the prison, and we interviewed and tested the prisoners and guards at various points throughout the study. Some of the videotapes of the actual encounters between the prisoners and guards were seen on the NBC News feature "Chronolog" on November 26, 1971.

At the end of only six days we had to close down our mock prison because what we saw was frightening. It was no longer apparent to most of the subjects (or to us) where reality ended and their roles began. The majority had indeed become prisoners or guards, no longer able to clearly differentiate between role playing and self. There were dramatic changes in virtually every aspect of their behavior, thinking and feeling. In less than a week the experience of impris-onment undid (temporarily) a lifetime of learning; human values were suspended, self-concepts were challenged and the ugliest, most base, pathological side of human nature surfaced. We were horrified because we saw some boys (guards) treat others as if they were despicable animals, taking pleasure in cruelty, while other boys (prisoners) became servile, dehumanized robots who thought only of escape, of their own individual survival and of their mounting hatred for the guards.

We had to release three prisoners in the first four days because they had such acute situational traumatic reactions as hysterical crying, confusion in thinking and severe depression. Others begged to be paroled, and all but three were willing to forfeit all the money they had earned if they could be paroled. By then (the fifth day) they had been so programmed to think of themselves as prisoners that when their request for parole was denied, they returned docilely to their cells. Now, had they been thinking as college students acting in an oppressive experiment, they would have quit once they no longer wanted the $15 a day we used as our only incentive. However, the reality was not quitting an experiment but "being paroled by the parole board from the Stanford County Jail." By the last days, the earlier solidarity among the prisoners (systematically broken by the guards) dissolved into "each man for himself." Finally, when one of their fellows was put in solitary confinement (a small closet) for refusing to eat, the prisoners were given a choice by one of the guards: give up their blankets and the incorrigible prisoner would be let out, or keep their blankets and he would be kept in all night. They voted to keep their blankets and to abandon their brother.

About a third of the guards became tyrannical in their arbitrary use of power, in enjoying their control over other people. They were corrupted by the power of their roles and became quite inventive in their techniques of breaking the spirit of the prisoners and making them feel they were worthless. Some of the guards merely did their jobs as tough but fair correctional officers, and several were good guards from the prisoners' point of view since they did them small favors and were friendly. However, no good guard ever interfered with a command by any of the bad guards; they never intervened on the side of the prisoners, they never told the others to ease off because it was only an experiment, and they never even came to me as prison superintendent or experimenter in charge to complain. In part, they were good because the others were bad; they needed the others to help establish their own egos in a positive light. In a sense, the good guards perpetuated the prison more than the other guards because their own needs to be liked prevented them from disobeying or violating the implicit guards' code. At the same time, the act of befriending the prisoners created a social reality which made the prisoners less likely to rebel.

By the end of the week the experiment had become a reality, as if it were a Pirandello play directed by Kafka that just keeps going after the audience has left. The consultant for our prison, Carlo Prescott, an ex-convict with 16 years of imprisonment in California's jails, would get so depressed and furious each time he visited our prison, because of its psychological similarity to his experiences, that he would have to leave. A Catholic priest who was a former prison chaplain in Washington, D. C. talked to our prisoners after four days and said they were just like the other first-timers he had seen.

But in the end, I called off the experiment not because of the horror I saw out there in the prison yard, but because of the horror of realizing that I could have easily traded places with the most brutal guard or become the

weakest prisoner full of hatred at being so powerless that I could not eat, sleep or go to the toilet without permission of the authorities. I could have become Calley at My Lai, George Jackson at San Quentin, one of the men at Attica or the prisoner quoted at the beginning of this article.

Individual behavior is largely under the control of social forces and environmental contingencies rather than personality traits, character, will power or other empirically unvalidated constructs. Thus we create an illusion of freedom by attributing more internal control to ourselves, to the individual, than actually exists. We thus underestimate the power and pervasiveness of situational controls over behavior because: a) they are often non-obvious and subtle, b) we can often avoid entering situations where we might be so controlled, c) we label as "weak" or "deviant" people in those situations who do behave differently from how we believe we would.

Each of us carries around in our heads a favorable self-image in which we are essentially just, fair, humane and understanding. For example, we could not imagine inflicting pain on others without much provocation or hurting people who had done nothing to us, who in fact were even liked by us. However, there is a growing body of social psychological research which underscores the conclusion derived from this prison study. Many people, perhaps the majority, can be made to do almost anything when put into psychologically compelling situations—regardless of their morals, ethics, values, attitudes, beliefs or personal convictions. My colleague, Stanley Milgram, has shown that more than 60 percent of the population will deliver what they think is a series of painful electric shocks to another person even after the victim cries for mercy, begs them to stop and then apparently passes out. The subjects complained that they did not want to inflict more

pain but blindly obeyed the command of the authority figure (the experimenter) who said that they must go on. In my own research on violence, I have seen mild-mannered co-eds repeatedly give shocks (which they thought were causing pain) to another girl, a stranger whom they had rated very favorably, simply by being made to feel anonymous and put in a situation where they were expected to engage in this activity.

Observers of these and similar experimental situations never predict their outcomes and estimate that it is unlikely that they themselves would behave similarly. They can be so confident only when they were outside the situation. However, since the majority of people in these studies do act in non-rational, non-obvious ways, it follows that the majority of observers would also succumb to the social psychological forces in the situation.

With regard to prisons, we can state that the mere act of assigning labels to people and putting them into a situation where those labels acquire validity and meaning is sufficient to elicit pathological behavior. This pathology is not predictable from any available diagnostic indicators we have in the social sciences, and is extreme enough to modify in very significant ways fundamental attitudes and behavior. The prison situation, as presently arranged, is guaranteed to generate severe enough pathological reactions in both guards and prisoners as to debase their humanity, lower their feelings of self-worth and make it difficult for them to be part of a society outside of their prison.

For years our national leaders have been pointing to the enemies of freedom, to the fascist or communist threat to the American way of life. In so doing they have overlooked the threat of social anarchy that is building within our own country without any outside agitation. As soon as a person comes to the realization that he is being imprisoned by his society or individuals in it, then, in the best American tradition, he demands liberty and rebels, accepting death as an alternative. The third alternative, however, is to allow oneself to become a good prisoner—docile, cooperative, uncomplaining, conforming in thought and complying in deed.

Our prison authorities now point to the militant agitators who are still vaguely referred to as part of some communist plot, as the irresponsible, incorrigible troublemakers. They imply that there would be no trouble, riots, hostages or deaths if it weren't for this small band of bad prisoners. In other words, then, everything would return to "normal" again in the life of our nation's prisons if they could break these men.

The riots in prison are coming from within—from within every man and woman who refuses to let the system turn them into an object, a number, a thing or a no-thing. It is not communist inspired, but inspired by the spirit of American freedom. No man wants to be enslaved. To be powerless, to be subject to the arbitrary exercise of power, to not be recognized as a human being is to be a slave.

To be a militant prisoner is to become aware that the physical jails are but more blatant extensions of the forms of social and psychological oppression experienced daily in the nation's ghettos. They are trying to awaken the conscience of the nation to the ways in which the American ideals are being perverted, apparently in the name of justice but actually under the banner of apathy, fear and hatred. If we do not listen to the pleas of the prisoners at Attica to be treated like human beings, then we have all become brutalized by our priorities for property rights over human rights. The consequence will not only be more prison riots but a loss of all those ideals on which this country was founded.

The public should be aware that they own the prisons and that their business is failing. The 70 percent recidivism rate and the escalation in severity of crimes committed by graduates of our prisons are evidence that current prisons fail to rehabilitate the inmates in any positive way. Rather, they are breeding grounds for hatred of the establishment, a hatred that makes every citizen a target of violent assault. Prisons are a bad investment for us taxpayers. Until now we have not cared, we have turned over to wardens and prison authorities the unpleasant job of keeping people who threaten us out of our sight. Now we are shocked to learn that their management practices have failed to improve the product and instead turn petty thieves into murderers. We must insist upon new management or improved operating procedures.

The cloak of secrecy should be removed from the prisons. Prisoners claim they are brutalized by the guards, guards say it is a lie. Where is the impartial test of the truth in such a situation? Prison officials have forgotten that they work for us, that they are only public servants whose salaries are paid by our taxes. They act as if it is their prison, like a child with a toy he won't share. Neither lawyers, judges, the legislature nor the public is allowed into prisons to ascertain the truth unless the visit is sanctioned by authorities and until all is prepared for their visit. I was shocked to learn that my request to join a congressional investigating committee's tour of San Quentin and Soledad was refused, as was that of the news media.

There should be an ombudsman in every prison, not under the pay or control of the prison authority, and responsible only to the courts, state legislature and the public. Such a person could report on violations of constitutional and human rights.

Guards must be given better training than they now receive for the difficult job society imposes upon them. To be a prison guard as now constituted is to be put in a situation of constant threat from within the prison, with no social recognition from the society at large. As was shown graphically at Attica, prison guards are also prisoners of the system who can be sacrificed to the demands of the public to be punitive and the needs of politicians to preserve an image. Social scientists and business administrators should be called upon to design and help carry out this training.

The relationship between the individual (who is sentenced by the courts to a prison term) and his community must be maintained. How can a prisoner return to a dynamically changing society that most of us cannot cope with after being out of it for a number of years? There should be more community involvement in these rehabilitation centers, more ties encouraged and promoted between the trainees and family and friends, more educational opportunities to prepare them for returning to their communities as more valuable members of it than they were before they left.

Finally, the main ingredient necessary to effect any change at all in prison reform, in the rehabilitation of a single prisoner or even in the optimal development of a child is caring. Reform must start with people—especially people with power—caring about the well-being of others. Underneath the toughest, society-hating convict, rebel or anarchist is a human being who wants his existence to be recognized by his fellows and who wants someone else to care about whether he lives or dies and to grieve if he lives imprisoned rather than lives free.

During the past few decades an incredible array of horrifying events has occurred in the modern world as the result of prejudice. Six million people were systematically exterminated in an attempt to rid the world of the "Jewish race"; several hundred thousand residents of Bangladesh were slaughtered in what was partly a religious war; blacks in our own country have been exploited, denied their civil rights, terrorized and murdered with impunity. When we consider these atrocities, and the less dramatic sufferings of millions of other people because of prejudice, it is easy to see why this topic is a major concern of social psychologists.

Prejudice is a broad phenomenon that encompasses many of the topics of social psychology—socialization, attitude formation and change, conformity, social influence and person perception. What is prejudice? The Oxford dictionary defines it as "preconceived opinion; bias favorable or unfavorable." In psychological usage, the term is typically used to refer to the possession of a stereotype (usually negative) of some class or group of people. By social stereotyping we mean the holding of certain categorical expectancies about the behavior and characteristics of a particular group. For example, there is the stereotype of blacks as lazy and unintelligent but possessing a "natural sense of rhythm"; the stereotype of women as passive, mindless and dependent; and the stereotype of hippies as radical, immoral and unwashed.

It is a human attribute to order the universe by making broad generalizations about classes of objects and individuals. And stereotypes need not be negative—after all, isn't it good to have a natural sense of rhythm? No. Not if such a characterization serves to rob the person of his individuality. When I am prejudiced against a group, I see all members of that class of persons as representatives of the stereotype, not as individuals with unique attitudes, tastes and characteristics. This "de-individuation"

Part Five

Prejudice and Scapegoating

viewing others through stereotypes

makes it easier for me, the prejudiced individual, to behave cruelly toward any member of that class.

Another problem with prejudiced attitudes lies in the accuracy of the generalizations made. We may praise an act when someone we like performs it but condemn the same behavior when it is carried out by a member of a disliked group. Closely related to this is the "halo effect" which is reflected in a tendency to see all behaviors and characteristics of a rejected group as negative. An excellent example of these mental gymnastics associated with maintaining prejudice is given in a dialogue reported by the late Gordon Allport in his book *The Nature of Prejudice:*

Mr. X: The trouble with the Jews is that they only take care of their own group.

Mr. Y: But the record of the Community Chest campaign shows that they give more generously, in proportion to their numbers, to the general charities of the community, than do non-Jews.

Mr. X: That shows they are always trying to buy favor and intrude into Christian affairs. They think of nothing but money; that is why there are so many Jewish bankers.

Mr. Y: But a recent study shows that the percentage of Jews in the banking business is negligible, far smaller than the percentage of non-Jews.

Mr. X: That's just it; they don't go in for respectable business; they are only in the movie business or run night clubs.

(Allport, 1954, pp. 13–14)

Just as it is difficult for the social psychologist to ignore any physical suffering caused by prejudice, people who are victims of prejudice and discrimination are not psychologically indifferent to the way they are treated. There is, it appears, a tendency for them to come to believe the expectations held by others and to act in a way that fulfills them—for example, by doing poorly in school, by failing to work. Prejudice can become a self-fulfilling prophecy.

People are not born with prejudiced attitudes. The acquisition of prejudice is very much a part of socialization. Because prejudiced attitudes comprise belief systems composed of highly related attitudes, often internalized during early socialization, they are quite resistant to change. Once a person has been indoctrinated, the subsequent use of reason, logic and education campaigns does not produce striking reductions in prejudice. Civil rights workers, for example, have discovered that integration or mere interracial proximity does not produce an immediate reduction in prejudice and may even lead to an increase in bigotry when individuals first come into close contact with members of minority groups.

The greatest reductions in prejudice seem to occur when individuals work together toward some common goal. This sharing of aim and effort, if successful, can lead to increased understanding and liking and hence to a significant change in attitude systems. But if the common effort ends in failure, the result may well be an increase in prejudice and intergroup hostility. Each group tends to blame the other for lack of success.

The tendency to attribute responsibility for a bad outcome to a disliked person or group is called "scapegoating." Scapegoating can serve a number of psychological functions: 1) it is usually accompanied by anger, which, of course, provides an outlet for accumulated frustration; 2) since we have someone else to blame, scapegoating enables us to shirk our own responsibility for failure; 3) scapegoating can also unify a group, as its members unite against a common target for hostility and punishment; the in-group increases its authority and control over the behavior of individual members by demonstrating the powerful sanctions it can bring to bear on outsiders or deviants; and 4) scapegoating is also employed in the hope of preventing a recurrence of accident or natural disaster. People seem prone to accept the magical belief that if the person "responsible" for a catastrophe can be located and punished, some gods will be placated and the probability of the recurrence of such an event will be greatly reduced.

The essays in this Part examine several forms of prejudice and scapegoating. Milton Rokeach discusses the paradoxical bigotry in religious beliefs—the idea that only some will be saved, that only one truth is available. It is important to note that prejudice can be associated with the highest ideals and can lead to tragic injustice in the service of worthwhile ends. Rokeach points out, however, that although there is a relationship between religious commitment and prejudiced behavior, this association is not inevitable.

Next, Gordon DeFriese and W. Scott Ford illustrate an important characteristic of attitudes—the discrepancy between verbal expressions of attitudes and actual behavior. The authors report that many persons may espouse liberal views but may be unwilling to make a behavioral commitment in support of these beliefs. Social pressures may operate to inhibit a desired correspondence between attitudes and behavior. This disparity has long been a serious problem in research on attitudes. Does the investigator accept verbal expressions as true indicators of beliefs, or is behavioral commitment necessary? There is no simple resolution; while actual behavior is the strongest indicator of attitude, expressed opinions do provide valid insights into the nature and interrelations of attitudes. Undoubtedly, both types of measures will continue to be employed, either singly or in combination.

James W. Clarke and John H. Soule report the results of a survey of southern children's reactions to the assassination of Martin Luther King. Their findings not only indicate the extent of racial prejudice in the late sixties but also provide information on the origins of prejudice. Their data strongly support the theory we suggested earlier: beliefs are internalized early, due mainly to the influence of parents. That is, Clarke and Soule found a high correspondence between children's attitudes and the perceived attitudes of their parents. Moreover, a large difference in attitude as a function of social class was indicated by the child's tendency to adopt and express racial views typical of the social class of his family. Because parents and the social milieu provide such strong sources of belief from infancy onward, it is not surprising that efforts to modify racial attitudes in schools have not been highly effective.

Lillian Rubin takes a personal view of the pervasiveness of racial stereotypes and prejudice. Describing the behavior of a group of committed and active liberals during their imprisonment after an anti-war demonstration, she makes it clear that even those who had adopted strongly anti-racist positions have internalized many of the stereotypes and practices of highly prejudiced persons. These liberals reinforced behavior in their fellow inmates that conformed to racial stereotypes and evinced discomfort at signs of actual equality among black and white prisoners. Again we see the difficulties in changing widely held beliefs reinforced through socialization.

That victims of prejudice internalize their own stereotype is shown in research on the attitudes of women toward women reported by Philip Goldberg. Female subjects were asked to evaluate several different articles, written in fact by one person, but attributed for experimental purposes to either a man or a woman. The female subjects downgraded the articles said to have been written by the woman. Apparently, women incorporate the idea that female intellectual endeavors are inferior to male efforts. The process by which these values are developed and the revolt against them have been discussed in Parts One and Two, by Freeman and Micossi respectively. Their data provide a stark indication of the distortions and misperceptions which are unconsciously acquired through societal influences.

Michael E. Brown presents an equally bleak view of the forces of prejudice in his essay on attitudes and behavior toward hippies in American society. He traces the increasing condemnation and persecution of those people labeled "hippie" and describes the mechanisms of control brought to bear upon them. The extent of reaction against this group is particularly interesting since, as Berger pointed out in Part One, hippie morality does not present a revolutionary breakthrough or breakdown in morality. Brown also notes the scapegoating of hippies in a time of national unrest. Their condemnation provides not only a release for frustrations and a repository for collective guilt, but is also a means of bolstering the power and authority of society.

Scapegoating of a different sort is described by Thomas E. Drabeck and Enrico Quarantelli, and, in the final essay, by Stephen P. Koff. Drabeck and Quarantelli discuss the need to personalize fault after a disaster. As they point out, the tendency to place blame for tragedies on an individual or group can hinder the development of reforms and structural changes needed to prevent a recurrence. Koff gives a specific example of the scapegoating of authorities in his recounting of reactions to a disastrous Italian flood.

As all of the research in this Part shows, the course of development produces in most or all of us attitudes that are inaccurate and that lead to misperceptions of experience. These prejudices impair our effectiveness and often result in tragic inequities for individuals subjected to them.

Paradoxes of Religious Belief

Milton Rokeach

All organized western religious groups teach their adherents, and those they try to convert, contradictory sets of beliefs. On the one hand, they teach mutual love and respect, the golden rule, the love of justice and mercy, and to regard all men as equal in the eyes of God. On the other hand, they teach (implicitly if not openly) that only *certain* people can be saved—those who believe as they do; that only *certain* people are chosen people; that there is only one real truth—theirs.

Throughout history man, inspired by religious motives, has indeed espoused noble and humanitarian ideals and often behaved accordingly. But he has also committed some of the most horrible crimes and wars in the holy name of religion—the massacre of St. Bartholomew, the Crusades, the Inquisition, the pogroms, and the burnings of witches and heretics.

This is the fundamental paradox of religious belief. It is not confined to history. In milder but even more personal forms it exists in our daily lives.

In 1949 Clifford Kirkpatrick, professor of sociology at Indiana University, published some findings on the relationship between religious sentiments and humanitarian attitudes. Professor Kirkpatrick investigated the oft-heard contention that religious feeling fosters humanitarianism; and, conversely, that those without religious training should therefore be less humanitarian. His conclusions were surprising—at least to the followers of organized religion. In group after group—Catholic, Jewish, and the Protestant denominations—he found little correlation at all; but what there was was negative. That is, the devout tended to be *slightly less* humanitarian and had more punitive attitudes toward criminals, delinquents, prostitutes, homosexuals, and those who might seem in need of psychological counseling or psychiatric treatment.

In my own research I have found that, on the average, those who identify themselves as belonging to a religious organization express more intolerance toward racial and ethnic groups (other than their own) than do non-believers —or even Communists. These results have been found at Michigan State University, at several New York colleges, and in England (where the Communist results were obtained). Gordon Allport in his book, *The Nature of Prejudice,* describes many of the studies that have come up with similar findings. In a recent paper he read at the Crane Theological School of Tufts University, he said:

On the average, church goers and professedly religious people have considerably more prejudice than do non-church goers and non-believers.

Actually, this conclusion is not quite accurate. While non-believers are in fact generally less prejudiced than believers toward racial and ethnic groups, it does not follow that they are more tolerant in every respect. Non-believers often betray a bigotry and intellectual arrogance of another kind—intolerance toward those who disagree with them. Allport's conclusion is valid if by "prejudice" we only mean ethnic and religious prejudice.

Organized religion also contends that the religious have greater "peace of mind" and mental balance. We have found in our research at Michigan State University—described in my book, *The Open and Closed Mind*—that people with formal religious affiliation are more anxious. Believers, compared with non-believers, complain more often of working under great tension, sleeping fitfully, and similar symptoms. On a test designed to measure manifest anxiety, believers generally scored higher than non-believers.

If religious affiliation and anxiety go together, is there also a relation between religion and serious mental disturbance? What is the relative frequency of believers and non-believers in mental hospitals, compared to the outside? Are the forms and courses of their illnesses different? I recently discussed this with the clinical director of a large mental hospital. He believes without question that religious sentiments prevail in a majority of his patients; further, that religious delusions play a major part in the illnesses of about a third of them.

It is pretty hard to conclude from such observations anything definite about the role religion plays in mental health. This is an area that needs much research, not only within our own culture but also cross-culturally. I am thinking especially of the Soviet Union. What is the relative frequency of mental disease in the Soviet Union as compared with western countries? To what extent could such differences be attributable to differences in religious sentiments? What is the proportion of believers and non-believers in Soviet mental hospitals? Many questions could be asked.

In a study in Lansing, Michigan, we found that when you ask a group of Catholics to rank the major Christian denominations in order of their similarity to Catholicism,

you generally get the following order: Catholic first, then Episcopalian, Lutheran, Presbyterian, Methodist, and finally Baptist. Ask a group of Baptists to rank the same denominations for similarity, and you get exactly the reverse order: Baptist, Methodist, Presbyterian, Lutheran, Episcopalian, and finally Catholic. When we look at the listings of similarities they seem to make up a kind of color wheel, with each one of the six major Christian groups judging all other positions from its own standpoint along the continuum. But actually it turns out that all these continua are basically variations of the same theme, with Catholics at one end and Baptists at the other.

Apparently people build up mental maps of which religions are similar to their own, and these mental maps have an important influence on everyday behavior. If a Catholic decides to leave his church and join another, the probability is greatest that he will join the Episcopalian church—next the Lutheran church—and so on down the line. Conversely, a defecting Baptist will more probably join the Methodist church, after that the Presbyterian church, and so on. The other denominations follow the same pattern.

The probability of inter-faith marriage increases with the similarity between denominations. When a Catholic marries someone outside his faith, it is more likely to be an Episcopalian, next most likely a Lutheran, and so on.

What of the relation between marital conflicts and inter-faith marriages? In general we find that the greater the dissimilarity, the greater likelihood of conflict both before and after marriage.

We determined this by restricting our analysis to couples of whom at least one partner was always Methodist. We interviewed seven or eight all Methodist couples; then another group in which Methodists had married Presbyterians; then Methodists and Lutherans; and on around. We not only questioned them about their marital conflicts, but also about their pre-marital conflicts. How long did they "go steady"? (The assumption is that the longer you go steady beyond a certain point, the more likely the conflict.) Did parents object to the marriage? Had they themselves had doubts about it beforehand? Had they ever broken off their engagement? For marital conflict, we asked questions about how often they quarreled, whether they had ever separated (if so, how many times), and whether they had ever contemplated divorce. From the answers we constructed an index of pre-marital and post-marital conflict.

These findings raise an issue of interest to us all. From

the standpoint of mental health, it can be argued that inter-faith marriages are undesirable. From the standpoint of democracy, is it desirable to have a society in which everyone marries only within his own sect or denomination? This is a complicated matter and cannot be pursued here. But these findings do suggest that somehow the average person has gotten the idea that religious differences—even minor denominational distinctions within the Christian fold —*do* make a difference; so much difference in fact that inter-faith marriages must result in mental unhappiness.

To pull together the various findings: I have mentioned that empirical results show that religious people are on the average less humanitarian, more bigoted, more anxious; also that the greater the religious differences, the greater the likelihood of conflict in marriage. Does a common thread run through these diverse results? What lessons can we learn from them?

It seems to me that these results cannot be accounted for by assuming, as the anti-religionists do, that religion is an unqualified force for evil; nor by assuming, as the pro-religionists do, that religion is a force only for good. Instead, as indicated at the beginning, I believe that these results become more understandable if we assume that there exist simultaneously, within the organized religions of the West, psychologically conflicting moral forces for good *and* evil—teaching brotherhood with the right hand and bigotry with left, facilitating mental health in some and mental conflict, anxiety, and psychosis in others. I realize that this seems an extreme interpretation; but the research bears it out.

Gordon Allport makes a similar point:

Brotherhood and bigotry are intertwined in all religion. Plenty of pious persons are saturated with racial, ethnic, and other prejudice. But at the same time many of the most ardent advocates of racial justice are religiously motivated.

We are taught to make definite distinctions between "we" and "they," between believer and non-believer; and sometimes we are urged to act on the basis of these distinctions, for instance in marriage. The category of man that comes to mind when we hear the word "infidel" or "heretic" is essentially a religious one. It is part of our religious heritage. But it is pretty difficult psychologically to love infidels and heretics to the same extent that we love believers. The psychological strain must be very great; and a major result must be guilt and anxiety.

This kind of dichotomy is not confined to religion. Gunnar Myrdal, in *The American Dilemma,* described the conflict between American ideals of democracy and practice of discrimination against minority groups, and the guilt, anxiety, and disorder it spawned. We are familiar in international affairs with the enormous psychological discrepancy between the humanitarian ideals of a classless society advocated by the Marxists and the anti-humanitarian methods employed by them for its achievement. No wonder there have been so many defections from the Communist cause in America and Europe! When the strain between one set of beliefs and another set of beliefs—or between belief and practice—becomes too great, one natural response is to turn away from the whole system.

I suspect that such contradictions lead often to defection from religion also. Most of the time, however, the result is psychological conflict, anxiety, and chronic discomfort arising from feelings of guilt. The contradictions in religious teachings are more subtle than those in politics and would, for the most part, be denied consciously. A conflict between ideological content and ideological structure—between *what* is taught and *how* it is taught—must be very subtle. A particular religious institution not only must disseminate a particular religious ideology; it must also perpetuate itself and defend against outside attack. It is this dual purpose of religious institutions, I hypothesize, which leads to the contradiction between the *what* and the *how*. It leads to the paradox of a church disseminating truly religious values to the extent possible, while unwittingly communicating anti-religious values to the extent necessary.

RESOLVING CONTRADICTIONS

Gordon Allport, writing on the relation between religion and bigotry, has suggested two types of religious orientation. He calls them the *extrinsic* and the *intrinsic.* The extrinsic outlook on religion is utilitarian, self-centered, opportunistic, and other-directed. The intrinsic, in contrast, includes basic trust, a compassionate understanding of others so that "dogma is tempered with humility" and, with increasing maturity, "is no longer limited to single segments of self interest." Allport does not imply that everyone is purely either intrinsic or extrinsic; rather, all range somewhere along the continuum from one pole to the other.

The extent to which a particular person has an intrinsic or extrinsic outlook depends largely on the way he is able to resolve the contradictory teachings of his religious group. This in turn depends on the particular quality of his experiences with others, especially with parents in early childhood. A person is more apt to be extrinsically-oriented if his early experiences included threat, anxiety, and punishment or if religion was used punitively, as a club to discipline and control him.

Good empirical evidence exists which supports Allport's distinctions. W. Cody Wilson has succeeded in isolating and measuring the extrinsic religious sentiment and in showing that it is closely related to anti-Semitism. Also, one of my collaborators, Dr. G. Gratton Kemp, has isolated two kinds of religiously-minded students, all enrolled in one denominational college. One group was open-minded and tolerant. The other group was closed-minded and highly prejudiced. Dr. Kemp studied their value orientations over a six-year period. He found that while they expressed similar values when in college, they diverged sharply six years later. Both groups ranked their religious values highest but then parted abruptly. The open-minded group put social values next and theoretical values third. The closed-minded group also ranked religious values highest, but political values were second in importance for them and economic values third. It is obvious that the total cluster of values is quite different between the open-minded and the closed-minded groups. These findings clearly suggest that religious people do indeed differ strongly in their orientations toward life to the extent that their religious outlook is, as Allport claims, extrinsic or intrinsic.

AN ANTI-HUMANITARIAN VICTORY?

All the preceding leads to the following tentative conclusions: the fact that religious people are more likely to express anti-humanitarian attitudes, bigotry, and anxiety and the fact that religious similarity and dissimilarity play an important role in marital conflict may both be interpreted as the end result of the emergence of the extrinsic rather than the intrinsic orientation toward religion. They also suggest that, in most people, the extrinsic orientation predominates. This greater prominence of extrinsic attitudes in turn seems to arise out of the contradictory beliefs trans-

mitted through organized religion: humanitarian on one side, anti-humanitarian on the other. One constructive suggestion that might be advanced is that ministers, rabbis, and priests should better understand the differences between the *what* and the *how* of belief, and the fact that contradictions between the *what* and the *how* can lead to excessive anxiety, pervasive guilt, and psychic conflict and, therefore, to all sorts of defensive behavior capable of alleviating guilt and conflict. Representatives of organized religion should consequently become more sophisticated about the unwitting contradictions introduced into religious teachings, and try to eliminate them—as the Catholics are doing now with belief in Jewish guilt for the crucifixion.

Parents are really the middlemen between the forces of organized religion and the child. What factors in rearing, in parental attitudes, in discipline techniques, in the quality of reward and punishment are likely to lead to what Allport has called the intrinsic orientation toward religion? What factors lead to the extrinsic? The data suggest that the more the parent encourages the formation and development of extrinsic attitudes toward religion, the more he hinders the growth of the child into a mature and healthy human being. The more he strengthens the intrinsic religious orientation, the more he helps his child grow healthy, mature, tolerant, and happy.

The conflict between the ideal and what seems to be the practical is widespread. But the current readjustment in racial relations, in which clergymen have taken so large a part, for all its upset and pain indicates that these dichotomies are neither eternal nor inevitable. Nor is the extrinsic orientation necessarily the "practical" one. Research and practice in race relations, criminology, and child-rearing have consistently shown that the non-punitive and accepting approach brings better results.

Change is underway, in the church and in the home, and brings with it, hopefully, greater emphasis on resolving the paradox between the what and the how of religious belief.

Open Occupancy— What Whites Say, What They Do

Gordon H. DeFriese and W. Scott Ford, Jr.

In recent years, the issue of "open occupancy" has become a source of fierce social conflict, particularly in urban areas where there are shortages of adequate housing for certain minority groups. Not only is this an important contemporary social issue, but it is an arena of behavior that involves some of the fundamental issues of social psychology—such as the question of an individual's readiness to translate his attitude into overt action.

Thus, suppose a white man says he is not prejudiced against Negroes. Would he also be willing to have Negroes of his same social class move into his neighborhood—and willing to let his anti-Negro neighbors *know* how he feels? Suppose we were aware of what his feelings about Negroes were, and also aware of what power social pressure had over him. Could we then accurately predict what he would say if asked to let his anti-Negro neighbors know about his feelings?

These questions can be rephrased as follows:
■ How are the attitudes that whites express about open occupancy related to their willingness to take clear, public stands for—or against—neighborhood desegregation?
■ How do social pressures affect a white person's willingness to do so?

Prior studies suggest that whatever people say they believe is strongly related to what they actually do. But there is no one-to-one relationship: You almost always find discrepancies.

173

In 1958, Melvin L. DeFleur and Frank R. Westie conducted a study that bears directly on the question of attitude versus action (*American Sociological Review*). They tried to find out how willing a number of college students were to be photographed with members of another race.

First, the students were given a verbal test that measured their general attitudes toward Negroes. Then they were asked to sign a series of "releases," indicating that they were willing to be photographed with Negroes—and that they would allow these photographs to be widely publicized. The researchers found that many of the students were inconsistent: One-third of those who had evinced liberal attitudes balked at signing the releases.

Next, each of the students was asked why he had signed, or refused to sign, the releases. From their answers, it appeared that most of the students were greatly influenced by social pressure—by whether they thought certain groups that they respected (parents, friends) would approve or disapprove of their signing. DeFleur and Westie concluded that this indirect pressure from reference groups is what intervenes between attitude and behavior—and brings about discrepancies.

Lawrence S. Linn used the DeFleur-Westie technique in a 1965 study (*Social Forces*), and found that over 50 percent of his subjects diverged in their attitudes toward Negroes and the way they behaved toward Negroes. In post-test interviews, his subjects told him they couldn't adjust their actions to their attitudes because of social and cultural pressures around them.

Yet, in one important way, Linn's findings differed from those of DeFleur and Westie. DeFleur and Westie concluded that social constraints intervened between attitudes and behavior—attitudes → social pressure → behavior. But Linn concluded that social and cultural influences are actually part of the background environment, and don't intervene *directly* in decision-making—social pressure → attitudes → behavior. In other words, social pressures help form attitudes, which influence behavior. Their effect, therefore, is indirect.

We ourselves agree with Linn—that when a person forms his attitudes, he "internalizes" the sentiments and values of other people who are important to him. But we also believe that social pressures *do* intervene directly between attitude and behavior. In short, social pressure → attitudes → social pressure → behavior. When people are in situations where they must make choices between conflicting demands, "what others will think or do" becomes a direct and important variable.

From the body of theory and research on attitudes and reference groups, we have formulated this proposition: In theory, a direct relationship exists between a person's expressed attitude and his likely behavior. But discrepancies do occur, and they are due to social constraints, which intervene between attitude and action and disturb the direct relationship.

For our study on open occupancy, we devised these hypotheses:

■ There is a direct relationship between the intensity of a person's verbal attitude toward Negroes and the way he behaves in regard to open occupancy.
■ There is a direct relationship between a person's response to open occupancy and the influence exerted by individuals and groups important to him.
■ These two variables—prior attitudes and influential groups—are better clues to a person's future behavior when measured together than when measured separately.

To Sign or Not to Sign?

To test these hypotheses, we interviewed some 400 whites in an urban area where housing values ranged between $10,000 and $15,000. There was an urgent need for Negro housing in that price range. But the study area was in a border state, and we knew of no Negroes who had bought or rented homes in middle- or upper-class white neighborhoods. Local real-estate agents resisted such sales or rentals, and many whites were afraid that their property values were threatened. Open occupancy had become an issue of bitter controversy.

From our individual subjects, we tried to learn three things:

■ What is his attitude toward Negroes?
■ Will he sign a statement indicating his willingness to endorse, or participate in, an interracial-housing policy for his neighborhood and town?
■ What groups might influence his attitudes and behavior—and how?

All the subjects took a test that measured their attitudes toward Negroes in general. Then they received two documents, each with a place for a signature. The first read:

"I, the undersigned, do hereby make public the declaration that I have *no objection* to having Negro families of social and economic characteristics similar to my own live in my neighborhood, and I *would,* in fact, uphold such practices within the community.

The second document read:

"I, the undersigned, do hereby make public the declaration that I *do object* to having Negro families live in my neighborhood, regardless of their social and economic characteristics, and I would *not,* in fact, uphold such practices within the community."

The subjects could sign either or neither. Of course, we put no pressure on them. But we told them that if they did sign, we would feel free to use these signatures in any way we wish, including *publicizing them through the news media.* Signing either document, therefore, was a real, meaningful, overt expression of a subject's stand on open occupancy.

After the subjects had either signed or not signed one of the documents, we gave them a list of groups that might have influenced them in their decision—immediate family, co-workers, neighbors, close relatives, and close friends. We then asked our subjects to indicate how much influence each group might have had on their decision to sign or not to sign ("great," "small," "no importance"). We also asked them to identify any other people or group *not* listed that might have influenced their decision. Finally, we asked them how they thought each of these groups felt about open occupancy, and how much these groups agreed with one another. (A subject's estimate of a group's attitudes might not be precisely accurate, of course, but we considered this less important than the fact that he *thought* his estimate was accurate. When people think something is true, it *is* true, for them, and they act accordingly.)

All the interviews were conducted over a single weekend—the short time-schedule was arranged to keep rumors from spreading that might affect the findings. Then too, we were afraid that, by interviewing people about open occupancy in a former slave-owning state with continuing problems of integration, there might be nasty incidents. Fortunately, no serious trouble arose. Some subjects, however, flatly refused to cooperate; some didn't supply important parts of the attitude tests; some had problems in communicating. Still,

TABLE I—How Attitudes Indicate Behavior—Responses to the Open Occupancy Documents

Attitude Scale Scores	Signed document for open housing	Did not sign	Signed document against open housing
0.00 to 0.99 (least prejudice)	1	1	1
1.00 to 1.99	8	36	5
2.00 to 2.99	5	50	7
3.00 to 3.99	1	47	30
4.00 to 4.99	0	31	23
5.00 to 5.99	0	6	10
6.00 to 7.00 (most prejudice)	0	0	0
Totals	15	171	76
Median Attitude Scale Scores	1.90	3.02	3.80

we obtained 262 fully completed, cooperatively obtained interviews.

Table I illustrates the relationship, in our study, between prejudice and overt behavior. Generally, the least prejudiced were the most likely to sign the first document; the most prejudiced were the most likely to sign the second document; those falling in between were most likely to sign neither.

Had we known in advance what a subject's attitude toward Negroes was, we could have increased the accuracy of predicting which document he would sign, or whether he would sign at all, by about 10 percent above chance. And if we consider only those subjects who signed one document—not those who signed neither—advance knowledge of *their* attitudes would have enabled us to increase our accuracy of prediction by as much as 40 percent above chance. Obviously, on the open-occupancy issue there is a definite connection between expressed attitude and overt behavior.

Table II indicates how much importance the subjects attributed to the influence of outside groups in trying to decide whether or not to sign either document. By and large, if we had known beforehand the importance our subjects attributed to social pressures, we could *not* have increased our accuracy of prediction very much beyond what knowledge of their attitudes had already provided. It might seem, then, that the influence of reference groups is minor: People responded to the question of open occupancy according to their own internal attitudes. However, the rest of the data allows another interpretation.

We had asked our subjects whether the groups that might influence them were "for," "against," or "neutral" about open occupancy (or whether they didn't know). We found that what a subject *thought* the reference groups thought about open occupancy was *as good* a predictor of how he would act as the attitudes he had expressed. Apparently our subjects were unwilling to acknowledge, or unconscious of, the power these outside groups had on their actions.

The Group Influence

Next, let's consider how a subject's views about the degree of consensus within his reference groups may have influenced his signing or not signing one of the documents. Clearly, social pressure from a group thought to be unanimous in outlook should be strongest. And here we found that we could predict which document a subject would sign, or whether he would not sign either, just as easily by measuring his belief about the amount of consensus in influence groups as by measuring his attitudes. There was a direct relationship between the subject's views on open occupancy and his conception of what his reference groups' views were.

Now, the third hypothesis was that attitudes and the influence of others, working together, would show a greater total effect on behavior than these two factors measured separately. This turned out to be true only when *all* choices (signing the first, signing the second, or signing neither) were considered. When only the signers of either the first or second document were considered, attitudes and influence groups together were *not* better predictors than each taken separately. This

may be because these people had the strongest opinions and resolve, and were the most inner-directed, so their attitudes were far more decisive than social pressures. In fact, the reference groups these people have may have been chosen according to their agreement with the subjects' own views.

That the behavior of those willing to take a stand could be predicted as easily from their attitudes or reference groups *taken singly* is, of course, significant. True, it is much simpler to learn people's attitudes than to learn what groups influence them, how much, and why, and then work out a combination of the two factors. But on an issue as touchy as open occupancy, the majority may well be unable or unwilling to state their preferences openly. In this study (Tables I and II), the number who signed neither paper was nearly twice as high as the number who signed either of the documents. There were over 11 times as many who signed neither as there were who took the unpopular course of signing the first document. And for this large, cautious group (and, therefore, for all groups put together), expressed attitude *plus* the pressure of influence groups is a better predictor of ultimate behavior than either factor alone.

Certainly, the nonsigner—the disengaged in general —warrants more attention from researchers. In this study, he was not strongly committed for or against open occupancy. In amount of prejudice against Negroes, he ranged between signers of the first document and signers of the second. Still, we will have a much better idea of how he will behave if we know what groups influence him than if we know only the attitudes he expresses. Outside pressures have a tremendous power over him, and when the winds of passion and social change rise, he leans with them.

All in all, our data confirm the hypothesis that a person's attitudes, and the social pressures on him, are better clues to his future behavior when measured together than when measured separately. These data certainly do not suggest that measuring attitudes alone is useless in this respect: Knowledge of a person's attitudes is important in our effort to make valid predictions about human behavior. But what our findings do suggest is that there are also definite advantages in measuring the force of social pressures when trying to predict how people will respond to significant social issues.

TABLE II—How Reference Groups Indicate Behavior— Responses to the Open Occupancy Documents

Attributed importance of reference groups (Index values*)	Signed document for open housing	Did not sign	Signed document against open housing
0-5 (little importance)	10	82	30
6-10	3	38	14
11-15	2	23	12
16-20	0	10	5
21-25	0	9	6
26-30 (great importance)	0	9	9
Totals	15	171	76

* For each reference group of "Great Importance," respondent was given 6 points; for each of "Some Importance," 3 points; and for each of "No Importance," no points were given. Maximum index value = 30 points.

How Southern Children Felt About King's Death

James W. Clarke and John W. Soule

Shortly after Martin Luther King's death on April 4, we set forth to investigate how Negro children and white children had reacted to the assassination. Our inquiry was conducted along lines similar to those charted by social scientists who had studied children's reactions to the assassination of John F. Kennedy.

There were parallels between King's death and the death of John F. Kennedy in 1963—and the death of Robert F. Kennedy in June of this year. In each case, a relatively young public leader was cut down during his prime years. All of these men had been associated with the civil-rights movement—King, the movement's spiritual leader; the two Kennedys, political leaders closely identified with and sympathetic to the cause of Negro equality.

The association between the three leaders began during the 1960 Presidential campaign when the Kennedys intervened after King had been jailed for his civil-rights activities in Atlanta, Ga. (King had been sentenced to four months' hard labor and was being held on a legal technicality. The Kennedy brothers telephoned to remonstrate with the judge who had

REACTIONS BY RACE TO KING'S ASSASSINATION (Table 1)

Initial Reactions	Negroes (Number: 189)	Whites (Number: 141)
Shocked, grieved, saddened, or angry	96%	41%
Indifferent or pleased	4	59
	100%	100%

sentenced King, and King was released from jail the following day.) The ties between them remained close until the assassinations. All three men were also unpopular with those who objected to the civil-rights movement.

Our study was designed to answer four questions:

■ How did schoolchildren react—intellectually and emotionally—to King's death?

■ Were their responses similar to those reported among children after President Kennedy's assassination?

■ Were there differences between the reactions of white children and Negro children? and

■ What effect did their parents' attitudes—as perceived by the children—have upon their own reactions?

Clearly, children are not exempt from political attachments; in fact, it is during childhood that people develop their most enduring values and preferences. Indeed, as the recent civil disorders show, young people may even become political actors of the first order —in Detroit, for example, 61.3 percent of the rioters were between 15 and 23 years of age. In China, teenagers were prominent in the recent Cultural Revolution.

Our subjects were students attending four public schools in two metropolitan communities in north and southeast Florida. They included 165 whites and 217 Negroes from seventh-, ninth-, and eleventh-grade

REACTIONS OF WHITES BY SEX TO KING'S ASSASSINATION (Table 2)

Initial Reactions	Males (Number: 70)	Females (Number: 71)
Shocked, grieved, saddened, or angry	27%	55%
Indifferent or pleased	73	45
	100%	100%

classes. Except for the eleventh-graders, all were attending schools that were essentially segregated.

In each class, the regular teacher distributed and administered our questionnaires. We, as two white university-professors, avoided any contact with the students in order to prevent any bias that might have been introduced by our presence. Every effort was made to keep from disrupting the normal classroom situation. And in selecting the sample, we tried to include a comparable number of Negro and of white students within each grade level.

Why were the sampling techniques not more rigorous? Simply because of time: We wanted to complete the survey as soon after the assassination as possible. As it was, the data were collected within 12 days after the assassination. This delay was caused by our having had to obtain the approval of school officials.

The data in Table 1 show a clear difference between the races in their reactions to King's assassination: Whites were distinctly less unhappy than Negroes.

The responses had been elicited by asking students the open-ended question, "How did you feel when you first heard of Dr. King's death?" Only two of the 382

PERCEIVED PARENTS' REACTIONS & CHILDREN'S REACTIONS (Table 3)

| Children's Reactions | Perceived Parents' Reactions | |
	Felt Bad (Number: 111)	Indifferent or glad (Number: 80)
Felt Bad	97%	17%
Indifferent or glad	3	83
	100%	100%

Note: Fully 50% of the sample were unable or unwilling to report their perceptions of their parents' attitudes.

respondents could not identify King. Fifty-two students answered "don't know" or "no response." (In investigating students' attitudes, particularly those of young students, a substantial number of "no responses" is to be expected.) Of those who did answer, reactions varied from a deep sense of sorrow to feelings of elation. Fifty-nine percent of the white students were indifferent or elated. Ninety-six percent of the Negro students expressed shock or grief.

What role, if any, did the sex of the respondents play in answering this question? Table 2 shows that white boys were appreciably less unhappy about King's assassination than white girls. Seventy-three percent of the white boys expressed either indifference or satisfaction—compared with 45 percent of the white girls. Virtually no difference was found between the reactions of Negro boys and Negro girls.

That parents transmit their attitudes and values to their children has been well documented. And with regard to King's assassination, we found a close correspondence between parents' responses (as interpreted by the students) and the students' own responses. (See Table 3.)

Previous research has also repeatedly found a link between racial prejudice and class—for example, more lower-status whites tend to be prejudiced than high-status whites. Our findings confirm this. (See table 4.) Indifference and pleasure after King's death were found among significantly more white students whose fathers were in clerical, sales, and laboring occupations (82 percent) than among white students whose fathers were in professional, managerial, or official occupations (35 percent). Further, 65 percent of these higher-status children expressed sadness or sympathy.

FATHER'S STATUS & WHITE STUDENTS' INITIAL REACTIONS   (Table 4)

Students' Initial Reaction	Father's Occupation Professional, Proprietors, Managers, Officials	Clerical, Sales, Laborers
	(Number: 65)	(Number: 51)
Shocked, grieved, saddened, or angry	65%	18%
Indifferent or pleased	35	82
	100%	100%

Additional evidence of class differences appears when the parents' race is considered, and then their reactions to the assassination are tabulated with regard to occupation. Table 5 (see next page), in conjunction with Table 4, shows that children evidently share the basic class biases of their parents. Sixty-three percent of the white children's fathers in lower-level occupations were either pleased by or indifferent about King's death —compared with 82 percent of their children. On the other hand, while it is hardly encouraging, fewer of the white children's parents in higher-level occupations shared these attitudes (25 percent of the parents, 35 percent of their children). The Negro students, however, were overwhelmingly saddened by the event without regard to class differences, as were their parents.

The students were also asked, "Did you say any special prayer or attend a memorial service for Dr. King?" Seventy percent of the Negroes said Yes, as opposed to only 17 percent of the whites. (Paul B. Sheatsley and Jacob J. Feldman reported that three-fourths of a national sample of adults said Yes to a similar question after President Kennedy's assassination.)

The Negro students, we learned, attend church more regularly than whites do. Yet the students' record of attending church in the past seemingly had little bearing on whether they prayed after King's assassination. Most Negroes did pray and most whites did not, regardless of their past record of attending church.

Another question was, "What do you think should happen to the person who shot Dr. King?" Sixty-five percent of the Negro students showed hostility toward the murderer or a desire for revenge (Table 6). Typical responses were:

Seventh-grade Negro—"He should be hanged by the neck on public TV."

Ninth-grade Negro—"He should be shot by Mrs. King or King's brother."

Eleventh-grade Negro—"He should be taken out and beaten. Why don't they set him loose on [a Negro university] campus? We would do the job on him, but good!"

Some 65 percent of the whites, conversely, felt that the assassin should be accorded due process of law. But 17 percent of the white students felt that the killer should be set free—or congratulated. Among such responses:

Seventh-grade white—"He should go free."

Ninth-grade white—"He should get the Congres-

| Parents' Reactions | Professional, Managerial, etc. | | Working-Class | |
	Negroes (Number: 40)	Whites (Number: 65)	Negroes (Number: 101)	Whites (Number: 56)
Felt bad	73%	34%	73%	12%
Indifferent or pleased	2	25	2	63
Not sure	25	41	25	25
	100%	100%	100%	100%

sional Medal of Honor for killing a nigger."

Eleventh-grade white—"We should try him in court and find him not guilty. He did what lots of us wanted to do, he had the guts."

Moreover, sympathy for the killer among whites increased with their grade level. Thus, about 30 percent of the white eleventh-graders wanted no punishment for the assassin, compared with only 4 percent of the white seventh-graders. As the grade level of the Negro

HOW SHOULD KING'S KILLER BE TREATED? (Table 6)

Proposed Treatment	Negroes (Number: 198)	Whites (Number: 151)
Tried, punished by courts, imprisoned	35%	65%
Killed	65	18
No punishment, congratulated	0	17
	100%	100%

children increased, however, they were much more likely to favor due process of law as opposed to extra-legal, violent, or revengeful punishments. While 74 percent of the seventh-grade Negroes wanted to treat the assassin violently, only 50 percent of the eleventh-grade Negroes did. Still, it is noteworthy—and alarming—that at all grade levels a majority of the Negro students favored some form of violent death for the killer, with no mention of normal legal procedures.

The students were also asked, "Who or what do you think is to blame for his [King's] death?" The data in Table 7 indicate that 35 percent of the Negro stu-

dents identified the assassin as a white man—as opposed to 12 percent of the whites. This may be evidence of the Negro students' racial suspiciousness and defensiveness. In this item of the questionnaire, 41 percent of the white students thought that King was to blame for his own death. Only 4 percent of Negroes felt this way. About 24 percent of all the students refused to speculate on who the assassin might be: 16 percent of the whites and 29 percent of the Negroes.

After President Kennedy's assassination, not one child—white or Negro—was reported as saying that "We are all to blame." Our findings are quite divergent. Some 27 percent of the Negroes blamed American society for King's death, as did 17 percent of the whites. But whereas whites tended to blame the ills of American society in general, the Negroes tended to blame specifically the racist character of American society.

When we analyzed these results by the grade level of the students, we found that, as their grade level increased, the Negroes were more likely to blame a racist society for King's death. Younger Negroes tended to

WHO WAS TO BLAME FOR KING'S DEATH? (Table 7)

Blame Placed Upon	Negroes (Number: 154)	Whites (Number: 138)
A white man	35%	12%
Killer's color not mentioned	34	30
King himself was to blame	4	41
A prejudiced, racist, sick society	27	17

Southern Children & Civil Rights

When we asked the children in our study how their parents felt about the civil-right movement, we made a startling discovery: Many of the Negro students either did not know or gave no answer. (See Table A.)

Forty-three percent of the Negroes whose parents were in high-status occupations fell into this category, as did 41 percent of the Negroes whose parents were in low-level occupations. Compared with white students of high-status parents, a somewhat greater number of Negro students of high-status parents were knowledgable (43 percent versus 48 percent); compared with white students of low-status fathers, many more Negro students of low-status parents were less knowledgable (41 percent versus 34 percent).

Since civil rights should be far more important to Negroes than to whites, these figures are somewhat surprising. Perhaps Negro parents fail to communicate their attitudes to their children: This may be a reflection of the apathy so commonly attributed to Southern Negroes. Or perhaps Southern Negro children are just afraid of admitting that their parents favor civil rights.

Just as we found that white parents in low-status occupations were less sympathetic to King's death than white parents in high-status occupations, we found essentially the same pattern with regard to the civil-rights movement. (Table A.) Among higher-status white parents, there was much more ambivalence toward the movement—or perhaps a greater reluctance on the part of their children to reveal their parents' attitudes on this issue.

We also discovered that there is a very high level of agreement between the students' values regarding the civil-rights movement and the values they view their parents as holding. (See Table B.) When we exclude the sizable "don't know" responses, from our knowledge of perceived parents' attitudes we can predict the children's attitudes with 73 percent accuracy.

OCCUPATIONAL STATUS & ATTITUDE ON CIVIL RIGHTS (Table A)

Parents' Attitudes on Civil Rights	Managers, Proprietors, Officials		Sales, Clerical, Laborers	
	Negroes (Number: 107)	Whites (Number: 73)	Negroes (Number: 102)	Whites (Number: 59)
Favorable	50%	16%	54%	2%
Unfavorable	7	36	5	64
No Answer	43	48	41	34
	100%	100%	100%	100%

CHILDREN'S & PARENTS' ATTITUDES TOWARD THE CIVIL-RIGHTS MOVEMENT (Table B)

Negro & White Children's Attitudes	Perceived Parents' Attitudes		
	Favorable (Number: 127)	Unfavorable (Number: 88)	Don't Know (Number: 160)
Favorable	79%	7%	26%
Unfavorable	6	73	24
Don't Know	15	20	50
	100%	100%	100%

view the event in a more limited way—to blame it on "a white man." Among the white students, as grade level increased, more of them put the blame on King himself. Over 66 percent of the white eleventh-graders blamed King for his own assassination.

Studies made after the assassination of President Kennedy also found that more Negroes, both adults and children, expressed sorrow over his death than whites did—like the Negro students in our study in response to King's death. Some of the items used in the study of reactions to President Kennedy's death were included in our questionnaire. (See Table 8.)

By and large, whites responded more emotionally to President Kennedy's assassination than to King's. More "felt the loss of someone very close" (a 54 percent difference), more "felt so sorry for his wife and children" (a 31 percent difference), more "felt angry that anyone could do such a terrible thing" (a 34 percent difference), more "hoped that the man who shot him would be killed" (a 16 percent difference), more "felt ashamed that this could happen in this country" (a 23 percent difference), and more were "so confused and upset I didn't know what to feel" (a 29 percent difference). On the other hand, more whites were "worried

CHILDREN'S REACTIONS TO THE TWO ASSASSINATIONS (Table 8)

This Is How I Felt

	King Reactions		Kennedy Reactions*	
	Negroes (Number: 217)	Whites (Number: 165)	Negroes (Number: 342)	Whites (Number: 1,006)
Felt the loss of someone very close	89%	15%	81%	69%
Worried what would happen to our country	88	85	74	63
Felt so sorry for his wife and children	98	63	91	94
Felt angry that anyone should do such a terrible thing	95	47	84	81
Hoped the man who killed him would be shot	76**	20**	54	36
Felt ashamed that this could happen in my country	77	63	75	86
Was so confused and upset I didn't know what to feel	40	15	40	44
Felt in many ways it was (King's) (Kennedy's) own fault	10**	49**	18	15

* Data from Roberta S. Sigel.
** The differences between these responses and the responses presented in Tables 6 and 7 are explained by the fact that a larger number of students responded to the items that appear in this table.

what would happen to our country" after King died (a 22 percent difference); and more "felt in many ways it was King's own fault" (a 34 percent difference).

The feelings of Negroes after the two assassinations were similar—but after King's death more were "worried what would happen to our country" (a 14 percent difference) and more "hoped that the man who shot him would be killed" (a 22 percent difference).

To be sure, these findings, in general, could have been foreseen. It can be argued that Negroes, because of their tragic history in this country, are more smitten by the death of any leader who seemed to be sympathetic to the cause of human equality. And it certainly could have been expected that a greater number of Negroes would feel unhappiness at the death of a Negro leader than whites would—just as more Catholics probably felt unhappy about Cardinal Spellman's death than Protestants and Jews did, and more Jews probably felt unhappy about Rabbi Wise's death than Christians did. But what is certainly significant here is the tremendous differences between whites and Negroes in their reactions to King's death: Only 15 percent of

the white students "felt the loss of someone close"; 49 percent of the white students "felt in many ways it was King's fault" (compared with only 15 percent of them feeling that way about Kennedy's death); 59 percent of the white students, as we have seen, felt indifferent about or pleased by King's death; and 17 percent of them felt that King's assassin should be freed or congratulated.

Yet perhaps the most disturbing findings of our study are that

1. among the white students, happiness about and indifference toward King's death increased with their grade level;

2. Negro students became more likely to blame a racist white society for King's death as their grade levels increased; and

3. over 50 percent of all Negro students expressed a desire for extra-legal revenge on King's assassin.

These findings, while only suggestive, certainly provide no basis for optimism in regard to race relations in the South.

The Racist Liberals —

An Episode in a County Jail

Lillian Rubin

"Get over here! What are you doing in *that* line? Are you looking to be put in a cell? You know you're not supposed to be in here with the demonstrators."

The place was the women's mess hall of the Alameda County (Calif.) jail (known as the Santa Rita Rehabilitation Center); the time, December 1967; the speaker, a prison guard. Her order had been directed at one of 70 women arrested for participating in an anti-war demonstration in Oakland. What was the difference between the woman shouted at and the rest of those in the line? She was black.

The white guard had responded to the symbol of blackness, not to the woman. For the guard, "demonstrators" were white; a black woman in the line could only mean that a "regular inmate" was violating the rules that the two groups be kept separated. (Both the jail officials and the prisoners distinguished between the "demonstrators" and the others in the prison, who were known as the "regular inmates.") That assumption was particularly inappropriate, however, since all the demonstrators—including the black woman—were easily differentiated from the rest of the prison population because they had been issued clothing that was distinctly unlike that of the others. But the guard had not even seen the woman's dress, only her black face.

That a racist society should have a racist prison guard should come as no surprise. Ironically, however, the incident also symbolizes the interaction between most of the white demonstrators and the black inmates. Defining themselves as political radicals or liberals, proclaiming their sympathy with the Negro, the demonstrators nonetheless responded not to a person but to a symbol; not to a subject but to an object. That story follows; but first a caveat.

Although this paper is written from the viewpoint of the participant observer, I was perhaps more participant than observer. I did not get arrested to "observe" the group, but to protest against the war in Vietnam. Thus, in a fundamental sense I was part of the group, identifying with its problems, responding subjectively to the behavior around me, and trying to influence the group's conduct. These observations, therefore, lay no special methodological claim to scientific rigor.

I do not mean to suggest that every member of the group participated—only that the interaction pattern I shall describe was the dominant one, and cut across the different political and ideological factions represented among the demonstrators.

Finally, nothing I shall say is meant to equate the overt racist response of the prison guards with the more subtle responses of the demonstrators, who sincerely believed that they had freed themselves from the consequences of being born and bred in a racist society. It is the American tragedy that the roots of racism reach into and infect every part of our institutional and psychological lives, conditioning and controlling our behavior in ways that we seldom recognize.

Of the 70 demonstrators, only one was black—a former student at the State University of New York in Albany. While many of the group resisted defining themselves as middle class, all, in fact, were—in edu-

cation, background, and orientation. Almost all had at least some college education; about 20 percent had attended graduate school. In fact, most of the group who were under 35 were students at Stanford, Santa Cruz, Berkeley, or San Francisco State. Of the 15 women over 35, every one was college-educated; all but three were either practicing professionals or graduate students. Their political and ideological orientations, however, were diverse. Although almost every one of the women defined herself as a "radical," the word was often used without the usual political content. To many it meant some abstract pitting oneself against the "system," without any positive ideological or political attachments. Several held themselves to be nonpolitical, equating politics with immorality. Their reasons for going to jail also varied, encompassing a deep need to make some symbolic gesture against the Vietnam war; the belief that this was one way to throw their bodies against the wheels that keep the system going; and the pragmatic conception that it was politically effective for middle-class people to affirm their opposition to the war in this way.

A Total Institution

An understanding of the events to be described requires some comprehension of the fact that a prison is a social system that controls—absolutely—authority, prestige, status, and rewards. Once a person is inside the walls, the outside recedes; his life depends on how well he acknowledges and understands that system and its power structure. Those who do so best are rewarded with positions of trust and status.

The institutional order at Santa Rita was a reversal of the usual social patterns. About 85 percent of the 90 regular inmates were black; every position of privilege and prestige available to inmates—trusties, guards' helpers, and so on—was occupied by a black woman. Thus, the Negroes had a numerical majority and occupied all the highest positions in the power, privilege, prestige hierarchy of the inmates. Perhaps the most striking thing about the interaction between white demonstrators and black inmates was the apparent compulsion on the part of the demonstrators to redress the balance of power between white and black—to restore it to the more familiar patterns of the outside world.

From our arrival on Tuesday until late Thursday, we were separated into four groups and locked in maximum-security dormitories, being allowed out—under guard—only for meals. Every article of personal property was taken from us; all privileges were suspended. Among us we had not even a comb, a toothbrush, or a Kleenex tissue. No one in authority would explain the reasons for this unusual treatment. And, since we had already spent two days in lockup in Oakland, we were tense, tired, frightened, and, worst of all for those who smoke, out of cigarettes. Our only solace during that time came from the trusties and guards' helpers, all Negro inmates, who appeared periodically in place of the guards and treated us with great kindness. Even though their privileged status was in jeopardy, they smuggled cigarettes and candy bars to us, brought us a few combs, delivered messages to the other dorms so we could be reassured about the welfare of the rest of the group, and brought whatever scraps of information they could gather about our fate.

It should be underscored that the black women's generosity was not related to our middle-class status. Regardless of color, people in jail quickly learn that their comfort, if not survival, depends upon their ability to stand together in times of crisis. To circumvent and subvert prison authority is more than just a game; often it is a necessity. No one is secure; no one is sure he will not be next in solitary. Reciprocity is, therefore, an accepted part of social life at Santa Rita; prisoners in lockup are sustained by those who are free. Favors will ultimately be paid back. So the inmates' only expectation was that, when able, we would participate in that system of reciprocity.

On Thursday we were released from lockup and moved into one of two large, unlocked dormitories. The regular inmates (who had formerly occupied both of these dorms) were moved together into the other one. While the rules proscribed visiting between the two dormitories, most of the time these rules were disregarded with impunity, and the attempt to keep the two groups separated was largely unsuccessful.

At the same time, our privileges were restored. This meant, among other things, commissary. Twice a week, on Monday and Thursday, all inmates not on punishment were permitted to place commissary orders for delivery the next day. We were by then indebted to the inmates who had sustained us in lockup. Using the rhetoric of gratitude and insisting on their obligation to pay their debts, almost every demonstrator ordered the maximum permissible amounts of cigarettes, chewing gum, and candy. And instead of just repaying the debt, for every cigarette and candy bar received the demonstrators returned ten. Moreover, they assured the others that they had "lots of money." "Just let us know what you want or need," they kept saying, "and we'll order it for you." "After all," the demonstrators said to each other, "they're too poor and deprived to have supported us so generously." When someone suggested that they should be wary of overcompensating—that perhaps it was good for these "deprived" people to be on the giving end of an experience with whites for a change—the suggestion was brushed aside. As a result, the black women were soon swarming about our dorm looking for handouts. Before long it became almost impossible to walk anywhere without being stopped by the call, "Hey, got a cigarette?" If, as sometimes happened, a demonstrator said, "No," the plea came, "Can't you find me one? Sure do need a cigarette." It became a game on both sides—the demonstrators vying to see who could give away the most, the other inmates trying to see just how successfully they could hustle us.

Almost overnight the status relations were reversed. The black women were returned to their accustomed "place"; they were transformed from givers to takers, reduced to testing the limits of the game. A benevolent paternalism reigned; the demonstrators gave far beyond anyone's expectations, and felt suitably ennobled. For the blacks, all the time-tested devices that protect them in interaction with whites were brought into play; the mask slipped into place. They were "on the make," "running a game," "putting on the Man"—always with the smile that acknowledged white "superiority," with deferential thanks, with the flashed V-for-peace sign that made the demonstrators feel so good, and with the comment, "Next time I'm going to be out there demonstrating with you." Now, it seemed, the demonstrators were satisfied. These were Negroes they could understand—pitiable and deprived. They could relate to these black women in their accustomed mode; they could feel sorry for them, discuss among themselves their terrible state of deprivation, shake their heads in wonder that anyone could have suffered so much and still be so "beautiful" with so much "soul."

Self-Conscious Nonviolence

It was remarkable, indeed, to hear these middle-class women—whose values and behavior were in such contrast with the expressive, aggressive, and often violent interaction of the regular inmates—describe the latter in such uncritical terms. By and large, the demonstrators were self-consciously nonviolent. They withdrew from physical contact, even the kind of half-playful pushing, shoving, and hitting that prevailed among the Negro women. They relied on words to express their feelings, displaying an extraordinary degree of control and restraint—both verbal and physical. While exhibitions of hostility were common among the regular inmates, many of the demonstrators saw such expressions as brutalizing and less-than-human. With calculated care they tried to repress any hostile feelings. Yet they made no similar demands on the black women with whom they came in contact. Instead, the blacks were defined as "beautiful people" or "free souls," never to be questioned, criticized, or called to account for their behavior.

The interaction with Alice, a very aggressive black inmate, was representative. Alice spent a great deal of time in our dormitory, swearing, swaggering, and posturing. While many of the demonstrators were uncomfortable in her presence, few dared acknowledge that discomfort even to themselves. Two incidents are worth recording.

On the Saturday before Christmas, the group met to discuss a fast for peace. Alice came to the meeting and entered the debate. Her comments were abrasive, divisive, disruptive, and irrelevant. The group became restive, and finally irritated. Alice, sensing that she had lost their attention and was about to lose her point (to dissuade us from fasting), said belligerently, "You goddamn owe me your attention. I'm giving up my breakfast to talk to you here, and you better listen." A shock wave went through the assemblage, followed by a murmured apology. Only one honest voice spoke up: "Why don't you go back and eat your breakfast? Nobody invited you here." Alice, enraged, jumped at the girl who had spoken, shouting: "You bitch—you just watch out, chick. I'll get you, I'll kill you!" A few demonstrators tried to assuage Alice's anger; a few tried to protect the girl who had been threatened. But generally the response was to protect Alice, to explain away her behavior, and to attempt to "re-educate ourselves" to avoid such confrontations in the future. Some women suggested that the group ought to explore these responses to the incident. Why, they asked, were so many of them so quick to redefine their standards for

human behavior when dealing with blacks? Not that white middle-class behavioral patterns should be imposed on others, they said, but people who abhor violence might naturally be expected to react negatively to its display. Moreover, it seemed reasonable to expect that the group would assume some responsibility to protect its members; or at least that Alice would be told firmly that an attack upon a demonstrator would not be tolerated. As if those who raised such questions were idiots, it was carefully explained that if "they" (the blacks) exhibited hostility and anger, it was incumbent on "us" to understand and accept it. After all, "they" had been "culturally deprived." It was not Alice's behavior that was to be judged, but that of the demonstrator who had spoken out. She, it was said, failed to understand and accept blacks; in fact, she owed Alice an apology. Interestingly, many of the same people who accepted Alice's behavior so uncritically rejected the black-power theme because they believed it to be a call to violence.

Two days later, on Christmas Day, Alice again barged into our dormitory, bounced down on a bed, and was quickly surrounded by about 10 or 12 admiring demonstrators. She carried on a monologue for about 10 minutes, then suddenly spied another prisoner —a white woman, not a demonstrator—entering the dorm. She jumped from the bed, rushed up, pushed the woman into the wall, and accused her of stealing something. Frightened, the white girl almost whimpered, "No, Alice, honest, I didn't take it." "Are you calling me a liar?" cried Alice. "Nobody gets away with talking like that to Alice." And she set upon the girl, beating her with her fists, pulling her hair, and kicking her. The demonstrators stood aghast—immobilized. Interminable moments later a few jumped into the fray and pulled Alice away from her victim. At that moment a guard arrived and removed her from the dorm. Twenty minutes later, Alice returned and resumed her favored position, surrounded by her admirers. Soon, about half the members of the group were surrounding her. But not one word of disapproval was spoken; not one person even hinted that her behavior had offended them. They acted instead as if they had accidentally witnessed an intimate family fight—the kind of situation from which nice middle-class people avert their eyes and pretend not to see.

The implicit racism of the demonstrators' stance toward Alice completely eluded them; explanations were of no avail. These radical white women were unable to understand that their definition of the situation, the very act of lowering expectations for a black woman, was a subtle acknowledgment of the theme of black inferiority. It said that "they" really could not be as good, as noble, as uplifted, as intelligent, as human as "we." Perhaps the epitome of this subtle derogation of the blacks came in their interaction with Betty.

Thirty-two years old, the mother of a 7-year-old son, Betty was filled with hatred for the white world "that's done me wrong." While only casually conversant with the rhetoric of militant black nationalism, she understood deep in her gut what it was all about and at Santa Rita was its most articulate spokesman. She often wandered into our dorm to see what the action was, and stayed around to talk of her desire to take her son to Africa so that he could be raised with "his own people and learn to respect hisself." Her proclamations were generally greeted with confusion and silence, sometimes broken by someone's saying, "Oh, Betty, you don't really mean you want to leave this country, do you?" To which Betty responded, "Damned right that's what I mean, girl."

One afternoon she came in to find a seminar in progress—about 25 women were sitting in a circle on the floor and talking about the meaning and importance of nonviolent resistance. Betty planted herself in the middle the group and shouted, "Shit, you don't know what you're talking about! Ain't no such thing as nonviolence. You're all violent, and you've done violence to me and mine for hundreds of years. Time's going to come soon when we'll pay you back. Black power, that's where it's at." For several minutes no one moved; no one spoke. Finally the group leader smiled sweetly and said, "Pooh, Betty, that black-power thing is nowhere; love's where it's really at. You know you don't mean that." "Shit, girl, I sure do mean it!" she shouted, then launched into a long and often incoherent tirade. The group sat quietly through her attack, wriggled self-consciously at her assertions that "black blood is stronger than your sickly white blood," and remained mute when she finished. Once again they responded with the eyes-averted-with-embarrassment pose. The seminar came to an abrupt end when everyone withdrew in self-conscious giggles and confusion.

What Could They Have Done?

One might ask: What else could they have done? Well, they could have responded to a flesh-and-blood woman instead of to a black symbol. Had she been white, her behavior would have been intolerable; she would probably have been stopped. In this case, however, the demonstrators might have acknowledged that her blackness afforded her special insights into the Negro response to nonviolence and the relationship between violence and black power, then shifted the discussion so she could share her experience and knowledge on an equal basis. Or they could have refused to permit her to disrupt their seminar by requesting that she join it but confine her comments to the subject under discussion.

Two hours later another group was meeting, this one discussing tactical alternatives to going to jail. Once again Betty intervened, loudly proclaiming her intention to "tell it like it is," just as she had to the first group. Again she stood in the middle of the group and began to berate them. This time, the group leader responded promptly. "Betty," she said, "this is a discussion about what other tactics the anti-war movement can devise besides going to jail. This is serious stuff to us. If everybody just hollers out, no one hears *anyone*. So, if you want to join the discussion, you'll have to sit down like the rest of us, wait for me to call on you, and try to stick to the subject when you talk." The black woman's response was gratifying. For the first time in her contact with the demonstrators she had been treated like an equal—and she knew it. She was held to the same behavioral expectations as every other member of the group—and she responded. In the end she made a significant contribution to the discussion, and the group to her understanding of the anti-war protest. On the day before our departure, she came to the woman who had led the seminar and said, "For a gray chick, you're O.K.; not many straight ones like you. You tell it like it is."

"Our Nigger"

Maggie, the lone black demonstrator arrested, tried to challenge the racial attitudes and behavior of the group. For technical legal reasons, Maggie and two others (both white) had been tried separately and arrived at Santa Rita 10 days after the rest of us. She was the center of attention from the moment she came.

While all three were greeted with warmth, it was dramatically apparent that almost all eyes and ears turned enthusiastically to the black woman.

It seemed as if everyone was determined to make contact with "our nigger." Her presence was a source of group pride; she enhanced their image of themselves as unprejudiced; and she symbolized the "integrated" nature of the anti-war movement. A great deal of chauvinistic, racist, and downright silly conversation ensued as people maneuvered to establish their credentials as racial liberals. They complained bitterly to her about the conditions in the jail for the regular inmates, especially the black ones. "They're so mean to black people," one girl said. "What makes you say that?" Maggie asked. "Look," another responded, "three out of the four girls in isolation are black." (The comments were particularly ludicrous in view of the fact, already mentioned, that all trusties and guards' helpers—positions with very high visibility—were black.) Maggie replied, "So what! I understand that nine out of ten of all the inmates are black, so those percentages don't sound bad to me." They recoiled in confusion and whispered among themselves, "Oh, maybe she's one of those middle-class Negroes who doesn't care about her *race.*"

Later, upon learning that Maggie was living in San Francisco, one of the girls, Sherry, rhapsodized, "I just love to go to the Fillmore district. It's so romantic and beautiful—the streets are filled with beautiful people who know how to *live,* who have *soul.* You're lucky to live there. I go there every chance I get." To which Maggie responded: "Oh, shit! I *don't* live there. It's ugly and dirty, and if you're not afraid to walk the streets of the Fillmore at night there's something wrong with you, girl, because *I* am." Sherry, confused, wounded, and uncomprehending, retreated. Later she said to another woman, Sarah, "What do you suppose is the matter with Maggie? She seems upset." Sarah replied, "Maybe all she's trying to ask is that we relate to her as a human being rather than as a Negro. Maybe she'd just like us to set the same standards for her and for other Negroes that we set for ourselves. Maybe it's hard for her to believe that people like you can find the behavior of a dope addict, a whore, a pimp, a mugger, or a thief beautiful. It's hard for me to accept that, too." Sherry said: "I don't understand what you mean. We have to accept that behavior—we've done it

to them. We've deprived them of their humanity. Now we have to take whatever they dish out."

So, under the aegis of tolerance, understanding, and acceptance Sherry stripped the Negro of human qualities and prepared to accept him—even to welcome him—as a second-class human being. For this kind of radical or liberal, the Negro has won the fight for first-class citizenship, only to face the next struggle—the fight for first-class human status.

Compensation without Degradation

It would have been easier and more comfortable to write these off as instances involving a few young innocents, unrepresentative of any large segment of the group. But neither truth nor the cause of racial understanding would be served. The attitudes and behavior to which I refer actually cross-cut the group at all ages and all levels of sophistication, from the 18-year-old college freshman to the 50-year-old school teacher, and included several who claim long experience in the civil-rights struggle.

These episodes serve to corroborate what many people have believed for some time—namely, that it is easier to cope with the overt racist than with the subtlety of the radical or liberal response. The racist admits his stance and defends it. Evidence brought to bear upon his racist philosophy might even change his mind. At worst, we know we can pass laws that prevent him from acting out the most vicious aspects of his beliefs. But what of the liberal or radical who starts with the most enlightened postulates about race, but who, as Jonathan Kozol so forcefully points out in *Death at an Early Age,* remains totally unaware of his own deep complicity in the racist structure and attitudes of this society? Somehow he must be helped to understand that his vision of the Negro as a beautiful albeit poor, deprived creature is as oversimplified and distorted as the one held by the racist. It should not be necessary to convince ourselves of the sublimity of the Negro—to invest him with idealized qualities of virtue, wisdom, and strength—in order to believe that his problems deserve our attention. It is enough to value human dignity and to recognize that for centuries this racist society has laid siege to it.

Yet I am aware of the dilemmas in this situation. I am not suggesting that it is inappropriate to respond to color. In fact, to talk about the ideal of color blindness is, in this racist society, to dodge the issue. Color barriers do exist. The problem is not to avoid seeing them but to find ways to cross them. The debate, for example, about whether compensatory programs for blacks are necessary, desirable, or democratic misses the mark. Of course such programs should exist. The paradox, simply stated, is this: How can we take account of the special conditions in the lives of Negros that call for compensatory programs, without the kind of gross lowering of standards described above that is actually a subtle form of racism—an implied acknowledgment of black inferiority? Sensitive teachers in ghetto schools see dramatic examples of the problems that derive from lowered expectations. Their experience has shown that children quickly learn to comply with the expectations set for them. When expectations in a classroom are high, many black children formerly thought to be incompetent rise to meet them; when ex-

pectations are low, the children respond accordingly. Despite these recent insights, the dilemma remains with us. How can we draw a line between legitimate compensatory programs and treatment that simply expects less of blacks because they are assumed (consciously or unconsciously) to be capable of less?

Similarly, the line is vague between a sympathetic understanding of the trials of the American Negro and the paternalistic response of many white radicals and liberals. At what point did the demonstrators' sympathy with the impoverishment of the black prisoners turn into a Lady Bountiful-type paternalism?

In sum: The aim is to respect the black man as a human being, granting him the usual quota of strengths and weaknesses; it is to accept him not just as a first-class citizen, but as a first-class man.

Are Women Prejudiced Against Women?

Philip Goldberg

"Woman," advised Aristotle, "may be said to be an inferior man."

Because he was a man, Aristotle was probably biased. But what do women themselves think? Do they, consciously or unconsciously, consider their own sex inferior? And if so, does this belief prejudice them against other women—that is, make them view women, simply because they *are* women, as less competent than men?

According to a study conducted by myself and my associates, the answer to both questions is Yes. Women *do* consider their own sex inferior. And even when the facts give no support to this belief, they will persist in downgrading the competence—in particular, the intellectual and professional competence—of their fellow females.

Over the years, psychologists and psychiatrists have shown that both sexes consistently value men more highly than women. Characteristics considered male are usually praised; those considered female are usually criticized. In 1957 A.C. Sheriffs and J.P. McKee noted that "women are regarded as guilty of snobbery and irrational and unpleasant emotionality." Consistent with this report, E.G. French and G.S. Lesser found in 1964 that "women who value intellectual attainment feel they must reject the woman's role"—intellectual accomplishment apparently being considered, even among intellectual women, a masculine preserve. In addition, ardent feminists like Simone de Beauvoir and Betty Friedan believe that men, in important ways, are superior to women.

Now, is this belief simply prejudice, or are the characteristics and achievements of women really inferior to those of men? In answering this question, we need to draw some careful distinctions.

Different or Inferior?

Most important, we need to recognize that there are two distinct dimensions to the issue of sex differences. The first question is whether sex differences exist at all, apart from the obvious physical ones. The answer to this question seems to be a unanimous Yes—men, women, and social scientists agree that, psychologically and emotionally as well as physically, women *are* different from men.

But is being different the same as being inferior? It is quite possible to perceive a difference accurately but to value it inaccurately. Do women automatically view their differences from men as *deficiencies?* The evidence is that they do, and that this value judgment opens the door to anti-female prejudice. For if someone (male or female) concludes that women are inferior, his perceptions of women—their personalities, behavior, abilities, and accomplishments—will tend to be colored by his low expectations of women.

As Gordon W. Allport has pointed out in *The Na-ture of Prejudice,* whatever the facts about sex differences, anti-feminism—like any other prejudice—*distorts perception and experience.* What defines anti-feminism is not so much believing that women are inferior, as allowing that belief to distort one's perceptions of women. More generally, it is not the partiality itself, but the distortion born of that partiality, that defines prejudice.

Thus, an anti-Semite watching a Jew may see devious or sneaky behavior. But, in a Christian, he would regard such behavior only as quiet, reserved, or perhaps even shy. Prejudice is self-sustaining: It continually distorts the "evidence" on which the prejudiced person claims to base his beliefs. Allport makes it clear that anti-feminism, like anti-Semitism or any other prejudice, consistently twists the "evidence" of experience. We see not what is there, but what we *expect* to see.

The purpose of our study was to investigate whether there is real prejudice by women against women—whether perception itself is distorted unfavorably. Specifically, will women evaluate a professional article with a jaundiced eye when they think it is the work of a woman, but praise the same article when they think its author is a man? Our hypotheses were:

■ Even when the work is identical, women value the professional work of men more highly than that of women.

■ But when the professional field happens to be one traditionally reserved for women (nursing, dietetics), this tendency will be reversed, or at least greatly diminished.

Some 140 college girls, selected at random, were our subjects. One hundred were used for the preliminary work; 40 participated in the experiment proper.

To test the second hypothesis, we gave the 100 girls a list of 50 occupations and asked them to rate "the degree to which you associate the field with men or with women." We found that law and city planning were fields strongly associated with men, elementary-school teaching and dietetics were fields strongly associated with women, and two fields—linguistics and art history—were chosen as neutrals, not strongly associated with either sex.

Now we were ready for the main experiment. From the professional literature of each of these six fields, we took one article. The articles were edited and abridged to about 1500 words, then combined into two equal sets of booklets. The crucial manipulation had to do with the authors' names—the same article bore a male name in one set of booklets, a female name in the other set. An example: If, in set one, the first article bore the name John T. McKay, in set two the same article would appear under the name Joan T. McKay. Each booklet contained three articles by "men" and three articles by "women."

The girls, seated together in a large lecture hall, were told to read the articles in their booklets and given these instructions:

"In this booklet you will find excerpts of six articles, written by six different authors in six different professional fields. At the end of each article you will find several questions. . . . You are not presumed to be sophisticated or knowledgeable in all the fields. We are interested in the ability of college students to make critical evaluations. . . ."

Note that no mention at all was made of the authors' sexes. That information was contained—apparently only by coincidence—in the authors' names. The girls could not know, therefore, what we were really looking for.

At the end of each article were nine questions asking the girls to rate the articles for value, persuasiveness, and profundity—and to rate the authors for writing style, professional competence, professional status, and ability to sway the reader. On each item, the girls gave a rating of from 1 (highly favorable) to 5 (highly unfavorable).

Generally, the results were in line with our expectations—but not completely. In analyzing these results, we used three different methods: We compared the amount of anti-female bias in the different occupational fields (would men be rated as better city planners, but women as better dieticians?); we compared the amount of bias shown on the nine questions that followed each article (would men be rated as more competent, but women as more persuasive?); and we ran an overall comparison, including both fields and rating questions.

Starting with the analysis of bias by occupational field, we immediately ran into a major surprise. (See box below.) That there is a general bias by women against women, and that it is strongest in traditionally masculine fields, was clearly borne out. But in other fields the situation seemed rather confused. We

had expected the anti-female trend to be reversed in traditionally feminine fields. But it appears that, even here, women consider themselves inferior to men. Women seem to think that men are better at *everything* —including elementary-school teaching and dietetics!

Scrutiny of the nine rating questions yielded similar results. On all nine questions, regardless of the author's occupational field, the girls consistently found an article more valuable—and its author more competent—when the article bore a male name. Though the articles themselves were exactly the same, the girls felt that those written by the John T. McKays were definitely more

---

Law: A Strong Masculine Preserve

These are the total scores the college girls gave to the six pairs of articles they read. The lowest possible score—9—would be the most favorable; the highest possible score—54—the most critical. While male authors received more favorable ratings in all occupational fields, the differences were statistically significant only in city planning, linguistics, and—especially—law.

Field of Article	Mean	
	Male	Female
Art History	23.35	23.10
Dietetics	22.05	23.45
Education	20.20	21.75
City Planning	23.10	27.30
Linguistics	26.95	30.70
Law	21.20	25.60

---

impressive, and reflected more glory on their authors, than did the mediocre offerings of the Joan T. McKays. Perhaps because the world has accepted female authors for a long time, the girls were willing to concede that the female professionals' writing styles were not *far* inferior to those of the men. But such a concession to female competence was rare indeed.

Statistical analysis confirms these impressions and makes them more definite. With a total of six articles, and with nine questions after each one, there were 54 points at which comparisons could be drawn between the male authors and the female authors. Out of these 54 comparisons, three were tied, seven favored the female authors—and the number favoring the male authors was 44!

Clearly, there is a tendency among women to downgrade the work of professionals of their own sex. But the hypothesis that this tendency would decrease as the "femaleness' of the professional field increased was not supported. Even in traditionally female fields, antifeminism holds sway.

Since the articles supposedly written by men were exactly the same as those supposedly written by women, the perception that the men's articles were superior was obviously a distortion. For reasons of their own, the female subjects were sensitive to the sex of the author, and this apparently irrelevant information biased their judgments. Both the distortion and the sensitivity that precedes it are characteristic of prejudice. Women—at least these young college women—are prejudiced against female professionals and, regardless of the actual accomplishments of these professionals, will firmly refuse to recognize them as the equals of their male colleagues.

Is the intellectual double-standard really dead? Not at all—and if the college girls in this study are typical of the educated and presumably progressive segments of the population, it may not even be dying. Whatever lip service these girls pay to modern ideas of equality between men and women, their beliefs are staunchly traditional. Their real coach in the battle of the sexes is not Simone de Beauvoir or Betty Friedan. Their coach is Aristotle.

The Condemnation and Persecution of Hippies

Michael E. Brown

This article is about persecution and terror. It speaks of the Hippie and the temptations of intimacy that the myth of Hippie has made poignant, and it does this to discuss the institutionalization of repression in the United States.

When people are attacked as a group, they change. Individuals in the group may or may not change, but the organization and expression of their collective life will be transformed. When the members of a gathering believe that there is a grave danger imminent and that opportunities for escape are rapidly diminishing, the group loses its organizational quality. It becomes transformed in panic. This type of change can also occur outside a situation of strict urgency: When opportunities for mobility or access to needed resources are cut off, people may engage in desperate collective actions. In both cases, the conversion of social form occurs when members of a collectivity are about to be hopelessly locked into undesired and undesirable positions.

The process is not, however, automatic. The essential ingredient for conversion is social control exercised by external agents on the collectivity itself. The result can be

benign, as a panic mob can be converted into a crowd that makes an orderly exit from danger. Or it can be cruel.

The transformation of groups under pressure is of general interest; but there are special cases that are morally critical to any epoch. Such critical cases occur when pressure is persecution, and transformation is destruction. The growth of repressive mechanisms and institutions is a key concern in this time of administrative cruelty. Such is the justification for the present study.

Social Control as Terror

Four aspects of repressive social control such as that experienced by Hippies are important. First, the administration of control is suspicious. It projects a dangerous future and guards against it. It also refuses the risk of inadequate coverage by enlarging the controlled population to include all who might be active in any capacity. Control may or may not be administered with a heavy hand, but it is always a generalization applied to specific instances. It is a rule and thus ends by pulling many fringe innocents into its bailiwick; it creates as it destroys.

Second, the administration of control is a technical problem which, depending on its site and object, requires the bringing together of many different agencies that are ordinarily dissociated or mutually hostile. A conglomerate of educational, legal, social welfare, and police organizations is highly efficient. The German case demonstrates that. Even more important, it is virtually impossible to oppose control administered under the auspices of such a conglomerate since it includes the countervailing institutions ordinarily available. When this happens control is not only efficient and widespread, but also legitimate, commanding a practical, moral and ideological realm that is truly "one-dimensional."

Third, as time passes, control is applied to a wider and wider range of details, ultimately blanketing its objects' lives. At that point, as Hilberg suggests in his *The Destruction of the European Jews,* the extermination of the forms of lives leads easily to the extermination of the lives themselves. The line between persecution and terror is thin. For the oppressed, life is purged of personal style as every act becomes inexpressive, part of the struggle for survival. The options of a life-style are eliminated at the same time that its proponents are locked into it.

Fourth, control is relentless. It develops momentum as organization accumulates, as audiences develop, and as unofficial collaborators assume the definition of tasks, expression and ideology. This, according to W. A. Westley's "The Escalation of Violence Through Legitimation," is the culture of control. It not only limits the behaviors, styles, individuals and groups toward whom it is directed, it suppresses all unsanctioned efforts. As struggle itself is destroyed, motivation vanishes or is turned inward.

These are the effects of repressive control. We may contrast them with the criminal law, which merely prohibits the performance of specific acts (with the exception, of course, of the "crime without victims"—homosexuality, abortion, and drug use). Repression converts or destroys an entire social form, whether that form is embodied in a group, a style or an idea. In this sense, it is terror.

These general principles are especially relevant to our understanding of tendencies that are ripening in the United States day by day. Stated in terms that magnify it so that it can be seen despite ourselves, this is the persecution of the Hippies, a particularly vulnerable group of people who are the cultural wing of a way of life recently emerged from its quiet and individualistic quarters. Theodore Roszak, describing the Hippies in terms of their relationship to the culture and politics of dissent, notes that "the underlying unity of youthful dissent consists . . . in the effort of beat-hip bohemianism to work out the personality structure, the total life-style that follows from New Left social criticism." This life-style is currently bearing the brunt of the assault on what Roszak calls a "counter-culture"; it is an assault that is becoming more concentrated and savage every day. There are lessons for the American future to be drawn from this story.

Persecution

Near Boulder, Colorado, a restaurant sign says "Hippies not served here." Large billboards in upstate New York carry slogans like "Keep America Clean: Take a Bath." and "Keep America Clean: Get a Haircut." These would be as amusing as ethnic jokes if they did not represent a more systematic repression.

The street sweeps so common in San Francisco and Berkeley in 1968 and 1969 were one of the first lines of attack. People were brutally scattered by club-wielding policemen who first closed exits from the assaulted area and then began systematically to beat and arrest those who were trapped. This form of place terror, like surveillance in Negro areas and defoliation in Vietnam, curbs freedom and forces people to fight or submit to minute inspection by hostile forces. There have also been one-shot neighborhood pogroms, such as the police assault on the Tompkins Square Park gathering in New York's Lower East Side on Memorial Day, 1967: "Sadistic glee was written on the faces of several officers," wrote the *East Village Other.* Some women became hysterical. The police slugged Frank Wise, and dragged him off, handcuffed and bloody, crying, "My God, my God, where is this happening? Is this America?" The police also plowed into a group of Hippies, Yippies, and straights at the April, 1968, "Yip-in" at Grand Central Station. The brutality was as clear in this action as it had been in the Tompkins Square bust. In both cases, the major newspapers editorialized against the police tactics, and in the first the Mayor apologized for the "free wielding of nightsticks." But by the summer of 1968, street sweeps and busts and the continuous presence of New York's Tactical Police Force had given the Lower East Side an ominous atmosphere. Arrests were regularly accompanied by beatings and charges of "resistance to arrest." It became clear that arrests rather than subsequent procedures were the way in which control was to be exercised. The summer lost its street theaters, the relaxed circulation of people in the neighborhood and the easy park gatherings.

Official action legitimizes nonofficial action. Private citizens take up the cudgel of law and order newly freed from the boundaries of due process and respect. After Tompkins Square, rapes and assaults became common as local toughs assumed the role, with the police, of defender of the faith. In Cambridge, Massachusetts, following a virulent attack on Hippies by the Mayor, *Newsweek* reported that vigilantes attacked Hippie neighborhoods in force.

Ultimately more damaging are the attacks on centers of security. Police raids on "Hippie pads," crash pads, churches and movement centers have become daily occurrences in New York and California over the past two and a half years. The usual excuses for raids are drugs, runaways and housing violations, but many incidents of unlawful entry by police and the expressions of a more generalized hostility by the responsible officials suggests that something deeper is involved. The Chief of Police in San Francisco put it bluntly; quoted in *The New York Times* magazine in May, 1967, he said:

Hippies are no asset to the community. These people do not have the courage to face the reality of life. They are trying to escape. Nobody should let their young children take part in this hippy thing.

The Director of Health for San Francisco gave teeth to this counsel when he sent a task force of inspectors on a door-to-door sweep of the Haight-Ashbury—"a two-day blitz" that ended with a strange result, again according to *The Times:* Very few of the Hippies were guilty of housing violations.

Harassment arrests and calculated degradation have been two of the most effective devices for introducing uncertainty to the day-to-day lives of the Hippies. Cambridge's Mayor's attack on the "hipbos" (the suffix stands for body odor) included, said *Newsweek* of Oct. 30, 1967, a raid on a "hippie pad" by the Mayor and "a platoon of television cameramen." They "seized a pile of diaries and personal letters and flushed a partially clad girl from the closet." In Wyoming, *The Times* reported that two "pacifists" were "jailed and shaved" for hitchhiking. This is a fairly common hazard, though Wyoming officials are perhaps more sadistic than most. A young couple whom I interviewed were also arrested in Wyoming during the summer of 1968. They were placed in solitary confinement for a week during which they were not permitted to place phone calls and were not told when or whether they would be charged or released. These are not exceptional cases. During the summer of 1968, I interviewed young hitchhikers throughout the country; most of them had similar stories to tell.

In the East Village of New York, one hears countless stories of apartment destruction by police (occasionally reported in the newspapers), insults from the police when rapes or robberies are reported, and cruel speeches and even crueler bails set by judges for arrested Hippies.

In the light of this, San Francisco writer Mark Harris' indictment of the Hippies as paranoid seems peculiar. In the September 1967 issue of *The Atlantic,* he wrote,

The most obvious failure of perception was the hippies' failure to discriminate among elements of the Establishment, whether in the Haight-Ashbury or in San Francisco in general. Their paranoia was the paranoia of all youthful heretics. . . .

This is like the demand of some white liberals that Negroes acknowledge that they (the liberals) are not the power structure, or that black people must distinguish between the good and the bad whites despite the fact that the black experience of white people in the United States has been, as the President's Commission on Civil Disorder suggested, fairly monolithic and racist.

Most journalists reviewing the "Hippie scene" with any sympathy at all seem to agree with *Newsweek* that "the hippies do seem natural prey for publicity-hungry politicians—if not overzealous police," and that they have been subjected to varieties of cruelty that ought to be intolerable. This tactic was later elaborated in the massive para-military assault on Berkeley residents and students during a demonstration in support of Telegraph Avenue's street people and their People's Park. The terror of police violence, a constant in the lives of street people everywhere, in California carries the additional threat of martial law under a still-active state of extreme emergency. The whole structure of repression was given legitimacy and reluctant support by University of California officials. Step by step, they became allies of Reagan's "dogs of war." Roger W. Heyns, chancellor of the Berkeley campus, found himself belatedly reasserting the university's property in the lot. It was the law and the rights of university that trapped the chancellor in the network of control and performed the vital function of providing justification and legitimacy for Sheriff Madigan and the National Guard. Heyns said: "We will have to put up a fence to re-establish the conveniently forgotten fact that this field is indeed the university's, and to exclude unauthorized personnel from the site. . . . The fence will give us time to plan and consult.

We tried to get this time some other way and failed—hence the fence." And hence "Bloody Thursday" and the new regime.

And what of the Hippies? They have come far since those balmy days of 1966-67, days of flowers, street-cleaning, free stores, decoration and love. Many have fled to the hills of Northern California to join their brethren who had set up camps there several years ago. Others have fled to communes outside the large cities and in the Middle West. After the Tompkins Square assault, many of the East Village Hippies refused to follow the lead of those who were more political. They refused to develop organizations of defense and to accept a hostile relationship with the police and neighborhood. Instead, they discussed at meeting after meeting, how they could show their attackers love. Many of those spirits have fled; others have been beaten or jailed too many times; and still others have modified their outlook in ways that reflect the struggle. Guerrilla theater, Up Against the Wall Mother Fucker, the Yippies, the urban communes; these are some of the more recent manifestations of the alternative culture. One could see these trends growing in the demonstrations mounted by Hippies against arrests of runaways or pot smokers, the community organizations, such as grew in Berkeley for self-defense and politics, and the beginnings of the will to fight back when trapped in street sweeps.

It is my impression that the Hippie culture is growing as it recedes from the eye of the media. As a consequence of the destruction of their urban places, there has been a redistribution of types. The flower people have left for the hills and become more communal; those who remained in the city were better adapted to terror, secretive or confrontative. The Hippie culture is one of the forms radicalism can take in this society. The youngsters, 5,000 of them, who came to Washington to counter-demonstrate against the Nixon inaugural showed the growing amalgamation of the New Left and its cultural wing. The Yippies who went to Chicago for guerrilla theater and learned about "pigs" were the multi-generational expression of the new wave. A UAWMF (Up Against the Wall Mother Fucker) drama, played at Lincoln Center during the New York City garbage strike—they carted garbage from the neglected Lower East Side and dumped it at the spic 'n' span cultural center—reflected another interpretation of the struggle, one that could include the politically militant as well as the culturally defiant. Many Hippies have gone underground—in an older sense of the word. They have shaved their beards, cut their hair, and taken straight jobs,

like the secret Jews of Spain; but unlike those Jews, they are consciously an underground, a resistance.

What is most interesting and, I believe, a direct effect of the persecution, is the enormous divergence of forms that are still recognizable by the outsider as Hippie and are still experienced as a shared identity. "The Yippies," says Abbie Hoffman, "are like Hippies, only fiercer and more fun." The "hippie types" described in newspaper accounts of drug raids on colleges turn out, in many cases, to be New Leftists.

The dimensions by which these various forms are classified are quite conventional: religious-political, visible-secret, urban-hill, communal-individualistic. As their struggle intensifies, there will be more efforts for unity and more militant approaches to the society that gave birth to a real alternative only to turn against it with a mindless savagery. Yippie leader Jerry Rubin, in an "emergency letter to my brothers and sisters in the movement" summed up:

Huey Newton is in prison.

Eldridge Cleaver is in exile.

Oakland Seven are accused of conspiracy.

Tim Leary is up for 30 years and how many of our brothers are in court and jail for getting high?

. . .

Camp activists are expelled and arrested.

War resisters are behind bars.

Add it up!

Rubin preambles his summary with:

From the Bay Area to New York, we are suffering the greatest depression in our history. People are taking bitterness in their coffee instead of sugar. The hippie-yippie-SDS movement is a "white nigger" movement. The American economy no longer needs young whites and blacks. We are waste material. We fulfill our destiny in life by rejecting a system which rejects us.

He advocates organizing "massive mobilizations for the spring, nationally coordinated and very theatrical, taking place near courts, jails, and military stockades."

An article published in a Black Panther magazine is entitled "The Hippies Are Not Our Enemies." White radicals have also overcome their initial rejection of cultural radicals. Something clearly is happening, and it is being fed, finally, by youth, the artists, the politicos and the realization, through struggle, that America is not beautiful.

Some Historical Analogies

The persecution of the Jews destroyed both a particular social form and the individuals who qualified for the Jewish fate by reason of birth. Looking at the process in the aggregate, Hilberg describes it as a gradual coming together of a multitude of loose laws, institutions, and intentions, rather than a program born mature. The control conglomerate that resulted was a refined engine "whose devices," Hilbert writes, "not only trap a larger number of victims; they also require a greater degree of specialization, and with that division of labor, the moral burden too is fragmented among the participants. The perpetrator can now kill his victims without touching them, without hearing them, without seeing them. . . . This ever growing capacity for destruction cannot be arrested anywhere." Ultimately, the persecution of the Jews was a mixture of piety, repression and mobilization directed against those who were in the society but suddenly not of it.

The early Christians were also faced with a refined and elaborate administrative structure whose harsh measures were ultimately directed at their ways of life: their social forms and their spiritual claims. The rationale was, and is, that certain deviant behaviors endanger society. Therefore, officials are obligated to use whatever means of control or persuasion they consider necessary to strike these forms from the list of human possibilities. This is the classical administrative rationale for the suppression of alternative values and world views.

As options closed and Christians found the opportunities to lead and explore Christian lives rapidly struck down, Christian life itself had to become rigid, prematurely closed and obsessed with survival.

The persecution of the early Christians presents analogies to the persecution of European Jews. The German assault affected the quality of Jewish organizations no less than it affected the lives of individual Jews, distorting communities long before it destroyed them. Hilberg documents some of the ways in which efforts to escape the oppression led on occasion to a subordination of energies to the problem of simply staying alive—of finding some social options within the racial castle. The escapist mentality that dominated the response to oppression and distorted relationships can be seen in some Jewish leaders in Vienna. They exchanged individuals for promises. This is what persecution and terror do. As options close and all parts of the life of the oppressed are touched by procedure, surveillance and control, behavior is transformed. The oppressed rarely retaliate (especially where they have internalized the very ethic that rejects them), simply because nothing is left untouched by the persecution. No energy is available for hostility, and, in any case, it is impossible to know where to begin. Bravery is stoicism. One sings to the cell or gas chamber.

The persecution of Hippies in the United States involves, regardless of the original intentions of the agencies concerned, an assault on a way of life, an assault no less concentrated for its immaturity and occasional ambivalence. Social, cultural and political resources have been mobilized to bring a group of individuals into line and to prevent others from refusing to toe the line.

The attractiveness of the Hippie forms and the pathos of their persecution have together brought into being an impressive array of defenders. Nevertheless theirs has been a defense of gestures, outside the realm of politics and social action essential to any real protection. It has been verbal, scholarly and appreciative, with occasional expressions of horror at official actions and attitudes. But unfortunately the arena of conflict within which the Hippies, willy-nilly, must try to survive is dominated not by the likes of Susan Sontag, but by the likes of Daniel Patrick Moynihan whose apparent compassion for the Hippies will probably never be translated into action. For even as he writes (in the *American Scholar*, Autumn, 1967) that these youths are "trying to tell us something" and that they are one test of our "ability to survive," he rejects them firmly, and not a little *ex cathedra*, as a "truth gone astray." The Hippie remains helpless and more affected by the repressive forces (who will probably quote Moynihan) than by his own creative capacity or the sympathizers who support him in the journals. As John Kifner reported in *The Times*, " 'This scene is not the same anymore,' said the tall, thin Negro called Gypsy. '. . . There are some very bad vibrations.' "

Social Form and Cultural Heresy

But it's just another murder. A hippie being killed is just like a housewife being killed or a career girl being killed or a hoodlum being killed. None of these people, notice, are persons; they're labels. Who cares who Groovy was; if you know he was a 'hippie,' then already you know more about him than he did about himself.

See, it's hard to explain to a lot of you what a hippie is because a lot of you really think a hippie IS something. You don't realize that the word is just a convenience picked up by the press to personify a social change thing beginning to happen to young people. (*Paul William, in an article entitled "Label Dies—But Not Philosophy,"* Open City, *Los Angeles, November 17-23, 1967.*)

Because the mass media have publicized the growth of a fairly well-articulated Hippie culture, it now bears the status of a social form. Variously identified as "counter-culture," "Hippie-dom," "Youth" or "Underground," the phenomenon centers on a philosophy of the present and takes the personal and public forms appropriate to that philosophy. Its values constitute a heresy in a society that consecrates the values of competition, social manipulation and functionalism, a society that defines ethical quality by long-range and general consequences, and that honors only those attitudes and institutions that affirm the primacy of the future and large-scale over the local and immediately present. It is a heresy in a society that eschews the primary value of intimacy for the sake of impersonal service to large and enduring organizations, a society that is essentialist rather than existentialist, a society that prizes biography over interactive quality. It is a heresy in a country whose President could be praised for crying, "Ask not what your country can do for you, but what you can do for your country!" Most important, however, it is heresy in a society whose official values, principles of operation and officials themselves are threatened domestically and abroad.

For these reasons the Hippie is available for persecution. When official authority is threatened, social and political deviants are readily conjured up as demons requiring collective exorcism and thus a reaffirmation of that authority. Where exorcism is the exclusive province of government, the government's power is reinforced by the adoption of a scapegoat. Deviant style and ideals make a group vulnerable to exploitation as a scapegoat, but it is official action which translates vulnerability into actionable heresy.

By contrast, recent political developments within black communities and the accommodations reached through bargaining with various official agencies have placed the blacks alongside the Viet Cong as an official enemy, but not as a scapegoat. As an enemy, the black is not a symbol but a source of society's troubles. It is a preferable position. The Hippie's threat lies in the lure of his way of life rather than in his political potential. His vulnerability as well as his proven capacity to develop a real alternative life permits his selection as scapegoat. A threatened officialdom is all too likely to take the final step that "brings on the judge." At the same time, by defining its attack as moderate, it reaffirms its moral superiority in the very field of hate it cultivates.

A Plausible Force

We are speaking of that which claims the lives, totally or in part, of perhaps hundreds of thousands of people of all ages throughout the United States and elsewhere. The number is not inconsiderable.

The plausibility of the Hippie culture and its charisma can be argued on several grounds. Their outlook derives from a profound mobilizing idea: Quality resides in the present. Therefore, one seeks the local in all its social detail—not indulgently and alone, but openly and creatively.

Vulnerability and improvisation are principles of action, repudiating the "rational" hierarchy of plans and stages that defines, for the grounded culture, all events as incidents of passage and means to an indefinitely postponable end—as transition. The allocation of reality to the past and the future is rejected in favor of the present, and a present that is known and felt immediately, not judged by external standards. The long run is the result rather than the goal of the present. "Psychical distance," the orientation of the insulated tourist to whom the environment is something forever foreign or of the administrator for whom the world is an object of administration, is repudiated as a relational principle. It is replaced by a principal of absorption. In this, relationships are more like play, dance or jazz. Intimacy derives from absorption, from spontaneous involvement, to use Erving Goffman's phrase, rather than from frequent contact or attraction, as social psychologists have long argued.

This vision of social reality makes assumptions about human nature. It sees man as only a part of a present that depends on all its parts. To be a "part" is not to play a stereotyped role or to plan one's behavior prior to entering the scene. It is to be of a momentum. Collaboration, the overt manifestation of absorption, is critical to any social arrangement because the present, as experience, is essentially social. Love and charisma are the reflected properties of the plausible whole that results from mutual absorption. "To swing" or "to groove" is to be of the scene rather than simply at or in the scene. "Rapping," an improvised, expansive, and collaborative conversational form, is an active embodiment of the more general ethos. Its craft is humor, devotion, trust, openness to events in the process of formation, and the capacity to be relevant. Identity is neither strictly personal nor something to be maintained, but something always to be discovered. The individual body is the origin of sounds and motions, but behavior, ideas, images, and reflective thought stem from interaction itself. Development is not of personalities but of situations that include many bodies but, in effect, one mind. Various activities, such as smoking marijuana, are disciplines that serve the function of bringing people together and making them deeply interesting to each other.

The development of an authentic "counter-culture," or, better, "alternative culture," has some striking implications. For one, information and stress are processed through what amounts to a new conceptual system—a culture that replaces, in the committed, the intrapersonal structures that Western personality theories have assumed to account for intrapersonal order. For example, in 1966, young Hippies often turned against their friends and their experience after a bad acid trip. But that was the year during which "the Hippie thing" was merely one constructive expression of dissent. It was not, at that point, an alternative culture. As a result, the imagery cued in by the trauma was the imagery of the superego, the distant and punitive authority of the Western family and its macrocosmic social system. Guilt, self-hatred and the rejection of experience was the result. Many youngsters returned home filled with a humiliation that could be forgotten, or converted to a seedy and defensive hatred of the dangerously deviant. By 1968 the bad trip, while still an occasion for reconversion for some, had for others become something to be guarded against and coped with in a context of care and experienced guidance. The atmosphere of trust and new language of stress-inspired dependence rather than recoil as the initial stage of cure. One could "get high with a little help from my friends." Conscience was purged of "authority."

Although the ethos depends on personal contact, it is carried by underground media (hundreds of newspapers claiming hundreds of thousands of readers), rock music, and collective activities, artistic and political, which deliver and duplicate the message; and it is processed through a generational flow. It is no longer simply a constructive expression of dissent and thus attractive because it is a vital answer to a system that destroys vitality; it is culture, and the young are growing up under the wisdom of its older generations. The ethos is realized most fully in the small communes that dot the American urbscape and constitute an important counter-institution of the Hippies.

This complex of population, culture, social form, and ideology is both a reinforcing environment for individuals and a context for the growth and elaboration of the complex itself. In it, life not only begins, it goes on; and, indeed, it must go on for those who are committed to it. Abbie Hoffman's *Revolution for the Hell of It* assumes the autonomy of this cultural frame of reference. It assumes that the individual has entered and has burned his bridges.

As the heresy takes an official definition and as the institutions of persecution form, a they-mentality emerges in the language which expresses the relationship between the oppressor and the oppressed. For the oppressed, it distinguishes life from nonlife so that living can go on. The they-mentality of the oppressed temporarily relieves them of the struggle by acknowledging the threat, identifying its agent, and compressing both into a quasi-poetic image, a cliche that can accomodate absurdity. One young man said, while coming down from an amphetamine high: "I'm simply going to continue to do what I want until they stop me."

But persecution is also structured by the they-mentality of the persecutors. This mentality draws lines around its objects as it fits them conceptually for full-scale social action. The particular uses of the term "hippie" in the mass media—like "Jew," "Communist," "Black Muslim," or "Black Panther"—cultivates not only disapproval and rejection but a climate of opinion capable of excluding Hippies from the moral order altogether. This is one phase of a subtle process that begins by locating and isolating a group, tying it to the criminal, sinful or obscene, developing and displaying referential symbols at a high level of abstraction which depersonalize and

objectify the group, defining the stigmata by which members are to be known and placing the symbols in the context of ideology and readiness for action.

At this point, the symbols come to define public issues and are, consequently, sources of strength. The maintenance of power—the next phase of the story—depends less on the instruction of reading and viewing publics than on the elaboration of the persecutory institutions which demonstrate and justify power. The relationship between institution and public ceases to be one of expression or extension (of a public to an institution) and becomes one of transaction or dominance (of a public with or by an institution). The total dynamic is similar to advertising or the growth of the military as domestic powers in America.

An explosion of Hippie stories appeared in the mass media during the summer of 1967. Almost every large-circulation magazine featured articles on the Hippie "fad" or "subculture." *Life's* "The Other Culture" set the tone. The theme was repeated in *The New York Times Magazine,* May 14, 1967, where Hunter Thompson wrote that "The 'Hashbury' (Haight-Asbury in San Francisco) is the new capital of what is rapidly becoming a drug culture." *Time's* "wholly new subculture" was "a cult whose mystique derives essentially from the influences of hallucinogenic drugs." By fall, while maintaining the emphasis on drugs as the cornerstone of the culture, the articles had shifted from the culturological to a "national character" approach, reminiscent of the World War II anti-Japanese propaganda, as personal traits were piled into the body of the symbol and objectification began. The Hippies were "acid heads," "generally dirty," and "visible, audible and sometimes smellable young rebels."

As "hippie" and its associated terms ("long-haired," "bearded") accumulated pejorative connotation, they began to be useful concepts and were featured regularly in news headlines: for example, "Hippie Mother Held in Slaying of Son, 2" (*The New York Times,* Nov. 22, 1967); "S Squad Hits Four Pads" (*San Francisco Chronicle,* July 27, 1967). The articles themselves solidified usage by dwelling on "hippie types," "wild drug parties" and "long-haired, bearded" youths (see, for example, *The New York Times* of Feb. 13, 1968, Sept. 16, 1968 and Nov. 3, 1967).

This is a phenomenon that R. H. Turner and S. J. Surace described in 1956 in order to account for the role of media in the development of hostile consciousness toward Mexicans. The presentation of certain symbols can remove their referents from the constraints of the conventional moral order so that extralegal and extramoral action can be used against them. Political cartoonists have used the same device with less powerful results. To call Mexican-Americans "zootsuiters" in Los Angeles, in 1943, was to free hostility from the limits of the conventional, though fragile, antiracism required by liberal ideology. The result was a wave of brutal anti-Mexican assaults. Turner and Surace hypothesized that:

To the degree, then, to which any symbol evokes only one consistent set of connotations throughout the community, only one general course of action with respect to that ob-

ject will be indicated, and the union of diverse members of the community into an acting crowd will be facilitated . . . or it will be an audience prepared to accept novel forms of official action.

First the symbol, then the accumulation of hostile connotations, and finally the action-issue: Such a sequence appears in the news coverage of Hippies from the beginning of 1967 to the present. The amount of coverage has decreased in the past year, but this seems less a result of sympathy or sophistication and more one of certainty: The issue is decided and certain truths can be taken for granted. As this public consciousness finds official representation in the formation of a control conglomerate, it heralds the final and institutional stage in the growth of repressive force, persecution and terror.

The growth of this control conglomerate, the mark of any repressive system, depends on the development of new techniques and organizations. But its momentum requires an ideological head of steam. In the case of the Hippie life the ideological condemnation is based on several counts: that it is dangerous and irresponsible, subversive to authority, immoral, and psychopathological.

Commenting on the relationship between beliefs and the development of the persecutory institutions for witch-control in the 16th century, Trevor-Roper, in an essay on "Witches and Witchcraft," states:

In a climate of fear, it is easy to see how this process could happen: how individual deviations could be associated with a central pattern. We have seen it happen in our own time. The "McCarthyite" experience of the United States in the 1950's was exactly comparable: Social fear, the fear of an incompatible system of society, was given intellectual form as a heretical ideology and suspect individuals were persecuted by reference to that heresy.

The same fear finds its ideological expression against the Hippies in the statement of Dr. Stanley F. Yolles, director of the National Institute of Mental Health, that "alienation," which he called a major underlying cause of drug abuse, "was wider, deeper and more diffuse now than it has been in any other period in American history." The rejection of dissent in the name of mental health rather than moral values or social or political interest is a modern characteristic. Dr. Yolles suggested that if urgent attention is not given the problem:

there are serious dangers that large proportions of current and future generations will reach adulthood embittered towards the larger society, unequipped to take on parental, vocational and other citizen roles, and involved in some form of socially deviant behavior. . . .

Dr. Seymour L. Halleck, director of student psychiatry at the University of Wisconsin, also tied the heresy to various sources of sin: affluence, lack of contact with adults, and an excess of freedom. Dr. Henry Brill, director of Pilgrim State Hospital on Long Island and a consultant on drug use to federal and state agencies, is quoted in *The New York Times*, Sept. 26, 1967:

It is my opinion that the unrestricted use of marijuana type substances produces a significant amount of vagabondage, dependency, and psychiatric disability.

Drs. Yolles, Halleck, and Brill are probably fairly representative of psychiatric opinion. Psychiatry has long defined normality and health in terms of each other in a "scientific" avoidance of serious value questions. Psychiatrists agree in principle on several related points which could constitute a medical rational foundation for the persecution of Hippies: They define the normal and healthy individual as patient and instrumental. He plans for the long range and pursues his goals temperately and economically. He is an individual with a need for privacy and his contacts are moderate and respectful. He is stable in style and identity, reasonably competitive and optimistic. Finally, he accepts reality and participates in the social forms which constitutes the givens of his life. Drug use, sexual pleasure, a repudiation of clear long-range goals, the insistence on intimacy and self-affirmation, distrust of official authority and radical dissent are all part of the abnormality that colors the Hippies "alienated" or "disturbed" or "neurotic."

This ideology characterizes the heresy in technical terms. Mental illness is a scientific and medical problem, and isolation and treatment are recommended. Youth, alienation and drug use are the discrediting characteristics of those who are unqualified for due process, discussion or conflict. The genius of the ideology has been to separate the phenomenon under review from consideration of law and value. In this way the mutual hostilities that ordinarily divide the various agencies of control are bypassed and the issue endowed with ethical and political neutrality. Haurek

and Clark, in their "Variants of Integration of Social Control Agencies," described two opposing orientations among social control agencies, the authoritarian-punitive (the police, the courts) and the humanitarian-welfare (private agencies, social workers), with the latter holding the former in low esteem. The Hippies have brought them together.

The designation of the Hippie impulse as heresy on the grounds of psychopathology not only bypasses traditional enmity among various agencies of social control, but its corollaries activate each agency. It is the eventual coordination of their efforts that constitutes the control conglomerate. We will briefly discuss several of these corollaries before examining the impact of the conglomerate. Youth, danger and disobedience are the major themes.

Dominating the study of adolescence is a general theory which holds that the adolescent is a psychosexual type. Due to an awakening of the instincts after a time of relative quiescence, he is readily overwhelmed by them.

Consequently, his behavior may be viewed as the working out of intense intrapsychic conflict—it is symptomatic or expressive rather than rational and realistic. He is idealistic, easily influenced, and magical. The idealism is the expression of a threatened superego; the susceptibility to influence is an attempt to find support for an identity in danger of diffusion; the magic, reflected in adolescent romance and its rituals, is an attempt to get a grip on a reality that shifts and turns too much for comfort. By virtue of his entrance into the youth culture, he joins in the collective expression of emotional immaturity. At heart, he is the youth of Golding's *Lord of the Flies,* a fledgling adult living out a transitional status. His idealism may be sentimentally touching, but in truth he is morally irresponsible and dangerous.

Youth

As the idealism of the young is processed through the

203

youth culture, it becomes radical ideology, and even radical practice. The attempts by parents and educators to break the youth culture by rejecting its symbols and limiting the opportunities for its expression (ranging from dress regulations in school to the censorship of youth music on the air) are justified as a response to the dangerous political implications of the ideology of developed and ingrown immaturity. That these same parents and educators find their efforts to conventionalize the youth culture (through moderate imitations of youthful dress and attempts to "get together with the kids") rejected encourages them further to see the young as hostile, unreasonable and intransigent. The danger of extremism (the New Left and the Hippies) animates their criticism, and all intrusions on the normal are read as pointing in that direction. The ensuing conflict between the wise and the unreasonable is called (largely by the wise) the "generation gap."

From this it follows that radicalism is the peculiar propensity of the young and, as Christopher Jencks and David Riesman have pointed out in *The Academic Revolution,* of those who identify with the young. At its best it is not considered serious; at its worst it is the "counter-culture." The myth of the generation gap, a myth that is all the more strongly held as we find less and less evidence for it, reinforces this view by holding that radicalism ends, or should end, when the gap is bridged—when the young grow older and wiser. While this lays the groundwork for tolerance or more likely, forbearance, it is a tolerance limited to youthful radicalism. It also lays the groundwork for a more thorough rejection of the radicalism of the not-so-young and the "extreme."

Thus, the theory of youth classifies radicalism as immature and, when cultivated, dangerous or pathological. Alienation is the explanation used to account for the extension of youthful idealism and paranoia into the realm of the politically and culturally adult. Its wrongness is temporary and trivial. If it persists, it becomes a structural defect requiring capture and treatment rather than due process and argument.

Danger

Once a life-style and its practices are declared illegal, its proponents are by definition criminal and subversive. On the one hand, the very dangers presupposed by the legal proscriptions immediately become clear and present. The illegal life-style becomes the living demonstration of its alleged dangers. The ragged vagabondage of the Hippie is proof that drugs and promiscuity are alienating, and the attempts to sleep in parks, gather and roam are the new "violence" of which we have been reading. Crime certainly is crime, and the Hippies commit crime by their very existence. The dangers are: (1) crime and the temptation to commit crime; (2) alienation and the temptation to drop out. The behaviors that, if unchecked, become imbedded in the personality of the suspectible are, among others, drug use (in particular marijuana), apparel deviance, dropping out (usually of school), sexual promiscuity, communal living, nudity, hair deviance, draft resistance, demonstrating against the feudal oligarchies in cities and colleges, gathering, roaming, doing strange art and being psychedelic. Many of these are defused by campaigns of definition; they become topical and in fashion. To wear bell-bottom pants, long side-burns, flowers on your car and beads, is, if done with taste and among the right people, stylish and eccentric rather than another step toward the brink or a way of lending aid and comfort to the enemy. The disintegration of a form by co-opting only its parts is a familiar phenomenon. It is tearing an argument apart by confronting each proposition as if it had no context, treating a message like an intellectual game.

Drugs, communalism, gathering, roaming, resisting and demonstrating, and certain styles of hair have not been defused. In fact, the drug scene is the site of the greatest concentration of justificatory energy and the banner under which the agencies of the control conglomerate unite. That their use is so widespread through the straight society indicates the role of drugs as temptation. That drugs have been pinned so clearly (despite the fact that many Hippies are nonusers) and so gladly to the Hippies, engages the institutions of persecution in the task of destroying the Hippie thing.

The antimarijuana lobby has postulated a complex of violence, mental illness, genetic damage, apathy and alienation, all arising out of the ashes of smoked pot. The hypothesis justifies a set of laws and practices of great harshness and discrimination, and the President recently recommended that they be made even more so. The number of arrests for use, possession or sale of marijuana has soared in recent years: Between 1964 and 1966 yearly arrests doubled, from 7,000 to 15,000. The United States Narcotics Commissioner attributed the problem to "certain groups" which give marijuana to young people, and to "false information" about the danger of the drug.

Drug raids ordinarily net "hippie-type youths" although lately news reports refer to "youths from good homes." The use of spies on campuses, one of the bases for the original protest demonstrations at Nanterre prior to the May revolution, has become common, with all its socially destructive implications. Extensive spy operations were behind many of the police raids of college campuses during 1967, 1968 and 1969. Among those hit were Long Island University's Southampton College (twice), State University College at Oswego, New York, the Hun School of Princeton, Bard College, Syracuse University, Stony Brook College and Franconia College in New Hampshire; the list could go on.

It is the "certain groups" that the Commissioner spoke of who bear the brunt of the condemnation and the harshest penalties. The laws themselves are peculiar enough, having been strengthened largely since the Hippies became visible, but they are enforced with obvious discrimination. Teenagers arrested in a "good residential section" of Naugatuck, Connecticut, were treated gently by the circuit court judge:

I suspect that many of these youngsters should not have been arrested. . . . I'm not going to have these youngsters bouncing around with these charges hanging over them.

They were later released and the charges dismissed. In contrast, after a "mass arrest" in which 15 of the 25 arrested were charged with being in a place where they knew that others were smoking marijuana, Washington's Judge Halleck underscored his determination "to show these long-haired ne'er-do-wells that society will not tolerate their conduct" (*Washington Post*, May 21, 1967).

The incidents of arrest and the exuberance with which the laws are discriminatorily enforced are justified, although not explained, by the magnifying judgment of "danger." At a meeting of agents from 74 police departments in Connecticut and New York, Westchester County Sheriff John E. Hoy, "in a dramatic stage whisper," said, "It is a frightening situation, my friends . . . marijuana is creeping up on us."

One assistant district attorney stated that "the problem is staggering." A county executive agreed that "the use of marijuana is vicious," while a school superintendent argued that "marijuana is a plague-like disease, slowly but surely strangling our young people." Harvard freshmen were warned against the "social influences" that surround drugs and one chief of police attributed drug use and social deviance to permissiveness in a slogan which has since become more common (*St. Louis Post-Dispatch*, Aug. 22, 1968).

Bennett Berger has pointed out that the issue of danger is an ideological ploy (*Denver Post*, April 19, 1968) : "The real issue of marijuana is ethical and political, touching the 'core of cultural values.' " *The New York Times* of Jan. 11, 1968, reports "Students and high school and college officials agree that 'drug use has increased sharply since the intensive coverage given to drugs and the Hippies last summer by the mass media.' " It is also supported by other attempts to tie drugs to heresy: *The New York Times* of Nov. 17, 1968, notes a Veterans Administration course for doctors on the Hippies which ties Hippies, drugs, and alienation together and suggests that the search for potential victims might begin in the seventh or eighth grades.

The dynamic relationship between ideology, organization and practice is revealed both in President Johnson's "Message on Crime to Insure Public Safety" (delivered to Congress on February 7, 1968) and in the gradual internationalizing of the persecution. The President recommended "strong new laws," an increase in the number of enforcement agents, and the centralization of federal enforcement machinery. At the same time, the United Nations Economic and Social Council considered a resolution asking that governments "deal effectively with publicity which advocates legalization or tolerance of the non-medical use of cannabis as a harmless drug." The resolution was consistent with President Johnson's plan to have the Federal Government of the United States "maintain worldwide operations . . . to suppress the trade in illicit narcotics and marijuana." The reasons for the international campaign were clarified by a World Health Organization panel's affirmation of its intent to prevent the use or sale of marijuana because it is "a drug of dependence, producing health and social problems." At the same time that scientific researchers at Harvard and Boston University were exonerating the substance, the penalties increased and the efforts to proscribe it reached international proportions. A number of countries, including Laos and Thailand, have barred Hippies, and Mexico has made it difficult for those with long hair and serious eyes to cross its border.

Disobedience

The assumption that society is held together by formal law and authority implies in principle that the habit of obedience must be reinforced. The details of the Hippie culture are, in relation to the grounded culture, disobedient. From that perspective, too, their values and ideology are also explicitly disobedient. The disobedience goes far beyond the forms of social organization and personal presentation to the conventional systems of healing, dietary practice and environmental use. There is virtually no system of authority that is not thrown into question. Methodologically, the situationalism of pornography, guerrilla theater and place conversion is not only profoundly subversive in itself; it turns the grounded culture around. By coating conventional behavioral norms with ridicule and obscenity, by tying radically different meanings to old routines, it challenges our sentiments. By raising the level of our self-consciousness it allows us to become moral in the areas we had allowed to degenerate into habit (apathy or gluttony). When the rock group, the Fugs, sings and dances "Group Grope" or any of their other songs devoted brutally to "love" and "taste," they pin our tender routines to a humiliating obscenity. We can no longer take our behavior and our intentions for granted. The confrontation enables us to disobey or to reconsider or to choose simply by forcing into consciousness the patterns of behavior and belief of which we have become victims. The confrontation is manly because it exposes both sides in an arena of conflict.

When questions are posed in ways that permit us to disengage outselves from their meaning to our lives, we tolerate the questions as a moderate and decent form of dissent. And we congratulate ourselves for our tolerance. But when people refuse to know their place, and, what is worse, our place, and they insist on themselves openly and demand that we re-decide our own lives, we are willing to have them knocked down. Consciousness permits disobedience. As a result, systems threatened from within often begin the work of reassertion by an attack on consciousness and chosen forms of life.

Youth, danger and disobedience define the heresy in terms that activate the host of agencies that, together, com-

prise the control conglomerate. Each agency, wrote Trevor-Roper, was ready: "The engine of persecution was set up before its future victims were legally subject to it." The conglomerate has its target. But it is a potential of the social system as much as it is an actor. Trevor-Roper comments further that:

once we see the persecution of heresy as social intolerance, the intellectual difference between one heresy and another becomes less significant.

And the difference, one might add, between one persecutor and another becomes less significant. Someone it does not matter who tells Mr. Blue (in Tom Paxton's song): "What will it take to whip you into line?"

How have I ended here? The article is an analysis of the institutionalization of persecution and the relationship between the control conglomerate which is the advanced form of official persecution and the Hippies as an alternative culture, the target of control. But an analysis must work within a vision if it is to move beyond analysis into action. The tragedy of America may be that it completed the technology of control before it developed compassion and tolerance. It never learned to tolerate history, and now it is finally capable of ending history by ending the change that political sociologists and undergroups understand. The struggle has always gone on in the mind. Only now, for this society, is it going on in the open among people. Only now is it beginning to shape lives rather than simply shaping individuals. Whether it is too late or not will be worked out in the attempts to transcend the one-dimensionality that Marcuse described. That the alternative culture is here seems difficult to doubt. Whether it becomes revolutionary fast enough to supersede an officialdom bent on its destruction may be an important part of the story of America.

As an exercise in over-estimation, this essay proposes a methodological tool for going from analysis to action in areas which are too easily absorbed by a larger picture but which are at the same time too critical to be viewed outside the context of political action.

The analysis suggests several conclusions:

■ Control usually transcends itself both in its selection of targets and in its organization.

■ At some point in its development, control is readily

institutionalized and finally institutional. The control conglomerate represents a new stage in social organization and is an authentic change-inducing force for social systems.

■ The hallmark of an advanced system of control (and the key to its beginning) is an ideology that unites otherwise highly differing agencies.

■ Persecution and terror go in our society. The Hippies, as a genuine heresy, have engaged official opposition to a growing cultural-social-political tendency. The organization of control has both eliminated countervailing official forces and begun to place all deviance in the category of heresy. This pattern may soon become endemic to the society.

Scapegoats, Villains, and Disasters

Thomas E. Drabek and Enrico L. Quarantelli

Disasters, such as the Montgomery, Alabama fire which killed 26 people in February, often bring out the best in individuals. Ability to endure suffering, desire to help others, and acts of courage and generosity come forth in time of crisis. But disasters can also evoke the worst in persons—a relentless search for scapegoats to blame for destruction and loss of life.

This tendency to seek the cause in a *who*—rather than a *what*—is common after airplane crashes, fires, cave-ins, and other catastrophes not caused naturally. Personalizing blame in this way is not only a standard response, but well in harmony with the moral framework of American society. Sin and crime are, after all, matters of personal guilt, by traditional Western legal and theological definitions.

However, social scientists differ in their explanations of what accounts for this personalizing of blame. This can be shown by consideration of three major disasters—the famed Cocoanut Grove night club fire in Boston which killed 498 persons in 1942; the strange sequence of three airplane crashes within three months at Elizabeth, New Jersey, in 1951-52; and the explosion which killed 81 persons in 1963 at the State Fairgrounds Coliseum in Indianapolis.

Social research on disasters has advanced two explanations for this personalizing of blame:

■ It is basically *irrational,* a form of "scapegoating" in which people can work off their frustrations and anxieties, as well as the feelings of guilt, anger, shock, and horror brought on by the disaster.

■ It is relatively *rational,* animated by a desire for prevention of future occurrences. Thus, personalization will take place only when it seems to be within human power to minimize or avoid such disasters, and when it is felt that punishing "the agents of responsibility" may bring forth the necessary remedial action.

The first approach is fully exemplified in a study conducted after the Cocoanut Grove fire. The second is generally illustrated by an analysis of the reactions to the plane crashes into Elizabeth, New Jersey. Following a brief exposition of these two viewpoints, we will suggest a possible new approach to the assessment of blame by considering a more recent disaster—the 1963 explosion in Indianapolis.

The scapegoating process is explicitly expounded by Helen Rank Veltford and George E. Lee in their study of the public reactions to the Cocoanut Grove tragedy. *(The Journal of Abnormal and Social Psychology,* April, 1943) The fire on November 28, 1942, was minor, being extinguished in less than 20 minutes. However, patrons trying to get out found two emergency doors unusable. Also, the major exit, a revolving door, was soon jammed with people. Many of the nearly 500 killed were trapped inside the club and died not only of burns but also of suffocation.

The reaction to this catastrophe was immediate and sharp. According to Veltford and Lee, the horror of the event gave rise to an outcry for avenging the victims and finding and punishing those responsible. Thus, there began a search not primarily for *what* had caused the tragedy, but simply *who* was responsible for it.

Veltford and Lee believe that the public fixing of blame primarily reflected an unconscious effort to relieve blocked emotional reactions or frustrations about what had occurred. There was no immediate public attack on Boston's lax and insufficient laws. Instead, members of the City Council and public officials were blamed for failure to pass more stringent legislation or to enforce existing statutes. After a month of investigation, the county grand jury indicted 10 men.

This personalization is viewed by Veltford and Lee as essential to scapegoating:

> The immediate and desired objective of the scapegoaters was to relieve their feelings of frustration, of fear, of hostility, of guilt, by legally fixing the responsibility on the guilty so that they might be punished.

Hence, the attempt to relieve unconscious guilt feelings resulted in irrational behavior; the selection of a series of scapegoats rather than demand for stricter and better laws.

Scapegoats and Bigwigs

However, the researchers point out that certain logical candidates were not chosen as scapegoats. For example, no blame was attached to the 16-year-old employee who actually started the fire by striking a match for light while replacing a missing bulb. Why not? According to Veltford and Lee it was because the public admired his straightforward voluntary admission of fault, because of his youth, and the fact that his mother was seriously ill. His teachers testified he was a model young man from an impoverished family. Of such things scapegoats are not made. The prankster who had presumably removed the bulb was not blamed either, because nobody knew who he was and because he was certainly not the direct cause of the fire, much less the deaths.

Those seeking someone to blame had "more satisfying" scapegoats to relieve their guilt feelings. Ten prominent persons and officials, including the owners of the club and the Boston Building Commissioner, were indicted and charged with a variety of offenses: conspiracy to violate building codes, failure to enforce fire laws, failure to report violations of the building laws, and so forth. Collectively they were "the rascals, for among certain elements of the public there is a deep-rooted, perhaps unrecognized latent hostility toward all political authority, toward those 'higher up.'" All accumulated past hostilities against "political bigwigs" and "money czars" could be focused on the two classes of scapegoats, owners and public officials: ". . . Elements of the public may have found opportunity to *enhance* their own self-conceived prestige; they could, by scapegoating, feel, momentarily, superior to these so-called 'higher ups.'"

Finally, as Martha Wolfenstein has documented in a review of the disaster literature, people find it difficult to blame the dead. It was the panic of the Cocoanut Grove victims that led to the blocked exit and a fatal crush—but no one blamed them for it. Wolfenstein found, in fact, that in a 1955 French race track disaster, a driver who crashed into the spectators was viewed as a savior rather than an "agent of destruction" because he saved the lives of other drivers by avoiding collisions. She concludes that an individual who survives disaster feels guilty for not having died himself. "Probably the more latent hostility there is present in an individual the greater will be his need to blame either himself or others for destructive happenings."

From this first perspective then, attribution of blame following disaster is typical and is motivated by unconscious guilt and related feelings. Such motivations produce a variety of irrational behaviors among which scapegoating is common. "Innocent" persons are selected on the basis of latent hostilities from a guilt-ridden populace.

In sharp contrast is the position advanced by Rue Bucher. (*American Journal of Sociology,* March, 1957) She analyzed reactions of residents of Elizabeth, New Jersey, in 1951-52 to three airplane crashes within a three-month period. Rather than being a *common feature* of disasters, Bucher suggests that individuals will be blamed only when *certain specific* conditions are present:

■ The situation must be defined sufficiently to assess responsibility. This occurs only when conventional explanations are not available. For example, in present day Western society, probably no person will be assigned direct responsibility for destruction caused by tornadoes, floods, and hurricanes. Damage and deaths from such events can be conventionally accounted for in non-personal and naturalistic terms.

■ ". . . Those who blame the agents of responsibility are convinced that the agents will not of their own volition take action which will remedy the situation."

■ ". . . Those responsible must be perceived as violating moral standards, as standing in opposition to basic values."

Bucher believes the primary motive is a desire to insure that it does not happen again. As a consequence, the attribution of responsibility tends to be shifted upward in the hierarchy of authority. Persons who may have had a direct hand in the catastrophe, such as the airline pilots, are not blamed. Bucher says that responsibility is ". . . laid where people thought the power resided to alleviate the conditions underlying the crashes. It was not instrumentality in causing the crashes which determined responsibility but ability to do something to prevent their recurrence. The problem was who had control over these conditions and who had the power to see that they were corrected."

In Elizabeth, specific blame was not placed—only a generalized "they" was held responsible for failure to take action. Bucher attributes this to the limited knowledge her lower and middle class respondents had about airlines, airports, and the industries and agencies that affect them.

From this perspective then, assessment of responsibility and personal blame has at least some subjective rationality. The chief desire is to prevent recurrence. Only when natural explanations are not enough will persons be blamed. If it is felt that appropriate action will not be taken by the "agents of responsibility," then blame will be assigned to those believed to have the power to change existing conditions. There are no buckshot accusations; specific names and charges depend on knowledge of persons and groups.

Actually, differences between the two viewpoints described above are primarily differences of interpretation of human behavior after disasters. There is a close parallel in the gross descriptions of that behavior. However, a study made by the authors of this article after the Indianapolis Coliseum explosion indicates the possibilities of a third explanation—one that places blame assessment into a much broader framework.

The Indianapolis Coliseum Explosion

At 11:06 p.m., on October 31, 1963, a performance of the "Holiday on Ice" show at the Indianapolis Coliseum was abruptly ended by a violent blast. Fifty-four persons were killed immediately, nearly 400 were injured. Twenty-seven of the injured died later, raising the final death count to 81, the largest toll in any Indiana disaster.

Press, radio, and television personnel went into action immediately. Initial coverage was on the rescue operations, identification of victims, and descriptions. But attention quickly focused on the cause and the responsibility. When liquid propane gas tanks found in the rubble were suspected of causing the explosion, the media quickly pressed forward on this trail.

Interest intensified throughout the night. The three major newspapers carried these headlines on their first editions after the disaster: "FIRE CHIEF RAPS GAS TANK USAGE IN THE COLISEUM"; "PROBE PRESSED BY BLAST THAT KILLED HERE"; "65 KILLED, HUNDREDS HURT IN COLISEUM GAS EXPLOSION." On November 1 the Marion County prosecutor requested the grand jury to begin an immediate investigation.

The spotlight was kept relentlessly focused on possible responsibility. For instance, the evening following the explosion the state fire marshal was pressed to admit in a televised interview that apparently no one had applied for or obtained the necessary permit to use liquid gas inside the Coliseum.

Formal investigations were conducted by at least nine different organizations. They included: the Indianapolis fire department, the Indianapolis police department, the state police, the Marion County sheriff's office, the State Administrative Building Council, the state fire marshal, the county coroner's office, and the company insuring the State Fair Board and the Indiana Coliseum Corporation. Mostly they concentrated on the physical cause of the explosion. This was a response at least in part to inquiries by the mass media trying to fix personal responsibility.

The grand jury completed its investigation in early December after five weeks of inquiry during which repeated trips to the scene of the disaster were made, and thirty-two witnesses were questioned. LP gas, illegally stored inside the Coliseum, was judged to have caused the explosion. Seven persons were indicted—three officials of the firm supplying the tanks, the general manager and the concession manager of the Indiana Coliseum Corporation, the state fire marshal, and the Indianapolis fire chief.

These events can effectively be interpreted within the framework suggested by Bucher. The illegal presence of the five LP gas tanks, and the quick identification by the media of the public and private officials who had been involved in their installation lent plausibility to a personal and non-naturalistic explanation of the explosion.

There were two additional elements. First, newspaper accounts suggested that previous warnings had not brought action. For instance, *The Indianapolis Star* reported that a check of official records indicated the fire marshal's office had been warned of leaking propane gas in the Coliseum on September 3, 1959. They stopped its use that day, but the next day inspectors were again notified of leaking LP gas at the Coliseum. This resulted in a declaration by the chief inspector from the fire marshal's office that he did not have an adequate staff to enforce fire regulations properly. Representatives from the Coliseum countered that LP gas tanks had been openly used for 10 years, but no one had ever told them they needed a permit. Hence, it was implied that the "agents of responsibility" could not be trusted to correct conditions.

It was even indicated that criticism by the grand jury would not bring about any change. The governor openly defended his fire marshal. He alleged that the grand jury had used public officials as "scapegoats," and added that the fire marshal had generally done a good job and would remain in office.

Of course, from a sociological viewpoint the issue is not whether the charges were true, but whether—and to what extent—they were made public and how people viewed them. It is, after all, an old axiom in sociology that "if a situation is defined as real, it is real insofar as consequences are concerned." Press reports clearly implied that some of those in power might not make changes necessary to prevent similar accidents in the future.

Further, words used in the indictments implied that the "agents of responsibility" were socially irresponsible if not immoral. The grand jury felt that some control over future uses of LP gas was needed to ". . . guarantee that the desire for profit on the part of a few will never again relegate the matter of public safety to a point of reckless indifference." The report further stated that "the fire marshal was considered (political) patronage, and he acted the part."

Thus, all of the elements suggested by Bucher as being necessary for blame were present.

Also, blame was focused high in the authority structures. Indictments were directed at the fire chief, not the city fire inspectors; the state fire marshal, not his agents; top executives of the firm supplying the tanks, not the individuals who actually installed them; and the executives of the Coliseum Corporation, not the concessionaires who used the tanks.

Thus, the facts seem to fit the Bucher interpretation. But could not these same facts be made to support the scapegoating theory? Those indicted for the Cocoanut Grove fire were also of high status. Could not those indicted as a result of the Coliseum explosion have really been selected because of irrational latent hostilities against "big shots"?

Changes, Not Charges

Closer reading of the grand jury report, however, renders such an interpretation improbable. Consistently there is reference to the need for changes in existing law, including on-site and possibly stand-by inspection during actual performances. The jury also labeled the permit system "archaic and useless," and wanted the entire state fire marshal's office reorganized "from top to bottom." Finally, it urged legislation to make violation of regulations by the fire marshal a crime.

Thus the prime interest of the grand jury was apparently for changes in organizations and laws to prevent similar disasters.

But in that case why did it not take specific steps to bring about such changes? Why did it merely indict persons? As we see it, personal blame assignment in American society cannot be avoided; it is rooted in the institutional framework. Investigative agencies are bound by laws that force them "to point the finger" only at persons who are potentially legally prosecutable. The grand jury might think the system to blame; but under the law it could only bring legal charges against human beings. Only individuals can be indicted and brought to trial—not social structures.

This was the situation at Indianapolis. There was some awareness that the problem touched the very roots of the system; but its solution was approached in the usual and almost necessary way. Only the traditional legal processes (i.e., a grand jury, indictments, trials and so forth) were utilized. The machinery for coping with these situations was not geared toward changing the social structure. The political-legal processes could only condemn individuals and ask for their punishment. The verbal assault in the mass media probably also served as another pressure on the grand jury to indict persons—and thereby weaken the call for other action.

The rationale is that punishment of the "guilty" deters others from committing similar acts. However, many sociologists suggest that this whole orientation with its focus on personal "guilt" and "innocence" may actually serve to delay necessary changes by concentrating on symptoms rather than causes. Paul B. Horton and Gerald R. Leslie note, for instance, that: "To many people, 'doing something' about a social problem means finding and punishing the 'bad' people." The consequence is that "punishing the 'bad' people, . . . will have very little permanent effect upon the problem." It may act to hinder its solution.

The way blame was fixed in Indianapolis illustrates this.

A basic structural element—the inspection procedure—was obviously inadequate. Only 12 investigators were expected to provide inspection for the entire state of Indiana. One had to cover 4,000 square miles. They only had power to issue impotent "cease and desist" orders. Both the fire marshal and the state inspectors were political appointees; no objective selection procedures existed for either position. Yet by blaming individuals, attention was taken away from all of this.

We believe that putting other persons into the same position could have made little difference. The fire marshal's staff, for instance, was so inadequate both in quantity and quality that meaningful preventive action by any fire marshal was impossible. Similarly, economic factors were alleged to have been responsible for inadequate safety training for the employees who installed or used the LP tanks.

In essence we are saying that the entire procedure used to remedy the conditions that caused the disaster may well be questioned. As Robert K. Merton and Robert A. Nesbit have pointed out, social problems may not always be recognized as such by those most intimately involved. Sociologists cannot restrict themselves to those social conditions that a majority of laymen regard as undesirable. The majority is not always knowledgeable enough to be a good judge of what is undesirable. Not all "processes of society inimical to the values of men are recognized as such by them."

Not only does individual blame draw attention from more fundamental causes, but it might actually give the illusion that corrective action of some sort is being taken. A spotlighting by the mass media may give the appearance of action and actually drain off the energy and time that might have led to action. As Merton and Paul F. Lazarsfeld have noted, greater information and publicity can actually create civic apathy. Public attention focused on punishment does not encourage action to correct structural flaws. In the example of the Indianapolis Coliseum, the inadequate inspection procedure remained submerged, hidden by the search for the guilty parties.

It is of more than passing interest that in another major disaster studied by the Disaster Research Center the absence of personal blame was accompanied by relatively rapid and major structural changes. On November 23, 1963, a nursing home fire in Ohio resulted in the death of 63 patients. Several investigations revealed many of the same, if not even greater, general weaknesses in the fire inspection procedures found in Indiana. However, there was little time spent looking for people to "blame" for the tragedy. A Grand Jury failed to indict anyone; no persons or officials were held responsible; and everyone connected with the event was exonerated. Yet within a few months, major and stringent new rules and regulations were put into effect throughout the state. Nursing homes not meeting the new standards were forced to close. Had this event not occurred, it is doubtful that new standards would have been enacted.

By contrast, in Indiana, more than three years after the disaster, not even personal blame had been settled. In early 1967 all legal cases were still pending except those against the owner and the general manager of the firm that supplied the tanks. The former had been found not guilty; the charge against the latter had been reduced from involuntary manslaughter to assault and battery, and he had

been fined $500. The charge against the Indianapolis fire chief had been dismissed quite early. The other four persons charged still remained under indictment.

As for any structural changes, even less had occurred. Some of the procedures—nothing substantial—had been altered in the fire marshal's office. In 1966, a seven-man bipartisan Fire Prevention Commission with supervisory power over the office had been established, but no major internal reorganization had occurred. For a time, fewer people attended events at the reopened Coliseum; but within a year, capacity and standing room audiences were back for some shows. Except for those most directly involved, the community had returned to its pre-disaster patterns.

The Impact of Disaster

It would be foolish to argue that personal blame assignment always prevents structural changes. There is indeed historical evidence to suggest that some disastrous events have an impact. For example, the first international code of maritime safety laws came in 1914, two years after the sinking of the *Titanic;* the latest in 1960, four years after the loss of the *Andrea Doria.* In the famous Triangle Shirtwaist factory fire in New York City (March 28, 1911), 145 workers were killed, and the owners were indicted for manslaughter; and yet within months new laws were passed, giving fire inspectors increased powers, establishing a division of fire prevention, and forcing changes in rules regarding fire prevention, drills, alarm systems, sprinklers, and fire escapes.

Even in Boston, three years after the Cocoanut Grove fire it could be written: "Under the impetus given by the worst fire in the city's history, the state is on its way to a system of building and inspecting regulations that may become a model." How much real change resulted and how much the basic structural flaws were affected, are of course matters that would have to be more fully studied. Yet these examples certainly suggest that punishment of "guilty individuals" *per se* does not automatically prevent some structural changes.

Personalizing fault—blaming our problems on the inadequacies or guilt of individuals rather than on systems or institutions—is not confined to disasters. Something akin to it has been observed in every aspect of American life from the content of movies dealing with social problems to the assumptions being made in the present day "war on poverty." Thus Herbert Gans has noted of certain kinds of contemporary films:

> Psychological explanations have replaced moral ones, but the possibility that delinquency, corruption and even mental illness reside in the social system is not considered, and the resolution of the problem is still left to a hero assisted by the everpresent *deus ex machina.*

S. A. Weinstock, on the approach to poverty problems: The underlying assumption here again is that poverty, social and economic deprivation, results from an inadequacy of the personality rather than an inadequacy in the socio-economic system. . . . Only measures aiming at individual rehabilitation . . . are encouraged, while measures designed to modify the *structure* of the economy . . . are rejected.

On race riots, Stanley Liberson and Arnold Silverman:

Accounts . . . attributing riots to communist influence, hoodlums, or rabblerousers . . . participants of this type are probably available in almost any community. What interests us is the community failure to see the . . . institutional malfunctioning or a racial difficulty which is not—and perhaps cannot—be met by existing social institutions.

As with blame after disasters, here too the fault-finding seems rooted in the very fabric of American society. Here also it distracts attention from structural flaws. If the individual is the source of all difficulties, why raise questions about the society?

Apparently it is not only in totalitarian societies that a "cult of personality" serves to protect existing structures, and keeps them from making rapid changes to meet important cultural values and goals—even if those changes might be vital to the welfare of the society.

Fall Guys in the Florentine Flood

Stephen P. Koff

All sorts of messages are painted or chalked on the walls of Florence. They include pro-Mao slogans, calls for a return to monarchy, accusations that President Johnson is a Hitler because of the war in Vietnam, and love notes to the latest rock 'n' roll favorite. After the tragic flood of Nov. 4, 1966, which caused enormous damage to the city, another phrase appeared: "The flood equals negligence equals crime." This equation is now found on the sides of buildings, in road tunnels, and on monuments. Many and perhaps most of the people of Florence, bitter toward their public authorities, agree with it.

The present-day Florentine is an intensely proud man who strongly identifies with the cultural riches of his historic Renaissance city. Even working-class political activists, who rarely or never visit a gallery or church, assume a certain air of superiority in conversation with foreigners, and drop the names of Dante, Michelangelo, Giotto, Botticelli, and others equally well-known in Florentine history.

The Florentine's pride in his cultural heritage carries over to his political culture. The glories of the Florentine Republic and the works of Machiavelli, Guicciardini, and other famous political writers still have special meaning for Florentine high-school students. One German scholar wrote: "Many circumstances combined to make Florence the center of a higher culture, of a more refined civilization, of greater literary and artistic activity. From the start a contribution was made by republican sentiment, and this gained great impetus as the capital of Tuscany [Florence], growing into one of the major Italian powers, was compelled to be alert to the threatening ambitions of the princes of both north and south. Without a sense of public duty, without political discipline, without material and cultural riches, this independent state would have had to succumb to the violence of the period."

Clearly, the concept of public duty is an important part of the political heritage of Florence. Republican sentiment and political discipline have been translated into ideas of local self-government—that is, rule by the citizens for the citizens. The local and national governments' handling of last November's cataclysmic flood has thus been one of the most hotly discussed aspects of the disaster.

November 4 was a national holiday. The nation was celebrating the forty-eighth anniversary of the end of World War I for Italy. In spite of heavy rains that swelled the Arno River on November 3, reviewing stands and bunting were put up around the city to prepare for the military parades scheduled for the following day. The people of Florence went to bed on November 3 totally unprepared for the flood that would engulf their city the next morning.

The cold statistics of the loss tell a great deal of the story. When the Arno rampaged over its banks, 5,000 families were left homeless, and many other families returned to homes unfit for habitation. The number of jobless at one point exceeded 50,000. More than half of the factories in the city and in the province were flooded. Eighty percent of the hotels in the city were forced to close. An even larger percentage of the restaurants were damaged. More than 6,000 stores were devasted. The famed artisan industry, centered in two of the sections most badly hit by the flood waters, took heavy losses. Several hospitals were isolated and lost valuable equipment. Churches, galleries, libraries, and parts of the University of Florence were hit, and several remain partially closed. Some 120 buses and more than 20,000 automobiles were destroyed. This recital can be considered a *short* list of damages. No one in a position of authority has been so foolhardy as to attempt a definitive assessment of the total cost of the disaster.

DISBELIEF, THEN ANGER

On that holiday morning, many Florentines had the frightening experience of being awakened by water rushing into their bedrooms. Others awoke from their sleep to the strange sounds of floating automobiles banging against one another or against buildings. The first reaction of many Florentines was disbelief.

Disbelief was quickly followed by anger—anger fired by the anguish of devastating personal losses. In Dante's day, bells on churches and other towers tolled to warn the people of invaders and other dangers. Couldn't the bells have been used, along with more sophisticated modern means like loudspeakers on cars, so evident during a recent election campaign?

And it is clear that, the night before the flood, a few people were warned about the danger. This fact contributed greatly to hardening the Florentines' attitudes toward their public authorities. The shopkeepers on the famed old Ponte Vecchio were warned by a night watchman, as seemed natural. The warning enabled them to save a good part of their valuable stocks. But why weren't others warned, too?

Widespread anger was provoked by reports that workers at the hydroelectric plants on the river outside the city had telephoned relatives and fellow employees in the city to alert them. Many Florentines demanded to know why the officers of the nationalized electric industry didn't follow suit and try to contact more people. If they couldn't give a general alert, why couldn't they at least notify the heads of the famed national library and the churches and museums situated near the river? Seemingly even more incredible was the fact that hospitals, firehouses, and public-record offices received no warning. Yet the workers at the dams said that they had notified the public authorities in Florence of the danger before midnight. Why didn't the city officials warn the people?

Now, it is true that, eight to ten hours before water struck the city, Florence's public officials knew that there was danger. But they had no idea of the enormousness of the threat. The Prefect, the representative of the national government to the local level, was the man responsible for sounding the general alarm. He was told of the danger. So was the Mayor, who went to his office in the city hall. But apparently neither made any effort to spread the warning.

The unofficial reason given for their not alerting the citizens was that such a warning might have caused panic and a loss of life. Florence, with a population of 250,000, is surrounded by hills. Many of its exits were blocked by the overflowing river. Hence a mass exodus by the available roads might have resulted in serious accidents and exposed those fleeing to the danger of drowning in traffic jams. The relatively small number of deaths (only 37) has been cited in support of the argument that, although more property might have been saved if a warning had been given, many more lives would probably have been lost.

Few Florentines fully accept this argument. Acknowledging that panic was a threat, they wonder why all emergency services were not put on a standby alert. If hospitals and fire stations had been prepared, these Florentines point out, they could probably have operated much more efficiently in the crisis.

After the flood waters receded on the morning of November 5, the stunned and bewildered Florentines began to take stock of their losses. One thing immediately seemed clear to them. They believed that they would have to carry out the salvage operation through their own efforts and that they would be foolish to count on massive government assistance. The solidarity and cooperation that flourished among the citizens reflected not only a positive attitude toward one another and toward their city, but also a common acceptance of the idea that public authorities could not be depended upon for aid.

The authorities did help, though. The national government sent military helicopters, which rescued people marooned on roofs; huge searchlights, which lighted areas that had lacked electricity for weeks; trucks and bulldozers, which helped with the heavy work or moved overturned cars and tree trunks; and thousands of foot soldiers, who worked in knee-deep, oil-stained mud. But the Florentines remained unimpressed. Their fundamental lack of faith in the authorities was reinforced by the evident lack of coordination in these public efforts (Florence had no civil-defense plan).

BITTERNESS TOWARD BUREAUCRACY

The poor image of the government was made worse by a November 4 telecast on the national network. As the flood waters still whirled destructively, a government news-commentator went on the air and declared that conditions in Florence were returning to normal.

In a few days, it became clear that the early accounts of the tragedy that had reached the United States, England, and the rest of Europe were more accurate than those circulated in Italy. Florentines returning to the city on

November 4 reported that workers manning the booths on the *autostrada* gave them no warning about conditions in the city. People traveling by train had a similar experience: They reached the city only to find that they were isolated in the station.

One official act, which under less trying circumstances might have elicited a favorable reaction among the populace, caused a minor storm. On Sunday, November 6, Giuseppe Saragat, the President of the Republic, visited Florence. As he rode through the most devasted areas, he was visibly shaken by what he saw. But he made a bad mistake. On encountering some children in the Santa Croce area, a working-class zone severely damaged by the flood, he handed out chocolates. Shouting curses and epithets, adults took the candies and hurled them back at the President. They shouted that they needed help, not chocolates.

Evidently the authorities in Rome had no idea of the gravity of the situation. Twice President Saragat tried to telephone Prime Minister Moro in Rome. Prime Minister Moro could not be reached. When this became known, the Florentines, with knowing glances, observed that the incident was typical. That the President spoke to the Minister of the Interior twice and alerted *him* to the need for massive aid seemed to be disregarded.

In their handling of the crisis, the local authorities were considered just as inadequate. The Mayor was a man without a solid administrative background—he had been chosen mainly because he had few political enemies. In fact, he was better known as an art historian and as an author of guidebooks than as a civic leader. The Mayor made the proper representations to the national government and gave out definitive statements to the press. He met with visiting firemen from all over the world, such as Massachusetts Senator Ted Kennedy and Governor John A. Volpe. But the population seemed to feel that, though he was trying his best, it was not good enough.

It was the Prefect, however, who emerged as the chief villain. One respected Communist Senator even brought involuntary-manslaughter charges against him. This elicited little open support for the Prefect, and some people with long anti-Communist records openly agreed with the charge. Legal action is still pending.

As the representative of the national government, the Prefect was considered (1) an outsider and (2) the agent of a governmental bureaucracy generally acknowledged to be inefficient and ineffectual. Ever since the unification of Italy one hundred years ago, local mistrust of the national government has been a serious political problem. The Fascist regime increased central control over the local governments. But the post-World War II era brought a sharp reaction. The Constitution of the Republic of Italy, written in 1946, specifically called for devolution of authority to regional units of government. This would have dealt the prefectural system a severe blow. As a result of political pressures, however, the constitutional provision calling for the creation of 19 regions has been implemented in only five cases. The handling of the Florentine flood strengthened the cause of those who called for setting up regional governments that, they argued, would be closer to the people.

Soon after the flood, there began a judicial inquiry into the role played by the dams along the Arno. The dams had been opened because there was fear that they might burst. The question being investigated was how much the opening of the dams contributed to the force of the water traveling toward Florence and also to the hugh waves that increased the destructiveness of the water. The Florentines feel that if the technicians at the dam were negligent, they should be prosecuted. On the other hand, there is some sentiment that punishing a few workmen and engineers would whitewash the real culprits—the higher government officials.

Even the historic visit of Pope Paul to Florence on Christmas Eve became associated with the public's attitude toward their officials. As the Pope acclaimed the efforts of the local public authorities, there was a stirring in the crowd. Some observers claim they even heard boos. Many felt that the Pope did not recognize that the Florentines themselves, not the government officials, deserved credit for Florence's rapid recovery. Had John XXIII still been Pope, some declared, he would not have waited until Christmas Eve to come and he would not have applauded the officials. He would have come to Florence the day after the flood and worked in the mud.

Another source of general complaint after the flood was the handling of public information. Wild rumors about epidemics and about the wholesale collapse of buildings began to circulate. To allay people's fears, the authorities placed public notices in the newspapers. But many flood victims failed to see them because they could not spend nine cents for a newspaper when nine cents would buy half a box of pasta. Signs were also put up on the sides of buildings. This was fine in the areas not hit by the flood waters, but walls in the damaged zones were still wet and muddy and the notices soon became illegible. People asked why centers of information had not been opened and why loudspeakers on cars had not been used.

In some areas, a confused system of distributing food and clothing in the first few days after the flood also caused severe hardship. It was in protest against this situation that a priest and a Communist led a march against city hall. There definitely was some collaboration between clerics and Communists in denouncing the government, and even grudging respect for each other's efforts.

The Florentines were proud that, in spite of the enormousness of the dislocation, there was little looting or black-market activity. In the very few instances observed, the police (employees of the national government in Italy) and the soldiers standing guard cracked down severely. Still, the people of Santa Croce argued that in their beleaguered zone of the city, they themselves forestalled such activities. For example, a station wagon filled with containers of drinking water, scarce at that time, reportedly came to the Santa Croce area soon after the flood. The owner of the car apparently wanted to sell the water. The local residents claim that some of their number turned over the car, rolled it into deep mud, then deposited it next to cars battered by the flood waters.

Throughout the crisis, the Florentines never really lost their composure and self-assurance. They would point with pride to the Ponte Vecchio, battered by the flood waters but still standing. It had been the only bridge not destroyed by the Germans during the Nazi occupation and had thus become a symbol of the Resistance in wartime. When the flood struck, the Ponte Vecchio once again became a symbol of resistance—the resistance of people who fully believed that their city would recover from the disaster through their own efforts, without reliance on the public sector of the nation.

We live in an age of violence. Nations are locked in conflict while within countries religious and political battles rage and violent crimes increase dramatically. The extent of conflict and violence and the consequences for society make this an urgent topic for research by social scientists. Were conflict simply a means of resolving ideological or territorial differences, understanding and controlling it would be difficult, but foreseeable. However, at an individual level, conflict seems to serve many complicated needs such as those for power, high self-esteem and prestige. Moreover, such needs are not always apparent even to participants. This factor introduces a great deal of complexity into the study of violence and conflict.

How do we approach the investigation of violence, conflict and conflict resolution? Research in this area employs all of the methodologies known to social science and faces all the problems inherent in attempting to comprehend multiple and interacting forces. Basically, the problems are similar whether the object of study is an individual, a group or a nation. Many social scientists have attempted to generalize from the experimental reactions of individuals or small groups to the behavior of societies. Whether this is justifiable or not remains an unanswered but crucially important question. In any case, the social turmoil of recent years has caused many social scientists to come to the conclusion that they must attempt to apply current knowledge, however imperfect, to the conflict and violence endemic in society. Criticism is leveled at the social scientist from both sides: on the one hand, he is accused of pursuing abstract and esoteric research while the society collapses around him; on the other, he is attacked for meddling in issues which many believe should be dealt with through political or judicial means. In this vein, Vice-President Agnew has issued a stinging attack on psychologists for attempting to control and shape behavior.

Part Six

Violence, Conflict, and Conflict Resolution

opposing and being opposed

When the social scientist does become a social activist, he must decide whether his proposals will be helpful or whether they will only exacerbate an already bad situation. It is possible, for example, that detailing psychological causes for an event such as the My Lai massacres may cause people to accept the inevitability of such occurrences and, for better or for worse, deemphasize and deny individual responsibility for them.

Finally, there has been little indication that those in positions of power will heed the findings and recommendations of social science. The recent bombing of North Vietnam provides a case in point. A great deal of money was spent after World War II on a survey of the effects of strategic bombing on morale and the will to continue fighting. The results generally indicated that bombing did not destroy morale but, conversely, often strengthened the will to resist. Although these data were readily available to planners of the Vietnam War, they were ignored in favor of a view that bombing would quickly bring North Vietnam to the negotiating table. As the Pentagon Papers show, this view was held for several years in the face of ever-mounting, disconfirming evidence.

The essays in this Part are examples of the kinds of investigations and analyses of conflict and violence undertaken by social scientists. In the first essay, James Short and Fred Strodtbeck discuss the causes of conflict among juvenile gangs. They studied several gangs intensively for a period of years. As they show, conflict is seldom based on simple disagreements over rights or territory or on retribution for real or imagined wrongs. Conflict has multiple causes and serves the psychological needs of individual members and of the group as a whole. Attempts to gain power and status and arguments over leadership often precipitate conflict. Combat can also serve to reaffirm the masculinity and self-esteem of gang members. The report can serve as a warning to those who seek a simple cause for every event and who tend to accept the first reasonable explanation for complex happenings.

The second essay describes one of the most widely seen conflicts in recent years—the riots surrounding the 1968 Democratic National Convention in Chicago, seen by millions on national television. The brutality and uncontrolled violence witnessed by so many resulted in widespread demands for an investigation into the causes of the riot and the exact events which transpired. The analysis reprinted here is an excerpt from the Walker Commission report; it shows how complex and difficult it is to isolate the precipitating factors in a violent confrontation. The reports of witnesses to the same event differed dramatically. The report also shows how conflict, once initiated, tends to polarize and dehumanize those involved and can easily escalate out of control.

Currently, the response to national tragedy seems to be the appointment of an investigative commission to seek out the "truth," to name the guilty, and to make recommendations for change and reform. Since 1963 we have had commissions to investigate political assassinations, race riots, violence, pornography and drugs. Much of the motivation behind the naming of a commission seems highly similar to the disaster scapegoating described by Drabeck and Quarantelli, in Part Five, where the reaction to a disaster was to attempt to fix blame on an individual in order to be able to relax and avoid worry about recurrences. Once a scapegoat has been found and punished, people can feel more secure. Commissions appear to be the best forum for the presentation of relevant data and recommendations from social science. However, the effects of these commissions on policy and official actions have been minimal. Jerome Skolnick, in this Part, provides a rare insider's look at the workings of a commission.

John R. Raser discusses another aspect of conflict—the individual's response to stress. Reasoning and performance are impaired when individuals are subjected to prolonged or extreme stress. Raser argues that in an era when individuals have control over devastating nuclear weapons, a panic response to stress could trigger a nuclear conflict despite the so-called fail-safe devices. He feels that the weaknesses of the human component of the arms systems have been seriously underestimated.

If Raser's fears about inadvertent atomic war are correct, the psychological proposals for reducing international tension by Muzafer Sherif and Milton Rosenberg assume additional importance. Sherif bases his proposals on research done on conflict between small groups. His research nicely illustrates the development of hostility and prejudice between groups and scapegoating in the event of failure to reach goals. Sherif sees the major route to conflict reduction as being through opposing groups working together toward superordinate goals. This is the same strategy which seems to be most effective in reducing prejudice *within* a society. Again, as in the case of prejudice, the failure to achieve a superordinate goal can lead to increased hostility.

Rosenberg applies psychological theories of individual attitude change to the problem of international distrust. He argues that both the instrumental learning model of attitude change and the consistency theories of cognition can be fruitfully employed as means of understanding and influencing national policy. He feels that such concepts as credibility, rewards and role-playing can have an impact on the attitudes of national leaders. He also contends that accentuating existing inconsistencies in leaders' belief systems as well as creating inconsistencies can result in real changes in attitudes and feelings.

To date, the influence of social science research on the control of violence and conflict and on international policies has been minimal. However, the continued failure of old and simplistic solutions to complex problems may motivate policy-makers to examine and test the data and recommendations of social psychology. In the meantime, it is encouraging to note that a sizable body of solid research and theory is accumulating.

Why Gangs Fight

James F. Short, Jr. and Fred L. Strodtbeck

Big Jake, leader of the Potentates, had been "cooling it" over the fall and winter. However Guy, leader of the Vice Kings, with whom the Potentates were often at war, warned: "Better watch Big Jake—he had to do *something*." Why? "He's *got* to build that rep again. He's been gone— now he's got to show everybody he's *back!*"

    —report from a director of detached workers with juvenile gangs

Like Big Jake, Duke, of the King Rattlers, had also been in jail. Before his internment he had been known for his self-possession—for being a "cool" leader. Although a capable and active fighter when he thought it necessary, he never lost his head and was very effective in negotiation, conciliation, and control. When he came out of jail his leadership and his personal future were threatened and uncertain, and he became belligerent, aggressive, and apparently reckless— with the approval of his gang. Once things settled down for him, however, he reverted to the cool behavior that had made him such an effective leader.

As with leaders of nations, the qualities that raise boys to the tops of juvenile gangs are not necessarily those that best qualify them to stay there, or to rule. "A good suitor may not make a good husband, or a good campaigner a good president." Moreover gangs, though they may admire the fighting campaigner, are often more difficult to control than nations; members who feel abused can sometimes simply drop out, as citizens cannot.

ON TO GLORY

These restrictions, however, do not limit fighting between gangs. Here a leader can work off his aggressions, show off his fighting prowess, and win prestige and popularity with his gang, making his position more secure. As with nations, tyrannizing outsiders is always more acceptable. A despot is someone who abuses his own people; if he attacks and tyrannizes other groups, he is a great and victorious leader, leading enthusiastic followers on to glory.

Juvenile gang leaders invest a great deal in their fighting reputations. Leadership and delinquency must therefore go together. In nearly all gangs we studied, over a three year period, we found that skill in fighting was highly valued, whether or not the gang itself had a fighting "rep." A fight often occurred because a gang, or its leaders, simply could not tolerate a real or implied threat to whatever reputation they had.

Some gangs are definitely "conflict oriented." Fighting is a major and necessary activity for them and a means of acquiring respect, admiration, and prestige within them. They must and do fight often. They have a heavy investment in—and therefore motivation toward—combat. Their leadership, reputation, and status are under constant challenge—anytime they falter some other gang will try to make them fall. They must be prepared for defense—indeed, they believe they must attack from time to time before others attack them, and to remind possible enemies to beware. "We are the mighty Vice Kings!" a leader will shout in challenge—much as Beowulf, using other names, might have done. The very titles and roles they create for themselves reflect the warlike stance—"war counselor," "armorer." These offices need not be clearly or formally defined or even performed; but they are recognized and given deference, and competition for them is fierce.

"Conflict" of course need not always involve major war—the primary purpose of battle is to prove oneself, not to capture anything. The kind of guerilla combat such gangs engage in was well illustrated in the following abstract of a detached worker's incident report:

"I was sitting talking to the Knights, re-emphasizing my stand on guns, because they told me they had collected quite a few and were waiting for the Vice Kings to start trouble. I told them flatly that it was better that I got the gun than the police. They repeated that they were tired of running from the Vice Kings and that if they gave them trouble they were fighting back.

"I looked out of the car and noticed two Vice Kings and two girls walking down the street. William then turned around and made the observation that there were about fifteen or twenty Vice Kings across the street in the alley, wandering up the street in ones or twos.

"The Vice Kings encountered Commando (the leader) Jones, and a couple of other Knights coming around the corner. The Vice Kings yelled across to Commando and his boys, and Commando yelled back. I got out to cool Commando down, since he was halfway across the street daring them to do something. I grabbed him and began to pull him back.

"But the Vice Kings were in a rage, and three came across the street yelling that they were mighty Vice Kings. At this point, along came Henry Brown with a revolver, shooting. Everybody ducked and the Vice Kings ran. I began to throw Knights into my car because I knew that the area was 'hot.'

"In the car the boys were extremely elated. 'Baby, did you see the way I swung on that kid?' 'Man, did we tell them off?' 'Did you see them take off when I leveled my gun?' 'You were great, baby . . .'

"The tension was relieved. They had performed well and could be proud. . ."

NOBODY LOSES?

No doubt the Vice Kings too felt the thrill of having faced conflict and come off well. They had met great danger bravely, and had a good alibi for not having won unquestioned victory—the enemy had a gun. The Knights, on their part also had an alibi—the worker had intervened. Both sides therefore won, and could mutually share satisfaction and enhanced reputation. Gang combat is not necessarily a winner-take-all game. No one need be defeated. The two gangs had "played the game" according to the standards of their "community"; they had been rewarded, and law and order were now restored. The larger society too profits from a no-loser game. Of course, results are not always so harmless. Boys and gangs are often beaten and people and property often injured in this "game."

Threats to the status of a leader can result in violence to whole gangs; but the process is more complicated than it seems. Threat to leadership is merely a special case of "status management," which involves all gang boys. How can high status best be achieved and maintained in the continuing and risky give and take of gang life?

HUMBUG

Several kinds of threats to status are covered by the broad conception of status management. They are well illustrated in the elements involved in a "humbug"—a general brawl— that our workers witnessed and recorded.

Jim, the detached worker, had taken his gang, the North Side Vice Kings, to a professional basketball game at the Chicago Amphitheater. The boys were in good spirits, but restless and volatile. Duke, the strongest leader, had been drinking. He sat near a younger group, the Junior Chiefs. He was friendly to them but obnoxious to venders and others, and was generally putting on a show for the younger boys.

Duke announced that he was going to buy some beer—he had recently turned twenty-one. The worker told him that beer was out when they were on an officially sponsored activity. Duke bought it anyway, and after an argument in which Duke kept mentioning his age, Jim took the beer from him. Duke became abusive to the worker and other spectators; and the other Vice Kings also acted up. Jim then announced that the entire group had to leave immediately.

On the way out they met another group, the South Side Rattlers. As they passed, Duke "fat-mouthed" one of them and blows were exchanged. The Rattlers, at first confused, retaliated and the humbug was on, while their workers, caught off guard, tried vainly to separate them.

A third group, the Cherokees, now happened on the scene. Having a grudge against the Vice Kings, they waited for no further invitation. "No one stopped to get an explanation of what was going on. The fellows just looked up, saw the fighting, and joined in." The Rattlers, apparently frightened by a couple of knives and a pistol, had started to run, and the fighting might have died had the Cherokees stayed out.

The police partially broke up the battle, but a new round of insults started it again. A fourth group, the Midget Vice Kings arrived; hearing challenge and counter-challenge, they too gave battle, siding with the Vice Kings.

After the combat, the detached workers reported that all three major groups involved talked about going home to get their "stuff" (weapons) and preparing to fight. The Rattlers, having been forced to retreat, were especially disturbed and made many threats. However, when the police came up and escorted them to their car, eliminating all possibility of further humbugs, they acted relieved and happy. On the way home they teased each other about running.

One group—the Junior Chiefs—had not been challenged, or otherwise received any "status threats." Not very surprisingly, they did not fight, and stayed and watched the basketball game.

STATUS AND MANHOOD

The other gangs, however, did feel their reputations and "manhood" threatened. Elements of threat included:

The worker publicly ignored and down-graded Duke's newly achieved adulthood.

Following this, he degraded him in the eyes of his special, younger, audience, the Junior Chiefs—and of his own gang, of which he was supposed to be a leader.

He publicly humiliated and degraded all the rest of the Vice Kings by ordering them to leave, like a bunch of kids who could not be trusted to behave in public. This too he did before the Junior Chiefs—an act which immediately downgraded them in the gang world— and before adults, who could immediately identify them as "kids."

Searching for an outlet for rage and frustration, and for a means to rebuild their shattered "reps," the Vice Kings encountered the Rattlers. They attacked them. Now the reputations of the Rattlers (and later of the Cherokees) were threatened, and *they* counter retaliated.

Yet, for all the ferocity, the fights were shortlived. Every group except the Vice Kings, who had been most threatened, were brought under control fairly quickly and stayed to see the basketball game—only the Vice Kings missed it. Moreover, despite talk of retaliation, the humbug was self-contained; in the following months there was no more humbugging between these groups. The fight served the usual purpose of upholding reputations and preserving the images of street warriors ready for combat.

Closer analysis, however, reveals more to the story. What happened to the ferocious warrior image after the fights were stopped? And why so easily stopped? Also, not all the boys fought. Except for the Vice Kings, each group contained some boys who stayed out. Careful review suggests that those most deeply involved in the fighting were the core gang-members—the leaders and those who wanted to be leaders. Not all gang members—and not all gangs—have the same investment in rep and status. Certainly no gang rules or standards, spoken or implied, require that *all* boys fight every time, even under these provocative circumstances.

Gang rules and expectations do influence the behavior of

members; but that influence is not clear cut, and depends mostly on the situation. Gangs are fluid; members change; boys come and go for days or weeks at a time, and unless they are leaders, or important core members, they are hardly missed. Under such circumstances, the group leaders cannot make members—especially fringe members—conform or give obedience by threatening expulsion or withdrawal of privileges. Most of the gang leaders we studied were surprisingly conciliatory within the group. But they had a special interest in making members want to belong to a gang with a good reputation.

"KICKS," NOT BLOWS

This article is concerned primarily with juvenile gangs whose status is built around conflict. But it must be emphasized that, despite prevalent stereotypes, juvenile gangs are not all conflict oriented, and value systems may vary among them as among other human groupings. A "retreatist" gang, which built its value system around the effect of dope, provides a dramatic contrast.

Although criticized and ridiculed repeatedly by other gangs for their cowardice and lack of manhood, the retreatists seldom responded to taunts, and always retreated from combat. They did not worry about their reputations as fighters—they had none—and did not think them important—in fact, they thought the conflict oriented gangs to be "square." Directly challenged to join other white gangs in repelling Negro "wade-in" demonstrators on a beach in Chicago, they got "high" on pills and unconcernedly played cards during the entire incident.

The basis of comaraderie—what was important—to the drug users was "kicks." Past and present exploits—their legends of valor—continually recounted, concerned "high" experiences and "crazy" behavior rather than bravery or toughness. "You get the feeling," a member of the team of research observers said, "that whatever the activity of the moment, the guys will talk about it in relation to dope— how taking dope affects their participation in the activity."

Even their humor revolved around the effect of dope— the antics of friends under the influence. They laughed about the boy who kept trying to start a junked car that had no motor. Another one, beaten by a Chinese laundryman he tried to rob, "was so doped out of his mind" that he asked the arriving police to arrest the other for beating him so. Some others climbed to a bedroom window and grabbed the leg of a girlfriend to wake her, but got the wrong window and the wrong leg—both of them her father's!

Not all gangs value combat. But each will protect what it does value. When the retreatists find what they value threatened, they withdraw, protectively. When a conflict oriented gang feels its status threatened, it fights.

PRESSURES FROM OUTSIDE

"Status threat" is a special case of the general status thesis—that people will tend to do what gives them standing and respect in society. But with adolescent boys in a gang "what gives them standing and respect" is contained in the limited compass of the face-to-face relationships within the gang, not—except indirectly—with the social class structure of society at large. Of course, directly and indirectly, pressures from outside do affect the gang boys. They come from at least three levels.

Adult sponsored and controlled institutions of the larger society. Schools, places of employment, social agencies, police, and other officials represent adult "authority." Their orientation is middle-class; they preach and perhaps believe that worth and success come from hard work, deferred gratification, self control, good grades, good behavior, saving money, and becoming a "leader" in approved organizations. Gang boys fail to achieve according to these standards. The hypothesis that, with legitimate channels closed to them they will choose the illegitimate, therefore does not disagree with our findings. But how this works precisely is not very clear, and other research indicates that these boys may not be as alienated as many think. Other pressures must also affect them more directly.

THE EXERCISE OF POWER

The lower classes have their own adult community institutions, which make their own patterns and exert their own pressures. There are poolrooms, parties, informal neighborhood gatherings, and the obvious social and political power manifested by the adults in rackets and politics.

At this level, standards of adult behavior most appropriate to everyday life for the boys are inferred and directly inculcated. Observation strongly suggests that the gang boys recognize and respect the exercise of power in their neighborhoods, whether from legitimate or illegitimate sources. But there is no demonstration of legitimate power they know that compares in drama and impact with the evidence of the power of organized crime—the numerous gang slayings of hoodlums, and even of politicians. Both Negro and white gang boys repeat as a by-word: "You can't beat the syndicate."

But modeling behavior after adults in order to "achieve adulthood" seems not to be as important a factor among Negros as among whites. Lower class Negro communities differ; there are fewer sharp age distinctions; all ages compete for excitement wherever it may be found—a bottle, a battle, or a broad. Poolhalls are frequented by young and old alike.

The adoption of adult lower class standards therefore cannot be the only, or even the major, cause of delinquency among adolescents. In the conflict-prone gangs especially, the next level must be the most important.

The Adolescent Gang World. The juvenile "delinquent"—especially the gang leader—is faced with a condition, not a theory. He must daily act out his role under the eyes of his fellow gang members, and the members and leaders of other gangs. Almost by definition, the destiny of a warlike gang is controlled by the actions, real or expected, of other gangs. How a gang defends or enhances its status depends on its judgment of the whole fluid situation. What is the state of peace or war with rival gangs? What old gangs are feuding? What new gangs are trying to carve out niches for themselves?

Even a group organized for criminal purposes, as one of ours was, will shift its goals to fighting if under threat or attack from outside—even though this might, for a criminal gang, bring on risk of exposure.

BRANCH GANGS

The interrelationships in the gang world are extensive. A gang will have "branches" across neighborhood lines (East Side Cobras and West Side Cobras); it will have Senior, Junior and Midget divisions within a neighborhood, with the younger members modeling themselves on the older, and expecting model behavior from them.

Even where pressures from outside make themselves manifest, they must filter down into and be expressed within the values of the gang itself. In fact the gang owes much of its reason for existence to its need to face and cope with such pressures, not losing status in the process—as would certainly happen if the adolescents had to face, nakedly, the censures, criticisms, and punishments of a middle-class or adult world they do not understand, and which does not understand them.

Each outside level represents forces which affect status within the gang—a boy can acquire "rep" by defiance of police, by vandalism of a neighborhood institution, or by showing "heart" in a gang fight. Whether or not the threat originated inside or outside the group, recognizing the existence of the gang and its internal dynamics is crucial to understanding how gang boys maintain status. The larger society is remote and abstract; even the neighborhood has indirect contact; the gang provides the face-to-face audience, the most direct and meaningful rewards and punishments.

Problems of status management are not confined to adolescent gangs. They affect us all—they rain on the just and the unjust alike, on parents, on delinquents, on corporation vice-presidents. And they rouse many besides juvenile gangs to violence.

In our work we noted that often merely assigning a worker to a gang, even before he had a chance to do anything, made the gang more docile, because being important enough to rate your own worker was such a mark of prestige that more energetic proof was not as necessary. Learning the techniques of status management—understanding the dynamics and importance of status considerations within juvenile gangs—provides a powerful lever by which gang behavior and deliquency can be grasped—and, perhaps, controlled.

Confrontation at the Conrad Hilton

The Walker Commission

A police riot. A reporter coined that phrase in at-tempting to capsulize the melee involving Chicago police and demonstrators in Chicago's Grant Park last August during the Democratic National Convention. Now the words have been immortalized by a Chicago study team on assignment from the President's Commission on the Causes and Prevention of Violence. The task of the study team was to find out what happened in Chicago and why. The result of its 53-day investigation was a documented report

*released December 1, entitled "Rights in Conflict,"
and bearing the name of a Chicago corporate attorney, Daniel Walker, who directed the investigation throughout and insisted on its immediate and un-
expurgated publication despite pressure from some
on the violence commission who wanted obscenity
in the report toned down and publication delayed
until at least next spring.*

*The report is based on 3436 statements of eyewit-
nesses and participants taken by the Walker committee and by the FBI. Those interviewed included
police officers, National Guardsmen, United States
Army personnel, demonstrators and their leaders,
government officials, convention delegates, news
media representatives and bystanders. The staff also
viewed about 180 hours of motion picture film provided by television networks and local stations, the
Chicago police department and others. More than
12,000 photographs were examined and official
police and National Guard records were reviewed.*

*It is important to note that although individual
members of Students for a Democratic Society, and
other allied organizations linked to the National
Mobilization Committee to End the War in Vietnam,*

*were interviewed, the organizations themselves re-
fused to cooperate with the study team. Thus, there
is a likelihood in the report of considerable under-
reporting of mass spontaneous violence.*

*Violence marked police-demonstrator relations
from beginning to end of the convention, but none
was so vicious as the bloody clash Wednesday evening, August 28, in front of the Conrad Hilton
Hotel, where many delegates were staying and where
the presidential campaign headquarters of Senator
Eugene J. McCarthy was located. The following
story is taken from the Walker Commission report.
It is the step-by-step, indeed—nearly blow-by-blow
account of events leading to the clash.—The editors*

By about 5 p.m. Wednesday the U.S. Attorney's report
says about 2000 persons, "mostly normally dressed," had
already assembled at the [Conrad] Hilton [Hotel]. Many
of these were demonstrators who had tired of waiting out
the negotiations and had broken off from the marchers
and made their way to the hotel. It appears that police already were having some difficulty keeping order at that location. Says the U.S. Attorney's report: "A large crowd had
assembled behind the police line along the east wall of the
Hilton. This crowd was heavily infiltrated with 'Yippie'

THE PARTICIPANTS

"There were of course, the hippies—the long hair and love
beads, the calculated unwashedness, the flagrant banners, the
open lovemaking and disdain for the constraints of conventional society. In dramatic effect, both visual and vocal, these
dominated a crowd whose members actually differed widely
in physical appearance, in motivation, in political affiliation,
in philosophy. The crowd included Yippies come to 'do their
thing,' youngsters working for a political candidate, professional people with dissenting political views, anarchists and
determined revolutionaries, motorcycle gangs, black activists,
young thugs, police and secret service undercover agents.
There were demonstrators waving the Viet Cong flag and the
red flag of revolution and there were the simply curious who
came to watch and, in many cases, became willing or unwilling participants.

To characterize the crowd, then, as entirely hippie-Yippie,
entirely "New Left," entirely anarchist, or entirely youthful
political dissenters is both wrong and dangerous. The stereotyping that did occur helps to explain the emotional reaction
of both police and public during and after the violence that
occurred.

Despite the presence of some revolutionaries, the vast
majority of the demonstrators were intent on expressing by
peaceful means their dissent either from society generally
or from the administration's policies in Vietnam.

Most of those intending to join the major protest demonstrations scheduled during convention week did not plan
to enter the Amphitheatre and disrupt the proceedings of
the Democratic convention, did not plan aggressive acts of
physical provocation against the authorities, and did not plan
to use rallies of demonstrators to stage an assault against
any person, institution, or place of business. But while it is
clear that most of the protesters in Chicago had no intention
of initiating violence, this is not to say that they did not
expect it to develop." From the summary of the Walker
Commission report.

types and was spitting and screaming obscene insults at the police."

A policeman on duty in front of the hotel later said that it seemed to him that the obscene abuses shouted by "women hippies" outnumbered those called out by male demonstrators "four to one." A common epithet shouted by the females, he said, was "Fuck you, pig." Others included references to policemen as "cock suckers" and "mother fuckers."

A short time later a reporter noticed a lot of debris being hurled from one of the upper floors of the Hilton. He climbed into a police squad car parked in the area and with the aid of police binoculars saw that rolls of toilet paper were coming from the 15th floor, a location he pinpointed by counting down from the top of the building. He then went to the 15th floor and found that the section the paper was coming from was rented by Senator McCarthy campaigners. He was not admitted to the suite.

If Dellinger's marchers in Grant Park now moved to the Hilton area, an additional 5000 demonstrators would be added to the number the police there would have to control.

The Crossing

At about 6 or 6:30 p.m., one of the march leaders announced by loudspeaker that the demonstrators would not be allowed to march to the Amphitheatre. He told the crowd to disperse and to re-group in front of the Conrad Hilton Hotel in Grant Park.

Police in the area were in a far from cheerful mood. A neatly dressed sociology student from Minnesota says he stepped off the sidewalk onto the grass and two policemen pulled their billy clubs back as though ready to swing. One of them said, "You'd better get your fucking ass off that grass or I'll put a beautiful goddam crease in your fucking queer head." The student overheard another policeman say to a "hippie-looking girl of 14 or 15, 'You better get your fucking dirty cunt out of here.' " The growing feeling of entrapment was intensified and some witnesses noticed that police were letting people into the park but not out. The marshals referred to the situation as a "trap."

As the crowd moved north, an Assistant U.S. Attorney saw one demonstrator with long sideburns and hippie garb pause to break up a large piece of concrete, wrapping the pieces in a striped T-shirt.

Before the march formally disbanded, an early contingent of demonstrators, numbering about 30 to 50, arrived at the spot where Congress Plaza bridges the Illinois Central tracks at approximately the same time as a squad of 40 National Guardsmen. The Guard hurriedly spread out about three feet apart across Congress with rifles at the ready, gas masks on, bayonets fixed.

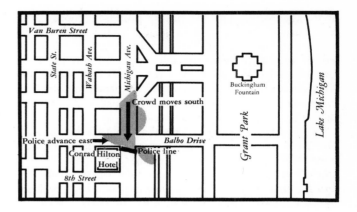

Now as the bulk of the disappointed marchers sought a way out of the park, the crowd began to build up in front of the Guard. "I saw one woman driving a new red late-model car approach the bridge," a news correspondent says: "Two demonstrators, apparently badly gassed, jumped into the back seat and hoped to get through the Guard lines. Guardsmen refused to permit the car through, going so far as to threaten to bayonet her tires and the hood of her car if she did not turn around. One Guardsman fired tear gas point blank beside the car."

The crowd's basic strategy, a medic recalled, was "to mass a sizeable group at one end of the line," as if preparing to charge. Then, when Guardsmen shifted to protect that area, a comparatively small group of demonstrators would push through the weak end of the line. Once the small group had penetrated the line, the medic says, members would "come up behind the Guardsmen and taunt them, as well as push and shove them from the rear." A Guard official said later that his men were attacked with oven cleaner and containers filled with excrement.

As the crowd swelled, it surged periodically towards the Guard line, sometimes yelling, "Freedom, freedom." On one of these surges a Guardsman hurled two tear gas canisters. Some of the tear gas was fired directly into the faces of demonstrators. "We came across a guy really badly gassed," a college coed says. "We were choking, but we could still see. But this guy we saw was standing there helpless with mucous-type stuff on his face, obviously in pain."

An Assistant U.S. Attorney says he saw "hundreds of people running, crying, coughing, vomiting, screaming." Some woman ran blindly to Buckingham Fountain and leaped into the water to bathe their faces. The Guard medic quoted earlier says he was again assaulted by demonstrators when he went into the crowd to treat a man felled by "a particularly heavy dose of tear gas."

"In Grant Park, the gassed crowd was angered . . .

more aggressive," says the history professor. Shortly after the gassing, says the Guard medic quoted earlier, "two forces of police arrived. They immediately waded into the crowd with clubs swinging indiscriminately, driving them off the bridge and away from the area." Once more, the Guardsman said, he was assaulted by demonstrators—this time when he tried "to treat an individual who received a severe head injury from the police."

Surging north from Congress Plaza to a footbridge leading from the park, the crowd encountered more Guardsmen. More tear gas was dispensed. Surging north from the site of the gassings, the crowd found the Jackson Boulevard bridge unguarded. Word was quickly passed back by loudspeaker "Two blocks north, there's an open bridge; no gas." As dusk was settling, hundreds poured from the park into Michigan Avenue.

The Crowd on Michigan Avenue

At 7:14 p.m., as the first groups of demonstrators crossed the bridge toward Michigan Avenue, they noticed that the mule train of the Poor People's Campaign was just entering the intersection of Michigan and Jackson, headed south. The wagons were painted, "Jobs & Food for All."

The train was accompanied by 24 policemen on foot, five on three-wheelers, and four in two squadrols. A police official was in front with the caravan's leaders. The sight of the train seemed to galvanize the disorganized Grant Park crowd and those streaming over the bridge broke into cheers and shouts. "Peace now!" bellowed the demonstrators. "Dump the Hump!" This unexpected enthusiastic horde in turn stimulated the mule train marchers. Drivers of the wagons stood and waved to the crowd, shouting: "Join us! Join us!" To a young man watching from the 23rd floor of the Hilton Hotel, "the caravan seemed like a magnet to demonstrators leaving the park."

The Balbo-Michigan Crowd Builds Up

When the crowd's first rank reached the intersection of Balbo and Michigan, the northeast corner of the Hilton, it was close to approximately 2000 to 3000 demonstrators and spectators. The police were armed with riot helmets, batons, mace, an aerosol tear gas can and their service revolvers (which they always carry). Behind the police lines, parked in front of the Hilton, was a fire department high pressure pumper truck hooked up to a hydrant. Pairs of uniformed firemen were also in the vicinity. The growing crowds, according to the U.S. Attorney's report, were a blend of "young and old, hippies, Yippies, straights, newsmen and cameramen," even two mobile TV units.

From within the crowd were rising the usual shouts from some of the demonstrators: "Hell no, we won't go!" . . . "Fuck these Nazis!" . . . "Fuck you, L.B.J.!" . . . "No more

war!" . . . "Pigs, pigs, pigs." . . . "The streets belong to the people!" . . . "Let's go to the Amphitheatre!" . . . "Move on, Move on!" . . . "You can't stop us." . . . "From the hotel," recalls a student, "people who sympathized were throwing confetti and pieces of paper out of the windows and they were blinking their room lights."

Isolated Incidents

Occasionally during the early evening, groups of demonstrators would flank the police lines or find a soft spot and punch through, heading off on their own for the Amphitheatre. On the periphery of the Hilton and on thoroughfares and side streets further southwest, a series of brief but sometimes violent encounters occurred.

For example, says the manager of a private club on Michigan Avenue, "a large band of long-haired demonstrators . . . tore down the American flag" overhanging the entrance to the club "and took it into Michigan Avenue attempting to tear it."

At about 7 p.m. from the window of a motel room in the 1100 block of South Michigan, a senator's driver noticed a group of demonstrators walking south, chanting: "Hell no, we won't go!" and "Fuck the draft." They were hurling insults at passing pedestrians and when one answered back, the witness says, "five demonstrators charged out of Michigan Avenue onto the sidewalk, knocked the pedestrian down, formed a circle around his fallen body, locked their arms together and commenced kicking him in a vicious manner. When they had finished kicking their victim, they unlocked their arms and immediately melted back into the crowd. . . ."

Back at the Conrad Hilton

Vice President Humphrey was now inside the Conrad Hilton Hotel and the police commanders were afraid that the crowd might either attempt to storm the hotel or march south on Michigan Avenue, ultimately to the Amphitheatre. The Secret Service had received an anonymous phone call that the Amphitheatre was to be blown up. A line of police was established at 8th and Michigan at the south end of the hotel and the squads of police stationed at the hotel doors began restricting access to those who could display room keys. Some hotel guests, including delegates and Senator McCarthy's wife, were turned away.

By 7:30 p.m. a rumor was passing around that the Blackstone Rangers and the East Side Disciples, two of Chicago's most troublesome street gangs, were on their way to the scene. (This was later proven to be untrue; neither of these South Side gangs was present in any numbers in either Lincoln Park or Grant Park.) At this point, a Negro male was led through the police line by a police officer. He spoke to the police officer, a city official and a deputy superintendent of police. He told them that he was

THE ARRESTS

Chicago police arrested 668 persons in connection with disturbances during the convention week. Fifty-two persons were in possession of weapons when arrested. The weapons consisted primarily of rocks and bricks, but police also arrested nine demonstrators with knives, two with guns, two with machetes and one with a bayonet.

Two-thirds of the Arrests Were Made of Persons From 18 to 25 Years Old, With Men Outnumbering Women 8 to 1.

Age	Arrested	Percentage of Total
17 and Under	64	9.6
18-20	221	33.1
21-25	221	33.1
26 and Over	157	23.5
Not Reported	5	0.8
	668	100.0%

Forty-three Percent of the Arrested Were Employed, Representing a Wide Range of Occupations Including Teachers, Social Workers, Ministers, Factory Laborers and Journalists.

Occupation	Arrested	Percentage of Total
Employed	287	43.0
Student	218	32.6
Unemployed	133	19.9
Not Reported	30	4.5
	668	100.0%

The Majority of Those Arrested Were Male Residents of Metropolitan Chicago, But Police Records Listed Persons From 36 States, Washington, D.C. and Five Foreign Countries.

Residence	Arrested	Percentage of Total
Chicago City	276	41.4
Out of State	291	43.5
Chicago Suburban	74	11.1
Other Illinois	14	2.0
Not Reported	13	1.9
	668	100.0%

Less Than 1/6 of Those Arrested Had Previous Records.

Sex	Age 17 and Under	Age 18-20	Age 21-25	Age 26 and Over	Total
Male	4	26	45	35	110
Female	0	2	4	2	8
	4	28	49	37	118

More Than 4/5 of the Previous Arrests Were For Misdemeanors.

Charge	Arrests	Percentage of Total
Felony	39	11.5
Misdemeanor	277	81.5
Narcotics	24	7.1
	340	100.0%

in charge of the mule train and that his people wanted no part of this mob. He said he had 80 people with him, that they included old people and children, and he wanted to get them out of the mob. The police officer later stated the group wanted to go past the Hilton, circle it, and return to the front of the hotel where Reverend Ralph Abernathy could address the crowd.

In a few minutes, Reverend Ralph Abernathy appeared and, according to the police officer's statement, "said he wanted to be taken out of the area as he feared for the safety of his group." The police officer directed that the train be moved south on Michigan to 11th Street and then, through a series of turns through the Loop, to the West Side.

A policeman on Michigan later said that at about this time a "female hippie" came up to him, pulled up her skirt and said, "You haven't had a piece in a long time." A policeman standing in front of the Hilton remembers seeing a blond female who was dressed in a short red minidress make lewd, sexual motion in front of a police line. Whenever this happened, he says, the policemen moved back to prevent any incident. The crowd, however, egged her on, the patrolman says. He thought that "she and the crowd wanted an arrest to create a riot." Earlier in the same general area a male youth had stripped bare and walked around carrying his clothes on a stick.

The intersection at Balbo and Michigan was in total chaos at this point. The street was filled with people. Darkness had fallen but the scene was lit by both police and television lights. As the mule train left, part of the group tried to follow the wagons through the police line and were stopped. According to the deputy superintendent of police, there was much pushing back and forth between the policemen and the demonstrators.

Continual announcements were made at this time over a police amplifier for the crowd to "clear the street and go up on the sidewalk or into the park area for their demonstrations." The broadcast said "Please gather in the park on the east side of the street. You may have your peaceful demonstration and speechmaking there." The demonstrators were also advised that if they did not heed these orders they would face arrest. The response from many in the crowd, according to a police observer, was to scream and shout obscenities. A Chicago attorney who was watching the scene recalls that when the announcements were broadcast, "No one moved." The deputy superintendent then made another announcement: "Will any non-demonstrators, anyone who is not a part of this group, any newsmen, please leave the group." Despite the crowd noise, the loud-speaker announcements were "loud and plainly heard," according to an officer.

While this was happening on Michigan Avenue, a separate police line had begun to move east toward the the crowd from the block of Balbo that lies between Michigan and Wabash along the north side of the Hilton.

Just as the police in front of the Hilton were confronted with some sit-downs on the south side of the intersection of Balbo and Michigan, the police unit coming into the intersection on Balbo met the sitting demonstrators. What happened then is subject to dispute between the police and some other witnesses.

The Balbo police unit commander asserts that he informed the sit-downs and surrounding demonstrators that if they did not leave, they would be arrested. He repeated the order and was met with a chant of "Hell no, we won't go." Quickly a police van swung into the intersection immediately behind the police line, the officers opened the door at the rear of the wagon. The deputy chief "ordered the arrest process to start."

"Immediately upon giving this order," the deputy chief later informed his superiors, "we were pelted with rocks, bottles, cans filled with unknown liquids and other debris, which forced the officers to defend themselves from injury. . . . My communications officer was slugged from behind by one of these persons, receiving injuries to his right eye and cheekbone."

The many films and video tapes of this time period present a picture which does not correspond completely with the police view. First, the films do not show a mob moving west on Balbo; they show the street as rather clean of the demonstrators and bystanders, although the sidewalks themselves on both sides of the street are crowded. Second, they show the police walking east on Balbo, stopping in formation, awaiting the arrival of the van and starting to make arrests on order. A total of 25 seconds elapses between

their coming to a halt and the first arrests.

Also, a St. Louis reporter who was watching from inside the Haymarket lounge agrees that the police began making arrests "in formation," apparently as "the result of an order to clear the intersection." Then, the reporter adds, "from this apparently controlled beginning the police began beating people indiscriminately. They grabbed and beat anyone they could get hold of."

"The crowd tried to reverse gears," the reporter says. "People began falling over each other. I was in the first rank between police and the crowd and was caught in the first surge. I went down as I tried to retreat. I covered my head, tried to protect my glasses which had fallen partially off, and hoped that I would not be clubbed. I tried to dig into the humanity that had fallen with me. You could hear shouting and screaming. As soon as I could, I scrambled to my feet and tried to move away from the police. I saw a youth running by me also trying to flee. A policeman clubbed him as he passed, but he kept running.

"The cops were saying, 'Move! I said, move, god dammit! Move, you bastards!'" A representative of the ACLU who was positioned among the demonstrators says the police "were cussing a lot" and were shouting, "Kill, kill, kill, kill, kill!" A reporter for the *Chicago Daily News* said after the melee that he, too, heard this cry. A demonstrator remembers the police swinging their clubs and screaming, "Get the hell out of here." . . . "Get the fuck out of here." . . . "Move your fucking ass!"

The crowd frantically eddied in a halfmoon shape in an effort to escape the officers coming in from the west. A UPI reporter who was on the southern edge of the crowd on Michigan Avenue, said that the advancing police "began pushing the crowd south." A cherry bomb burst overhead. The demonstrators strained against the deputy superintendent of police's line south of the Balbo-Michigan intersection. "When I reached that line," says the UPI reporter, "I heard a voice from behind it say, 'Push them back, move them back!' I was then prodded and shoved with nightsticks back in a northerly direction, toward the still advancing line of police."

"Police were marching this way and that," a correspondent from a St. Louis paper says. "They obviously had instructions to clear the street, but apparently contradicting one another in the directions the crowd was supposed to be sent."

The deputy superintendent of police recalls that he ordered his men to "hold your line there" . . . "stand fast" . . . "Lieutenant, hold your men steady there!" These orders, he said, were not obeyed by all. He said that police disregarded his order to return to the police lines—the beginning of what he says was the only instance in which he personally saw police discipline collapse. He estimates that ten to 15 officers moved off on individual forays against demonstrators.

The Clash

Thus, at 7:57 p.m., with two groups of club-wielding police converging simultaneously and independently, the battle was joined. The portions of the throng out of the immediate area of conflict largely stayed put and took up the chant, "The whole world is watching," but the intersection fragmented into a collage of violence.

Re-creating the precise chronology of the next few moments is impossible. But there is no question that a violent street battle ensued.

People ran for cover and were struck by police as they passed. Clubs were swung indiscriminately.

"I saw squadrons of policemen coming from everywhere," a secretary said. "The crowd around me suddenly began to run. Some of us, including myself, were pushed back onto the sidewalk and then all the way up against . . . the Blackstone Hotel along Michigan Avenue. I thought the crowd had panicked."

"Fearing that I would be crushed against the wall of the building . . . I somehow managed to work my way . . . to the edge of the street . . . and saw police everywhere.

"As I looked up I was hit for the first time on the head from behind by what must have been a billy club. I was then knocked down and while on my hands and knees, I was hit around the shoulders. I got up again, stumbling and was hit again. As I was falling, I heard words to the effect of 'move, move' and the horrible sound of cracking billy clubs.

"After my second fall, I remember being kicked in the back, and I looked up and noticed that many policemen around me had no badges on. The police kept hitting me on the head."

Eventually she made her way to an alley behind the Blackstone and finally, "bleeding badly from my head wound," was driven by a friend to a hospital emergency room. Her treatment included the placing of 12 stitches.

A lawyer says that he was in a group of demonstrators in the park just south of Balbo when he heard a police officer shout, "Let's get 'em!" Three policemen ran up, "singled out one girl and as she was running away from them, beat her on the back of the head. As she fell to the ground, she was struck by the nightsticks of these officers." A male friend of hers then came up yelling at the police. The witness said, "He was arrested. The girl was left in the area lying on the ground."

A *Milwaukee Journal* reporter says in his statement, "when the police managed to break up groups of protesters they pursued individuals and beat them with clubs. Some police pursued individual demonstrators as far as a block . . . and beat them. . . . In many cases it appeared to me that when police had finished beating the protesters they were pursuing, they then attacked, indiscriminately, any civilian who happened to be standing nearby. Many of these were not involved in the demonstrations."

In balance, there is no doubt that police discipline broke during the melee. The deputy superintendent of police states that—although this was the only time he saw discipline collapse—when he ordered his men to stand fast, some did not respond and began to sally through the crowd, clubbing people they came upon. An inspector-observer from the Los Angeles Police Department, stated that during this week, "The restraint of the police both as individual members and as an organization, was beyond reason." However, he said that on this occasion:

There is no question but that many officers acted without restraint and exerted force beyond that necessary under the circumstances. The leadership at the point of conflict did little to prevent such conduct and the direct control of officers by first-line supervisors was virtually nonexistent.

The deputy superintendent of police has been described by several observers as being very upset by individual policemen who beat demonstrators. He pulled his men off the demonstrators, shouting "Stop, damn it, stop. For Christ's sake, stop it."

"It seemed to me," an observer says, "that only a saint could have swallowed the vile remarks to the officers. However, they went to extremes in clubbing the Yippies. I saw them move into the park, swatting away with clubs at girls and boys lying in the grass. More than once I witnessed two officers pulling at the arms of a Yippie until the arms almost left their sockets, then, as the officers put the Yippie in a police van, a third jabbed a riot stick into the groin of the youth being arrested. It was evident that the Yippie was not resisting arrest."

"In one incident, a young man, who apparently had been maced, staggered across Michigan . . . helped by a companion. The man collapsed. . . . Medical people from the volunteer medical organization rushed out to help him. A police officer (a sergeant, I think) came rushing forward, followed by the two other nightstick-brandishing policemen and yelled, 'Get him out of here; this ain't a hospital.' The medical people fled, half dragging and half carrying the young man with them. . . ."

During the course of arrests, one girl lost her skirt. Although there have been unverified reports of police ripping the clothes from female demonstrators, this is the only incident on news film of any woman being disrobed in the course of arrest.

While violence was exploding in the street, the crowd wedged, behind the police sawhorses along the northeast edge of the Hilton, was experiencing a terror all its own.

Early in the evening, this group had consisted in large part of curious bystanders. But following the police surges into the demonstrators clogging the intersection, protesters had crowded the ranks behind the horses in their flight from the police.

From force of numbers, this sidewalk crowd of 150 to 200 persons was pushing down toward the Hilton's front entrance. Policemen whose orders were to keep the entrance clear were pushing with sawhorses. Other police and fleeing demonstrators were pushed from the north in the effort to clear the intersection. Thus, the crowd was wedged against the hotel, with the hotel itself on the west, sawhorses on the southeast and police on the northeast.

Films show that one policeman elbowed his way to where he could rescue a girl of about ten years of age from the vise-like press of the crowd. He cradled her in his arms and carried her to a point of relative safety 20 feet away. The crowd itself "passed up" an elderly woman to a low ledge.

"I was crowded in with the group of screaming, frightened people," an onlooker states, "We jammed against each other, trying to press into the brick wall of the hotel. As we stood there breathing hard . . . a policeman calmly walked the length of the barricade with a can of chemical spray [evidently mace] in his hand. Unbelievably, he was spraying at us." Photos reveal several policemen using mace against the crowd. "Some of the police then turned and attacked the crowd," a Chicago reporter says. A young cook caught in the crowd relates that:

"The police began picking people off. They would pull individuals to the ground and begin beating them. A medic wearing a white coat and an armband with a red cross was grabbed, beaten and knocked to the ground. His whole face was covered with blood."

As a result, a part of the crowd was trapped in front of the Conrad Hilton and pressed hard against a big plate glass window of the Haymarket Lounge. A reporter who was sitting inside said, "Frightened men and women banged . . . against the window. A captain of the fire department inside told us to get back from the window, that it might get knocked in. As I backed away a few feet I could see a smudge of blood on the glass outside."

With a sickening crack, the window shattered, and screaming men and women tumbled through, some cut badly by jagged glass. The police came after them. "A patrolman ran up to where I was sitting," said a man with a cut leg. "I protested that I was injured and could not walk, attempting to show him my leg. He screamed that he would show me I could walk. He grabbed me by the shoulder and literally hurled me through the door of the bar into the lobby. . . .

"I stumbled out into what seemed to be a main lobby. The young lady I was with and I were both immediately set upon by what I can only presume were plainclothes police. . . . We were cursed by these individuals and thrown through another door into an outer lobby." Eventually a McCarthy aide took him to the 15th floor.

In the heat of all this, probably few were aware of the Haymarket's advertising slogan: "A place where good guys take good girls to dine in the lusty, rollicking atmosphere of fabulous Old Chicago. . . ."

There is little doubt that during this whole period, beginning at 7:57 p.m. and lasting for nearly 20 minutes, the preponderance of violence came from the police. It was not entirely a one-way battle, however.

Firecrackers were thrown at police. Trash baskets were set on fire and rolled and thrown at them. In one case, a gun was taken from a policeman by a demonstrator.

"Some hippies," said a patrolman in his statement, "were hit by other hippies who were throwing rocks at the police." Films reveal that when police were chasing demonstrators into Grant Park, one young man upended a sawhorse and heaved it at advancing officers. At one point the deputy superintendent of police was knocked down by a thrown sawhorse. At least one police three-wheeler was tipped over. One of the demonstrators says that "people in the park were prying up cobblestones and breaking them. One person piled up cobblestones in his arms and headed toward the police." Witnesses reported that people were throwing "anything they could lay their hands on. From the windows of the Hilton and Blackstone hotels, toilet paper, wet towels, even ash trays came raining down." A police lieutenant stated that he saw policemen bombarded with "rocks, cherry bombs, jars of vasoline, jars of mayonnaise and pieces of wood torn from the yellow barricades falling in the street." He, too, noticed debris falling from the hotel windows.

A number of police officers were injured, either by flying missiles or in personal attacks. One, for example, was helping a fellow officer "pick up a hippie when another hippie gave [me] a heavy kick, aiming for my groin." The blow struck the officer partly on the leg and partly in the testicles. He went down, and the "hippie" who kicked him escaped.

In another instance, a Chicago police reporter said in his statement, "a police officer reached down and grabbed a person who dove forward and bit the officer on the leg. . . . Three or four fellow policemen came to his aid. They had to club the demonstrator to make him break his clamp on the officer's leg." In another case, the witness saw a demonstrator "with a big mop of hair hit a police officer with an old British Army type metal helmet." The reporter said he also heard "hissing sounds from the demonstrators as if they were spraying the police." Later he found empty lacquer spray and hair spray cans on the street. Also he heard policemen cry out, "They're kicking us with knives in their shoes." Later, he said, he found that demonstrators "had actually inserted razor blades in their shoes."

By 8:15 p.m., the intersection was in police control. One group of police proceeded east on Balbo, clearing the street and splitting the crowd into two. Because National Guard lines still barred passage over the Balbo Street bridge, most of the demonstrators fled into Grant Park. A Guardsman estimates that 5,000 remained in the park across from the Hilton. Some clubbing by police occurred; a demonstrator says he saw a brick hurled at police; but few arrests were made.

Wild in the Streets

Now, with police lines beginning to re-form, the deputy superintendent directed the police units to advance north on Michigan. He says announcements were again made to clear the area and warnings given that those refusing to do so would be arrested. To this, according to a patrolman who was present, "The hippie group yelled 'fuck you' in unison."

Police units formed up. National Guard intelligence officers on the site called for Guard assistance. At 8:30 the Secret Service reported trucks full of Guard troops from Soldier Field moving north on Michigan Avenue to the Conrad Hilton and additional units arrived about 20 minutes later. The troops included the same units that had seen action earlier in the day after the bandshell rally and had later been moved to 22nd Street.

By 8:55 p.m., the Guard had taken up positions in a U-shaped formation, blocking Balbo at Michigan and paralleling the Hilton and Grant Park—a position that was kept until 4 a.m. Thursday. Although bayonets were affixed when the troops first hit the street, they were quickly removed. Explains a Guardsman who was there: "The bayonets had gotten in our way when we were on the Congress Street bridge." At one point, a demonstrator tried to "take the muzzle off" one of the Guardsmen's rifle. "All the time the demonstrators were trying to talk to us. They said 'join us' or 'fuck the draft.' We were told not to talk to anyone in the crowd." One Guard unit followed behind the police as a backup group.

With the police and Guard at its rear, the crowd fractured in several directions as it moved away from Balbo and Michigan. Near Michigan and Monroe another casualty center had been set up in the headquarters of the Church Federation of Greater Chicago. This, plus the melding of the crowds northbound on Michigan and east-bound on Monroe, brought about 1,000 persons to the west side of Michigan between Adams and Monroe, facing the Art Institute. There were few demonstrators on the east side of Michigan.

At 9:25 p.m., the police commander ordered a sweep of Michigan Avenue south from Monroe. At about this same time the police still had lines on both the west and east sides of Michigan in front of the Hilton and additional National Guard troops had arrived at 8th Street.

At 9:57 p.m., the demonstrators still on Michigan Avenue, prodded along by the southward sweep of the police, began marching back to Grant Park, chanting "Back to the park." By 10:10 p.m., an estimated 800 to 1,000 demonstrators had gathered in front of the Hilton.

By then, two city street sweeping trucks had rumbled up and down the street in front of the hotel, cleaning up the residue of violence—shoes, bottles, rocks, tear gas handkerchiefs. A police captain said the debris included: "Bases and pieces of broken bottles, a piece of board (1″ × 4″ × 14″), an 18-inch length of metal pipe, a 24-inch stick with a protruding sharpened nail, a 12-inch length of ½-inch diameter pipe, pieces of building bricks, an 18-inch stick with a razor blade protruding . . . several plastic balls somewhat smaller than tennis balls containing approximately 15 to 20 sharpened nails driven into the ball from various angles." When the delegates returned to the Hilton, they saw none of the litter of the battle.

As the crowd had dispersed from the Hilton the big war of Michigan and Balbo was, of course, over. But for those in the streets, as the rivulets of the crowd forked through the areas north of the hotel, there were still battles to be fought. Police violence and police baiting were some time in abating. Indeed, some of the most vicious incidents occurred in this "post-war" period.

The U.S. Attorney states that as the crowd moved north on Michigan Avenue, "they pelted the police with missiles of all sorts, rocks, bottles, firecrackers. When a policeman was struck, the crowd would cheer. The policemen in the line were dodging and jumping to avoid being hit." A police sergeant told the FBI that even a telephone was hurled from the crowd at the police.

In the first block north of the Hilton, recalls a man who was standing outside a Michigan Avenue restaurant, demonstrators "menaced limousines, calling the occupants 'scum,' telling them they didn't belong in Chicago and to go home."

As the police skirmish line moved north, and drew nearer to the squad cars, the lieutenant said, he saw several persons shoving paper through the cars' broken windows—in his opinion, a prelude to setting the cars on fire. A theology student who was in the crowd states that "a demonstrator took a fire extinguisher and sprayed inside the car. Then he put paper on the ground under the gas tank. . . . People shouted at him to stop." To break up the crowd, the lieutenant said, he squirted tear gas from an aerosol container and forced the demonstrators back.

"Two or three policemen, one with a white shirt, advanced on the crowd," one witness said, "The white-shirted one squirted mace in arcs back and forth before him."

A cameraman for the *Chicago Daily News* photographed a woman cowering after she had been sprayed with mace. A *News* representative states that the officer administering the mace, whom the photographers identified as a police lieutenant, then turned and directed the spray at the cameraman. The cameraman shot a photograph of this. The police lieutenant states that he does not remember this incident.

A priest who was in the crowd says he saw a "boy, about 14 or 15 white, standing on top of an automobile yelling something which was unidentifiable. Suddenly a policeman forced him down from the car and beat him to the ground by striking him three or four times with a nightstick. Other police joined in . . . and they eventually shoved him to a police van."

A well-dressed woman saw this incident and spoke angrily to a nearby police captain. As she spoke, another policeman came up from behind her and sprayed something in her face with an aerosol can. He then clubbed her to the ground. He and two other policemen then dragged her along the ground to the same paddy wagon and threw her in.

"At the corner of Congress Plaza and Michigan," states a doctor, "was gathered a group of people, number between 30 and 40. They were trapped against a railing by several policemen on motorcycles. The police charged the people on motorcycles and struck about a dozen of them, knocking several of them down. About 20 standing there jumped over the railing. On the other side of the railing was a three-to-four-foot drop. None of the people who were struck by the motorcycles appeared to be seriously injured. However, several of them were limping as if they had been run over on their feet."

Reporter Witnesses Attack

A UPI reporter witnessed these attacks, too. He relates in his statement that one officer, "with a smile on his face and a fanatical look in his eyes, was standing on the three-wheel cycle, shouting, 'Wahoo, wahoo,' and trying to run down people on the sidewalk." The reporter says he was chased 30 feet by the cycle.

A few seconds later he "turned around and saw a policeman with a raised billy stick." As he swung around, the police stick grazed his head and struck his shoulders. As he was on his knees, he says someone stepped on his back.

A Negro policeman helped him to his feet, the reporter says. The policeman told him, "You know, man I didn't do this. One of the white cops did it." Then, the reporter quotes the officer as saying, "You know what? After this

is all over, I'm quitting the force."

An instant later, the shouting officer on the motorcycle swung by again, and the reporter dove into a doorway for safety.

Near this same intersection, a Democratic delegate from Oklahoma was surrounded in front of his hotel by about ten persons, two of them with long hair and beards. He states that they encircled him for several minutes and subjected him to verbal abuse because they felt he "represented the establishment" and was "somewhat responsible for the alleged police brutality." The delegate stood mute and was eventually rescued by a policeman.

At Van Buren, a college girl states, "demonstrators were throwing things at passing police cars, and I saw one policeman hit in the face with a rock. A small paddy wagon drove up with only one policeman in it, and the crowd began rocking the wagon. The cop fell out and was surrounded by the crowd, but no effort was made to hurt him."

At Jackson, says the graduate student quoted earlier, "People got into the street on their knees and prayed, including several ministers who were dressed in clerical garb. These people, eight or ten of them, were arrested. This started a new wave of dissent among the demonstrators, who got angry. Many went forward to be arrested voluntarily; others were taken forcibly and some were beaten. . . . Objects were being thrown directly at police, including cans, bottles and paper."

"I was in the street," a witness who was near the intersection states, "when a fire in a trash basket appeared. . . . In a few minutes, two fire engines passed south through the crowd, turned west on Van Buren and stopped. They were followed by two police wagons which stopped in the middle of the block. As I walked north past the smaller of the two wagons, it began to rock." (The wagon also was being pelted by missiles, the U.S. Attorney states, and "PIGS" was painted on its sides.)

"I retreated onto the east sidewalk," the witness continued. Two policemen jumped out of the smaller wagon and one was knocked down by a few demonstrators, while other demonstrators tried to get these demonstrators away. The two policemen got back to the wagon, the crowd having drawn well back around them." The U.S. Attorney's report states that one of the policemen was "stomped" by a small group of the mob.

A young woman who was there and who had attended the bandshell rally earlier in the afternoon states that the crowd rocked the wagon for some time, while its officers stayed inside. "Then," she says, "the driver came out wildly swinging his club and shouting. About ten people jumped on him. He was kicked pretty severely and was downed. When he got up he was missing his club and his hat."

A police commander says that at about this moment he received "an urgent radio message" from an officer inside the van. He radioed that "demonstrators were standing on the hood of his wagon . . . and were preparing to smash the windshield with a baseball bat," the commander recalled. The officer also told him that the demonstrators were attempting to overturn the squadrol and that the driver "was hanging on the door in a state of shock." The commander told the officer that assistance was on the way.

"I heard a '10-1' call on either my radio or one of the other hand sets being carried by other men with me," the U.S. Attorney states, "and then heard, 'Car 100-sweep!' [Car 100 was assigned to the police commander.] With a roar of motors, squads, vans and three-wheelers came from east, west and north into the block north of Jackson."

"Almost immediately a CTA bus filled with police came over the Jackson Drive bridge and the police formed a line in the middle of the street," says a witness. "I heard shouts that the police had rifles and that they had cocked and pumped them. Demonstrators began to run."

"I ran north of Jackson . . . just as police were clearing the intersection and forming a line across Michigan," says the witness quoted above. "The police who had formed a line facing east in the middle of Michigan charged, yelling and clubbing into the crowd, running at individuals and groups who did not run before them."

"As the fray intensified around the intersection of Michigan and Jackson, a big group ran west on Jackson, with a group of blue-shirted policemen in pursuit, beating at them with clubs," says the U.S. Attorney's report. "Some of the crowd ran up the alleys; some north on Wabash; and some west on Jackson to State with the police in pursuit."

An Assistant U.S. Attorney later reported that "the demonstrators were running as fast as they could but were unable to get out of the way because of the crowds in front of them. I observed the police striking numerous individuals, perhaps 20 or 30. I saw three fall down and then be overrun by the police. I observed two demonstrators who had multiple cuts on their heads. We assisted one who was in shock into a passer-by's car.

"A TV mobile truck appeared . . . and the police became noticeably more restrained, holding their clubs at waist level rather than in the air," a witness relates. "As the truck disappeared . . . the head-clubbing tactics were resumed."

One demonstrator states that he ran off Michigan Avenue on to Jackson. He says he and his wife ran down Jackson and were admitted, hesitantly, into a restaurant. They seated themselves at a table by the window facing onto Jackson and, while sitting at the table, observed a group of people running down Jackson with policemen

following them and striking generally at the crowd with their batons. At one instance, he saw a policeman strike a priest in the head with a baton.

At the intersection of Jackson and Wabash, said a student whose wife was beaten in the race from Michigan, "the police came from all four directions and attacked the crowd. Demonstrators were beaten and run to the paddy wagons. I saw a black policeman go berserk. He charged blindly at the group of demonstrators and made two circles through the crowd, swinging wildly at anything."

An Assistant U.S. Attorney watching the action on various side streets reported, "I observed police officers clearing people westward . . . using their clubs to strike people on the back of the head and body on several occasions. Once a policeman ran alongside a young girl. He held her by the shoulder of her jacket and struck at her a few times as they were both running down the sidewalk.

A traffic policeman on duty on Michigan Avenue says that the demonstrators who had continued north often surrounded cars and buses attempting to move south along Michigan Avenue. Many males in the crowd, he says, exposed their penises to passers-by and other members of the crowd. They would run up to cars clogged by the crowd and show their private parts to the passengers.

To men, the officer says, they shouted such questions as, "How would you like me to fuck your wife?" and "How would you like to fuck a man?" Many of the demonstrators also rocked the automobiles in an effort to tip them over. A policeman states that bags of feces and urine were dropped on the police from the building.

As the crowd moved south again on Michigan, a traffic policeman, who was in the vicinity of Adams Street, recalls, "They first took control of the lions in front of the Art Institute. They climbed them and shouted things like, "Let's fuck" and "Fuck, fuck, fuck!" At this same intersection, an officer rescued two Loop secretaries from being molested by demonstrators. He asked them, "What are you doing here?" They replied, "We wanted to see what the hippies were like." His response: "How do you like what you saw?"

Old Town: The Mixture as Before

While all that was going on in and around Grant Park, Lincoln Park on Wednesday was quiet and uncrowded; but there was sporadic violence in Old Town again that night. Two University of Minnesota students who wandered through the park in the morning say they heard small groups of demonstrators saying things like "Fuck the pigs," and "Kill them all," but by this time that was not unusual. They also heard a black man addressing a group of demonstrators. He outlined plans for the afternoon, and discussed techniques for forming skirmish lines, disarming police officers, and self defense.

Also during the morning Abbie Hoffman was arrested at the Lincoln Hotel Coffee Shop, 1800 North Clark, and charged with resisting arrest and disorderly conduct. According to Hoffman's wife, Anita, she and her husband and a friend were eating breakfast when three policemen entered the coffee shop and told Hoffman they had received three complaints about an obscene word written on Hoffman's forehead. The word was "Fuck." Hoffman says he printed the word on his forehead to keep cameramen from taking his picture.

Most of the violence against police, from all reports, was the work of gang-type youths called "greasers." They dismantled police barricades to lure squad cars down Stockton Drive, where one observer says "punks engaged in some of the most savage attacks on police that had been seen." Ministers and hippies in the area were directing traffic around the barricades and keeping people from wandering into the danger area. Two ministers in particular were trying to "keep the cool."

Back at The Hilton

By 10:30 p.m., most of the action was centered once more in Grant Park across from the Hilton, where several hundred demonstrators and an estimated 1,500 spectators gathered to listen to what one observer describes as "unexciting speeches." There was the usual singing and shouting. Twice during the evening police and Hilton security officers went into the hotel and went to quarters occupied by McCarthy personnel—once to protest the ripping of sheets to bandage persons who had been injured and a second time to try to locate persons said to be lobbing ashtrays out of the windows. But compared to the earlier hours of the evening, the rest of the night was quiet.

In Grant Park, the sullen crowd sat facing the hotel. Someone with a transistor radio was listening to the roll call vote of states on the nomination and broadcasting the count to the rest of the throng over a bullhorn. There were loud cheers for Ted Kennedy, McCarthy, McGovern and Phillips ("He's a black man," said the youth with the bullhorn.) Boos and cries of "Dump the Hump" arose whenever Humphrey received votes. "When Illinois was called," says the trained observer, "no one could hear totals because of booing and the chant, 'To Hell with Daley.' "

During this time the police line was subject to considerable verbal abuse from within the crowd and a witness says that both black and white agitators at the edge of the crowd tried to kick policemen with razor blades embedded in their shoes. Periodically several policemen would make forays into the crowd, punishing demonstrators they thought were involved.

At about "Louisiana," as the roll call vote moved with quickening pace toward the climax of Humphrey's nomi-

nation, the crowd grew restless, recalls a trained observer. About this same time, according to the Log, the police skirmish line began pushing the demonstrators farther east into the park. A report of an officer being struck by a nail ball was received by police. Film taken at about this time shows an officer being hit by a thrown missile, later identified as a chunk of concrete with a steel reinforcement rod in it. The blow knocked him down and, as he fell, the crowd cheered and yelled, "More!" The chant, "Kill the pigs," filled the air.

"At 'Oklahoma,' " recalls an observer, "the Yippie on the bullhorn said, 'Marshals ready. Don't move. Stay seated.' "

"The front line rose [facing the police] and locked arms, and the others stayed seated. Humphrey was over the top with Pennsylvania, and someone in the Hilton rang a cow bell at the demonstrators. Boos went up, as did tension. A bus load of police arrived. Others standing in front of the Hilton crossed Michigan and lined up behind those in front of the demonstrators.

"The chant of 'Sit down, sit down' went out. An American flag was raised on a pole upside down. Wandering began among demonstrators and the chant continued.

Shortly before midnight, while Benjamin Ortiz was speaking, National Guard troops of the 2/129 Inf. came west on Balbo to Michigan to replace the police in front of the Hilton. "For the first time," says an observer, "machine guns mounted on trucks were pulled up directly in front of the demonstrators, just behind the police lines. The machine guns, and the Guard's mesh-covered jeeps with barbed wire fronts made the demonstrators angry and nervous. Bayonets were readied. In films of this period the word "pig" can be seen written on the street.

"Ortiz continued, 'Dig this man, just 'cause you see some different pigs coming here, don't get excited. We're going to sleep here, sing here, sex here, live here!' "

As the police moved off, one of the first Guard maneuvers was to clear demonstrators from Michigan's east sidewalk. This was done to allow pedestrian traffic. The crowd reacted somewhat hostilely to the maneuver, but by and large, the demonstrators semed to view the Guard as helpless men who had been caught up in the events and did not treat them as badly as they had the police. Having secured the sidewalk, the guards shortly retired to the east curb of Michigan Avenue. A line of "marshals" sat down at the edge of the grass at the feet of the guards. Access to the hotel was restored and people began to move from the hotel to the park and vice versa. By now, there were an estimated 4,000 persons assembled across from the Hilton. Most of the crowd sat down in a mass and became more orderly, singing "America" and "God Bless America." McCarthy supporters joined the crowd and were welcomed.

By 12:20 a.m., Thursday, the crowd had declined to 1,500 and was considered under control. By 12:33 a.m., the police department had retired from the streets and the Guard took over the responsibility of holding Michingan from Balbo to 8th Street. At 12:47 a.m., another contingent of Guard troops arrived at the Hilton. Delegates were returning and were being booed unless they could be identified as McCarthy or McGovern supporters. Those delegates were cheered and asked to join the group.

The crowd grew in number. By 1:07 a.m., the Secret Service estimated 2,000 persons in the park across from the hotel. Ten minutes later the crowd had grown by another 500. Those in the park were "listening to speeches—orderly" according to the log.

The Violence Commission: Internal Politics and Public Policy

Jerome H. Skolnick

The 1960s are already infamous for assassinations, crime in the streets, student rebellion, black militancy, wars of liberation, law and order—and national commissions. We had the Warren Commission, the Crime Commission, the Riot Commission and the Violence Commission; and the point about them was that they were among the major responses of government to the social dislocations of the decade. Millions of people followed the work of these commissions with interest and gave at least summary attention to their reports. Social scientists were also interested in commissions, though skeptical about their value. Most would probably agree with Sidney and Beatrice Webb's description of Royal Commissions, "These bodies are seldom designed for scientific research; they are primarily political organs, with political objects."

I share this view, yet I have worked with three commis-

sions, albeit under very special arrangements guaranteeing freedom of publication. The discussion that follows is partly analytical and partly autobiographical, especially where I discuss my work as director of the task force on "Violent Aspects of Protest and Confrontation" for the Violence Commission. If the autobiography stands out, that is because I did not participate in commissions to observe them. I studied the phenomena at issue—crime, police, protest and confrontation—not commissions. Still, my experience may be helpful in understanding commission structures, processes and dilemmas.

Constituencies

Commissions have three functioning groups: commissioners, the executive staff, the research staff, with overlapping but distinctive interests.

Andrew Kopkind has recently written that President Lyndon B. Johnson chose the 11 commissioners for his National Advisory Commission on Civil Disorders because of their remarkable qualities of predictable moderation. The Violence Commission, chaired by Dr. Milton Eisenhower, was perhaps even more predictably "moderate" than the Riot Commission. It included a member of the southern and congressional establishment, Congressman Hale Boggs; Archbishop, now Cardinal, Terence J. Cooke, Francis Cardinal Spellman's successor; Ambassador Patricia Harris, standing for both the political woman and the Negro establishment; Senator Philip A. Hart, Democrat of Michigan, associated with the liberal establishment in the Senate; Judge A. Leon Higginbotham, a Negro and a federal judge from Philadelphia; Eric Hoffer, the president's favorite philosopher, presenting the backlash voice of the American workingman; Senator Roman Hruska, Republican of Nebraska, a leading right-wing Republican; and Albert E. Jenner, Jr., prominent in the American Bar Association and in Chicago legal affairs. In addition, there was Republican Congressman William M. McCulloch of Ohio, who had served on the Kerner Commission and was the only overlapping member of both commissions. In response to criticisms that the Riot Commission contained no social scientists, Dr. W. Walter Menninger was appointed, although he is a practicing psychiatrist and not a social scientist. Finally, there were Judge Ernest W. McFarland, the man whom Lyndon Baines Johnson had replaced in the House of Representatives, and another Texan, Leon Jaworski, a close personal adviser to the president and a prominent and conservative lawyer.

Obviously, the commissioners themselves cannot perform the investigative and analytical work of the commission. Commissioners are chosen because apparently they represent various economic and political interests, not because they have distinguished themselves as scholars or experts. In fact, they do not "represent" anyone. What they best mirror is a chief executive's conception of pluralist America.

Moreover, even if a commissioner should have the ability to do the research, he or she usually has other demands on their time. Inevitably, then, the staff of the commission does the work—all of the leg work and the research and most of the writing of the final report, with, of course, the commission's approval.

The staffs of both the Riot Commission and the Violence Commission were similar. The executive staff, working out of Washington, was charged with getting the research and writing job done and with organizing the time of the commission. In each case, the director of the executive staff was a leading Washington attorney who had ties with the Johnson administration, David Ginsburg for the Riot Commission, Lloyd Cutler for the Violence Commission. Moreover, younger attorneys were named as their closest associates.

There had been considerable friction in the Riot Commission between the research staff and the executive staff, as well as between both and the commissioners. According to Andrew Kopkind, the social scientists under Research Director Robert Shellow drafted a document called "The Harvest of American Racism" which went further than most top staff officials thought prudent in charging that racism permeated American institutions. "Harvest" characterized the riots as the first step in a developing black revolution in which Negroes will feel, as the draft put it, that "it is legitimate and necessary to use violence against the social order. A truly revolutionary spirit has begun to take hold . . . and unwillingness to compromise or wait any longer, to risk death rather than have their people continue in a subordinate status." According to Kopkind, both Ginsburg and Victor Palmieri, his deputy director, admitted that they were appalled when they read "Harvest." Shortly after its submission many of the 120 investigators and social scientists were "released" from the commission staff in December 1967 (on public grounds that money was needed to pursue the war in Vietnam). But Kopkind says that there is every reason to believe that the "releasing" was done by Palmieri (with Ginsburg's concurrence) because of the failure of Shellow's group to produce an "acceptable" analytical section. The commissioners themselves are reported to have known little of the firing or of the controversy surrounding it but were persuaded by Ginsburg to go along with it.

I tell this story only because it bears on the central question of what effects, if any, informed researchers and writers can have on the final reports of commissions, the public face they turn to the world. Kopkind, for example, argues that the "Harvest" incident proves that the *Kerner Report* would have been "liberal" regardless of events preceding its final writing. He concludes, "The structure of the Commission and the context in which it operated suggest that its tone could have hardly been other than 'liberal.' The finished product almost exactly reproduced the ideological sense given it by President Johnson more than half a year earlier. The choice of Commissioners, staff, consultants and contractors led in the same direction." Yet that outcome is not at all evident from the rest of Kopkind's analysis, which argues, for example, that the commissioners were selected for their predictable moderation, that one commissioner, Charles Thornton, attempted to torpedo the report just before its launching and that the findings of the report were patently offensive to President Johnson. It is at least arguable that the "liberalism" of the final report was not inevitable, that it might have been far more on the conservative side of "moderate" and that the "Harvest" document had something to do with moving it to the Left.

The Eisenhower Violence Commission

When Senator Robert F. Kennedy was assassinated and the president appointed yet another commission, many observers were suspicious. Was this the only response that Washington could give to domestic tragedy? Even the press gave the Violence Commission unfavorable publicity. The commissioners seemed even more conservative than the riot commissioners. Some considered the commission a devious plot by President Johnson to reverse or smudge the interpretation of civil disorders offered by the Riot Commission.

Furthermore, what could the Violence Commission say that hadn't already been said by the Riot Commission? The distinction between civil disorder and violence was not, and still isn't, self-evident. Moreover, because of the flap over the firing of the social scientists on the Kerner Commission, many of that community were deeply and understandably dubious about the possibility of doing an intellectually respectable job under commission auspices.

The executive staff saw this problem and coped with it, first, by establishing the position of research director, so that social scientists (James F. Short, Jr., jointly with Marvin Wolfgang, as it turned out) occupied a place in the hierarchy of the executive staff, a club usually limited to corporation lawyers. Authority still rested with the executive director, but the research directors performed four important functions; they initiated the commission policy of independent task forces with freedom of publication; they helped select the social science staff; they served as liaison between the social scientists, the executive staff and the commissioners; and they served as good critics and colleagues.

Furthermore, they promoted another departure from Kerner Commission practice, namely that social scientists and lawyers are the co-directors of task forces.

Some additional comments are warranted here because organizational structures and rules may seriously influence intellectual autonomy. University social scientists with little legal or governmental experience may assume that freedom to write and publish follows from well-intentioned assurances of future support. Yet as one experienced man with whom I shared a panel recently put it: "He who glitters may one day be hung."

The social scientist must understand the ways he can be hung and protect himself accordingly. First, his materials can be used and distorted. Second, his name can be used, but his material and advice ignored. This is particularly possible when social scientists hold highranking but relatively powerless titles on the commission. Ultimately, they are placed in the dilemma of seeming to endorse the final product. (In the Violence Commission, for example, the names of James F. Short, Jr., and Marvin Wolfgang seemingly "endorse" the scholarly merit of the final report. In addition, the presence of a recognized social science staff does the same. To this extent, we were all "co-opted," since none of us, including Short and Wolfgang, were responsible for the final report.) Third, he may experience subtle (sometimes not so subtle) pressures to shape or present his findings in favored directions. Finally, his work may be suppressed.

In general, one receives maximum protection with a *written* contract guaranteeing freedom of publication. Beyond that, however, experienced Washington hands can be quite charming—which holds its own dangers for one's intellectual independence.

From the very beginning, the executive staff expressed some doubts about the ultimate impact the commission's own report would have on public policy, or even the shape it would take. Recall that this was the summer of 1968, following the assassination of Senator Kennedy and before the national conventions of both parties. Who could foretell what future event would have what future impact on national politics? Who could, with confidence, predict the nominees for the presidency, the victor and his attitude toward the commission?

Task Force Reports

Like the able corporation lawyers they are, the executive staff came up with a prudent primary goal, a set of books called *Task Force Reports,* which they hoped could be a solid contribution to understanding the causes and prevention of violence in America. I call this goal prudent because it set a standard that was at least possible in theory. From these studies, it was felt, the commission would write its own report; the initial idea was to have each task force report provide the materials for a summary chapter for the commission report.

Modest as this plan was, it soon ran into difficulty. Commissions are usually run at a gallop. With all the best intentions and resources in the world, it is virtually impossible to complete eight books of high quality in five months, particularly when no central vision controls the research and writing. Our own report, *The Politics of Protest,* was completed on time, but we worked under enormous pressure. Still, we had several advantages.

First, a shared perspective among key staff members contributed to a fairly consistent analysis. We shared a deep skepticism about counterinsurgency views of civil disorder as a form of "deviant" pathology that needed to be stamped out as quickly as possible. On the contrary, we assumed that insurgents might conceivably be as rational as public servants. Our approach was influenced, first, by subjectivist and naturalistic perspectives in sociology, which lead one, for instance, to take into account both the point of view of the black rioter and to assume his sanity, and to assume as well the sanity of the policeman and the white militant. Second, we were influenced by revisionist histories of America, which see her as a more tumultuous and violent nation than conventional histories have taught us to believe. Finally, we were influenced by social historical critiques of the theory of collective behavior, which interpret seemingly irrational acts on the part of rioters as forms of primitive political activity, and by an emphasis upon social history in understanding such collective behavior as student protest, rather than upon analysis of "variables."

Another advantage in favor of our task force was that our headquarters was at the Center for the Study of Law and Society at Berkeley. This kept us away from the time-consuming crises of Washington, although the tie-line kept us in daily touch with events there. In addition, the center and the Berkeley campus offered a critical mass of resources that probably could not be duplicated anywhere else. Our location, then, combined with my status as independent contractor with the commission, offered a degree of independence unavailable to the other task force directors. For example, the staff members of our task force were not required to have a White House security clearance.

Finally, the staff was far from unhappy about working for a national commission. Those involved, regardless of expressions of skepticism, were not opposed to making a contribution to a national understanding of the issues involved. My contract with the government, and its contract with me, assured the staff that its best understanding of the issues would be made public.

Given time limitations, it was impossible to undertake the original research one would need for a large-scale social science project. My inclination, shared by the research directors and the executive staff, was to recruit a staff experienced in research on the areas under study. We saw the five-month period as an opportunity to summarize findings rather than to undertake original investigation.

We did, however, conduct original interviews with black militants and with police. As can be imagined, these interviews were not easily obtained. For black militants our interviewer was a man with extensive connections, but who stipulated that he would interview only if we agreed to listen to and not transcribe the tapes and make no notations of who was being interviewed. The interviews substantiated much that we suspected and served to sharpen our analytical outlook. Similarly, the interviews we held with policemen—conducted, incidentally, by a former policeman—served to fill gaps in our thesis that the police were becoming an increasingly politicized force in the United States.

I should also add that our emphasis on social history and political analysis seemed to violate some of the expectations of some portions of our audience.

Audiences and Hearings

The Politics of Protest staff worked with three audiences in mind. First, we were concerned with trying to persuade the commissioners of the validity of our findings and the validity of our analysis. They were our primary audience. Our second was the general public, an audience we had little confidence in being able to influence except,

perhaps, through persuading the commissioners. Most reports have a limited readership—and *The Politics of Protest* isn't exactly *The Love Machine.* So our third audience was the academic community and the media representatives. In the long run, the university had to be our major audience, since the report is scholarly and the media treated with publication as news, quickly displaced by other stories.

The audience for the hearings was both the commissioners and the general public. Several members of the executive staff believed that one reason the Kerner Commission failed to gain public acceptance was its failure to educate the public along the way. The "predictably moderate" commissioners had been emotionally moved in the hearings, especially by representatives of the black communities of America, but the public had never been allowed to hear this testimony. Consequently, the Violence Commission hearings were made public, and each task force was given three days for hearings.

Hearings are a form of theater. Conclusions must be presented to evoke an emotional response in both the commissioners and the wider television audience. In this respect, the planners of the hearings can be likened to the author and director of a play with strategy substituting for plot. Yet strategies can and do go awry, and so the outcome of the play is not determined, nor can one guarantee whether the effect on the audience will be tragic or comedic.

A staff tries to get across a point of view on the subject matter. At the same time, however, it is also expected to be "objective," that is, lacking a point of view. The expectation is that staff and commissioners will walk along fresh roads together, reaching similar conclusions. This expectation derives from the image of a trial. Such an adjudicatory model must, however, be largely fictional. The "judges," the commissioners, already have strong views and political interests, though they are supposed to be neutral. The staff, too, is supposed to lack opinions, even though it was selected because of prior knowledge.

Since strategy substitutes for plot, there really are only three possible outcomes. The play may be a flop, that is, the staff perspective is not communicated; or the perspective is communicated, but unemotional so as to merely make a record; or emotional engagement is achieved. Here social science as theater reaches its ultimate art.

Commissioners are used to hearings, are used to testimony and probably cannot be moved in any new direction unless emotionally engaged. Commissioners are culturally deprived by the privatized life of the man of power. Whatever may have been their former backgrounds, commissioners are now the establishment. They may be driven to and from work, belong to private clubs and remain out of touch with the realities of the urban and political worlds they are assumed to understand. They are both protected and deprived by social privilege.

Moreover, their usual mode of analysis is legalistic and rationalistic. Not intellectuals, they are decision makers interested in protecting the record. Furthermore, they are committed to the prevailing social, economic and political structures, although they will consider reforms of these structures and may well be brought to see contradictions within them. In addition, they are affiliated with certain political and social interests. Consequently, there are practical limits to the possibilities of persuading any of them to a novel position.

The public is another audience for the hearings, but there are also constraints on teaching the public. All that "public hearings" means is that the media are present, not the mass of the public, and the media reports only the most dramatic messages. Also, commissioners themselves become part of the cast. The TV will register an exchange between a witness and a commissioner. So a strategist (director) must anticipate what that exchange might be.

Finally, the presence of the press alters the atmosphere of the hearing room. We held mostly public hearings and some hearings in executive session. With the television cameras and the radio people and the newspaper people present, the commissioners were stiff and formal. When the press left, the commissioners visibly relaxed.

Given these conditions, how does one go about casting? First, we tried to present witnesses who represented a variety of points of view. That was elementary. But within that framework we had to decide: what kinds of witnesses representing what kinds of points of view will bring the most enlightened position with the greatest effect both on the commissioners and on the general public?

There are practical limitations in hearings. Obviously, it may not be possible to get the witness you want, or to get him for a particular day. Ira Heyman, general counsel, and I were given three days for hearings to discuss the antiwar and student movements, black militancy and the responses of the social order. This was not enough time for any of these topics to be adequately discussed. The one day of hearings on black militancy was especially inadequate, although undoubtedly the most exciting. It was also the most difficult to arrange, the most trying and the most rewarding.

Hoffer vs. the Black

First, there was some question as to whether any well-known black militant would have anything to do with the Violence Commission. Even if he should want to, anybody who stepped forward to represent the militant black community could be charged with playing a "personality" game and disavowed as representing even a segment of the black community. After much thought, we decided on Huey P. Newton, minister of defense of the Black Panther party as a widely acceptable representative of black militancy. He was willing to cooperate, politically minded and seeking opportunity to present his point of view.

Herman Blake, an assistant professor of sociology at the University of California at Santa Cruz, joined me in interviewing Newton and was to present the interview to the commissioners. Although Blake would not officially be representing the Panthers, Newton knew him, knew of his work and trusted him to make an accurate analysis of the tape of the interview that was to be played to the commission.

As it turned out, there was no problem at all. Both Blake and I, in Charles Garry's presence, interviewed Newton in the Alameda County Courthouse Jail where he was being held while standing trial for the alleged murder of an Oakland policeman.

The Newton tape, and Blake's testimony, produced an emotionally charged confrontation between Blake and Eric Hoffer and a dignified censure of Hoffer by Judge Higgin-

botham, vice-chairman of the commission.

Mr. Hoffer: I tell you there is rage among the Negroes on the waterfront. It is at the meetings when they get together. Suddenly they are repeating a ritual. A text. You are repeating it. Now I have . . . I don't know of these people, where they were brought up. All my life I was poor and I didn't live better than any Negro ever lived, I can tell you. When I was out picking cotton in the valley the Negroes were eating better than I did, lived in better houses, they had more schooling than I did . . .

Mr. Blake: Have you ever been called a nigger?

Mr. Hoffer: Let me finish it. By the way, the first man in the U.S. I think who wrote about the need to create a Negro community was in 1964 when I . . .

Mr. Blake: Why do you stop calling it a community then?

Mr. Hoffer: I say that you have to build a community. You have to build a community and you are not . . .

Mr. Blake: We can't build a community with white people like you around telling us we can't be what we are.

Mr. Hoffer: You are not going to build it by rage. You are going to build it by working together.

Mr. Blake: You are defining it.

Mr. Hoffer: They haven't raised one blade of grass. They haven't raised one brick.

Mr. Blake: We been throwing them, baby, because you been out there stopping them from laying bricks and raising grass.

Judge Higginbotham: Mr. Chairman . . .

Dr. Eisenhower: Mr. Blake . . .

Mr. Jenner: Would you do me a personal favor and stay for a moment, Mr. Blake?

Judge Higginbotham: Mr. Chairman, if I may, I feel compelled because I trust that this Commission will not let statements go in the record which are such blatant demonstrations of factual ignorance that I am obliged to note on the record how totally in error Mr. Hoffer is on the most elementary data.

The McCone Commission, headed by the former director of Central Intelligence, who I assume while he may not be the philosopher which Mr. Hoffer is, that he is at least as perceptive and more factually accurate. The McCone Commission pointed out that in Watts, California, you had unemployment which ran as high as 30 and 40 percent. Sometimes 50 percent among youth. It pointed out in great detail [that] in the Watts area you had the highest percent of substandard housing any place in L.A.

If my colleague, Mr. Hoffer, who I would like to be able to call distinguished, would take time out to read the data of the McCone Report, which is not challenged by anyone, based on government statistics, at least the first portion of his analysis would be demonstrated to be totally inaccurate, and I am willing, as a black man, to state that what I am amazed at is—that with the total bigotry, patent, extensive among men who can reach fame in this country —[not] that there has been as little unity as there has been. It is surprising that there has been as much.

I think that Mr. Hoffer's statements are indicative of the great racist pathology in our country and that his views are those which represent the mass of people in this country. I think that what Toynbee said that civilizations are destroyed from within, that his comments are classic examples of proving that.

Dr. Eisenhower: Mr. Blake, only because we have two other distinguished persons to testify this afternoon, I am going to conclude this part of our testimony. I want you to know that I personally had some questions to ask you but my good friend Judge Higginbotham asked precisely the questions in his part that I had intended to do. So on behalf of the Commission I thank you for your willingness to come, for your candor, for being with us and I accept the sincerity and truth of what you said to us.

Mr. Blake: Thank you.

That day, I think it is fair to say, was the most emotional day of the hearings for the Violence Commission. Eric Hoffer was an exemplary witness for the depth of racism existing in this country. No wealth of statistics could have conveyed as well to the other commissioners and to the public in general what racism meant to the black man.

Yet Hoffer is also a popular public figure. Moreover, only a minute or so of the hearings was shown on national television. There, Hoffer was seen shouting at a bearded black man in a dashiki. It is doubtful that much enlightenment was achieved by the televising of that exchange. I believe that in the long run the reports themselves will have a far greater impact than the TV time allocated to the hearings.

A first draft of *The Politics of Protest* was sent off to the executive staff of the commission on 27 December 1968, approximately five months after the initial phone call from Washington. They received the report with mixed feelings. They were, I know, impressed with the magnitude and quality of the report, but it violated the kinds of expectations they had about commission reports. We were clearly less concerned about "balance" and "tempered" language than we were about analytical soundness, consistency and clarity. Some of the commissioners were described to me as "climbing the walls as they read it." And this did not make an easy situation for the executive staff. They suggested in January that it be toned down, and I did *not* tell them to go to hell. I listened carefully to their suggestions and accepted most of them concerning language and tone. But I did not alter the analysis in any of the chapters. I.F. Stone was later to call our analysis "Brilliant and indispensable," and a *Chicago Tribune* editorial ranked it alongside the *Walker Report* as "garbage."

The Impact of Commission Reports

Since the report was published, I have often been asked the question: Of what use is all this? Does it actually contribute to public policy? My answer is, I don't know. *The Politics of Protest* apparently made little impact on the commission itself. It was cited only once in the final report of the commission, and then out of context. But the book has been given considerable publicity, has been widely and favorably reviewed and has been widely adopted for classroom use. The major audience for *The Politics of Protest* will probably be the sociology and political science class, although more than most books on this subject it will find its way into the hands of decision makers.

The Politics of Protest will also provide an alternative analysis to the main report of the Violence Commission. Naturally, we think our analysis is more pointed, more consistent, more scholarly and more directed to the historical causes of American violence than the commission's own report, which adopts a managerial, counterinsurgency perspective that looks to symptoms rather than causes. But history will tell. Reports sponsored by commissions are ultimately intellectual documents subject to the criticism that any book or investigation might receive.

Yet they are something more as well. Despite the increasing tendency among radicals and intellectuals to challenge the usefulness and integrity of commission reports, they do tend to create an interest over and above that of similar work by individual scholars. One can even point to a series of commission reports that have had an enormous impact—those used by Karl Marx in developing his critique of capitalist production. Without the narrative provided by these commissions, Marx's *Capital* would have been a much more abstract and predictably obscure document and simply would not have attracted the readership it did. Marx himself, in his preface to *Capital,* offers an accolade to these investigative commissions.

Commission reports, whatever their analytical strictures, defects or omissions, come to have a special standing within the *political* community. If a social scientist or a journalist gathers "facts" concerning a particular institution, and these facts are presented in such a way as to offer a harshly critical appraisal of that social institution, the gathering and the analysis of such facts may be called "muckraking." But if the same or a similar set of facts is found by a commission, it may be seen as a series of startling and respectable social findings.

And herein lies the essential dilemma posed by the commission form of inquiry. On the one hand, we find a set of high-status commissioners whose name on a document will tend to legitimize the descriptions found therein; and on the other hand, precisely because of the political character of the commissioners, the report will be "bal-anced" or "inconsistent" depending on who is making the judgment. A commission, upon hearing one expert testify (correctly) that there is darkness outside and another testify (incorrectly) that the sun is shining will typically conclude that it is cloudy.

Nevertheless, whatever facts are gathered and are presented to the public, they are in the public domain. No set of facts is subject only to one interpretation and analysis. Surely it was not in the minds of the commissioners of inquiry in nineteenth-century England to provide the factual underpinning for a Marxist critique of capitalist production. Yet, there was no way to stop it. So my point is simply this: to the extent that a commission of inquiry develops facts, it necessarily has done something of social value. Its interpretations can be challenged. How those facts and how those interpretations will be met and used depends upon the integrity and ability of the intellectual community.

The Failure of Fail-Safe

John R. Raser

"We have defiled our intellect by the creation of such scientific instruments of destruction that we are now in desperate danger of destroying ourselves. Our plight is critical and, with each effort we have made to relieve it by further scientific advances, we have succeeded only in aggravating our peril. As a result, we are now speeding inexorably toward a day when even the ingenuity of our scientists may be unable to save us from the consequences of a single rash act or a lone reckless hand upon the switch of an uninterceptible missile"

General of the Army Omar N. Bradley, Nov. 5, 1957

Every man—whether poet or pimp, philosopher or philanderer—likes to believe that the work to which he applies his energies is of some value. He may define that value in any number of ways: It uplifts the spirit of man, it serves basic human cravings, it increases man's comprehension of the universe, or it fulfills his own indisputable drives. Most of us, lauding consistency more than living it, claim all of the above things at some time, and rationalize our work in terms of any or all of the named values. And like Jeremy Bentham, or like Max Spielman in John Barth's novel *Giles Goat Boy,* we are likely to measure our work by "examining each moment whether what we are doing just now is likely to add to, or detract from, the sum of human misery." It's a tricky and uncertain rule, but it may be the best we can find.

Students of human behavior—behavioral scientists—have special problems in these areas, both because what we study (humankind) is the most precious and volatile element in our world, and because what we discover in our studies can have such a potent effect on the destiny of the very object of study—human beings. Because the study of human behavior is so crucial, and so poorly understood, I should like to outline what behavioral scientists do.

Briefly, we try to understand how human beings act in a variety of situations, by studying them in laboratories and clinics, by using interviews and questionnaires, and by examining historical cases. Some of us go a step further. We interpret what we have learned and apply it to problems of human existence—child-rearing, marital relations, racial tensions, poverty, the population explosion, educational policy, or war.

It is this last—war—that is my major interest, and that I wish to discuss. I should like to report on several studies of what happens to human beings in a crisis, then apply the findings of those studies to some aspects of modern warfare. In doing so, I have two objectives. First, I hope to demonstrate that those of us who engage in these difficult and frequently maligned analyses of human behavior sometimes have good reason to believe that our work *is* of value and *does* contribute to the alleviation of human misery; and second, I hope to furnish insights into the crucial role that various assumptions about human behavior can have upon questions of the design of weapons and upon modern military strategy.

I should like to begin by summarizing the findings of several research projects. The first, by James A. Robinson, a professor of political science at Ohio State University, is "Simulating Crisis Decision-Making." The second, "Crises in Foreign Policy Making: A Simulation of International Politics," is by Charles F. Hermann of Princeton University. The third, written at Stanford by Ole R. Holsti, is "Perceptions of Time and Alternatives as Factors in Crisis Decision-Making." The last is a book by physiological psychologist Walter Cannon, *Bodily Changes in Pain, Hunger, Fear and Rage.*

Now, these are jaw-breaking titles and it is obvious from just listing them—without reference to their contents, which are larded with graphs, tables, and formulas—that this is not the type of literature that one keeps on one's coffee table for light reading. Nor are they the kind of document likely to be found in a Congressman's briefcase, a President's chambers, or a general's quarters. But they *are* worth knowing about.

The first two, by Robinson and Hermann, are reports

of a complicated laboratory experiment in which military officers acted out the roles of national and military decision-makers in "games" of international affairs. The experimenters introduced crises into the games at various stages—crises that suddenly confronted the officers with intense threats to the achievement of their goals. In studying the officers' behavior in such crises, the experimenters were able to determine that, as a crisis became more intense, the men lost some of their ability to evaluate information, were able to consider fewer alternative courses of action, and tended to be less flexible. In short, as threat increased and time for response decreased, their ability to cope with the situation was lessened.

War Messages Reveal Human Deterioration

Holsti's study applied a sophisticated technique of computer analysis to the six-weeks'-long period preceding the outbreak of World War I. His study of the pattern of message flow, and his analysis of the contents of the messages, show plainly that as the crisis intensified, the key governmental and military decision-makers of Austria-Hungary, Germany, ·England, France, and Russia responded in the same manner as the officers in Robinson and Hermann's laboratory experiment. The decision-makers saw fewer alternatives, they distorted their position in relationship to others, their messages became more stereotyped, and they began to lose the ability to think in long-range terms, focusing their attention instead on extricating themselves from the current problem—and damn the long-range consequences. Thus, as threat intensified, their ability to think and act rationally degenerated, as was true of the officers in the laboratory study.

These studies are among the most recent analyses of the effects of a crisis on decision-making in international relations. Other studies indicate that in most areas of human concern—child-rearing, domestic relations, driving, business, and, indeed, all human activity—conditions of crisis generate similar effects. Panic, terror, hysteria, confusion, anger, and even merely "being rattled" or "upset" can produce these lapses in a person's mental ability. According to the late Harry Stack Sullivan, even the mildest forms of a crisis create

" . . . a considerable degree of imperception, an arrest of constructive, adaptive thinking, and a high degree of suggestibility to almost anything that seems simple and a way out of the difficult situation. There is complete insensitivity to elaborate, difficult suggestions; but the person is relatively impotent to ward off or to resist any simple idea that is given to him."

The point to keep in mind from these three studies, then, is that in times of crisis one is just not able to function as well mentally as one normally does.

The book by Walter Cannon records over 40 years of research on people from several races and cultures. When fear or anger are aroused, he reports, our bodies change. Adrenaline shoots into the bloodstream, the heart speeds up and pumps faster, the muscles expand, the nerves and muscles in the back tense, blood sugar increases, and strength becomes measurably greater. In brief, when faced with a sudden threat, people become—physically—superb fighting machines, far more capable of meeting that threat than otherwise—*if the threat is immediate and physical, and if physical violence is needed to counter it!* Like a cornered rat suddenly transformed into a screeching bundle of fury, launching itself with bared teeth at a man 100 times its size, a desperate and afraid human being turns into a frightening engine of destruction. But as Cannon also points out, while the body gorges itself with strength on account of fear, the mind loses its focus. We think less clearly, we lose our perspective, vision becomes centered on the source of our fear—we are "in a blind rage." Like the rat, we may launch ourselves against an overwhelming adversary, only to go down in "glorious" defeat.

These studies, then, give us a picture supported by much other research. Threat, fear, and rage (crises) *stimulate* us physically but *impair* our mental powers. That's the way we are built, that's how the evolutionary process has coded our glands to operate.

Weaponry Changes War, Not Men

Now I want to change the subject momentarily and discuss the nature of war. Not its value or morality, but its nature. I simply want to describe what it has been like to fight in a war, and how this has changed as we have created sophisticated weaponry to serve our dreams and fears.

Centuries ago, men fought on foot or from horseback, from behind walls and towers. They fought with clubs, knives, spears, swords, bows and arrows, slings, and axes. The Greek or the Hun charged into battle with his every cell inflamed with rage, his heart pounding, adrenaline surging through his veins, his muscles bulging. The defender, too, crouching in his fortress or dashing for his weapon, was suddenly hit with terror, and then rage as he saw the slaughter begin, and he too was transformed into a madly fighting animal. For both, their physiological responses served them well, and their heroic actions became the stuff of epic literature.

More recent developments in weapons mean that the combatants often face one another with guns and flaming jellies. When the man in the trench is suddenly shaken by an exploding shell, or watches his friend's face shattered by a well-placed bullet, rage hits him, his body responds, and his thinking blanks. Screaming vengeance, he may charge suicidally into a hail of machine-gun fire, or dash to toss a grenade into a gunnery nest, or singlehandedly disarm a tank with stones or Molotov cocktails. Again, occasional success is the result. More often, on account of such new death-dealing devices, the outcome is horrible death. Man's instinctual reactions are beginning to conflict with his own cleverness in creating weapons—and are serving him less well. But usually only a few die, so, such incidents, while sad, are probably not important in the scheme of the universe.

But with some types of modern weapons, infinitely greater power has been placed in the hands of the individual. The strategic-bomber pilot over Germany or North Vietnam with his load of TNT or napalm, winging towards his industrial or military target, consults a hundred instruments, a dozen charts, groggily remembers a morning briefing, co-ordinates his crew. Now the defenders react—fighters dive from above, flak and missiles ascend from below. Fear clutches the pilot's heart, rage clouds his vision, he is less able to think clearly, he forgets his information, he tries desperately to get out of trouble—his pounding heart, pulsing veins, and tense muscles are not an aid to him at all, but a hindrance, while his impaired mental power makes him a less, not more, effective fighting man. The result may be, and often is, a blanket of death dumped in fury or error on an innocent hamlet, an empty field, or on the pilot's own troops. No longer is the man whose reasoning power collapses in a crisis the only one to suffer; now others must pay the price. And if the man whose judgment falters under pressure is not a bomber pilot but a chief of

state, as in 1914, the world might be plunged into war and several million people might die. But again, in a limited war using conventional weapons, the destruction is nowhere near total. Fifty years after the armistice, the war has lost its sharp outlines, new problems have plagued the world, and the race of man goes on.

When untold nuclear firepower is added to the equation, however, the outcome is different. In our preoccupation with jungle and paddy war in Vietnam, we have let this fact recede to the backs of our minds, but there is another—and all-encompassing—spectre of violence dominating our world. That spectre consists of arsenals of nuclear destruction designed to deter the very holocaust they render possible. To the brains and judgments of individual men has been coupled the power of the suns. Belligerents confront one another across the world—hostile, angry, fearful, threatening and being threatened—and the world is always on the brink of crisis. No longer does the nuclear warrior face his enemy man to man; now he is tangled in a vast complex of gadgets. He is expected to be a servomechanism to electronic devices, a brain plugged into a vast machine, a single circuit in an endlessly complex chain of command. He has been physically emasculated and intellectually extended. His is the brain, the decision unit; but the mechanical extensions of his senses and of his muscles embrace the globe.

Having now reported some behavioral-science research findings on human reactions to threat and crisis, and having sketched the changing nature of man's role in warfare, I should like to combine the two discussions. In doing so, I hope to show how these human reactions may confound the intent and functioning of these weapons systems. I will use just one example—that of the nuclear submarine, usually considered the most reliable deterrence instrument in the American arsenal.

Forty-one of these Polaris submarines prowl the depths of the oceans, each carrying more explosive power than has been expended in the history of warfare. Each is linked to headquarters by radio waves. Each is commanded by officers chosen for their reliability. In 1964 some strategists began to question that reliability, suggesting that it might be safer if there were some kind of electronic lock-up of the missiles, a lock-up that could be released only by radio signal from headquarters—a Permissive Action Link, as it was designated. The Navy's response was an outraged assertion that these officers had been carefully selected, painstakingly trained, and continually tested, and that they could be totally trusted to behave responsibly— *never* to fire unless ordered to and *always* to fire if ordered to. And the admirals won the dispute. The PAL proposal was dropped and, following a large-scale rescreening program of the Strategic Air Command and Navy personnel who occupied key positions, the assumption was "bought" that the men were a totally reliable component in the decision system.

As we have seen, this very assumption may have been wrong. It may be wrong even with the safeguard of the most sophisticated selection and testing programs. Bruno Bettelheim, a psychiatrist who spent two years in Dachau and Buchenwald, reports of his fellow-prisoners that:

"The way a person acted in a showdown could not be deduced from his inner, hidden motives, which, likely as not, were conflicting. Neither his heroic nor his cowardly dreams, his free associations or conscious fantasies permitted correct predictions as to whether, in the next moment, he would risk his life to protect the life of others, or out of panic betray many in a vain effort to gain some advantage for himself."

The same is true of military officers. Roy Grinker and John Spiegel, psychiatrists who conducted studies of aircraft combat crews during World War II, reported the results of interviews, as well as the results of their intensive testing program. They concluded:

". . . no matter how 'normal' or 'strong' an individual is, he may develop a neurosis if crucial stress impinging on him is sufficiently severe. . . . Furthermore, it has been learned that the important psychological predispositions to 'operational fatigue' are usually latent and therefore difficult to detect until they are uncovered by catastrophic events. It must be concluded that for the vast majority the *only test for endurance of combat is combat itself.*"

They go on to state that military-security regulations prohibit their giving statistics as to how often soldiers collapse during combat!

Surely, you might say, the skills of selection boards and psychiatric procedures have been improved in the more than 20 years since the end of World War II. But not according to two of the men responsible for the Navy's selection and testing program. Captain R.L. Christy and Commander J.E. Rasmussen write that:

". . . the information which is available suggests that the present-day program is not nearly as effective as it was during World War II. . . . Moreover, the general training and experience level of psychiatrists and clinical psychologists assigned to these activities has generally decreased since the end of the Korean War."

They point out that "the program is least effective with high-level personnel where the examiner is faced with complex personality structures and sophisticated defense mechanisms," and conclude that:

"In simplest terms, it is unrealistic to expect any examiner to identify a reasonably well integrated individual's Achilles' heel and the unique combination of emotional and situational factors which could render him ineffective in the unforeseeable future."

What are the implications of this for nuclear weapons systems and their control personnel? The authors state that:

"When the manpower supply is plentiful, it well may be wise to adopt rather high and rigid psychiatric assessment standards for use with men assigned to nuclear weapons. *Some adjustment of the standards becomes necessary during periods of critical manpower shortage.*" (Emphasis added.)

And finally:

"Isolated instances exist, such as those recently reported in the press releases on the human-reliability problem, where obviously unfit individuals have been assigned to nuclear-weapons systems and subsequently have been responsible for potentially disastrous situations. There is no question that the majority of these individuals would have been disqualified for such an assignment if they had undergone psychiatric assessment prior to assuming their duties in a nuclear-weapons system. However, it has been the authors' experience that *the most potentially dangerous situations in the Navy have involved personnel who demonstrated no evidence of psychiatric disturbance at the time of their initial assignment to militarily sensitive duties.* Moreover, as a rule these individuals function in a highly effective fashion for a considerable length of time prior to developing psychiatric illness. Quite frequently, in retrospect, one could not have anticipated that the illness would have developed in this particular group of patients even though the presence of certain underlying psychopathology might have been recognized."

This, then, is the reality behind the military public-relations programs that would persuade us that we can "sleep tight tonight" since our fates are in the hands of infallibly reliable guardians. But behind the public facade, the military has also apparently recognized the frailty of man, for most weapons systems have been hedged with some sort of "fail-safe" arrangement. With the Polaris, for example, only after receiving a sequence of radio signals may a submarine commander fire his missiles at predetermined targets. And this firing requires that several men perform coordinated tasks. The captain and his crew are *never* supposed to decide on their own to fire those missiles. They *can*—it's technically possible—but they aren't supposed to. The captain must *coordinate* the efforts of a group of subordinates in order to fire the missiles, the assumption being that if the captain loses his judgmental ability, the others will retain theirs and thus prevent a mistaken firing.

Officers Rarely Questioned

Yet this assumption, too, is probably wrong. These are men who are chosen for compatibility, who have worked and thought and reasoned together. Chances are very good that they will react in the same way to any crisis. Grinker and Spiegel discuss the intense emotional bonds that grow among combat crews and the almost mystical sense of trust and interdependence that develops, concluding that "From a psychological point of view, the combat leader is a father and the men are his children." And even if the subordinates have doubts, there is research showing that they will most probably obey their captain's order. Paul Torrance has conducted research on B-26 crews and finds that when there is disagreement among them on a correct solution to a problem, the captain nearly always carries the others with him, regardless of whether his decision is "objectively" right or wrong. German officers obeyed, almost to the last man, even though many of them could not have truly accepted Hitler's doctrines. Laboratory subjects will obey an experimenter's instructions to the point of inflicting (so they think) intense electrical shocks on another subject, simply because an experimenter instructs them to do so "for the purposes of the research." When asked later why they did it, the subjects responded, with surprise at the question, "Why, we were told to." The drive to obey an authority seen as legitimate is almost overwhelming—even among students! How much stronger it must be for a military man not to behave mutinously when the "authority" is his senior officer.

My main point, however, is that these men control immense destructive power—and that they alone can check its use. Nothing but the sanity and cool judgment of *all* such key men in the world keep us alive today. Not only submarine commanders, but heads of state, secretaries of defense, radar observers, generals, and bomber-wing and missile-complex commanders must be able to think rationally, interpret information correctly, and act responsibly—keep cool heads in crisis after crisis, and wait patiently and soberly during times of calm. And it must be *all* of them.

This is the way the world is—poised on the brink of destruction because of the assumption that we can rely on the wisdom and cool judgment of these men at all times. Let me sketch a playlet demonstrating the possible consequences of our having failed to make an examination of that assumption before we acted on it.

Both the Soviet Union and the United States (not to mention France, Great Britain, China, and a dozen other countries that may soon join them) have long-range bombers, intercontinental missiles, shorter-range bombers and missiles, and fleets of submarines, all carrying arsenals of nuclear weapons and all under the control of men who must use their good judgment about striking or holding. Let's place our cast of actors on the submarines, since we started with them and since they are often touted as the most error-proof weapons system. If it's *conceivable* that an accident could occur with Polaris, leading to a decision that leads to an unintended war, then the danger is even greater with B-52s, Minuteman missile complexes, and short-range strike forces operating in the European corridors.

The United States and the Soviet Union also have been trying very hard to find ways of detecting these submarines so they cannot remain invulnerable in war. Suppose that in about 1970—in the midst of a Pueblo-like crisis—the Soviet Union responds by asserting that its own intelligence efforts are not inferior to those of the United States, that it has just perfected a radical new means of detecting submerged Polaris submarines. The United States, unwilling to believe this and afraid of domestic and allied reaction, denies that the Soviet Union has succeeded. The Soviet leaders, facing internal critics of the country's unaggressive stance over Vietnam, decide to demonstrate their military potency to the United States, the power of their technology to the world, and their vigorous leadership to their own people. They daringly plan to knock out one Polaris in such a way that everyone will be pretty certain that they did it, but no one could prove it. (Recall the Thresher incident if you like.) They track a submarine with one of their location ships (a fishing trawler); they find its range in the depths of the Indian ocean; they launch a salvo of long-range torpedoes. What they don't know is that the United States has made some recent sonic advances of its own. The submarine detects the oncoming torpedoes and takes evasive action, so it is not the "clean kill" upon which the attacker had relied, but a "near miss." The torpedoes explode, the submarine's hull is damaged, water begins to flood in, panic hits the crew. All is chaos. The men know they will die in a few minutes. The officers, on the basis of instrument readings, are certain that the Polaris has been hit by the Russians, but due to the damage, the depth at which they are cruising, and the attacker's jamming, they cannot establish radio contact with headquarters. Visions of mushroom clouds turning their families into ashes, visions that have haunted their minds for months, suddenly well to the surface; rage explodes in their bodies. Their hearts begin to pound, adrenaline shoots into their blood streams, their muscles expand, their breathing rates accelerate, their blood-sugar levels increase, their muscular strength nearly doubles—but . . . to what end? There is no charging foe, no soul-curdling yell to let out; there are only rows of cold buttons to push. Their reasoning falters, they can't think of alternatives, their memories function inadequately, they can't accurately process information coming in over their meters, they lose track of the long-term perspective and begin to act reflexively. The captain gives the command—"We must accomplish our mission. We will not die in vain." The crew, stunned and equally irrational, obeys.

The final act thus begins. The submarine is desperately trimmed for firing. The missiles lift from their capsules. Suddenly every decision level is in crisis, from radar observer to premier, and reflexes replace reflection. The Soviet Union, now under real attack, despairingly begins to retaliate; the United States orders its counterforce strike; the macabre dance of death unfolds, and in a few hours the world has been reduced to radioactive rubble. There are survivors, but the final curtain of dust does its work well; in a few generations the genetic key has been cruelly twisted, the race of man retreats into mutant extinction, the insects begin their rule of the next geological epoch.

This particular scenario is dramatic and unlikely. It is also tragic and possible. Five nations have thousands of separate weapons systems spread over the world, each with individual command units. As early as 1960, an authoritative report indicated that U.S. nuclear systems had already suffered 10 major accidents and about 50 minor ones—and this, of course, did not include the Thresher incident, the U-2 crashes, Vietnam activities, or nuclear bombs dropped off Spain and Greenland. Premier Khrushchev reportedly told Richard Nixon about an erratic Soviet missile that was destroyed by a signal from the ground as it headed toward Alaska, and on another occasion he implied that military commanders, on their own initiative, could order an attack on American U-2 bases. And these realities obtain in only a short period of time, and with the most "responsible" and sophisticated nuclear powers! In a few years there will be many more such nations. How much compounded will the chance of such crises be when Indonesia, Egypt, Israel, or South Africa have their own primitive nuclear complexes to reinforce their local quarrels? And we may be sure that the experience and technology of every other country will not match the expertise that provides the safeguards incorporated into a Polaris.

How to Control for Human Flaws

Coupling the individual human being to the power of the suns has meant that man's physiological response to crisis may no longer be functional—it may be a tragic flaw. He has become an unwitting victim of his own clever machinations. Now that we have attached our brains to intricate machines of near limitless power, and swaddled our tumescent bodies in frustrating physical inaction, even in the thick of warfare, man may become a self-destroying misfit.

This conceivable scenario with even the relatively foolproof Polaris highlights two basic assumptions on

253

whose accuracy the fate of the world may rest: (1) that carefully selected men will retain cool judgment in an intense crisis, and (2) that even if one man fails, others will act as a "fail-safe" device. Yet, as I have demonstrated, *behavioral-science research shows that both assumptions are almost certainly false.*

We have been trapped, trapped by our egos, into believing that under any conditions we human beings can control both ourselves and the limitless machines to which we attach ourselves. This belief grew out of 17th-century rationalism, and has been reinforced by our spectacular success in mastering our environment. And we *are* good—damned good—at creating a world in our image and in controlling that world. But there are little foxes, fragile seams, weak links, Achilles' heels, endemic to the human condition, and it well behooves us to lower our ego defenses enough to hear the voices of those who have examined human behavior at its extremes—the kind of extremes that can face decision-makers upon whose infallibility we rely. Sometimes these voices can tell us not only where we are making mistakes, but how we might rectify them.

In 1965 I suggested that the Polaris submarines retain their 1200-mile range missiles rather than getting 2500-mile range missiles; and that they be kept "off-station" or out of range of their targets by several hours' sailing time. This would mean that they *could* be used as retaliatory threats (which is what we claim they are for), but that they would *not* be in the provocative position of being able to strike first without warning, and that they could *not* cause a terrible escalation of the kind of incident I have just described. The responses from military and governmental personnel were that this was an intriguing idea, but since it would mean that Polaris could not be used in a "counterforce" role, the idea could not be taken seriously (as if the use of Polaris in counterforce targeting were somehow decreed by God, or as if counterforce strategies themselves had been proven desirable); or that it was "too late," since the long-range missiles were already in production; or that it would be pointless unless all of our weapons systems could receive the same treatment. In short, the reaction was one of unwillingness to cope with the really difficult problems, a response of fatalistic resignation to the uncontrollability of our destinies, and of detachment from the horror that we may be hastening.

National decision-makers must decide how to build weapons systems; they must decide whether to rely on "nuclear deterrence" or some other strategy. They must make endless assumptions (often unconsciously) about what people are like, how people will respond to crisis, to threat, to rage, to boredom, to too much or too little information, and so on and on. But it is not their business to read endless and often badly written research reports; it is beyond their scope to understand the complex scientific methods used in exposing the intricate dynamics of human behavior. Thus, these decision-makers often act in ignorance—they make false assumptions.

The scholar—the serious student of human behavior, like Robinson, Hermann, Holsti, Cannon, and myself—believes that someone must be responsible for examining policy in the light of the things we are learning about how human beings function. We believe we are failing in our mission unless we tap the policy-maker on the shoulder and tell him we have reason to believe that he is making an unjustified assumption or an erroneous decision. And if he fails to respond to the tap, some of us believe we need to use whatever skills we can generate to collar and shake him, to shout in his ear—to *make* him listen. Otherwise, we are being irresponsible in our role as scholars.

What I have said in the last few pages is just one "minor" illustration of the kind of contribution we can make. Polaris *has* been improved over the years, on the basis of the designers' better understanding about the complexities of human behavior. It is far more difficult to devise a credible "accidental war" scenario now than it was in 1960—or 1965.

But many issues—from other, less stable weapons systems to negotiating strategies, from our policy towards China, or in Vietnam, to race relations or population growth—are crying for analysis and understanding. We behavioral scientists are not simply teaching industry how to administer personality tests better, or teaching the Defense Department how to design a bomber cockpit better, or teaching the Peace Corps how to train a volunteer better.

In many instances we are digging up information that is revolutionary—information that may suggest that a radical revision is necessary in the basic policy assumptions of our nation's decision-makers, and of decision-makers throughout the world.

Creative Alternatives to a Deadly Showdown

Muzafer Sherif

For some years, the world has lived in the ominous shadow of a deadly showdown. The consequences of such a tragic climax have been vividly described by the creators of weapons themselves. These grim consequences have led many to search for measures to avoid a showdown and to reduce the conflicts which are at its roots.

Among the various measures advocated are the following:

Various models of deterrence, that is, up-to-date models of the old "balance of power."

Conferences of leaders and their representatives to negotiate differences.

Programs of person-to-person contact, such as exchange of persons and conferences of students, scientists, businessmen, artists and teachers.

Dissemination of information designed to correct erroneous views of each other held by the parties in conflict.

There is at least one condition necessary if any of these measures are to be effective—the provision of a broad *motivational* basis for contacts, communication, and negotiation. If such a broad motivational basis is created any one of these measures, except the first, permits creative alternatives to a deadly showdown. I will touch on these measures and their variants in context. First, however, I should make it clear why I do not regard the first—namely, deterrence—as a creative solution.

As C. N. Barclay, British military author, stated in the *New York Times Magazine* of May 5, 1963 (p. 17): "The deterrent is the modern version of the balance of power, employed in the past—not very successfully—to keep the peace in Europe. The difference lies in the fact that failure to keep the peace in the days of conventional weapons . . . was not universally fatal. Failure with nuclear weapons, on the other hand, would be catastrophic for all mankind". Let us not be misled by new trappings or the use of high speed computers. A rose by any other name smells as sweet, and deterrence smells like a preliminary to war. In contrast, the aim of the other measures is to reduce con-conflict, not maintain it.

THE RESEARCH BACKGROUND

Whatever a social psychologist such as myself can contribute to the search for alternatives to a headlong plunge into mass destruction must rest on the research and theory in his specialty. I will, therefore, mention briefly the factual basis for my conclusions.

Fifteen years ago, we began a program of research on conflict between human groups and its resolution. Hunches, or hypotheses if you like, were based on existing research and on cases of conflict between groups of all sizes and description. Our hunches concerned conditions *sufficient* for the development of conflict between groups, along with the hostile acts and attitudes that accompany it, and conditions *necessary* for the subsequent reduction of the conflict and change of the participants' attitudes. Three experiments were conducted, each continuing 24 hours a day for nearly a month.

Here, I will not go into details of the experiments, which will be of interest mainly to fellow social psychologists and which are readily available in print. A brief summary, however, may be in order as a point of departure for the focus of this paper.

The experiments started with two bunches of unacquainted and very similar individuals, brought to a summer camp. By presenting them with situations where pulling together with one's fellows led to desired ends, we soon had two genuine groups—each with its own recognized leader, name, and local customs. Once the groups formed, a series of events was introduced in which the victory of one group inevitably meant defeat for the other. Over a period of time, as predicted, the two groups became hostile toward each other; they called each other names; they disliked each other intensely, and they began to fight. This unfortunate outcome was a necessary preliminary to the study of various measures in reducing conflict between groups.

GROUP CONFLICTS AND STEREOTYPES

In the course of encounters between the groups, each individual—whether leader or appointed representative or rank-and-file—acted as a loyal, responsible member of his group. Being loyal and responsible, in this case, meant that he directed his energies and efforts against the rival. The unfavorable qualities, the derogatory stereotypes attributed to the other group, as derogatory stereotypes were the *products* of this process, and were not an initial condition for it. One's own group was endowed with favorable qualities which were self-justifying and even self-glorifying. The rival group was assigned stereotyped traits which justified its treatment as an enemy. Since this is a *product* of intergroup conflict, and is not its initial cause, attempts to remove the stereotyped conceptions in and of themselves—through information, pleas for fair-mindedness or justice—are ordinarily rather futile and fruitless.

Once hostile attitudes and unfavorable stereotypes of another group are stabilized, they influence the manner in which individual members see and size up events. Each side sees the actions of the other through the colored glasses of hostility, which filter out the favorable colors in which we see ourselves and our friends. Undoubtedly, this filtering process affects the judgment of *negotiators* and *representatives*. For example, in one experiment, an individual holding a high position in his own group decided, with the best of motives, that the time had come to negotiate peaceful relations with the hostile group. He was received by them as an enemy who sought to mislead them with pretended expressions of reconciliation. His departure was accompanied by a hail of "ammunition" collected by the group "in case" they were attacked—in this case, green apples.

THE LEADER REJECTED

Equally interesting was the fate of this individual, who had made reasonable attempts at reconciliation, when he returned to his own group. Far from being received as a hero, he was chastised for even making the attempt. This is but one of many examples of the fact that leadership, representation, and negotiation between groups are governed primarily by and operate within the bounds acceptable in each group. If he is to negotiate effectively, a leader or his delegate must remain a part of his own group. In order to do so, he must act in ways that his fellow members regard as acceptable and decent, in terms of their group's definitions. The realistic alternatives that a leader or negotiator can consider, therefore, are limited. Not all possible alternatives that are logically conceivable, or even rational, are realistically available. The realistic alternatives are those that are clearly acceptable to members of his own group at the time. In large groups, where negotiations may be conducted in secret, a leader has somewhat more latitude. But there is not one leader in the world today who could long remain in power after committing his group to a course clearly unacceptable to the members.

How can the blinding stereotypes and self-justifications of groups in conflict change, and how can the vicious circle stop, if the groups do not accept the regulation of some still larger body? Many methods are effective in the context of a series of superordinate goals, which are felt as urgent by *all* parties involved.

NEW COMMUNICATION POSSIBLE

When contacts between persons involve superordinate goals, communication is utilized to reduce conflict in order to find means of attaining common goals. True and favorable information about the other group is seen in a new light, and then the probability of this information being effective is enormously enhanced.

When groups cooperate toward superordinate goals, their leaders are in a position to take bolder steps toward greater mutual understanding and trust. Lacking superordinate goals, however, genuine moves by a leader to reduce intergroup conflict may be seen by his own group as out-of-step and ill-advised. He may be subjected to severe criticism and even to a loss of faith. Where there are superordinate goals, however, these encourage a leader to make moves to advance cooperative efforts. He can more freely delegate authority, and negotiation can proceed more effectively. The decisions reached are more likely to receive support from other group members.

There are some similarities between these experiments and real life. First, the entire experience was very natural for the individuals studied, and the problems they faced were very real to them. They cared a great deal about their groups and their vicissitudes. Second, like many groups in real life, behavior toward the other group was not regulated by rules enforced by some superior authority. The groups formulated their own ways of relating to each other.

Being experiments, however, these studies were necessarily in miniature. The groups were small, as they had to be to have experimental control of their habitat. The members were young boys; since then, however, similar results have been obtained by other investigators working with adults.

Still, there is a genuine problem of whether or not one is justified in drawing analogies between what happened to these small groups and what happens to large and powerful nations. I leave this to your judgment and, ultimately, to the outcome of future research conducted on a larger scale.

SUPERORDINATE GOALS

I shall now venture to state some things we learned from these experiments about intergroup conflict and its reduction. A variety of measures were proposed for the reduction of conflict and were tried out in the experiments. One of these turned out to be a *necessary* condition for the avoidance of violent alternatives.

This necessary condition is the existence of "superordinate goals." Superordinate goals are those ends greatly desired by all those caught in dispute or conflict, which cannot be attained by the resources and energies of each of the parties separately, but which require the concerted efforts of all parties involved. Even in our miniature experiments, we found that a *series* of superordinate goals was required if concerted effort was to become general, and if hostility was to turn to friendly interchange between groups. Even at this level, the reduction of intergroup conflict is not a one-shot affair. A series of superordinate goals has a cumulative effect, which provides a broad motivational base on which person-to-person contacts, information, and conferences between leaders or representatives can become effective.

Communication must be opened between groups before prevailing hostilities can be reduced. But person-to-person contact and communication without goals which are urgent, compelling, and highly appealing to *all* groups involved frequently serve only as mediums for further accusations and recriminations. The discussion or the negotiation gets bogged down, directly or indirectly, in the fruitless question of "Who's to blame?" for the existing state of affairs.

The experiments revealed a dynamic sequence resulting in a vicious circle, with each side justifying its own actions and casting blame on the other side. For this to happen, it was sufficient to have two groups, each pitted against the other for a goal that can be won only if one group fails. It is also pertinent to note that individual members need not in any way be neurotic or sinful for the vicious circle to occur.

In the experiments, the groups were from the same culture and the members were as similar in background and appearance as possible. Shall we then, attribute their behavior to universal human nature? Since we arranged the conditions which started this vicious circle and since we later successfully altered it, there is no justification for assuming that this is "just the way of human nature."

When the groups in our experiments were in conflict, considering each other as enemies, each adopted a policy of deterrence. In addition to security measures designed to conceal their possessions and locations, weapons were improvised from available resources and were hoarded "in case" they were needed. Banners were destroyed and raids on each other's property were conducted in stealth as a show of power. It may be, therefore, that deterrence is a way of conducting conflict rather than a preserver of the peace, as it is sometimes represented.

Various measures suggested for reducing intergroup conflict acquire new significance and effectiveness when they become part and parcel of joint efforts directed toward goals with real and compelling value for all groups concerned. The development of such superordinate goals provides the necessary motive. It is needed to lift the heavy hand of the past, with its entrenched stereotypes and vicious circle of "Who's to blame?", and to work out procedures for cooperation.

Over a period of time, the procedures of groups working toward superordinate goals are generalized to new problems and situations. In time, the process should assume organizational forms. If the tasks of building such organizations seem formidable, they are certainly no more formidable than those which a modern war would impose. There can be no doubt that man's potentialities can be realized better in the course of such efforts than in the vicious circle of assigning blame for the present state of affairs, in pursuing old fears, old hostilities, old conflicts—with their awesome possibilities in this present world.

BEYOND THE EXPERIMENTS

In considering the possibility of superordinate goals in international affairs, we must pass beyond our experiments. For in our experiments, superordinate goals emerged in problem situations that involved the deprivation of vital necessities or the achievement of a venture much-desired by all. They were not matters for interpretation, and they did not require experts with different opinions about the "facts" to offer conjectures. The conditions giving rise to superordinate goals in our experimental groups were compelling and immediate—right in front of their eyes, a naked necessity for all to see and feel.

DEBATING HUMAN SURVIVAL

In the thousand-fold complex problems engulfing the people of the world today, there seems to be a debate about one goal which should be overriding—human survival. There is debate among scientists as well as policy-makers about the range of weapons of destruction and their carriers; about the radius of destruction in population centers; about whether 100 million or 500 million people would perish or be mutilated; about which peoples and places would be involved; about how many and what kind of shelters are required for survival as human beings, if they survive; about the effects of radiation on the present and future generations of children. Such debates continue as though we were splitting hairs instead of talking about millions of human lives.

In the midst of these debates, the problem of human survival is obscured; instead of human survival emerging as an all-embracing superordinate goal, its urgency is muffled. Yet human survival is the most inclusive superordinate goal. It provides the needed motivational basis for:

> making possible the effective negotiations of leaders toward the abolishment of nuclear warfare as an alternative;
> communication and information to be effective toward abandonment of war as a means of furthering national or ideological policy — *any* national or ideological policy;
> exchange of persons across national lines to be occasions for understanding rather than promoting the vicious circle of "Who's to blame?"

But, for all of these, human survival has to be felt as a necessity—like the air we breathe, the food we eat, the danger sign that we heed when near high explosives.

A DECLARATION FOR HUMAN SURVIVAL

One effective first step toward the recognition of human survival as a superordinate goal may be a universal *declaration* for human survival and development, including in vivid word and picture, the horrors of nuclear war, its cost in life, its destruction of human civilization and culture, and the ever-present dangers of radiation to those who survive. Some experts on communication conclude that people do not listen to threats, pointing to studies showing that the threat of cancer is not sufficient to cause people to stop smoking. However, we know that when people of a country learn of a genuine threat to the lives and well-being of their country, even in the newspapers, they do have a strong desire for survival and removal of the threat; and all sectors of society pull together for this purpose. Human survival is a positive goal for all peoples, and the common threat to all today has not been presented with comparable urgency.

As we all know, declarations have been made by groups of scientists, by professional bodies, and even by heads of governments and military men of stature. What is intended here is not just another declaration at a single conference, or in a few newspapers, or in an occasional policy statement. What is intended here is an agreement—especially by policy makers of the major powers—that a universal declaration for human survival, which also conveys in understandable terms what nuclear warfare means, has their full support. Of course, even this is not sufficient.

Such a universal declaration for human survival as a recognized superordinate goal needs the support of all religious bodies which ask for prayers for peace, so that the universal declaration for human survival will be part of their daily and weekly exercises. All organizations, boards and regents directing policies at university, high school and grade school levels in every country, who profess to have at heart the well-being and development of the younger generation as civilized human beings, should make such a universal declaration an integral part of their educational programs. Owners and directors of the mass media of communication in all countries—who profess public responsibility in enlightening and informing—should feature prominently and repeatedly such a universal declaration for human survival as a cherished goal. At the cost of appearing naive, I also propose that political parties in all countries who profess their concern with peace on earth and the brotherhood of man should include this universal declaration as an integral part of their platforms—even if this be the only plank they share in common.

If through these means, human survival becomes a superordinate goal for the majority of peoples of the world, then nuclear war may be out-of-bounds in their eyes as an alternative in national or ideological policies. Being out-of-bounds in terms of cherished goals of the people for survival and development as human beings, the attempts of demagogues to fish in muddied waters, to dramatize issues and events out of all proportion, will fall on deaf ears. Leaders will be charged with staying within the bounds of the cherished goals of their peoples.

A NEW FRAMEWORK FOR COOPERATION

I do not suggest at all that a universal declaration could settle the problems underlying international conflicts. I do propose it as a *first* step toward eliminating nuclear war as an alternative that any leader could consider. The under-lying conflicts, however, can be affected to the extent that the nations of the world and their citizens engage in common enterprises which each sees as being for the benefit of all, regardless of their differences.

The differences between nations may seem so great today that the possibility of common concerns seems slim. I am inclined, however, to find merit in the observation by Eugene Rabinowitch (*Bulletin of the Atomic Scientists,* February, 1963) that there are such areas, and that "the cultural and scientific areas are the least controversial and most suitable for international cooperation" at present (p. 7). The implications of our own research also support his contention that such cooperation should be, not merely an exchange of persons, but "common enterprises" jointly initiated and carried out on a large scale.

In brief, the implications of our research is that when superordinate goals are concretely perceived and emotion-ally felt by members of groups in conflict, they do tend to cooperate, to pull together their resources and energies to attain them. A series of such efforts over a period of time is effective in reducing their hostilities, changing their un-favorable images of each other, and producing a climate in which creative alternatives to mutual extinction can be explored. The exploration of creative alternatives may be more effective than the prevailing policy of contending parties at present, in which strategists attempt to figure out probabilities of deterrence. This policy of deterrence contains the constant hazard of getting out of hand because of even a small miscalculation or misinformation at this or that particular point.

INTER-NATION UNIVERSITIES

A final word on committing the knowledge, resources, and efforts of major parties in conflict to common, large-scale projects, as part of a process directed toward the superordinate goal of human survival on the level of the cultures attained through centuries. Such common and interdependent projects could include, for example, joint efforts by cosmonauts, technicians, and researchers of nations aimed at the conquest of space. Such projects could include inter-nation universities, in which the faculty consists of scholars and scientists who have outgrown the 19th century conception of national ways of life and ideo-logical divisions as closed systems. These are only examples already proposed by various authors such as Charles E. Osgood and Eugene Rabinowitch. In joint meetings of scholars and scientists dedicated to human survival, and the survival of human cultures across national and ideological lines, a whole series of such common and interdependent ventures could be imaginatively worked out.

The involvement of talents, resources and effort in joint and interdependent *new* projects is less liable to misinter-pretations as trickery or propaganda moves. In the more direct political and military areas where parties already have entrenched stands, sometimes fixed as national norms or stereotypes, the likelihood of misinterpreting the motives and moves of the other side is greater. However, once a new series of joint and interdependent projects is underway, active involvement in it is likely to be conductive to an atmosphere of good faith, in which the negotiating parties will not be suspect at every turn and twist of occasion.

New Ways to Reduce Distrust Between the U.S. and Russia
Milton J. Rosenberg

"Nations are not people, and therefore the troubles between them cannot be understood through psychology." So runs a complaint that psychologists often hear from political scientists these days.

This point of view strikes me as both justified and unjustified, depending upon the kind of psychological approach being considered. Worthy of condescension

is the sort of shallow psychologizing that suggests that national frustration leads directly to national aggression, or that attempts to explain particular wars as due to the madness of some specific historical figure or the basic personality structure of a whole people.

Another approach to the psychology of international relations, however, has been quietly maturing over the last decade. This approach assumes that the interests of various nations are frequently in real conflict—but that it is also common for international rivalries of the war-risking kind to be based largely upon attitudes that have no clear factual support. A guiding purpose in this new approach is to achieve a better understanding of the psychological forces that tend to drive both types of conflict toward limited, and then unlimited, war.

One important development is the attempt to focus some of the major theories of attitude change upon the relations between national élites. This may point ways out of dangerous international antagonisms that are rooted mainly in attitudes. And even where the clash of national interests is apparently "intractable," the alteration of background attitudes may still point ways out of the dilemma.

In this article, I hope to show how two of the major theories of attitude change might be applied in lowering some of the barriers to realistic settlement of international issues.

For simplicity I shall deal mainly with the interaction between the American and Soviet policy élites. But what is suggested here could be readily applied to aspects of the U.S.-Chinese or the Soviet-Chinese relationships—or, for that matter, to those of Israel and Egypt or any other set of national élites locked into mutual disdain and suspicion but not yet caught in long-term regression to active war, as we now are in Vietnam.

The Power of Positive Reinforcement

The *instrumental-learning* model of attitude dynamics was developed by Carl I. Hovland and Irving L. Janis and their associates, first in field experiments conducted for the Army during World War II and then at Yale. At its core is the idea that we learn to like or dislike (or to trust or distrust) someone or something by *reinforcement*—that is, because in the past the expression of our like or dislike has brought us rewards or reduced our needs.

The largest amount of experimental study has been devoted to two types of rewards. One is tied directly to what a person can gain if he changes some specific attitude—for instance, a person could reduce his anxiety over his health if he adopted an uncompromisingly negative attitude toward smoking. The second type of reward is due to increased social acceptance gained by moving one's attitudes toward the attitudinal standards set by others. Usually this happens not through mere cynical compliance, but through a gradual and "internalized" reorientation.

Changing the attitude of another person, according to this model, requires a series of steps:
—attract the attention of the person or groups whose attitudes you want to change;
—establish your credibility and trustworthiness;
—provide well-planned and informative communications that cast doubt upon the reasons and rewards that bolster the present attitude, and make change seem desirable by highlighting the rewards associated with the new, advocated attitude; and
—get the person or group to "rehearse" the new attitude for a while—to make its promised rewards seem more real and immediate.

Experimental work conducted by the Yale group and others has identified a number of factors that determine the success with which the various stages are negotiated. Among them are the basic credibility of the source of the persuasive communication; the way in which the communication is structured; the use of anxiety arousal; "role-playing" as a way of getting the person to consider the arguments and incentives that support the new attitude; the importance to the person of groups that support his attitude or its opposite; and personality factors making for general persuadability or rigidity.

Clearly, this model is relevant to changing the attitude pattern of distrust that continues to hamper movement toward true American-Soviet conciliation. The policy élites involved are composed of men playing roles that reduce flexibility. What limits these men most is that they feel *required* to distrust the opposing power and the assurances offered by its élite. Yet each side recognizes that the other's attitude of distrust must be converted toward trust if anything better than an easily-upset détente is to be achieved. Specifically, each side faces the problem of getting the other to believe its assurances that it will refrain from a surprise nuclear attack; that it will abide by arms-control and disarmament agreements (even when these cannot be effectively policed); that it will scrupulously adhere to sphere-of-influence agreements; and that it will accept necessary limitations of sovereignty as new and powerful international institutions are developed.

How are such attitudes of trust to be cultivated while policy élites still pursue and protect national interests? How can the Soviet-American "credibility gap" be closed?

The Yale experiments on credibility indicated that what seems to count most are the communicator's apparent status and expertise. But these have little bearing upon relations between policy-élite representatives, who are usually perceived by their opposite numbers as possessing both of these qualities in more than sufficient degree.

Closing the Credibility Gap

At this level there is, however, a more direct route toward cultivating attitudes of trust. Though difficult to pursue, it must be taken, even while each nation strives to preserve and advance its own national interests. That route, to speak bluntly, is to stop posturing, faking, and lying.

Is it possible—even conceivable—that nations, in their relations with one another, can abandon the deceit that, since Machiavelli, has seemed essential to statecraft? Many specialists would immediately answer, in the tones of revealed doctrine, "As it was in the beginning, is now, and ever shall be, world without end. Amen." But at the risk of sounding naive, I believe that we need take a fresh look.

I suggest that the present international system is so inadequate and dangerous that the American and Soviet leaders have very compelling reasons to go beyond the limits of conventional *Realpolitik* and impose some moral order on their relationships. The exploration of this radical possibility could best begin with a direct assault upon the attitudinal problem of international distrust. There are probably many ways in which the behavioral sciences might help to mount such an assault. One would be the use of inter-nation gaming and simulation techniques—to provide "dry run" tests of an international system based upon a principle of generalized trust. Such studies might clarify just how feasible, how resistant to breakdown, a system of this sort would be, and how it might best be instituted.

But we need not wait. Immediate initiatives in honesty and self-revelation are now available for the seizing. Even though a great deal remains secret, even though the international system remains more closed than open, much could still be revealed to an antagonist under conditions that would allow him the opportunity for verification. There are possibilities in the direct revelation of data about arms technology, economic plans, the policy-formulation process itself. Such candor might well invite reciprocation. It might, in fact, set in motion expanding cycles of reciprocity that could eventually encompass most of the matters now surrounded by suspicion.

Another way of attempting to reduce attitudes of distrust would be, simply, to seek occasions that will require promises to be given—particularly promises that seem to incur some disadvantage for the promiser —and then to make sure that they are conscientiously fulfilled. This serves as almost incontrovertible evidence of reliability and credibility.

Additional useful suggestions can be drawn from the work of the Hovland group when we consider their emphasis (well backed by many experimental studies) upon appeals to the motives and incentives of individuals. How does this translate to the situation of one élite communicating with another? It highlights the importance of conducting diplomatic interaction so as to make clear to the other side the gains that are available if it will undertake an accommodating shift on some issue under negotiation.

This recommendation applies not so much to the general goal of reducing attitudes of distrust as to the conciliation of more specific issues. What if the United States offered the Soviet Union something it wanted in return for an arms quarantine of the Middle East? Or what if the Soviet Union offered us some equally meaningful reward for a U.S. guarantee that West Germany would not be allowed access to nuclear arms? In either instance the consequence might be conciliatory yielding. This would be due to changes of attitudes on the particular issues. But an exchange of such yieldings, particularly if accompanied by the recurring experience of promises kept, could alter the more basic attitudes of distrust that still persist between the American and Soviet policy-making groups.

Why, then, has this approach to conciliation rarely been used? One reason: Ingrained attitudes of mutual distrust inhibit easy exploration and flexible exchanges of conciliatory shifts. Another: The incentives occasionally offered to change attitudes are usually negative, not positive—threats and harassment, not attractive rewards. Leaders on either side may sometimes be forced to bow to such pressures, but their distrust and hostility will hardly diminish. Just the opposite: The élite group forced to yield, especially if humiliated, will await its opportunities for retribution.

The United States and Russia will continue to try to control each other's attitudes and actions by negative means as long as their leaders view their relationship as an extended zero-sum game—one side can win only if the other loses. Some issues, of course, are zero-sum; but many can be so structured that mutual gain *is* possible. Peace itself, after all, is a mutual gain.

Trading Off the Advantage

Still, it is clear that possibilities for mutual gain cannot be found in each and every conflict. It would be better, therefore, to systematically rely on cross-trading. In other words, the advantage in one interest conflict is given to one side, while the advantage in another conflict is given to the other side. For example, the Soviet Union's refusal to allow unlimited inspection of its atomic facilities, and the United States' commitment to some form of nuclear force within NATO, are both seemingly unbudgeable stances. Might full, unscheduled inspections in the Soviet Union be traded for the permanent cancellation of plans for a NATO nuclear force?

The opportunities are vast. Both sides could continually review their priorities. How strongly do they desire particular concessions? What are they willing to offer in trade? Permanent trade-off negotiations could lead to large and thoroughgoing patterns of settlement.

After some initial success in trade-off negotiations, both groups would have experienced gains: The reduction of tensions, and domestic improvements made possible by shifting economic resources away from the defense sector. These gains would probably foster additional significant change in the attitudes of competitiveness and distrust that presently impede progress in American-Soviet conciliation. And this, in turn, would be likely to produce, on both sides, the strengthened conviction that trade-off negotiations are generally profitable even though they require abandonment of some earlier policy goals.

It would also be very useful if the United States and the Soviet Union were to immediately expand the search for shared problems that do *not* raise the apparent or fundamental issues of the lingering Cold War—problems in such comparatively manageable areas as technological development, scientific techniques, urban design, educational methods, crime con-

trol, and administrative organization. An institutionalized system that would foster greater East-West cooperation in the solution of such cross-national, domestic problems would probably be of clear benefit to both nations, as well as to the members of their respective blocs. And this, too, would further invalidate basic attitudes of competitiveness and distrust and foster further progress in resolving issues that have persisted in the framework of Cold War competition.

At least one other recommendation can be drawn from the instrumental-learning model of attitude change. Studies at Yale and elsewhere have shown that role-playing is a direct and effective method of changing attitudes. The subject becomes a kind of devil's advocate: He is required to argue for a viewpoint quite different from his own. In laboratory experiments, this often leads to attitude change—though exactly why and how this happens remains controversial.

In discussions between opposing groups of policy-makers, one would not expect or desire such facile shifts of attitude. But there is good reason to expect that role-playing techniques could help policy-makers of opposed groups to reexamine and, where necessary, revise the attitudes of suspicion and distrust they approach one another with. Further formal research on this process, and real-life experiments with it, would add considerably to the development of a technology of conciliation.

A word of warning is required. When a formerly hostile and untrusting opponent is beginning to change his attitudes, when he is letting his guard down, the temptation to take advantage of his new and tentative trust will often be great. Though short-run strategic and political gains may beckon in such a situation, they must be completely rejected—for nothing will so easily destroy the credibility of conciliatory communications and actions than a lapse into even a single unscheduled seizure of advantage.

The Search for Consistency

The *consistency* theories represent a second major approach to attitude change, and they can add a good deal to our understanding of how to reduce distrust between policy élites. Though they differ in important ways, all these theories see an attitude as a combination of elements bound together in a kind of internal balance, so that any sizable disruption will bring into play a self-regulating dynamic that restores the original harmony. The basic assumptions, then, are that human beings need attitudinal consistency and are intolerant of inconsistency—and that when this consistency is disrupted, they often restore it through the process of attitude change.

So goes the general consistency-theory analysis. But to show its relevance to the problem of inter-élite distrust, we must get down to the particulars of one of the major theories of this type. The one that I will use is my own, though it reflects aspects of a related theory developed in cooperation with Robert Abelson. The fact that I use it here does not mean that it is superior to the other consistency models of attitude change, but simply that it is convenient for probing deeper into the problem of cross-élite attitude change.

Basic to this model is the definition of an attitude as a kind of psychological stance in which elements of *affect* and *cognition* are intimately related. The affective core of the attitude is simply the person's habitual feeling of like or dislike toward some "object," be that a person, an issue, a proposal, an institution, or an event. The cognitive component is simply his total set of beliefs about that liked or disliked object, particularly beliefs about how it is related to other things he is interested in and has feelings about.

To exemplify just what we mean by affective-cognitive consistency, and by the kind of inconsistency that fosters a change of attitude, we need to work through a concrete illustration. Let us take a hypothetical U.S. Senator standing on the periphery of the American decision-making circle just before the ratification of the atmospheric nuclear test-ban treaty. He approves of the treaty and plans to vote for it. This reflects his affective component—how he *feels* about the treaty.

In public debate he gives some of his reasons—the cognitive component: "The ban will slow the nuclear race. It will protect us from radioactive poisoning of the air. It will show the world that we mean it when we say we want peace." Privately, he adds other considerations: "It will probably freeze the nuclear race where it is now, while we still have a big advantage. Also, it should eventually open up some Eastern European markets we can use." Still another of his private reasons: "Judging by the latest polls, my stand should go over well with the liberal church and women's groups back home. Anyway, it should get the White House off my back and maybe get me better support from the National Committee in my next campaign."

If we check all of these reasons (technically, each is a cognition about the relationship between the attitude object and some other emotionally significant object), we find an interesting fact: The attitude object (the test-ban treaty) toward which the Senator has a positive feeling is, to him, positively related to such welcome developments as "opening up some Eastern European markets" and negatively related to such unwelcome possibilities as "radioactive poisoning of the air." This demonstrates a general principle: A positively-evaluated attitude object will typically be seen as bringing about desired goals or preventing undesirable ones; a negatively-evaluated object will be seen as blocking the way to desired goals, or fostering undesirable ones. Such affective-cognitive consistency has often been shown to be characteristic of stable attitudes. Furthermore, research has shown that the stronger and more extreme the basic positive or negative feeling toward the attitude object, the greater will be the person's certainty about the supporting beliefs.

How then, according to this model, can attitudes be changed? One must begin by trying to break up the internal harmony of beliefs and feelings—by inducing, or increasing, inconsistency. Most often, this is attempted by presenting arguments, data, and "facts" from sources that are seen as authoritative because of their prestige or expertise. The purpose is either to undermine beliefs that support the affective core of the attitude ("Experts say we can't be sure of our test-detection system, so how can we know the Russians won't keep testing and get far ahead of us?"), or to introduce new assertions that cast a different light—and thus induce contrasting feelings—on the subject ("If we stop testing, we simply cannot develop a good low yield, antimissile missile").

Introduce enough inconsistency and the subject will no longer be able to tolerate it. How much internal inconsistency a person can stand varies from attitude to attitude, situation to situation, and person to person. But everyone must reach a point where the piling up of inconsistency forces him to try to do something about it.

When a person's internal inconsistency becomes unbearable, one of three things will usually happen:

■ He will simply retreat from the conflict. He will try to find some way to disregard the whole area of inconsistency.

■ He will reject and expel the new cognitions that

are upsetting the old balance, and restore the initial attitude. (Incidentally, we may assume that this is what our hypothetical Senator did, since it is just what many real Senators did. The arguments *against* the nuclear test-ban treaty were simply not so telling and credible, or so important in the values they referred to, as were the arguments in favor of the treaty. In this case, the easiest route to reducing internal inconsistency was, ultimately, to reject the arguments that had generated, it.)

■ He will yield to the new inconsistency-arousing cognitions, and—by changing his feelings about the attitude object—restore consistency.

This last is, of course, what is usually meant by attitude change.

Consistency theory also predicts, and has experimentally demonstrated, that the reverse form of attitude change is possible: *Feelings* can be altered first, and cognitions will follow. But, in real life, affect change resulting from prior cognition change is far more common.

What determines whether internal inconsistency brings about an overall change of attitude? First, the nature of the attitude itself. An attitude will probably be more easily changed by inconsistency if:

■ The number of beliefs that support the attitude is small.

■ The attitude object is believed to serve comparatively unimportant goals.

■ The person already holds a few beliefs that are inconsistent with his overall attitude.

■ The original attitude is isolated from most of the other attitudes of the individual—is itself, therefore, in a sense an inconsistency. (An example with a real Senator: Everett M. Dirksen's support of an earlier civil-rights bill was on the periphery of his essentially conservative concerns; his stance on civil rights has since undergone several sea changes.)

A second factor determining whether inconsistency leads to attitude change is how important the attitude is to a person's needs and essential motivations. The less the holding of the attitude serves to meet his real needs, the more easily—if threatened by inconsistency—it can be changed. Similarly, his attitudes are more easily altered when he does not need them for the roles he plays, or for maintaining good standing in the groups he identifies with.

From the foregoing, it is apparent why changing the attitudes of national leaders has been so difficult during the Cold War—even though both sides wanted to find some way out. The core attitudes of distrust, hostility, and competition have been so thoroughly anchored and buttressed by supporting beliefs, so strongly influenced by what leaders think their positions and "roles" require of them, that there has been very little room for flexibility.

This does not mean that evidence of good will or pacific intentions has been totally useless. But what usually happens is that these gestures are reinterpreted in ways that reduce their power to generate inconsistency and thus their power to affect attitudes. For example, an American offer of wheat sales would typically be interpreted by the Russians as a tactic to help the U.S. economy. And American leaders are likely to interpret Soviet offers to share information about industrial nuclear technology as a ploy to save the costs of research—rather than really to further general cooperation. Many leaders traditionally interpret gestures for peace as a mask for hostile intent—and bellicose gestures as proof of it.

Perhaps, therefore, the greatest positive good that came from the few very dangerous confrontations between the United States and the Soviet Union—particularly the Cuban missile crisis—has been that they gave the leaders of both nations some appreciation of how deeply each wanted to avoid stumbling into nuclear war. Since then, a number of steps toward avoiding danger have been taken, and they have probably thrown some inconsistency into the attitudes of mutual distrust. As a result, there is probably a fair opportunity today for each side to act in ways that could ultimately bring about changed attitudes. How can this best be done? The consistency approach offers some leads.

Sorting Out the Real Issues

One clear recommendation is that, before the competing policy groups undertake to revise each other's attitudes, they study what these attitudes really are, and what beliefs are built into them. Too often policymakers seem confused about the perceptions and purposes that lie behind the policy positions taken by the competing power. "Riddles wrapped in mysteries inside enigmas" lie more often in the eye of the observer than the observed. Surely, within the great mass of white papers, diplomatic conversations, propaganda releases, and policy rationalizations that flow from Washington or Moscow there should be enough material for an educated reconstruction of how opposing leaders really think and feel about an issue, and how they structure policy around it. Close study of this sort would help isolate the issues on which the other side would be comparatively receptive to actions and messages that could generate internal inconsistency.

Obviously these issues, at the present time, would be on the outer edge of major policy and have little immediate effect on important conflicts. But the real purpose of such early efforts is to lower the opposing side's defense against information and action that might create inconsistency in more central attitudes. If either side could convince the other that it really *does* favor cultural exchange in order to reduce tension, rather than to make propaganda—or that it really *wants* disengagement in Central Europe to avoid military confrontations, rather than to gain some devious advantage—then the day will be much closer when the very center of the web of distrust and competition can be directly assaulted.

But can such direct assault succeed when the core issues still seem virtually irreconcilable? How is this to be done? This is where the consistency approach is especially pertinent. It suggests strongly that *there are no truly intractable, unchangeable attitudes.* Instead, there are less resistant and more resistant ones. Where resistance is high, this is because the affective portion of the attitude is supported by a large number of detailed beliefs that are consistent with it—and also because the attitude itself is consistent with the role demands and ideologies that leaders must live up to. For such an attitude to be changed it must be bombarded with a continuing, unrelenting stream of inconsistency-generating communications and events— and the more peripheral attitudes to which it is tied must also be exposed to pressures for change.

To reverse the attitudes of distrust with which the Soviet and American élites approach and misinterpret each other, either or each of them must undertake an unflagging display of trustworthiness—and give strong, unequivocal evidence that its paramount desire is conciliation. In this light Charles Osgood's GRIT strategy is very relevant. Osgood recommends a long series of unilateral, tension-reducing initiatives on the part of the United States, even if no sign of reciprocation appears from the Soviets for some time. He also maintains

that concrete actions speak much louder—and less ambiguously—than words.

For too long both the United States and the Soviet Union have been lagging in this regard. On the American side, occasional actions in the Kennedy years and in the last period of the Eisenhower era may have worked, whether by intention or not, to generate some inconsistencies in Soviet core attitudes of distrust. But these actions were never designed as part of a strong, well-focused plan for reducing tension. Today the situation is worse. What probably stands out most to the Soviets is our past escalation of the Veitnam war and our continuing rejection of those opportunities for realistic settlement that are apparently available.

Finding the Opinion Leaders

Still other recommendations can be drawn from the consistency approach, particularly from the variants developed by other authors. Here is one example out of a number of possibilities: Both Fritz Heider and Theodore Newcomb have studied the kind of consistency that is found *between* rather than *within* the attitudes of separate people. And both have reported considerable supporting evidence for this proposition: People who are tied together by friendship or more formal role relationships tend toward mutual consistency on important attitude issues. Nevertheless, they will sometimes encounter inconsistency between their separate attitudes. When this happens, the formally or emotionally subordinate person will usually alter his attitude to bring it into consistency with that of the other person.

This proposition is not surprising, but put this way it does have considerable practical value. What it suggests is that attempts to produce attitude change through arousing inconsistency will work best if we first learn as much as possible about members of the "target group" and their relationships with one another. Who are the key men, why, and what are they like?

The most influential, in governmental as in business élites, are not always the most visible. When we know who the crucially placed people in the opposing élite are—and, particularly, when their importance is based upon their analytic or strategic skills—we have found the people toward whom our initial attempts at inconsistency arousal ought to be especially directed. If *their* attitudes begin to shift, the effect may spread across the élite group more rapidly than could otherwise happen.

Forces Against Innovation

In all that I have said up to now I have been urging greater adventurousness in the attempt to reduce inter-élite distrust. But, of course, real-life constraints and responsibilities often inhibit the taste for adventure and innovation. The policy-élite groups of the contesting powers are still limited by their attitudes of distrust toward one another, and by concerns over the domestic political consequences of a too rapid or dramatic movement toward international conciliation. Also they are sometimes hampered by the "prudential" (the word is borrowed from certain strategic analysts) definition of their roles—that is, they sometimes take it as their obligation to imagine the worst they can about the opposing power's motives and intentions and then to act on the assumption that what they have imagined is accurate.

Thus most of the suggestions made here would probably not be acceptable to typical members of the policy élites of the contesting powers. However, desperation over the impasse imposed by the Cold War, and fear of escalation, have moved some leaders to re-examine their own attitudes about the plans and intentions of their opposite numbers. This development had, in fact, progressed quite far—until it began to languish and lose relevance in the wake of the Vietnam war.

If the Vietnam war should end with a setback for those American policy-makers still committed to the John Foster Dulles "roll-back of Communism" and "brinksmanship" doctrines, we may see an energetic renewal of the search for meaningful conciliation. Awareness of the possibilities discussed here could make that search much more productive. And in the meantime it can foster preparation for new peace initiatives and help to keep alive the prospect of ultimate conciliation.

In a society where the secret ballot of individual citizens determines national policy and occasionally even life or death, an understanding of the dynamics of the political process is of vital importance. Politicians, political scientists and psychologists have become increasingly interested in gaining an understanding of the psychological processes governing individuals' political behavior.

Our understanding of the psychology of politics is growing rapidly, although the amount to be learned far outweighs current knowledge. The avowed goal of such research is *not* to develop techniques of influencing voters by playing upon their psychological needs and anxieties, but rather to create an environment where political decisions are openly and rationally reached.

A discussion of political behavior is, of course, an inquiry into attitude systems and the relationship between attitudes and overt behavior. The research strategies employed to investigate political attitudes and behavior are well represented by the reports in this Part. Robert Abelson, in the first essay, dispels much of the mystery surrounding the use of computers and public opinion polls to predict voting behavior. As he shows, the careful study of small groups of voters who are representative of larger blocs such as cities or states can lead to highly accurate and rapid predictions of voting trends. It is the development of computer programs to deal with polls and early returns from these groups that has led to the projections shown in television coverage of elections. Studies of the relations between expressed opinions on major issues and voting patterns in presidential elections indicate that there is a powerful relationship between expressed political attitudes and political behavior. Abelson's data also show that tendencies toward cognitive consistency (which have been discussed by Aronson in Part One and by Rosenberg in Part Six) both influence political behavior

Part Seven

Political Behavior

sharing in collective decision-making

and make the prediction of this behavior quite accurate. What cognitive consistency implies is that attitudes tend to be interrelated and consistent with one another. Thus our knowledge of only one attitude held by an individual often makes it possible for us to predict his attitudes and behavior on a wide variety of related issues. Consistency theory also suggests that change in one attitude will be associated with the modification of other beliefs. For example, a change in a person's attitude about integrated schooling should bring about subsequent shifts in his attitudes toward integrated housing and minority groups in general.

Fred Greenstein, in the second essay, takes a different approach to politics by examining the psychological significance of the presidency. He finds that the office of president has several kinds of psychological meaning for citizens. His data imply that despite partisan hostility and disapproval of specific acts, the president is perceived as a national figure with qualities which transcend individual characteristics. The overwhelming sorrow expressed at the death of any president reveals some of the psychological aspects of the office. Another reaction noted is a marked increase in the popularity and influence of the president in times of sudden national crisis. The latter represents a typical response to psychological stress. When individuals face severe threats the response to such a situation is usually to show increased dependency on members of their peer group and to show greatly increased reliance on leaders and other figures. It is likely that the enormous influence of Adolf Hitler in his early days was a function of the great stress imposed on the German people by the depression and social upheaval of the times.

In another vein, Lawrence Schiff reports on the psychological characteristics of young conservatives. He seeks to understand the adoption of a particular political philosophy through uncovering the personality dynamics of individuals. Schiff finds that there are three types of youth who are attracted to conservatism and that the same political philosophy serves very different needs for each group. One group simply embraces the right-wing beliefs of their parents without questioning them. The other two groups, who have undergone a conversion experience into militant conservatism, form distinct classes based on whether the conversion occurred shortly after puberty or during late adolescence. Early converts appear to be attracted to conservatism as a means of obtaining security and concrete answers while coping with the turmoil of adolescence. Late converts, on the other hand, seem to internalize conservatism out of a sense of repulsion at the ways of society and seem to be motivated by a fear that they cannot live up to their own or their parents' high standards and ambitions.

Other research has aimed at isolating similar personality needs among young radicals. While inquiry into personality factors provides considerable insight into the nature of those holding extreme political positions, it is probable that those holding less extreme views are more influenced by situational factors than by personality needs.

In the final essay, James Wright examines the relationship between media reports about Vietnam and public opinions about the war. Contrary to most theories of media impact, he finds the greatest influence and change among the elite—the well-educated upper classes; the media have relatively little impact on the opinions of the working classes. At the same time, it seems apparent from Wright's data that the media do influence the attitudes of a significant segment of the population.

Computers, Polls, and Public-Opinion — Some Puzzles and Paradoxes

Robert P. Abelson

Despite a number of unpredictable happenings on the political scene in 1968, public-opinion polls and computers, the twin symbols of voter predictability, seem to be more frequently employed than ever. Indeed, although he had little success with it, Nelson Rockefeller built his whole campaign to impress the Republican delegates on his showing in the polls. In this article I will review several past applications of computers to the study of public opinion, particularly those activities in which I myself have been involved. In the process of this review, a picture of the nature of public political opinion will emerge, a picture that may help resolve the paradox that voter opinion, in response to a political campaign, can be simultaneously predictable and unfathomable.

A couple of years prior to the 1960 Presidential election, the heady notion was in the air of using computers for analysis of voter reactions. Limited funds were available within the Democratic Party to support a foray by Ithiel de Sola Pool, myself, and others into the computerization of public opinion. Our proposal involved two steps: first, we would assemble from archives covering the previous decade a massive public-opinion data bank, tabulating the position of many different types of voters on many different public issues; second, using these data, we would try to predict the consequences of a potential emphasis by the Democratic candidate on any of a number of issues.

Opponents of the project (most of them political experts who felt very uncomfortable at the prospect of computers invading their domain of expertise) freely expressed opinions about the impossibility of doing anything sensible by computer, and the immorality of trying, even if the project were guaranteed not to succeed. Ethics aside, expressions of doubt about the feasibility of our computer project could be summarized by six skeptical questions:

1. *The Validity Question:* Can responses on public-opinion surveys be trusted; that is, do people tell the interviewer what they really think?

2. *The Obsolescence Question:* Don't survey data rapidly become outdated, so that as you accumulate new data in a data bank, the old data grow useless?

3. *The Completeness Question:* How do you know that the surveys are asking the right questions? Or, to put it differently, what happens when a new political issue comes up for which there are no banked data?

4. *The Relative-Importance Question:* How can you tell how important a given issue is for a voter, relative to all the other issues or factors that might be involved in a political campaign?

5. *The Quantitative Prediction Question:* Even if attention is confined to a single issue, how can you predict *how many* voters will be exposed to, and influenced by, an appeal to that issue? Finally,

6. *The Marketing Question:* Even if one knows how many voters might be won over on a given issue, how will that help a candidate to phrase particular appeals on this issue?

It is interesting that these six major questions express no intrinsic doubts about computer technology. To ask whether a computer prognostication of electoral behavior is possible is not to ask whether the *computer* can do it, but rather whether it is possible to solve the technical questions raised in setting up the computations. The role of the computer has been grossly magnified, however, even to the point where *Harper's* Magazine published a mystical account entitled "The People Machine," a sinister title that has since provided gleeful reference material for several anti-Kennedy books including a recent unkind biography of the late Robert F. Kennedy.

But while the answers to the six key questions depend very little upon the nature of computers, they depend a great deal upon the nature of public opinion. Let us take up the thread of the 1960 election project again, to outline our procedures and the results.

From public-opinion survey materials preserved in the Roper Public Opinion Research Center, we accumulated the responses of approximately 100,000 people to an average of about 20 interview items. On the basis of face-sheet information, each respondent was classified as a "voter type," such as, "Eastern, small-town, high-status occupation, white Protestant, male Republican." There were 480 such voter types, the basis upon which, incidentally, Eugene Burdick titled his novel of a computerized candidate *The 480*. We tabulated the percentage of respondents of each voter type favoring, opposing, or having no opinion on each of 50 different issues or candidates. Thus, for any given issue or cluster of issues, for example civil rights, our data bank provided a profile across all 480 voter types of the probable extent of support of the opposing sides on the general issue.

Although we had initially intended to use the data bank for dynamic analyses of many issues in the 1960 campaign, the major task finally commissioned and carried out was the full-scale analysis of the so-called Catholic issue, the effect of John F. Kennedy's Catholicism on the voters.

Obviously, a common-sense analysis of this issue would suggest that a certain number of normally Republican Catholics would vote for Kennedy because of his Catholicism and that a certain number of normally Democratic Protestants would vote against Kennedy because of their anti-Catholicism. These were precisely the two major assumptions incorporated into our computer simulation of the outcome of a hypothetical election based entirely on the Catholic issue.

But note that these assumptions are quantitatively vague, specifying only that "certain numbers" of key voter types should defect to the other side. How did

we know *how many* voters would be influenced in the two directions by the Catholic issue? For one direction, defection *away* from the Democrats, we used the part of the data bank containing responses reflecting anti-Catholicism. The usual survey question had been, "If your party nominated an otherwise well-qualified candidate for President who happened to be a Catholic, would you vote for him?" Over 20 percent of Protestant Democrats had said No. Despite some speculation among political analysts about an extra burst of secret anti-Catholicism expressed not to pollsters, but later inside the voting booth, we chose to believe that the percentages expressed in surveys were accurate.

On the other side of the coin, the major survey organizations had neglected to ask the corresponding *pro*-Catholicism question, namely, "If the *other* political party nominated an otherwise well-qualified candidate for President who happened to be a Catholic, would you vote for him?" Since we had no solid information by which to set the rate of defection of Catholic Republicans to the Democrats, we—and here a blush is appropriate—we *guessed*.

Our guess was that one-third of all Republican Catholics would vote for John F. Kennedy. As it turned out, this was not far wrong, being a slight underestimate. In any case, estimates for defection rates on the Catholic issue were available among all voter types. These estimates were aggregated state by state, to generate the predicted effect of the Catholic issue on the entire electorate. Two things were done with these prognostic figures: first, we compared them with Kennedy-Nixon poll standings early in the campaign; second, we compared them with the final vote tallies. Both comparisons led us to the conclusion that the 1960 election could indeed be largely understood as the superposition of the Catholic issue onto traditional party loyalties, since our simple prognoses corresponded well with reality.

On the basis of the comparison with earlier poll results, we had advised Kennedy that by August the Catholic issue had already taken hold with the voters to the full predicted extent, and that therefore (if all our assumptions were correct) he had nothing to lose by calling further attention to his religion with an appeal to fair play. Kennedy followed this kind of advice, which was also available to him from half a dozen other sources, including his own natural inclinations.

The success of our computer simulation suggested

that some of the skeptical questions that had been raised against predictions of this sort could be answered quite satisfactorily.

The Validity Question

The validity question was perhaps the most dramatic. Why wasn't there considerably more anti-Catholic voting than the amount predicted by surveys? Don't social psychologists recognize a clear and large potential discrepancy between public and private attitudes when the private attitude is of low public acceptability, such as religious prejudice? And isn't a public-opinion interview indeed a *public* situation, and voting a private situation?

Admittedly the good fit of our computer prediction to the actual results is not a strong direct test of all the assumptions of the model. Compensating errors are a logical possibility. But in the case of the so-called hidden anti-Catholic vote, there are independent sources of evidence that what anti-Catholic vote there was, was not concealed from pollsters. Why not?

Before attempting a speculative answer, I might note that a comparable conundrum arises in reviewing the 1964 Presidental election. There was supposed to be a secret Goldwater vote unbeknownst to public-opinion interviewers, but that vote did not materialize either.

Let us consider two types of anti-Catholic voters in 1960, the overt and the latent. The overt type had a set of arguments or slogans with which he could convince himself about the danger of a Catholic in the White House. There seems to be no reason why he would have hesitated to express his prejudices, along with supporting argumentation, to an interviewer. Even an attitude that might be unpopular nationally would not seem unpopular to a local enthusiast in contact with many like-minded neighbors. In this connection, it should be noted that public-opinion interviewers run heavily to passive, middle-aged, middle-class local women. These women can readily be perceived by the person with strong opinions as obliging neutral vessels who will carry his messages to City Hall or the state capital or to some vague national consciousness beyond. The interviewers are more likely seen this way than as loyal representatives of an authoritative Establishment that will punish people with unpopular views. Of course, if the interviewee holds strange, idiosyncratic opinions for which he doubts he can count on social support—let us say that he thinks that dolphins should be sent into Haiphong harbor to secretly sabotage Russian ships—then he might hesitate at the prospect of making a fool of himself before the interviewer. But sizable minority opinions are not of this character, since social support is available from friends and neighbors.

These remarks have applied to the case of the confident, overt anti-Catholic. Now imagine another vintage-1960 voter with some suspicion and distrust of Catholics, but also with some uncertainty as to the fairness and propriety of such feelings, some doubt of their relevance to the choice of a President, and no confidence that he could command wholehearted social support for his anti-Catholic feelings. Given the stimulus of a sweet lady interviewer asking whether he, the voter, would be willing to vote for a Catholic nominated by his own party, his response might well be the "fair" answer—that he would of course vote for the good man, Catholic or no. Now picture this voter's twin brother, not exposed to the lady interviewer, but instead to the stimulus of the voting booth presenting his party's Catholic versus the other party's Protestant. Will his suspicion of Catholics now triumph over both fairness and party loyalty because the voting booth is private? To assume that he will is to predict a discrepancy between poll and vote. But since a discrepancy did not appear in our study, this assumption is presumably not correct. Here I submit that the voting booth is not psychologically very private. The voter's family and close friends and perhaps a few acquaintances have probably asked him in advance how he intends to vote and will probably ask afterwards how he *did* vote. A socially undesirable decision in the booth must therefore be cast at the cost of an intent to dissemble when asked about the decision later.

The man who doesn't feel he has a real justification for holding a socially undesirable attitude is therefore in much the same psychological position in the voting booth as he is in the interview situation, albeit one is by appearances more private than the other. In both cases, he must either allow himself to be trapped into making the socially desirable response, or else suffer the social discomfort associated with making an undesirable response.

I do not mean to assert that there are no differences at all between interview and voting-booth situations. There might be a number of people who would vote differently from the way they would poll, but not necessarily all would vote in favor of the less socially desirable response. Some individuals might even use the privacy of the voting booth to guiltily register a conforming response (for example, a pro-minority group vote) that they would be too embarrassed to support in public. This orientation might especially apply to moderate Negro candidates such as Massachusetts Senator Edward Brooke and Cleveland Mayor Carl Stokes. The matter deserves further analysis and study, but I hope I have made one major point successfully, namely that there is no evidence for massive "secret votes" in recent Presidential campaigns. I would further assert that in general the validity of surveys is quite high, although there is a certain kind of exception to which I refer below.

Obsolescence of Data Banks

Returning now to other skeptical questions about computer-aided political prognosis, we come to the possible obsolescence of data banks. Do old surveys really help predict present trends? In our main 1960 simulation, none of the data were gathered later than 1958. Yet the predictions did not substantially suffer on this account, as later replications of the simulation made clear. Of course, the key predictive factors were party loyalty and religion, both highly stable, but still it may be surprising that anti-Catholic sentiments expressed prior to 1958 were germane and predictively valid two years later.

Further surprises were provided by a simulation of the 1964 election results. With data no newer than two years old, we produced a prediction of state-by-state outcomes that was substantially as accurate as the prediction of the 1960 election. More intricate use of the data bank was required, however. For the 1964 election we used data on not one but three political issues: civil rights, nuclear policy, and social-welfare policy.

In brief, we assumed that Republicans who did not support Goldwater on at least two of the three issues would defect to the Democrats, and that Democrats who did not support Johnson on civil rights would defect to the Republicans. The data bank, however, did not contain responses to direct questions such as, "Do you support Goldwater on civil rights?" Instead, the questions on each issue spanned a decade of possibly miscellaneous topical concerns. On civil rights, for example, the questions dealt largely with aspects of the

Supreme Court desegregation ruling of 1954, like "Should the schools in Little Rock, Ark., be integrated now, or should integration be postponed?" Now, one would not *necessarily* expect a high correlation between an anti-integration stand in 1957 and sympathy seven years later with Goldwater's vote against the 1964 Civil Rights Act, to say nothing of the actual behavior of voting for Goldwater. Yet the fairly good predictive accuracy of the 1964 simulation suggests that, at least on the national level, rather old survey items can serve reasonably well as indicators of enduring group dispositions toward stable themes in political life.

With two types of local elections, though, the up-to-dateness of survey data can be a much more serious question. In party primaries, the stabilizing effect of party loyalty is not a factor, and very volatile shifts of candidate strength can appear at the last moment, particularly when discussion of issues is nebulous or absent. In local referenda, likewise, the issues are often unfamiliar and unclear until the 11th-hour introduction of strong arguments. Thus, both primaries and referenda present special difficulties in applied analysis.

Many of the most spectacular apparent failures of polls have been in primaries. "Pollsters Fooled Again," declared the *New York Times* on page 1 of its News of the Week section the Sunday after Eugene McCarthy's stunning showing in the New Hampshire primary, which began the incredible 1968 political season. The idea that pollsters have been tricked by a shrewd electorate makes appealing journalism, but it can tend to perpetuate a serious misrepresentation, as I shall try to show.

In 1964, there were three key Republican primaries, and the polls were wrong in all three cases. In New Hampshire, Rockefeller was supposed to be slightly ahead, but Lodge won easily. In Oregon, Lodge was supposed to be ahead, but Rockefeller won easily. And in crucial California, the final poll had Rockefeller the winner but, of course, Goldwater won.

In 1968, only one primary winner was miscalled by the polls (Robert Kennedy's loss to McCarthy in the close Oregon race), but the percentage predictions were occasionally way off, as in New Hampshire.

The percentage errors in two of the three 1964 cases were much too large to be accounted for by sampling variation, but the clue to what might have gone wrong was that the eventual winner gained five percentage points between the next-to-last poll and the last poll. A late trend was also evident in McCarthy's New Hampshire showing in 1968. This is the basis for what I like to call the First Law of Poll-Watching: *If in a dull primary you see a trend in the polls a week before the election, extrapolate to the result by tripling this trend in the final week.*

The psychological basis for this carefree, slightly tongue-in-cheek rule of thumb is that unless the issues are sharply drawn early, the attributes of the candidates do not usually make a clear impression until the last two weeks before the election. As the day of decision nears, however, any compelling, pithy argument may create a wave of social endorsement for the lucky candidate in whose behalf the argument can be made. With Lodge in the 1964 New Hampshire primary, the pithy argument was that Lodge, unlike the other candidates, was after all a New Englander. With Rockefeller in Oregon, it was that Rockefeller was at least campaigning while Lodge wasn't even clearly interested. In California, the situation was rather more complicated. The campaign commanded sharper interests and loyalties, and no sweeping overall trend was discernible just before the last poll, so the First Law did not apply.

In 1968 in New Hampshire, the simple idea of registering a protest against President Johnson gained rapid currency (though less than half of the voters knew that McCarthy was a "dove"). And in Oregon and elsewhere Robert Kennedy apparently suffered near voting time from the charge that he was ruthless.

Local Referendum Campaigns

With local referendum campaigns, similarly, there is every indication that a strong last-minute amplification of simple, possibly trivial, arguments occurs, carrying the day for one side or the other. Here, too, there are some notable examples of polls seeming to be incorrect. National samples typically show sentiment in favor of water fluoridation at around 60 percent. Yet three out of four local fluoridation referenda lose. The explanation seems to be that before the referendum campaign starts, more positive than negative arguments are known, but during the last two weeks the negative arguments gain wider currency, and a sufficient number of people change from weak pro to weak anti opinions to ensure defeat. I have some very detailed data from a study I did of the water-fluoridation referendum in Berkeley in 1964, which clearly showed this effect.

Two other cases, both notorious, in which polls were accurate in predicting the referendum outcome but were seriously incorrect in calling the percentage margin of victory, were the Proposition 14 vote against fair housing in California in 1964, and the repeal in New York of a civilian police review board in 1966. And lest anyone think from these examples that the illiberal side always wins referenda when the chips are down, I hasten to mention a contrary instance: In California in 1966, a very strict provision (called CLEAN) against obscene literature was leading slightly in the polls yet lost on election day, even while Reagan was romping away with the governorship.

These examples suggest a Second Law of Poll-Watching: *If in a referendum an abstract principle is pitted against a very concrete fear or desire, the concrete side will gain heavily as the campaign nears its conclusion.*

Ordinarily, polls are not taken frequently enough in referendum campaigns to allow extrapolation of last-minute trends. If they were, the experienced poll-watcher could add to this Second Law the triple-trend principle of the First Law—that is, take the percentage gain of the concrete side of the issue in the next-to-last week of the campaign and triple it to predict the final outcome. The reason I suspect that this would work is that the psychological processes involved in last-minute trends are probably similar in referenda and primaries: Just when public attention finally begins to focus lazily on the imminence of voting on a complex matter, a compelling little summarization of what it's all about makes the social rounds.

The feelings involved may range widely in intensity, and the arguments may vary in content from one issue to the next, without disturbing the generalization that in a public confrontation the concrete side of an issue gains voters from the abstract side. The principle of preventive dental hygiene is rather abstract, whereas the various alarms that can be conjured up about fluoride poisoning and impure water are immediate and concrete. In parallel fashion, it is all well and good to declare in principle against pornography, but if it means that someone is going to censor what you read, or worse, take away your copy of *Playboy,* well, then one must stand and be counted.

Now, the discrepancies between abstract and concrete can, to the outside observer, look like sheer hypocrisy, and, on racial issues, conniving bigotry as well.

Yet the voter himself may be blissfully unaware of a discrepancy as he switches from his bland early endorsement of a general principle in an interview to his later concerned support of an application of its contrary, under the stimulus of a pointed campaign exposing him largely to the latter side. Even if he is aware of the discrepancy, it may not disturb him. As political scientist Robert Dahl puts it, "[It is] a common tendency of . . . mankind . . . to qualify universals in application while leaving them intact in rhetoric."

As my preceding remarks have indicated, local campaigns possess a volatility not characteristic of national campaigns. Computerizing local public opinion is therefore more hazardous than computerizing national public opinion. Furthermore, it is an expensive proposition because data-bank information cannot be transferred from one locale to another. Extensive background on the local issues and voters in Berkeley doesn't help you much in predicting the outcome of an election in Indianapolis.

There are quite a number of very interesting psychological questions to be investigated in local referenda or mass public controversies, however, and the construction of computer models whose predictions can be checked against responses from local survey panels is at least one useful way to proceed with such an investigation. To check the predictions of one computer model devised a few years ago by Alex Bernstein and me, I have assembled intensive data from three cities on fluoridation and school-segregation controversies. In this endeavor, we have encountered one peculiar problem that deserves mention, though I will not explore it in detail here. In a local computer model, it is necessary to predict *individual* rather than group opinion changes because there are not enough respondents to construct a large bank of voter types; but when we examine some of these individual changes, however, we find strong evidence of unreliable pseudo-change. Many respondents hop wildly back and forth on the attitude scales from one time to the next, while reporting no exposure to any conversations or persuasive appeals on the issue. It is as if their interview responses are given randomly. This is the phenomenon that sociologists Paul Lazarsfeld and James Coleman refer to as "turnover," and political social psychologists Philip Converse and Milton Rosenberg call "non-attitudes." It is especially prevalent on topics that for uninformed voters

are essentially "nonsense issues," such as water fluoridation, but it occurs to some extent on all issues. And computer simulation models, obviously, will have difficulty in tracing something that isn't there.

Most of what I have said thus far paints a picture of public opinion as disorganized and wishy-washy. But in fact I believe that there are definite simple patterns at work. The forces acting upon public opinion may be viewed as gravitational masses pulling upon a shallow body of water. If more than one force is applied, then the resultant response is often a simple sum of the various appropriate responses. Thus, although the published account of our 1960 and 1964 computer analyses invoke so-called cross-pressure theory, the theory that opposing decisional elements impinging on the voter interact to produce strong motivational effects, I am much more inclined in retrospect to take the view that different issues superpose upon one another *without* mutual interference. Characterizing this view are four simple assumptions:

1. Most issues have so little effect that for practical purposes one may ignore them;

2. One or two issues may have the same effect across all voter types;

3. One or two issues may have different effects across major voter types, effects proportional to measurable susceptibilities to the issue among the various types; and

4. These effects combine additively to determine the final outcome.

What convinces me most strongly of the accuracy of this simple "gravitational" model is the great success of another kind of computer analysis—the election-night computer projections by the television networks of final vote outcomes. (See "How Computers Pick an Election Winner," November, 1966.) In the early projection attempts, a number of pratfalls occurred, but in 1964 and again in 1966 the speed and accuracy of projection were awesome. In the 229 races called in those two election years, each of the two major networks made but two errors. The successful pattern is by now familiar: The bemused announcer, without the slightest understanding of how it's done, and not knowing whether he should believe it himself, reports, "With the polls closed only 20 minutes, and 0 percent of the vote tabulated, the computer already predicts that incumbent Governor Sam Smurch of Idaho will lose to his opponent, Runaway Roberts." And sure enough, when the tabulation is finally in four hours later, Sam Smurch loses.

Observation in a Few Key Districts

On the basis of my experience at NBC in 1964, I can suggest how these minor miracles can be performed. One basic and extremely simple supposition is that a trend observed in a few districts to a large portion of states or even to the whole state. Since the early observation of trends is clearly important to early projection, key districts can be chosen from among those known to have early returns available. But another crucial property of key districts is whether their shifts in voting from election to election have corresponded to the state's shifts over corresponding elections—that is, whether these districts are "swingometric." Suppose that in a state that voted 47 percent Democratic in a previous comparable election, a swingometric precinct that last time went 30 percent Democratic now goes 38 percent Democratic, and one that went 50 percent Democratic now goes 58 percent Democratic. On the basis of only these two pieces of early information, the best guess about the outcome would be a statewide 8 percent swing toward the Democratic side from the previous state results; thus, if in the previous election the Democrats had captured 47 percent of the statewide vote, they would now be predicted to capture 55 percent. Of course, the accuracy depends upon whether these key precincts are in some sense representative of the state, unless *all* precincts have swung the same 8 percent, in which case it doesn't matter which ones you choose for early projection.

If one party's campaign exerts equal attraction on all voter types, it will produce roughly the same amount of swing in all precincts. The projection procedure will then be very "robust," that is, insensitive to the choice of key early precincts. But consider the slightly more subtle situation where the campaign exerts different effects across the state's major population types, say urban versus rural. In that case, the key precincts must be carefully selected to give a balanced picture of swings in both groups. Ideally the selection of key precincts should be deliberately balanced on the basis of the population characteristics known or thought to be important in a swing. Thus, if the state is divided 50-50 between urban and rural population, and key precincts show a 4 percent swing to the Democrats in urban areas and a 6 percent swing to the Republicans

in rural areas, then the projected swing in the state as a whole would be 2 percent in favor of the Republicans.

There are many variations on this basic scheme. Instead of previous voting records, polls throughout the state and in the key precincts can provide the baseline for calculating a probable swing. This polling approach is especially useful in party primaries lacking a historical precedent. The networks have managed to project primary results as well as final election results, although in 1964 and again in 1968 CBS almost goofed in mercurial California with overly quick declarations based too heavily on Southern California key precincts.

That rather simple election-night projection models can work so well is testimony to the simplicity of the major forces operating on the electorate. If a unique constellation of many different forces combined to produce the vote outcome in each separate district, then geographical variation of outcomes would be so high and so apparently unsystematic that any prediction would be hazardous.

Is the view of public opinion I am espousing, with its emphasis on bland simplicity, an unusual view? No, indeed. Professional politicians, and lay and academic analysts of the public mind, have long sounded closely related themes. Herbert McClosky, following an analysis that revealed weak and self-contradictory clusters of public beliefs about democratic norms and practices, put the matter quite sharply. He said, "As intellectuals and students of politics we are disposed both by training and sensibility to take political ideas seriously. . . . We are therefore prone to forget that most people take them less seriously than we do, that they pay little attention to issues, rarely worry about the consistency of their opinions, and spend little or no time thinking about the values, presuppositions and implications which distinguish one political orientation from another."

It seems to me that we can understand and perhaps even sympathize with the general public's failure to organize the political world very well if we realize that there are limits on the typical man's intellectual reach —that his organizing capacities and efforts are usually applied only over a small content area.

Opinion Molecules

To see this pattern, let us postulate the existence of self-contained cognitive units called opinion *molecules*. Each molecule functions for the person holding it by serving most of the purposes an opinion serves. Much has been written about the expressive purposes of opinions and about the psychodynamic functions of more general attitude orientations, but there is a more homey and widespread function that opinions satisfy. Opinions bestow conversational and cognitive security —they give you something to say and think when the topic comes up. To serve this function, as well as some of the deeper psychological functions, the usual minimum-sized, stable opinion molecule seems to require a *fact,* a *feeling,* and a *following*—that is, some item of "information" (which may or may not be objectively correct); some emotional orientation; and some sense that there are others who hold the same opinion.

It is easy to give examples of such molecules: "It's a fact that when my Uncle Charlie had back trouble, he was cured by a chiropractor. You know, I feel that chiropractors have been sneered at too much, and I'm not ashamed to say so, because I know a lot of people who feel the same way." Or again, "Nobody on this block wants to sell to Negroes, and neither do I. The property values would decline." These sorts of opinions are often quite impervious to other levels of argumentation because of their complete, closed, molecular character. It is as if the opinion-holder were saying, "What else could there possibly be to add?"

Certainly the opinion molecule's size will vary, from individual to individual, depending upon habit, education, intelligence, personality, and social context. Sometimes a molecule will have only two components, say just a fact and feeling with no following, as in private little delusions, or a feeling and a following with no essential dependence on variations in fact, as in "Burn, baby, burn." On the other hand, it is quite possible to have larger molecules that include arguments to counter the opposition, qualifications of the opinion, and an organized account of the facts, feelings, and following on the other side.

How elaborate the structure housing an opinion will be depends upon how elaborate the individual requires it to be to serve his purposes. For example, if no counter-arguments are expected, then there is no need to prepare for them. But this is also a matter of cognitive style, varying according to a self-imposed question, "How much do I have to know to be entitled to an opinion?" Presumably, highly educated individuals feel some embarrassment when and if their opinions are revealed as superficial, and therefore are at pains to try to construct them well. But most of the general public feels no such pressure, and there is no realistic reason why they should. Without question, this is a source of great frustration to all those who in some way work to try to increase the public's level of sophistication.

It is possible, as we have seen, to get a lot of mileage out of very simple computer models because the drifts in mass public opinion usually follow simple patterns. In the last analysis, however, despite the fact that any given pattern may be simple, the question of which particular pattern will emerge in a given election campaign is still something of an imponderable. The interpretations placed upon crucial events and personalities —the labels or images, or call them what you will— determine the components available for people's opinion molecules, and these components are never either completely predictable or completely under the control of powerful political figures.

Thus there will always be margin for error in computer prognosis of public opinion, particularly prognoses that try to project too far forward in time. For those still ethically troubled by the political advent of computer analysis, let me add that potential protection against the trivialization of the electoral process is the same as it has always been: an electorate that responds to complex issues in a complex way, a way that defies sterotypes and formulas—and the computers.

The Best-Known American

Fred I. Greenstein

People in the streets around Times Square could hardly believe the news. A man in evening dress said, "It can't be true." There was a steady stream of telephone calls to newspaper offices by persons seeking to verify the news.

(A congressman of an opposing party said): "Oh what a calamity. This is a tremendous shock. . . . Politics are now forgotten in the love all factions had for him as a man."

(On the official day of mourning) . . . public activity was suspended; banks, stores, theaters, and movie houses were closed. At noon, the entire nation observed two minutes of silence in honor of the dead President.

The President described in this newspaper account was not John F. Kennedy, it was Warren G. Harding. Harding was not considered a romantic figure; he was not young, not dead from other than natural causes. But he was the President.

Very similar shock and disturbance was also recorded when Franklin D. Roosevelt died in office in 1945 and there have been reports of similar public reaction to every Presidential death since Lincoln's. The descriptions of psychological responses to presidential deaths are, in general, so identical as to be interchangeable. In each instance the same sense of shock and loss, the public weeping, people acting dazed and disoriented, and showing the symptoms of anxiety.

The public reaction to Kennedy's death is certainly freshest in memory, and was the most completely recorded. It was extensively documented in a national survey conducted immediately after his assassination, three years ago this month. A large majority of the respondents (79 percent) reported that their immediate and "deeply felt" reaction was to think of the President's death as "the loss of someone very close and dear." Half of the national sample acknowledged having wept, many reported such symptoms as loss of appetite (43 percent), insomnia (48 percent), general feelings of nervousness and tension (68 percent). Throughout the following weekend, people were unable or unwilling to carry on normal activities. The average adult spent eight hours on Friday, ten hours on Saturday, eight hours on Sunday, and another eight hours on Monday tuned in on television and radio reports of the assassination and its aftermath.

Of course, Kennedy's comparative youth, his personality, the times, and the tragic manner of his death had much to do with this strong reaction. But Roosevelt, a much older man, died of natural causes, and the effect on the public was in most respects identical.

It may be pointed out that both Kennedy and Roosevelt were colorful, attractive, and controversial men, Presidents in time of crises, men associated with strong policies who tended to rouse passion in both partisans and critics. But what of Harding?

The deaths of other public figures—political leaders, ex-Presidents, religious leaders, entertainment celebrities—do not produce similar reactions, except in very specialized segments of the population.

These extraordinary outbursts of public emotion toward the President are one side of a striking paradox in American political behavior. The other side is the remarkable indifference of most Americans to the sphere of society in which the President is a key actor. This indifference has been documented in endless ways in public opinion surveys:

—80 percent of the electorate do not usually discuss politics.

—90 percent never write public officials.

—45 percent do not know how many senators there are from each state.

—53 percent do not know how long congressmen are elected for; few voters even know who their state congressman is.

How do we account for the seeming inconsistency between public indifference to politics and the profound emotional outpouring that results when the nation's chief political figure dies in office?

There are a number of information sources which shed some light on the matter. First, we possess a good deal of research on public opinion among adults. Then recently there have been significant investigations into children's attitudes toward political authority. Finally, an interesting, if uneven, collection of psychiatric case histories has accumulated over the years, detailing what psychiatric patients have thought, said, and felt about subjects touching on high ranking authorities. Tied together, these three sources—even

if they do not fully resolve the inconsistency—can lead us to some enlightening, if speculative, conclusions about the psychological meaning of the presidency to Americans.

Adult Views about the President

The polls make clear that the President is the best known political figure in the United States. Indeed, he must be the best known person in the nation. This, as we have seen, is not true of other authorities and politicians. More than half of all voters are typically unable to name—or even to recognize the names of—such leading figures as cabinet secretaries, governors of major states, and Supreme Court Justices. In September 1963, less than a year before he received the Republican presidential nomination, Barry Goldwater was unknown to a full 42 percent of a Gallup Poll national sample.

Public officials are less well known than most mass entertainment figures (motion picture stars, television celebrities, athletes), many of whom are familiar to 90 percent or more of the public. But nearly everyone (95 percent) knows the President's name. For many Americans the President provides virtually the sole cognitive link to the political system, a fact related to the consistent ability of twentieth century Presidents to be reelected. (Only two have been defeated; one, Hoover, during a major depression, and the other, Taft, as a result of a major party split.)

A second poll finding is that high public officials are greatly respected in American society. Americans commonly express dislike and distrust of "politicians." But when they are asked to rank occupations according to "general standing," they regularly place such positions as Supreme Court justice, governor, and senator at the top of their rankings, ahead of even the most prestigious civilian role (which happens to be that of physician). Curiously, the presidency itself has never been included in such studies, but, if it were, everything we know would lead us to expect it to be ranked on top.

A third poll finding is that most incumbent Presidents, on most occasions, receive considerably more approval than disapproval. In the case of Presidents Roosevelt, Eisenhower, Kennedy, and Johnson, the regular Gallup Poll assessments of "how good a job the President is doing" *never* found more people disapproving than approving. The only exception has been President Truman; when he took office after Roosevelt's death he received the highest favorable rating ever recorded by the Gallup Poll (87 percent), but at a later point was rated favorably by only 23 percent of the electorate.

A remarkable range of presidential public decorum has proved to be consistent with public approval of the incumbent President—Roosevelt's aristocratic bearing, Eisenhower's folksiness, Kennedy's detached intellectuality and wit, Johnson's use of the idiom of the American Southwest. Yet there evidently are limits to what is considered consistent with the dignity of the presidential role, limits which very probably were transcended in Truman's scrappy partisanship and his occasional public displays of temper.

Fourth, we may note the consistent readiness of citizens to come to the President's support in times of crisis, particularly international crisis. While assessments of the President's performance are generally more positive than negative, his public esteem does fluctuate. Very often the increases in presidential popularity follow fast upon some major presidential action. When the decision was made to resist the Communist invasion of South Korea, President Truman's popularity rose—within the period of a single month—from 37 percent approval to 46 percent approval. Eisenhower's popularity rose from 67 percent to 75 percent during the month of the Suez crisis, and from 52 percent to 58 percent after sending the marines to Lebanon in 1958. Roosevelt's popularity rose from 72 to 84 percent after Pearl Harbor.

More recently, President Johnson's popularity, after suffering a steady erosion during the intensified Vietnamese fighting in the first half of 1966, rose from 50 to 56 percent following the bombing of oil supply dumps in the area of Hanoi and Haiphong.

Even unsuccessful international actions have led to increased presidential popularity. Eisenhower's popularity went up by 6 percentage points after the U-2 incident and the collapse of the Paris summit meetings; Kennedy's by 10 points after the Bay of Pigs invasion. Typically, a rally-around-the-President effect also takes place just after election or reelection, indicating that there is a substance to the familiar metaphor which sees public office as a "mantle" of majesty and authority that has been placed on his shoulders, changing his image. John F. Kennedy had the support of only a fraction of 1 percent more than half of the electorate in November 1960; but by the time of his inauguration, only two months later, 69 percent approved of him.

Finally, there is evidence that citizens perceive and judge the President largely in personal terms. In early 1948 a three-state sample of voters who had already indicated who they wanted elected were asked: "What are the qualities that you think would make him the best man (for President)?" Personal qualities exceeded ideological references more than fourfold. When people were asked during the 1950's what they liked or disliked about President Eisenhower, they most commonly referred to his personal characteristics, conscientiousness, warmth or coldness, physical vigor, sincerity and integrity, religious background and practice. There also were references to policy positions and leadership or lack of it—but together these were less frequent than statements about personal qualities. Comparable evidence exists about Kennedy and Nixon in the 1960 campaign. For both there were substantially fewer references to policy commitments than to the man.

In summary, the surveys show that the President is almost universally known, standing out with far greater clarity than other actors on the political scene; his role seems to be highly respected; his personal popularity fluctuates, but tends generally to be high; support for him increases when he takes decisive action, particularly actions which commit the nation in the international arena; he is perceived and judged to a considerable extent in personal terms.

Children's Views about the President

The President normally is the first public official of whom children become aware. By the age of nine (and usually earlier) virtually every child knows the name of the incumbent President. Like the least informed adults, however, they know very little else about government and politics. But they already share the adult conception of the importance of high political office. Nine-year-olds, asked to rank occupations in terms of importance, place the President at the top, well above such groups as physicians, school teachers, and clergymen. In addition, young children see the President in overwhelmingly favorable terms, thinking of him as benevolent and helpful. The following statements are typical:

—"The President is doing a very good job of helping people to be safe."

—"The President . . . takes care of the U.S."

—"The President has the right to stop bad things before they start."

These early childhood attitudes provide a fascinating problem for analysis. They evidently develop quite subtly, in ways not easy to untangle or explain. Young children are apparently not *taught* to believe the President important and virtuous. In fact, they ordinarily are not explicitly taught about the presidency at all in the early school years. Rather, the notion that the President is "very important" seems unconsciously to build up in the child's mind from casual exposure to such sources as the mass media and adult conversations. The firmness of a young child's belief in the importance of the President, despite absence of accurate information about what he really does, can be seen in this interview conducted in the 1950's, with a seven-year-old:

INTERVIEWER: Have you heard of the President of the United States?

ROBERT: Yes.

I: What is his name?

R: Eisenhower.

I: What does he do?

R: Well, sometimes he . . . well, you know . . . a lot of times when people go away he'll say good-bye and he's on programs and they do work.

I: What kind of work does he do? Do you know any more about it?

R: (After thought) Studying.

I: What sort of things does he study?

R: Like things they gotta do . . . like important . . . what's happening and the weather and all that.

I: Now tell me this. Who is more important, the President of the United States or a doctor?

R: (Pause) The President.

I: Who do you think is more important, the President of the United States or a school teacher?

R: (Emphatically) President!

I: Why is the President more important?

R: They do much more work and they're much importanter. School teacher isn't.

I: (After being told in response to further questions that the President is also more important than a storekeeper and than a general in the army): Who do you think is more important than the President?

R: (Long pause) Lemme see . . . I don't know.

What "information" Robert does have about the Presidency is largely imaginative. It is assembled from the important activities of Robert's older brother, who studies his homework, and from a hazy recollection of the television news broadcasts that transmit somewhat mysterious communications to the adults of the family in the intervals between the children's shows. Yet Robert's basic disposition toward the presidency (which only later will be filled in with specific information) is already well formed.

A rather similar course can be found in the development of political party loyalties. Here also the basic emotional stance—the underlying attitude that "I am a Democrat" or "I am a Republican"—comes first and then gradually the information upon which we might expect such attitudes to be based develops and falls into line.

It has been argued that children's early conceptions of the presidential role provide them with "perceptual filters," which shape their later learning about politics; and that the positive nature of these early conceptions should contribute to a generally favorable orientation toward the political system.

Deeper Feelings About the President

Another source of insight into the psychological meaning of the President to citizens comes from psychiatric literature. Although not very well documented, the suggestions from this source are intriguing and merit further study.

As Freud saw it, the mind tends to thrust out of consciousness distasteful thoughts—such as emotionally painful memories of childhood experiences and unacceptable impulses, many of which are sexual or aggressive. But what is repressed often reappears in other guises—in dreams and neurotic symptoms, and as latent meaning underlying and coloring much of everyday life.

Early conflicts with parents, who are the ultimate authorities in a young child's life, produce much of this repression. Typically there are two inconsistent (in psychiatric jargon "ambivalent") impulses toward family authority that the child forces out of consciousness—the need to be excessively submissive and the need to express hostility, to rebel. In later life, according to this line of psychiatric reasoning, these repressed feelings toward the private authorities of childhood are expressed in citizens' reactions to public authorities such as the President.

There are two reasons why this still imperfectly documented psychiatric reasoning is of interest.

First, psychiatric explanations are especially geared to deal with the seeming paradox of emotional reactions that are out of proportion to the individual's prior attitudes and behavior—for example, intense mourning at the death of an individual one had expressed little feeling toward. In such a case the psychiatrist expects to find that unconscious feelings had been present all along.

Second, even if one does not accept the underlying theory, psychiatric case histories of patients in treatment give unusual insight into feelings and responses that cannot readily be observed in more formal interviews. For example, when President Roosevelt died a number of psychoanalysts reported that their patients reacted in ways that clearly indicated they identified him with one or both of their parents. One analyst found similar associations among his patients even during the less extreme circumstances of the election campaigns of 1948, 1952, and 1956. President Kennedy—in spite of his youth—affected some patients in the same manner, both before and after his death.

What Does the Presidency Mean?

Drawing on the three kinds of research findings, we can suggest several ways in which the President seems to have psychological meaning for citizens:

■ By virtue of being a single highly publicized figure who combines the roles of political leader and head of state the President *simplifies perception* of government and politics. Just as the modern American President has come to be the main source of energy and initiative in the actual workings of the government, he also serves as the main "handle" for providing busy citizens with a sense of what their government is doing. For some citizens the President is virtually the only vehicle for following government and politics, and for children he serves as an instrument of civic learning.

■ The President provides citizens with an *outlet for emotional expression*. In addition to his obvious uses in partisan politics, there are his ceremonial duties and the publicized aspects of his (and his family's) private life. Here again we have an equivalent to the more dignified displays of symbolic activity associated elsewhere in the world with monarchs. In these aspects of his role the President competes for attention very favorably with such professional celebrities as film stars.

■ The President serves as a *symbol of unity*. The public reaction to a presidential death is a grim instance of the unifying power of the presidency. Despite strong political partisanship, the overwhelming impression that comes through is of the homogeneity of public support. Regret at President Kennedy's death was shared by pro-Kennedy Northern Negroes and anti-Kennedy Southern whites. Another instance, already noted, is the rally-round spirit—the tendency of citizens to come to the support of their President in time of international crisis, regardless of the merits of the dispute.

■ It may well be that in times of crisis, the President serves still another function, providing citizens with a *vicarious means of taking political action*. It seems quite likely that at such times numerous people find themselves "identifying" with the President, at least in the superficial fashion in which we find ourselves taking the part of the hero of a motion picture or novel. To the degree that the President's actions are effective, citizens who identify themselves with him may experience heightened feelings of strength—of being in a world which is not completely dependent upon external circumstances and events.

■ Finally, whether or not one psychically takes the part of the President, it is clear that he serves as a reassuring *symbol of social stability*. For many people, one of the most disturbing aspects of President Kennedy's assassination was the implication that went with it of lack of control—of possible national and international disaster. (As a college student put it, "We're always pushing how civilized we are . . . then here in the United States a President gets assassinated.") This, in effect, is the direct opposite of the crisis situation in which a calm and decisive President by seeming to be in firm command, enhances the citizens' feelings of confidence and security.

It is a caricature of the complex, sprawling, uncoordinated nature of the American political system to see it as a great ship of state, sailing on with the President firmly at the helm. But a great many people find comfort in this oversimplified image.

Dynamic Young Fogies—Rebels on the Right

Lawrence F. Schiff

From the bearded poet to the motorcycle delinquent, American adolescents usually go through a period of uncertainty and search, of trying to break away from old controls and standards, and of trying to establish their own identities and personalities.

As psychiatrist Erik H. Erikson puts it, youth searches for "fidelity"—"something and somebody to be true to"—and "often tests extremes before settling on a considered course." This period in adolescence often involves the rejection of things as they are, or as society says they should be.

So it seems an amazing paradox that many young people today, in a small but apparently growing movement, have dedicated themselves to promoting *greater* conservatism, *more* tradition, and *more* devotion and adherence to the values not only of an older generation, but apparently even of an older century.

The conservative movement began in 1960 on the wave of enthusiasm generated by the abortive attempt to get the vice-presidential nomination for Barry Goldwater. The excitement, the spontaneous appearance of so many young conservatives, led to the formation of the Young Americans for Freedom—or YAF. Since then, fed by the rise of other non-affiliated but similarly oriented local college groups, the campus conservative movement has become a fairly successful and going concern. There is no doubt that, paradoxical or not, a small but sizable segment of our young people have found something in this movement to which they respond, and that seems to meet their internal and external demands.

In my study I found that about two-thirds of those interviewed had undergone such a strong change in belief and behavior in coming to conservatism that it could properly be said that they had experienced a form of "conversion." (The other third had simply followed comfortably along the right-wing paths already set by their parents.) These converts, I discovered, had gone through crises and events that were very revealing about their development as adolescents and their total development as human beings.

Specifically, I have found that at the various stages of adolescence different kinds of persons were attracted by conservatism, for different reasons, and in response to different needs. It matters a great deal whether the conversion occurred *immediately following puberty* (between 12 and 17), or in *late adolescence* (beyond 17). There is some overlap; but the two groups are distinctive, each with its own dynamics and style.

The Obedient Rebels

The late converts—whom I call "the obedient rebels"—were the ones most representative of campus conservative activists. Typically they were from homes very much concerned with high status and achievement. In almost all cases their early experiences were dominated by a determined parent, or parents, with detailed and ambitious expectations for their children. All but one were eldest or only sons and the burden of parental ambition fell on them. The obedient rebels (at least in the early years and again after conversion) were usually considered the "good boys" of their families.

Each "rebelled"—sometimes because he felt he could not live up to or realize himself under such pressure—or departed to some degree from the path set out for him. But the revolt was not without peril. Suddenly he would be horrified to discover (on the campus, in the armed services, or among the lower-classes) that he was surrounded by "radicalism," "immorality," or personal hardship—something for which his comfortable background had not prepared him. He would reject the new environment totally and become converted to a conservatism not much different from the one he had left in the first place—but which, superficially at least, he had accepted on his own initiative and conviction.

Psychologically, in essence, his conversion was a reaction to the threat of genuine personality change—which allows great creative possibilities, but also involves dangers. In effect he had come to the pit of change, looked down into it, and turned back, rejecting all alternatives beyond the reaffirmation of obedience; if the non-convert conservatives had never left home, the obedient rebels had returned home.

The *early* adolescent converts, however, exhibited a strikingly different and even more interesting pattern—one signifying a very different way of coping with adolescence. Their conversions were made during, and as part of, the turbulent and formative center of adolescence, and were intertwined, warp and woof, with the demands, potentialities, problems, and limits of that period. The personality changes were reflected in the conversion experience itself.

Where the obedient rebel came to conversion as a result of shock and repulsion (a negative reaction), the early convert came as a result of attraction, or recognition, because he saw something that seemed to meet his needs (for positive reasons). The late convert came to escape from and to deny real change; the early convert came seeking answers and seeking change. His conversion was change itself.

The late convert identified with the overall posture and prestige of the new conservatism, rather than with its detailed content. He was concerned mostly with status, with position, with social identification, with respectability and role—not with passionate belief. As such he could accept its doctrine totally, without much quibble, since what counted was what it stood for, rather than what it was. But the early convert's acceptance of conservatism was specific, personal, immediate, discriminating, and emotional; and he was much more interested in content, as he understood it, than in form.

To understand the contrasts between early and late conversion it is best to go back to the beginnings, in boyhood, and follow the process through time.

As noted, the late converts typically came from families with great determination to see that their children rose in the world. They were under great pressure to achieve and conform—as the interviews revealed.

—Herron's father, a highly successful independent lawyer, early and ardently began to infuse his young son with the spirit of his "adherence to strict moral standards" . . .

—Finestock's immigrant father received a primary school education here and then in true Horatio Alger fashion, rose . . . to put together a fabulously successful business. He intended that his son would actualize his success. . . .

Under such pressure they bent; each in his own way, always covertly and at times involuntarily, they veered from the too high and too rigid parental blueprint.

—Herron . . . chafing under . . . his father's tutelage, began to channel his energies into activities only marginally related to the development of intellect or character. . . . Throughout his adolescence he managed to balance off his resentment against his father by avoiding overt disobedience, always maintaining the form but not the substance of his father's preachments.

—Finestock's father had "pulled strings" to get him into a first-rate college, but after two unhappy years there he flunked out.

Their conversions, when they came, were a reaction to the new standards to which their rebellion had exposed them. They rejected this new environment totally—and as individuals, rather than as a result of being solicited by other conservatives. While it may have set them apart for a time from most of their immediate fellows it did give them a reassuring image and identity, and it led them back toward their parents.

—Herron's conversion took place while he was stationed abroad in the Navy. Disturbed by the "slothfulness" and "self-indulgent habits" of the local citizenry, he had a sudden realization of "the consequences of not subscribing to a strict moral code."

—Manning reacted to his college's total climate. He found himself "appalled and amazed" about some of the college newspaper editorials . . . "disappointed" with the college's moral climate. . . .

Attack Toward the Rear

Conversion for the early adolescents presents a striking contrast. They did not turn from what they found in adolescence to go back to a childhood pattern. In fact, just the opposite—their adolescent conversions were a rejection of their beginnings.

Typically, the early convert came from a family where relationships were intense, and often stressful, unsettling, or full of strife:

—For O'Hara, childhood was . . . far from tranquil. His father (was) a man with a "quick temper" and "quick to criticize" . . . there were always "big arguments." "At one time I looked upon him as the oppressor of both me and my mother, and now I look on them both as in the same boat."

—Mann recalls himself as "a rather uncontrolled" kid, "disciplined from above. But inside I was rebellious . . . I was probably a pretty wretched kid."

—Arnold relates a persistent "inferiority complex. . . . I didn't conform to my mother's beliefs. . . . She kept repeating how no-good I was and how she wished I'd never been born. (This) had quite a dire effect on me."

Two of the young converts had alcoholic fathers; two others came from homes in which chronic instability kept things "wound up and involved."

In all of these cases, the child's emotional life was hyperactive and somewhat uncontrolled. Unlike the late converts, childhood experiences stimulated, rather than molded, character. They would not, or could not, silently conform. These early converts entered adolescence with still smoldering, unsettled infantile residues that had to be worked out some way.

Not surprisingly therefore, virtually all experienced during adolescence a sharp break with the past.

O'Hara: "I was flamboyant originally and a social guy, and then all of a sudden, snap! After sophomore year (high school) I became an introvent, a searcher. . . . I realized I didn't want to be anything like my father was —not his profession, not his personality—and that's just what I was going to be. . . . I wanted to go out on my own—I couldn't stand my dad."

Others went through a social dislocation that served as the break between childhood and what followed:

—Howard, after years of wandering . . . with his Army doctor father . . . at the onset of high school . . . settled into . . . an upper-middle-class suburban community where the family's style of living rose sharply. (He) felt "a little out of place for the first couple of years" . . . in "a rebellion against the accepted ideas I found around me."

—Mann was cut off from his Jewish past in New York City when he became a congressional page. . . . Assigned to the Republican side of the House, he became thoroughly involved in "contacts with those with another point of view."

Three boys came from working-class homes. They broke away from parental patterns and chose their own college-bound paths early—and alone. No brothers or sisters followed.

My mother wasn't even sure I should go to college. I just told her I was going.

Parental values—and even parental models—become irrelevant as each pursued his own road to self-realization.

Our society, with its lack of ritualized organization, does not make the path of growth easy for the young. Peter Blos (*On Adolescence,* The Free Press, 1962) points out: "Where tradition and custom offer no unchallenged influence over the individual, the adolescent has to achieve by personal resourcefulness the adaptation that institutionalization does not offer him. On the other hand, this lack of institutionalized pattern opens up the opportunity for individual development, for the creation of a unique, highly original, and personal variation on tradition."

Thus, finally, this breakaway, whatever handicaps it imposed, also allowed the early converts to work out their own highly individual fates without the inhibitions of family control or tradition. And their conversions played key roles in this working-out.

For some, separation from their families began with the

Forty-seven conservatives from nine college campuses (all but one in New England) were extensively interviewed and given a variety of tests. Geographically the sample included students from every region in the country; academically, from college drop-outs to Rhodes scholars; economically, from families with incomes from $5,000 to $75,000; politically, from moderate Republicans through John Birch enthusiasts to unreconstructed royalists; in religion from atheism to extreme orthodoxy.

About two-thirds of them, in becoming conservatives, had made such a strong break with their previous attitudes and behavior that it would be legitimate to call them "converts"; and it was on these that the study concentrated. The other conservatives were simply following along in footsteps already well worn by parents or community in expected and familiar ways. But the converts—whether by changing from indifference to commitment or by moving sharply to the right—had undergone changes and experiences important not only to their development as adolescents, but to their total life cycles.

A more detailed study of the obedient rebel-type converts has been published in the *Journal of Social Issues*.

---

pain of severe withdrawal—"a self-inflicted purgatory."

—O'Hara: "I don't remember those years—I try to forget—don't think about it that much." Through his second year in high school he alternated between the "good works" of a Catholic social action group and quasi-delinquency, then suddenly "realized that there was hypocrisy in my life" and literally "pulled out . . ." spending much of the next two years trying to "settle it by lying down and thinking about myself."

—For Griffith the marriage of his sister (who had served as a mother substitute) brought on a depressive state for several years. . . . Through high school he was "introverted, very, very quiet. . . . (the kids') middle-class outlooks repulsed me. . . ."

—For Arnold and Wilson the challenge of adjustment proved unmanageable and led to . . . enlistment in the armed forces. . . .

For other converts the transition was more benign, but just as decisive.

From this "purgatory," this searching, they found and embraced conservatism.

—(Griffith's) exposure to and developing enthusiasm about the writings of Ayn Rand and Goldwater conservatism crystallized soon after . . . the death of his father and a year of emotional turmoil for his widowed mother.

—O'Hara: "I wanted to spread out. I almost became a priest; but it's a much greater task to do it on your own. That's what I'm working on now." During two summers

. . . away from home he made his first contacts with conservatism. "Things were so completely different . . . just remade me—my dad wasn't around—I made friends fast —everything else was forgotten."

For working-class converts the conversion came when they had replaced their family ties with outside middle-class and conservative models.

In sum, these early conversions came about because they served to meet and answer the challenges of adolescence for these young men. They fit Blos's contention that: "Adolescence, not only in spite of, but rather because of, its emotional turmoil, often affords spontaneous recovery from debilitating childhood influences. . . ." and Erickson's suggestion that: "We look at adolescence not as an affliction, but as a normal phase of increased conflict characterized by a high growth potential."

Follow the Hero

Typically, the early convert had a "hero," who had great influence, both as recruiter and example.

There was a counselor there, a man who appealed to me. It turned out he had a ranch in Arizona, he was born on it and he was a conservative . . . that's where I first became interested . . . he was a cool guy and he seemed reasonable. . . . Naturally this transferred into the policies he put forth.

William F. Buckley, the popular and vocal editor of the *National Review,* is a key hero:

Well, my romance with him—first of all I think he has tremendous style—secondly he's a more complete man . . . he doesn't hedge—he says it, he's not afraid to say it. Lord, that is a tremendous quality in this age.

The archetypal heroes for the early convert, of course, are those that Ayn Rand creates—and Miss Rand herself. She, too, is "not afraid to say it." Her creations are heroic in the fullest and most uninhibited sense of the word. Existing outside of time, history, and social circumstance, they are unfettered men, free of any social or personal responsibilities or knowledge that might slow down their single-minded pursuit of their self-interest (which, as it happens, is also the greatest public good, since they are a unique breed of supermen whose genius is all that keeps the world moving). Miss Rand's unabashed "philosophy" is outside the conservative mainstream. It is avowedly atheistic and egotistical and is meant to shock the conventional, so it is taboo to the obedient rebels. But how many teen-agers, smarting under parental, social, and school controls which they find false and binding, would not thrill to the story of an architect who refused to compromise with his paying clients and blew up a building development because someone tampered with his design?

Unlike the "lone wolf" obedient rebel, the early convert is usually converted *by* somebody or *with* somebody—it is a social process. He becomes part of a group of similar persons who give support both to him and his belief. Conservatism is woven into the fabric of his relationships:

—Madding "got hold of the (John Birch) *Blue Book* and passed it on to my friends; nearly all were very much impressed. . . ."

—Riley joined his campus YAF chapter because "I liked the people in it."

The early adolescent undergoes a deep conversion. His whole "self-system" is involved. His personality and emotions have been expressed in the act, not just his public face.

—O'Hara (had) an experience of intense self examination which lasted through several "extremely turbulent years, psychologically and emotionally." He now sees conservatism as the only philosophy "congruent with my whole philosophy of life." For O'Hara to arrive at this point required a "personal experience of God" . . . "Inspiration first and examination later."

—Griffith found himself adopting political ideas that were the opposite of his father's. "I suppose there's some deep psychological basis."

—Mann's response to a suggestion of his mother that he would have to become a Democrat in order to be elected. . . . "She doesn't understand that this would mean changing me as a person."

Gung-ho Among the Conservatives

Commitment among adolescents tends to be "all out." Among the conservatives this takes the form of "gung-ho" anti-communism (a strange use of the old Chinese Communist slogan). With the older converts this was often directed most harshly at what they suspected were anti-anti-Communists in their midst—the enemy within—which may, psychologically, be an overt rejection of forbidden internal impulses. The early converts on the other hand seemed to have no such internal conflicts. The enemy was outside their ranks—distinct, identifiable, and real. "Gung-ho" meant to them what it did to Carlson's Raiders.

Conversion did, however, in other ways shed revealing lights on their deep inner needs and impulse life:

People are afraid of nuclear weapons (but) I don't fear the bomb . . . in a way I think it'd be an interesting experience . . . (I) would've enjoyed being a part of the Korean War. . . . I would've enjoyed shooting a few of those guys—they're our enemies.

The process of differentiating the self from the surrounding environment, a crucial part of self-realization, received dramatic form among the early converts. As Edgar Friedenberg describes it: "The oppositional, rebellious, and restive strivings, the stages of experimentation, the testing of the self by going to excess—all these have a positive usefulness . . . for self-definition." For several the conversion was a part of the means through which these strivings were expressed:

—Mann, aware of the unpopularity of his views, particularly back home, reacted with "a kind of strange and exaltative joy that someone was finding what I was saying especially incomprehensible."

—Griffith: "It's 'in' to be liberal. . . . Every once in a while, sitting at a table, everybody nods in agreement—and it's a little bit difficult to dissent. That's a very nice word, 'dissent,' and I think it should be preserved."

—Howard's original conservative thinking was formulated as a part of "a rebellion against the accepted ideas I found around me." He became, "by way of argument," a proponent of Herbert Hoover.

—O'Hara enjoys thinking of himself . . . as someone . . . able to "throw everything out."

Note the ease—indeed the relish and pride—in accepting the image of the self as iconoclast. They often seemed equally as concerned with what was "not me" within the spectrum of conservatism (a concern significantly different from that of the obedient rebels, who repudiated dissension within the ranks). What is distinctive is the emphasis on defining the self as in conflict with and yet as part of surrounding influences.

These young men are, more than most, "tuned in" on themselves—they have a heightened awareness of themselves.

—O'Hara reports feeling "as a man alone" after he "jumped out on my own, suddenly."

—Mann . . . thinks "everyone is basically insular . . . I am . . . everyone is distinct from everyone else deep inside. . . . There are many times when the most precious thing to me is to just sit down and think my own thoughts."

Important in this process of self-realization is the early convert's emphasis on the he-man self-image of conservatism—the rugged individualist, the combat soldier, Ayn Rand's hypermasculine heroes—an identification that might serve also to still any secret doubts about his own masculinity.

The early convert is at this stage still an unstable and incomplete human being—disengaged and aggrandized—a volatile configuration of conflicting strivings, tendencies, growth potentialities, and neurotic dangers. Since he is unfinished, only on rare occasions in the present sample did the political beliefs formed at conversion not undergo further important change.

Finally therefore, and most significantly, the early convert is engaged in a dynamic open-end process of alteration—similar, in this respect, to almost all other adolescents. He is on the "right track," but he is also traveling, and the end is neither in sight nor completely known. The obedient rebel has arrived; his beliefs and posture are round, firm, and fully packed. His conversion resulted in reduced tension and resolved conflict, and he will not again willingly risk uncertainty. Change is suspect and may be abhorrent. But to the early convert change is not at all unwelcome; he looks forward to it as another adventure. He delicately balances tentativeness and commitment:

I feel that every student is essentially an observer in that he need not be committed to too many things. I have definitely not committed to conservative politics. . . . I'll give you my tendency, not my opinion. Opinion implies commitment.

In many cases he shows himself flexible, open to outside influences:

Madding . . . is unsure if the economics course in which he is currently enrolled might not be "liberalizing me." . . . "Right now I'm just feeling my way along."

Actual changes take place:

Howard began as a Randian disciple and then . . . "found I was looking for some 'new departure' in politics in the individualist direction, something not a revolt or return to the past."

In short and in summary, early conversion for these boys was a part of continuing development. It contributed substantially to self-definition; it helped integrate the entire personality; it helped the adolescent toward positive sexual identity, and the ability to have close relationships with other people. The conversion of the typical obedient rebel restored and bound him to his original role. The overall effect of the conversion of the young adolescent was emancipation.

But it is apparently true even of the young converts that, compared to the non-conservatives, they feel a need for all-inclusive answers, spelled out. Our society, according to Erik Erikson, requires of its youth many contradictory things, necessitating, therefore, "a distaste for ideological explicitness." The young conservatives need more than that: as convert Mann put it, "you must have a point of view . . . a basic premise . . . or everything is senseless."

Against the anti-hero of the modern novel with his existential despair, the analytic critic who debunks old traditions, and the disillusioned old radicals from the depression, the far right throws the heroic novel, the embattled and engaged young critic, and the refurbished old radical who has found another New Jerusalem—this one on the road back to Adam Smith. The new convert may not understand all of this, but it does give him something with sharp edges on which to shape himself, something more than the simple necessity to "get along." In this strident ideology and movement, he can find an object able to take on his fantasies and fears, to allow extreme possibilities to be tested, to provide space to work out problems, and room to grow or to regress.

The young converts found in conservatism a way to bring internal needs and fears into the open in the form of ideas and actions, there to communicate them, to shape them, to face them consciously and render them amenable to control. But the obedient rebels were more interested in restriction, in cutting off internal debate and conflict. It is paradoxical, therefore, but inevitable, that the obedient rebel demanded total and rigid conformity to conservative doctrine but was not emotionally involved in it very much; while the young converts cared passionately, but kept straying from orthodoxy.

Significantly then, the end for the young converts is not yet:

O'Hara: "Where I go from here I don't know. Terms like 'truth' and 'right' and 'wrong' are fine . . . except in the sense that they've come to be pretty much meaningless. . . . But I think we can give them some meaning."

Life,Time,and the Fortunes of War
James D.Wright

Unquestionably, the public's attitude toward the Vietnam war has changed greatly in recent years. Commercial polls, media reports and academic studies bear the same message: the war has lost support. But these trend-spotters have left unanswered many questions about the nature of this change. Have the political sentiments articulated at the country club bridge table changed more radically than those voiced at the neighborhood tavern? And if they have, who or what is responsible?—the mass media? Certainly, their editorial viewpoints have undergone concurrent shifts.

But just how powerful are the media? Does a jolting photo-essay of war dead unlock closed minds or lose subscribers? Conversely, could a series of prowar editorials whip up support for a waning cause? Is one medium more effective than another? Is the work-weary lower-income T.V.-watcher any more affected by the evening newscast than the commuting stockbroker is by the news magazine he leafs through enroute to his upper middle-class suburb?

The change in attitudes toward the war coupled with the change in how the war has been reported offers a unique opportunity for social scientists to investigate how mass media and public opinion interact: who influences whom; which is a cause of change and which is a reflection of it.

The period under review here is that from 1964, when President Johnson was swept into office by a huge majority, to 1968 when President Nixon took office, promising to end the war. It was a time when the United States commitment in Vietnam was vastly escalated. The number of troops involved in the war jumped from 40,000 "advisers" to a half-million combat personnel, and in the process, the war was brought home to ever-increasing numbers of people.

Another major phenomenon of the period (no doubt related to the continued escalation) was the rise of large-scale protest against the war. Beginning as a relatively restricted and nonviolent movement in the fall of 1966 with the first big march on Washington, the Movement had taken on a more radical coloration by the summer of 1968. The demands of the protesters changed from the mere end of a senseless war to the end of United States "imperialism" abroad and even the overthrow of "the system" at home. The prominence given to protests in the media cannot but have had an effect on mass sentiment toward the conflict itself.

During the four years from 1964 to 1968, the major media in the country shifted their editorial stance markedly, from a prowar to a fairly obviously antiwar position. This change in the media stance creates an unusual and desirable research situation, because most studies of the influence of the media are forced to deal with them as a constant rather than as a variable.

Fortunately, the University of Michigan's Survey Research Center (SRC) made comprehensive election studies in 1964 and 1968, and the data from them make possible a detailed analysis of the shift in attitudes over the period and of the extent to which the media were responsible.

Before examining these studies, however, it is important to realize the theoretical background against which the analysis must be set, because, in my view, the conclusions to be drawn upset the traditional patterns of speculation about the attitudinal and behavioral impact of the so-called mass media.

There are two characteristic forms of social scientific theory in this area. First, there is the tradition of mass society theorizing. This view links the advance of industrialization and urbanization with breakdowns in the primary social bonds. Upward occupational mobility, a situation presumably endemic to industrial society, is seen as destroying a person's ties with the past—with his parents, his friends and other primary social groups. Meanwhile, increasing urbanization locates individuals in new and unfamiliar milieux in which their old values and attitudes will be inappropriate. These demographic and social

psychological processes result in the creation of "mass man," the so-called rootless individual. Lacking strong informal ties to primary social networks, a society of such mass men will be manipulable and public opinion in such a society is believed to be largely "uncrystallized," or, as sociologist William Kornhauser puts it, "available" for manipulation by national political elites. The mass media, then, function mainly as the propaganda arms of these elite groups, with the capability of reaching out and mobilizing mass opinion in support of the elites' goals, whatever these may be.

The second theory contrasts Kornhauser's view. Founded by Paul Lazarsfeld and his associates at Columbia University in the 1940s and early 1950s, it springs from a tradition of political analysis and media research which we may profitably call the "group bases" theory of politics. Lazarsfeld's conception of the relationship between political attitudes and the mass media is summed up in the slogan: reinforcement rather than conversion. In other words, the media are basically successful at reinforcing and articulating already existing opinions or even at creating opinions in areas where none previously existed, but are not so successful at converting individuals from a firmly held opinion to a new one. Lazarsfeld's concept involved a resurrection of the classical sociological image of man as being located amid an array of social and informational networks or primary groups and deriving the major portions of his political ideology and support from those networks. In sharp contrast to the mass-society view, which was then dominant, Lazarsfeld hypothesized that these networks would override the impact of the formal media. Hence, a situation of reinforcement rather than conversion would exist.

Concentric Circles

In 1964, Johan Galtung published an article in *The Journal of Peace Research* which attempted a quasi-synthesis of these two views. In it, Galtung speculates that society, for purposes of political analysis, can best be conceptualized as a series of concentric circles. At the center is a small decision-making nucleus; this is surrounded by a social center, constituted by a core of the well-informed and articulate mass public; these are both finally enclosed by the social periphery, consisting of the majority of the mass public who remain relatively unconcerned with and uninformed about matters of public policy. On its simplest level, Galtung's view is that mass-society theories will tend to describe the state of politics in the periphery and that "social bases" theories will tend to describe politics in the center. Hence, the center (i.e., the middle-aged, males, the well-educated, the high-income, white-collar workers) will consist of a fairly stable and well reinforced body of informed public opinion anchored in ideological communities, which will consequently be immune to overtures made by the media. Those on the periphery (that is the young and the old, females, the poor, the poorly educated, blue-collar workers) will be characteristically amorphous, unconcerned, unreinforced, uncrystallized—in short, more susceptible to media manipulation.

A number of political and social scientists have recently extended the analyses I have outlined above specifically to attitudes toward the war. Seymour Martin Lipset, for example, in an article on Vietnam published in the September-October 1966 issue of *trans*action, asserted that "in the area of foreign policy, most Americans know very little and are only indirectly involved," while Sidney Verba and associates in a 1967 article in *The American Political Science Review,* noted that "most recent academic studies of public attitudes have demonstrated that the public has little information on most issues and that most people do not have thought-out, consistent and firmly held positions on most matters of public policy." Yet in the same article Verba admitted: "We found that the war in Vietnam was a salient problem" and later, "It is our opinion that [these data] represent fairly high levels of information on an issue of foreign policy." Concerning the hypotheses about uncrystallized opinion and manipulability, Lipset asserted that "when it comes to Vietnam basically the opinion data indicate that national policy-makers, particularly the President, have an almost free hand to pursue any policy they think correct and get public support for it." This uncrystallization hypothesis was also elaborated in a 1970 article for *Scientific American* by Philip Converse and Howard Schuman. Finally, Milton Rosenberg joined Verba and Converse in extending these lines of reasoning into specific hypotheses about the role of the media, in their *Vietnam and the Majority: A Dove's Guide:*

> In the early years of our Vietnam involvement the news and opinion media fell into voluntary alignment with the government, lending ready support and popularization to the rationale for our overall stance in the international sphere. However, in the last four or five years much media content has been increasingly critical of the Vietnam war. This has probably both reflected and helped to deepen the gradual erosion of the general public's approval (or acceptance) of our involvement in Southeast Asia.

At this point we should take a look at the national print media in the period under review, and clarify exactly how much of a shift occurred in their editorial attitudes. A few illustrations will give an idea of the nature and size of this change. Fortunately, it is readily assessable because approximately 90 percent of the total United States magazine readership (for political information as distinct from entertainment) was concentrated, as of 1968, in seven major magazines: *Life, Look, Time, Newsweek, U.S. News & World Report, Reader's Digest* and the *Saturday Evening Post.*

Until 1966, *Life* magazine was under the editorial direction of that avid Cold Warrior, Henry Luce. Mr. Luce's politics were well reflected in the pages of his magazines: witness the following from a *Life* editorial of early 1963:

> We too have some national interests to further. . . and there are lots of places where the average American would like to ease by unilateral action the pains and frustrations of a decade of "alliance diplomacy." In Vietnam, the ghoulish pessimism of the French, plus a deteriorating war, has goaded Washington to reconsider the possibility of stepping up the war. It would also be a pleasure to respond more loftily and unilaterally to the pigmy insults of Castro, of Ghana.

An editorial in the January 8, 1965 issue of *Life* spoke of negotiations as "a euphemism for American withdrawal and a Communist takeover"; in February of 1966, the magazine published an article supporting an escalation, under the title "The War is Worth Winning" (February 25, 1966).

Similar sentiments occurred constantly in Mr. Luce's other major magazine, *Time,* in the same period. From a "non-editorialized" news article of early 1964:

> The key to the situation remains the United States struggle to keep South Vietnam from falling to Communism. . . . It has been clear for a long time what would happen if South Vietnam gave way to Communism: the reaction described by the famous "domino theory" would undoubtedly set in (April 3, 1964.).

A mid-1965 *Time* "Essay" clarified the magazine's position still further:

> It is sometimes forgotten that Communism still remains an international and aggressive movement, that "infiltration" and "subversion" remain realities. . . . [If the United States were to be pushed out of Vietnam], Americans would only have to make another stand against Asian Communism later, under worse conditions and in less tenable locations (May 14, 1965).

The "Essay" was entitled, "Vietnam: the Right War at the Right Time."

Yet by 1968, both *Time* and *Life* had taken markedly more conciliatory stances. From *Life:*

> We urge that this campaign be de-escalated—that the U.S. suspend for the time being the general air attack against the Hanoi-Haiphong industrial and transport system (January 5, 1968).

> (Quoting Edwin Reischauer, ambassador to Japan): "We have lost this war in terms of our original objectives. . . . " Is it defeatism to say that? Perhaps: but it is mainly a confession that all the military power in the world can be muscle-bound and useless in some revolutionary situations. Force has its limits and kill ratios are

not the measure of its efficiency (February 23, 1968).

By the middle of 1969, *Life* had published the photographs of the previous week's war dead, hardly a clarion call to escalation.

And from *Time*, in August, 1968:

Not all the basic goals of either the U.S. or North Vietnam policy are likely to survive a genuine settlement. . . . Through some combination of a cease-fire, withdrawal and supervision, the guns will eventually fall silent in Vietnam.

The same essay spoke favorably of "integrating the Communists into South Vietnam politics" and described the war as "messy and formless."

Look, too, showed a substantial shift away from support for the war in the four-year period. From an article published early in 1964:

For should South Vietnam be so internally weakened by incessant nightly guerrilla attacks that North Vietnam could absorb it, the bountiful rice harvests of the Mekong delta would well out in life-giving gushers to industrially emerging, but chronically starving, North Vietnam and Red China. Cambodia, Laos, and Thailand would fall like dominoes, and India would be exposed to an Asian Communist bloc for once well-fed and economically viable (January 28, 1964).

Yet by the middle of 1968, *Look* had taken a markedly different stand. In an editorial following seven pages of horrifying war photographs, the editors commented:

Look publishes these photographs to remind you of some things that many Americans seem to have forgotten: that people and nations make mistakes. . . . The Vietnam war has been a mistake, destroying something precious in the word, "America" (May 14, 1968).

The editorial concluded with a call to "wind up our involvement as quickly and as honorably as possible." By late 1969, even the "honorably" qualification was dropped: "We should get out of Vietnam immediately" (J. Robert Moskin, foreign editor, *Look*, November 18, 1969).

Similar shifts are also apparent in *Newsweek* and the *Saturday Evening Post*. (*Newsweek,* for instance, on the occasion of Ho Chi Minh's death in September, 1969, spoke of him as "the George Washington and Abraham Lincoln" of the Vietnamese people.) In the middle of 1964, the *Saturday Evening Post* ran an editorial which included the following:

To pull out of South Vietnam or to accept some glib "solution" as "neutralization" would, as Secretary Rusk has suggested, very likely bring a "major shift in the balance of power." The militant, predatory, and bellicose Communist Chinese regime would be greatly strengthened in power and prestige. . . . The government of the United States in the past has bought untold trouble for future generations of Americans by its failure

to appreciate the true dimension of the Communist menace in Asia (June 13, 1964).

Yet by early 1967, the magazine came around to a decidedly different position. Editorializing about President Johnson's professed lack of alternatives in the conduct of the war, the *Post* editors wrote:

The alternative to war is peace; the alternative to bombing civilian villages is to stop bombing civilian villages; the alternative to complaining that one has no choice is to investigate what the choices are (February 11, 1967).

In the same editorial, the *Post* editors endorsed a "permanent and unconditional" bombing halt. In April of 1967 they wrote, "One of the chronic embarrassments of our struggle for Vietnam is that we have been fighting on behalf of a government that doesn't really represent anybody" (April 22, 1967).

Of the Big Seven magazines, only *Reader's Digest* and *U.S. News & World Report* remained relatively hawkish on the war throughout the period. See, for example, the article by Walter Judd in the September 1968 *Reader's Digest,* entitled "No 'Surrender' in the Vietnam Peace Talks," or the *U.S. News* editorial of September 23, 1968. I have not separated the readers of these two magazines—they represent about 15 percent of the total magazine readership—from readers of the more dovish magazines in the analysis that follows.

Obviously, the shifting position of national newspapers is much more difficult to assess. Many of the national circulation newspapers had, however, come out against the war sometime before 1968, among them, the *New York Times*, the *Washington Post*, the *Christian Science Monitor*, the *Atlanta Constitution*, and the *St. Louis Post-Dispatch*. (The *Boston Globe* did an informal study in 1968 of many major American newspapers and found much shifting to more dovish positions. This study is cited in James Aronson's *The Press and the Cold War*, Bobbs-Merrill, 1970.) It is, of course, practically impossible to assess the editorial content of the countless small-town newspapers across the country, but in any case the high-status urban groups are more likely to be attentive to papers such as the *Times*, the *Post*, and so on. And it is, as we shall see, the high-status groups who are our major concern here.

This quite clear and extensive shift on the part of the chief national print media, then, has created a situation highly favorable to the assessment of media impacts on political attitudes. At the most basic level, if the media's editorial opinions do have decisive effects on the public's political attitudes, then we should expect groups with high media attention to be relatively more hawkish in 1964, when the major media were noisily rattling sabres than in 1968, when they had taken a markedly more conciliatory stance. Correlatively, groups with low attention to the media should show considerably less shifting in the four-year period. On the other hand, if the media cannot achieve the easy conversion of that audience, then attention to the media should be basically unrelated to the content and character of a person's opinions about the war in Vietnam.

In November of 1964 (just after the national elections) and in October of 1968 (just prior to the national elections), the Survey Research Center asked the following questions:

Which of the following do you think we should do *now* in Vietnam?

☐ Pull out of Vietnam entirely.

☐ Keep our soldiers in Vietnam but try to end the fighting.

☐ Take a stronger stand, even if it means invading North Vietnam.

The SRC also asked the following questions concerning patterns of media attention in each of the two study years:

We're interested in finding out whether people paid much attention [to the elections].... Take newspapers, for instance—did you read about the campaign in any newspaper? [IF YES] How much did you read articles about the election—regularly, often, from time to time, or once in a great while?... How about the radio? ... How about magazines? ... How about television?

In 1968 the SRC asked, along with which of the three options the United States should pursue in the conduct of the war, whether the respondent thought our original involvement in Vietnam a mistake. It is interesting to note how markedly dove sentiment varied depending on which question one examines. More than half the sample, for instance, thought the original commitment a mistake, but less than one-fifth chose the pull-out option. Even among the supposedly dovish group who thought we should have stayed out of Vietnam, only one-third favored a pull-out, while about one-fourth chose the stronger stand. An answer that the United States "did the wrong thing" by getting into Vietnam, then, gives the researcher no indication of whether the respondent thinks United States objectives there are worth a further sacrifice of life; the support given the stronger stand is a better indication. Who are the members of the population who would support a further sacrifice of life in the Southeast Asian effort? In order to find out, this report focuses on the third response to the SRC survey question.

The basic distributions for the Vietnam question are presented in Table I.

As the table indicates, the percentage of respondents offering "no opinion" expectedly declined from 41 percent in 1964 to 10 percent in 1968. Part of this decline is because the question was asked in the *post*-election

Sampling Public Opinion on the War

The SRC studies are based upon stratified and clustered probability samples of households of the noninstitutionalized American population of voting age in the contiguous states. The analyses given here are based on the white, non-South responses only. The reason for this is not in any way one of bias. The facts are that both the blacks and the white South are considerably more stable in their support for escalation than is the rest of the population. Among these with an opinion, for instance, escalation received the support of 25 percent (N = 67) of the black respondents in 1964, and 20 percent (N = 153) in 1968. Similarly, among white southerners with an opinion, escalation received the support of 47 percent (N = 202) in 1964, 50 percent (N = 321) in 1968. The reasons for the greater stability of these two groups are interesting but not germane here, and the analysis of trends in support, the inclusion of these groups artificially deflates the actual amount of shifting on the war issue. Consequently, I have omitted them from this analysis with the exception of Table I where the data included represent responses from throughout the nation, and of both races.

Most of the accounts based upon the SRC studies present the second option ("Keep our soldiers in Vietnam but try to end the fighting") as the "status quo" option. There is, however, some question as to whether this is an accurate interpretation. The alternative does rather explicitly specify an attempt to "end the fighting"; insofar as "end the fighting" is taken to mean a cease-fire, then the option is considerably more peace-oriented than the conventional "status quo" label would indicate.

segment of the interview in 1964 and in the *pre*-election interview in 1968; but undoubtedly, another part of the decline reflects a growing public awareness of the war in the four-year period.

One question worth asking is in which camp the "newly awakened" show up; the evidence indicates that they are

Table I — Change in Support for Policy Alternatives in Vietnam from 1964 to 1968

	Pull Out	Stay, End Fighting	Stronger Stand	Don't Know, Other
	Total Sample			
1964	8%	22%	29%	41%
1968	19%	37%	34%	10%
	Of Those With an Opinion			
1964	13%	37%	49%	—
1968	22%	41%	37%	—

likely to be numbered in the anti-war columns. From 1964 to 1968 the stronger stand gained the support of an additional 4.5 percent of the total population compared with a 15-point gain for "end the fighting" and an 11.5-point gain for a pull-out. Although the evidence does not allow a definitive answer, it does suggest that a good portion of the newly awakened reject the stronger stand.

In any case, the substantial differences in the percentage of people responding "don't know—other" makes raw percentage comparisons difficult or misleading. Consequently, the results have been recomputed on the basis of those in the sample who did express an opinion (see the bottom half of Table I), and the remaining tables in this report are based on these recalculations.

One problem with the technique of repercentaging on this basis is that it tends to overestimate the actual hawkish sentiment because, in effect, it assumes that the "don't knows" would be equally distributed across all three response categories, were they to have an opinion. Yet, as I suggested earlier, those without an opinion are in fact more likely to show up in the first and second categories than in the third. Nonetheless, since our concern is with support for the stronger stand, it seems appropriate to overestimate rather than underestimate that support, in keeping with the scientific tradition of erring, if at all, on the conservative side.

Removing those without an opinion leaves us with a reasonably satisfactory portrait of the "more active" public, the group which had at least formulated *some* opinion on a major foreign policy issue, and which comprised 90 percent of the population sampled in 1968. What conclusions can we draw from a comparative analysis of this group in terms of its attention to the national print media?

As indicated in Table I, the overall population shift among those who expressed an opinion on the Vietnam issue was about 12 percentage points over the four-year period. The expectation that the bulk of this shift might be located among the groups with the highest print media attention receives considerable support in Table II. As this clearly indicates,
the 12 percentage-point shift nationwide is caused almost exclusively by major shifts among those segments of the population who pay the greatest attention to the print media. The evidence is particularly persuasive with regard to the magazine readers. As the table suggests, about 25 percent of the population pays more than casual attention to the national newsmagazines. Among that 25 percent, support for escalation declines 20 percentage points. Among the remainder of the population, however, support for escalation declines only marginally (2 percentage points). The indication, then, is that most of the national shifting on the war issue was concentrated in those groups

Table II — Decline in Support for the Stronger Stand by Magazine and Newspaper Readers between 1964 and 1968

	Read Magazines		Read Newspapers	
	Good Many/ Several	Less than Good Many/ Several	Regularly/ Often	Less than Regularly/ Often
1964	54%	41%	56%	43%
1968	34%	39%	39%	36%
Percentage difference	20%	2%	17%	7%

Respondents include white, non-South only, as percentage of those with an opinion.

with the highest print media attention.

Attention to the media, however, is also correlated with a number of other factors, notably social class. A study made by *Newsweek* in 1960, for instance, claimed that almost 90 percent of its male readers were either students or those in white-collar occupations, and reported similar figures for *Time* and *U.S. News & World Report.* My own data indicate that about 34 percent of the total magazine reading is done by college graduates, who represent some 14 percent of the population. Or, to put the argument in another form, about half of the college-educated population in 1968 were accustomed to reading magazines regularly or often for political purposes, as compared to about one-fifth of high-school graduates and about one-tenth of those who had less than a high-school education. And even these figures probably underestimate the gap between the high-status groups and the low-status groups as measured on the media attention variable. For example, "a good many" magazine articles may mean, for the poorly educated, five or six a year, for the better educated, five or six a month, or even a week. There are also probably significant differences in the fashion in which the articles are read and the purposes for which they are used.

But there is little to be gained by belaboring the obvious, that the high-status groups are much more likely to be attentive to the print media than the low-status groups. The possibility that the results displayed in Table II are merely artifacts of an underlying class dimension is addressed in Table III, which deserves detailed inspection.

As an aid to interpretation, I suggest focusing on the "multiple media" variable, listed third. As the table headings indicate, the left-hand side of the table compares those who read both magazines and newspapers regularly or often in 1964 and 1968, while the right-hand side of the table compares those who read neither medium more than occasionally in the two study years. The evidence summarized here clearly indicates an interaction between social class and media attention in their effect on attitudes towards Vietnam.

Table III — Decline in Support for the Stronger Stand by Magazine and Newspaper Readers from the Upper Middle Class (UMC), Lower Middle Class (LMC) and Working Class (WC) from 1964 to 1968

| | Read Magazines | | | | | |
| | Good Many/ Several | | | Less Than Good Many/Several | | |
	UMC†	LMC	WC	UMC	LMC	WC
1964	67%	44%	55%	60%	60%	46%
1968	34%	19%	51%	39%	39%	40%
Percentage difference	33%	25%	4%	21%	21%	6%

| | Read Newspapers | | | | | |
| | Regularly/ Often | | | Less Than Regularly/Often | | |
	UMC	LMC	WC	UMC	LMC	WC
1964	69%	59%	50%	52%	39%	46%
1968	37%	35%	46%	36%	33%	38%
Percentage difference	32%	24%	4%	16%	6%	8%

| | Read Multiple Media | | | | | |
| | Both Newspapers and Magazines | | | Neither Newspapers nor Magazines | | |
	UMC	LMC	WC	UMC	LMC	WC
1964	78%	50%	55%	59%	41%	45%
1968	40%	19%	48%	41%	33%	38%
Percentage difference	38%	31%	7%	18%	8%	7%

Respondents include white, non-South only, as a percentage of those with an opinion.

†Social class as used in the present study involves both an occupational and an income distinction. The working class consists of those in blue-collar occupations; the remaining white-collar workers have been split into upper and lower middle class on the basis of an income distinction with the cutting line at $10,000.

Consider, first, workers who read both media regularly or often. The group indicates a meager 7-percentage-point shift away from support for escalation, which compares to an identical 7-percentage-point shift among the non-reading workers and a 12-percentage-point shift in the population as a whole.

Now, compare the working-class pattern with the pattern shown by the high-status group. Among the reading members of the latter, some 38 percent shifted their position from support for escalation, as contrasted to only an 18-percentage-point shift among the nonreading upper middle class. Clearly, class and media attention interact, or in less technical terms, it can be said that the high-status groups appear to be particularly susceptible to media manipulation. The evidence surely is that the high-status groups "got the message" in both 1964 and in 1968, whereas the low-status groups were barely affected by the changes that had taken place in the media stance.

The introduction of further statistical controls only intensifies the basic finding. For instance, among upper middle-class white Protestant Republicans who read both magazines and newspapers frequently—hardly a peripheral group by any criterion—support for an escalation in Vietnam dropped a full 60 percentage points, from 91 percent support in 1964 to 31 percent support in 1968. Comparable data for the reading section of the working class show that support for escalation ran to 48 percent in 1964 and dropped only 2 percentage points to 46 percent in 1968. This again reaffirms the conclusion that the general drop in support for escalation is mainly caused by the peculiar susceptibility of the upper middle class to media influence.

A possible alternative explanation for these findings might be that the high-status shift occurred independently of the media shift and that the high-status groups simply sought out media consonant with their new beliefs. But there is no evidence to indicate any substantial shifting around for a medium consonant with some newfound political attitudes. Twenty-eight percent of the nonmanual workers in both 1964 and 1968 chose the newspaper as their most important source of political information; 11 percent of the group in 1964 and 12 percent in 1968 chose magazines. The magazine readers' attention to particular magazines was not quite so stable: among the nonmanual group, *Life* dropped 9 points (from 20 percent of the total magazine readers who mentioned *Life* as their most important magazine in 1964 to 11 percent who so mentioned it in 1968), *Saturday Evening Post* dropped 7 points, *Reader's Digest* and *Look* stayed the same, *Time* gained 4, *Newsweek* gained 6, and *U.S. News* gained 7. But if the figures do indicate some shifting around among magazines, the shift is by no means decisively in favor of the dovish magazines. Indeed, the hawkish *U.S. News* gained 7 points, while the more dovish *Life* lost 9. If the decline in hawkish sentiment among the high-status groups is the result of some outside factor and those groups have sought out media consonant with this new attitude (a situation which in itself would render the association spurious), there is no sign of such an occurrence in the available data.

At any rate, it is transparently clear that the trend away from a "tougher" stand in the population as a whole is mainly seen in those within the high-status groups who pay close attention to the print media. The argument is highlighted by the virtual absence of any shifting among the working-class population, irrespective of their media attention. This again suggests that the general drop in support for escalation is in fact mainly caused by the special susceptibility of the high-status groups to media influences. To be sure, the high-status groups are more likely to be attentive to print media, but the dramatic shift away from support for escalation is not to be found even among the

297

(admittedly) fewer low-status readers. It is true that the upper middle-class nonreaders also drop considerably in their support for escalation, but the drop is by no means as spectacular as the corresponding one among their more attentive cohorts.

A brief digression is in order here on the question of party identification and city size. Between 1964 and 1968 support for the stronger stand among Republicans fell 29 percentage points, more than twice the 14-point drop for Democrats. The data indicate that this disproportionate Republican shift is chiefly caused by the concentration of white Protestant upper middle-class readers in the GOP ranks. Among working-class Republican newspaper readers, for instance, support for escalation declined only 4 percentage points, by comparison. The examination of support for escalation by party identification, however, uncovers some interesting trends, particularly along the city-size dimension.

As Table IV indicates, urban Democrats show very little shift away from the stronger stand; for every level of media attention, the shift does not substantially differ from the national mean. Rural Democrats who read neither newspapers nor magazines regularly similarly show little shift; 13 points compared to a population mean shift of 12 points. Among Democrats, then, the only disproportionate shift is among rural newspaper readers. The Republican pattern, however, is markedly different. Both urban and rural Republicans with high media attention shift substantially (47 and 38 points respectively); urban nonreaders and rural newspaper readers shift only slightly when compared to the national mean.

This suggests that the Democratic milieu might be called a protective or reinforcing milieu. Urban Democrats appear particularly impervious to media influences, which is to suggest that their environment or the conditions of their existence are likely to be a more important source of political attitudes than, for instance, the media. Or, to put it another way, urban Democrats are likely to exhibit fairly "rational" political attitudes, in that those attitudes appear either to derive from or at least be maintained by their milieu. It is significant that among Democrats, the only group to show any marked shift in the four-year period, is that of rural newspaper readers, who are for all practical purposes without a political milieu which might serve as a source of political attitudes.

Republicans, on the other hand, appear to obtain very little reinforcement from their milieu. Indeed, the only areas of relative stability among the Republican ranks are the urban nonreaders and the rural newspaper readers, and it is a safe bet that the rural Republican newspapers have not "come around" on the war to the extent that the urban newspapers and magazines have. This, then, suggests that Republicans derive less of their attitudes (or reinforcement of their attitudes) from the conditions of their existence, or, again, that Republicans are likely to be relatively less "rational" in their choice of political attitudes. Indeed, the stereotypical Republican monolith appears to be less a function of some special sense of community or class consciousness than a result of their reading more of the same media.

Opinion Conversion

To my mind the relationship between the media and political attitude change needs radical rethinking by social scientists. All the currently held positions are challenged by the evidence I have put forward here. Contrary to the Lazarsfeldian position, the media appear in this instance, at least, to have succeeded in effecting enormous opinion conversions among the high-status groups. In contrast to the claims of the mass-society theory, some segments of the population—notably the supposedly peripheral working class—seem unusually resistant to media manipulation. As for Galtung's theory of a stable center and a volatile periphery, it appears to have things precisely backwards: as

Table IV – Change in Support for the Stronger Stand According to Size of Residential Community, Party Identification and Readership of Magazines and Newspapers from 1964 to 1968

	1964			1968		
	Read Both Magazines & Papers	Read News-papers Only	Read Neither	Read Both Magazines & Papers	Read News-papers Only	Read Neither
Democrats						
Urban	45%	52%	36%	35%	39%	28%
Rural	—	68%	51%	—	43%	38%
Republicans						
Urban	74%	62%	50%	27%	34%	33%
Rural	73%	46%	54%	35%	39%	29%

Urban means a population greater than 10,000.
Respondents include white, non-South only, as a percentage of those with an opinion.

far as the Vietnam issue is concerned, stable opinion lies in the periphery and the manipulable opinion in the center.

One of the first questions to come up is why the high-status groups should be so vulnerable to impressions from the media. Perhaps there may be a greater ability for self-deception among members of the high-status groups, an ability—or perhaps a liability—to pick attitudes and positions out of the media and subsequently convince oneself that they are self-generated. Or it may simply be that the upper middle class attends to the media more seriously than its lower-status cohorts.

Another possibility is that the segment of the national elite which controls the media has very little interest in manipulating the working-class mass and simply concentrates its efforts, apparently most effectively, on the upper middle class. It is, after all, the upper middle class which supports the local and national elites, and whose resources, both financial and technical, are potentially beneficial to the elite group. In the same way that factory foremen are given the "errand boy" tasks of carrying out managerial directives, the upper middle class may be given the task of implementing elite decisions. Even if the metaphor is not apt, it is suggestive.

A third possibility is that, while the media elite may have an *interest* in manipulating the working-class mass, their ability to do so may be severely limited. All of the editorializing in the world, for example, is certain to leave unaffected groups who do not read the editorial page. Even beyond that limitation, the media have to contend with a strongly reinforcing or protective working-class milieu. If, as I have suggested, workers respond mainly to alterations in the basic conditions of community and environment, then it is clear that the media will encounter major difficulties in making inroads among the low-status groups.

A fourth possibility is that the better educated upper middle class is also better trained to be sensitive to predominant elite ideologies. This hypothesis would view the universities more or less as elite-controlled institutions which train an "available" cadre of quasi-political functionaries, the upper middle class, who can be called upon to support the policies of the national elite. This would give the media the mass-society function of serving as the communications and propaganda arm of the elite group, or, to return to the earlier metaphor, simply as foremen who give attitude and policy directives to the upper middle class masses.

There is also the puzzling question of why, given the conventional formulation of working-class attitudes as volatile and unstable, the data presented here indicate precisely the reverse. One possibility, of course, is that the conventional formulation is simply wrong. Another, more conspiratorial in nature, is that the media, seeking to cover their tracks, have hoodwinked their audience—which in-

---

TV—The Common Man's Medium & The Vietnam War

Interestingly enough, attention to television—the poor man's medium—apparently makes very little difference in working-class attitudes toward the war. Like the other media, television leaves the working class largely unaffected. In 1964, for instance, 50 percent of the workers with high television attention (N = 202) supported an escalation, as compared with 48 percent support among those who watched the television infrequently or not at all for political purposes (N = 58). The comparable percentages for 1968 are 41 percent (N = 211) and 40 percent (N = 77) respectively, decreases of 9 and 8 percentage points. Hence, the differences between the working-class watchers and the working-class nonwatchers are minimal for both years. In the middle class, however, the nonwatchers stay about the same for the two study years (46 percent in 1964 [N = 38] and 46 percent in 1968 [N = 65]), while the watchers drop 28 percentage points (from 62 percent support in 1964 [N = 175] to 34 percent in 1968 [N = 217]). Again, this attests to the particular susceptibility of the middle classes to media influences.

---

cludes, obviously, most social scientists—into believing that they are most adept at reaching the low-status groups, all the while secretly manipulating the attitudes of the national upper middle class.

A third possibility, and one I personally think the most likely, is that the data for this report were gathered in times of relatively high political awareness, either just before or just after the national elections. Such a report taps the "mass" when it is, so to speak, at its political best, when attitudes have been most carefully considered, and when information on the major issues is most readily available. It is this more politically aware milieu which exposes the essential stability of mass or working-class opinion on, in this case, the war issue. The suggestion is that, at least among the working-class masses, the widely flaunted "free hand" of the president becomes severely tied down as the election approaches.

A final question remains: Given the degree of acceptance for the "no conversion" hypothesis in the social scientific community, why does the present study find significant media effective—even if localized in high-status groups—when the bulk of the previous evidence has suggested that none are?

First of all, this study considers trends in public opinion and the long-term accumulation of what might otherwise appear to be insignificant opinion changes. Walter Weiss (in a review of media research in the *Handbook of Social Psychology* edited by Gardner Lindzey and Elliot Aronson) has suggested that the "pervasive influence of the media may lead to small, cumulative changes between campaigns. . . the net result may be to affect the dispositions themselves, or to set the perceptual frame in which the campaign is interpreted and responded to." This would suggest that simple cross-sectional surveys may overlook the cumulative influence of the media, i.e., that the media's impact is relatively slight in the short run and hence remains untapped by the standard social science methodology.

But more importantly, examining the issue of the Vietnam War makes it possible to treat the media as a variable rather than as a constant. The major print media have shifted in their position on the war, and it is precisely that shift that makes the conversion hypothesis approachable. But on what other major national issue has such a media shift been apparent? The point, of course, is that in the absence of such a shift, research into the possible conversion effects of the media must leave at the level of speculation the question of what would have happened had the media taken a different position.

To be sure, far too many events occurred in the period from 1964 to 1968 for it to be even remotely a situation where all other things were equal. However, despite the impossibility of a true "ceteris paribus" assumption, the documented media shift still allows us to come much closer to a legitimately controlled research situation than has hitherto been possible with media research.

If the media shift on the war issue is truly indicative of a change in sentiment among one segment of the national elite, then the continuance of the war into the present (and, from all indications, well beyond the present) is indicative of a lack of change in sentiment among another segment of the national elite. This serves to emphasize the existence of significant lines of cleavage, even within the elite group, which is a useful corrective for those accustomed to thinking of the national elite in monolithic terms.

The continuance of the war despite the opposition of the media contains other important lessons, in that it shows the scant power wielded by elites who control mass opinion rather than the major decision-making institutions. Kornhauser, for instance, has stressed the importance of competing elites in maintaining mass access to the elite groups and, although he offers no example, presumably competition between the media elite and the governmental elite would be one such case. Yet, such competition is fairly meaningless when only the one elite controls the decision-making power. The Republican upper middle class, for instance, declined markedly in support for escalation from 1964 to 1968; still, there was virtually no pressure at the Republican convention to nominate a "peace" candidate. The Democrats' attempt to nominate a "peace" candidate needs no further comment here.

For Further Reading

PART ONE. SOCIALIZATION

Psychosexual Development (W. Simon and Gagnon)

The Development of Motives and Values in the Child by Leonard Berkowitz (Basic Books, 1964).

The Sexual Scene by John Gagnon and William Simon (Aldine-Atherton, 1970).

The Moral Judgment of the Child by Jean Piaget (Free Press, 1960).

An Outline of Psychoanalysis by Sigmund Freud, translated by James Strachey (W. W. Norton, 1970).

Men in Groups by Lionel Tiger (Random House, 1969).

Nature, Man, and Woman by Alan Watts (Pantheon Books, 1958).

Threat and Obediance (Aronson)

The Social Animal by Elliot Aronson (W. H. Freeman, 1972), pp. 89–140.

"Effect of the Severity of Threat on the Devaluation of Forbidden Behavior" by Elliot Aronson and J. M. Carlsmith (*Journal of Abnormal and Social Psychology*: 66, 1963, 584–588).

"Long-Term Behavioral Effects of Cognitive Dissonance" by J. L. Freedman (*Journal of Experimental Social Psychology*: 1, 1965, 145–155).

"Some Conditions of Obedience and Disobedience to Authority" by Stanley Milgram (*Human Relations*: 18, 1965, 57–76).

"Effects of Severity of Threat and Perceived Availability on the Attractiveness of Objects" by E. A. Turner and J. C. Wright (*Journal of Personality and Social Psychology*: 2, 1965, 128–132).

Body Image (Kurtz)

Physique and Character by Ernest Kretschmer (Routledge & Kegan Paul, 1936).

The Image and Appearance of the Human Body by Paul Schilder (International Universities Press, 1950).

The Body Percept edited by Seymore Wapner and Heinz Werner (Random House, 1965).

The Social Construction of the Second Sex (Freeman)

"Current Patterns in Sex Roles: Children's Perceptives" (*Journal of the National Association of Women Deans and Counselors* 25:

October 1961, 3–13) and "Sex-Role Identification: A Symposium" (*Merrill-Palmer Quarterly* 10: 1964, 3–16), both by Ruth E. Hartley.

Roles Women Play: Readings Toward Women's Liberation edited by Michelle Garskof (Brooks-Cole Publishing Co., 1971).

Testing Masculinity in Boys Without Fathers (Barclay and Cusumano)

"Effects of Early Father Absence on Scholastic Aptitude" by Lyn Carlsmith (*Harvard Educational Review*: 34, 1964, 1–21).

"Children's Perceptions of Adult Role Assignments: Father-Absence, Class, Race and Sex Influences" by Joan Aldous (*Journal of Marriage and the Family*: 34, February 1972, 55–65).

PART TWO. BELIEFS, ATTITUDES, AND CONVERSION

Hippie Morality (B. Berger)

The Electric Kool-Aid Acid Test by Tom Wolfe (Farrar, Straus, and Giroux, 1968).

It's Happening by J. L. Simmons and Barry Winograd (Marc-Laird Publications, 1966).

Looking Forward: The Abundant Society by Walter A. Weisskopf, Raghavan N. Iyer et al. (Center for the Study of Democratic Institutions, 1966).

The Next Generation by Donald N. Michael (Random House, Vintage Books, 1965).

The Failure of History by Robert J. Heilbroner (Grove Press, 1961).

Authority in the Comics (A. Berger)

"Comics and Culture" by Arthur A. Berger (*Journal of Popular Culture,* Fall, 1971).

"Eroticomics: Or What Are You Doing with that Machinegun, Barbarella?" by Arthur A. Berger (*Social Policy:* November-December, 1970).

Murder, Juries, and the Press (R. Simon)

"The Influence of the Character of the Criminal and His Victim on the Decisions of Simulated Jurors" by D. Landy and Elliot Aronson (*Journal of Experimental Social Psychology*: 5, 1969, 141–152).

"Attribution of Fault to a Rape Victim As a Function of Respectability of the Victim" by Cathaleene Jones and Elliot Aronson (*Journal of Personality and Social Psychology,* in press).

"Observers' Reactions to the Innocent Victim" by M. J. Lerner and C. H. Simmons (*Journal of Personality and Social Psychology*: 4, 1966, 203–210).

The Jury and the Defense of Insanity by Rita James Simon (Little, Brown, 1967).

"Assignment of Responsibility for an Accident" by Elaine Walster (*Journal of Personality and Social Psychology:* 3, 1966, 73–79).

Flying Saucers Are for People (Buckner)

Is Another World Watching? by Gerald Heard (Harper & Row, 1951).

Behind the Flying Saucers by Frank Scully (Holt, Rinehart & Winston, 1950).

A Psychiatrist Joins the Movement (Coles)

Children of Crisis: A Study of Courage and Fear by Robert Coles (Little, Brown, 1967).

The Desegregation of Southern Schools: A Psychiatric Study (Anti-Defamation League of B'nai B'rith, 1963).

The Making of a Black Muslim (Howard)

Outsiders: Studies in the Sociology of Deviance by Howard S. Becker (Free Press, 1963).

Black Nationalism: A Search for an Identity in America by E. Essien-Udom (University of Chicago Press, 1962).

The Black Muslim in America by C. Eric Lincoln (Beacon Press, 1961).

The Autobiography of Malcolm X by Malcolm Little (Grove Press, 1965).

The Social Psychology of Social Movements by Hans Toch (Bobbs-Merrill, 1965).

Conversion to Women's Lib (Micossi)

The Second Sex by Simone de Beauvoir (Alfred A. Knopf, 1953).

The Feminine Mystique by Betty Friedan (W. W. Norton, 1963).

The Female Eunuch by Germaine Greer (McGraw-Hill, 1971).

Woman in a Man-Made World edited by Nona Glazer-Malbin and Helen Youngelson Waehrer (Rand McNally, 1972).

PART THREE. INDIVIDUAL AND GROUP INFLUENCES ON BEHAVIOR

Conformity and Commitment (Kiesler)

Conformity and Deviation edited by Irwin A. Berg and Bernard M. Bass (Harper & Row, 1961).

The Presentation of Self in Everyday Life by Erving Goffman (Basic Books, 1971).

The Social Psychology of Groups by J. Thibalt and H. Kelly (John Wiley, 1959).

Flattery Will Get You Somewhere (Jones)

Ingratiation: A Social Psychological Analysis by E. E. Jones (Appleton-Century-Crofts, 1964).

"Some Variables Affecting the Use of Conformity As an Ingratiation Technique" by D. R. Kauffman and I. D. Steiner (*Journal of Experimental Social Psychology:* 4, 1968, 400–414).

"Ingratiation and the Use of Power" by D. Kipnis and R. Vanderveer (*Journal of Personality and Social Psychology:* 17, 1971, 280–286).

"Self-Persuasion, Social Approval, and Task Success As Determinants of Self-Esteem Following Impression Management" by A. S. Upshaw and L. A. Yates (*Journal of Experimental Social Psychology:* 4, 1968, 143–152).

The Applied Art of One-Downsmanship (Weinstein)

The Complete Upmanship by Stephen Potter (Holt, Rinehart & Winston, 1971).

Games People Play by Eric Berne (Grove Press, 1964).

Relations in Public by Erving Goffman (Basic Books, 1971).

White Gangs (W. Miller)

Delinquency and Opportunity: A Theory of Delinquent Gangs by Richard A. Cloward and Lloyd E. Ohlin (Free Press, 1960).

Delinquent Boys: The Culture of the Gang by Albert K. Cohen (Free Press, 1955).

Group Process and Gang Delinquency by James F. Short and Fred L. Strodtbeck (University of Chicago Press, 1965).

Street Gangs and Street Workers by Malcolm W. Klein (Prentice-Hall, 1971).

The Gang: A Study of 1313 Gangs in Chicago by Frederick M. Thrasher (University of Chicago Press, 1927).

Putting the Business World into a Test Tube (Vaughan and Bass)

Training in Industry: The Management of Learning by Bernard M. Bass and James A. Vaughan (Wadsworth Publishing Co., 1966).

Swinging in Wedlock (Palson and Palson)

Group Sex by Gilbert D. Bartell (New American Library, 1971).

PART FOUR. CLOSED ENVIRONMENTS

Responses to Life in a Mental Hospital (Shiloh) *and* The Mental Hospital As a Sane Society (Talbot and S. Miller)

Social Class and Mental Illness by August B. Hollingshead (John Wiley, 1958).

One Flew Over the Cuckoo's Nest by Ken Kesey (Viking Press, 1969).

Being Mentally Ill by Thomas Schedd (Aldine-Atherton, 1966).

The Mind That Found Itself by Clifford W. Beers (Doubleday, 1948).

Human Problems of a State Mental Hospital by Ivan Belknap (McGraw-Hill, 1956).

Moral Treatment in American Psychiatry by J. Sanbourne Beckoven (Springer Publishing Co., 1963).

From Custodial to Therapeutic Patient Care in Mental Hospitals by Milton Greenblatt (Russell Sage Foundation, 1955).

A Case of Ostracism (Plath and Sugihara)

"The Laws of Buraku" by Minoru Kida (*Japan Quarterly*: 4, 1957).

"The Fate of Utopia: Adaptive Tactics in Four Japanese Groups" by David W. Plath (*American Anthropologist*: 68, 1966).

"The Japanese Rural Community: Norms, Sanctions, and Ostracism" by Robert J. Smith (*American Anthropologist*: 63, 1961).

Local Government in Japan by Kurt Steiner (Stanford University Press, 1965).

Sensei and His People: The Building of a Japanese Commune by Yoshie Sugihara and David Plath (University of California Press, 1968).

Together in Isolation (Haythorn and Altman)

Sensory Restriction: Effects on Behavior by D. P. Schultz (Academic Press, 1965).

Personal Space by R. Summer (Prentice-Hall, 1969).

The Social Psychology of Groups by John W. Thibaut and Harold H. Kelley (John Wiley, 1959).

Hidden Society by Vilhelm Aubert (Bedminster, 1965).

Isolation: Clinical and Experimental Approaches by C. A. Brownfield (Random House, 1965).

Theory and Experiment in Social Communication by Leon Festinger (University of Michigan Research Center for Group Dynamics, 1950).

The Machiavellians by Stanley S. Guterman (University of Nebraska Press, 1970).

Environmental Stress and the Maintenance of Self-Esteem (Helmreich and Radloff)

Men Under Stress by R. R. Grinker and J. P. Spiegel (Blakiston, 1945).

The Antecedents of Self-Esteem by S. Coopersmith (W. H. Freeman, 1967).

"Dishonest Behavior as a Function of Differential Levels of Induced Self-Esteem" by Elliot Aronson and D. Mettee (*Journal of Personality and Social Psychology*: 9, 1968, 121–127).

"Stress and Frustration" by I. L. Janis in his edited collection, *Personality: Dynamics, Development, and Assessment* (Harcourt Brace Jovanovich, 1969).

Groups Under Stress: Psychological Research in SEALAB II by Roland Radloff and Robert Helmreich (Appleton-Century-Crofts, 1968).

The Psychological Power and Pathology of Imprisonment (Zimbardo)

Asylums by Erving Goffman (Doubleday, Anchor Books, 1961).

PART FIVE. PREJUDICE AND SCAPEGOATING

Paradoxes of Religious Belief (Rokeach)

The Nature of Prejudice by Gordon Allport (Addison-Wesley, 1966).

Prejudice and Racism by James Jones (Addison-Wesley, 1972).

The Open and Closed Mind by Milton Rokeach (Basic Books, 1960).

The Three Christs of Ypsilanti by Milton Rokeach (Alfred A. Knopf, 1964).

Open Occupancy (DeFriese and Ford)

"Prejudice: Causes and Cures" by Richard Ashmore in B. Collins' *Social Psychology* (Addison-Wesley, 1970).

Social Change and Prejudice by Bruno Bettelheim and M. Janowitz (Free Press, 1964).

"Social Psychology and Desegregation Research" by Thomas Pettigrew (*American Psychologist*: 16, 1961, 105–112).

Studies in Housing and Minority Groups edited by Nathan Glazer and Davis McEntire (University of California Press, 1960).

Prejudice and Society by Earl Raab and Seymour M. Lipset (Anti-Defamation League of B'nai B'rith, 1959).

Strangers Next Door: Ethnic Relations in American Communities by Robin M. Williams (Prentice-Hall, 1964).

Are Women Prejudiced Against Women? (Goldberg)

"Who Likes Competent Women?" by J. Spence and Robert Helmreich (*Journal of Abnormal and Social Psychology*, in press).

The Prisoner of Sex by Norman Mailer (Little, Brown, 1971).

"Evaluation of the Performance of Women As a Function of Their Sex, Achievement, and Personal History" by Gail I. Pheterson, Sara B. Kiesler, and P. A. Goldberg (*Journal of Personality and Social Psychology*: 19, 1971, 114–118).

"Sex-role Stereotypes and Self-Concept in College Students" by P. Rosencrantz, S. Vogel, et al. (*Journal of Counseling and Consulting Psychology*: 3, 1968, 287–295).

Masculine/Feminine: Readings in Sexual Mythology and the Liberation of Women edited by Betty Roszak and Theodore Roszak (Harper & Row, 1969).

The Condemnation and Persecution of Hippies (Brown)

The Destruction of the European Jews by Raul Hilberg (Quadrangle Books, 1961).

Revolution for the Hell of It by Abbie Hoffman (Dial Press, 1968).

The Religions of the Oppressed by Vittorio Lanternari (Alfred A. Knopf, 1963).

Bomb Culture by Jeff Nuttall (MacGibbon and Kee, Ltd., 1968).

Scapegoats, Villains, and Disasters (Drabek and Quarentelli)

Communities in Disaster by Allen Barton (Doubleday, 1969).

Social Organization Under Stress: A Sociological Review of Disaster Studies by Allen Barton (National Academy of Sciences, 1963).

Disaster in Aisle 13 by Thomas Drabek (The Ohio State University College of Administrative Science, 1968).

Law and the Lawless by Thomas Drabek and Gresham Sykes (Random House, 1969).

Complex Organizations: A Sociological Perspective by Thomas Drabek and J. E. Haos (Macmillan, in press).

Disaster, Disaster, Disaster: Catastrophes Which Changed Laws edited by Douglas Newton (Franklin Watts, 1961).

Tornado by James B. Taylor et al. (University of Washington Press, 1970).

PART SIX. CONFLICT AND CONFLICT RESOLUTION

Why Gangs Fight (Short and Strodtbeck)

Street Corner Society by William Whyte (Unviersity of Chicago Press, 1959).

Confrontation at the Conrad Hilton (The Walker Commission)

Miami and the Siege of Chicago by Norman Mailer (World Publishing Co., 1968).

Rights in Conflict: Convention Week in Chicago, August 25-29, 1968: A Report by Daniel Walker (E. P. Dutton, 1968).

The Violence Commission (Skolnick)

The Politics of Protest (The Report to the National Commission on the Causes and Prevention of Violence) by Jerome H. Skolnick (Simon and Schuster, Clarion Books, 1969).

The Failure of Fail-Safe (Raser)

Fail Safe by Eugene Burdick (McGraw-Hill, 1962).

Arms Control for the Late Sixties by James E. Dougherty and J. F. Lehman, Jr. (Princeton University Press, 1967).

Sanity and Survival: Psychological Aspects of War and Peace by Jerome D. Frank (Random House, 1968).

Nuclear Weapons, Missiles, and Nuclear War by Charles A. McClelland (Chandler Publishing Co., 1960).

Creative Alternatives to a Deadly Showdown (Sherif)

Groups in Harmony and Tension: An Integration of Studies on Intergroup Relations by Muzafer Sherif and Carolyn W. Sherif (Harper & Row, 1953).

Intergoup Conflict and Cooperation: The Robbers' Cave Experiment by Muzafer Sherif et al. (University of Oklahoma Book Exchange, 1961).

New Ways to Reduce Distrust Between the U.S. and Russia (Rosenberg)

"The Effect of Threat on Interpersonal Bargaining" by Martin Deutsch and R. M. Krauss (*Journal of Abnormal and Social Psychology:* 61, 1960, 181-189).

A Theory of Cognitive Dissonance by Leon Festiner (Harper & Row, 1957).

Communication and Persuasion by Carl I. Hovland and Irving L. Janis (Yale University Press, 1953).

International Behavior: A Social Psychological Analysis edited by Herbert C. Kelman (Holt, Rinehart & Winston, 1965).

An Alternative to War or Surrender by Charles Osgood (University of Illinois Press, 1963).

Attitude Organization and Change by Milton Rosenberg et al. (Yale University Press, 1960).

PART SEVEN. POLITICAL BEHAVIOR

Computers, Polls, and Public Opinion (Abelson)

"Political Behavior" by David O. Sears in Gardner Lindzer and Elliot Aronson's edited series, *The Handbook of Social Psychology*, Vol. 5 (Addison-Wesley, 1968).

Candidates, Issues, and Strategies: Computer Simulation of the 1960 and 1964 Presidential Elections by Ithiel de Sola Pool and Samuel Popkin (M.I.T. Press, 1965).

"Simulation of Social Behavior" by Robert P. Abelson in Lindzey and Aronson's *The Handbook of Social Psychology*, Vol. 2 (Addison-Wesley, 1968).

Theories of Cognitive Consistency: A Sourcebook edited by Robert P. Abelson, Elliot Aronson, et al. (Rand McNally, 1968).

The 480 by Eugene Burdick (McGraw-Hill, 1964).

American Voting Behavior edited by Eugene Burdick and Arthur Brodbeck (Free Press, 1959).

The Best-Known American (Greenstein)

Children and Politics by Fred I. Greenstein (Yale University Press, 1965).

Children and the Death of a President by Martha Wolfenstein and Gilbert Kliman (Doubleday, 1965).

Rebels on the Right (Schiff)

They'd Rather Be Right by Edward Cain (Macmillan, 1963).

Identity, Youth, and Crisis, edited by Erik Erikson (W. W. Norton, 1968).

The Vanishing Adolescent by Edgar Z. Friedenberg (Beacon Press, 1959).

Life, Time and the Fortunes of War (Wright)

The Press and the Cold War by James Aronson (Bobbs-Merrill, 1970).

The Political Beliefs of Americans by Lloyd Free and Hadley Cantril (Simon and Schuster, 1968).

Public Opinion and Foreign Policy by James H. Rosenau (Random House, 1961).

The Contributors

ROBERT ABELSON ("Computers, Polls and Public Opinion") is professor of psychology at Yale University and associate director of the Yale Program in Communication and Attitude Change. He is a member of the Research Board of Simulmatics Corp. and has been a fellow at the Center for Advanced Study in the Behavioral Sciences, 1957-58 and 1965-66.

IRWIN ALTMAN ("Together in Isolation") is professor and chairman of the department of psychology at the University of Utah. He is director of the Association for the Study of Man-Environment Relations, a contributor to numerous professional journals and author (with J.F. McGrath) of *Small Group Research.*

ALLEN G. BARCLAY ("Testing Masculinity in Boys Without Fathers") is professor of psychology at St. Louis University, associate director of the Child Development Clinic at St. Louis University's School of Medicine, and director of psychological services at the Cardinal Glennon Memorial Hospital for Children.

BERNARD M. BASS ("Putting the Business World into a Test Tube") is professor of business and of psychology at the University of Pittsburgh. He is also director of the Management Research Center there. He has headed research groups studying human stress tolerance, Air Force R.O.T.C. leadership and transnational managerial differences. With James A. Vaughan he is author of *Training in Industry: The Management of Learning.*

ARTHUR A. BERGER ("Authority in the Comics") is associate professor in the social science department of San Francisco State College. He is the author of *Li'l Abner: A Study in American Satire, The Evangelical Hamburger* and *Pop Culture.* He collaborated with S. I. Hayakawa and Arthur Chandler on the third edition of *Language in Thought and Action.*

Robert P. Abelson

Irwin Altman

Allan G. Barclay

Bennett M. Berger

Arthur A. Berger

BENNETT M. BERGER ("Hippie Morality") is professor of sociology at the University of California at Davis. He is engaged in research on communes. Among his recent publications is a collection of his essays, called *Looking for America.*

MICHAEL E. BROWN ("The Condemnation and Persecution of Hippies") is assistant professor of sociology at Queens College and regional secretary of the New University Conference. He is co-author of *Collective Behavior: Unauthorized Social Action.*

H. TAYLOR BUCKNER ("Flying Saucers Are for People") is associate professor of sociology at Sir George Williams University in Montreal. He served as research consultant to the School of Criminology at the University of California at Berkeley. His interests include deviant behavior, social psychology and the techniques of participant observation research.

JAMES W. CLARKE ("How Southern Children Felt About King's Death") is associate professor of government at the University of Arizona. His research covers a broad range of American political behavior and has appeared in several journals and books.

ROBERT COLES ("A Psychiatrist Joins the Movement") is a research psychiatrist at Harvard University. He has worked in Appalachia and was a consultant to the Appalachian Volunteers. He has published widely in the field of child psychiatry and is the author of several books, including *Children of Crisis: A Study of Courage and Fear.*

DONALD R. CUSUMANO ("Testing Masculinity in Boys Without Fathers") is assistant professor of psychology at Forest Park Junior College, St. Louis, Missouri.

GORDON H. DeFRIESE ("Open Occupancy") is assistant professor of sociology and research at the Health

305

Michael E. Brown

Robert Coles

H. Taylor Buckner

Donald R. Cusumano

Thomas E. Drabek

Jo Freeman

John Gagnon

Fred I. Greenstein

Services Research Center of the University of North Carolina at Chapel Hill. His research interests lie in work-role alienation among white-collar and professional workers, and institutional dependency within the military.

THOMAS E. DRABEK ("Scapegoats, Villains, and Disasters") is associate professor of sociology at the University of Denver. His recent publications include *Disaster in Aisle 13*; *Laboratory Simulation of a Police Communication System Under Stress*; *Law and the Lawless* (with Gresham M. Sykes); and *Complex Organizations: A Sociological Perspective* (with J. E. Haos).

W. SCOTT FORD ("Open Occupancy") is assistant professor of sociology and research associate in the Institute for Social Research at Florida State University. His research interests are race and ethnic relations and urban studies. He is the author of *Interracial Public Housing in Border City* and co-author of *The Demand for Higher Education*.

JO FREEMAN ("The Social Construction of the Second Sex") is working on her doctorate at the University of Chicago. She has been an organizer in the women's liberation movement and is also a free-lance writer and photographer. She has published several articles on women in magazines and anthologies.

JOHN GAGNON ("Psychosexual Development") is associate professor in the department of sociology at the State University of New York at Stony Brook. His work is in the areas of criminology, deviant behavior, youth, the community, and marriage and the family. Among his books are *Sex Offenders: An Analysis of Types*, with Paul H. Gebhard, Cornelia V. Christenson and Wardell B. Pomeroy, and *The Sexual Scene* and *Sexual Deviance: A Reader*, both edited with William Simon.

PHILIP GOLDBERG ("Are Women Prejudiced Against Women?") is associate professor of psychology at Connecticut College in New London. His research, which he describes as "scattered and profane," has centered on the socio-clinical areas of psychology. He is presently conducting research on the cognitive and personality variables associated with voting behavior.

FRED I. GREENSTEIN ("The Best Known American") is professor and chairman of the department of government at Wesleyan University in Middletown, Connecticut. He is the author of *Introduction to Political Analysis* (with R.E. Lane and J.D. Barber); *The American Party System and the American People*; *Children and Politics, Personality and Politics* (with M. Lerner); and *A Source Book for the Study of Personality and Politics*. In September 1973 he will be Henry Luce Professor of Politics, Law and Society at Princeton University.

WILLIAM W. HAYTHORN ("Together in Isolation"), a social psychologist, is professor of psychology at Florida State University. He was director of the behavioral sciences department of the Naval Medical Research Institute where he headed a program of research on the effects of isolation and confinement of small groups.

JOHN R. HOWARD ("The Making of a Black Muslim") is Dean of Social Science at the State University of New York at Purchase. He has co-edited *Where It's At: Radical Perspectives in Sociology* and co-authored *Life Styles in the Black Ghetto*. He is currently doing research on structural supports for black mobility and is editor of *Awakening Minorities: American Indians and Puerto Ricans*, published by Transaction Books.

EDWARD E. JONES ("Flattery Will Get You Somewhere") is professor and chairman of the department of psychology at Duke University. Many of his articles appear in *Attribution: Perceiving the Causes of Behavior* (with D. Kanouse, H. H. Kelley et al.)

CHARLES A. KIESLER ("Conformity and Commitment") is professor and chairman of the psychology department at the University of Kansas. He is author of *The Psychology of Commitment* and senior author of *Attitude Change: A Critical Analysis of Theoretical Approaches* and *Conformity*. He is editor of a series, *Topics in Social Psychology*, and is

John R. Howard

Edward E. Jones

Charles A. Kiesler,

Richard Kurtz

associate editor of the *Journal of Personality and Social Psychology*.

STEPHEN P. KOFF ("Fall Guys and the Florentine Flood") is associate professor of political science at the Maxwell Graduate School of Citizenship and Public Affairs at Syracuse University. He is editor and contributor to a volume entitled *The Political Force of Italy*. Currently he is studying executive power in Italy and the impact of political instability.

RICHARD M. KURTZ ("Body Image—Male and Female") is associate professor of clinical psychology at Washington University. His research interests include body image, psychiatric decision-making processes and measurement theory.

ANITA MICOSSI ("Conversion to Women's Lib") is pursuing a doctorate in sociology at the University of California at Berkeley. She has completed studies at the University of Padua and was an instructor at the College of San Mateo, California. Her research emphasizes social psychology and social movements.

STUART C. MILLER ("The Mental Hospital as a Sane Society"), a psychoanalyst, is a member of the senior psychiatric staff at the Austen Riggs Center in Stockbridge, Massachusetts, and a member of the group research team at the hospital there.

WALTER B. MILLER ("White Gangs") is senior research associate at the Joint Center for Urban Studies of Massachusetts Institute of Technology and Harvard University, and is director of the Roxbury Delinquency Research Project.

CHARLES PALSON ("Swinging in Wedlock") is a doctoral candidate in anthropology at the University of Chicago. He also teaches marriage and family relations at Immaculata College in Immaculata, Pennsylvania. He is national president of the Student Evaluation Project, which publishes student evaluations of graduate departments of anthropology.

REBECCA PALSON ("Swinging in Wedlock") has studied anthropology and art. Co-author with her husband of several articles on the culture of sex and the structure of swingers'

Anita Lynn Micossi

relationships, she is working with him on a book, *Friends and Lovers: A Study in the Use and Meaning of Sex.*

DAVID W. PLATH ("A Case of Ostracism and Its Unusual Aftermath") is professor of anthropology and Asian studies at the University of Illinois at Urbana-Champaign. He has done field research on adult socialization in Japan.

ENRICO L. QUARANTELLI ("Scapegoats, Victims, and Disasters"), professor of sociology at Ohio State University, is co-director of the Disaster Research Center. He is currently doing research on organization functioning in stress situations, focusing particularly on the emergence of new groups in disaster settings.

ROLAND RADLOFF ("Environmental Stress and the Maintenance of Self-Esteem") is Program Director for Social Psychology of the National Science Foundation. He taught at Yale University before working as a research psychologist at H.E.W. and at the Naval Medical Research Institute. His most extensive publication on his major research interest is *Groups Under Stress: Psychological Research in SEALAB II* (with Robert Helmreich).

JOHN R. RASER ("The Failure of Fail-Safe") is associate professor of international relations and government at the Claremont Graduate School in Claremont, California. He has been research associate and project director at the Western Behavioral Sciences Institute in La Jolla, California.

MILTON ROKEACH ("The Consumer's Changing Image") is a social psychologist presently teaching in the psychology department at the University of Western Ontario in London, Canada. He is the author of *The Open and Closed Mind* (with Richard Bondi), *Beliefs, Attitudes and Values* and *The Three Christs of Ypsilanti.*

MILTON J. ROSENBERG ("New Ways to Reduce Distrust Between the U.S. and Russia") is professor of psychology at the University of Chicago. A large part of his experimental work has focused on the process of attitude

Stuart C. Miller

Walter B. Miller

Charles Palson

Rebecca Palson

David W. Plath

Roland Radloff

308

change. His most recent book is *Beyond Conflict and Containment: Critical Studies of Military and Foreign Policy*, published by Transaction Books.

LILLIAN RUBIN ("The Racist Liberals") is a member of the Graduate Division faculty at the Wright Institute in Berkeley, California. She is the author of *Busing and Backlash: White Against White in an Urban School District*. Her current research interests are class differences in sex-role socialization and identification among women, and the problems of urban education.

LAWRENCE F. SCHIFF ("Dynamic Young Fogies") is director of the Adolescent Service at Boston State Hospital, and psychological consultant for the Freeport Foundation, Inc., in Newton, Massachusetts. His research centers on the psychology of adolescents.

MUZAFER SHERIF ("Creative Alternatives to a Deadly Showdown") is professor of social psychology and director of the Psycho-social Studies Program at Pennsylvania State University. He is co-author of *Reference Groups* and is author of *In Common Predicament: The Social Psychology of Intergroup Conflict* and *Social Interaction*.

AILON SHILOH ("Sanctuary or Prison") is professor of anthropology and public health in the Graduate School of Public Health at the University of Pittsburgh. He is the author of *Studies in Human Sexual Behavior: The American Scene* and *Alternatives to Doomsday*.

JAMES F. SHORT, JR. ("Why Gangs Fight") is professor of sociology at Washington State University. His books include *Gang Delinquency*, *Delinquent Subcultures* and *The Social Fabric of the Metropolis*. He is the editor of *Modern Criminals*, published by Transaction Books.

RITA JAMES SIMON ("Murder, Juries, and the Press") is professor and head of the department of sociology at the University of Illinois. A member of the Institute of Communications Research, she is the author of *The Jury and the Plea of*

John R. Raser

Milton Rokeach

Milton J. Rosenberg

Lillian Rubin

Ailon Shiloh

Insanity, As We Saw the Thirties and *Readings in the Sociology of Law*.

WILLIAM SIMON ("Psychosexual Development") is program supervisor in sociology and anthropology at the Institute for Juvenile Research in Chicago. At the Institute for Sex Research at Indiana University he collaborated with John H. Gagnon in the preparation of many articles on sexual behavior. With Gagnon and Paul H. Gebhard he has written *A Technical Report on the Marginal Tabulations of the Institute for Sex Research*. He is co-editor of *The Sexual Scene*, published by Transaction Books.

JEROME H. SKOLNICK ("The Violence Commission") is professor at the University of Chicago School of Criminology and research sociologist at the Center for the Study of Law and Society there. He was director of the Task Force on Violent Aspects of Protest and Confrontation of the National Commission on the Causes and Prevention of Violence, and he has published a book on *The Politics of Protest*.

JOHN W. SOULE ("How Southern Children Felt About King's Death") is associated with the department of political science at San Diego State College in California.

FRED L. STRODTBECK ("Why Gangs Fight") is a social psychologist at the University of Chicago and co-author of *Group Process and Gang Delinquency* (with James Short). He is the author of numerous articles dealing with marriage and the family, small group interaction, jury deliberations and juvenile gangs.

YOSHIE SUGIHARA ("A Case of Ostracism and Its Unusual Aftermath") collaborated with David Plath on *Sensei and His People: The Building of a Japanese Commune*. She is interested in adult socialization in Japan.

EUGENE TALBOT ("The Mental Hospital as a Sane Society") has a private practice in psychotherapy and is a consulting clinical psychologist at Williams College in Williamstown, Massachusetts.

JAMES A. VAUGHAN ("Putting the Business World into a Test Tube")

309

Rita James Simon

James L. Short, Jr.

William Simon

is associate professor of business administration and associate director of the Management Research Center at the University of Pittsburgh. He is co-director of a grant to study the effects of electronic data processing on managerial and organizational behavior. With Bernard M. Bass, he is co-author of *Training in Industry: The Management of Learning.*

EUGENE WEINSTEIN ("The Applied Art of One-Downmanship") is professor and chairman of the department of sociology at the State University of New York at Stony Brook.

JAMES D. WRIGHT ("Life, Time and the Fortunes of War") is a doctoral candidate in sociology at the University of Wisconsin. His research interests include social mobility and political ideology, the sources of right-wing political support, and the extent and causes of popular political cynicism.

PHILIP G. ZIMBARDO ("Pathology of Imprisonment"), professor of social psychology at Stanford University, is currently a Fellow at the Center for Advanced Study in the Behavioral Sciences. He is the author of numerous articles in the area of social psychology.

John W. Soule

Jerome Skolnick

Fred L. Strodtbeck

Yoshie Sugihara

Eugene Talbot

James D. Wright

PHILIP G. ZIMBARDO

Elliot Aronson

Robert Helmreich

ELLIOT ARONSON (Co-editor of this collection and author of "Threat and Obedience") is a social psychologist and professor of psychology at the University of Texas at Austin. The recipient of the annual award of the American Association for the Advancement of Science for creative research in social psychology in 1970, he is co-editor of *The Handbook of Social Psychology* (with Gardner Lindzey) and *Theories of Cognitive Consistency: A Sourcebook*, as well as editor of *Voices of Social Psychology* and author of *The Social Animal*. His current research interests include social influence, interpersonal attractiveness and encounter groups.

ROBERT HELMREICH (co-editor, and co-author of "Environmental Stress and the Maintenance of Self-Esteem") is professor of psychology at the University of Texas at Austin. The co-author of *Groups Under Stress: Psychological Research in SEALAB II* (with Roland Radloff), he is interested in problems of field research in social psychology and has studied the reactions of individuals and groups in isolated and stressful environments. He is also collaborating with Janet Spense in research on sex roles and attitudes toward women.